Global Governance of Food and Agriculture Industries

Global Governance of Food and Agriculture Industries

Transatlantic Regulatory Harmonization and Multilateral Policy Cooperation for Food Safety

Edited by

Reba A. Carruth

George Washington University, USA

Edward Elgar

Cheltenham, UK • Northampton, MA, USA

Published by
Edward Elgar Publishing Limited
Glensanda House
Montpellier Parade
Cheltenham
Glos GL50 1UA
UK

Edward Elgar Publishing, Inc.
136 West Street
Suite 202
Northampton
Massachusetts 01060
USA

A catalogue record for this book
is available from the British Library

Library of Congress Cataloguing-in-Publication Data

Global governance of food and agriculture industries: transatlantic regulatory harmonization and multilateral policy cooperation for food safety/
Reba A. Carruth [editor].
p. cm.
Includes bibliographical references and index.
1. Food industry and trade—Government policy. 2. Agricultural industries—Government policy. 3. Food industry and trade—Safety regulations. 4. Agricultural industries—Safety regulations. 5. Food—Safety measures—International cooperation. I. Carruth, Reba Anne, 1955– .
HD9000.6.G54 2006
363.19'26—dc22 2005044195

ISBN-13: 978 1 84376 196 9
ISBN-10: 1 84376 196 3

Printed and bound in Great Britain by MPG Books Ltd, Bodmin, Cornwall

Contents

PART III REGIONAL AND GLOBAL REGULATORY HARMONIZATION AND GOVERNANCE OF FOOD SAFETY

PART IV REGULATED COMPETITION IN GLOBAL FOOD AND AGRICULTURE INDUSTRIES

PART V CONCLUSIONS

Contributors

Dr Reba A. Carruth specializes in Transatlantic Policy Cooperation and Global Market Governance, and directed the Transatlantic Project at The George Washington University in Washington, DC, and is full-term member of the Council on Foreign Relations.

Dr Genaro Garcia, Coordinator of Food Safety in the Veterinary Public Health Unit of the Pan American Health Organization/World Health Organization (PAHO/WHO) in Washington, DC.

Linda R. Horton served in the Food and Drug Administration (FDA) and is now the Head of Food and Drug Law Department, Hogan & Hartson Law Firm, Washington, DC.

Dr Lee Ann Jackson, Professor of International Economics, Center for International Economic Studies, School of Economics, Adelaide University, Australia.

Dr Ariane König, Pew Fellow at the Center for Risk Management and Kennedy School of Public Affairs at Harvard University and Advisor to the European Commission on Food Safety regulations and policies.

Dr Cheikh Ndiaye, Senior Food and Nutrition Officer, Head of Economic and Social Department, Food and Agriculture Organization (FAO) Regional Office For Africa, Ghana.

Dr Fernando Robles, Professor of International Marketing and International Business at the George Washington University. Dr Robles specializes in Latin American and Western Hemisphere market and trade issues such as MERCOSUR (Southern American Common Market) and the pending Free Trade Area of the Americas (FTAA).

Dr Jørgen Schlundt, Director of the Department of Food Safety, Zoonoses and Foodborne Diseases in the World Health Organization, Geneva, Switzerland.

Dr Grace Skogstad, Professor of Political Science at the University of Toronto where she specializes in international political economy.

Foreword

If nothing is so certain as death and taxes, then nothing is so essential as food and regulation – perhaps especially the regulation of food safety. Food safety regulation is vital for protecting human health and maintaining confidence in a sector that fills one of the most fundamental human needs. Yet in today's globalized economy, with rapidly growing international trade in agricultural products, the problems with regulating food safety have only grown more difficult and controversial. This book comes at an important time and offers much needed attention to the transnational challenges of regulating food safety.

The need for food safety regulation is evident. Consumers are unable to know the ingredients in their food or the conditions under which it is produced and distributed. Even with existing forms of domestic regulation in developed countries, food-processing facilities continue to exhibit inadequate sanitation in their operations. Moreover, today's dangers are often less visible than the gross abuses observed by Upton Sinclair in the United States around the turn of the twentieth century. Many of the 5000 food-related deaths, and 75 million cases of food-borne illnesses that occur in the US each year, come from exposure to invisible pathogens that are impossible for consumers to detect in their food. Certain of these micro-organisms – such as *listeria* – can even grow when perishable products are kept refrigerated. Perhaps most vexing of all, potential dangers from genetically engineered agricultural products remain unknown.

The need for regulation of agriculture extends beyond the need to protect consumers from hidden dangers. It also stems from the fact that food markets can easily spread disease. For example, when Foot-and-Mouth disease broke out at a single farm in north-east England, it led rapidly to an epidemic that devastated Great Britain's livestock industry, and prompted extensive efforts to halt its spread to other countries. More recently, an outbreak of a highly deadly form of avian influenza has been spreading throughout many parts of Asia – threatening both poultry industries and public health. Communicable diseases simply cannot be confined to those parties engaged in business transactions with each other. Both the overall industry and the public are vulnerable if even one farm or food processor fails to act responsibly.

The trend toward the concentration of certain agricultural businesses into the hands of a small number of large firms gives rise to yet a final need for government regulation. If agricultural and food production industries become highly concentrated, firms can exploit their market power at the expense of the consumer. For example, recent reports allege that Monsanto, a multinational biotechnology company, has tried to fix prices for some of its leading agricultural products, such as its popular herbicide Round-Up, and various strains of genetically modified seeds. Further advances in biotechnology may lead to new agricultural technologies that are hard to replicate, or are designed in ways that make it hard for others to compete. If so, then antitrust oversight may be needed to counter the ill effects of these new opportunities for market power.

Whether to address market power, externalities, or information asymmetries, regulation is vital in the food and agricultural sectors. Yet to be effective, regulation must be created and enforced through robust governmental institutions. While many developed countries possess the necessary regulatory capacity, even these countries' institutions will prove insufficient to respond to some of the most pressing food safety challenges that lie ahead. With hundreds of billions of dollars worth of international trade in food each year, the local grocery store has literally become a global marketplace. As a result, regulatory authorities must also respond globally. Local and national regulators must increasingly work with counterparts from around the world to coordinate international regulatory responses.

This book addresses the numerous regulatory challenges created by the globalization of food markets. The broadened scope of economic activity only exacerbates the kinds of problems that create the need for food safety regulation. Diseases that once might have been confined within the borders of a country now spread easily around the world, and the speed at which perishable products move in international trade makes it imperative that regulatory institutions respond just as speedily to outbreaks of disease or signs of contamination. In addition to complicating traditional regulatory problems, globalization also makes it harder for regulatory institutions to intervene effectively. Information asymmetries that once existed mainly between producers and consumers now exist between exporting and importing countries, forcing regulators and purchasers in importing countries to trust the quality of food – and the quality of the regulatory infrastructure – found in distant lands. Language and cultural differences compound the challenges of ensuring food safety and maintaining accuracy in labeling practices.

In the absence of a unified global government, regulatory governance depends on extensive international coordination and cooperation – with plenty of competition and conflict along the way. As the chapters in this book make clear, the solutions to today's food safety problems must depend on more than just setting the right policy standards. They also depend on creating the right kinds of international institutions to establish and enforce those standards. Regulatory governance in a global economy requires new thinking about institutional arrangements that go beyond reliance on the power of the nation-state. Food safety regulation must now involve efforts to harmonize standards, craft mutual recognition agreements, develop treaties, and enhance the authority and capacity of international institutions such the Codex Alimentarius Commission.

The regulatory challenges addressed in this book are vital not merely because they involve a subject – namely, food – that is critical to human survival, but also because they strike at the core of the institutional and regulatory challenges created by a globalized economy. By focusing on the transnational regulatory governance of food safety, this book succeeds not only in offering valuable insight into one of the most pressing international problems of today, but also casts important light on much larger questions about governance in a global economy.

Cary Coglianese
Regulatory Policy Program,
John F. Kennedy School of Government,
Harvard University

Acknowledgments

The editor would like to acknowledge the generous sponsorship and support of the German Marshall Fund of the United States. Through the leadership and support of the German Marshall Fund, the 'Transatlantic Regulatory Harmonization and Global Industry Standards: 21st Century Challenges and Opportunities for Regulatory Cooperation, Cross Border Competition, and Global Market Governance Conference' was convened at the George Washington University in 1999, and served as the basis for the Global Biotechnology Policy and Market Governance Working Group, and this book. In addition, the editor would like to thank the World Health Organization in Geneva, Switzerland, and the Pan American Health Organization/World Health Organization (PAHO/WHO) in Washington, DC, for their continual help and support on the conference, working group and the book series project. Finally, the editor wishes to thank Carlos Lara of Lara and Associates (formerly from the Embassy of Mexico) for all his help and assistance with the conference and the book project.

The editor also wishes to thank the following participants and presenters in the Global Biotechnology Policy and Market Governance Working Group: His Excellency Ambassador Aziz Mekouar – Embassy of Morocco in Washington, DC; Tom Billy – US Codex Committee; Dr Siphiwe Mkhize – Embassy of South Africa in Washington, DC; Tony Van der Haegen – Delegation of the European Commission in Washington, DC; Takahashi Kazuhisa – Embassy of Japan in Washington, DC; Dr Samuel Juarez – Embassy of Spain in Washington, DC; Dr Sebastian Heath – PAHO/WHO in Washington, DC; Dr Sergei Strokov – Embassy of the Russian Federation in Washington, DC; Hannele Tikkanen – Embassy of Finland in Washington, DC; Charlotte Beaglehole – Embassy of New Zealand in Washington, DC; Jose Molina – Embassy of Argentina; Jan Adriennsens – Embassy of Belgium in Washington, DC; James Hughes – Embassy of Britain in Washington, DC; Inge Hamid – Embassy of the Netherlands; Dr Philip Corrigan – Embassy of Australia in Washington, DC; Ron Krystynak – Embassy of Canada in Washington, DC; Friedrich Wacker – Embassy of Germany in Washington, DC; and Dr Carol Buy – Embassy of France.

In addition, the editor extends her gratitude to Linda Horton – Head of Food and Drug Law Division, Hogan & Hartson Law Firm, Washington,

DC Office; Walter Batts – Office of International Programs, US Food and Drug Administration; Dr Albino J. Belotto – Chief of the Veterinary Public Health Unit of the Pan American Health Organization/World Health Organization; and his colleagues Dr Genaro Garicia – Regional Adviser on Food Safety/Veterinary Public Health Unit, PAHO/WHO, and Dr Raul Vargas – Veterinary Public Health Consultant/Professor of Veterinary Medicine and Public Health, Faculty of Veterinary Medicine, National Autonomous University of Mexico, for their support and assistance on the book project. Likewise, special thanks are due to Dr Jørgen Schlundt – Director, Department of Food Safety, Zoonoses and Foodborne Diseases, WHO, Geneva, Switzerland; Dr Charles Riemenschneider – North American Liaison, United Nations Food and Agriculture Organization in Washington, DC; Dr Jean Louis Jouve – FAO Headquarters in Rome, Italy; Tom Buis – National Farmers Union Office in Washington, DC; and Dr Michael Rodenmeyer – Pew Institute in Washington, DC.

Finally, the editor thanks Professor Amiti Etzioni, Professor F.A.M. Alting von Geusau and Professor Frank Delmartino for their intellectual support and training. I would also like to thank Professor Ernie Englander, Professor William H. Becker and President Stephen Joel Trachtenberg at The George Washington University for their support of the Transatlantic Policy and Global Market Governance Project, and Matthew Lieber, Geoffry Antell, Luis Villafana, Bestami Biljcek, Grant Allyn Couch, Shahram Ahmadzadegan, Chris Seubert and Harvey D. Moore for their assistance in editing this book.

PART I

Global Governance and Regulation of Food Safety

1. Socio-economic foundations of food safety regulation and the governance of global agri-food industries

Reba A. Carruth

I ROLES AND RESPONSIBILITIES OF GOVERNMENTS IN THE GOVERNANCE OF FOOD SAFETY IN GLOBAL AGRI-FOOD INDUSTRIES

Introduction

At the start of the twenty-first century, national governments are engaging in regulatory policy cooperation to govern food safety in global agri-food industries. The major goals of collective policy action by national governments and regulatory authorities are to increase food safety, protect consumers, promote animal and plant health, and safeguard the public health in national food systems and global agri-food industries.[1] To a large extent, these regulatory policy and market governance goals are driven by growing national food demand, the transformation of traditional farming systems and agricultural production, the rise of modern biotechnology and the globalization of agri-businesses, food companies and industries.

As the decade unfolds, the structure of national food systems and global agri-food industries are rapidly changing. In turn, food safety is at risk due to growing reliance on global food trade and integrated global agri-food industries to meet consumer demand, and the food security needs of nations.[2] The sources of these national food system changes and food safety threats in global agri-food industries are as follows:

- the growing integration of local and national farming systems, farming cooperatives and food supply chain industries through contract farming agreements with global agri-businesses, food companies and biotechnology firms, and

- the consolidation of food production, processing and retailing food companies across global food supply chain industries.[3]

In this global food system, small farmers in developing nations and independent family-owned farms in developed countries are contracted by large agri-businesses and food companies. In turn, branded food and feed products are manufactured and sold across many countries and regions in the global food system. Through this strategy, many global agri-businesses and food companies have regulatory arrangements that permit the importation of foreign food products under a local company name. The result of the integration of farming and food supply chains is the consolidation of national food systems and the concentration of global agri-food industries. Consequently, national governments must regulate the growing food safety risks that arise from the integration of national food systems, food companies and global agri-food industries.[4]

Food Safety Regulation in Historical Perspective

The regulation of food safety, and the governance of agricultural trade markets can be traced back to antiquity.[5] At that time, food safety regulation and laws covering agricultural trade began to appear in the Roman Empire and Judeo-Christian civilizations.[6] Eventually, the use of Roman civil law by emerging European empires and nation-states resulted in the adoption of food safety and trade regulations for weights and measures, food purity and false product labeling.

By the thirteenth century, English and other European guilds moved to regulate food safety and agricultural trade to protect consumers and traders from food product risks and unsafe commercial practices. During this period, guild regulations and food trade standards served as a source of monopoly power, market protection from competitors, and strategic competitive advantage for guild members.[7] Throughout the Middle Ages in Europe, laws were passed to regulate food safety in regard to the sale and consumption of eggs, sausages, cheese, beer, wine and bread.[8]

By the nineteenth century, the dangers of chemical contamination of food became known. As a result of this new public health threat, new scientific knowledge and understanding of food chemistry emerged and created a professional discipline for food safety. As the century progressed, the regulation of food safety and food purity, based on the analysis of chemical and food composition, provided the basis for modern food sciences and food safety regulation. At the end of the nineteenth century, new technologies for food preservation and conservation were developed in response to international food trade and growing consumer demand for processed food.

At the start of the twentieth century, food consumption and demand changed dramatically due to technological innovation, and changing patterns of food conservation and storage. Consequently, national governments were concerned over conflicting food safety regulations and food trade laws.[9] By the inter-war period, food and agriculture products were produced and sold with little or no additives, preservation or processing.[10] Eventually, in the early post-Second World War period, growing dependence on processed and preserved foods increased government and citizen concerns over food safety. At the end of the twentieth century, governments, food regulators and consumers became increasingly concerned about food safety risks from pesticide, microbial, chemical and environmental contamination.[11] Therefore, in the twenty-first century, the following food safety issues are emerging relative to the protection of consumers and public health in global agri-food industries:

- the rise in food contamination through traditional and new food pathogens such as *Escherichia Coli* and other microbial, bacteria and viral sources of food contamination
- the emergence of genetically modified crops, animals, microbes and nutrients which require new scientific and public policy frameworks for consumer protection, animal livestock and plant health, public health and food safety regulation
- the growing consumer demand for high-quality fresh produce and unprocessed fruits and vegetables for year-round consumption and purchase
- the increasing demand for imported food to support changing domestic food consumption trends, food security and the nutritional needs of nations
- the increasing consumption of meals away from home with increased risk of food contamination by food handlers and workers
- the declining number of global food suppliers, processors and agri-food retailers which provide more food for ever larger numbers of consumers within and between nations in the global food system.[12]

The source of many food safety and public health risks are global animal livestock diseases such as avian flu, animal feed contamination and the BSE (Mad Cow) infection of beef cattle.[13] In each case, regulations for veterinary public health, animal livestock health, and food and feed safety were undermined by delayed policy action on the part of national governments, farmers, food regulators, agri-businesses and agri-food industries. In the case of Mad Cow disease and avian flu, the failure to immediately cull infected animal livestock, denials of the magnitude of the problem, and government and businesses alliances to control publicity over the national food safety crisis resulted in the systemic contamination of global meat and poultry industries.[14]As a result, the transmission of animal livestock diseases and food-borne illnesses to humans through contaminated food and exposure is a growing threat to public health and consumer safety.

Bioterrorism and Food Safety Sabotage

The deliberate criminal and bioterrorist contamination of national food supply chains, regional food systems and global agri-food industries present a growing threat to food safety. However, there are past and present examples of the deliberate contamination of food crops and farming systems. For example, Nationalist Afrikaner forces in the Apartheid government of South Africa secretly developed chemical and biological weapons for the deliberate contamination of food systems. In this instance, biotechnology and chemical agents were used to contaminate the food supplies and farm crops in the Black African townships. In some cases, deliberate food contamination was carried out through the injection of chemicals and poisons into canned foods, water supplies and farmland.[15]

In a more recent example in the United States, during the September 11th 2001 terrorist attacks, one of the terrorists attempted to purchase a crop duster in the Midwest region. Since the Midwestern part of the United States is the 'breadbasket for the world' and the home base of global agribusinesses such as Cargill and ConAgra, national food supply chains and global agri-food industries can easily be contaminated. Consequently, terrorists now have the capability to contaminate national food crops and animal livestock in one of the largest and most regulated agricultural food systems in the world.[16]

In this regard, the deliberate microbial and chemical contamination of plants and food crops, and unregulated GM food production represent growing sources of food safety and public health risks in national food markets and global agri-food industries. However, many developing countries have poor infrastructure for pre- and post-crop harvesting and storage, and limited regulatory capacity. Consequently, many developing countries are unprepared for food safety hazards arising from the deliberate and accidental contamination of food crops, animal livestock and processed foods. Therefore, global consumers are exposed to growing food safety risks.

At the present time, the United States and other developed nations are implementing national and regional food safety programs to prevent, identify and neutralize the effects of bioterrorist attacks on food systems. For example, new biotechnologies are being developed and used for the early detection of food pathogens and chemical agents. Concurrently, national governments are working to ensure that legally binding animal livestock and plant health regulations are enforced across the entire food chain and global agri-food industries.

In spite of these efforts, consumers face increasing food safety risks due to the consolidation of national farming systems, food supply chains and agri-business and the concentration of global agri-food industries. While the deliberate contamination of animals and livestock products can also occur, vast amounts of planted crop fields are easier to sabotage. Therefore, national governments and multilateral organizations, such as the Food and Agriculture Organization (FAO) and the World Health Organization (WHO), are working to strengthen the safety and early detection system for plant, crop and animal livestock contamination.

Finally, national governments increasingly face growing food safety risks due to unregulated competition in national food markets and the globalization of food trade. For example, in the United Kingdom, there is growing concern over the introduction of Foot-and-Mouth disease and food safety risks through the illegal importation of meat.[17] In a number of cases, illegal shipments of meat are purposely labeled as fruit or non-meat products to escape close inspection. Furthermore, the UK food safety authorities note that large quantities of illegal and unregulated meat products arrive through freight shipments and passenger luggage. As a result, food safety and animal livestock health are at risk due to the spread of disease through unregulated meat trade.

II STRUCTURAL CHANGE, MARKET CONCENTRATION, CORPORATE POWER AND THE REGULATION OF FOOD SAFETY IN GLOBAL AGRI-FOOD INDUSTRIES

The Changing Role of Farming and Agriculture in Global Food Production

Throughout history, farming and agri-food industry sectors serve as the basis for socio-economic development, capitalist market transformation, and the integration of nations into the global market system.[18] By the end of the twentieth century, many national governments implemented policies to accommodate World Trade Organization (WTO) agricultural trade liberalization, and cross-border foreign direct investment (FDI) by large agri-businesses and global food companies. In many cases, national governments implemented the following policy changes which weakened the position of small independent farmers:

- the shift away from strong public sector support and government policy interventions away from traditional farming and agricultural systems to private sector and global agri-food industry interests
- the decentralization and privatization of government services for traditional farmers, rural communities and agricultural sectors which resulted in the marginalization of the agri-food industry sector
- the decline and termination of public investment and policy support for traditional farming, agricultural industries and rural infrastructure.[19]

As the globalization of agri-food industries accelerates, the central role of independent farmers, conventional agriculture and rural communities in the production of safe food is now under threat. Therefore, the roles of traditional farmers and rural communities as custodians of the land, crop and livestock managers and protectors of the environment are being lost due to globalization. Unfortunately, these negative trends are occurring at a time when the risks of national food system and global food supply chain industry contamination from plant, crop, fish and animal livestock diseases are increasing.

For example, during the initial outbreak of BSE in the United Kingdom, and the avian flu in Asia, national governments were under pressure by farmers and meat and poultry industries to protect their market interests.[20] In each case, concerns over the economic impacts of food safety crises on national food producers and industries delayed the enforcement of risk management and food safety measures. Therefore, the protection food safety requires strict government regulation and enforcement of farming and animal livestock health standards in global meat, poultry and livestock product industries.[21]

In the case of plant crop health, the first line of defense for food safety historically consists of traditional farmers, farming cooperatives and rural communities. However, farmers need plant health inspection infrastructure and capital for the prevention, identification, management and eradication of plant pests and dangerous fungal contaminants such as mycotoxins. In this context, farmers are needed to protect conventional food plant and crop species, and to oversee biotech agriculture and GM food production.[22] Unfortunately, the rapid integration of national food supply chains through contract farming, regional free trade agreements and cross-border competition by agri-businesses and food companies, are increasing the food safety risks in global agri-food industries.[23] Ultimately, the role of small and independent farmers must be strengthened as the first line of food safety protection in national food systems and global agri-food industries.[24]

In response to the central role and needs of independent farmers, the National Farmers Union (NFU) serves as a powerful policy advocate for the regulation of food safety. Over time, the NFU is mobilizing public policy to support and strengthen the position of independent farmers in the US and transatlantic food systems, and in global agri-food industries. Through its independent farmer centered public policy approach, the NFU supports mandatory food safety standards and regulations for agri-business, global food trade and agri-food industries.

In this regard, the strengthening of traditional farming systems is viewed by the NFU as a requirement for food safety, animal livestock and plant health and consumer protection. However, the growing resistance of large agri-business, food processors and some developing countries to mandatory food traceability, and country-of-origin labeling confirm the magnitude of this problem. Furthermore, the use of offshore food sourcing to produce and re-import branded food underscore the true nature of competing regulatory and industry interests. On this point, the NFU and other consumer and farmer organizations are calling for stricter enforcement of food safety and antitrust regulation of the domestic and offshore operations of global food companies.[25]

Global Consolidation and Integration of Global Agri-Food Industries

The globalization of food production, cross-border merger and acquisitions, and consolidation of food supply chains through contract farming agreements are integrating global agri-food industries.[26] In response to these policy and market trends, large US and European Union (EU) based agri-businesses and food companies are rapidly integrating lower-cost farmers and food producers in developing countries into global food supply chain industries. Ultimately, transatlantic and Organization for Economic Cooperation and Development (OECD) based food conglomerates are pre-empting emerging competitors in developing countries through cross-border acquisitions, FDI, contracts and regional free trade agreements.

As the decade unfolds, effective competition by independent farmers and food producers is weakened in a growing number of countries.[27] In a similar way, the retail branding of food with private labels results in strong brand loyalty. As a consequence, global food retailers are exerting increasing control over farmers, food producers and food processors across national food supply chains and global agri-food industries. In turn, product differentiation and competition by local and national competitors is decreasing as global agri-food industries consolidate across nations and regions.

Finally, the supplier power of global food processors and retailers is growing through 'preferred suppliers' that subcontract production through vertically integrated food production chains, and concentrated global agri-food industries. In this food system, global food retailers dictate the terms of trade and sale to farmers and food processors that compete for shelf space in supermarkets and grocery stores around the world. As a result, consumer food product choices are increasingly shaped and controlled by powerful agri-business, food processors and food retailers in networked global agri-food industries.[28]

III BUSINESS AND PUBLIC POLICY FRAMEWORKS FOR THE GOVERNANCE OF FOOD SAFETY IN GLOBAL AGRI-FOOD INDUSTRIES

The globalization of agri-food industries is creating major business and public policy challenges for national governments and multilateral organizations in the twenty-first century. As the role of market forces increase in national, regional and global food production, government regulation of food safety requires a multi-level business and public policy framework. The basis for this business and public policy framework for the governance of food safety in global agri-food industries is as follows:

- National governments are under increasing moral, legal and political pressure to protect consumers and the public health from unsafe food and food safety risks in food systems and global agri-food industries.
- Nations are under increasing risks from the environmental, accidental and intentional contamination of food products, and threats of bioterrorist attacks on national food systems, food supply chains and global agri-food industries.
- National governments are under increasing pressure to protect the public health, animal health and plant health through use of science-based risk assessment, risk communication and risk management measures and precautionary regulations.
- National governments are responsible for ensuring food security and food safety for all citizens in spite of increasing dependence on large multinational agri-businesses, food conglomerates and global agri-food industries.
- National governments are under increasing pressure to regulate the nature and conduct of food market competition between independent farmers and industrial agri-business, as well as competition

between conventional food production, organic agriculture and foods derived from biotechnology in national food systems and global agri-food industries.

- National governments are responsible for the regulation of agribusiness, food companies and the impact of agri-food industry globalization on food safety, consumer protection and public health.

From a business and public policy perspective, many nations lack the regulatory capacity, public health infrastructure and industry standards needed to govern food safety in agri-food industries. On this point, the EU Food Standards Authority confirms the growing risks associated with EU enlargement, and the noted increase in illegal food imports. In some cases, the food-processing plants in the new member countries are not in compliance with EU food safety standards. As a result, the food-processing plants will have to be upgraded or closed. Nevertheless, the risk of food fraud is increasing since products are being sold illegally, due to the need for new inspection points on the enlarged EU external borders.[29]

At the present time, many governments in developing nations are increasingly concerned about the food safety risks from contaminated food imports, and the deliberate sale of adulterated, mislabeled and expired branded processed foods. For example, reports from African governments show that imported processed foods, from both developed and developing nations, are sometimes dumped in countries with limited regulatory and food inspection capacity.[30] In some cases, food products are purposely mislabeled, are past their expiration dates and, therefore, cannot be sold in highly regulated transatlantic and OECD markets. Furthermore, many governments are increasingly concerned about growing food safety risks from food product fraud. In the United Kingdom, for example, there are growing threats to food safety from contaminated meat that is deliberately shipped into the country under false cargo labeling. In other cases, local meat and poultry fraud is used to recycle rotting and contaminated meat and poultry to restaurants, food retailers and consumers.[31]

In light of the growing complexity of food safety as a business and public policy issue, national governments and multilateral institutions must govern the growing interrelationships between multi-level food market interests. The market interests, that is, corporations, shareholders, industry actors and lobbyists, and public policy interests, that is, governments, consumers, citizens, civil society and food industry stakeholders, must be addressed on a multi-level basis (Baron 2003). In this regard, the public policy and market forces that encase national food systems and global agri-food industries can be understood as follows:

Business and Public Policy Context of Food Safety Regulation in Global Agri-Food Industries

Issues

Regulation of food safety relative to agri-food product safety, public health, food quality, consumer protection, biosecurity, modern biotechnology, environmental protection, animal health, plant health, consumer welfare and product liability.

Interests

Individuals, consumers, citizens and public interest groups with food safety concerns and preferences for agri-food and biotechnology products/ National Farmers Union, Public Citizen, Transatlantic Consumer Dialogue, Consumers Union, Arab Federation of Consumers and the International Dairy Federation.

Institutions

Local, national, regional and multilateral policy institutions, governments, public health organizations, regulatory agencies and industry standards organizations with legal authority and responsibility for food safety regulation, policy cooperation, standards harmonization and the governance of agri-food firms, industries and the biotechnology sector in the global food system/US FDA, United States Department of Agriculture (USDA), EU Commission/Food Safety Authority of the European Union, Association of South East Asian Nations (ASEAN), Asia-Pacific Economic Cooperation Conference (APEC), South African Development Community (SADC), North American Free Trade Agreement (NAFTA), MERCOSUR, South Asian Association for Regional Cooperation (SAARC), World Trade Organization (WTO), Codex Alimentarius, International Standards Organization (ISO) and OECD.

Information

Public institutions, private agri-food organizations, public health agencies, non-governmental organizations (NGOs), farmer organizations, consumer groups, national, regional and global regulatory authorities with food safety information collection, risk assessment, risk management, and risk communication responsibilities for product safety, consumer protection, animal health, plant health, public health and governance of food safety in agri-food industries and the biotechnology sector, for example, the National Institute of Health (NIH), US Center for Disease Control (CDC), EU Food Safety Authority, Food and Agriculture Organization (FAO), International Plant Protection Convention (IPPC), International

Office of Epizootics (OIE)/World Animal Health Organization – WHO/World Health Organization.[32]

In this framework, the roles and responsibilities of governments, food safety regulators, farmers, agri-businesses and global agri-food industries are embedded in an overarching meta-framework of socio-economic goals for citizens, civil society and nations. As globalization, regional free trade and market integration accelerate, the normative basis for national regulatory policy and market governance are converging across nations (Eisner 1991). The boxed text shows the overarching socio-economic framework for normative consensus on the goals for food safety regulation in national food systems and global agri-food industries in the twenty-first century.

To achieve these food safety goals, national governments increasingly rely on public interest models of regulation based on precaution and science-based risk assessment. At the present time, national governments are engaging in collective regulatory policy cooperation to enforce product liability and corporate responsibility for food safety and consumer protection.[33]

BOX 1.1 GOVERNANCE OF FOOD SAFETY IN GLOBAL AGRI-FOOD INDUSTRIES

GLOBAL FOOD SYSTEM – UN/MULTILATERAL INSTITUTIONS

REGIONAL FOOD SYSTEM – REGIONAL POLICY SYSTEMS

NATIONAL FOOD SYSTEM – NATIONAL GOVERNMENTS

PUBLIC HEALTH – ANIMAL HEALTH – PLANT HEALTH – FOOD SAFETY REGULATORS

AGRI-FOOD COMPANIES – INDUSTRIES

MODERN BIOTECHNOLOGY

ANIMAL LIVESTOCK – FISH – PLANT – CROP HEALTH

FARMERS AND AGRICULTURE

STATE/PROVINCIAL/LOCAL GOVERNMENT

CITIZENS – CONSUMERS – CIVIL SOCIETY – MORAL COMMUNITY

Furthermore, national governments are harmonizing regional and multilateral regulatory standards to govern food safety across free trade areas and global agri-food industries.[34] Therefore, the governance of food safety in global agri-food industries requires convergence of business and public policy systems.[35]

Regulatory Competition and Regulatory Harmonization: Emerging Paradigms for the Governance of Food Safety in Global Agri-Food Industries

In response to challenges posed by globalization, free trade and regional market integration, two diverging schools of thought are evolving. In each conceptual framework of regulation, the central issue is the role of regulatory and industry standards harmonization as public policy and market governance mechanisms for national governments. In both schools of thought, the issues of consumer protection, consumer welfare maximization and the collective good of nations in the global market system emerge as central themes. The following summaries highlight this debate relative to the regulation of food safety in an age of agri-food industry globalization.

Regulatory harmonization: collective governance of food safety in global agri-food industries

The regulatory harmonization school argues that the governance of firm, market and industry globalization requires normative consensus, policy cooperation and legal convergence among nations to protect consumers, public health and the public interest. Consequently, governments are using Memorandums of Understanding (MOUs), Mutual Recognition Agreements (MRAs), regional and global product certifications and conformity assessments, and multilateral frameworks for the harmonization of regulatory standards to govern consumer safety and public health.[36] Ultimately, market globalization and regional free trade agreements requires multi-jurisdictional cooperation and regulatory harmonization to prevent market failure. Therefore, extraterritorial and multi-jurisdictional frameworks for consumer protection, public health and public safety regulation are needed to govern economic globalization through international treaties and international laws (Maier 1982).

The growing trend in regulatory harmonization is important given the fact that firm and industry globalization surpassed the governance of global markets in the twentieth century.[37] In this respect, regulatory harmonization, and antitrust policy cooperation through international laws and multilateral policy agreements serve as welfare enhancing measures for consumers and nations in the global market system.[38] Furthermore, regulatory harmonization and industry standards are needed to control the negative externalities of supplier power and cross-border competition in national markets and global industries.[39] Therefore, national governments must increasingly engage in regional and multilateral policy cooperation to strengthen regulations and industry standards for consumer protection, public health and public safety.[40]

On this point, Public Citizen, a leading consumer protection and public interest group in the United States, reports that food safety is now at risk due to globalization. In many cases, foreign produced foods are re-imported as 'domestic food products' through legal and technical exceptions to national food safety regulations.[41] For example, consumer organizations argue that the global food market and regional free trade interests of agri-businesses, and meat processors in the US, are weakening national food safety regulations. In this context, Public Citizen believes that NAFTA, the pending Free Trade Area of the Americas (FTAA) and other free trade agreements are driven to meet the global market expansion goals of agri-business such as Cargill, ConAgra, Perdue, and Tyson Foods.

In the Western Hemisphere region, Public Citizen and other consumer protection groups argue that globalization and free trade are undermining food safety, consumer protection and the public health of citizens in the US, Mexico and Brazil. For example, US agri-business, food company and agri-food industry mobilization against the highest levels of food safety regulation, that is, country of origin labeling and food traceability, are reducing consumer protection. Instead, food companies rely on weaker labor, environmental and food safety regulations to produce and process food in other countries, which is then re-imported and marketed as US meat.[42] In response to this trend, consumer protection and independent farmer organizations are calling for stronger enforcement of food safety standards.

In the past, competing models of regulation and market governance resulted in diverging product certifications and industry standards. Therefore, mutual recognition agreements, regulatory harmonization and mandatory industry standards are required (Albert 1993; Dezalay1992).[43] To achieve these goals, the global firm and industry regulation model can be applied to the governance of food safety in global agri-food industries (Drahos and Braithwaite 2000) (see Box 1.2).

As the decade unfolds, the governance of global agri-food industries requires normative consensus on the public policy and market governance goals of food safety regulations. However, normative consensus on regulatory standards for consumer protection, public health, animal and plant safety, biosecurity and the collective good must be achieved at the national, regional and multilateral levels.[44] Ultimately, normative consensus on the fundamental socio-economic goals of national food systems and global

BOX 1.2 GOVERNMENT POLICY MODEL OF GLOBAL AGRI-FOOD FIRM AND INDUSTRY REGULATION

1. Definition of the global agri-food industry business and public policy problem
2. Governments move to reach normative agreement on core food safety principles
3. Agreement on regulations, public policies, laws and principles for global agri-food firm and market governance
4. National and cross-border enforcement of food safety regulations and rules through ratification and harmonization of multilateral agreements
5. Globalization of food safety regulatory standards to govern global agri-food firms and industries

agri-food industries is now a requirement for the multilateral harmonization of food safety standards and regulations.

As globalization intensifies, national governments are responsible for ensuring that food market failures, consumer information gaps and the externalities of food production are effectively managed in national food systems and global agri-food industries.[45] In this respect, the regulatory harmonization school advocates policy and institutional convergence to govern national market systems as they integrate through regional free trade agreements such as NAFTA, ASEAN, MERCOSUR, the EU and the pending FTAA. Therefore, national governments must work through multilateral frameworks to harmonize regulations for consumer protection, public health and the collective good of nations in the twenty-first century.

Regulatory competition challenges for food safety in global agri-food industries

The regulatory competition school argues that consumer choice and product safety can be achieved through reliance on self-correcting market forces in diverse market environments. Furthermore, the regulatory competition school argues that decentralized policy-making, and national regulation of firms and industry are preferable to the harmonization of regulatory and market governance systems.[46] In this respect, advocates of regulatory competition argue that when consumers and firms have alternatives and choices of business environments across national market jurisdictions, a Pareto-superior outcome can be achieved.[47] When this occurs, the harmonization of regulatory policies, industry standards, antitrust and economic laws can create new problems and inefficiencies (Daniels 1991).[48]

According to this view, national governments should avoid attempts to harmonize regulations since consumer welfare and product safety can be weakened.[49] In the case of regional free trade areas such as NAFTA, APEC and the EU, 'races to the bottom' are seen as the result of idealistic attempts to harmonize regulatory standards.[50] Therefore, regulatory competition is more efficient and welfare enhancing in competitive markets and global industries.[51]

In the case of food safety, the challenge for national governments is transatlantic, regional and multilateral regulatory harmonization and institutional convergence. In the transatlantic region, the basis for regulatory competition between the United States and the European Union is divergent assessment of consumer protection, animal health, plant health and public health risks.[52] For example, US and EU regulation of food safety risks from GM food production, novel food products and the use of veterinary drugs, often involves competing and diverse models of regulation. Therefore, transatlantic regulation of consumer protection, animal health, plant health, biotechnology, economic efficiency and the public health requires the convergence of US and EU regulatory systems.

To summarize, regional free trade agreements and agri-food industry globalization requires increasing regulatory, antitrust and competition policy capacity by national regulators.[53] However, many governments of developing nations lack the regulatory capacity and antitrust policy frameworks needed to govern food safety in agri-food industries. As a result, regulatory competition is now a source of consumer safety, animal and plant health, public health and biosecurity risks in global agri-food industries.[54] Moreover, the dangers of regulatory and industry standards 'races to the bottom' increase the need for multilateral regulatory standards harmonization.[55] Consequently, regulatory harmonization, industry standards convergence, mutual recognition, antitrust and competition policy cooperation, are required to regulate food safety in global agri-food industries.[56]

IV GOVERNMENT REGULATION OF AGRI-BUSINESS, FOOD COMPANIES AND GLOBAL AGRI-FOOD INDUSTRIES

Consumer Protection and Welfare Maximization

The fundamental goals of government regulation of firm and industry competition are as follows: to protect consumers and the public health, support market efficiency, increase consumer welfare maximization, ensure public safety and to uphold the collective good of nations. In this regard, regulation theory tries to explain the public versus private interest, public goods and institutional structure aspects of regulatory policy enforcement and reform.[57] Therefore, the goals of government regulation of agri-food industries can be summarized as follows:

- to compensate for inadequate information by consumers and competitors within domestic, regional and global food market systems
- to control the impact of supplier monopoly and oligopoly power of large agri-businesses, food companies and biotechnology firms on food product choice, consumer safety, competition and technological innovation in national, regional and global agri-food industries
- to control the externalities of domestic and cross-border competition by global food companies, agri-businesses and biotechnology firms
- to control windfall profits by world class agri-food companies, agri-businesses and biotechnology firms
- to strengthen consumer power and assert the collective good of society and the nation in the global food system, food and agriculture markets, and food supply chain industries [58]

In many cases, the absence and failure of effective firm and industry competition historically leads to regulatory interventions by governments on behalf of consumer protection, public health and the public interest. However, market forces and reliance on private firms for the delivery of public goods such as food, pharmaceutical and biotechnology products, is driving the process of firm and industry regulation (Vietor 1994). At the same time, market globalization increases the need for more effective regulation of firms and industries, and the governance of markets by national governments.[59] Therefore, the globalization of firms and industries requires multi-jurisdictional policy cooperation for the enforcement of regulations.[60]

Regulating Consumer Choice and Industry Structure: Antitrust and Competition Policy

The regulation of antitrust and competition in domestic markets and global agri-food industries on behalf of consumer protection, food product safety and the public health, are legitimate and necessary goals of national governments.[61] By the end of the twentieth century, institutional competition between national regulatory, antitrust and competition policy authorities emerged to protect domestic firms and industries.[62] As market globalization accelerates in the twenty-first century, the Antitrust Division of the US Department of Justice warns that national laws and regulations are now inadequate to govern firms and markets.[63] Furthermore, the globalization of markets requires collective policy action by governments to regulate firms and industries.[64] Ultimately, multi-jurisdictional cooperation among regulatory, antitrust and competition policy authorities is required in an age of globalization, to govern consumer protection, product safety and choice, public health and the public interest (Fox 2001).[65]

The Structural School

The Structural School argues that supplier power prevents consumer access to adequate product information, and restricts product choice through the restriction of competition. According to the Structural School model of government regulation and industry structure, threats to consumer protection, product safety and public health arise from the lack of effective firm competition in markets. To be more specific, the concentration of markets and industries through powerful companies that engage in collusive pricing strategies, exclusive production arrangements and marketing alliances ultimately results in decreasing consumer welfare, competition, product safety and innovation. In turn, supplier power weakens consumer welfare, product safety and the collective good of nations in domestic markets and global industries.[66]

In order to achieve the regulatory policy goals of the Structural School, national governments must intervene and aggressively regulate competition to ensure food safety in national food supply chains and global agri-food industries. For example, complete food product and food safety information is needed for optimal purchasing decisions in global food trade and agri-food markets. Therefore, mandatory regulation of food labeling, that is, country of origin labels, and GM content and production data is needed to protect consumers in national markets and global agri-food industries. Box 1.3 provides an overview of the Structural School approach to the regulation of food safety in national and global agri-food industries:

In this context, food safety standards and regulations provide rules and guidelines for food production, processing, packaging, labeling, transport, storage, trade and marketing. At the same time, food safety standards provide rules and guidelines for consumer protection, food product labeling information and food product choice through the regulation of agribusiness, food company and global agri-food industry competition. In turn, food safety regulations can drive consumer demand and product choice in national and global agri-food industries.[67]

BOX 1.3 STRUCTURAL SCHOOL OF REGULATION, INDUSTRY STRUCTURE, AND MARKET GOVERNANCE

Social and political as well as economic objectives are needed to regulate food markets.

Food and agricultural commodities markets are fragile and prone to failure without regulation.

Government must protect society from supplier power in national and global agri-food markets.

Government must protect food consumers from others and from themselves, for example, unsafe food practices.

Government must protect competitors to prevent monopoly; avoid foreclosing opportunities for competitors.

More agri-food competitors means more competition and food product choices.

High barriers to entry reduce efficiency; potential entry may not limit the power of incumbent firms.

Market power derives from horizontal power and from vertical arrangements in agri-food industries.

Increased profits encourage firms to collude in concentrated agri-food markets.

Concentration in agri-food industries reduces market efficiency and increases profits.

Efficiency and fairness in agri-food markets requires government protection and regulation.

Source: Baron (2003, p. 281: see Figure 9-3 – Structural and Chicago Schools and New IO Perspective chart).

The Chicago School

According to the Chicago School framework of industry structure, mandatory regulation of firm and market competition often creates economic inefficiency, and reduces consumer welfare. At the same time, consumer choice is decreased due to the distortion of market forces, and the subjugation of corporate strategy, technological innovations and product development to the goals of governments and interest groups. Therefore, the Chicago School advocates minimal regulation on behalf of consumer protection and competition. Instead, self-regulating firms and industries

BOX 1.4 CHICAGO SCHOOL OF FIRM, INDUSTRY AND MARKET GOVERNANCE

Economic objectives; agri-food industry efficiency with a focus on prices.

Agri-food markets are resilient; food market imperfections can be addressed through incentives.

Competition is the best protector of consumers, public health and safety, and economic efficiency.

Consumers are responsible for their own food safety decisions and will protect themselves.

Conditions for perfect competition are sufficient but not necessary in agri-food markets and industries.

Competition can be effective with only a few agri-businesses and food company competitors.

Few barriers to entry; barriers are few due to the efficiency of incumbent agri-businesses and food companies; potential entry limits the economic power of incumbents.

Market power can only arise from horizontal power agri-food markets and industries.

Industry concentration is more likely due to lower costs of larger agri-businesses and food companies.

Judge agri-business and food conglomerate practices in terms of their effects on efficiency and prices; use the rule of reason.

Economic efficiency; individual choice and responsibility should be used to regulate food safety and consumer protection.

Source: Baron (2003, p. 281: see Figure 9-3 – Structural and Chicago Schools and New IO Perspective chart).

that rely on market forces and product demand is the best way to ensure consumer protection, product safety and quality. In the few instances where market interventions are needed, the scale and scope of government regulation and industry standards enforcement should be limited.[68]

In global agri-food industries, government regulation of agri-business and food companies should be pro-competitive, market friendly and rely on self-correcting market forces. For example, shifting supplier and product choices of consumers will punish agri-businesses and food companies that produce substandard, fraudulent and unsafe food and feed products.

Therefore, multilateral food safety standards may result in the reduction of consumer welfare, product choice, and market competition. As Box 1.4 shows, the Chicago School advocates the 'survival of the fittest' in national food markets and global agri-food industries, unhampered by burdensome regulations.

In terms of industry structure, the Chicago School recommends that food safety standards and regulatory harmonization should not be used to protect less competitive farming and food production systems in national and global agri-food industries. Moreover, large agri-businesses and food companies should not be forced to comply with burdensome and expensive regulations for food safety. In this regard, food safety regulations should not be used to restrict the product innovation strategies of world-class agri-businesses, food companies and biotechnology firms that produce GM and processed foods. On the contrary, market power and market share in national and global markets reflect consumer sentiments, and buyer and seller satisfaction in global agri-food industries.

The New Industrial Organization School

The New Industrial Organization (New IO) model of industry structure, argues that market globalization is resulting in strategic firm alliances and networked industries.[69] As economic globalization intensifies, converging technologies and product developments result in the cross-border integration of firms and networked industries. In turn, mergers and acquisitions, joint ventures and strategic marketing alliances result in fewer differentiated product choices. Therefore, strategic alliances between food, pharmaceutical and biotechnology companies present regulatory challenges in global agri-food industries. Box 1.5 summarizes the New IO perspectives of regulation in networked global agri-food industries.

As the globalization of food markets accelerates, national governments and food safety regulators face the threat of regulatory capture by powerful networked companies and agri-food industries. In turn, powerful companies and networked agri-food industry interests can challenge the global enforcement of mandatory food safety regulations.[70] Therefore, governments must collectively regulate oligopolistic competition and monopoly power in networked global agri-food industries.

Management-Based Regulation and Global Food Industries

The globalization of industries requires firm and industry self-regulation and standards enforcement to ensure consumer protection, product safety and protection of the public health. The benefits of firm and industry

BOX 1.5 NEW IO SCHOOL OF INDUSTRY REGULATION, COMPETITION POLICY AND MARKET GOVERNANCE

Economic objectives; static and dynamic efficiency in agri-food industries.

Most agri-food markets are resilient, but some have imperfections such as network externalities: strategic behavior can limit efficiency due to oligopolistic competition and restriction of product choice.

Competition is the best protector of consumers, but government interventions can be required to regulate competition in accordance with food safety and food product standards.

Consumers can protect themselves when they have true food choices.

Both agri-food product innovation and competition are required for efficiency in agri-food industries.

Competition can be effective with a small number of agri-businesses and food company competitors.

Barriers to entry can be present, for example, the economics of food safety and food product standardization which prevent agri-food products from small and medium-sized companies and developing countries from complying with mandatory regulations.

Market power derives from horizontal factors but can be extended through vertical arrangements and strategic behavior. Collusion is possible with repeated encounters between agri-businesses, biotechnology firms and food companies.

Industry concentration can be due to lower costs, market power, or strategic opportunities.

Judge agri-business practices in terms of impact on present and future agri-food industry competition; use rule of reason except for cases such as price fixing.

Economic efficiency; individual and collective responsibility for food safety.

Source: Baron (2003, p. 281: see Figure 9-3 – Structural and Chicago Schools and New IO Perspective chart).

self-regulation and industry standards within the context of mandatory government regulation are as follows: corporate management and industry can move faster, are more flexible, economically efficient, technologically innovative and responsive to production, processing and manufacturing problems. Consequently, firm and industry self-regulation, is increasingly needed to strengthen consumer protection and product safety in national and global industries.

At the national and global levels, firm and industry self-regulation requires cooperation among competitors to achieve the collective good.[71] Nevertheless, there is a perception that corporate management and industry are more knowledgeable of the technical aspects of products and production processes than government regulators, consumers or third-party actors. However, reliance on firm and industry self-regulation as a substitute for mandatory government regulation is increasingly challenged due to perceptions of economic efficiency and profitability overriding consumer protection, public health and the public interest.[72] Therefore, management-based regulation must be implemented within a broader socio-economic context of mandatory government policies, embedded markets, industries and corporations within society and nations.[73]

In global agri-food industries, product liability risks for agri-businesses and food companies are growing.[74] As a result of growing demands for stricter food safety standards in global agri-food industries, corporate management and food industry leaders are adopting management-based regulations.[75] In turn, corporations and industry standards organizations are attempting to balance mandatory government regulation with management-based regulation.[76] In this context, national food firms must address the following food safety issues in global agri-food industries:

- changing environments and cultural contexts of food safety
- changing consumer food choices and food cultures
- relatively small investment in health education and food safety in comparison to large food marketing and food advertising budgets for branded foods
- emergence of multi-level and multilateral frameworks for the regulation of food contamination and nutrition-based food safety issues
- inability of HACCP process inspection systems to detect non-communicable diseases
- emerging systems of mandatory government and management based regulation of food supply chain firms and industries in the transatlantic and OECD countries, with little or no impact on developing countries.[77]

In response to changing trends in global agri-food industries, new paradigms of management-based regulation are emerging which move from reliance on technology and performance-based policies. In the new paradigm, management is required to use its informed position and intricate knowledge of food production, manufacturing and processing industries to protect consumers and the public health from food safety hazards in global agri-food industries (Coglianese and Lazer 2002a). To accomplish these goals, management is increasingly required to develop and implement on-site process inspections and standards to support mandatory government regulation of agri-food industries.[78]

As food safety risks in global agri-food industries grow, management-based regulation is a critical and necessary component of food firm, industry and global market governance.[79] In a growing number of developed and developing nations, the adoption of proactive HACCP process inspection and Food Pathogen Reduction Programs are mandatory for food safety regulation. However, management-based regulations for food production and food-processing must be customized to meet the local requirements of farmers and food producers in developing countries. Therefore, transatlantic regulators and multilateral food safety organizations are assisting governments and agri-food industries in Africa, Asia, Latin America, Eastern Europe and the Middle East to implement management-based regulations.

At the present time, global food companies now face growing liability exposure from food contamination as well as nutrition-based food safety risks. In response to these challenges, the leading global food retailers such as Royal Ahold, Kroeger, Wal-Mart and others launched a Global Food Safety Initiative (GFSI). Through this collective action at the firm and industry level, global food retailing companies are developing management-based regulations in parallel with national, regional and multilateral

BOX 1.6 GLOBAL AGRI-FOOD FIRM AND INDUSTRY MODEL OF FOOD SAFETY SELF-REGULATION

1. Definition of a global corporate strategy and agri-food industry problem or threat
2. Selected firms change market strategy to resolve food safety or regulatory problem
3. Other global agri-food firms and other industries adopt 'Good Manufacturing Practice' (GMP) or Best Practices
4. Global voluntary adoption of new standards to avoid or manage emerging multi-level and multilateral government regulation of food safety in global agri-food industries[80]

food safety standards.[81] Box 1.6 summarizes the self-regulation process in global agri-food industries.

In summary, Good Agricultural, Manufacturing, Retail and Distribution Practices are increasingly used to strengthen self-regulation in global agri-food industries. In turn, many global food supply chain industries are adopting management based regulations. The growing role of mandatory HACCP programs and Best Practices in the regulation of global seafood, meat, poultry, grain and processed food industries confirms the importance of management-based regulations in the governance of food safety.[82]

V NETWORKS OF MULTILATERAL INSTITUTIONS, REGULATORY HARMONIZATION AND GLOBAL MARKET GOVERNANCE SYSTEMS

In an age of globalization and regional free trade, United Nations specialized agencies, that is, the Food and Agricultural Organization (FAO) the World Health Organization (WHO), and their subsidiary body Codex Alimentarius, are the core multilateral system for food safety regulation. In this system, FAO, WHO and Codex Alimentarius provide the scientific, technical and regulatory framework for national, transatlantic, regional and multilateral harmonization of food safety standards. In the unfolding network of multilateral food safety institutions, the World Animal Health Organization (formerly the Office of Epizootics) (OIE), and the International Plant Protection Convention (IPPC) are working in cooperation with FAO, WHO and Codex Alimentarius. In this regard, OIE and IPPC serve as the multilateral frameworks for animal livestock health and plant health standards harmonization for food safety in cooperation with Codex Alimentarius.

WTO Sanitary and Phytosanitary and Technical Barriers to Trade Agreements

The regulation of food safety in global food trade is provided for in the market governance provisions of the General Agreement on Tariffs and Trade (GATT) and WTO rules and agreements. However, the GATT rules permitted exceptions for governments and national regulators to enact strong laws and to enforce standards on domestic and foreign products to protect human, animal and plant health. By the 1970s, the Tokyo Round of GATT trade negotiations (1974–79) resulted in the creation of the Agreement on Technical Barriers to Trade (TBT).[83] In the 1980s and 1990s, the following global trade, food safety and intellectual property rights agreements were adopted by member countries; the Agreement on the Application of Sanitary and Phytosanitary Measures (SPS), the Agreement on Technical Barriers to Trade (TBT) and the Agreement on Trade Related Aspects of Intellectual Property Rights (TRIPS).[84] The WTO SPS and TBT agreements are designed to promote fair competition in domestic and international food and agriculture markets, while protecting consumer safety, animal and plant health and the public health against food safety hazards.[85]

The WTO SPS agreement strengthens the ability of national governments to regulate food safety in cross-border food trade, and competition in global agri-food industries.[86] In this regard, the regulation of national food systems and global food trade through the WTO SPS agreement confirms the growing trend in regulatory policy harmonization and the multilateral governance of food safety.[87] The core goals and objectives of the WTO SPS food safety regulations and inspection standards for global food trade are as follows:

- protection of humans and animals from the health risks associated with additives, contaminants, toxins or disease-causing organisms in food and agriculture products
- protection of humans, as citizens and consumers, from animal- or plant-borne diseases
- protection of animals or plants from pests, diseases or disease causing micro organisms, and finally
- prevention or reduction of economic damages and costs to society and nations as a result the spread of contaminated food and agricultural products.[88]

The scope of WTO SPS agreement includes domestic food products, as well as food and agriculture products that are traded in global markets and imported from foreign countries.[89] In this context, regulatory standards and inspection transparency are included in the WTO SPS agreement as risk assessment measures for food safety.[90] Furthermore, national food safety regulations must be based on science, and enforced only to the level needed to protect public health, animal livestock and plant health and consumer safety.[91] Finally, the WTO SPS agreement calls for national governments to harmonize their food safety regulations with Codex Alimentarius, OIE and the IPPC for plant and crop health standards.[92]

The Role of FAO, WHO and Codex Alimentarius

International food safety standards cooperation for the multilateral governance of food trade and agri-food industries predates the twenty-first century.

The following chronology of food standards in Box 1.7 highlights the growing role of the FAO, WHO and Codex Alimentarius in the development of a multilateral institutional framework for food safety standards harmonization.

BOX 1.7 FAO AND WHO FOOD SAFETY REGULATION AND GLOBAL FOOD TRADE STANDARDS TIMELINE

1. In history, ancient civilizations codify the preparation and trade of food and agriculture products.
2. In the mid-1800s, the first general food laws are adopted and enforcement agencies are created. During this period, food sciences and chemistry gain credibility as reliable methodologies are developed to test food safety.
3. The Austro-Hungarian Empire compiles a collection of standards and product descriptions for a broad range of food and agriculture products entitled Codex Alimentarius Austriacus for the governance of food safety.
4. In the late 1800s the first shipment of frozen meat from Australia and New Zealand to the United Kingdom marks the start of a new phase of international food transport and trade.
5. In the early 1900s food trade associations push for the globalization of agri-food trade through the harmonization of food safety regulations and trade laws.
6. In 1903 the International Dairy Federation (IDF) creates international standards for milk and milk products, and eventually becomes a strong advocate for the creation of the Codex Alimentarius Commission.
7. In 1945, the United Nations Food and Agriculture Organization (FAO) is given responsibility for nutrition and international food standards.
8. By 1948, the United Nations World Health Organization (WHO) is founded, and given responsibility for public health and a mandate to establish food standards.
9. In 1949, the government of Argentina pushes for the creation of a regional Latin American food code entitled Codigo Latino-Americano Alimentos.
10. In 1950, joint FAO/WHO expert meetings begin to examine nutrition, food additives and related food safety and trade standard issues.

11. In 1953 the World Health Assembly, the highest governing body in WHO, publicly states that increasing use of chemicals in the food industry is a new public health problem that requires the attention of governments, regulators and public health officials.
12. From 1954 to 1958 the Austrian government pushes for the creation of a regional food code, the Codex Alimentarius Europaeus or the European Codex Alimentarius.
13. In 1961 the first FAO Regional Conference for Europe officially endorses the need for an international agreement (instead of a regional arrangement) on minimum food standards and invites the Director-General to submit proposals for a joint FAO/WHO program for food standards to the FAO Conference.
14. The first regional FAO conference, the Council of the Codex Alimentarius Europaeus adopted a resolution to request that FAO and WHO take over and globalize its food safety standards work.
15. During the same year, WHO, the Economic Commission for Europe (ECE), the Organization for Economic Cooperation and Development (OECD) and the Council of the Codex Alimentarius at the FAO conference created the Codex Alimentarius and agrees to launch an international food standards program.
16. In 1961, the FAO Conference creates a Codex Alimentarius Commission and requests early approval by WHO of a joint FAO/WHO food standards program.
17. In 1962, the Joint FAO/WHO Food Standards Conference requests that the Codex Alimentarius Commission implement a joint FAO/WHO food standards program and create the Codex Alimentarius.
18. In 1963, the World Health Assembly accepts the importance of WHO's role in food safety and public health, and approves the creation of the Joint FAO/WHO Programme on Food Standards and adopts the statutes of the Codex Alimentarius Commission.[93]

In the multilateral system, FAO, WHO and Codex Alimentarius develop food safety standards for national food systems, global food trade and agrifood commodities. Through the harmonization of Codex Alimentarius food safety standards, national governments are strengthening consumer protection and public health in the global food system. In this regard, FAO, WHO and Codex Alimentarius now provide the multilateral framework for food safety standards harmonization and mutual recognition in the global food system.

Plant Health and Food Safety in Global Agri-Food Industries: The Role of IPPC

The International Plant Protection Convention (IPPC) is an international treaty that provides a regulatory standards framework for the identification, control and eradication of plant pests, crop contamination and food safety hazards. Through the ratification of the International Plant Protection Convention in 1997, and the WTO SPS Agreement on the Application of Phytosanitary and Sanitary Measures, a multilateral regulatory framework now exists for the harmonization of plant and crop safety standards. In its role as the main multilateral agreement for the protection of plant and crop health and food safety, the IPPC developed the International Standards for Phytosanitary Measures (ISPMs) through the work of the Interim Commission on Phytosanitary Measures (ICPM).[94] Through the implementation of these agreements, national governments are able to exchange information for the identification, eradication and inspection of plants and crop products.

The IPPC secretariat is based in the FAO headquarters in Rome. The main activities of the IPPC are plant and crop health standard-setting, information exchange and technical assistance on the inspection, quarantine and management of plant diseases and pest infestations. In addition to the work of the secretariat, the IPPC works through National Plant Protection Organizations (NPPOs). In this regard, NPPOs work to ensure that pest-free places of plant, crop and food production are in compliance with IPPC phytosanitary regulations and standards. The NPPOs must meet the following requirements:

- provision of systems to establish pest freedom
- provision of systems to maintain pest freedom
- verification that pest freedom is attained and maintained
- verification and certification of plant and crop identity, consignment integrity and phytosanitary security
- creation of buffer zones for pest-free zones and pest-free production sites.[95]

The achievement of these plant health and food safety goals requires effective pest risk analysis, risk assessment, risk management and agreement on phytosanitary regulations.[96] As global demand for foods produced from plants, cereals and grain crops increases, the importance of this multilateral food safety agreement is rapidly growing. In this respect, food safety and public health risks are from plant diseases and contamination of cereals and grains with mycotoxins, aflatoxins and other diseases that threaten food and feed safety. Therefore, the IPPC also works through Regional Plant Protection Organizations (RPPOs), and their contracting parties to carry out the plant health standards work. The regional plant protection organizations are as follows:

- Asia and Pacific Plant Protection Commission (APPPC)
- Caribbean Plant Protection Commission (CPPC)
- Comite Regional de Sanidad Vegetal para el Cono Sur (CONSAVE)
- Comunidad Adina (CA)
- European and Mediterranean Plant Protection Organization (EPPO)
- Inter-African Phytosanitary Council (IAPSC)
- North American Plant Protection Organization (NAPPO)
- Organismo Internacional Regional de Sanidad Agropecuraria (OIRSA)
- Pacific Plant Protection Organization (PPPO).

In support of international food trade, and the globalization of food production systems, the IPPC is working to establish pest-free areas and zones to ensure the containment and eradication of harmful plant diseases and crop pests. Through the concept of 'pest freedom', exporting countries provide assurances to importing countries that plants, crops and related food products are free from pests and dangerous diseases. In turn, pest freedom also confirms that crops and plants used for food and feed production meet the phytosanitary regulations and safety standards.

OIE and Animal Health: Food Safety, Veterinary Public Health and Livestock Products

The OIE is a multilateral organization dedicated to the promotion of veterinary public health standards and regulatory harmonization in the area of animal health protection. The organization was created in January 1924 by 28 founding countries, and is based in Paris, France. The official mission of OIE in the area of food safety regulation, animal health and veterinary public health is as follows:

- to guarantee the transparency of animal disease status on a global basis

- to collect, analyze and disseminate veterinary scientific information
- to provide expertise and promote international solidarity for the control of animal diseases
- to guarantee the safety of global food trade and global meat and livestock industries by developing sanitary rules for the production, marketing and trade of animals and livestock products.[97]

In light of the importance of animal diseases and veterinary public health for food safety, the OIE is increasing its role and collaboration with FAO, WHO and Codex Alimentarius for the harmonization of animal health, and food and feed safety standards. In this new capacity, OIE is increasing its focus on scientific standard-setting, animal livestock production and food safety. Through this food safety initiative, the OIE is working on the linkage between zoonoses and diseases transmitted to humans through food, regardless of whether or not the animals and livestock are affected. In this new OIE activity, food safety hazards and risks will be identified, assessed, communicated and managed prior to the primary processing of meat, fish and livestock food products by agri-food companies and industries.

The OIE has a formal Working Group on Animal Production and Food Safety that provides technical assistance and regulatory standards guidelines for food safety and farm livestock management. In addition to the International Animal Health Code, the OIE is intensifying its efforts for animal health, public health and consumer protection relative to *tuberculosis*, *brucellosis*, *cysticercoses* and *trichinellosis*. Animal livestock diseases that do not always affect animals, but can be transmitted to humans through the food chain such as *campylobacteriosis*, *salmonellosis*, *listeriosis* and *enterotoxigenic Escherichia coli* are also included in this effort.[98]

The OIE Working Group is reviewing the following Codex Alimentarius Commission food safety codes relative their implications for animal health and livestock management:

- Draft Code of Practice for Meat and Poultry Hygiene
- General Principles of Food Hygiene
- Code of Practice for Milk and Milk Products
- Draft Code of Practice for Animal Feeding
- Use of Veterinary Drugs
- Draft Code of Practice for Fish and Fishery Products
- Draft Code of Practice for Aquaculture.[99]

Finally, the OIE in cooperation with Codex Alimentarius is working to improve the knowledge and understanding of food safety and veterinary public health in animal production by farmers and veterinarians. In this regard, OIE is working in cooperation with Codex Alimentarius on the issues of antibiotic resistance, 'Good Farming Practices', and the safety of animal livestock derived from modern biotechnology.[100]

VI CONCLUSION: REGULATORY HARMONIZATION AND FOOD SAFETY IN GLOBAL FOOD AND AGRICULTURE MARKETS AND INDUSTRIES

In conclusion, the globalization of food systems, agri-food firms and industries, and the growth of international food trade are increasing the need for the multilateral harmonization of food safety regulations. In this regard, many developing countries and regions lack the regulatory policy, market governance capacity and food safety infrastructure needed to govern food safety and competition in national and global agri-food industries. As a result, consumers in developed and developing countries are exposed to increasing food safety risks from unsafe food, bioterrorism and contaminated food crop and animal livestock products in global agri-food industries.[101]

As the threat of bioterrorism and the deliberate contamination of integrated food supply chains and networked global agri-food industries grows, national governments must harmonize food safety regulations to protect citizens and nations. In response to these regulatory challenges, the governance of food safety requires stronger regulatory control of cross-border competition and food chain integration by global agri-businesses, food companies and biotechnology firms. Likewise, traditional farming, food crop, livestock and fish production, animal and plant health, GM food production and food-processing must be regulated in accordance with WTO SPS and Codex Alimentarius standards.

In this respect, national governments must regulate the food safety impacts of firm and market competition in global food supply chain industries. However, many agri-business, food companies and biotechnology industry interests are pushing for 'market friendly' regulations that promote economic efficiency and profits over the primacy of consumer protection and public health. Nevertheless, overreliance on market forces and self-correction mechanisms for the protection of food safety increases the risks to consumers and nations. Furthermore, the systemic effects of market failure, and regulatory capture by large agri-business and food companies, can endanger consumer safety, public health and food product choice. Ultimately, national governments must regulate firm and industry competition to ensure food safety in national food systems and global agri-food industries.

As the decade unfolds, regional free trade, market integration and globalization of agri-food firms and networked food supply chain industries can result in regulatory harmonization or regulatory competition by national governments. In the case of regulatory competition, destructive patterns of food safety regulation and institutional competition by nations can occur in an attempt to gain competitive advantage in global food markets and agri-food industries. In turn, consumer protection, public health and effective competition in national food systems and global agri-food industries can be weakened through the use of less than optimal regulations and divergent food safety standards.[102] Consequently, concerns over food safety standards 'races to the bottom or the top' must be addressed through regulatory harmonization, policy cooperation, institutional convergence and multilateral organizations.

Finally, collective policy action by national governments, and normative consensus on regulatory standards harmonization through multilateral organizations such as FAO, WHO and Codex Alimentarius, the WTO, OIE and the IPPC is the new framework for the global governance of food safety. In this multilateral framework for the regulation of food safety in national food systems and global agri-food industries, governments are engaging in multi-level and multi-jurisdictional policy cooperation to establish a 'rule of soft food safety regulatory law'.[103] Therefore, the regulation of food safety in national food systems, regional food supply chains and global agri-food industries requires harmonization through networks of multilateral institutions in the twenty-first century.

NOTES

1. United States Department of Justice – Antitrust Division (2000), *International Competition Policy Advisory Committee to the Attorney General and Assistant Attorney General for Antitrust Final Report* Washington, DC: Department of Justice – Antitrust Division, pp. 1–7.
2. WHO (2000), *WHO Global Strategy for Food Safety*, Geneva, Switzerland: WHO.
3. Bruinsma, Jelle (ed.) (2003), *World Agriculture: Towards 2015/2030 – An FAO Perspective*, Earthscan, Rome, Italy: FAO.
4. WHO (1999), *Food Safety by the Director-General*, 2 December, EB 105/10, Geneva, Switzerland: WHO.
5. See 'Origins of Codex Alimentarius', p. 1, www.fao.org/docrep. In fact, Assyrian tablets have been found that document the methods of food weights and measures, while ancient Egyptian scrolls discuss food labeling of specified foods and agriculture products.
6. Braithwaite, J. and P. Drahos (2002), *Global Business Regulation*, Cambridge, MA: Cambridge University Press.
7. Ibid.

8. Ibid.
9. Ibid., p. 3.
10. Institute of Medicine and National Research Council (1998), *Ensuring Safe Food: From Production to Consumption*, Washington, DC: National Academy Press, p. 18.
11. Ibid., p. 3–4.
12. Ibid., p. 19.
13. BSE has now been found in goats in France.
14. In the case of BSE, avian flu and dioxin contamination of chicken feed, the governments delayed action, and consequently delayed the risk management process in an effort to protect national economic and food trade interests.
15. The full report of the South African chemical and biotechnology program (Project Coast) can be found in the Truth and Reconciliation trial final reports. In addition, the information can be found on the www.nti.org/e_researchSAfrica.
16. In this instance, the use of crop dusters is now heavily monitored in the US, given the easy access of the terrorist to agricultural system prior to the 11 September terrorist attacks.
17. 'Review for imported meat laws', BBC, 29 March 2003.
18. Dixon, J., A. Gulliver and D. Gibson (2001), *Global Farming Systems Study: Challenges and Priorities to 2030 – Synthesis and Global Overview*, Rome, FAO/World Bank, pp. 5–15. From the 1980s onwards, international food markets grew as national governments in developed and developing countries moved to comply with GATT and WTO policies for the global liberalization of agricultural trade. Eventually, by the 1990s, the structural adjustment requirements of the World Bank and IMF resulted in decreasing public sector investment in domestic farming, agriculture, food production and rural infrastructure.
19. Ibid., p. 16.
20. The Governments of Thailand and Britain moved to protect their respective poultry and beef industries and delayed food safety action and risk communication and management of Mad Cow disease and avian flu. Therefore, good farming and agriculture production practices for animal health and animal feed standards, and state-of-the-art veterinary public health programs are required for the prevention, early detection and eradication of animal livestock diseases and to protect food safety.
21. OIE (2002), *Report of the Meeting of the OIE Working Group on Animal Production and Food Safety*, November, Paris, p. 3.
22. The segregation of GM food crops is needed to ensure that unsafe GM foods can traced and recalled. Likewise, plant and crop species preservation are also needed to protect the safety of the food system.
23. See official website of the International Plant Protection Convention, International Phytosanitary Portal (IPP), http://www.ippc.int/ipp/EN/default.jsp.
24. The decline of independent farming systems and small farmers across the globe represents a growing threat to the integrity and safety of national food systems, and global agri-food industries.
25. The consolidation of global agri-businesses, food companies and food supply chain industries, is raising regulatory concerns over food safety. As a result of these trends, national governments are under increasing pressure in the OECD countries and developing nations to regulate competition in food supply chains and global agri-food industries.
26. Bruinsma, Jelle (ed.) (2003).
27. Eaton, Charles and Andrew W. Shepherd (2001), *Contract Farming – Partnership for Growth*, FAO Agricultural Series Bulletin 145, Rome: FAO, p. 1–6.
28. Venturini, Luciano (2002), *The Food System in Transition: An EU Perspective*, Working Paper WP02-2, presented at the Joint Conference on Food, Agriculture and the Environment, 25–28 August, Red Cedar Lake, Wisconsin.
29. 'Food "risks" of EU expansion', *BBC News*, Wednesday, 15 January 2003.
30. See WHO Annual African Food Safety Reports.
31. See Meat Fraud examples on BBC News Online – Thursday, 21 December 2000,

'Condemned meat conspiracy exposed', http://news.bbc.co.uk/1/hi/uk/108154.stm, Friday, 29 August 2003, 'Illegal meat trade's "drug profits"', http://newsbbc.co.uk/hi/uk news/England/nothinghamshire/3190889.stm, BBC Online – 3 January 2005, Food "police" fight illicit trade', http://news.bbc.uk.zhi/uk/news/wales 4220949.stm.

32. Baron, David P. (2003), *Business and its Environment*, 4th edition, Upper Saddle, NJ: Prentice Hall, pp. 3–6
33. Moore, Mark H. (2001), 'The market versus the forum', in John D. Donahue and Joseph S. Nye Jr (eds), *Governance Amid Bigger and Better Markets*, Washington, DC: Brookings Institution, pp. 324–5.
34. WHO (2002), *WHO Global Food Strategy for Food Safety*, Geneva, Switzerland, p. 6.
35. Cox, Robert W. (1994), 'Global restructuring: making sense of the changing international political economy', in Richard Stubbs and Geoffrey R.D. Underhill (eds), *Political Economy and the Changing Global Order*, New York: St. Martin's Press, pp. 45–57.
36. Mutual recognition agreements are increasingly used as a first step to regulatory harmonization and market integration through bilateral and regional free trade agreements.
37. Braithwaite, J. and P. Drahos (2002).
38. United States Department of Justice – Antitrust Division (2000).
39. Regulatory harmonization requires the reform and realignment of national laws for consumer protection, public health, the maximization welfare and the public safety in response to regional free trade, market integration and globalization. The European Union is the most advanced model of regional market integration and regulatory harmonization as a result of the creation of the Single Market in 1992. Since that time, regulatory harmonization is achieved through the use of mutual recognition of national regulations and industry standards, the identification of core health, consumer protection and product safety requirements, and the use of technical specifications by national standards and conformity assessment bodies. See Majone, pp. 3–4.
40. Etzioni, Amitai (2004), *From Empire to Community: A New Approach to International Relations*, New York and Basingstoke: Palgrave Macmillan.
41. In the 'post-Fordist' system of flexible manufacturing, agri-businesses and food companies increasingly shift food production and processing outside of their home countries. As a result, the regulatory jurisdiction of national food safety, public health, antitrust and competition policies, laws and regulations are unable to govern food firm and industry competition and food standards enforcement beyond a nation's borders. See Majone (2001).
42. Public Citizen (2003), *The WTO Comes to Dinner – US Implementation of Trade Rules Bypasses Food Safety Requirements*, Washington, DC: Public Citizen, pp. I–v, 1–8.
43. See Picicciotto, Sol (1996), 'Interaction between jurisdictions and networks', in Joseph McCahery, William Bratton, Sol Picciotto and Collin Scott (eds), *International Regulatory Competiton and Coordination*, Oxford: Clarendon Press.
44. See Etzioni, Amitai (1968), *The Active Society: A Theory of Societal and Political Processes*, New York and London: Free Press/Macmillan, p. 106. According to Amitai Etzioni, the state is mechanism for top-down control of socio-economic and market forces versus an 'upward' system of consensus formation. Therefore, regulatory harmonization within and between nations should be viewed and understood as market governance and control processes that are part of a multilateral network of local and federal government systems in an age of globalization.
45. Donahue, John D. and Joseph S. Nye Jr (2001), *Governance Amid Bigger, Better Markets*, Washington, DC: Brookings Institution, pp. 5–9.
46. See Murphy, Dale D. (2004), *The Structure of Regulatory Competition*, Oxford and New York: Oxford University Press. Also see Esty and Geradin (2001), pp. xxiii. Also see Charles Tiebout (1956) 'A pure theory of local expenditures', *Journal of Political Economy*, **64** (5), pp. 416–24.
47. See Picicciotto (1996).
48. This view is also important since classical and neoliberal theories argue against strong

government regulation and policy interventions to protect consumers from market failures. Instead, market forces are viewed as the optimal mechanism for the correction of problems and deficiencies that arise during the course of firm and industry competition. See Daniels (1991).

49. Ibid.
50. Public Citizen (2003), *WTO Comes to Dinner – US Implementation of Trade Rules Bypasses Food Safety Requirements*, A Special Report by Public Citizen's Global Trade Watch and Critical Mass Energy and Environment Program, Washington, DC, pp. 5–8. Also see Lucinda Sikes (1998), *The Impact of Harmonization on US Food Standards*, twenty-first Annual National Food Policy Conference, 24 March, http://www.publiccitizen.org/trade/harmonization/comments/articles.cfm? ID=4355. See Public Citizen Global Trade Watch publications on globalization and free trade, http://www.publiccitizen.org/trade.
51. In some cases, national governments may end up weakening optimal regulatory environments to accommodate nations with limited or non-existent regulatory capacity. In fact, this is typically, the argument used by opponents of the EU, regional free trade agreements, that is, NAFTA, and WTO market liberalization.
52. The BSE crisis increased the focus of governments and food safety regulators on veterinary public health and animal health as the starting point of consumer protection and food safety regulation in global agri-food and animal feed industries.
53. Daniel Esty and Damien Geradin (eds) (2001), *Regulatory Competition and Economic Integration*, New York and London: Oxford University Press, pp. 32–40. Esty and Geradin argue that competitive pressures alone are insufficient mechanisms to ensure the effective governance of firms and markets.
54. Esty and Geradin (2001), pp. xxi.
55. Picciotto (1996), p. 91.
56. Esty and Geradin (2001), pp. xxi, 351–3.
57. Vietor, Richard (1994), *Contrived Competition: Regulation and Deregulation in America*, Cambridge, MA: Belknap/Harvard University Press, pp. 310–11.
58. Baron, D. (2003), *Business and its Environment*, 4th edn, Upper Saddle River, NJ: Prentice-Hall, p. 281.
59. Donahue and Nye (2001), pp. 1–9
60. See Vogel, David (1981), 'The "New" social regulation in historical and comparative perspective', in Thomas K. McCraw (ed.), *Regulation in Perspective: Historical Essays*, Boston, MA: Harvard Business School Press, pp. 155–85.
61. See Majone, Giandomenico (1990), *Deregulation or Re-Regulation: Regulatory Reform in Europe and the United States*, London: Pinter, p. 2.
62. Through the process of regulatory and market competition between nations the effective governance of firms and markets is weakened to successfully attract corporate investment, trade and FDI. Therefore, the regulation of firms and industries were national in focus and territorial scope.
63. Collective action by national and regional antitrust, competition and regulatory authorities is now required to govern domestic and global markets and industries.
64. US Department of Justice (2000), pp. 33–85.
65. In response to market globalization, the US, EU and Japanese governments, as well as other regulatory and market governance authorities, are coordinating the regulation of firm and industry competition in the global industries. In a growing number of cases and industry sectors, antitrust and regulatory policy cooperation occurs through multilateral institutions in accordance with international public laws, and legally binding treaty agreements between nations.
66. Beckert, Jens (2002), *Beyond the Market: The Social Foundations of Economic Efficiency*, Princeton, NJ: Princeton University Press.
67. See Amitai Etzioni (1988), *The Moral Dimension: Toward a New Economics*, New York and London: Free Press/Macmillan Press, pp. 199–216. According to Etzioni, competition is in fact conflict that must be managed with clear rules in market economy and society to protect the collective good.

68. Chicago School has limitations as a model for competition and government regulation of firms and industries.
69. New IO perspectives attempt to update the Chicago School, but fails to address the fundamental issues identified in the Structural School.
70. This is illustrated by the efforts of WHO to reduce salt and sugar consumption to fight the global obesity crisis.
71. In the context of self-regulation, governments are involved and monitor the effectiveness of voluntary industry standards and codes of practice. The moral implications of government regulation are often weighed against the economic efficiency and rational choice aspects of global neoliberal market and trading systems (ibid., pp. 364–80), According to the authors, industrial morality is an important factor for challenging the status quo, and launching the discussion and development of rules of conduct for firms in an industry. See Gunningham and Rees (1997).
72. Ibid. p. 366.
73. Muller, Karl H. (2002), 'On socio-economic embeddedness', in J. Rogers Hollingsworth, Karl H. Muller and Ellen Jane Hollingsworth (eds), *Advancing Socio-Economics – An Institutional Perspective*, Lantham, MD: Rowman & Littlefield, pp. 59–78.
74. Ibid., p. 2. Through the growing public health campaign against obesity, food companies are facing a growing risk of product liability. Finally, some food industry observers are warning about the growing threat of class-action law suits and regulatory control of world class food companies along the lines of the tobacco industry case in the United States.
75. 'Under fire, food giants switch to healthier fare', Bruce Horovitz, *USA Today*, Tuesday, 1 July 2003, pp. 1–2. For example, Kraft Foods, the largest food company in the United States, is responding to public pressure, consumer health concerns and WHO warnings on the global obesity epidemic by changing the portions, packaging, fat content and calorie counts of its products.
76. Breyer, Stephen (1982), *Regulation and its Reform*, Cambridge, MA: Harvard University Press, pp. 115–16.
77. Professor Tim Lang, International Food Safety Conference 'CIES – The Food Business Forum, Executive Summary, Food Safety – A Risky Business', 29–30 January 2004, Barcelona, p. 3.
78. Cary Coglianese and David Lazer (2002a), *Management Based Regulation: Prescribing Private Management to Achieve Public Goals*, Joint Center, AEI-Brookings Joint Center for Regulatory Studies, Working Paper 02–11, Washington, DC: Brookings Institution, pp. 3–8.
79. Coglianese, Cary and David Lazer (2002b),'Management-based regulatory strategies', in John D. Donahue and Joseph S. Nye (eds), *Market Based Governance*, Cambridge, MA: Visions of Governance in the Twenty-First Century, and Washington, DC, Brookings Institution Press, pp. 201–19.
80. International Food Safety Conference (2004), welcome address by Fons Schmid-Royal Ahold, the Netherlands, p. 3.
81. See Drahos and Braithwaite (2002), discussion of the role of industry and regulatory standards. According to the authors, regulatory standards can be manipulated by competing government and corporate business and public policy interests.
82. Institute of Medicine and National Research Council (1998), p. 5.
83. Ibid.
84. Ibid.
85. Ibid.
86. In many ways, the Uruguay Round served as a major and permanent turning point in the globalization of food and agricultural industries.
87. The formal agreement on the Sanitary and Phytosanitary Measures (SPS agreement) came into force with the creation of the WTO on 1 January 1995. This agreement was specifically designed to establish legally binding rules and regulations for the governance of food safety in global agri-food industries. Through this international agreement, national governments of over 132 countries reached normative consensus and

took collective regulatory action to create a 'rule of law' for food safety regulation in global food trade and agri-food products.

88. The WTO Agreement on the Application of Sanitary and Phytosanitory Measures (SPS Agreement), http://www.org/english/tratop_e/sps_e/spagr_e.htm.
89. Ibid.
90. Ibid.
91. Ibid. See Article 5 on the Assessment of Risk and Determination of the Appropriate Level of Sanitary and Phytosanitary Protection.
92. Ibid. See Article 3 on Harmonization and Article 4 on Equivalence.
93. FAO/WHO (1999), *Understanding the Codex Alimentarius, Food and Agriculture Organization of the United Nations and the World Health Organization*, Rome. See the Origins of the Codex Alimentarius, p. 2, http://www.fao.org/documents/show_cdr.asp?url_file=docrep/w9114e/w9114e03.htm.
94. International Phytosanitary Portal (IPP) – official website for the International Plant Protection Convention, International Standards for Phytosanitary Measures, http://www.ippc.int/ipp/en/default/.jsp. ISPM No. 01: Principles of Plant Quarantine as Related to International Trade – February 1995. ISPM No. 02: Guidelines for Pest Risk Analysis – April 1996. ISPM No. 04: Requirements for the Establishment of Pest Free Areas – February 1996. Also see Draft International Standards for Phytosanitary Measures for Country Consultation (ISPMS) for 2005 at http://www.ippc.int/servlet/cosservlet?status=NDOXM50syZpwVujjMzPsomMzc9a29z.
95. IPPC (1999), *Requirements for the Establishment of Pest Free Places of Production and Pest Free Production Sites*, Publication Number 10, October 1999, pp. 6–9. Main IPPC Website – National Reports and Information on NPPOs, http://www.ippc.int/ipp/en /default/.jsp.
96. FAO-IPPC (1995), *International Standards for Phytosanitary Measures – Principles of Plant Quarantine Related to International Trade*, Number 1, February 1995, p. 3, FAO, Rome. See Main IPPC Website – Regional Reports and Information on RPPOs, http://www.ippc.int/ipp/en/default/.jsp.
97. OIE official website – The OIE at a Glance http://www.ote.int/eng/oie/en_objectifs/hem. OIE (2002), *Report of the Meeting of the OIE Working Group on Animal Production Food Safety, Paris*, 18–20. November 2003, www.oie/int/eng/sewsanitaire/enintroduction. htm, OIE (2003), *Report of the Second Meeting of the OIE Working Group on Animal Production Food Safety*, Rome, 8–9 July, pp. 15–24.
98. OIE (2002), pp. 2–3.
99. Ibid., p. 4.
100. Ibid.
101. Institute of Medicine and National Research Council (1998). p. 46.
102. Ibid., p. 350.
103. Picciotto (1996), pp. 120–23.

REFERENCES

Albert, M. (1993), *Capitalism Against Capitalism*, London: Whurr Publishers, pp. 101–13 and 226–9.

Baron, David P. (2003), *Business and its Environment*, 4th edition, Upper Saddle River, NJ: Prentice Hall.

Beckert, Jens (2002), *Beyond the Market: The Social Foundations of Economic Efficiency*, Princeton, NJ: Princeton University Press.

Breyer, Stephen (1982), *Regulation and Its Reform*, Cambridge, MA: Harvard University Press.

Bruinsma, Jelle (ed.) (2003), *World Agriculture: Towards 2015/2030 – An FAO Perspective*, Earthscan Rome: FAO.

CIES – International Food Safety Conference (2004), 'CIES – The Food Business Forum, Executive Summary, Food Safety – A Risky Business', 29–30 January, Barcelona.

Coglianese, Cary and David Lazer (2002a), *Management Based Regulation: Prescribing Private Management to Achieve Public Goals*, Joint Center, AEI-Brookings Joint Center for Regulatory Studies, Working Paper 02–11, Washington, DC: Brookings Institution.

Coglianese, Cary and David Lazer (2002b),'Management-based regulatory strategies', in John D. Donahue and Joseph S. Nye (eds), *Market Based Governance*, Cambridge, MA: Visions of Governance in the Twenty-First Century, and Washington DC: Brookings Institution Press.

Cox, Robert W. (1994), 'Global restructuring: making sense of the changing international political economy', in Richard Stubbs and Geoffrey R.D. Underhill (eds), *Political Economy and the Changing Global Order*, New York: St. Martin's Press.

Daniels, R.J. (1991), 'Should provinces compete? The case for a competitive corporate law market', *McGill Law School Journal*, **36** (1), 130–90.

Dixon, J., A. Gulliver and D. Gibson (2001), *Global Farming Systems Study: Challenges and Priorities to 2030 – Synthesis and Global Overview*, Rome: FAO/World Bank.

Donahue, John D. and Joseph S. Nye Jr (2001), *Governance Amid Bigger, Better Markets*, Washington, DC: Brookings Institution.

Drahos, P. and J. Braithwaite (2000), *Global Business Regulation*, Cambridge, MA: Cambridge University Press.

Eaton, Charles and Andrew W. Shepherd (2001), *Contract Farming – Partnership for Growth*, FAO Agricultural Series Bulletin 145, Rome: FAO, pp. 1–6.

Eisner, M. (1991), *Antitrust and the Triumph of Economics, Institutions, Expertise and Policy Change*, Chapel Hill: University of North Carolina Press.

Esty, Daniel and Damien Geradin (2001), *Regulatory Competition and Economic Integration*, New York and London: Oxford University Press.

Etzioni, Amitai (1968), *The Active Society: A Theory of Societal and Political Processes*, New York, and London: Free Press/Macmillan.

Etzioni, Amitai (1988), *The Moral Dimension: Toward a New Economics*, New York and London: Free Press/Macmillan.

Etzioni, Amitai (2004), *From Empire to Community: A New Approach to International Relations*, New York and Basingstoke: Palgrave Macmillan.

FAO (2003) *World Agriculture: Towards 2015/2030 – An FAO Perspective*, edited by Jelle Bruinsma, Earthscan, Rome: FAO.

FAO-IPPC (1995), *International Standards for Phytosanitary Measures – Principles of Plant Quarantine Related to International Trade*, Number 1, February 1995, p. 3, FAO, Rome.

Fox, Eleanor M. (2001) 'Anti trust law on a global scale: races up, down and sideways', in Daniel Esty and Damien Geradin (eds), R*egulatory Competition and Economic Integration*, New York and London: Oxford University Press.

Gunningham, Neil and Joseph Rees (1997), 'Industry self-regulation: an institutional perspective', *Law & Policy*, **19** (4), pp. 364–80.

Institute of Medicine and National Research Council (1998), *Ensuring Safe Food: From Production to Consumption*, Washington, DC: National Academy Press.

IPPC (1999), *Requirements for the Establishment of Pest Free Places of Production Sites*, Publication Number 10, October 1999, pp. 6–9.

Maier, H.G. (1982), 'Extraterritorial jurisdiction at a crossroads: an intersection

between public and private international law', *American Journal of International Law*, **76** (2), 280–320.
Majone, Giandomenico (1990), *Deregulation or Re-Regulation: Regulatory Reform in Europe and the United States*, London: Pinter.
Majone, G. (2001), 'Regulatory legitimacy in the United States and the European Union', in Kalypso Nicolaidis and Robert House (eds), *The Federal Vision: Legitimacy and Levels of Governance in the US and the European Union*, Oxford University Press, pp. 252–74.
Moore, Mark H. (2001), 'The market versus the forum', in John D. Donahue and Joseph S. Nye Jr (eds), *Governance Amid Bigger and Better Markets*, Washington, DC: Brookings Institution.
Muller, Karl H., (2002), 'On socio-economic embeddedness', in J. Rogers Hollingsworth, Karl H. Muller and Ellen Jane Hollingsworth (eds), *Advancing Socio-Economics – An Institutional Perspective*, Lantham, MD: Rowman & Littlefield, pp. 59–78.
Murphy, Dale D. (2004), *The Structure of Regulatory Competition*, Oxford and New York: Oxford University Press.
OIE (2002), *Report of the Meeting of the OIE Working Group on Animal Production and Food Safety*, Paris: OIE.
OIE (2003), *Report of the Second Meeting of the OIE Working Group on Animal Production Food Safety*, Rome, 8–9 July, pp. 15–24.
Picicciotto, Sol (1996), 'Interaction between jurisdictions and networks, in Joseph McCahery, William Bratton, Sol Picciotto and Collin Scott (eds), *International Regulatory Competiton and Coordination*, Oxford: Clarendon Press.
Public Citizen (2003), *The WTO Comes to Dinner – US Implementation of Trade Rules Bypasses Food Safety Requirements*, A special Report by Public Citizen's Global Trade Watch and Critical Mass Energy and Environment Program, Washington, DC: Public Citizen.
Sikes, Lucinda (1998), 'The impact of harmonization on US food standards', 21st Annual National Food Policy Conference, 24 March, www.publiccitizen.org/trade/hormonization/comments/articles.cfm?ID=4355.
Tiebout, Charles (1956), 'A pure theory of local expenditures', *Journal of Political Economy*, **64** (5), pp. 416–24.
United States Department of Justice (2000) *International Competition Policy Advisory Committee To the Attorney General and Assistant Attorney General for Antitrust Final Report*, Washington, DC: US Department of Justice Antitrust Division.
Venturini, Luciano (2002), *The Food System in Transition: An EU Perspective*, Working Paper WP02-2, 25–28 August, Red Cedar Lake, Wisconsin, presented at the Joint Conference on Food, Agriculture and the Environment.
Vietor, Richard (1994), *Contrived Competition: Regulation and Deregulation in America*, Cambridge, MA: Belknap/Harvard University Press.
Vogel, David (1981), 'The "new" social regulation in historical and comparative perspective', in Thomas K. McCraw (ed.), *Regulation in Perspective: Historical Essays*, Boston, MA: Harvard Business School Press, pp. 155–85.
WHO (1999), *Food Safety Report by the Director General*, 2 December 1999, EB105/10, Geneva: WHO.
WHO (2002), *WHO Global Strategy for Food Safety*, Geneva: WHO.
The WTO Agreement on the Application of Sanitary and Phytosanitary Measures (SPS Agreement), http://www.wto.org/English/tratop_e/sps_e/spagr_e.htm.

2. Globalization and food safety in global agri-food industries

Reba A. Carruth

I GLOBALIZATION OF AGRI-FOOD MARKETS AND INDUSTRIES

Introduction

From a historical perspective, the globalization of agri-food industries evolved over several centuries of agricultural commodity and animal livestock trade (Braithwaite and Drahos 2002). During this period, the Silk Road in Asia, Dutch trade in the Spice Islands and European colonial trading systems resulted in a global system of East–West and North–South trade. From the fifteenth century onwards, British, French, Portuguese, Dutch and Spanish colonies and trading companies were established to secure vast supplies of agricultural commodities from the fifteenth century onwards. Over time, European colonies in the African, South Asian, Asia-Pacific and American regions were integrated into a vast system of global agricultural commodity trade and food supply chain industries.

In this system, a core and periphery structure was established in which the European colonial powers controlled and sourced vital agricultural commodities out of South Asia, Africa, the Asia-Pacific and the Americas at very little cost. The primary agricultural commodities were processed and transformed into value-added agri-food products for trade, commerce and financial market speculation in Europe, North America and Japan.[1] By the nineteenth century, the expansion of transatlantic and colonial networks of agricultural commodity trade in Asia, Africa, the Caribbean and Latin America led to the creation of modern agri-businesses and food companies. Through this process, powerful buyer and food supply chains emerged in Europe, the United States and Japan by the end of the century. The result of this phenomenon was the rapid integration of agricultural commodity chains into emerging global agri-food industries.

By the early twentieth century, new systems of agricultural production and food-processing emerged, and created a new phase of agri-food industry globalization. During this period, more complex systems of agricultural commodity trade, and modern corporate systems for agricultural and industrial food production emerged. As the century progressed, competition in national and global agri-food industries was dominated and controlled by specialized grain and commodity traders and agri-food merchants based in the transatlantic countries (Porter 1986). For example, powerful agri-businesses, such as Cargill emerged as powerful industry actors and forces of socio-economic change in the United States. Eventually, large agri-businesses in the United States and Europe became drivers of corporate innovation and powerful drivers of agri-food industry globalization.[2]

In the early post-Second World War period, the multinational corporations grew in response to explosive consumer demand in the 1960s.[3] In many cases, international expansion of sales, processing and manufacturing operations through foreign direct investment provided access to markets, and a structure for global industry production. However, global marketing, research and development (R&D) innovations in biotechnology and cross-border competition increasingly weakened the regulatory control of national governments over agri-food industries.[4] From the 1980s, onwards, neoliberal paradigms of global trade, market liberalization, deregulation, structural adjustment and privatization of agricultural commodity chains and markets in Africa, Asia and Latin America weakened the negotiation power of local farmers and food producers.[5]

By the end of the twentieth century, the rise of flexible manufacturing in the transatlantic region, Australia and Japan resulted in the rise of powerful agricultural commodity buyer and food supply chains.[6] During this period, consolidation of global companies and market systems gave rise to powerful agri-businesses, food companies, food retailers and global agri-food industries. But more important, globalization weakened the regulatory effectiveness of national governments. Instead, national governments were forced to negotiate with powerful transatlantic and global food companies for direct investment, technology transfer and job creation.[7]

As a result of the implementation of structural adjustment policies in many African, Latin American and Asian countries, the supplier power of world-class agri-businesses and food companies in the transatlantic region and OECD countries was strengthened.[8] For example, during the 1980s and 1990s, consolidation of the US food retailing industry accelerated. From the period from 1987 to 1998, most merger and acquisition strategies were well under way among the top 20 food retailers in the United States.[9] At the start of the twenty-first century, large vertically integrated agri-businesses, food companies and biotechnology firms continue to consolidate agri-food industries through FDI, strategic alliances and contract farming systems.[10]

II GLOBAL FOOD COMMODITY CHAIN AND AGRI-FOOD INDUSTRY CONCENTRATION

Global Food Commodity Chain Integration

By the start of the 2000s, the structure of global agricultural commodity chains and global agri-food industries had changed rapidly (Raufman et al. 2000). During this period, the comparative advantages of agricultural commodity producers and independent farmers rapidly declined relative to knowledge, capital and information based systems of global competition by corporate agri-business. As a result, transatlantic and Asia-Pacific based food companies were able to concentrate their supplier and buyer power in global agricultural commodity chains.[11]

By the year 2000, processed foods accounted for approximately 68 per cent of global food trade with concentration occurring with the following products; cereals, fruit and vegetables, pulses, tropical juices and beverages and poultry products. Furthermore, the concentration of global food-processing industries by a small number of agri-businesses, food processors and retailers based in transatlantic and OECD countries occurred during this period.[12] In contrast, developing countries which provide the primary agricultural commodities are less integrated in the value-added segments of the global agri-food industry.[13] Instead, developing countries were able to position their agri-food products for the lower price segments of the global poultry, fruit and vegetable, tree nut, diary and spice markets.[14]

Since the start of the 2000s, many developing countries have increased their dependence on preferential trade and regional free trade agreements as policy and market strategies for agri-food industry growth and diversification. In contrast, transatlantic and OECD food producers, agri-businesses, food processors and food retailers are rapidly consolidating global agricultural commodity chains. Moreover, these companies which are based in the transatlantic region and Japan now control food product development, R&D and access to value-added processed and branded agri-food products in the following ways:

- consolidation of international market systems
- control over the structure of global food trade
- dictation of parallel management based food retail standards.

After a period of global food industry consolidation by US, EU and Japanese based agri-businesses and food processors from the 1960s to the 1980s, many agri-food industries experienced structural change.[15] Eventually, the rise of bilateral, regional and multilateral free trade agreements and cross-border mergers and acquisitions, increased the integration of networked global agri-food industries (United States Department of Justice 2000). As a result of these trends, developing nations are increasingly forced to adopt growing food safety regulations and food quality standards of the transatlantic region and OECD countries.[16]

The globalization and integration of agricultural commodity chains based in Africa, Asia and Latin America reflect the power of world-class agri-businesses and food companies based primarily in the US and the EU.[17] As a result of the globalization of agricultural commodity chains, the regulation of food safety is emerging as a complex and important issue for transatlantic, OECD and developing countries.[18] Nevertheless, US, EU and Asian-Pacific food companies and food retailers are under increasing consumer and regulatory pressure to assume food product liability across the entire food supply chain.

Consolidation of Global Food-Processing Industries

By the 1980s, the growing demand for branded foods and rising incomes in Asia and Latin America gave rise to foreign direct investment by multinational food companies. In many instances these companies initiated cross-border contract farming agreements, branded food product introductions and food distribution strategies to develop new customers and global markets. Eventually, branded processed and convenience foods supported the global franchise expansion of companies such as McDonald's, Kentucky Fried Chicken (KFC), Pizza Hut, Domino's Pizza, Taco Bell, TCBY Yogurt, Popeye's Chicken, TGI Friday, A&W Subway, Dairy Queen and Wendy's.[19]

In the 1990s, food processors in the transatlantic and Asia-Pacific regions consolidated their supplier power across agricultural commodity chains in developing countries and global agri-food industries.[20] Throughout this period, contract farming agreements, global sourcing of agricultural commodities and strategic FDI grew rapidly in the Latin American and Asia-Pacific regions. By the start of the 2000s, the structure of global food-processing industries was permanently changed due to the following market trends:

- home market saturation in the transatlantic region and OECD countries
- merger and acquisitions by national and international food retailers and wholesalers
- technological innovation, modern biotechnology and GM food production

- changing consumer demand and food product preferences, the growth of food service companies and global competition in world food and agricultural markets.[21]

In many cases, food-processing companies use a combination of price and quality competition, food production innovation, and food product line expansion strategies to integrate national markets into global agri-food industries.[22] By the start of this decade, the branded and processed foods segments of global agri-food industries continued to grow. Table 2.1 charts the top 100 global food processors in 2002 and illustrates the growing geographical diversity of agri-food industry production in the twenty-first century.

The sheer size, market power and supplier power of US, European and Japanese food and beverage companies underscore the growing challenge facing national food safety regulators and governments. In terms of rankings, US companies held seven of the top ten position in the list of top 100 largest food and beverage companies in 2002. However, Nestlé SA of Europe held the number one position and continues to expand across the globe. In contrast, Kraft Foods in the US holds the number two position in the global 100 rankings.[23] Currently, the US market is the largest for food and beverage marketing and production. However, emerging markets in Latin America, Eastern Europe, South Asia and the Asia-Pacific region are becoming the sources of growth, profitability and competition for transatlantic food-processing companies.[24]

Food Retailing Industries

The global consolidation of food retailing industries is the result of structural changes in buyer and food supply chains. In the past, primary agricultural commodities and food products were distributed across long intermediary chains that included traders, brokers, buyers, and so on. However, the rapid globalization of food trade, and growing international competition resulted in the rationalization of food retailer strategies and supply chains in the 1990s. In many cases, global food sourcing, long-term agreements, contract farming and strategic alliances between suppliers, are driving the global consolidation of food retailing companies. In turn, food retailers globally source prepared, processed and fresh foods.[25]

As a result of this market strategy, networks of national and regional food producers and distributors are integrating global agri-food industries.[26] Through the development of global food retailing chains and supermarket networks, companies such as Wal-Mart and Ahold are developing multi-channel food retail strategies. In this strategy, consumers have a

Table 2.1 Top 100 global food processors

Rank	Company	Headquarters	Food sales (US millions)	Change %	Period ending	Product type
1	Nestlé S.A.	Vevey, Switzerland	46 628	20	31/12/01	Diversified
2	Kraft Foods Inc.	Northfield, III.	38 119	11.9	31/12/01	Diversified
3	ConAgra Inc.	Omaha, Neb.	27 630	1.6	31/5/01	Diversified
4	PepsiCo Inc.	Purchase, NY	26 935	31.8	31/12/01	Beverages and snack foods
5	Unilever plc	London, England and Rotterdam, the Netherlands	26 672	2.5	31/12/01	Diversified
6	Archer Daniels Midland Co.	Decatur, III.	23 454	17	30/6/02	Ingredients, grain-based products
7	Cargill Inc.	Minneapolis, Minn.	21 500	2.8	31/5/02	Grain-based foods
8	The Coca-Cola Co.	Atlanta, Ga.	20 092	−1.8	31/12/01	Beverages
9	Diageo plc	London, England	16 644	0.7	30/6/01	Alcoholic beverages
10	Mars Inc.	McLean, Va.	15 300	7.1	31/12/01	Confections
11	Anheuser-Busch Inc.	St Louis, Mo.	12 262	5.3	31/12/01	Brewery
12	Groupe Danone	Paris, France	12 184	−4.1	31/12/01	Diary, biscuits water
13	Kirin Brewery Co. Ltd	Tokyo, Japan	11 287	−1.2	31/12/01	Beverage
14	Asahl Breweries Ltd	Tokyo, Japan	11 050	2.4	31/12/01	Brewery
15	Tyson Foods	Springdale, Ark.	10 751	45.1	29/9/01	Meat and poultry
16	Dean Foods Co.	Dallas, Texas	9700	66.3	31/12/01	Dairy
17	H.J. Heinz Co.	Pittsburgh, Pa.	9431	0	1/5/01	Frozen and shelf-stable foods

Table 2.1 (continued)

Rank	Company	Headquarters	Food sales (US millions)	Change %	Period ending	Product type
18	Sara Lee Corp.	Chicago, Ill	9219	25.6	29/6/02	Meats, bakery, beverage
19	Kellogg Co.	Battle Creek, Mich.	8853	27.3	31/12/01	Grain-based foods
20	Snow Brand Milk Products Co. Ltd	Tokyo, Japan	8511	2.1	31/3/02	Diary
21	Helneken N.V.	Amsterdam, the Netherlands	8233	11.5	31/12/01	Brewery
22	Cadbury Schweppes plc	London, Englad	8070	17.5	31/12/01	Beverages, confections
23	General Mills Inc.	Minneapolis, Minn.	7949	46	26/5/02	Grain-based foods
24	Diary Farmers of American Inc.	Kansas City, Mo.	7902	20	31/12/01	Diary
25	Nippon Meat Packers Inc.	Osaka, Japan	7589	3.8	31/3/02	Meat processor
26	Parmalat Finanziaria SpA	Milan, Italy	7392	−0.1	31/12/01	Diary, bakery
27	Interbrew	Brussels, Belgium	6918	−15.9	31/12/01	Brewery
28	Campbell Soup Co.	Camden, NJ	6664	6.3	29/7/01	Shelf-stable and baked goods
29	Suntory Ltd	Osaka, Japan	6227	−34.3	31/12/01	Food and liquor
30	Maruha Corp.	Tokyo, Japan	6078	−5.6	31/03/02	Seafood processor
31	Smithfield Foods Inc.	Smithfield, Va.	5900	14.5	29/4/01	Pork processor
32	Associated British Foods	London, England	5618	1	16/9/01	Bakery, fats and oils

33	Fonterra Cooperative Group	Hamilton, New Zealand	5540	31.9	31/5/02	Dairy
34	Yamazaki Baking Co. Ltd	Tokyo, Japan	5417	−0.5	31/12/01	Bakery
35	Ajinomoto Co. Ltd	Tokyo, Japan	5151	3.9	31/3/02	Diversified
36	Danish Crown	Randers, Denmark	5100	8.8	30/9/01	Beef and pork processor
37	Tate and Lyle plc	London, England	5060	−4.2	31/3/02	Sweeteners and starches
38	Meiji Milk Products Co. Inc.	Tokyo, Japan	4929	0.8	31/3/02	Dairy
39	Hershey Food Corp.	Hershey, Pa.	4557	8	31/12/01	Confections
40	Groupe Lactalls	Laval, France	4500	−0.1	31/12/02	Dairy
41	Scottish and Newcastle plc	Edinburgh, Scotland	4495	−3.5	30/4/02	Brewery
42	Aria Foods group	Arhus, Denmark	4453	118.5	30/9/01	Dairy
43	Dole Food Company Inc.	Westlake Village, Calif.	4449	−6.6	31/12/01	Canned fruits and vegetables
44	Carisberg Breweries A/S	Copenhagen, Denmark	4383	26.5	31/12/01	Beverages
45	SABMiller plc	Johannesburg, S Africa	4364	4.3	31/3/02	Brewery
46	CHS Cooperatives	St Paul, Minn.	4270	−9.5	31/8/01	Grain-based foods
47	Morinaga Milk Industry Co. Ltd	Tokyo, Japan	4162	−1.5	31/12/01	Diversified
48	FEMSA de C.V.	Monterrey, Mexico	4147	0	31/12/01	Beverages
49	Hormel Foods Corp.	Austin, Minn.	4124	12.2	27/10/01	Meat and food
50	Royal Numico NV	Zoetermeer, the Netherlands	4110	−3.4	31/12/01	Infant formula

Table 2.1 (continued)

Rank	Company	Headquarters	Food sales (US millions)	Change %	Period ending	Product type
51	ContiGroup Companies Inc.	New York, NY	4000	N/A	31/12/01	Pork, poultry and seafood
52	Sapporo Breweries Ltd	Tokyo, Japan	3890	−1.2	31/12/01	Beverage
53	Südzucker AG	Mannheim, Germany	3825	−3.4	28/2/02	Sweeteners, ice cream
54	Friesland Coberco Diary Foods Holding N.V.	Meppel, the Netherlands	3818	−0.1	31/12/01	Diary
55	The Procter and Gamble Co.	Cincinnati, Ohio	3801	2.5	30/6/02	Food and beverage
56	Koninklijke Wessanen NV	Amstelveen, the Netherlands	3764	−5.1	31/12/01	Natural and specialty foods
57	McCain Foods Ltd	Florenceville, NB, Canada	3750	−7.5	30/6/01	Frozen foods
58	Itoham Foods Inc.	Hyogo, Japan	3737	−2.1	31/3/02	Meat products
59	Farmland Industries	Kansas City, Kan	3720	−3.9	31/12/01	Beef processor
60	Nichirei Corp.	Tokyo, Japan	3706	−0.3	31/3/02	Frozen foods
61	Campina Melkunie BV	Zaltbommel, the Netherlands	3703	0.2	31/12/01	Dairy
62	Grupo Bimbo S.A. de C.V.	Mexico City, Mexico	3687	13.1	31/12/01	Baked goods
63	Allied Domecq pic	Bristol, UK	3562	9.7	31/8/01	Spirits and wine
64	Interstate Bakeries Corp.	Kansas City, Mo.	3532	1	2/6/02	Baked goods

65	Nippon Suisan Kaisha Ltd	Tokyo, Japan	3527	4.1	31/3/02	Seafood processor
66	Bongrain SA	Viroflay, France	3500	−2.3	31/12/01	Cheese processor
67	Grupo Modelo SA de CV	Mexico City, Mexico	3440	15.3	31/12/01	Brewery
68	CSM NV	Diemen; the Netherlands	3142	37.4	30/9/01	Ingredients
69	Maple Leaf Foods Inc.	Toronto, Canada	3106	14.1	31/12/01	Meat, bakery
70	Land O'Lakes Inc.	Arden Hills, Minn.	3062	14.1	31/12/01	Diary
71	Schwan's Sales Enterprises Inc.	Marshall, Minn.	3000	−10.4	31/12/01	Frozen foods
72	Pernod Ricard Co.	Paris, France	2970	−2.2	31/12/01	Wine and spirits
73	Novartis International AG	Basil, Switzerland	2955	−11.4	31/12/01	Ingredients
74	International Multifoods Corp.	Minnetonka, Minn.	2849	12.8	2/3/02	Grain-based foods
75	Constellation Brands Inc.	Fairport, NY	2821	17.7	31/3/02	Wine, beer, spirits
76	American Beverage Co.	Sao Paulo, Brasil	2796	6.6	31/12/01	Brewery
77	Perdue Farms Inc.	Salisbury, Md.	2700	8	31/3/01	Poultry
78	QP Corp.	Tokyo, Japan	2666	3.2	30/11/01	Diversified
79	Panamerican Beverages Inc.	Panama City, Panama	2651	2	31/12/01	Beverage
80	Keystone Foods LLC	Philadelphia, Pa.	2643	1.9	31/12/01	Meat and poultry
81	Kerry Group plc	Kerry, Ireland	2605	7.7	31/12/01	Ingredients
82	Fosters Group Ltd	Victoria, Australia	2577	12.1	30/6/01	Beverage
83	Nisshin Seifun Group Inc.	Tokyo, Japan	2575	−1.4	31/3/02	Flour milling
84	George Weston Ltd	Toronto, Canada	2 490	4	31/12/01	Baked goods

Table 2.1 (continued)

Rank	Company	Headquarters	Food sales (US millions)	Change %	Period ending	Product type
85	Nissin Food Products Co. Ltd	Osaka, Japan	2476	2.5	31/3/02	Soy sauce, frozen foods
86	Wm Wrigley Jr Co.	Chicago, Ill.	2430	13.2	31/12/01	Confections
87	Adolph Coors Co.	Golden, Colo.	2429	−0.6	30/12/01	Brewery
88	National Dairy Holdings LP	Dallas, Texas	2400	N/A	30/4/02	Dairy
89	Le Groupe SODIAAL	Paris, France	2875	15.7	31/12/01	Diary
90	Nordmilch	Bremen, Germany	2860	8.8	31/12/01	Diary
91	Glanbia plc	Kilkenny, Ireland	2254	2.8	31/12/01	Diary, ingredients
92	Chiquita Brands Int'l. Inc.	Cincinnati, Ohio	2242	−0.5	31/12/01	Produce
93	Pilgrim's Pride	Dallas, Texas	2215	47.7	29/12/01	Poultry
94	Prima Meat Packers	Tokyo, Japan	2212	−2.1	31/3/02	Meat
95	Saputo Inc.	Montreal, Canada	2167	60	31/3/02	Diary
96	Barilla	Parma, Italy	2088	4.8	31/12/01	Pasta
97	Uniq plc	London, England	1991	45.3	31/3/02	Convenience foods
98	Meiji Selka Kaisha Ltd	Tokyo, Japan	1779	1.4	31/3/02	Confections
99	Corn Products International Inc.	Bedford Park, Ill.	1887	1.2	31/12/01	Ingredients
100	Gold Kist Inc.	Atlanta, Ga.	1811	16.1	30/6/01	Poultry

Source: Global Food Market Database. Leather Food RA, Surrey, UK.

declining number of food companies and local suppliers.[27] For example, in the United States, Kroger, Albertson's, Wal-Mart, Safeway and Ahold USA controlled 43 per cent of all food retailing operations in the US by 2001.[28] Consequently, the global food retailing industry is projected to decrease to six or fewer companies from the set of leading global food retailers in Table 2.2 in a few years.

The consolidation of the global food retailing industry is supported by the centralization of operations by information technology and infrastructure. Through the use of information technology, consumer purchases, inventories and business transactions are managed and controlled. As a result of this trend, food retailing and food supply chain management is occurring across regional and global markets.

Table 2.2 Global top 25 food retailers 2002

Store rank	No. of stores	Sales in billion$
1. Wal-Mart Stores/USA	5 164	244.50
2. Carrefour/France	10 704	64.70
3. Ahold/Netherlands	9 407	59.20
4. Kroger/USA	3 667	51.80
5. Metro/Germany	2 411	48.50
6. Tesco/United Kingdom	2 294	39.50
7. Costco/USA	400	38.00
8. Albertson/USA	1 688	35.60
9. Rewe/Germany	12 077	35.20
10. Aldi/Germany	6 609	37.70
11. Safeway/USA	1 887	32.40
12. ITM/France	12 863	31.50
13. Ito-Yokado/Japan	23 700	27.20
14. Edeka/Germany	14 374	27.00
15. Auchan/France	1 120	25.90
16. Sainsbury/United Kingdom	681	25.90
17. Aeon/Japan	8 120	24.60
18. Tengelmann/Germany	7 015	24.40
19. Schwartz Group/Germany	5 342	21.60
20. Casino/France	9 056	21.50
21. Delhaize Group/Belgium	2 520	19.40
22. Leclerc/France	535	19.20
23. Supervalu/USA	1 220	19.20
24. Daiei/Japan	4 086	17.70
25. Publix/USA	756	15.90

Source: M&M Planet Retail, www.planetretaail.net, Supermarket News Research.

III GLOBALIZATION OF FRUIT, VEGETABLE, CEREALS AND LIVESTOCK INDUSTRIES

Globalization of Fruit and Vegetables Industries

The globalization of fresh fruit and vegetable commodity chains is accelerating due to rising consumer demand in the NAFTA, EU and APEC regions. In turn, food company exports and FDI are growing in developing countries and emerging regions in the Western Hemisphere, Eastern Europe, Africa, South Asia and the Middle East. In this agri-food industry, global trade in fresh fruits and vegetables from developing countries in Africa, the Western Hemisphere and Asia-Pacific regions provide year-round supplies of a wide variety of fresh produce.[29]

At the present time, the EU is the leading destination, consumer and supplier of fresh fruit and vegetable commodities and processed products. A large amount of EU fresh produce originates in Africa, the Caribbean and the Pacific (the ACP countries), the Mediterranean and North African regions.[30] Since countries in these regions have preferential trade agreements with the EU, local fruit and vegetable commodity chains are integrating into global agri-food industries.

In a similar way, the NAFTA region is a major consumer, producer, importer and processor of fruit and vegetable products. In the Western Hemisphere, Central America and South America are now the main fruit suppliers for the United States. In this context, Guatemala, Ecuador, Colombia and Chile are strategic fresh fruit commodity suppliers for North American food processors and food retailers. In this regard, the United States is number one, Mexico is in seventh position and Canada ranks tenth in global fruit and vegetable export markets.

The Asia-Pacific region is rapidly evolving as a large consumer, competitor and producer of fresh fruits and vegetables (Pacific Economic Cooperation Council 2002). In the region, Japan is a major global importer and consumer of fresh fruit and vegetable products.[31] In this regard, Japan is a major driver of competition and food safety regulatory standards in global fruit and vegetable industries. In spite of these strict food quality and food safety challenges, Japanese food companies are rapidly creating supplier agreements outside Japan to ensure stable and secure supplies of fresh produce.

As the twenty-first century unfolds, China is emerging as a major consumer, producer and trader of fresh fruit and vegetable products for the Japanese and global food markets.[32] For example, China is now the world's largest apple producer. In this capacity, China's major apple markets are Russia for low-cost apples, and the ASEAN countries and Hong Kong for high-priced apples.[33] In turn, China is now the world's second largest exporter of frozen vegetables (excluding frozen French fried potatoes) after Belgium which holds the first place. Furthermore, China is a major producer of processed food products, including juices, which now account for over two-thirds of the country's fruit and vegetable exports. Currently, Japan purchases approximately half of China's processed food products. Tables 2.3 and 2.4 confirm the integration of fruit and vegetable commodity chains into transatlantic and Asian processed food products.

As the tables show, the transatlantic countries and regions are major consumers, producers and marketers of fresh and processed fruit and vegetable products. However, African, Western Hemisphere and South Asian nations are increasingly the 'countries of origin' and fresh fruit and vegetable commodity suppliers to food companies and agri-food-processing industries in the NAFTA, EU and APEC regions.

Changing structure of fresh fruit and vegetable supply chains

Very often, intermediaries in the global produce industry, such as grower-shippers in developing countries, harvest and prepare fresh fruits and vegetables for OECD food retail markets. As the first phase in the global fruit and vegetable chain, grower-shippers often supply food wholesalers, retailers, food service companies and direct consumer markets.[34] As a result of this trend, controlled atmosphere (CA) technologies are used to increase the shelf life of fresh fruit and vegetables sourced from developing countries to the EU, NAFTA and APEC regions.[35] In many cases, shipping technologies increase the ability of food processors and food retailers to source food around the globe on a year-round basis. The benefits of these transport, food preservation and other CA technologies are as follows:

- lower respiration rates of fruits and vegetables
- the ability to directly or remotely monitor and adjust oxygen, carbon dioxide and nitrogen levels of refrigerated containers that ship fresh fruits and vegetables
- delayed ripening, retardation of food discoloration and freshness monitoring of produce, that is, lettuce, asparagus, peaches, mangoes and avocadoes which perish in traditional refrigeration storage and ocean transport containers
- the ability to control humidity and ethylene gas levels that accelerate the ripening of fruits and vegetables
- the ability to use remote monitoring systems for refrigerated containers to warn about pending spoilage of fresh produce, and to control product liability through the verification of the dates and times of cargo quality and food safety changes.[36]

Table 2.3 Top 30 global exporters of fresh and processed fruit and vegetables, 1999–2001

Exporting group	Fresh fruits	Fresh vegetables	Processed fruits and veg.	Fruit and veg. juices
EU	Belgium	Belgium	Belgium	Austria
	France	France	Denmark	Belgium
	Germany	Germany	France	Denmark
	Greece	Greece	Germany	France
	Italy	Ireland	Greece	Germany
	Netherlands	Italy	Italy	Ireland
	Spain	Netherlands	Netherlands	Italy
		Spain	Portugal	Netherland
		United Kingdom	Spain	Spain
			United Kingdom	United kingdom
NAFTA	Canada	Canada	Canada	Canada
	Mexico	Mexico	Mexico	Mexico
	United States	United States	United States	United States
Asia	China	China	China	China
	Philippines	India	India	Philippines
	Thailand	Korea, South	Indonesia	Thailand
		Malaysia	Philippines	
		Thailand	Thailand	

Southern hemisphere	Argentina Australia Brazil Chile New Zealand South Africa	Argentina Australia New Zealand Peru	Argentina Australia Chile New Zealand Peru South Africa	Argentina Australia Brazil Chile South Africa
Banana-exporting countries	Colombia Costa Rica Côte d'Ivoire Ecuador Guatemala Honduras Panama	Guatemala	Costa Rica	Costa Rica Ecuador
Others	Israel Morocco Poland Turkey	Egypt Hungary Israel Jordan Kenya Morocco Poland Turkey	Hungary Morocco Poland Turkey Yugoslavia	Belize Hungary Israel Poland Switzerland Saudi Arabia Turkey

Souce: *Global Trade Patterns in Fruits and Vegetables*, Washington, DC: ERS/USDA, p. 9.

Table 2.4 Top 30 global importers of fresh and processed fruit and vegetables 1999–2001

Exporting group	Fresh fruits	Fresh vegetables	Processed fruits and veg.	Fruit and veg. juices
EU	Austria	Austria	Austria	Austria
	Belgium	Belgium	Belgium	Belgium
	Denmark	Denmark	Denmark	Denmark
	Finland	Finland	Finland	Finland
	France	France	France	France
	Germany	Germany	Germany	Germany
	Ireland	Greece	Greece	Greece
	Italy	Ireland	Ireland	Ireland
	Netherlands	Italy	Italy	Italy
	Portugal	Netherlands	Netherlands	Netherlands
	Spain	Portugal	Portugal	Portugal
	Sweden	Spain	Spain	Spain
	United Kingdom	Sweden	Sweeden	Sweden
		United Kingdom	United Kingdom	United Kingdom
NAFTA	Canada	Canada	Canada	Canada
	Mexico	Mexico	Mexico	Mexico
	United States	United States	United States	United States
Asia	China	Hong Kong	China	Hong Kong
	Hongo Kong	Indonesia	Hong Kong	Japan
	Indonesia	Japan	Japan	Korea, South
	Japan	Malaysia	Korea, South	Singapore
	Korea, South	Singapore	Singapore	
	Singapore			

Others	Argentina	Algeria	Argentina	Australia
	Brazil	Brazil	Australia	Botswana
	Czech Republic	Czech Republic	Brazil	Czech Republic
	Norway	Norway	Norway	Israel
	Poland	Poland	Poland	Norway
	Russian Federation	Russian Federation	Russian Federation	Poland
	Saudi Arabia	Saudi Arabia	Saudi Arabia	Russian Federation
	Switzerland	Switzerland	Switzerland	Saudi Arabia
				Switzerland

Souce: *Global Trade Patterns in Fruits and Vegetables*, Washington, DC: ERS/USDA, p. 10.

As the globalization of fruit and vegetable commodity chains and industries accelerates, agri-businesses and food companies are increasing the price, quality and safety of their products.[37] Since over 80 per cent of all fruit and vegetable products are imported to the EU, NAFTA and APEC regions, state-of-the-art shipping and conservation technologies are used to preserve fresh produce from developing countries.[38]

Meat, Fish and Livestock Industries: Beef, Pork, Broiler Chicken and Fish

Since the 1980s, the globalization of meat and animal livestock industries accelerated in response to rising consumer demand, growing production and processing in developing countries and global food trade. In this context, rising incomes in developing countries, and the growing shift of meat and poultry production to China, Brazil and Thailand, are accelerating the global integration of the meat and poultry industries.[39] In terms of production, the United States, the European Union, Australia, Canada, Brazil and Argentina are the leading producers and exporters in the global meat and poultry industries. In contrast, Russia, Japan, China, Mexico and the United States are the leading consumers in the global meat and poultry industries.[40]

The global meat and poultry industries are divided into the following segments: fresh, chilled, frozen, specialty cuts, and prepared meals.[41] As a result, technological innovation is increasingly used to improve the safety and quality of meat and poultry products. For example, the Japanese are developing new controlled atmosphere technologies, refrigerated containers, vacuum packaging and improved microbial controls to protect meat safety and quality. Through these innovations, transpacific and transatlantic shipping of meat and poultry products across regions and global transport routes is becoming more efficient.[42]

The global meat and poultry industries are now dominated by large producers and processing companies. While small and medium-sized companies compete in the global meat and poultry industries, economies of scale and scope are necessary for success. By the start of the twenty-first century, the 50 firms in Table 2.5 led the global meat and poultry industry.

At the present time, the leading global meat producers and processing companies have foreign operations in the Americas, Europe and the Asia-Pacific regions. Through these foreign sales offices and processing plants, multinational meat and poultry companies are able to develop new customers and markets. Furthermore, multinational companies can service large regional and global markets with more efficiency and lower costs. In response to the changing patterns of consumer demand in Asia, US meat and poultry producers supply the Japanese markets through their processing plants in Thailand.[43]

Table 2.5 Top 50 global meat processors

Rank	Firm	Country	Sales (mil $)	Year ended	Comments
1	Tyson Foods, Inc.	US	24 000	Sept. 2001	Sales increase reflects acquisition of IBP, Inc., Dakota Dunes, S.D.
2	ConAgra Foods	US	13 894	May 2001	Sales decrease represents sale of the firm's fresh beef and pork operations to Swift and Co.
3	Excel Corp.	US	12 000	May 2002	Beef, pork and turkey processor
4	Nestle SA	Switzerland	10 150	Dec. 2001	Company has total sales of $56 billion – the $10 1 billion figure represents sales for the firm's prepared dishes division
5	Swift and Co.	US	8 000	May 2001	Represents acquisition of ConAgra's fresh meat operations
6	Nippon Meat Packers	Japan	7 853	March 2002	Japan's largest fresh meat manufacturer
7	Smithfield Foods, Inc.	US	7 400	April 2002	Sales increase reflects acquisition of Packer land Packing and Moyer Packing
8	Farmland Refrigerated	US	4 754	N.A.	Company is currently reorganizing under Chapter 11 protection
9	Danish Crown	Denmark	4 534	Sept 2001	Denmark's largest meat company
10	Sara Lee Packaged Meats	US	4 166	June 2001	Diversified processed meats manufacturer
11	Hormel Foods Corp.	US	4 124	Oct. 2001	Diversified processed meats manufacturer
12	Itoham	Japan	3 883	March 2002	Red meat manufacturer
13	Oscar Mayer and Pizza	US	3 653	Dec. 2001	Diversified processed meats manufacturer
14	Perdue Farms, Inc.	US	2 700	March 2001	Family-owned poultry processor

Table 2.5 (continued)

Rank	Firm	Country	Sales (mil $)	Year ended	Comments
15	Nutreco Holding NV	The Netherlands	2 506	Dec. 2001	Total company sales were $3.74 billion However, only 67 per cent of total sales represent meat and poultry interests
16	Prima Meat Packers	Japan	2 297	March 2002	Fresh meat manufacturer
17	Dumeco B.V.	The Netherlands	2 254	Dec. 2001	Red meat slaughterer and processor
18	Pilgrim's Pride Corp.	US	2 215	Sept. 2001	Poultry processor with strong foothold in the US and Mexico
19	Uniq PLC	United Kingdom	2 136	March 2002	Convenience food manufacturer
20	OSI Group	US	2 100	N.A.	Sales figure is an estimate. The company is a meat manufacturer with global interests
21	Maple Leaf Meats Group	Canada	2 015	Dec. 2001	Canada's largest meat company
22	Golden State Foods	US	2 000	Dec. 2001	Diversified processed meat and liquid products manufacturer
23	Keystone Foods L.L.C.	US	2 000	N.A.	Beef and chicken supplier to McDonald's
24	A. Moksel AG	Germany	1 846	Dec. 2001	German meal processor
25	Marudai Food Co. Ltd	Japan	1 838	March 2002	Fresh and processed meats manufacturer
26	Gold Kist, Inc.	US	1 811	June 2001	Poultry processor
27	CG Nordfleisch AG	Germany	1 742	Dec. 2001	German meat processor
28	Starzen Co. Ltd	Japan	1 727	March 2002	Meat processor with significant wholesale operations in Japan
29	Veronesi Group	Italy	1 487	Dec. 2001	Sales figure includes Agricola Italiana Alimentare poultry and Montorsi park operations

30	Camporfrio Alimentacion SA	Spain	1 475	Dec. 2001	Spanish processed meat manufacturer
31	Doux SNC	France	1 333	Dec. 2001	France's largest poultry processor
32	Glanbia PLC	Ireland	1 332	Dec. 2001	Total company sales were $2562 billion Fifty-two per cent come from the food processing sector
33	Grampian Country Foods	Scotland	1 327	May 2001	Scottish agri-business firm
34	Westfleisch	Germany	1 208	Dec. 2001	Estimate CG Nordfleisch and Westfleisch will merge Jan. 2003
35	Foster Poultry Farms	US	1 200	Dec. 2001	The largest poultry processor in the Western US
36	Charoen Pokphand	Thailand	1 196	Dec. 2001	Sales figure reflects 68 per cent of the company's business in meat and poultry processing
37	Sadia Alimentos SA	Brazil	1 160	Dec. 2001	Brazil's largest meat company
38	Cremonini SPA	Italy	1 138	Dec. 2001	Sales figure includes the company's beef, processed meats and distribution business, which total approximately 87 per cent of sales
39	LDC Societe Anonyme	France	1 022	Feb. 2001	Poultry processor and convenience food manufacturer
40	Wayne Farms/Dutch	US	880	March 2001	Poultry processor
41	Irish Food Processors Ltd	Ireland	879	March 2002	Cooperative of Irish beef processors
42	Swedish Meats	Sweden	870	Dec. 2001	Sweden's largest meat processor
43	Yonekyu Corp.	Japan	855	Feb. 2002	Meat processor manufacturing ham, sausages, and other meat products

Table 2.5 (continued)

Rank	Firm	Country	Sales (mil $)	Year ended	Comments
44	House of Raeford Farms	US	850	April 2001	Chicken and turkey processor
45	Olymel Ltd	Canada	845	Oct. 2001	Canadian pork and poultry processor
46	Rosen's Diversified	US	800	Sept. 2001	Beef slaughterer and processor
47	Perdigao SA	Brazil	783	Dec. 2001	Holding company with interests in vertically integrated meat and poultry operations
48	Seaboard Corp.	US	772	Dec. 2001	Pork processor
49	Colorado Boxed Beef	US	740	March 2001	Full-service meat and poultry processor
50	Greater Omaha Packing Co.	US	725	Nov. 2001	Nebraska beef packer

Source: *Structure of the Global Markets for Meat*, Washington, DC: ERS/USDA, pp. 16–17.

The success of global meat and poultry producers is due to their production and cost efficiencies in the processing and distribution across domestic and foreign markets. For example, Danish Crown in Denmark is the ninth largest meat company in the world. While the Danish market is very small, large state-of-the art pig farms in Denmark allow the company to sell pork products in Europe, North America and the Asia-Pacific region. In a similar way, the Brazilian companies, Sadia and Perdigao, are world-class producers of poultry and pork, which are sold in South America, Japan, the Middle East and Europe.[44]

Beef industry

The global beef industry is driven by growing consumer demand, cross-border trade and competition, rising animal livestock productivity and increasing meat-processing capacity. As globalization of the beef and cattle industry accelerated, the concentration of cattle production and processing in large plants and slaughterhouses emerged as a global industry trend.[45] The production of beef starts on farms and ranches with animal livestock management capacity. The animals are raised and sold for slaughter and processing to food retailers who distribute the beef products to final consumers.[46] Therefore, technological innovations in beef processing, animal feed additives, computerized feed mill operations, and meat transport systems are changing the structure of national and global beef industries.[47]

The pork industry

By the 1990s, the consolidation of the US and global pork industries was well under way. During this period, the growing use of contracts between pig farmers and pork wholesalers, and the vertical consolidation of pork markets drove the globalization of pork meat industries.[48] The use of veterinary medicine, modern biotechnology innovation, productivity gains in pig farming, and economies of scale and scope in pork meat production are rapidly changing the structure of the global pork industry.[49] In contrast to earlier periods, the global pork industry segments industrial pig farming into specialized operations.[50]

The global pork industry is growing due to the rise of fast-food restaurants and new menu choices that increasingly include mixed meat offerings.[51] For example, the sale of hamburgers and sandwiches with bacon illustrate the interrelationships between red meat industries. In addition, the red meat industries are strategically repositioning pork as a 'healthy' food choice. Eventually, genetic engineering and farming innovations produced branded lean pork products by Smithfield Foods Inc. that earned the American Heart Association seal of approval as a healthy food choice. Through this strategy, the red meat industries work together to counter consumer concerns about the health impacts of beef and pork consumption.[52] In response to the growing demand for high-quality pork products, pig producers are working to ensure a large supply of standard quality pigs to meet global consumer demand.[53]

The broiler chicken industry

The consolidation of the global broiler chicken industry is driven by the introduction of labor and cost saving technologies, the investment of capital, and the genetic modification of poultry as a source of food and nutrition for humans. As the decade unfolds, vertical coordination and consolidation in the global broiler chicken industry is increasing in response to growing consumer demand for poultry products.[54] Through selective breeding, quality improvement and poultry industry research, chicken production became a year-round process to support the growing global demand for poultry meat.[55] Furthermore, chicken processors use poultry farming contracts, and vertical coordination with chicken producers, processors and food retailers, to meet growing global demand for safe, high-quality, nutritious and safe chicken products.[56]

Fish and aquaculture products

The global fish and aquaculture industry represent a major sector of the global food market system. During the period form 1980 to 2000, global fish and aquaculture trade grew from $15 billion in 1980 to $56 billion by 2001 (Vannuccini 2004).[57] At the start of this decade, approximately 40 per cent of the global fish industry represented fresh fish products, followed by frozen fish which accounted for approximately 30 per cent of the market. The remainder of the global fish industry consisted of canned fish which represented approximately 14 per cent of the market, and cured fish which accounted for an estimated 12 per cent of the global fish and aquaculture industry.[58]

The global seafood industry consists of wild, farmed, fresh and processed products. In many cases, seafood products are smoked, canned, salted, dried, frozen and raw.[59] In contrast to the past, a growing share of the global seafood industry is farm raised instead of wild. Currently, developing countries provide approximately three-quarters of the products for the global seafood industry. A large share of the global fish and seafood industry is imported by the US, EU, Japan and other OECD countries which have high food safety and consumer protection standards.[60]

By the late 1990s, Thailand was ranked as the leading global exporter of fish and aquaculture products, followed by Norway, China, the United States, Denmark and Canada. During this period, approximately 80 per cent of all fish and aquaculture exports went to the transatlantic region or the OECD countries.[61] By the start of this decade, Japan, the United States and the European Union increased their share of global fish and aquaculture imports.[62]

In terms of global demand and consumption trends, FAO reports that approximately 75 per cent of all fish produced is used for human food. The remaining 25 per cent is used to make fishmeal and oils. According to FAO, over half of all fish and aquaculture products originate in developing countries, and the FAO estimates that approximately 50 per cent of all global fish and aquaculture products come from developing nations. However, developing country fish and aquaculture producers are concentrated in the fresh and unprocessed segment of the global industry.[63]

Global Cereals and Grain Industries

In response to growing consumer demand and the national food security requirements, the global grain and cereal industries are projected to grow in the next decade.[64] In the global wheat industry, the greatest increase in production is projected to occur in developing countries in Africa, the Middle East and Asia. However, the demand for wheat and processed wheat products is strongest in Brazil, China, Indonesia, Egypt, Mexico, Pakistan and sub-Saharan Africa. In terms of industry structure, the following countries account for 75 per cent of the total world production in the global wheat industry: the United States, the European Union, Canada, Argentina and Australia. However, India produces and exports a large amount of lower-quality wheat in the global grain and cereals markets. Likewise, the Ukraine, Kazakhstan and Russia, as well as Eastern Europe, are increasing their production in the global wheat industry.

In the global corn industry, the following countries are the leading producers of corn for food and feeds: the United States, Argentina, Central and Eastern Europe and China. At the present time, Brazil and South Africa are also emerging as significant corn producers. However, in the case of South Africa, most of the export crops are sold to SADC countries. In the case of Brazil, non-GM corn is produced for export to niche markets that reject GM food production. In the next decade, the US share of the global corn industry is projected to increase from 60 per cent to 70 per cent of the world market.

In the global rice industry, diversification into the production of high-quality premium rice varieties is driving the demand for rice products. For example, long grain rice is sold in South and Southeast Asia, the Middle East, sub-Saharan Africa and Latin America. Currently, the largest markets for long grain rice are as follows: Indonesia, Nigeria, Iran, Iraq, the Philippines and Saudi Arabia. In contrast Japan, South Korea, Taiwan, Turkey and Jordan are major markets for the short and medium grain segment of the global rice industry. Finally, in the case of aromatic rice products, such as jasmine and basmati varieties, Thailand, Vietnam, the United States, India and China are the major producers.

Globalization and Modern Biotechnology Innovation in Global Agri-Food Industries

At a very basic level, genome science and biotechnology are branches of scientific knowledge that are used to selectively breed micro-organisms, plants and animals for human consumption and industrial use. Eventually, these new biotechnology innovations gave rise to the Green Revolution, and the development of novel plant and animal products by agri-business and global agri-food industries. Since the 1980s, genome science and biotechnology have been used by agri-businesses and pharmaceutical companies to develop new food and drug products.

GM seeds

The starting point for GM food production is the global seed industry. The goal of GM seed production is to apply genome science to the preservation and improvement of food plant and crop species (Joint FAO/WHO Food Standards Programme 2000). In global agri-food industries, GM seeds are used to preserve and improve the genetic base of food plants and crops that are under threat due to over cultivation, pest destruction and microbial contamination. In terms of benefits, GM seeds offer the possibility of improving agricultural productivity and food production through the removal of food plant and crop vulnerabilities.[65] At the start of this decade, the largest markets for seed production were as follows: the United States, China, Japan, CIS countries, France, Brazil, Germany, Argentina, Italy and India.[66]

GM crop production

Modern biotechnology is used to create novel crops, livestock and micro-organisms through the manipulation of plant, fish and animal genes. Through the adoption of biotechnology, farmers and food-processing companies can improve crop and livestock quality, and reduce plant and animal losses from insects, parasites and microbial diseases.[67] In spite of resistance, GM food producers, that is, agri-businesses and food companies, are working to increase acceptance of modern biotechnology by consumers, animal feed producers and food safety regulators.[68]

According to proponents of GM food production, economic efficiency and consistent product quality are the major benefits for both consumers and producers.[69] In contrast, most agri-food companies and producers cite the following commercial benefits from GM plants and crops: insect resistance, herbicide tolerance, plant and crop quality, plant oil quality, virus and microbial resistance, longer shelf life, low allergenicity and delayed ripening.[70] In terms of consumer and public benefits, it is argued that plant and crop reproduction termination through gene suppression can result in food quality control, species preservation and the prevention of 'out crossing' to non-GM crops. However, this strategy can have a restrictive effect on farming strategies and consumer choice for conventional food production.[71]

GM animal livestock and global agri-food industries

As the controversy over GM crops and foods accelerated in the 1990s, biotechnology companies quietly moved to commercialize animal livestock for global agri-food industries.[72] In some cases, cloned animals and fish can

BOX 2.1 GOALS OF ANIMAL CLONING FOR PRODUCERS AND INDUSTRIES

1. Preservation of the high value of rare animals.
2. Increase the biosecurity and risk management strategy of producers, farmers and ranchers.
3. Development and preservation of selected gene pools for future livestock management and industrial food production.
4. Preservation and support of genetic diversity.
5. Preservation of cell lines for future cloning of animals and livestock.

PROJECTED BENEFITS OF ANIMAL CLONING FOR CONSUMERS

1. Development of safer meat and milk supplies.
2. Increased quality of meat and milk.
3. Optimalization of R&D and test herds.
4. Reduction of unwanted animals such as veal calves.
5. Reduction of livestock and environmental impacts.

Sources: Slides by Ron D. Gillespie, Cyagra, Inc.[73]

increase productivity, economic efficiency and competitiveness in global meat, fish and related livestock product industries. Therefore, animal semen sellers, meat and dairy producers and livestock industries anticipate higher product quality and increased profitability through animal-cloning biotechnology. Box 2.1 shows benefits of animal livestock cloning for meat, fish and livestock producers and global agri-food industries.

In spite of high production cost and growing regulatory challenges, meat, fish and livestock producers are moving to commercialize animal biotechnology for livestock management, breeding and food production.[74] Therefore, the new 'animal livestock biotechnologies' are an emerging product strategy for national and global agri-food industries.[75] However, the risk of conventional animal and plant species contamination pose food safety risks. For example, GM cows that are bred to produce drugs and pharmaceutical products in their milk, cannot to be sold for meat or milk production. In this respect, the contamination of conventional cattle livestock populations and food allergy risks are growing in global meat and livestock industries.[76]

Organic Farming and Food Products

Organic farming and agriculture is a rapidly growing segment of the global agri-food industry. In contrast to foods produced with modern biotechnology, organic food is natural and contains less additives, and chemical contaminants. Moreover, organic farming supports and sustains the natural biological and ecological system through the use of environmentally friendly method of weed, pest and disease control. Finally, organic farming relies on the use of organic materials for the fertilization of soil, stresses animal welfare, relies on biological control of pests, and manual, mechanical and thermal weeding techniques.[77]

As a growing segment of the global agri-food industry, organic farming and food production are under way in over 100 countries. The growing consumer demand for organic food provides product choice and alternatives to GM crops and livestock products.[78] The following organic food products are now available in national supermarkets and global agri-food industries: fresh fruits and vegetables, dried fruits and nuts, processed fruit and vegetables, coffee, tea and cocoa, spices and herbs, oils, sweeteners, grains, dried vegetables, meat, dairy products and eggs, alcoholic beverages, processed foods, that is, juices, essential oils, marmalades, pickled and candied peels, grains and animal feeds.[79]

The organic food segment is growing in the European Union, North America, Japan and Australia. In turn, global food retailers, food processors and agri-businesses are moving to compete in this small but growing segment of the global agri-food industry. In response to this trend, some developing nations are producing organic foods to increase their competitiveness in the value-added segment of the global agri-food industry. However, countries must certify the organic origin, quality standards and compliance with food safety regulations.[80]

VI GLOBAL FOOD INDUSTRY INTEGRATION AND THE GLOBALIZATION OF FOOD SAFETY RISKS

In the twenty-first century, the global integration of national food systems, agricultural commodity chains, food trade and agri-food industries are driven by regional and multilateral free trade agreements. In turn, regional free trade agreements, and trade liberalization through the WTO, are integrating global agri-food industries. As the decade unfolds, the following food safety risks are emerging in national food systems and global agri-food industries:

- growing consumption of meals away from home
- the growing dependence of consumers and nations on global food trade
- the growing use of GM crops and biotechnology for livestock production
- the concentration of global food production, processing and distribution through a decreasing number of transatlantic and OECD based agri-businesses, food companies and global agri-food industries
- the growing trend in foreign food sourcing and offshore food-processing by global agri-business and food companies
- the growing threat of terrorist sabotage of farming and agricultural sectors and food supply chain industries
- the emergence of global veterinary public health threats such as BSE, antibiotic resistance, dioxin contamination of animal feed, and avian flu
- limited mandatory enforcement of HACCP process controls systems, food pathogen control programs and industry standards across national food systems and global food supply chain industries
- the rapid growth of food exports and the sourcing of food by global agri-businesses and food companies from developing countries with limited regulatory capacity for the harmonization of Codex and SPS food safety standards.[81]

The globalization of agri-food industries and food trade are now the context for mandatory regulation of food safety.[82] Furthermore, consumers are exposed to increasing food safety risks through food contamination, unregulated GM food production, and bioterrorist sabotage of food systems and supply chain industries.[83] Therefore, farmers, agri-business and food companies face increasing product liabilities for illness and death caused by adulterated food products.[84]

Animal Health and Food Safety Hazards in Global Agri-Food Industries

Bovine Spongiform Encephalopathy (BSE) and the global beef industry

The relationship between animal livestock health and food safety is well known due to the highly publicized Mad Cow crisis in the United Kingdom. Eventually, the food safety crisis spread to the European Union, Japan, Canada, the United States and the global beef and meat industries.[85] In Asia, the first reported case of mad cow disease occurred in Japan. The Japanese government and Consumers Union-Japan now acknowledge that the BSE outbreak in Japan is directly linked to the importation of approximately 300 tons of Mammalian Meat and Bone Meal (MBM) animal feed from the United Kingdom prior to 1996. By 2004, BSE was found in North America, and is linked to the use of contaminated animal feeds. Eventually, BSE was also found in goats in France, and increases concerns about food safety risks in global meat and livestock industries.

The linkage between the health of cattle, consumer safety and public health now extends to the consumption and exposure to infected cattle parts and derivative food and non-food products. As the decade unfolds, there is growing evidence of a linkage between BSE and contamination of blood with Creutzfeldt-Jakob disease (CJD) pathogens (WHO 2002). According to reports from the United Kingdom, there is growing surveillance of blood transfusions in response to reports of deaths of patients who were later found to have contracted CJD.[86] As a result, there are now BSE threats to public health from CJD transmission in contaminated blood products.

In some cases, the threat to consumer safety and public health is growing due to the diverse use of cattle tissue and body parts across several industries. In this context, there is increasing surveillance of the following human and animal products derived from cattle: cosmetics, hides, gelatin, diary products, human medicines, animal medicines, animal feed, hormones for humans and animals, cells for transplantation, vaccines, confectionary products, cakes, biscuits, prepared foods, and meat stock for human food and soup.[87]

Food safety and the global poultry industry: the case of avian flu

In the global poultry industry, the outbreak and rapid spread of the avian flu is a growing threat to animal health, public health and food safety in global food industries. According to WHO, all birds and poultry are susceptible to avian flu, but some species are less able to resist the virus. As a result, these birds can become the source of deadly infections that spread from poultry to humans.[88]

The current avian flu epidemic in the global chicken and poultry industry originated in the Asia-Pacific region. The first case was reported in November 2003, as an outbreak of 'chicken cholera' by the government of Thailand. By December 2003, the government of South Korea reported an outbreak of avian flu at a chicken farm near the capital city of Seoul. By the start of 2004, several more reported cases of avian flu were reported by the governments of Vietnam, Japan, Taiwan and Laos.[89] In China, cases of new and suspected outbreaks of the H5N1 strain of avian flu were found in several provinces, including Xian, which has a lot of tourism related to the famous terracotta warriors.

The spread of the avian flu epidemic to North America has serious implications for food safety, animal livestock health and veterinary public health in global poultry and egg industries. For example, the first reported cases of avian flu in the United States had a serious impact on the domestic and global broiler chicken industries. Initial confirmation of avian flu in large poultry farms in Rhode Island and Connecticut in 2003, eventually spread to Delaware and Maryland early in 2004.[90] In response to the outbreak of avian flu in major poultry-producing states, approximately 35 countries banned the importation and sale of US chickens.

Currently, the USDA is working to convince other countries to scale back the chicken and poultry bans to specific regions in the US with avian flu outbreaks. However, many countries refused to lift the bans on US poultry imports until containment and eradication of avian flu are verified.[91] For example, the Japanese government banned the importation of US chickens as a precautionary measure. The importation of US poultry could not resume from the infected areas until Japanese food safety regulators carried out US plant inspections.[92]

In response to the outbreak and subsequent spread of avian flu to poultry farms and humans, WHO and FAO called for the immediate culling (killing of entire flocks of poultry) of chicken and other poultry livestock to prevent the spread of the disease.[93] For example, in 1997, an outbreak of a similar avian influenza, H5N1, required the culling of the entire poultry flock of Hong Kong. In this case approximately 1.5 million birds were slaughtered in three days to prevent the spread of the disease.[94]

In South Korea, approximately 2 million chickens and ducks were slaughtered as a precautionary measure as a result of two confirmed cases of avian flu near the capital city of Seoul.[95] In a similar case, the Netherlands experienced a serious outbreak of H7N7 avian flu in 2003. In response to this contamination of the Dutch poultry industry, 30 million birds were culled to stop the spread of the virus. As a result, the confidence of Dutch consumers, public health authorities and, ultimately, the national poultry industry was strengthened due to the rapid response of the government and producers.[96]

In Canada, avian flu spread to over 12 poultry farms in British Columbia in a 24-hour period. Within a few days, over 18 poultry farms were infected, resulting in the loss over 200 jobs, the culling of approximately 400 000 chickens, and illness in at least two workers. In response to the outbreak of avian flu in Canada, the Canadian Food Inspection Agency and Ministry of Agriculture ordered the slaughter of 19 million chickens, turkeys and ducks over a two-week period. The goal of this risk management measure is to contain the disease, and prevent further contamination of the Canadian and North American poultry industry.[97]

In a similar way, contamination of chicken and poultry products with *Campylobacter* is a major food safety and public health threat for the food industry. The source of food contamination is poultry, and can be spread through broiler chicken flock feces. Eventually, the pathogen grows in the gut of chickens. As a result, food contamination occurs during transport from poultry farms to processing plants and during the slaughtering, evisceration and de-feathering phase. Consumers are exposed through inadequate preparation and cooking of poultry products.[98] The industrial production of broiler chickens and the unregulated disposal and management of manure waste are increasing global food safety risks.[99]

In many countries, animal livestock health and veterinary public health are rapidly growing areas of food safety regulation.[100] As a consequence, the meat processors and animal livestock producers face growing food safety and product liability risks.[101] Table 2.6 ranks countries relative to the presence or absence of BSE, swine fever, Newcastle disease and other animal diseases that affect global meat and livestock industries.

In this regard, the role of veterinary public health in the regulation of meat and livestock industries, consumer protection and food safety is growing. Therefore, increasing focus on farming and livestock management, animal health and animal welfare is now an important area of food safety regulation in global agri-food industries (OIE 2002).

Animal feeds, veterinary drugs and food safety

Historically, antibiotics and other animal feed additives are used to enhance the quality of meat products, and to improve the detection, treatment and prevention of livestock diseases. Through the proactive use of fortified livestock feed, veterinary pharmaceutical products, and disease management practices with vaccines, the safety of meat and livestock products is

Table 2.6 Certification of meat and poultry disease free zones

Country area	Countries/ areas affected (A) with African swine fever	Countries/ areas affected with Bovine Spongiform Encephalopathy (A)	Countries/ areas that are considered to have a substantial risk (R) associated with BSE	Countries/ areas free of classical swine fever (F)*	Countries/ areas free of exotic Newcastle disease (F)	Countries/ areas free of Foot-and-Mouth disease and rinderpest (F)**
Africa – all countries on the continent (see also Rep of South Africa)	A					
Albania			R			
Andorra			R			
Australia				F	F	F
Austria		A		*		**
Bahama Islands						**
Barbados						F
Belgium		A		*		**
Belize						F
Bermuda						F
Bosnia-Herzegovina			R			
Brazil	A					
Bulgaria			R			
Canada		A		F	F	F

Table 2.6 (continued)

Country area	Countries/ areas affected (A) with African swine fever	Countries/ areas affected with Bovine Spongiform Encephalopathy (A)	Countries/ areas that are considered to have a substantial risk (R) associated with BSE	Countries/ areas free of classical swine fever (F)*	Countries/ areas free of exotic Newcastle disease (F)	Countries/ areas free of Foot-and-Mouth disease and rinderpest (F)**
Channel Islands						**
Chile					F	**
Costa Rica					F	F
Croatia			R			
Cuba	A					
Czech Republic		A				**
Denmark		A		F		**
Dominican Republic						F
El Salvador						F
Estonia						**
Federal Republic of Yugoslavia			R			
Fiji				F	F	F
Finland		A		F	F	**
Former Yugoslav Republic of Macedonia			R			
France		A				**
Germany		A				**

Germany (except for a list of specific arcas, see APHIS website)				*		
Greece		A		*	F	**(rinderpest)
Greenland						F
Guatemala						F
Haiti	A					F
Honduras						F
Hungary			R			**
Iceland				F	F	F
Ireland, Republic of		A		F	F	**
Israel		A				
Italy (except for Emilia-Romagna, Piemonte, and Sardinia)		A		*		**
Emilia-Romagna and Piemonte		A				**
Sardinie	A	A				**
Jamaica						F
Japan		A				**
Liechtenstein		A				
Luxembourg		A				**
Malta	A				F	
Mexico (except States of Sonora Sinaloa and Yucatan)						F
Sonora				@	#	F
Sinaloa					#	F
Yucatan				@		F
Monaco			R			
Netherlands		A				**

Table 2.6 (continued)

Country area	Countries/ areas affected (A) with African swine fever	Countries/ areas affected with Bovine Spongiform Encephalopathy (A)	Countries/ areas that are considered to have a substantial risk (R) associated with BSE	Countries/ areas free of classical swine fever (F)*	Countries/ areas free of exotic Newcastle disease (F)	Countries/ areas free of Foot-and-Mouth disease and rinderpest (F)**
New Caledonia						**
New Zealand				F	F	F
Nicaragua						F
Norway			R	F		**
Oman		A				
Panama						F
Papua New Guinea						**
Poland		A		A		**
Portugal		A				**
Romania			R			
San Marino			R			
Slovakia/Slovenia		A				
South Africa, Republic of	A					(rinderpest)
Spain		A			F	**
Sweden			R	F	F	**
Switzerland		A			F	**

Territory of St Pierre and Miquelon					F
Tobago					F
Trinidad					F
Trust Territories of the Pacific Islands			F		F
United Kingdom of Great Britain and Northern Ireland					
Northern Ireland	A		F		**
Scotland, Wales, Isle of Man	A		F	F	**
England (except Essex, Norfolk, Suffolk counties)		A		F	F**
Essex, Norfolk, Suffolk counties	A			F	**
Falkland Islands	A				

Source: *Structure of the Global Markets for Meat*, Washington, DC: ERS/USDA, pp. 16–17.

increasing. Therefore, in the near future, farmers will be able to use antibiotics, vaccines and sophisticated veterinary pharmaceutical products to combat Foot-and-Mouth disease, avian flu, classical swine fever and BSE.

Nevertheless, consumers are increasingly concerned about the growing use of food additives, veterinary drugs, antibiotics and chemicals in meat, livestock and crop production. Furthermore, increased meat, livestock and agri-food product risks for pregnant women, children and the elderly are posing new consumer protection challenges for governments and corporate management. For example, small amounts of arsenic used in poultry feed are traditionally used by poultry farmers to control intestinal parasites in chicken. However, increasing consumption of chicken, and growing exposure to larger amounts of arsenic are linked to cancers of the bladder, lungs, skin, kidneys, liver and prostate glands, as well as cardiovascular, pulmonary, immunological, neurological and endocrine system problems.[102]

In some cases, temporary bans on the sale and importation of meat and livestock products that test positive for antibiotic drug residues reduce the competitiveness of farmers and food producers in global agri-food industries. For example, the EU Veterinary Committee occasionally recommends temporary restrictions on the importation of US poultry and Chinese meats and seafood due to the use of antimicrobial chemicals and agents.[103] Finally, food safety risks are increasing as a result of growing antibiotic resistance by food pathogens to veterinary drugs. Very often, veterinary drugs are used to prevent infection and to accelerate animal livestock growth.[104]

Food safety in global fish and seafood industries

In the twenty-first century, industrial fisheries and aquaculture are major segments of the global food industry. However, concerns over food safety risks associated with contaminated feed are emerging as new information becomes available. For example, two independent research studies conducted in Canada and England revealed that food contamination with chemicals, including polychlorinated biphenyls, were ten times higher in farmed salmon. In some instances, farmed salmon had higher levels of pesticide contamination than wild species of the same fish. Consequently, the growing chemical contamination of farmed salmon and other cultivated fish species, and the adulteration of fish feeds with toxic agents, are creating food safety risks.[105]

In response to the confirmation of these findings by consumer and food safety authorities in the US and EU, governments are issuing consumer advisories that warn against high levels of Scottish salmon and albacore white tuna consumption by pregnant women, nursing mothers and young children.[106] In addition, shrimp, canned light tuna, salmon, pollack and catfish were recommended as safe with limited daily and weekly consumption.[107] In the United States, a joint FDA/EPA (Environmental Protection Agency) consumer advisory was issued for the first time in history to warn against overconsumption of shark, swordfish, king mackerel, tilefish and albacore tuna. As one of the most popular fish in the American diet, the FDA and EPA warned about the risk of high levels of mercury consumption via albacore white tuna, and the risk of nervous system deformity in unborn babies and young children.

In spite of this controversy, WHO and FAO confirm that larger amounts of dioxin and polychlorinated biphenyl (PCBs) are present in farmed salmon than their wild counterparts. In order to correct this food safety problem, WHO recommends regulation to limit the levels of dioxin and PCBs allowed in food and animal feeds. While the levels of PCBs and dioxins in farmed salmon are still below the maximum levels allowed, a comprehensive risk assessment of the total consumption of these chemical contaminants must be taken into account. Therefore, FAO and WHO warn that the nutritional benefits of farmed salmon must now be weighed relative to the risks posed by the consumption of contaminated fish.[108]

Finally, there are growing food safety risks in the global fish and seafood industries due to food pathogens such as *Vibrio vulnificus*, and *Salmonella*.[109] For example, even in the United States, which highly regulates food safety in fish and seafood industries, salmonella contamination is a problem. In 2001 FDA fish detention and rejection reports showed that approximately a quarter of all detentions and over half of all violations were for wild and farmed shrimp and prawns.[110] In some cases antibiotic residues and feed additives in seafood exceed the maximum levels allowed by transatlantic and multilateral food safety standards.

Food additives and chemical contamination in global agri-food industries

Food additives are an important component of modern food production and processing industries. In global agri-food industries a wide variety of chemicals are added in the form of enzymes, vitamins, minerals, food coloring and flavor enhancers to improve the appearance, attractiveness and taste of food for consumers. In many instances, food companies and agri-food industries use food additives such as gums and fibers to improve the bulk weight and textures of food products.

Over time, there is growing concern by food safety regulators over the safe use of additives in the production, processing and marketing of food products. Furthermore, expanding knowledge of the impact of food additives and chemicals on the suppression of immune, hormonal and endocrine and nervous systems provides the scientific basis for the regulation of food additives and chemicals used in food production, processing and retailing.[111] In this context, there is increasing regulation for full disclosure of food additives through mandatory product labeling. For example, a class action suit was filed against the three largest grocery food chains in the US over the sale of artificially colored salmon. In this instance, farmed salmon is dyed pink to give the impression that the fish was the same as free-swimming salmon that is offered as a competitive product in supermarkets and grocery stores.[112]

Another area of food safety concern are macronutrients and substitutes such as no-calorie sweeteners, fat replacements and so on, which can pose serious health risks to consumers who are poorly informed about the benefits of these food additives.[113] In a similar way, there is a growing trend in biofortification to increase the nutritional value of foods. In this market segment, dietary supplements, nutraceuticals and pharma foods are sold to supplement nutrition. However, consumer and public health risks are growing from the unregulated sale and use of herbal additives and health supplements ingredients from India and China.

Finally, the risk of chemical and pesticide contamination of food is growing as a result of global food sourcing, contract farming and food-processing in developing countries. Very often, food contamination with chemical pesticides is directly linked to agricultural productivity and pest management strategies of farmers and agri-business. In many cases, environmental contamination occurs through the absorption of dangerous chemicals by animal livestock, plant crops and fish. For example, in the United States, food safety concerns were raised due to presence of rocket fuel in fresh lettuce.[114] In this case, over 300 drinking water sources and farm wells in California, and other sources in 15 states, were contaminated with perchlorate, an ingredient used in rocket fuel. As a result, contaminated lettuce contained several thousand times the recommended level of perchlorate which originated from Lockheed Martin.

Microbial contamination of food products in global agri-food industries

In many developing countries, food is produced, distributed and consumed locally, and fresh food and produce is cooked in traditional ways.[115] As globalization intensifies, governments and consumers are concerned about food contamination by traditional and new food pathogens. The meat, poultry and seafood pathogens in Table 2.7 pose serious food safety risks for consumers and public health, as well as tourism and global agri-food industries.[116]

The surveillance of food contamination across the entire food chain, requires mandatory regulation of food safety and food hygiene in global agri-food industries.[117] For example, the threat to fast-food restaurants and

Table 2.7 Food pathogen and food safety risks in global meat and produce industries

Pathogen	Food industry	Consumer safety risk
1. Pirons (BSE)	Cattle and meat	Variant Creutzfeldt-Jakob disease (vCJD)
2. Campylobacter	Cattle and pork	Reactive arthritis/Guillain-Barré syndrome
3. Escherichia coli	Cattle	Hemalytic uremic syndrome
4. Listeriosis monocytogenes	Meat and poultry	Sepsis, meningitis, bacterimia, acute febrile gastroenteristis
5. Salmonella (non-typhoid)	Poultry, eggs, seafood, cattle fruits and vegetables	Reiter's syndrome and reactive arthritis
6. Yersinia	Pork	Joint pain
7. Toxoplasma gondi	Pork and cattle	Reactive arthritis, miscarriage, birth defects

the meat processing industry is often due to the outbreak of *enerohaemorrhagic E.coli 0157:H7*, which causes illness and death in children. In this instance, the purchase and consumption of ground beef and hamburger products, unpasteurized apple cider, milk, lettuce, alfalfa sprouts and drinking water are sources of food hazards. In addition, strains of *Salmonella typhimurium DT 104* were found to have a genetically encoded resistance to five commonly prescribed antibiotics, which in turn, resulted in the spread of this food-borne pathogen throughout the global food system.[118]

According to the WHO, food contamination in the production, processing, and distribution process results in public health costs as well as economic costs to nations.[119] In global grain and cereals industries, food safety risks due to mycotoxin contamination are very high. In fact, the USDA estimates that approximately a quarter of the global food and feed industry output is contaminated with mycotoxins.[120] In turn, there are increased risks of cancer, immune system suppression and death from prolonged consumption of contaminated grain and agricultural commodity products.[121] Consequently, 'farm to table' strategies for Good Agricultural Practices (GAP), Good Hygienic Practices (GHP) and Good Manufacturing Practices (GMP) inspections are required to monitor food contamination and adulteration.[122] In the meantime, farmers, agri-businesses and food companies face growing product liability and the collapse of agri-food markets due to food contamination incidents.[123]

Bioterrorism and food crime in global agri-food industries

The monitoring of food safety by national governments is now a major regulatory policy and national security goal. The urgency of food safety regulation in the twenty-first century is reinforced by the growing risk of bioterrorist sabotage, and deliberate contamination of national food systems and global food supply chain industries.[124] Through the use of dangerous biological and chemical agents, terrorists can release deadly contaminants into national food systems and global agri-food industries.[125] In this regard, the integrity of national food systems and global agri-food industries must be protected through 'farm to table' and 'boat to throat' food safety infrastructure.[126]

The deliberate contamination of food is a growing problem in many countries. For example, in China, a food vendor poisoned his competitor's food products in an effort to increase his profits and gain control over the local market. As a result of this act of food sabotage, several people died as a result of food poisoning. While the scale and scope of this incident is relatively small, food crime poses serious systemic threats to food safety in global agri-food industries.[127]

Pharming agriculture and food safety: pharmaceutical products in food production

At the start of the twenty-first century, modern biotechnology increasingly focuses on the production of medicines and pharmaceutical products in food crops and animal livestock. Through the use of genome science, agri-food crops and animal livestock can produce anticoagulants, blood substitutes, hormones and edible vaccines to fight against measles, polio, diptheria, yellow fever and viral diarrhea. In this context, the use of genome science to produce pharm foods that contain medicines and pharmaceutical products is a new phase in industrial agri-food industry production.

In reality, agri-food industries have multiple uses that must be regulated to ensure food safety. As the decade unfolds, dual purposes for farming and agriculture are driven by the growing role of pharmaceutical companies in biotechnology markets and global agri-food industries. While pharm crops and livestock are in the early phases of development, there are concerns over contamination of animals and food. In this new area of agriculture and modern biotechnology, GM crops and livestock are used to produce drugs and enzymes to treat and cure illnesses and diseases such as anemia, liver cirrhosis, cystic fibrosis, HIV and hepatitis B and C.[128] While pharm crops and livestock are in the early phases of development, there are food safety concerns over the contamination of animals and food.

At the present time, transgenic corn is the most important pharm crop plant in the global agri-food industry.[129] However, other grain and cereal crops such as GM alfalfa are being developed to increase the efficiency of global pharmaceutical drug production.[130] For example, in the past, microbial fermentation was used to industrially produce medicines and pharmaceutical products. However, new varieties of GM alfalfa produce pharmaceutical products from their plant leaves.

Ultimately, new GM pharm crops are increasing the cost and production efficiencies of global pharmaceutical industries. Therefore, tomatoes, fruit and corn will be used increasingly to produce pharmaceutical products by drug firms that are also integrated agri-food and biotechnology companies. For example, in 2004, the EU announced the launch of a new 12 million euro project to develop vaccines from GM food crops.[131] The project, called Pharma Planta, consists of EU scientists and networks of laboratories that are working to produce vaccines and pharmaceutical products for global diseases such as HIV/AIDS, rabies and tuberculosis (TB). The results of this project are expected by 2009. In this project, GM corn, potatoes, tomatoes and tobacco will be investigated for their ability to produce human proteins and low-cost vaccines for developing countries.[132]

Currently, world-class agri-businesses and pharmaceutical companies such as Monsanto (USA), Meristem (France) and biotechnology companies like ProdiGene and Epicyte have global market and strategic interests in pharm crops and livestock products. In turn, long-term competitive advantage relative to patent rights and the profitable production of drugs and vaccines in food crops and livestock are at stake. Therefore, pharm food production is emerging as a new high-value niche market for farmers, agribusiness and food companies.[133]

In summary, pharm crops can contaminate food supplies through the introduction of bioactive agents intended for use as pharmaceutical products. In the case of corn, contamination can occur through uncontrolled cross-pollenation. When this occurs, farmers with conventional crops can mistakenly introduce pharm crops into food-processing and retail outlets. In addition, contamination can occur during seed production and transport. Therefore, the production of these hybrid crops increases the food safety risks for humans, as well as animals, which may eat toxic GM pharm plants by accident. Therefore, multi-purpose agriculture, and the growing trend in GM micro-organisms, food crops and animal livestock for pharmaceutical production, pose serious food safety risks through accidental mingling during the production, processing and distribution processes.

VII CONCLUSIONS: GOVERNANCE FOOD SAFETY IN GLOBAL AGRI-FOOD INDUSTRIES

The globalization of agri-food industries is accelerating the integration of agricultural commodities chains and national food systems. In turn, transatlantic and Asian-Pacific food companies and agri-food industries increasingly rely on growing customer bases and food production capacity of developing countries. As OECD and developing countries increase food security through regional free trade and WTO agricultural market liberalization, food safety risks are growing in global agri-food industries.

In this respect, genome science, biotechnology and the use of agriculture and animal livestock for pharmaceutical production present new markets for global food and pharmaceutical companies. However, governments, consumers and farmers are increasingly concerned about food safety risks in global agri-food industries. In this respect, the limited regulatory capacity, food inspection and biosecurity infrastructure in developing countries, which increasingly source food for transatlantic and other OECD countries, increases food safety risks. In turn, developing countries face socio-economic hardships due to their incomplete integration into value-added food markets.

Finally, the regulation of food safety must address the systemic risks posed by the global consolidation and vertical integration of agri-food companies in networked agri-food industries. If the current trends continue in global agri-food industries and agricultural commodity chains, farming, modern biotechnology, food-processing and food retailing will be controlled by a small number of privately held corporations. In turn, the driving force for management will continue to be return on investment for shareholders, and corporate profitability. As a consequence, the mandatory regulation of food safety in national food systems, regional food supply chains and global agri-food industries is a food security and national security priority for all nations in the twenty-first century.

NOTES

1. Historically food trade, shipping innovations and colonial expansion set into motion the current system of core and periphery structure which is currently undergoing a rapid phase of centrifuge.
2. Brohel, Wayne G. (1992), *Cargill-Trading the World's Grain*, Dartmouth, NH: University Press of New England, pp. 746–9.
3. Barnet, Richard J. and Ronald E. Muller (1974), *Global Reach: The Power of Multinational Corporations*, New York: Simon & Schuster.
4. Chandler, A.D. Jr (1990), *Scale and Scope: The Dynamics of Industrial Capitalism*, Cambridge, MA: Harvard University Press.

5. Gereffi, G. (1995), 'Global production systems and Third World development', in B. Stallings (ed.), *Global Changes, Regional Response: The New International Context of Development*, Cambridge: Cambridge University Press, pp. 100–42.
6. See Whitely, R. (1999), *Divergent Capitalisms: The Social Structuring and Change of Business Systems*, New York and Oxford: Oxford University Press.
7. Strange, Susan (1988), *States and Markets*, Oxford: Basil Blackwell.
8. Porter, Michael (ed.) (1986), *Competition in Global Industries*, Boston, MA: Harvard Business School Press, pp. 405–47.
9. Ibid., p. 10.
10. Mody, Ashoka (2004), 'Is FDI integrating the world economy?', *The World Economy*, **27** (8), pp. 1195–222.
11. FAO (2003), *Major Policy Issues and Market Factors Having Implications for the Long-Term Performance of Agricultural Exports*, Committee on Commodity Problems, Sixty-fourth Session, 18–21 March, Rome: FAO.
12. Fold, N. (2002), 'Lead firms and competition in 'bi-polar' commodity chains: grinders and branders in global cocoa-chocolate industries', *Journal of Agrarian Change*, **2** (2), pp. 228–47.
13. Ibid.
14. Ibid.
15. Rugman, A.M. and A. Verbeke (2004), 'A perspective on regional and global strategies of multinational enterprises', *Journal of International Business Studies*, **35** (1), pp. 3–18.
16. Rauch, J.E. (1999), 'Networks versus markets in international trade', *Journal of International Economics*, **48**, pp. 7–35.
17. Phyne, J. and J. Mansilla (2003), 'Foraging linkages in the commodity chain: the case of the Chilean salmon fishing industry 1987–2001', *Sociologica Ruralis*, **43** (2), pp. 108–27.
18. Clancy, M. (1998), 'Commodity chains, services and development: theory and preliminary evidence from the tourism industry', *Review of International Political Economy*, **5** (1), pp. 122–48.
19. Ibid., pp. 24, 90–96.
20. Ibid., pp. 7–8.
21. Ibid.
22. Ibid., pp. 20–21.
23. Food Engineering, 'The world's top 100 food & beverage companies', http://www.food-engineering.org, 1 October 2002.
24. Ibid.
25. In addition to greater economic efficiency, marketing costs are reduced by enlisting the support of food suppliers and distributors into the design, category management, advertising, packaging and in-store promotion of food.
26. Ahold presentation to ERS/ USDA.
27. Ibid.
28. Ibid.
29. Huang, Sophia Wu (2004), 'Global trade patterns in fruits and vegetables', *Global Trade Patterns in Fruits and Vegetables*, ERS, WRS-04-06, Washington, DC: USDA, pp. 1–2.
30. The EU is sourcing fresh produce through its preferential trade arrangements, and will shift to bilateral free trade strategies by the end of the decade to secure and stabilize the supply of fresh fruits and vegetables.
31. Dyck, John H. and Kenzo Ito (2004), 'Japan's fruit and vegetable market', *Global Trade Patterns in Fruits and Vegetables*, ERS, WRS-04-06, Washington, DC: USDA pp. 72–3.
32. Shields, Dennis and Sophia Wu Huang (2004), 'China's fruit and vegetable trade', *Global Trade Patterns in Fruits and Vegetables*, ERS, WRS-04-06, Washington, DC: USDA pp. 52–63.
33. Ibid., p. 55.
34. Ibid., p. 6.
35. Ibid., pp. 14–18.

36. Ibid.
37. Ibid., p. 2.
38. *Global Trade Patterns in Fruits and Vegetables* (2004), ERS, WRS-04–06, Washington, DC: USDA, p. 14.
39. Ibid., pp. 1–15.
40. MacDonald, James M., Michael E. Ollinger, Kenneth E. Nelson and Charles Hardy (1999), *Consolidation in the US Meatpacking Industry*, AER, # 785, USDA, Washington, DC: USDA, pp. 4–5.
41. Ibid.
42. Ibid., p. 14.
43. Ibid., pp. 13–15.
44. Ibid., p. 15. Also see Zylbersztajn, D. and C.A.P.M. Filho (2003), 'Competitiveness of meat and agri-food chain in Brazil', *Supply Chain Management*, **8** (2), pp. 155–65.
45. Hayes, Dermot J., John R. Green, Helen H. Jensen and Adrienne Erbach (1991), 'Measuring international competitiveness in the beef sector', *Agribusiness*, **7** (4), pp. 357–74.
46. Ibid., p. 14.
47. Ibid., pp. 4–5.
48. Martinez, Steve W. (1999), *Vertical Coordination in the Pork and Broiler Industries-Implications for Pork and Chicken Products*, AER, #777, USDA, Washington, DC: USDA.
49. Ibid, p. 8. Also see Hayenga, Marvin (1998), 'Cost structures of pork slaughter and processing firms: behavioral and performance implications', *Review of Agricultural Economics*, **20** (2), pp. 574–83.
50. Martinez (1999).
51. Ibid.
52. Ibid.
53. Ibid., p. 25.
54. Dyck, John H. and Kenneth E. Nelson (2003), *Structure of Global Markets for Meat*, ERS 785, Washington, DC: USDA, p. 5.
55. Ibid., p. 2.
56. Ibid., pp. 21–3.
57. Vannuccini, S. (2004), *Overview of Fish Production, Utilization, Consumption and Trade – Based on 2002 Data Fishery Information*, Data and Statistics Unit, Rome: FAO, p. 2.
58. FAO (2002), *The State of World Fisheries and Aquaculture (SIFIA) 2002*, Rome: FAO, p. 2.
59. Alshouse, Jane, Jean Buzby, David Harvey and David Zorn (2004), 'Seafood safety and trade', *International Trade and Food Safety*, AER 828 Washington, DC: USDA, pp. 48–68.
60. Ibid.
61. Vannuccini, op. cit. pp. 11–13.
62. Ibid.
63. FAO (2004), 'Fish trade as success story for developing countries, but is the field level enough?', FAO Press Release, FAO Newsroom, www.fao.org/newsroom/en/news/2004/37147/, 13 February 2004.
64. Trostle, Ronald, Paul Westcott and Edwin Young (2004), 'Agricultural baseline projections – global agricultural trade 2004–2013', ERS Briefing Room, www.USDA.gov.
65. Fernandez-Cornejo, Jorge (2004), *The Seed Industry in US Agriculture*, ERS, Washington, DC: USDA, pp. 5–6 and 29–34.
66. See the global seed industry statistics on the International Seed Federation website, International Seed Federation, http://www.worldseed.org/.
67. Ibid. Also see WHO (2005), *Modern Food Biotechnology, Human Health and Development: An Evidence Based Study*, Geneva, pp. 1–10.
68. Traxler, G. (2004), *The Economic Impacts of Biotechnology-Based Technological*

Innovations, Agriculture and Developments Economics Division, Rome: FAO, pp. 8–13.
69. In this respect, genome technology serves as a major factor input which revolutionized corporate strategy and competitiveness both in low-income countries in Asia, Africa and Latin America, and in the OECD countries.
70. James, Clive (1998), *Global Review of Commercialized Transgenic Crops*. ISAAA, #8–1998, Ithaca, NY: Cornell University, pp. 10–11.
71. Ibid., p. 33.
72. FDA/PEW (2002), *Animal Cloning and the Production of Food Products: Perspectives From the Food Chain*, Proceedings from a Workshop, Dallas, Texas, 26 September, sponsored by the PEW Initiative on Food and Biotechnology and the Center for Veterinary Medicine and the US Food and Drug Administration, Rockville, MD and Washington, DC: FDA and Pew Initiative on Food and Biotechnology, pp. 12–14.
73. In ibid., p. 14.
74. BBC News website, 'Cloned animals "safe to eat" ', by Richard Black, http://news.bbc.co.uk/2/hi/science/nature/2207697.stm, 21 August 2002.
75. Bruinsma, Jelle (2002), *World Agriculture: Towards 2015/2030 – An FAO Perspective*, Rome: FAO/Earthscan, pp. 173–4.
76. National Research Council (2002), *Committee on Defining Science Based Concerns Associated with Products of Animal Biotechnology, Committee on Agricultural Biotechnology, Health and the Environment*, Washington, DC: National Academies Press.
77. UNCTAD/WTO – FAO (1998) *Market Prospects for Organic Food and Beverages*, International Trade Center Committee on Commodity Problems – Intergovernmental Group on Citrus Fruits, Valencia, 22–25 September, Geneva: WTO, pp. 1–2.
78. FAO press release 99/33, Rome, 25 January 1999.
79. Bruinsma (2002), op.cit., pp. 312–14.
80. UNCTAD/FAO, op.cit., p. 5.
81. As the decade unfolds, many developing nations generate foreign exchange revenue from cross-border food trade, and integration into global agri-food industries. In this respect, the food and agricultural industry sector are critical for the socio-economic development of all nations in the global system.
82. Roberts, D. (1998), 'Preliminary assessment of the effects of the WTO Agreement on Sanitary and Phytosanitary Trade Regulations', *Journal of International Economic Law*, **1** (3), pp. 377–465.
83. WHO (1999), *Food Safety Report by the WHO Director General, Executive Board 105th Session*, 2 December, Geneva: WHO.
84. WHO (2002b), *Global Strategy for Food Safety*, Food Safety Program, Geneva: WHO, pp. 4–5.
85. BSE started in the United Kingdom, spread to the European Union and eventually the global food system through the integration and cross-border competition in global agri-food industries.
86. BBC News website, 'Blood donor "may have passed on CJD" ', http://news.bbc.co.uk/1/hi/health/3327745.stm. 17 December 2003.
87. Baros, L.O. (2001), 'Recent developments in animal identification and the traceability of animal products in international trade', *Review of Science and Technology – Office of Epizootics*, **20** (2), pp. 640–51.
88. WHO Media Center Fact Sheet, Number 277, 15 January 2004.
89. BBC News website, 'Time line: avian flu', http://news.bbc.co.uk/1/hi/world/asia-pacific/3429547.stm, 20 February 2004.
90. *Washington Post*, 'Md. bans live poultry sales as a precaution – avian flu prompts calls for federal help', 12 February 2004.
91. *Washington Post*, 'Beef production down after mad cow', 17 March 2004.
92. BBC News website, 'US chicken imports suspended', http://news.bbc.co.uk/1/hi/world/americas/3469795.stm, 8 February 2004.

93. Orden, D., T. Josling and D. Roberts (2002), 'Product differentiation, sanitary barriers and arbitrage in world poultry markets', in B. Krissof (ed.), *Global Food Trade and Consumer Demand for Quality*, New York: Kluwer Academic/Plenum, pp. 147–64.
94. See WHO (2005), *Avian Influenza: Assessing the Pandemic Threat*, Geneva, pp. 7–20. WHO (2004), 'Avian Influenza – Fact sheet', http://www.who. int/csr/don/2004_01_15/en/, 15 January. WHO (2004), Avian Flu influenza update #5 – Avian Influenza – HSNI infection in Humans: Urgent Weed to Eliminate the Animal Reservoir', http://www.who.int/csr/ don/2004_01_22/en/index.html.
95. BBC News website, 'US chicken imports suspended', http://news.bbc.co.uk/1/hi/world/americas/3469795.stm, 8 February 2004.
96. See 'WHO Avian Flu Influenza Update #5 – Avian Influenza – HSNI infection in Humans: Urgent Need to Eliminate the Animal Reservoir', http://www.who.int/csr/don/ 2004_01_22/en/index.html.
97. BBC News website, 'Bird flu prompts huge Canadian cull', http://news.bbc.co.uk/2/hi/americas/3603807.stm, 6 April 2004.
98. Joint FAO/WHO Food Standards Programme (2001), *Expert Consultation on Risk Assessment of Microbiological Hazards in Foods*, 23–27 July, Geneva: WHO, pp. 12–17.
99. WHO (2002b), p. 3.
100. Animal health is directly related to food safety and veterinary public health is now a growing area of global agri-food industry regulation.
101. Henson, S. and M. Mazzocchi (2002), 'Impact of Bovine Spongiform Encephalopathy on agribusiness in the United Kingdom: results of a study of equity prices', *American Journal of Agricultural Economics*, **84** (2), pp. 370–86.
102. Organic Consumers Association, 'Eating chicken may boost arsenic exposure', from Karen Pallarito, Health Day Reporter, www.organicconsumer.org/foodsafety/arsenic 12304.cfm, 19 January 2004.
103. Mathews, Kenneth H., Jason Bernstein and Jean C. Buzby (2004), 'Animal diseases and pathogens and food safety', *International Trade of Meat and Poultry Products and Food Safety*, Washington, DC: USDA, p. 66.
104. Ibid.
105. Organic Consumers Association, 'Toxic salmon from fish farms', from Thomas Garvey May, Natural Foods Merchandiser, www.organicconsumer.org/toxic/salman072202.cfm, July 2002.
106. BBC News website, 'Scare over farmed salmon safety', http://news.bbc.co.uk/2hi/health/3380735.stm, 8 January 2004. MSNBC.COM (2004), 'Toxic or not? Reel in our safe fish guide', 9 September, http://msnbc.msn.com/id/5932670. EPA Consumption Advice – Joint Federal Advisory for Mercury in Fish – 2004 FDA/EPA Consumer Advisory – What You Need to Know About Mercury in Fish And Shellfish, http://www.epa.gov/ waterscience/fishadvice/factsheet.html.
107. See WHO Geneva website, http://www.who.int/foodsafety/chem/pcbsalmon/en/.
108. WHO (2004) 'PCBs and dioxin in salmon', http://www.who.int/foodsafety/chem/pcb-salmon/en/index.html, 20 January.
109. Alhouse et al. (2004).
110. Ibid.
111. WHO (2002b), p. 5.
112. Organic Consumers Association – Supermarket Campaign, 'Lawsuits seek labeling of farmed salmon as artificially dyed', Linda Ashton, http://www.organicconsumer.org/ge042503.salmon.cfm, 24 April 2003.
113. Institute of Medicine and National Research Council (1998), *Ensuring Safe Food: From Production to Consumption*, Washington, DC: National Academy Press, pp. 58–9.
114. Organic Consumers Organization, 'Rocket fuel residues found in lettuce', Oakland, CA http://www.organicconsumers.org/toxic/lettuce042903.cfm, 2 January 2003.
115. Ibid., p. 178.
116. Mathews et al. (2004), p. 52.
117. Codex Alimentarius, pp. 3–4.

118. See WHO (1999), *Food Safety Report by the WHO Director General, Executive Board 105th Session*, 2 December, Geneva: WHO.
119. Motarjemi, Y., F. Kaferstein, G. Moy, K. Miyagishima, S. Miyagawa and A. Reilly (1995), *Food Safety Issues – Food Technologies and Public Health*, WHO/FNU/FOS/95.12-Food Safety Unit-Program of the Food and Nutrition – World Health Organization, Geneva: WHO, pp. 2–5.
120. See Dohlman, Erik (2004), 'Mycotoxin regulations – implications for international agricultural trade', *International Trade and Food Safety*, ERS, Washington, DC: USDA.
121. Ibid.
122. FAO/WHO Global Forum of Food Safety Regulators (2002), 'Introductory Remarks', Hartwig de Haen, Assistant Director-General, Economic and Social Development, *Global Forum for Food Safety Regulation, Conference Proceedings*, Rome: FAO/WHO Food Safety Regulators Secretariat, pp. 69–72.
123. FAO/WHO Global Forum of Food Safety Regulators (2002), 'Capacity building and technical assistance – new approaches and building alliances', Deepak Gupta Ministry of Health and Family Welfare, Government of India, *Global Forum for Food Safety Regulation, Conference Proceedings*, Rome: FAO/WHO Food Safety Regulators Secretariat, p. 178.
124. Bioterrorism is now a major concern for the United States and other nations. Therefore food safety is increasingly incorporated in national security, homeland security and industry regulation.
125. WHO (2002a), *Food Safety Issues, Terrorist Threats to Food – Guidance for Establishing and Strengthening Prevention and Response Systems*, Food Safety Department, Geneva: WHO, p. 1.
126. Ibid., p. 12.
127. In this case, the Chinese government executed the guilty party. However, the incident sent shock waves around the world since the food was sabotaged by another food vendor.
128. Mellon, Margaret (2002), 'Who's minding the pharm?', *Catalyst, The Magazine of the Union of Concerned Scientists*, **1** (2), pp. 3–4.
129. Ibid., p. 4.
130. See Comis, Dan (1999), 'Transforming pollen for better plants for the "pharm"', USDA Agriculture Research Service, www.ars.usda.gov/is/pr/1999/990629.htm.
131. BBC News website, 'EU funding for GM plant vaccines', http://news.bbc.co.uk/2/hi/science/nature/388_7517.stm, 12 July 2004.
132. Ibid.
133. PEW Initiative on food and Biotechnology (2002), *Pharming the Field: a Look at the Benefits and Risks of Bioengineering Plants to Produce Pharmaceuticals*, Proceeding from a Workshop Sponsored by the PEW Initiative on Food and Biotechnology, the US Food and Drug Administration and Cooperative State Research Education and Extension Service of the US Department of Agriculture, Washington, DC: USDA, pp. 4–16.

REFERENCES

Alshouse, Jane, Jean Buzby, David Harvey and David Zorn (2004), 'Seafood safety and trade', *International Trade and Food Safety*, AER 828, Washington, DC: USDA, pp. 48–68.

Barnet, Richard J. and Ronald E. Muller (1974), *Global Reach: The Power of Multinational Corporations*, New York: Simon & Schuster.

Baros, L.O. (2001), 'Recent developments in animal identification and the

traceability of animal products in international trade', *Review of Science and Technology*, Office of Epizootics, **20** (2), pp. 640–51.
BBC News website (2002), 'Cloned animals "safe to eat"', by Richard Black, http://news.bbc.co.uk/2/hi/science/nature/2207697.stm, 21 August 2002.
BBC News website (2003), 'Blood donor "may have passed on CJD"', http://news.bbc.co.uk/1/hi/health/3327745.stm, 17 December 2004.
BBC News website (2004a), 'Bird flu prompts huge Canadian cull', http://news.bbc.co.uk/2/hi/americas/3603807.stm, 6 April 2004.
BBC News website (2004b), 'EU funding for GM plant vaccines', http://news.bbc.co.uk/2/hi/science/nature/3887517.stm, 12 July 2004.
BBC News website (2004c), 'Scare over farmed salmon safety', http://news.bbc.co.uk/2/hi/health/3380735.stm, 8 January 2004.
BBC News website (2004d), 'Time line: avian flu', http://news.bbc.co.uk/1/hi/world/asia-pacific/3429547.stm, 20 February 2004.
BBC News website (2004e), 'US chicken imports suspended', http://news.bbc.co.uk/1/hi/world/americas/3469795.stm, 8 February 2004.
Braithwaite, J. and P. Drahos (2002), *Global Business Regulation*, Cambridge: Cambridge University Press.
Brohel, Wayne G. (1992), *Cargill – Trading the World's Grain*, Dartmouth, NH: University Press of New England.
Bruinsma, Jelle (2002), *World Agriculture: Towards 2015/2030 – An FAO Perspective*, FAO/Earthscan, Rome: FAO.
Chandler, A.D. Jr (1990), *Scale and Scope: The Dynamics of Industrial Capitalism*, Cambridge, MA: Harvard University Press.
Clancy, M. (1998), 'Commodity chains, services and development: theory and preliminary evidence from the tourism industry', *Review of International Political Economy*, **5** (1), pp. 122–48.
Comis, Dan (1999), 'Transforming pollen for better plants for the "pharm"', USDA Agriculture Research Service, http://www.ars.usda.gov/is/pr/1999/990629.htm.
Dohlman, Erik (2004), 'Mycotoxin regulations – implications for international agricultural trade', *International Trade and Food Safety*, ERS, Washington, DC: USDA.
Dyck, John H. and Kenzo Ito (2004), 'Japan's fruit and vegetable market', *Global Trade Patterns in Fruits and Vegetables*, ERS, WRS-04-06, Washington, DC: USDA, pp. 72–3.
Dyck, John H. and Kenneth E. Nelson (2003), *Structure of Global Markets for Meat*, ERS 785, Washington, DC: USDA.
EPA (2004), 'EPA Consumption Advice – Joint Federal Advisory for Mercury in Fish – 2004 FDA/EPA Consumer Advisory – what you need to know about mercury in fish and shellfish', http://www.epa.gov/waterscience/fishadvice/factsheet.html.
Esty, Daniel and Damien Geradin (eds) (2001), *Regulatory Competition and Economic Integration*, New York and London: Oxford University Press.
FAO (2002), *The State of World Fisheries and Aquaculture (SIFIA) 2002*, Rome: FAO.
FAO (2003), *Major Policy Issues and Market Factors Having Implications for the Long-Term Performance of Agricultural Exports*, Committee on Commodity Problems, Sixty-fourth Session, 18–21 March, Rome: FAO.
FAO (2004), 'Fish trade as success story for developing countries, but is the field

level enough?', Press Release, FAO Newsroom, 13 February 2004, FAO Press Release www.fao.org/newsroom/en/news/2004/37147/.
FAO-IPPC (1995), *International Standards for Phytosanitary Measures – Principles of Plant Quarantine Related to International Trade*, Number 1, Rome: FAO.
FAO/WHO (2002a), 'Capacity building and technical assistance – new approaches and building alliances', Deepak Gupta Ministry of Health and Family Welfare, Government of India, *Global Forum for Food Safety Regulation, Conference Proceedings*, Rome: FAO/WHO Food Safety Regulators.
FAO/WHO (2002b), *Global Forum of Food Safety Regulators: Improving Efficiency and Transparency in Food Safety Systems – Sharing Experiences*, Marrakesh, 28–30 January, Conference Proceedings, Rome: FAO/WHO.
FAO/WHO Global Forum of Food Safety Regulators (2002), Introductory Remarks, Hartwig DE Haen, Assistant Director-General, Economic and Social Development, *Global Forum for Food Safety Regulation, Conference Proceedings*, Rome, Italy: FAO/WHO Food Safety Regulators Secretariat.
FDA/PEW (2002), *Animal Cloning and the Production of Food Products: Perspectives from the Food Chain*, proceedings from a workshop sponsored by the PEW Initiative on Food and Biotechnology and the Center for Veterinary Medicine and the US Food and Drug Administration, Dallas, Texas, 26 September Rockville, MD. and Washington, DC: FDA and Pew Initiative on Food and Biotechnology.
Fernandez-Cornejo, Jorge (2004), *The Seed Industry in US Agriculture*, ERS, Washington, DC: USDA.
Fernandez-Cornejo, Jorge and William D. McBride (2002), *Adoption of Bioengineered Crops*, Washington, DC: USDA.
Fold, N. (2002), 'Lead firms and competition in "bi-polar" commodity chains: grinders and branders in global cocoa-chocolate industries', *Journal of Agrarian Change*, **2** (2), pp. 228–47.
Food Engineering (2002), 'The world's top 100 food & beverage companies', www.foodengineering.org, 1 October 2002.
Gereffi, G. (1995), 'Global production systems and Third World development', in B. Stallings (ed.), *Global Changes, Regional Response: The New International Context of Development*, Cambridge: Cambridge University Press, pp. 100–42.
Global Trade Patterns in Fruits and Vegetables (2004), ERS, WRS-04-06, Washington, DC: USDA.
Government of India (2002), *Global Forum for Food Safety Regulation*, Conference Proceedings, Rome: FAO/WHO Food Safety Regulators Secretariat.
Hayenga, Marvin (1998), 'Cost structures of pork slaughter and processing firms: behavioral and performance implications', *Review of Agricultural Economics*, **20** (2), pp. 574–83.
Hayes, Dermot J., John R. Green, Helen H. Jensen and Adrienne Erbach (1991), 'Measuring international competitiveness in the beef sector' *Agribusiness*, **7** (4), pp. 357–74.
Hendrickson, Mary, William D. Heffernan, Phillip H. Howard and Judith Heffernan (2001), *Consolidation in Food Retailing and Dairy: Implications for Farmers and Consumers in a Global Food System*, Washington, DC: National Farmers Union.
Henson, S. and M. Mazzocchi (2002), 'Impact of Bovine Spongiform Encephalopathy

on agribusiness in the United Kingdom: results of a study of equity prices', *American Journal of Agricultural Economics*, **84** (2), pp. 370–86.

Huang, Sophia Wu (2004), 'Global trade patterns in fruits and vegetables', *Global Trade Patterns in Fruits and Vegetables*, ERS, WRS-04–06, Washington, DC: USDA, pp. 1–2.

Institute of Medicine and National Research Council (1998), *Ensuring Safe Food: From Production to Consumption*, Washington, DC: National Academy Press.

IPPC (1999) *Requirements for the Establishment of Pest Free Places of Production and Pest Free Production Sites*, Publication Number 10, Rome: FAO.

James, Clive (1998), *Global Review of Commercialized Transgenic Crops*. ISAAA, #8–1998, Ithaca, NY: Cornell University.

Joint FAO/WHO Food Standards Programme (2000), *Safety Aspects of Genetically Modified Foods of Plant Origin, Report of a Joint FAO/WHO Expert Consultation on Foods Derived from Biotechnology*, 29 May – 2 June, Geneva: WHO.

Joint FAO/WHO Food Standards Programme (2001), *Expert Consultation on Risk Assessment of Microbiological Hazards in Foods*, 23–27 July Geneva: WHO.

Kaufman, Phil R., Charles R. Handy, Edward W. McLaughlin, Kristen Park and Geoffrey M. Green (2000), *Understanding the Dynamics of Produce Markets – Consumption and Consolidation Grow*, Washington, DC: USDA.

MacDonald, James M., Michael E. Ollinger, Kenneth E. Nelson and Charles Hardy (1999), *Consolidation in the US Meatpacking Industry*, AER, # 785, Washington, DC: USDA.

Martinez, Steve W. (1999), *Vertical Coordination in the Pork and Broiler Industries – Implications for Pork and Chicken Products*, AER, #777, Washington, DC: USDA.

Mathews, Kenneth H., Jason Bernstein and Jean C. Buzby (2004), 'Animal diseases and pathogens and food safety', *International Trade of Meat and Poultry Products and Food Safety*, Washington, DC: USDA, p. 52.

Mellon, Margaret (2002), 'Who's minding the pharm?', *Catalyst, The Magazine of the Union of Concerned Scientists*, **1** (2), pp. 3–4.

Mody, Ashoka (2004), 'Is FDI integrating the world economy', *The World Economy*, **27** (8), pp. 1195–222.

Motarjemi, Y., F. Kaferstein, G. Moy, K. Miyagishima S. Miyagawa and A. Reilly (1995), *Food Safety Issues – Food Technologies and Public Health*, WHO/FNU/FOS/95.12-Food Safety Unit – Program of the Food and Nutrition, Geneva: WHO.

MSNBC.com (2004), 'Toxic or not? Reel in our safe fish guide', http://msnbc.msn.com/id/5932670, 9 September.

National Research Council (2002), *Committee on Defining Science Based Concerns Associated with Products of Animal Biotechnology, Committee on Agricultural Biotechnology, Health and the Environment*, Washington, DC: National Academies Press.

OIE (2002) *Report on the Meeting of the OIE Working Group on Animal Production Food Safety*, Paris: OIE.

Orden, D., T. Josling and D. Roberts (2002), 'Product differentiation, sanitary barriers and arbitrage in world poultry markets', in B. Krissof (ed.), *Global Food Trade and Consumer Demand for Quality*, New York: Kluwer Academic/Plenum, pp. 147–64.

Organic Consumers Association (2002), 'Toxic salmon from fish farms', Thomas Garvey May, Natural Foods Merchandiser, http://www.organicconsumer.org/foodsafety/arsenic12304.cfm, July.

Organic Consumers Association-Supermarket Campaign (2003), 'Lawsuits seek labeling of farmed salmon as artificially dyed', Linda Ashton, http://www.organicconsumer.org/ge042503.salmon.cfm, 24 April.

Organic Consumers Association (2004), 'Eating chicken may boost arsenic exposure', Karen Pallarito, Health Day Reporter, http://www.organicconsumer.org/foodsafety/arsenic12304.cfm, 19 January.

Pacific Economic Cooperation Council (2002), *Pacific Economic Cooperation Council Outlook 2002–2003, Making the Region's Food Supply Safer*, Singapore: Pacific Economic Cooperation Council.

PEW Initiative on Food and Biotechnology (2002), *Pharming the Field: A Look at the Benefits and Risks of Bioengineering Plants to Produce Pharmaceuticals*, Proceedings from a Workshop Sponsored by the PEW Initiative on Food and Biotechnology, the US Food and Drug Administration and Cooperative State Research Education and Extension Service of the US Department of Agriculture, Washington, DC: USDA.

Phyne, J. and J. Mansilla (2003), 'Foraging linkages in the commodity chain: the case of the Chilean salmon fishing industry 1987–2001', *Sociologica Ruralis*, **43** (2), pp. 108–27.

Porter, Michael (ed.) (1986), *Competition in Global Industries*, Boston, MA: Harvard Business School Press, pp. 405–47.

Rauch J. E. (1999), Networks versus markets in international trade', *Journal of International Economics*, **48**, pp. 7–35.

Roberts, D. (1998), 'Preliminary assessment of the effects of the WTO Agreement on Sanitary and Phytosanitary Trade Regulations', *Journal of International Economic Law*, **1** (3), pp. 377–465.

Rugman, A.M. and A. Verbeke (2004), 'A perspective on regional and global strategies of multinational enterprises', *Journal of International Business Studies*, **35** (1), pp. 3–18.

Shields, Dennis and Sophia Wu Huang (2004), 'China's fruit and vegetable trade', *Global Trade Patterns in Fruits and Vegetables*, ERS, WRS-04–06, Washington, DC: USDA, pp. 52–63.

Strange, Susan (1988), *States and Markets*, Oxford: Basil Blackwell

Traxler, G. (2004), *The Economic Impacts of Biotechnology-Based Technological Innovations*, Agriculture and Developments Economics Division, Rome: FAO.

Trostle, Ronald, Paul Westcott and Edwin Young (2004), 'Agricultue baseline projections – global agricultural trade 2004–2013', ERS Briefing Room, http://www.USDA.gov.

UNCTAD/WTO – FAO (1998), *Market Prospects for Organic Food and Beverages, International Trade Center Committee on Commodity Problems – Intergovernmental Group on Citrus Fruits*, Valencia, 22–25 September, Rome: FAO.

United States Department of Justice (2000), *International Competition Policy Advisory Committee to the Attorney General and Assistant Attorney General for Antitrust – Final Report*, Washington, DC: US Department of Justice AntiTrust Division.

Vannuccini, S. (2004), *Overview of Fish Production, Utilization, Consumption and Trade – Based on 2002 Data Fishery Information*, Data and Statistic Unit, Rome: FAO, p. 2.

Washington Post (2004), 'Maryland bans live poultry sales as a precaution – avian flu prompts calls for federal help', http://www.washingtonpost.com/wp-dyn/articles/A39514-2004mar 8.html, 12 February.

Washington Post (2004), 'Beef production down after mad cow', 17 March.
Whitely, R. (1999), *Divergent Capitalisms: The Social Structuring and Change of Business Systems*, New York and Oxford: Oxford University Press.
WHO (1999), *Food Safety Report by the WHO Director General, Executive Board 105th Session*, 2 December, Geneva: WHO.
WHO (2002a), *Food Safety Issues, Terrorist Threats to Food – Guidance for Establishing and Strengthening Prevention and Response Systems*, Food Safety Department, Geneva: WHO.
WHO (2002b) *Global Strategy for Food Safety*, Food Safety Program, Geneva: WHO.
WHO (2002c), *WHO Consultation on Public Health and Animal Transmissible Spongiform Encephalopathies: Epidemiology, Risk and Research Requirements – With the Participation of the Office International des Epizooties*, 1–3 December 1999, Geneva: WHO.
WHO (2004), 'Avian Influenza – Fact Sheet' http://www.who.int/csr/don/2004_01_15/en/, 15 January.
WHO (2004), 'PCBs and dioxin in Salmon', http://www.who.int/foodsafety/chem/pcbsalmon/en/index.html, 20 January.
WHO (2004), 'Avian Flu Influenza Update # 5 – Avian Influenza – H5N1 Infection in Humans: Urgent Need to Eliminate the Animal Reservoir', http://www.who.int/csr/don/2004_01_22/en/index.html.
WHO (2005), *Avian Influenza: Assessing the Pandemic Threat*, Geneva, pp. 7–20.
Zylbersztajn, D. and C.A.P.M. Filho (2003), 'Competitiveness of meat and agri-food chain in Brazil', *Supply Chain Management*, **8** (2), pp. 155–65.

PART II

Transatlantic Food Safety Regulation and the Governance of Global Agri-Food Industries

3. Transatlantic governance of agri-food and biotechnology industries: regulatory cooperation and competition in food safety

Reba A. Carruth

I GLOBALIZATION OF FOOD AND AGRICULTURE INDUSTRIES: EMERGING CHALLENGES FOR TRANSATLANTIC FOOD SAFETY REGULATION

Introduction

At the start of the twenty-first century, the transatlantic region is a driving force in the globalization of food trade and global agri-food industries. In turn, transatlantic food systems and agri-food industries are governed by mandatory consumer protection, food safety, animal and plant health, and public health regulations and standards. As a consequence, the US and EU have well-developed regulatory policies and industry standards for the governance of food safety.

At the present time, the transatlantic region represents the largest regulatory cooperation, trade and market system in the world.[1] In support of this relationship, the Transatlantic Economic Partnership (TEP), Transatlantic Consumers Dialogue (TACD) and Transatlantic Business Dialogue (TABD) serve as formal mechanisms for regulatory cooperation and convergence.[2] Furthermore, the creation of mutual recognition, product certification and market agreements between the US and EU are deepening regulatory cooperation in the transatlantic region. In the case of food safety, the US and EU are converging regulations for food production, processing, retailing and inspection.[3] Consequently, the US and EU are central actors in the development of global food safety standards for global agri-food industries.[4]

Transatlantic Agricultural Production and Global Food Trade

At the start of the twenty-first century, the US and the EU represented two of the largest global food and agricultural industries, farming and consumer interests in the global market system.[5] During that period, the EU was the world's largest importer of agri-food products, while the US held the second position. Tables 3.1 and 3.2 reflect the central position of the transatlantic region in global food trade and markets at the start of this decade.

In this context, Figures 3.1 and 3.2 show that the US and EU have considerable food market interests with Japan and other Asian-Pacific nations.

Table 3.1 Shares of US–EU in selected global food export markets in 2000 (percentages)

Product	US	EU[1]
Grains	28	19
Wheat	27	14
Corn	63	1
Barley	6	54
Rice	14	3
Oilseeds	43	2
Soybeans	59	0
Soybean oil	11	18
Soybean meal	19	5
Olive oil	1	76
Sugar	1	20
Tobacco	32	19
Wine	8	56
Milk (total)[2]	5	38
Butter	1	25
Cheese	4	44
Dry milk	4	36
Meat	27	15
Beef and veal	30	6
Pigmeat	24	36
Poultrymeat	30	13
Fruit and vegetables	17	11

Notes:
1. Excludes intra-EU exports.
2. Milk equivalent.

Source: FAO data (unadjusted), in Normile and Leetman (2004, p. 9).

However, the US has growing agri-food trade and food industry interests with other East Asian countries, most notably, South Korea, China, Taiwan and Hong Kong. At the regional level, the United States has strong agri-food market interests with its NAFTA partners, that is, Canada and Mexico, in North America. In contrast, the EU has strong food trade ties with Central and Eastern Europe, Russia, the Mediterranean and the Near Eastern/Middle Eastern regions.

The composition of US and EU food imports converge in the following categories; coffee, tea, spices, fruits, nuts, meats, vegetables and tubers.[6] By the start of the 2000s, the EU's largest food import categories were edible

Table 3.2 Shares of US–EU in global food import markets in 2000 (percentages)

Product	US	EU[1]
Grains	6	5
Wheat	2	4
Corn	2	5
Barley	3	0
Rice	3	6
Oilseeds	2	28
Soybeans	0	29
Soybean oil	1	1
Soybean meal	0	41
Olive oil	34	23
Palm oil	1	16
Sugar	7	10
Tobacco[2]	4	9
Wine	32	23
Milk (total)[3]	11	10
Butter	3	18
Cheese	20	14
Dry milk	0	3
Meat	14	12
Beef and veal	23	10
Pigmeat	14	2
Poultrymeat	1	12
Fruit and vegetables	21	25

Notes:
1. Excludes intra-EU imports.
2. Includes tobacco products.
3. Milk equivalent.

Source: FAO data (unadjusted), in Normile and Leetman (2004, p. 10).

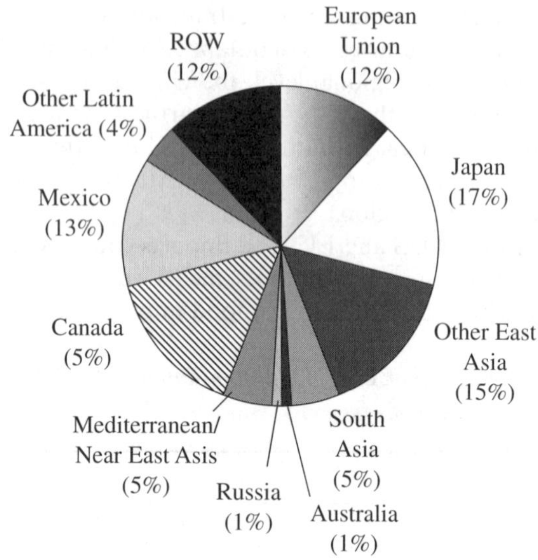

Source: UDA, FATUS, in Normile and Leetman (2004, p. 9).

Figure 3.1 Major US markets for agricultural exports in 2000

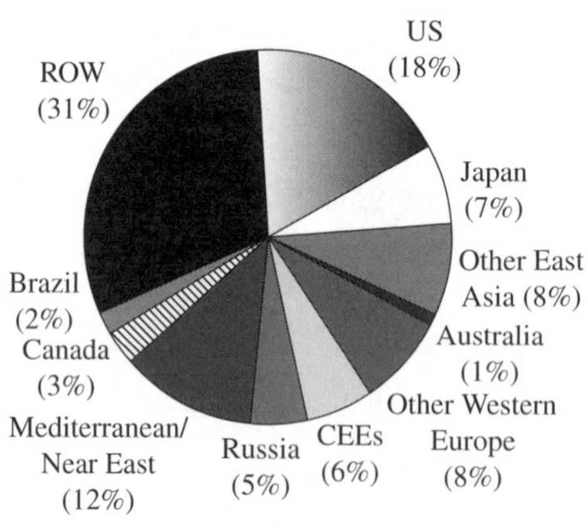

Source: European Commission data, in Normile and Leetman (2004, p. 10).

Figure 3.2 Major EU markets for agricultural exports in 2000

fruits, nuts, coffee, tea and spices. During the same period, the US imported approximately 34 per cent of the global trade in olive oil, and 20 per cent of the global trade of beef and veal. In addition, the US imported over 20 per cent of the global trade in wine, tobacco, fruits and vegetables.[7] In contrast, the US imported a smaller share of global oilseeds, soybeans and soybean meal. Nevertheless, the US and EU import specialty categories and qualities of meat, year round fruits and vegetables, wine, beer and fruit juices.

II US AND EU FARMING, AGRICULTURAL POLICY AND INDUSTRIES

The Role of Farmers and Agriculture in the US Agri-Food System

Historically speaking, agriculture provided the socio-economic basis for wealth creation in the American colonies. By the nineteenth century, the agricultural sector provided the resources required for capitalist market transformation, and industrial development. By the post-Second World War period, American agri-food production changed dramatically as a result of technological innovation, structural change in national industries and the growth of manufacturing as the base of the national economy.

In the EU, farming units are smaller than their counterparts in the US. In contrast, the US has approximately three times as much arable land as the EU prior to enlargement in May 2004. While there are fewer farms in the US, the units are larger in terms of acreage and output. In contrast, EU farmers and food producers are primarily focused on intra-EU and regional agri-food markets.[8] As globalization intensified in the 1980s, consolidation of farming and agricultural production by large agri-business and food companies increased.[9] By the 1990s, global food trade and cross-border FDI prompted concerns about competition in transatlantic agri-food industries.[10]

Independent Farming, Globalization and Transatlantic Food Safety

As the globalization of food markets accelerates, the National Farmers Union (NFU) and other allied farmer organizations in the transatlantic region are working to prevent regulatory capture by large agri-business and food company interests in national food systems and global agri-food industries (National Farmers Union 2003). Therefore, the NFU and consumer organizations such as Public Citizen are working to increase the market access of independent farmers and farming cooperatives in national, transatlantic and global agri-food industries.[11] Moreover, the NFU and other consumer and farmer organizations are calling for increased enforcement, enhancement and strengthening of farming, agri-food trade and food safety regulations in the US, transatlantic and global food markets.[12]

EU Farmers and the Common Agricultural Policy in Food Safety

Historically, farming and agriculture played a central role in the socio-economic development of Europe, the industrial revolution, and the rise of European nations as world powers in the global market system. As a central force in the socio-economic development of European nations, traditional farmers and agricultural production are protected within larger policy frameworks. In this respect, the protection of European farmers and rural communities provides the basis for agri-food industry structure, food trade and food safety regulation in the EU.[13]

In the EU, the formal protection of farmers and agricultural industry interests is provided for in the Treaty of the European Community through the Common Agricultural Policy (CAP). In turn, the CAP protects EU farmers and agri-food industry interests by giving subsidies for livestock farming through production and compensatory payments. However, in contrast to the US, the CAP shifted Europe's farming and food production to focus exclusively on national food security and intra-regional food trade. In turn, global food markets were not a primary consideration for the EU. By the end of the twentieth century, the CAP covered approximately 90 per cent of all EU farming and agri-food industry production in the following sectors: cereals, pork/beef/sheep/goat/poultry meat, eggs, fruits and vegetables, bananas, wine, milk products, rice, oils and fats, sugar, flowers, processed fruit and vegetables.[14]

In regard to food exports to third markets and the global food markets, the CAP refunds farmers and agri-food producers for exports, and ensures that EU agri-food products are competitive relative to world price levels. Finally, in the case of food-processing industries, EU industries are protected through the regulation of foreign food-processing companies. In this context, the CAP allows for restriction of FDI, and the re-importation of non-EU processed food.[15]

Converging Transatlantic Farming, Agricultural and Agri-Food Industries

As the century unfolds, the US and EU share mutual socio-economic, commercial and strategic policy interests in transatlantic food trade and agri-food industries.[16] In this regard, the NAFTA, MERCOSUR and EU enlargement to EU-25 in May 2004 are historical turning points in transatlantic food markets, food trade and agri-food industry integration. However, US agri-business and food exporters increasingly rely on value-added foods for the European markets due to competition from new EU member states in primary commodity markets. For example, new member countries such as Poland, will emerge as major producers of pork, feed grains and beef, and competitors in regional and global food markets. Moreover, the continued rejection of GM foods, and growing consumer demand for organic and conventional food products will favor EU farmers and agri-food industries.[17] As a result of EU enlargement, Europe will have a larger share of global food trade, markets and agri-food industries.[18]

At the start of this decade, reform of the CAP emerged as a major area of transatlantic and global food trade conflict. By June 2003, the EU adopted a framework for the reform of the CAP. Through this reform of the EU farming, agriculture and food industry sector, the following changes to the CAP are under way:

- reduction and elimination of selected price supports for rye, rice and dairy products
- reduction of payments to large farms and agri-businesses and increased funding of rural development programs
- increasing focus on food quality, with special focus on new premium quality durum wheat, and food producer incentives for high-quality agricultural products and food production processes
- funding and support of animal and plant health, environmental protection, animal welfare and occupational health and safety
- linkage of farmer and agri-food producer payments to compliance with food safety, animal health and welfare and environmental standards
- provisions for EU farmers to have more control and flexibility over their choice of food and feed crops excluding crops, fruits and vegetables for which they receive payments in sectors yet to be reformed, or crops that have restricted planting regulations.[19]

The current EU reform of the CAP is designed to make agri-food markets and the agriculture sector in Europe more responsive to global food market forces, more efficient, and more responsive to EU consumer demands for safe food.[20] In this regard, the US and EU farming and agricultural industry systems are converging on the following policy dimensions:

- direct price supports for commodities and food products
- income support for farmers and food producers through the use of direct payments
- planting flexibility for program crops
- production and food supply controls
- reduction of surpluses and large agri-food stocks
- protection of commodities and food products with tariffs

Table 3.3 US–EU agricultural trading volumes[1,2]

Commodity	Europe	United States
Cocoa	1831080	2079980
Coffee	554274	2718508
Sugar	1027382[3]	6314773[4]
Corn	46237	18132447
Wheat	107677	6872891
Hogs	2731	1931260

Notes:
1. European futures and option trading volumes were converted to US equivalent trading volumes by adjusting for differences in contract sizes between European and US futures and option contract sizes.
2. By volume, including ATA, BCE, LIFFE and MATIF.
3. Includes white and raw sugar.
4. Includes world (# 11) and domestic (# 14) contracts.

Source: Futures Industry Association, International Report, December 2002 and Monthly Volume Report, December 2002; Dismukes et al. (2002, p. 31).

- the use of export subsidies
- federal budget support.[21]

At the present time, the socio-economic and national security aspects of food self-sufficiency, and competitiveness, in global agri-food markets serve as strong policy drivers for transatlantic competition.[22] As Table 3.3 shows, the US surpassed the EU in terms of agricultural commodity trading volumes at the start of this decade.

In the past, transatlantic policy conflicts over the socio-economic and political goals of government protection of farmers, and agricultural industries increased US and EU food standards tensions.[23] As market globalization intensifies, transatlantic farmers, agri-business and food producers are competing on the basis of high-quality and safe agri-food products. Therefore, reliance on high-quality and safe agricultural commodities and livestock products underscores the need for technological innovation in competitive transatlantic food markets and global agri-food markets.

Global Competition and Transatlantic Food-Processing and Retailing Industries

At the start of this decade, US and EU food retailers increased the scale and scope of their strategies in global agri-food markets and industries. In this regard, FDI in transatlantic and global agri-food sectors, merger and acquisitions, and the development of niche markets for value-added and branded food products are accelerating (Dunning 1999). As a consequence, defensive merger and acquisitions by US and EU food-processing companies are consolidating transatlantic food-processing and retailing industries.[24]

In the EU, food retailing industries are now driven by grocery store chain consolidation and concentration at the regional and global levels (Veturini 2003). The structural changes in European food retailing industries reflects the convergence of agri-food markets in the transatlantic region, and growing consumer demand in the global food markets. In response to the globalization of food markets, defensive mergers and acquisitions by EU based food retailers such as Carrefour and Promodes are reflections of the ongoing consolidation in European food industries. Furthermore, EU food retailers are rapidly expanding into Asian and Latin American food retailing markets and food industries. Through this global expansion strategy, EU food retailers are increasing sales revenue, corporate profits, and customer bases in developing countries and emerging markets.

In the case of US food retailing industries, globalization increasingly requires global expansion and direct competition with EU-based food retailers to achieve economies of scale and scope. In many cases, the acquisition of local product lines and grocery chains are required to increase market share, profitability and global customer bases. Therefore, US food processors are increasing manufacturing efficiency, plant productivity, product lines and market share in global processed food markets.[25]

By the start of this decade, US food-processing companies and industries were among the leading importers and exporters of processed food in the global food system (see Table 3.4). In this context, food and beverage industries accounted for approximately 1/6 of the entire US manufacturing sector (Harris 2002). In response to market forces, US food processors are increasing sales, profitability and market share through value-added products, information technology, automated production, and aggressive expansion into transatlantic and foreign markets through exports, FDI and joint ventures.[26]

III TRANSATLANTIC REGULATORY COOPERATION: VETERINARY PUBLIC HEALTH IN MEAT AND ANIMAL LIVESTOCK INDUSTRIES

The meat sector is a leading agri-food industry in the transatlantic region and the global food market. In this context, the US and EU are major

Table 3.4 Leading US and EU food producers: top global food and beverage companies, 1999

Company	Sales (in US M$)
Nestlé SA	41 422
Philip Morris Companies	31 139
ConAgra Inc.	24 594
PepsiCo Inc.	20 367
Unilever	20 310
The Coca Cola Company	19 805
Cargill, Inc.	17 143
Diageo, PLC	16 419
Mars, Inc.	14 500
ADM	14 283

Source: *Food Engineering*, October 2000, ibid., National Farmers Union.

competitors in the global beef, poultry and meat industries. Consequently, the US and EU have a strong influence in the regulation of animal livestock health, veterinary public health and food safety in the global beef and meat processing industries.[27] However, at start of this decade, food safety regulators in the United States and European Union faced growing challenges to their animal livestock health and food safety regulatory policies.

Poultry Inspection Conflict and US–EU Chicken Trade Wars

In the 1990s, the US and the EU experienced regulatory competition and market conflict over poultry inspection standards. At that time, the EU Commission decided that antimicrobial treatment of poultry with harmful chemical agents should be banned to protect food safety, consumer protection and public health. Due to the food safety and poultry meat inspection regulations adopted by the European Union in 1997, the US authorities were no longer able to sign export certificates for compliance with EU poultry import standards and regulations.[28] As a result of the refusal of the EU Commission to reverse this decision, US poultry imports to the European Union were banned as of April 1997, and resulted in the loss of approximately $50 million per year by US poultry exporters and industries.[29]

In 1998, the EU agreed to carry out a scientific study on the use of antimicrobial treatments. The study concluded that veterinary antimicrobial drugs should only be used as part of a larger strategy for food pathogen control across the entire food chain. However, the EU noted that TSP and lactic acid were more acceptable as chemical antimicrobial agents. Nevertheless, reliance on low concentrations of chlorine by US poultry farmers and producers continued to be unacceptable for EU food safety and meat inspection regulators.

Eventually, in May 2002, the US government and EU Commission agreed to work on the renewal of US poultry imports to the European Union. By June 2003, progress was made by US and EU food safety and poultry industry authorities on the resolution of this inspection standard conflict that ended the annual $21 million transatlantic poultry trade in 1997. In 2003, a study on poultry contamination was conducted by the Scientific Committee on Veterinary Measures and Public Health (SCVPH) in the EU. At that time, it was agreed that antimicrobial treatments are needed within the context of a broader system of food pathogen reduction.[30]

The report noted that antimicrobial treatments were useful for the slowing down the food spoilage process, and the reduction of poultry pathogens. However, the report noted that chemical antimicrobials, such as low concentrations of chlorine, cannot eliminate all pathogens from poultry. Therefore, management-based regulation of poultry inspection, and poultry processing through HACCP and food pathogen reduction programs are needed. As a result of this finding, and the need to resume transatlantic poultry trade, the USDA and the EU food inspection authorities are developing mutually acceptable and recognized poultry inspection systems.

Beef Hormones: Food Additives for Livestock Growth Acceleration

The beef hormone market dispute started in 1981, when the EC Council Directive 81/602 was enacted to prohibit the use of hormones in beef. In an attempt to reach a compromise, the European Commission proposed that natural hormone use be authorized for therapeutic uses and treatment of livestock. Nevertheless, the US beef producers continued to use synthetic hormones to accelerate weight gain in cattle, and to increase their competitiveness in global markets. Through this strategy, US beef and cattle producers increase their competitiveness and the value of their meat and livestock products in global food markets. However, the European Parliament adopted a resolution to ban synthetic hormones in the EU in 1985. Eventually, US exports of beef to the EU were halted due to the lack of compliance with the EU ban of synthetic hormones in beef.

In June 1987, a Joint WHO and FAO Expert Committee on Food Additives (JECFA) was convened. The Expert Committee ruled that the hormones in questions were not dangerous in terms of daily intakes and exposure from the consumption of US beef products. Nevertheless, the hormone ban against US beef went into affect, and was renewed by the

European Parliament in 1996. In the case of Canada, differences in food safety measures with the European Union increased transatlantic trade and regulatory conflict. For example, the dispute over Canadian and American hormone-fed beef was, in fact, a North American and European food safety conflict. In 1998, the US, Canada and New Zealand filed a joint complaint against the EU in the WTO. As a result of the US complaint, the WTO ruled against the EU. By 1999, the EU was given a deadline for compliance with the WTO decision, and to avoid fines for market injury.[31]

To summarize, the WTO dispute settlement process was used to settle the food safety dispute over artificial growth hormone fed beef.[32] In this instance, the United States and Canada jointly launched a formal complaint against the EU for banning the importation of North American hormone-fed beef. In response to this joint complaint, the WTO Panel and Appellate Bodies ruled that the EU ban on US and Canadian beef violated WTO trade rules because it was not based on scientific risk analysis. Moreover, there was insufficient scientific evidence to support the ban. However, the EU rejected the WTO decision, and continued to ban North American beef from the US and Canada. As a result, the US and Canada won the right to compensation.[33]

Contaminated Animal Feeds and BSE

In 1996, the BSE food safety hazard was positively linked to a brain-wasting syndrome in humans known as Creutzfeldt-Jakob disease (CJD). More important, the cause of the BSE or Mad Cow crisis was the use of animal feeds contaminated with mammal tissues from the spinal cord and neurological systems of infected livestock. At the time, the EU faced a serious crisis in the regional food system and global agri-food industry. Moreover, the contamination of animal feeds represented a double failure in the protection of animal health and public health. Nevertheless, the British government rejected calls to issue warnings for the consumption of British beef. Instead, the British government declared British beef safe to eat in the UK. As a result, the BSE crisis in the UK grew into an EU-wide threat to consumer protection, food safety and the public health in global beef and cattle industries and national food systems.

During this period, EU food safety regulators and agri-food industries were under increasing scrutiny and consumer pressure due to the BSE and dioxin crises.[34] In both cases, European consumers believed that large EU agri-business, poultry and beef industry interests in Belgium and the United Kingdom put profits ahead of food safety, animal livestock health and public health. Therefore, the need for a European 'farm to table' and 'boat to throat' approach to food safety regulation emerged as the institutional response to these EU animal livestock health and food safety crises. As a result, the *White Paper on Food Safety* was officially published and released in January 2000, announcing the following reforms of EU food safety regulations and consumer protection policies:

- creation of a European Food Safety Authority for independent scientific advice, risk assessment, risk management and risk communication
- comprehensive regulation and legal enforcement of product safety, consumer protection, animal health and welfare and environmental protection across the agri-food production chain
- harmonization of national regulations, laws and industry standards for the production, processing, inspection, transport and retailing of food in the EU
- increased consumer and stakeholder dialogue and cooperation
- application of the precautionary principle in risk management to include traceability of food and their ingredients across the food chain.[35]

In response to the demands for regulatory reform, the European Foods Standards Agency (FSA) was created in April 2000. The goal of this regional food safety agency is to protect the public health of consumers and citizens in the European Union. Through the 'farm to table' regulation of the FSA, food production, processing and preparation, and the impact of GM foods and biotechnology are regulated at the regional level.

Transatlantic Regulatory Cooperation and Mutual Recognition

In response to the growing food safety and veterinary public health risks in the transatlantic beef and global meat industries, the US and EU developed a bilateral MRA agreement for regulatory cooperation and product certification verification.[36] In July 1999, the US and EU signed the veterinary health *Agreement Between the United States of America and the European Community on Sanitary Measures to Protect the Public and Animal Health in Trade in Live Animals and Animal Products*. Through this transatlantic regulatory cooperation framework, live animals, meat and edible meat offal, fish and crustaceans (shellfish and seafood), dairy products, natural honey, lard animal fat and oils, wool grease including lanolin, and other animal oils are covered in this Mutual Recognition Agreement (MRA).[37]

In this transatlantic MRA, the US and EU agree to recognize the sanitary regulations of each other, and to increase the efficiency of food safety inspection and verification systems in the region. As signatory parties to this mutual recognition agreement, the US FDA and the EU Commission 'agree to safeguard public health and animal health and to facilitate trade in animals and animal products between the US and the EU'. By taking into full account the risk of animal diseases, measures to control and eradicate the diseases, and prevention of the disruption of trade, the US and EU agree to uphold their rights and obligations under the WTO SPS agreement.[38]

The transatlantic veterinary public health agreement covers trade in live animals and animal products. However, it does not include sanitary measures as they relate to food additives, processing aids, flavors, color additives, sanitary stamps, irradiation (ionization), contaminants (including pesticides, chemical residues, mycotoxins, natural toxins, physical contaminants and animal drug residues), chemicals from the migration of substances from packaging materials, labeling of foods (including nutritional labeling), feed additives, animal feeds, medicated feeds and premixes.

Article 7 of the MRA agreement on the trade of live animals and animal products, calls for the determination of equivalence in sanitary regulations by the importing and exporting parities. Article 9 of this agreement calls for the verification of the safety and health of live animals and animal products. Likewise, Article 11 specifies the procedures for notification of public health and animal health risks to food safety, and food inspection and processing emergencies. In terms of food safety inspection, animal livestock health and meat safety, the transatlantic agreement states that international standard-setting organizations such as FAO, WHO, Codex Alimentarius, OIE and IPPC, are to be used as the reference and source of standards and guidelines. Therefore, US and EU compliance with meat safety regulations are carried out in accordance with WTO, FAO, WHO, Codex Alimentarius, OIE and IPPC standards.

A major requirement of this transatlantic MRA is that on site food safety verifications and inspections must take into account all aspects of the livestock and meat-processing industries in the transatlantic food chain. In this respect, the transatlantic agreement addressed the following issues of agri-food firm and industry governance:

- regulations for the protection of food safety
- structure and operations of inspection and product safety certification
- assessment of livestock production, meat- and food-processing facilities structure, layout, operations and working procedures
- public health statistics, sampling methods and results (for science-based risk assessment)
- compliance mechanism for food safety standards

- reporting and compliance procedures, and
- training programs.[39]

Through this agreement, the US and EU agree to acknowledge their mutual consumer protection, public health, animal health and global agri-food industry interests. During this period, Canada and the EU also signed a Veterinary Agreement in December 1998. This agreement covers two-way trade in animal products as well as fish and fish products, and serves as a starting point for future mutual recognition of sanitary measures programs between Canada and the EU.[40]

IV TRANSATLANTIC GOVERNANCE OF BIOTECHNOLOGY INDUSTRIES

Regulatory Competition in GM Crop Production and Agriculture

The case of modern biotechnology and GM food production is now a major point of reference for transatlantic regulatory competition and global market conflict. By the mid-1990s, US agri-businesses and food companies moved to commercialize biotechnology and genetically modified foods in the transatlantic and global food markets. In 1996, genetically modified crops derived from modern biotechnology were industrially produced in the United States, and approved through voluntary FDA regulatory guidelines.

By the start of this decade, GM corn, soybeans and cotton were a major component of US agri-food commodity exports. According to the Pew Foundation on Food and Biotechnology, GM crops accounted for 69 per cent of all cotton, 68 per cent of soybeans and 26 per cent of all corn grown in the United States by 2001. While other countries such as Argentina, Brazil and China are also using GM seeds and crops, the US is the leading source of GM food products, and accounts for approximately 3/4 of all GM agriculture in the world.[41]

From the view of the EU regulatory authorities, the US adopted GM food and biotechnology agriculture to support the global product development and agri-food market expansion strategies of leading US agri-businesses like Monsanto. In turn, these companies own the patents for many of the early novel seed and crop products.[42] Therefore, EU food safety regulators placed the burden of GM food safety verification onto the FDA, US agri-businesses and agri-food industries.

In this regard, transatlantic regulatory conflicts over the safety of GM food can be viewed as a consumer protection, public health and competition policy issue. For example, in contrast to the EU, US government regulators and agri-food companies supported a Chicago School perspective of industry regulation. Through this regulatory framework, the US government and agri-food industry interests stressed the need to reward large successful innovative companies like Monsanto, Novartis, Adventis, and so on for their biotechnology, GM food product innovation and market success. Ultimately, market forces and consumer choice should be allowed to drive GM food production.

In contrast, the EU Commission used scientific risk assessment and the precautionary principle to support the Structural School approach to strong agri-food firm and industry regulation. In this instance, the ability of consumers to make safe food choices relative to GM foods derived from modern biotechnology was called into question. Furthermore, the EU Commission stressed the need for mandatory regulation, traceability and segregation of novel foods from their conventional counterparts to protect consumer choice. Eventually, a moratorium on GM food production and novel food approvals was implemented until a precautionary science-based system of risk assessment for food safety could be developed.[43]

EU regulation of GM food and novel food products

In response to regulatory competition and growing transatlantic food trade conflict, the EU adopted the 'Novel Foods Regulation' in May 1997. This regulatory policy requires agri-businesses, food producers and food companies to submit formal requests to member state governments, and the European Commission for the introduction of novel foods. In this regulatory policy framework, novel foods are products which contain, or are produced from GM crops and animals. As part of the Novel Foods Regulation, the European Commission also introduced provisions for special food labeling of GM foods and agri-food ingredients. Through the introduction of the following regulatory policies, the European Commission increased food safety regulation in Europe:

- mandatory regulation and documentation to trace the presence of GM foods in the EU food system from the farm, processors, manufacturers and retail stores, that is, supply and distribution chain traceability regulation of agri-food companies and industries
- mandatory labeling of GM animal feed by agri-food producers and processing companies
- mandatory labeling of GM food including agri-food products derived from GM seeds and crops regardless of the presence of GM DNA or protein in final product for consumers

- rationalization and centralization of GM food authorization and approval processes for GM crops and food ingredients and their release into the environment and markets.[44]

In the US, food safety regulators also faced growing pressure from consumers and environmental groups for mandatory regulation of GM food production.[45] In spite of US agri-business and food industry lobbying against mandatory GM food regulations, an ABC news poll confirmed the growing rejection of GM foods by US consumers.[46] Nevertheless, US agri-businesses, biotechnology food companies and food industry associations such as the American Soybean Association and the Grocery Manufacturers Association of America, warned that the EU regulations served as non-tariff trade barriers. Furthermore, compliance with mandatory EU regulations for traceability, labeling and the segregation of GM food could result in billions of dollars in lost revenue for US agri-food companies and industries. As a result, the FDA and USDA formally stated US government and agri-food industry objections to mandatory EU regulations for GM food safety.[47]

The FDA published a 'Guidance for Industry' document for GM product labeling. In this guidance document, agri-food producers are requested to voluntarily notify the FDA at least four months before the product goes to market. During this period, the scientific description of the product should be posted on the internet. While the FDA, USDA and EPA share regulatory oversight of biotechnology and GM food safety, agri-food producers can voluntarily label, or not label, their GM food products.[48] As a result, voluntary regulations and guidelines left much to be desired by anti-GM food and biotechnology interests in the US and EU.

Food Traceability and GM Foods

StarLink GM corn for animal feed

By 2000, the United States produced 43 per cent of the world corn crop. During this period, the United States had the largest volume of corn production, and was the largest exporter of this popular grain. However, the markets for US corn products are increasingly affected by EU regulations on GM corn for human and animal feed. For example, Aventis, a large biotechnology company, was notified of the entry of StarLink Bt corn into the human food system in the United States, and later in Japan. At that time, the Consumers Union in the United States challenged a request by Aventis to have a temporary exemption from the EPA regulations for it GM corn.

The main food safety concern of the EPA was the fact that StarLink corn was not proven to be safe for human consumption. Instead, it was only approved as animal feed due to the risk of food allergy for humans, and genetic pollution of conventional corn crops. According to the Consumers Union, Aventis failed to meet the 'reasonable certainty of no harm' requirement of the Food Quality Protection Act. Therefore, consumer protection and environmental safety groups pushed to have GM corn segregated from the human food supply. Through these findings, the regulatory weakness in the US and global food safety system was highlighted, and supported the growing demand for more aggressive regulation of US agri-food companies and biotechnology in the EU.[49]

As the transatlantic regulatory conflict spread across nations in the global food system, US farmers, agri-business and large corn and grain industry producers faced increasing rejection of GM food. During this period, US agri-food companies and industries complained about the decline in corn exports to the European Union. While the export of corn gluten for animal feed was not affected by the labeling regulations, corn for human consumption was restricted by EU regulations. In contrast, GM soybeans were approved by the US and EU, and were not affected by the GM food safety regulations.[50]

GM wheat

In contrast to other agriculture sectors, US wheat producers showed pragmatic concern over the growing regulation of GM crops and the role of consumer opposition in the mandatory controls on novel food approvals. For example, in the run-up to the introduction of Monsanto's Roundup Ready Wheat, the National Association of Wheat Growers, the US Wheat Associates and the Wheat Export Trade Education Committee wanted to be certain that an acceptable strategy was in place to segregate GM wheat from traditional non-GM wheat crops. In turn, US agri-businesses and agri-food industry associations also support the development of a threshold level for accidental inclusion of GM traits in bulk wheat or food products.[51]

In the US, large agri-businesses and food companies concede that transatlantic consumers and global markets are suspicious of GM wheat. In fact, the USDA was petitioned by US consumer and farm groups to stop the development of Roundup Ready Wheat by Monsanto in the US.[52] Moreover, consumer and regulatory rejection of GM food in the EU, other countries and regions could result in the loss of US wheat and other global grain and cereal markets to strong competitors such as Argentina, Australia, Canada, the EU and the former Soviet Union countries. Therefore, the National Grain and Feed Association in the US concedes that international acceptance is necessary for the adoption of GM wheat and other food products derived from biotechnology.[53] In order to achieve regulatory acceptance, a secure segregation and traceability plan for GM wheat is required before Monsanto can release the new product in national and global markets.[54]

In response to these GM traceability, segregation and labeling issues, US farmers and agri-business now face transatlantic and global agri-food market challenges. Initially, cross-contamination drove the need to separate GM food crops from traditional non-GM crops and agriculture. However, the USDA is now strengthening regulations on the production and segregation of GM crops that produce drugs and pharmaceutical products. The new USDA regulations require mandatory buffer zones between GM pharm crops, increased training of farmers and employees in biotechnology companies, stricter harvesting requirements and a significant increase in the number of annual inspections for biotechnology companies.[55]

Multilateral dimensions of transatlantic regulatory competition in GM foods

As the century unfolds, US regulators and agri-food industry leaders believe that EU regulations for GM food protect EU farmers, agri-food industries and government interests. In this respect, the Bush administration positioned world famine and food insecurity in Africa as the result of unfounded and unscientific fears and GM food safety regulations by European governments (Paarlberg 1997). Consequently, US government and agri-food industry leaders believe that African governments are under pressure to block the production and trade of GM food from their EU trading partners.[56]

In an effort to resolve the growing transatlantic regulatory conflict, the United States and Canada requested the creation of a working group on biotechnology at the WTO Ministerial Conference in Seattle, Washington in December 1999. The members of the working group included the EU Joint Research Center (JRC), and the USDA Grain Inspection Packers and Stockyards Administration (GIPSA). The major goal of this working group was to reach agreement on agri-food product testing, and food safety certification of GM food imports to promote trade. Through this framework, efforts were made to reach a regulatory compromise on GM food regulation through the Joint EU–US Biotechnology Working Group. Unfortunately, the basic regulatory policy and market positions of the US and EU continued to diverge, and eventually led to growing international concern over the safety of foods derived from modern biotechnology. Therefore, in 2001 the US refused to continue, and eventually filed a formal WTO complaint against the EU in May 2003.[57]

Eventually, Canada also rejected the EU regulation of GM agri-food products. As the world's largest producer of GM canola, Canada opposed the de facto moratorium on the licensing of GM products that the EU had in place since June 1999. At that time, Canadian farmers and government officials criticized the EU for imposing significant costs on GM food producers with regulations that are difficult to enforce. On the contrary, the Canadian government believes the EU food safety and biotechnology regulations may lead to fraud and discriminate against GM products.

By 2003, the US filed a formal complaint against the EU to the WTO. In this complaint, the US successfully mobilized major trading countries to support the WTO case against the EU. While Canada did not have an aggressive trade dispute strategy for resolving the GM food conflict, it eventually joined the US complaint at the WTO, and challenged the legality of the EU moratorium on GM foods and the related regulatory policies. More important, the regional alignment of all the NAFTA countries – the United States, Canada and Mexico – against the EU in this trade complaint to the WTO, reflects the converging regulatory policy and agri-food industry interests of the North American region in global food markets (Shaffer 2004).

As the century unfolded, transatlantic regulatory conflict over GM food derived by modern biotechnology emerged as an important new issue for the multilateral food safety standards and public health organizations such as FAO, WHO and Codex Alimentarius. For example, in light of the potential food safety and environmental risks of agriculture, the Cartegena Protocol on Biosafety was implemented through the United Nations. The goal of this UN protocol is to provide a multilateral framework for the governance of food system safety and the environmental impacts of GM food and biotech agriculture in the global food system. Through the ratification of the UN Biosafety Protocol, the traceability of bulk GM commodities sold in the global agri-food markets and industries is a growing regulatory requirement.

In 2003, the proposal for the introduction of GM wheat confirmed the importance of multilateral agreement on food safety standards for novel food products. In this instance, several US companies invested in R&D for the development and commercialization of GM wheat that is resistant to herbicides and common pathogens. While the development of GM wheat was slower than that of GM crops due to its complicated genetic makeup, the EU moratorium on GM foods and multilateral expert consultations on food safety and risk assessment delayed the launch of this novel food crop.[58]

In spite of these challenges, Monsanto led the way by completing the submission for Roundup Ready GM wheat to Canadian and US regulators for market approvals. Pending approvals by North American regulators, and Japan, which is one of the largest importers of wheat and other agri-food products, Roundup Ready Wheat will be the first GM wheat to enter the US agri-food market and the global food system.[59] Nevertheless, there is growing concern among US consumers and farmers about the long-term safety and commercial acceptance of GM food crops.

By fall 2003, the EU agreed to approve new GM foods and has since moved to approve new novel food products and GM crops. In this regard, the EU now has a food safety regulatory system in place to manage risks to consumer protection, animal health and welfare, GM food production, public health and environmental protection. Nevertheless, strong consumer and farmer resistance to GM wheat forced Monsanto to drop its plans to market Roundup Ready wheat in the EU.[60] In the future, Monsanto hopes to market GM wheat. However, strong rejection of GM wheat illustrates the significance of EU biotechnology and food safety regulations for the governance of global agri-food industries.

V CONSUMER PROTECTION, GM FOOD AND TRANSATLANTIC REGULATION

At the start of the twenty-first century, the power of transatlantic consumer interests groups in the regulation of food safety, animal livestock and plant health and GM food production is rapidly growing.[61] In response to the perceived threat to consumer safety and the public health, the Trans-Atlantic Consumer Dialogue (TACD) emerged as the first US/EU consumer organization to formally articulate converging citizen opposition to GM food products.[62] As the umbrella organization for powerful consumer groups on both sides of the Atlantic, the TACD challenges the power of corporate agri-businesses and biotechnology company interests over the regulation of national food systems and global agri-food industries.

During this period, Public Citizen, and the Consumers Union reported that transatlantic agri-business and global agri-food industry interests were able to weaken national food safety regulations. For example, Public Citizen cites the growing role of regional free trade agreements and WTO market liberalization goals in the decision to grant regulatory cooperation and MRAs to countries with limited food safety capacity.[63] In this context, regulatory standards 'races to the bottom' and their impact on food safety, consumer protection and public health in the US and EU are major business and public policy issues. Consequently, the Consumers Union issued the following recommendations to strengthen consumer protection, food product safety and environmental protection:

- GM foods should be subject to mandatory human safety tests and pre-market reviews.
- Regulators should be notified when GM food is being imported.

- Consumers have a fundamental right to know what they are eating.
- USDA should set single national standards to certify that organic food is free of all GM ingredients and genetic materials.
- Industry must be held liable for economic, environmental and biological damage, that is, genetic pollution and contamination.
- The use of antibiotic marker genes, which increase antibiotic resistance in humans, must be stopped.[64]

In February 2000, the TACD formally stated its position on transatlantic consumer protection, food safety concerns and the potential public health risks potentially posed by GM foods.[65] For example, the creation of new food allergies due to the mixing of genetic material from different organism, such as peanuts, fish, and so on could cause fatal anaphylatic shock.[66] In a similar way, GM food production is causing transatlantic consumer and public health concerns over the potential creation of new food toxins, increased food toxicity and antibiotic resistance as a result of genome manipulation.

In the case of antibiotic resistance, the TACD noted that GM food and biotechnology can result in the use of antibiotic resistant marker genes. In turn, the altered genes can lead to increased resistance of bacteria and microbes to antibiotics in humans and animals. As a result, new and more virulent strains of disease can emerge to cause consumer illness and global public health pandemics. Therefore, mandatory pre- and post-market risk assessments, and food safety regulation are required to protect US and EU consumers, and the global public health.

By the start of the 2000s, the risks of food allergies, antibiotic resistance, toxicity and nutritional content issues emerged as areas for transatlantic regulatory cooperation and food safety guidance through Codex.[67] On this point, the TACD cites consumer concerns about the potential for decreased nutritional content and food benefits due to the alteration of protein, starch, vitamin and fatty acids levels in GM foods.[68] In light of the importance of food safety and consumer protection, transatlantic regulatory policy harmonization must address the following issues:

- GM food and ingredient labeling
- GM food and animal feed traceability
- GM food crop and livestock segregation
- removal of hormones and antibiotics as animal growth promoters
- assertion of consumer and public health as the primary goal of food safety regulation
- the use of science-based risk assessment, risk management and risk communications as the basis for regulatory harmonization and

industry standards convergence through the WTO SPS Agreement, FAO, WHO, Codex Alimentarius, OIE and IPPC.

Finally, the consumers' 'right to know' the origin, content and production details of their food emerged as a rallying point for US and EU consumer organizations. However, consumers' 'right to choose' non-GM food over GM food is increasingly threatened by the mixing of GM and conventional agri-food products in transatlantic and global agri-food industries.[69] In this respect, the TACD argues that agri-business and food industries, particularly in the United States, are violating the rights of transatlantic consumers by refusing to segregate GM crops and by their strong resistance to mandatory GM labeling. In light of these consumer protection and product choice concerns, the TACD puts forth the following recommendations for transatlantic regulation of GM food:

1. The immediate establishment of mandatory regulations for human health evaluation and risk assessment of GM food through the Codex ad hoc Intergovernmental Task Force on Biotechnology.
2. The development of substantial equivalence criteria for the risk assessment of GM food and agri-food products.
3. Increased consumer research on attitudes toward the current and potential future use of genome science and biotechnology in agri-food industries, and their acceptance in national, regional and global food systems.
4. The implementation of strong science-based evaluation of environmental safety to identify and manage the long-term impacts of GM food and agriculture on public health, toxic pollution, pesticide resistance, wildlife endangerment and reduced biodiversity.
5. An immediate ban on antibiotic resistance genes in GM crops.
6. Mandatory regulation of GM food labeling in the US and EU, including ingredients in processed food and foods where the GM ingredients are used but are no longer present in the final food product, including animal feeds.
7. The development of a government to government notification system for the shipment and commercial introduction of GMOs and GM agri-food products in global markets and national food systems.
8. Stricter enforcement of corporate liability and mandatory insurance for companies that release GM plants, crops and animals into the environment.
9. The development of common standards to ensure the protection of non-GM foods, traditional farming and conventional agricultural systems.
10. The monitoring of the long-term consumer safety and public health affects of GM food and ingredients in human and animal diets.[70]

By 2004, the transatlantic policy mobilization of the TACD resulted in mandatory pre-market safety approvals for GM products in 35 countries. In addition, the TACD is calling for the US and EU to adopt common EU-type regulations for consumer protection and environmental safety to counter the exclusive patent rights, market control and lobbying power of agri-business, food company and global agri-food industry interests. Finally, the TACD called for the US to drop its WTO case against the EU since all countries have the right to develop domestic food safety policies and national regulations without the threat of WTO trade sanctions.[71]

Resolution of the GM food moratorium

In response to growing transatlantic and international pressure, the EU is responding to calls from the US, Canada, Australia, Latin America and some developing countries to remove the ban on GM food. At the same time, the EU is under increasing pressure to reform the CAP and remove tariff and regulatory barriers to food trade. After a period of regulatory and institutional reform of food safety policies and agencies, the EU lifted the six-year moratorium on biotechnology and GM food production in 2004.[72] In May 2004, the EU Commission announced the approval of Bt-11 sweet corn, which is produced by Syngenta, a Swiss biotechnology company, for human consumption. According to the EU Commission, Bt-11 GM sweet corn is scientifically evaluated and considered as safe as conventional corn.[73]

During the vote by EU member countries on the final approval of the GM corn, there was a notable shift towards consideration for approval versus outright rejection of the novel food product. For example, Spain, Belgium and Germany abstained, while Italy, the UK, the Netherlands, Ireland, Sweden and Finland voted to lift the ban on GM food. However, France, Portugal, Austria, Luxembourg, Greece and Denmark voted against the lifting of the ban on GM food. In response to the decision, EU consumer organizations expressed strong outrage against the approval of the Bt corn. Nevertheless, the EU Commission is now satisfied that a strong precautionary regulatory framework is now in place to protect consumer safety, public health and the environment in Europe.[74]

In 2004, the German government announced that GM food is safe when marketed under a strict regulatory framework. As a result of this decision, GM foods were available in German and European supermarkets by 2005.[75] In contrast to Germany, there is still strong consumer rejection and farmer mobilization against GM food and agriculture in the United Kingdom. Therefore, Bayer Crop Science, the only biotechnology company allowed to grow herbicide-tolerant corn in the UK was forced to delay the introduction of the GM food product in the UK.[76]

According to the company, the UK government continues to place regulatory barriers that prevent the full commercialization of GM food production. Likewise, strong consumer resistance in the UK requires the delay of the GM corn products until 2008. However, Bayer Crop Science is working on the introduction of rape oilseed, while Monsanto and Syngenta are competing for the approval of GM sugar beets in the UK in spite of the current resistance to GM food production. In this respect, GM food production in the UK and the rest of EU is delayed, but will move forward under the auspices of the European Food Safety Authority before the end of the current decade.

To summarize, EU government, policy-makers and industry leaders are examining the economic and strategic role of global biotechnology industries. Over time the brain drain from the EU to the US caused by the flight of biotechnology scientists, and the growing power of US companies and industries in the biotechnology sector is increasingly viewed as a long-term economic risk for the EU.[77] In response to this reality, a comprehensive multi-year strategy is now in place to help the EU gain ground in the emerging biotechnology sector. In this context, the EU Commission, published the *Life Sciences and Biotechnology – A Strategy for Europe* report which provides the 'strategic vision' for agri-food and industrial applications of biotechnology in the European Union as the twenty-first century unfolds.[78]

VI CONCLUSIONS: THE NEW TRANSATLANTIC REGULATORY COOPERATION AND GLOBAL FOOD SAFETY

Transatlantic Regulatory Cooperation and Global Agri-Food Industry Governance

As the twenty-first century unfolds, regulatory policy and institutional competition between the US and EU governments undermines food safety, animal health, public health and the collective good nations. Furthermore, transatlantic regulatory and market competition have a negative effect on multilateral frameworks for food safety standards harmonization.[79] Therefore, transatlantic regulatory harmonization is critical for the governance of food safety in national food systems, regional food supply chains and global agri-food industries.[80]

In this context, food safety standards and regulations for animal livestock health and welfare, plant health, animal feeds, meat hygiene, HACCP food inspections, GM food safety, food traceability and environmental protection are critical areas for transatlantic regulatory harmonization.[81] In the years ahead, the transatlantic region's central role in the acceleration of multilateral food safety harmonization will continue to grow. Therefore, transatlantic and multilateral food safety standards harmonization is urgently needed to address emerging threats to food safety in global agri-food industries.

In the transatlantic agri-food industry sector, the regulation and governance of food safety are now entering a new phase of cooperation and regulatory convergence. For example, the reform of the EU Common Agriculture Policy is viewed as a positive step in the right direction by the US and the WTO. However, the role of precaution in the regulation of GM food, animal livestock and plant health, and sustainable agriculture for the protection of food safety continues to be an area of transatlantic regulatory competition. Therefore, the US and EU are developing transatlantic regulatory policy cooperation and Mutual Recognition Agreements for consumer protection, public health, animal health and food safety.[82]

The strengthening of transatlantic regulatory harmonization is the major goal of the Transatlantic Economic Partnership that serves as the formal mechanism for US and EU regulatory policy cooperation. Through transatlantic 'government to government' and 'regulator to regulator' cooperation, common regulatory policies, legal standards harmonization and market governance frameworks can be implemented on behalf of the public interest and collective good of the US, EU, and the multilateral system.[83]

As the century unfolds, the EU is gaining respect and support among other nations, regional groups and multilateral institutions who now acknowledge the need for science-based and precautionary risk assessment in the regulation of food safety. In this context, there is now growing pressure for mandatory multilateral regulation of food safety, animal livestock health, plant heath, food traceability and compliance with HACCP process inspection standards in global agri-food industries.[84]

In the European Union, regional and transatlantic policy cooperation and institutional convergence is occurring through the European Food Safety Authority. Through this institutional reform, the US FDA and USDA now have centralized regulatory authorities that can more effectively develop common food safety regulations and standards. As a result, the US FDA and USDA will be able to work on the resolution of risk assessment and risk management, poultry and meat inspection, food traceability, GM food segregation and biosecurity systems with the European Food Safety Authority. Ultimately, the US and EU are now in a stronger position to achieve regulatory policy harmonization and institutional convergence for food safety, consumer protection, animal health, plant health, public health and the regulation of effective competition in transatlantic markets and global agri-food industries.

In the case of the United States, there are notable victories relative to the role of independent food safety regulatory agencies based on the FDA institutional model. Prior to the transatlantic food safety conflicts of the 1990s, the role and importance of independent, precautionary, market friendly and science-based regulators was not an issue for many countries in Europe, and across the globe. However, various regulatory and market governance conflicts confirmed the power of the US model of food safety.

The near collapse of the EU food safety system in the wake of the dioxin and Mad Cow crises confirms the need for an independent centralized authority. Furthermore, the need for regulations that support true consumer choice and protect the public health within the context of food trade and agri-food industry globalization can now be viewed as positive contributions of the US regulatory model. The reinforcement of the US position through the WTO complaint procedures further confirms the challenge of unilateral food safety standards and regulatory policies as non-tariff trade barriers.

Finally, the globalization of agri-food firms and industries is decreasing the competitiveness, market power and policy influence of small and independent farmers. In this regard, transatlantic regulatory harmonization must strengthen and reassert the power of independent farmers and consumers relative to powerful agri-business and agri-food industry interests in the US and EU. Furthermore, the US and EU governments must work together to assist developing countries in the development of regulatory capacity for food safety compliance with FAO, WHO, Codex Alimentarius and WTO SPS standards.[85] In this respect, the integration of US and EU market systems increases the need and urgency for common transatlantic frameworks for food safety and regulated competition in regional and global agri-food industries.[86]

NOTES

1. Historically, the United States and Europe are linked through agriculture trade that started during the colonization of the Americas in the fifteenth century. By the nineteenth century, the transatlantic trade relationship expanded to include agricultural and non-agricultural goods and products.
2. Transatlantic Economic Policy (TEP), Transatlantic Business Dialogue (TABD) and Transatlantic Consumer Dialogue (TACD) are formal institutional mechanism for regulatory, consumer protection and commercial policy cooperation between the US government and regulatory agencies and the European Commission and European regulatory authorities.

3. Quinlan, Joseph P. (2003), *Drifting Apart or Growing Together? The Primacy of the Transatlantic Economy*, Center for Transatlantic Relations, Paul H. Nitze School of Advanced International Relations, Johns Hopkins University, Washington, DC: SAIS, pp. 3–5.
4. Berman, George A. and Mathias Heideger (eds) (2000), *Transatlantic Regulatory Cooperation: Legal Problems and Political Prospects*, Oxford: Oxford University Press.
5. Normile, Mary Anne and Susan E. Leetman (2004), *US–EU Food and Agriculture Comparisons*, WRS-04-04, ERS, Washington, DC: USDA, pp. 3–10.
6. Ibid., p. 10.
7. Ibid., p. 10.
8. Ibid., pp. 3–12.
9. Normile, Mary Anne, B.W. Effland and C. Edwin Young (2004), *US–EU Farm Policy – How Similar?* WRS-04-04, ERS, Washington, DC: USDA, pp. 20–2.
10. Artuso, A. (2003), 'Risk perceptions, endogenous demand and regulation of agricultural biotechnology', *Food Policy*, **28** (2), pp. 131–45. According to the author, it may be more economically efficient to have strong and costly regulations to assure consumers of the safety of GM products. In turn, production costs can be replaced through increased demand in highly regulated biotech food and agriculture markets.
11. Ibid.
12. The NFU advocates regulated competition and antitrust enforcement on behalf of independent farmers in national markets and global food trade. The NFU works to protect the interests of independent farmers and food safety. See NFU, Comments on Antitrust Letter, 15 July 2005 to the Antitrust Modernization Commission in Washington, DC (NFU 2005a). Also see NFU letter and position paper to the Antitrust Modernization Commission on behalf of the National Council of Farmer Cooperatives on 15 July 2005 (NFU 2005b).
13. The leading EU Consumer Organization (BEUC) and National Farmer Unions support traceability and labeling legislation. The farmers are concerned about the need for stiff regulation of the product and corporate liability of biotech companies for damage to the environment, public health and animal health.
14. EUROPA website Common Agriculture Policy Document, http://europa.eu.int/comm/agriculture/index en.htm.
15. Ibid.
16. Normile, Mary Anne and Jason Price (2004), 'The United States and the European Union-Statistical overview', in M.A. Normile and S. Leetman, *US–EU Food and Agriculture Comparisons*, WRS-04-04, ERS, Washington, DC: USDA, pp. 1–13.
17. Ibid., pp. 10–16.
18. Ibid., p. 3.
19. Ibid., p. 26.
20. See *The New Reformed Agricultural Policy*, 26 June 2003, Luxembourg: Europa.
21. Normalie and Leetman (2004), p. 20.
22. Dismukes, Robert, John L. Bird and Fred Linse (2002), 'Risk management tools in Europe: agricultural insurance, futures and options', in *US–EU Food and Agricultural Comparisons*, WRS-04-04, ERS, Washington, DC: USDA, pp. 28–9.
23. Ibid., pp. 24–6.
24. Ibid.
25. Ibid., p. 10
26. Harris, J. Michael (2002), *Food Manufacturing*, ERS, USDA, US Food Marketing System, AES-811, Washington, DC: USDA.
27. Stephen Woolcook (1996), 'Competition among rules in the Single European market', in Joseph McCahery, William Bratton, Sol Picciotto and Collin Scott (eds), *International Regulatory Competition and Coordination – Perspectives on Economic Regulation in Europe and the United States*, Oxford: Clarendon Press. According to Woolcock there is a balance that must be managed relative to regulatory harmonization and competition between standards and market rules inside the EU and in the transatlantic region, (ibid., pp. 281–305).

28. See EU Directive 97/79/EC which bans use of antimicrobial treatment of US poultry exports to EU.
29. Poultry Decontamination-GAIN Report E23111 (June 2003).
30. Report of the Scientific Committee on Veterinary Measures and Public Health (SCVPH) (2003), europa.eu.int/comm./useu.be/agri/usda.html/food/fs/sc/scu/out63_en.pdf.
31. 'The US–EU Beef Hormone Dispute', http://www.fas.usda.gov/itp?policy/hormone1.html, 24 February 1999.
32. The WTO is not the correct multilateral institution or authority to govern the regulation of domestic markets, citizens and society.
33. See FAO (2003), *World Agriculture: Toward 2015/2030 – an FAO Perspective*, ed. Jelle Bruinsma/Earthscan, Rome: FAO. Agriculture technologies and biotechnologies are driving regulatory and market policies in the transatlantic and global agri-food system.
34. Vos, Ellen (2000), 'EU food safety regulation in the aftermath of the BSE crisis', *Journal of Consumer Policy*, **23** (3), pp. 227–55. According to Professor Vos, the BSE crisis marked the end of ad hoc regulation of food safety and reliance on European Court of Justice provisions.
35. European Commission (2000), *White Paper on Food Safety*, Commission of the European Communities, Brussels: European Commission, pp. 14–34.
36. According to Braithwaite and Drahos, mutual recognition occurs when full regulatory harmonization is not possible in the short term. However, MRAs are important for the harmonization of regulations to occur through the systematic convergence and verification of acceptable standards. Braithwaite, J. and P. Drahos (2000), *Global Business Regulation*, Cambridge: Cambridge University Press, pp. 511–12.
37. In addition, lactose and lactose syrup, pasta and couscous (except products that are non-animal origin), soups and broths, ice cream and other edible ices except products not made of animal origin, glands and other animal organs used for organic and theraputic uses, animal blood, vaccines, cultures of micro-organisms (excluding yeasts), animal and vegetable fertilizers, casein derivatives, enzymes (except those of non-animal origin), hides, raw furskins, wool, fine or coarse animal hair and animal collections of zoological interest. See Annex I of the agreement.
38. On 20 July 1999, in the wake of the spreading BSE crisis and contamination of the global beef and meat industry, the United States and the European Union signed the *Agreement Between the United States of America and the European Community on Sanitary Measures to Protect Public and Animal Health in Trade in Live Animals and Animal Products*.
39. Annex VI of the agreement covers Guidelines for Conducting an Audit of Livestock, Meat and Food Processing industry compliance in the US and EU.
40. In response, the Government of Canada made new investments to enable better detection of residues in live animals and meat as well as to re-evaluate the safety of certain growth hormones. See Wilson, Barry (2001a), 'Food inspection gets money', *The Western Producer*, 1 March: 103.
41. Ibid.
42. 'Biotech-genetically modified organisms – European Union', prepared for the EU–US Summit, Washington, DC, Brussels, http://europe.eu.int/comm/food/fs/gmo/gmo_index_en.html, 25 June 2003.
43. By the end of 1998, the moratorium on the approval of GM food crops emerged as a major point of regulatory competition and trade conflict in the transatlantic agri-food market.
44. Pew Foundation (2002), 'US vs EU: explanation of trade issues surround genetically modified foods', Washington, DC: Pew Foundation Food and Biotechnology Initiative.
45. Taylor, Michael R. and Jody S. Tick (2003), *Post-Market Oversight of Biotech Food*, Washington, DC: Pew Initiative for Food and Biotechnology, pp. 13–38 and 67–71. According to this report, there is weak regulatory oversight of 'deregulated' biotechnology food and technologies. In spite of the fact that US FDA, USDA/APHIS and EPA are given regulatory authority, there is no formal or mandatory post-market control or testing.

46. Pew Initiative on Food and Biotechnology (2003), 'More than half of Americans would avoid GM food if so labeled', News Service, Washington, DC: Pew Initiative on Food and Biotechnology.
47. Pew Foundation, USDA Letter to Secretary Venneman.
48. See Rodenmeyer, Michael (2001), *Harvest on the Horizon*, Washington, DC: Pew Initiative on Food and Biotechnology, pp. 19–50 and 53–54. According to the Pew Foundation, biotechnology was promoted by industry in terms of benefits such as increased food production, increased nutrition and food energy, pharmaceutical development, plant and animal management, environmental upgrading. However, none of the socio-economic impacts and costs of this technology were addressed in the mid-1990s.
49. Hanson, Michael (2000), *Comments on the Assessment of Scientific Information Concerning StarLink Corn*, Consumer Policy Institute, New York: Consumers Union.
50. Pew Initiative on Food and Biotechnology, 'Brazilian officials burn GM Soy', http://pewagbiotech.org/buzz/display.story ID=50, 13 August 2005.
51. Ibid.
52. Ibid.
53. Pew Initiative on Food and Biotechnology, 'A Wheaty issue: GM wheat enters the regulatory area', http://pewagbiotech.org/buzz/display.php 3? storyID=96, 28 March 2003 and 'Are the markets ready for GM wheat?', Keith Kendell, 'Markets wary of GM wheat', and John Bloomer, 'Preparing the market for GM wheat', http://pewagbiotech.org/buzz/display.php 3?storyID=97.
54. Kendell, op. cit.
55. Pew Initiative on Food and Biotechnology, 'USDA tightens oversight of biopharmed plants', News in Brief, see AgBiotech Buzz, http://pewagbiotech.org/buzz/display.php 3?ID=99, 28 March 2003.
56. Brinkley, Joel (2003), 'Europe and US trade jabs on modified foods', *International Herald Tribune/The New York Times*, 25 June, pp. 1 and 6.
57. Pew Initiative for Food and Biotechnology (2003), *US vs EU: An Examination of the Trade Issues Surrounding Genetically Modified Food*, Washington, DC: Pew Initiative on Food and Biotechnology, pp. 6–23.
58. Josling, Tim, Donna Roberts and David Orden (2004), *Food Regulation and Trade – Toward a Safe and Open Global System*, Washington, DC: Institute for International Economics, pp. 156–81.
59. Pew Initiative on Food and Biotechnology, 'A wheaty issue: GM wheat enters the regulatory arena', op. cit.
60. *BBC News* (2004b), 'Monsanto drop plans for GM wheat', 11 May.
61. The growing threat of a virulent and lethal pandemic from Asian avian flu is increasing concern.
62. Pew Initiative on Food and Biotechnology (2000), 'Consumer concerns about biotechnology and genetically modified organisms (GMOs)', *Trans Atlantic Consumer Dialogue Doc. No. Food-5PP-00*, Brussels: TABD.
63. Public Citizen (2003b), *The WTO Comes to Dinner – US Implementation of Trade Rules Bypasses Food Safety Requirements*, Global Trade Watch and Critical Mass Energy and Environment Program, Washington, DC: Public Citizen.
64. Hanson, Michael (1999), 'A regulatory patchwork with big holes', *The Forum*, New York: Consumers Union.
65. Pew Initiative on Food and Biotechnology (2000), op. cit.
66. Ibid.
67. Ibid.
68. Ibid., p. 2.
69. Ibid., p. 1.
70. Ibid., p. 5.
71. Public Citizen (2003c), 'TACD asks US government to drop WTO case against the EU GM policy', *TACD – Public Citizen*, Washington, DC: Public Citizen.
72. *BBC News* (2004c), 'European Union lifts GM food ban', 19 May.

73. Ibid.
74. Ibid.
75. *BBC News* (2004a), 'Germany ready to legalise GM corn', 12 January.
76. *BBC News* (2004d), 'Bayer deals blow to UK GM crops', 31 May.
77. *Food Chemical News* (2003), 'EU official urges transatlantic agreement on biotechnology co-existence', 12 May, **45** (13), According to Tony Van der haegen, Minister Counsleor of Agriculture in the EU Delegation on Washington, DC, the US and EU must move to a common position on the regulation of biotechnology and conventional organic crops. Minister Van der Haegen warned that the EU is facing serious brain drain to the US, and exclusion from the strategic biotechnology industry.
78. European Commission (2002), *Life Sciences and Biotechnology – a Strategy for Europe*, Brussels: European Commission, pp. 5–11. In this vision, the application of biotechnology to food quality, sustainable agriculture and pesticide use, as well as pharmaceutical and manufacturing applications is discussed relative to government, business and society in the EU and transatlantic competition in emerging global biotechnology industries.
79. Adversarial approaches to non-market aspects of food safety in the United States and the importance of social democracy in Europe are resulting in competition for support by third countries and regions in the formation of multilateral frameworks for the regulation of global agri-food industries. Therefore, the escalation of regulatory competition in the transatlantic area between the US and the EU must be encapsulated to contain damage to the socio-economic goals in accordance with normative consensus on the collective good in the global food system.
80. Council on Foreign Relations (2004), *Renewing the Atlantic Partnership – Report of an Independent Task Force Sponsored by the Council on Foreign Relations*, Henry A. Kissinger and Lawrence H. Summers Co-Chairs, and Charles A. Kupchan, Project Director, New York: Council on Foreign Relations, p. 10.
81. Normalie, Mary Anne, Arun B.W. Effland and C. Edwin Young (2004), *US–EU Food and Agriculture Comparisons*, WRS-04-04, Washington, DC: USDA, pp. 14–27.
82. See White House (2003), 'US–EU Summit: Transatlantic Cooperation and Trade', US Department of States Fact Sheet, Office of the Press Secretary, Washington, DC: The White House, 25 June. Also see US–EU Reach Agreement on Veterinary Equivalence, US Mission to the European Union, 4/30/97. The US and EU were locked in conflict over EU poultry inspection regulations and US refusal to comply with prescriptive regulations that lacked a foundation in health and science. In turn, the US tried to show that the EU poultry was not able to meet the requirements and standards of the Pathogen Reduction/Hazard Analysis and HACCP programs that were in place for the US inspection of poultry. Eventually, the US and EU moved to reach agreement that would allow the importation of US poultry since its ban in 1997. At the time of the ban, US poultry imports to the EU represented approximately $21 million in trade revenue for US poultry producers.
83. Hamilton, Stephen F., David L. Sunding, and David Zilberman (2003), 'Public goods and the value of product quality regulation: the case of for food safety', *Journal of Public Economics*, **87** (3–4), pp. 799–817. According to the authors, consumers are also citizens who want private good as well as public goods. Therefore, the authors argue that private consumption trends and market behavior are inadequate and poor predictors of policy preferences for the regulation of product safety and product quality.
84. Congressman Cary Kucinich (D)Ohio, introduced a package of six bills in the House of Representatives to enact a comprehensive and strict framework for the regulation of all GM plants, animals, micro-organisms, and so on, and to reform the US food safety system.
85. Public Citizen (2003a), *Mutual Recognition Agreements (MRAs)*, Global Trade Watch, Washington, DC: Public Citizen.
86. Devuyst, Youri (2000), 'Towards a multilateral competition policy regime', *Global Governance*, **6** (3), pp. 19–33.

REFERENCES

Artuso, A. (2003), 'Risk perceptions, endogenous demand and regulation of agricultural biotechnology', *Food Policy*, **28** (2), pp. 131–45.

BBC News (2004a), 'Germany ready to legalise GM corn', 12 January.

BBC News (2004b), 'Monsanto drop plans for GM wheat', 11 May.

BBC News (2004c), 'European Union lifts GM food ban', 19 May.

BBC News (2004d), 'Bayer deals blow to UK GM crops', 31 May.

Berman, George A. and Mathias Heideger (eds) (2000), *Transatlantic Regulatory Cooperation: Legal Problems and Political Prospects*, Oxford: Oxford University Press.

Braithwaite, John and Peter Drahos (2000), *Global Business Regulation*, Cambridge: Cambridge University Press.

Brinkley, Joel (2003), 'Europe and the US trade jabs on modified foods', *International Herald Tribune/The New York Times*, 25 June, pp. 1 and 6.

Council on Foreign Relations (2004), *Renewing the Atlantic Partnership – Report of an Independent Task Force Sponsored by the Council on Foreign Relations*, Henry A. Kissinger and Lawrence H. Summers Co-Chairs, and Charles A. Kupchan, Project Director, New York: Council on Foreign Relations.

Devuyst, Youri (2000), 'Towards a multilateral competition policy regime', *Global Governance*, **6** (3), pp. 19–33.

Dismukes, Robert, John L. Bird and Fred Linse (2002), 'Risk management tools in Europe: agricultural insurance, futures and options', in *US–EU Food and Agriculture Comparisons*, WRS-04-04, ERS, Washington, DC: USDA.

Dunning, John H. (1999), *Governments, Globalization and International Business*, Oxford: Oxford University Press.

European Commission (2000), *White Paper on Food Safety*, Commission of the European Communities, Brussels: European Commission.

European Commission (2002), *Life Sciences and Biotechnology – a Strategy for Europe*, Brussels: European Commission.

European Commission (2003a), *The New Reformed Agricultural Policy*, 26 June, Luxembourg: EUROPA.

European Commission (2003b), *Report of the Scientific Committee on Veterinary Measures and Public Health (SCVPH)*, europa.eu.int/comm./user.be/agri/usda.html/food/fs/sc/scu/out63_en.pdf.

FAO (2003), *World Agriculture: Toward 2015/2030 – an FAO Perspective*, ed. Jelle Bruinsma/Earthscan, Rome: FAO.

FDA (1999), *Agreement Between the United States of America and the European Community on Sanitary Measures to Protect Public and Animal Health in Trade in Live Animals and Animal Products*, Rockville, MD: FDA.

Food Chemical News (2003), 'EU official urges transatlantic agreement on biotechnology co-existence', 12 May, **45** (13).

Hamilton, Stephen F., David L. Sunding and David Zilberman (2003), 'Public goods and the value of product quality regulation: the case of for food safety', *Journal of public Economics*, **87** (3–4), pp. 799–817.

Hanson, Michael (1999), 'A regulator patchwork with big holes', *The Forum*, New York: Consumers Union.

Hanson, Michael (2000), *Comments on the Assessment of Scientific Information Conserning StarLink Corn*, Consumer Policy Unit, New York: Consumers Union.

Harris, J. Michael (2002), *Food Manufacturing*, ERS, USDA, US Food Marketing System, AES-811, Washington, DC: USDA.

Josling, Tim, Donna Roberts and David Orden (2004), *Food Regulation and Trade – Toward a Safe and Open Global System*, Institute for National Economics, Washington, DC, pp. 156–81.

National Farmers Union (2003), *2003 Policy of the National Farmers Union, Adopted by Delegates to the National Farmers Union's 101th Anniversary Convention*, Anaheim, CA, Washington, DC: National Farmers Union.

National Farmers Union (2005a), Letter with comments to the Antitrust Modernization Commission, 15 July, Washington, DC.

National Farmers Union (2005b), Letters and positions paper for the National Council of Farmer Cooperatives to the Antitrust Modernization Commission, 15 July, Washington, DC.

Normile, Mary Anne and Susan E. Leetman (2004), *US–EU Food and Agriculture Comparisons*, WRS-04-04, ERS, Washington, DC: USDA.

Normile, Mary Anne, B.W. Effland and C. Edwin Young (2004), *US–EU Farm Policy – How Similar?* WRS-04-04, ERS, Washington, DC: USDA.

Paarlberg, R. (1997), 'Agricultural policy reform and the Uruguay Round: synergistic linkage in a two-level game?', *International Organization*, **51** (3), pp. 413–44.

Pew Initiative on Food and Biotechnology (2000), 'Consumer concerns about biotechnology and genetically modified organisms (GMOs), *Trans Atlantic Consumer Dialogue Doc. No. Food-5PP-00*, Brussels: TACD.

Public Citizen (2003a), *Mutual Recognition Agreements (MRAs)*, Global Trade Watch, Washington, DC: Public Citizen.

Public Citizen (2003b), 'TACD asks US government to drop WTO case against the EU GM policy', *TACD – Public Citizen*, Washington, DC: Public Citizen.

Public Citizen (2003c), *The WTO Comes to Dinner – US Implementation of Trade Rules Bypasses Food Safety Requirements*, Global Trade Watch and Critical Mass Energy and Environment Program, Washington, DC: Public Citizen.

Quinlan, Joseph P. (2003), *Drifting Apart or Growing Together? The Primacy of the Transatlantic Economy*, Center for Transatlantic Relations, Paul H. Nitze School of Advanced International Relations, Johns Hopkins University, Washington, DC: SAIS.

Report of the Scientific Committee on Veterinary Measures and Public Health (SCVPH) (2003), europa.eu.int/comm./useu.be/agri/usda.html/food/fs/sc/scu/out63_en.pdf.

Rodenmeyer, Michael (2001), *Harvest on the Horizon*, Washington, DC: Pew Initiative for Food and Agriculture.

Shaffer, G. (2004), ' Recognizing public goods in WTO dispute settlement: who participates? Who decides?', *Journal of International Economic Law*, **7** (2), pp. 459–82.

Taylor, Michael R. and Jody S. Tick (2003), *Post-Market Oversight of Biotech Food*, Washington, DC: Pew Foundation Food and Biotechnology Initiative.

The New Reformed Agricultural Policy (2003), 26 June, Luxembourg: Europa.

US beef hormone case, www.FAS.usda.

US–EU Summit: Transatlantic Cooperation and Trade (2003), US Department of States Fact Sheet, Office of the Press Secretary, 25 June, Washington, DC: The White House.

Venturiano, Luciano (2003), *The Food System in Transition: An EU Perspective*,

Working Paper WPO3-1, Center for International Food and Agricultural Policy, St Paul, Minnesota, http://www.agecon.lib.umn.edu/mn/wpo3-01.pdf.
Vos, Ellen (2000), 'EU food safety regulation in the aftermath of the BSE crisis', *Journal of Consumer Policy*, **23** (3), pp. 227–55.
White House (2003), 'US–EU Summit: Transatlantic Cooperation and Trade', US Department of State Fact Sheet, Office of the Press Secretary, 25 June, Washington, DC: The White House.
Wilson, Barry (2001a), 'Food inspection gets money', *The Western Producer*, 1 March: 103.
Wilson, Barry (2001b), 'US vs EU: explanation of trade issues surround genetically modified foods', Washington, DC: Pew Initiative on Food and Biotechnology.
Woolcook, Stephen (1996), 'Competition among rules in the Single European Market', in Joseph McCahery, William Bratton, Sol Picciotto and Collin Scott (eds), *International Regulatory Competition and Coordination – Perspectives on Economic Regulation in Europe and the United States*, Oxford: Clarendon Press.

4. Governance of food safety in the European Union

Ariane König*

I INTRODUCTION

Over the past decade, the development of common policies and laws on food safety has become a priority issue in the European Union. Several factors that have influenced these developments stand out. In the 1980s, the main motivation for establishing a Common Food Policy was the creation of the Single Market, which required harmonizing member state standards and labeling requirements that could serve as barriers to trade. In the 1990s, EU policy processes responded to a broader set of forces of change. These forces of change include a series of food safety crises, new consumer concerns and preferences, and changes in the structure of the food industry.

The Bovine Spongiform Encelopathy (BSE) crisis was the single most important trigger for regulatory reform of the food safety system in the European Union. First, it highlighted the need for improved coordination in the adoption of risk management measures in the area of food safety across the member states. The BSE crisis, and the use of a dioxin-contaminated chicken feed batch, highlighted the need for a vertically integrated approach to the governance of animal feed and food safety that addresses all stages of production 'from farm to table'. The crises also undermined consumer confidence in Europe's food safety systems, and resulted in a complete overhaul of the EU food safety system. The goals of this institutional reform are to increase the effectiveness of the food safety regulatory system and to re-establish consumer trust.

In the period 1997 to 2003 the establishment of a simpler and more effective food safety system was a priority for all European institutions. Regulation EC No 178/2002 on the General Principles of Food Law and the Establishment of the European Food Safety Authority (henceforth the General Food Law) sets out the general principles of food law in the European Union, and serves to establish a European Food Safety Authority (EFSA). The law defines the European institution's role in the governance of food safety; this was seen as essential for future crisis management and to rebuild consumer trust. The new law also clarifies accountability in matters of food safety for member state public sector authorities implementing food law and private firms handling foods.

This chapter describes the development of policies and laws on food safety in the European Union. The chapter has three parts. Part II provides an overview on the legislative process at the EU level, and the mechanism through which policy stakeholders can influence the decision processes. Part III describes food law in the European Union, as it stands today. The fundamental differences between the EU and US food safety systems, such as provisions on labeling, traceability and the precautionary principle are also highlighted. Finally, Part IV describes the implications of enlargement and the international dimension of the EU food safety system.

II THE EU LEGISLATIVE PROCESS IN THE AREA OF FOOD LAW

The Role of European Agri-Food Industries and Consumer Interest Groups in EU Policy-Making Processes

European Union food law was developed in tandem with wider legal, structural and political transformations in the EU. Since the ratification of the 1957 Treaty of Rome on the creation of the European Economic Community, the remit of the Community has expanded from a purely economic focus to encompass increasingly political realms. The legal basis for European Community health and environmental policy was granted with the Single European Act of July 1987. The Act added powers to the Treaty providing for community competence in matters of the environment, health, consumer protection and safety at work.

The trend over successive treaties, first in the 1992 Treaty of Maastricht and then in the 1997 Treaty of Amsterdam, is to give increasing emphasis to health and environmental concerns, consumer protection and product information. Since the adoption of the Treaty of Amsterdam in 1997, EU food law is largely based on the following three Articles in the Treaty on the European Union: Article 95 on the completion of the internal market; Article 152 on the EU's commitment to a high level of public health; and Article 153 on the provision of a high level of consumer protection.[1]

There are two distinct levels of policy-making in the EU: consensus-driven procedures on policy instruments and guidelines at the level of the European institutions; and the transposition and/or implementation of the legal instruments by the member states.[2] All legislation that serves to implement Articles of the Treaty of the European Union on the Single

Market, including legislation relating to food safety, is developed through the co-decision procedure.[3] In this decision-making procedure, Parliament can propose amendments to the law. The Parliament has two readings to amend the draft legislation proposed by the Commission. The Council brings forward a common position of the member states that is based on the Commission initiative and Parliament's proposed amendments.[4] The success of policy proposals at EU level (as anywhere else) often depends on constructive dialogue and the readiness to develop mutually acceptable solutions between groups holding diverse interests.

Interest groups including trade, environmental, consumer groups and industry associations have a number of lobby opportunities at the EU and member state levels. At the EU level there are few, if any, legal obligations that specify concrete procedural mechanisms for stakeholder involvement in policy processes.[5] Therefore, consultation with stakeholders, if it occurs, is much less formal and transparent than in the US, and there are no procedures to ensure that 'all' viewpoints are considered.[6]

Even though their involvement is less formal than in the US, stakeholders have important opportunities to influence EU level policy processes. First, the European Commission in initiating the legislative process usually consults stakeholders, such as associations representing European industry sectors or consumer groups, on early draft policies and proposals for legislation. European Parliamentarians, playing active roles in the legislative process, often welcome information from those they think represent the interests of their major constituents. In addition, EU level interest groups also lobby the permanent representatives of member states at the Council of Ministers.[7]

The main stakeholders in the governance of food safety include consumer groups and food industry associations. The main consumer group active in the area of food safety at EU level is the BEUC, the European Consumers' Organization. The BEUC is a Brussels-based federation of 36 independent national consumer organizations from EU countries, from countries of the European Economic Area, such as Norway and Switzerland, and from countries that acceded to the EU in May 2004. The activities of the BEUC are financed mainly by contributions from its member organizations.

The European Commission also provides funds for the BEUC under the general framework program for financing activities in support of consumers. The BEUC will defend interests relating to product safety and quality, and societal and ethical issues. The BEUC's vision is one of shared responsibility towards these ends among all stakeholders. A shift of consumer preferences towards obtaining more information, and willingness to pay for organic produce and value-added food products by large segments of the population, influence and are influenced by, the commercial and market strategies of the major food retailers and producers.

The food industry in Europe has contributed to establishing four main lobby groups that aim to influence European policy processes: the Association of the European Retail and Distribution Industry (EuroCommerce); the European Food and Drinks Federation (CIAA); the European Crop Protection Association (ECPA); and the European Biotechnology Industry Association (EuropaBio). The members of EuroCommerce and CIAA contribute significantly to EU exports and employment. A brief profile of each is provided, including, in some cases, their positions on the more controversial issues of EU food law such as labeling, traceability and the regulation of foods derived from genetically modified crops.

The European retail and distribution sector consists of 4.7 million enterprises, contributing 13 per cent of European added value, and 22.5 million jobs. Food retailers and distributors represent a significant proportion of this. The top four policy priorities of EuroCommerce are to: promote free trade; facilitate EU enlargement; ensure the movement of goods and services within the EU; and ensure a high level of food safety and appropriate information on food products. Interestingly, the association supports policies on traceability and, in particular, the segregation of foods derived from genetically modified organisms in the US and the EU.[8] However, the association voiced concerns on the European Union labeling provisions, stating that there is confusion between safety, traceability, labeling and information. It advocates agreeing on a rationale for labeling and key messages that need to be conveyed to consumers first, before developing any further ad hoc legislation that tackles individual labeling issues.

Food processing is one of the most important industrial sectors in the EU. The European food and drink industry transforms over 70 per cent of the raw materials produced in Europe. It is responsible for 133 billion euros (11 per cent) of the total industrial added value created in the EU in 2001, for about 2.7 million (12 per cent) of all industrial jobs. There are over 26 000 food processing companies. In the EU, each household spends on average 13 per cent of its total spending on food and drink. In 2000 food and drink exports amounted to about 43 billion euros, with a positive balance of trade of 8 billion euros. (Exports of primary agricultural produce only amounted to under 10 billion euros, with a negative balance of trade.) The largest share of European food and drink products were exported to the United States (21 per cent). (See also Tables 4.1 and 4.2.) The structure of the industry is changing with new and increasingly effective technologies for production, transport, and logistical and information management.[9]

The European food and beverage industries both create and adapt to changes in consumer preferences, and changes in the food safety system.

Table 4.1 EU food and drinks trade (M euros)

	2000	2001	% of 2001	% of 1998
Export	42 862	45 015	5	12.5
Imports	34 821	38 369	10.2	12.5
Balance	8 041	6 646	−17	12.3

Source: CIAA website from Eurostat. CIAA is the European confederation of the food and drinks industry, website: http://www.ciaa.be.

Table 4.2 The European food and drink industry in the EU economy

	2000	1998
EU production (bn euros)	593	545
Employees (mn)	2.7	2.6
Companies	26 095	24 823
Value added (bn euros)	133	123

Source: CIAA website from Eurostat. CIAA is the European confederation of the food and drinks industry, website: http://www.ciaa.be.

The industrial structure of the sector is subject to similar changes as in the US, albeit these developments of concentration and vertical integration are slower. In the food sector, large multinationals are increasingly out-competing smaller businesses, and have an increasingly important voice in influencing evolving food safety systems. The largest five European food processors are Nestlé, Unilever, Diageo, Danone, and Cadbury-Schweppes (see Table 4.3).

Food retailers and processors had significant influence in shaping European attitudes to foods derived from genetically modified crops. Major European food retailers committed proactively to avoid the use of foods derived from genetically modified crops in their own private label produce (often marketed exclusively in their stores).[10] In the retail sector, shelf space is a concern, and labeling and duplication of private label products with and without ingredients derived from genetically modified crops to provide consumer choice did not seem of economic interest. Food processors such as Nestlé and Unilever followed suit. As a consequence of these commitments, the firms had to actively work to establish supply chains of food ingredients free from genetically modified crops; this involved lobbying in countries from which agricultural produce is imported.

Table 4.3 Major European food processors

Name and country	Food/ drink sales (billion euros)	Sales in Europe (billion euros)	Food/ drink sales in Europe (billion euros)	Total employees (000s)	European employees (000s)	Food/drink sectors
Nestlé Switzerland	52.6		17.7	230	92	Cereal, dairy, beverages, confectionery
Unilever NL/GB	32.1	20.2		279	75	Dairy, beverages, dressings, frozen foods, cooking products
Diageo GB	19.0	4.1		72		Alcoholic beverages
Danone France	14.5	9.2	9.2	101	38	Dairy, beverages, biscuits, and cereals
Cadbury-Schweppes GB	8.9			38	17	Beverages, confectionary

Source: CIAA website. CIAA is the European confederation of the food and drinks industry, website: http://www.ciaa.be.

The policy interests of the more specialized associations such as the ECPA and EuropaBio carry less weight. Syngenta and Aventis (recently acquired by Bayer and now named Bayer Crop Sciences), the two largest European-based companies active in the area of agricultural biotechnology, have lower stakes in the rapid market adoption of genetically modified crops than those for example of the US-based multinational Monsanto, as they have more diverse product portfolios. The ECPAs activities largely focus on pesticide regulation. Issues relating to foods derived from genetically modified crops are often not pursued under this platform, since there can be conflicting interests between the agro-chemical and agricultural biotechnology industries.

EU Food Safety Regulations, Policies and Laws

Until the 1990s, the harmonization of food law across the EU member states proceeded in a fragmented fashion, mainly driven by the need to protect the free movement of goods in the creation of the European Community's Single Market.[11] This was also evidenced by the rulings of the European Court of Justice in a series of court cases that served to strike down national measures protecting national food industries, such as the ruling striking down the German beer purity laws and Germany's attempt to prevent imports of the French blackcurrant liquor Cassis de Dijon.[12] The early cautious approach to harmonization of food law of the EU member states resulted in a large number of fragmented laws, which include horizontal framework directives with general provisions on food additives, labeling and hygiene of foods, and vertical product-specific directives such as those with hygiene provisions for specific animal-derived food products.[13] The late 1980s and early 1990s also saw the implementation of directives for the regulation of food additives, pesticide residues in foods, genetically modified organisms and contaminants in foods.[14]

The most fundamental changes in institutional structures, law and policy, both in the member states and at the EU level, occurred in and after 1997. The rapid adoption of common provisions by the member states, driven by the European Commission, was largely precipitated by the BSE crisis. The recognition of the need for improved integration of food safety systems across member states, and human food and animal feed production sectors, provided a common basis for consensus among stakeholders. Institutional changes included the creation of the European Commission Directorate General for Health and Consumer Protection, also called DG SANCO, in 1997, and the creation of the European Food Safety Authority (EFSA) in 2002.

Legislative changes include the final agreement between member states, the Commission, Parliament, and the Council on the long negotiated Regulation EC No 258/97 on novel foods and food ingredients (henceforth Novel Foods Regulation).[15] The Novel Foods Regulation gave the European Commission a clear role in the governance of food safety. This role was strengthened with the publication of the General Food Law. The General Food Law has also established clear accountability for public and private sector entities involved in implementation of, and compliance with, EU food law. Further consolidation of the as yet fragmented legislative provisions on food hygiene and labeling is also ongoing.

The deliberations on a common EU food safety policy by the European Commission, the member states and the European Parliament helped to define three overarching common objectives in the governance of food safety: to protect human life and health and consumer's interests with due regard to the protection of animal and plant health and the environment; to safeguard the EU-wide free movement of human food and animal feed; and to consider existing and planned international standards.

The General Food Law

The General Food Law provides for an integrated approach to ensuring food safety across the EU member states and the food and animal feed sectors.[16] General principles of EU food law state that risk analysis is based on scientific risk assessment conducted by the recently instituted European Food Safety Authority and establishes an EU level authorization procedure (this section). Other general principles include the protection and information of consumers through comprehensive labeling schemes; provisions for traceability, that is, the ability to trace back to the origin and to understand the distribution of foods and food ingredients; and the application of the precautionary principle in instances of significant uncertainty in the risk assessment (all of which are addressed in subsequent sections of this document). Most important, however, the new law clarifies accountability of all legal entities involved in food production and regulation in the EU. The new law describes general food safety requirements that are imposed on both the member states and food companies.

The primary responsibility for compliance with the food safety requirements is placed on food companies at all stages of the production, processing, manufacturing or distribution of food. This is to be achieved through implementation of self-regulation provisions relying on the Hazard Analysis Critical Control Points systems (HACCP).[17] The member state authorities are to monitor and verify compliance of private sector entities with the law. This provision complements the existing EC liability legislation for defective products which establishes the principle that the producer will be liable for a defect of his product; the directive was amended in 1999 to cover primary agricultural produce such as meat, eggs and grains.[18]

The law also provides a legal basis for the Commission's coordination of an EU-wide rapid alert system and crisis management system network of national institutes and competent authorities, in which the European Commission Directorate General for Health and Consumer Protection plays an important role. Furthermore, the General Food Law provides for one policy-making procedure for all products that require EU level approvals, such as food additives, pesticide residues in food, and novel foods, including foods derived from genetically modified organisms. The policy process is as follows: the European Commission Directorate for Health and Consumer Protection administers the review process. As provided for in the General Food Law, the European Food Safety Authority reviews the risk assessment submitted by applicants intending to place a novel food on the European market. The General Food Law emphasizes the importance of

Note: *Before the implementation of the Treaty of Amsterdam with revised rules for regulatory committees, unanimity in Council was required in order to reject a Commission proposal. After the EU enlargement on 1 May 2004, voting rules have changed.

Figure 4.1 Decision-making processes under the General Food Law

separating risk assessment, risk management,[19] implementation and enforcement of the law.[20]

The regulatory authorities in the European Commission Directorate General for Health and Consumer Protection are responsible for drafting proposals based on risk assessment and other broader considerations that may affect choice of policy options (see Figure 4.1). A regulatory committee comprised of representatives of member states' authorities then decides, through a weighted voting system, whether to accept the Commission's proposal. If the regulatory committee's opinion is not in accordance with the proposed measure, or if no opinion is delivered, the question is referred to the Council of Ministers. The Council of Ministers can approve or reject a Commission proposal with a qualified majority of member states' votes. If rejected, the European Commission prepares a new proposal. If the Council of Ministers takes no decision within three months, or lacks a qualified majority to oppose the proposal, the European Commission will adopt the proposal.

Unlike the broad decision-making powers that are conferred on the US Food and Drug Administration, the EFSA's mandate is restricted to providing risk assessments.[21] There are two main reasons: first, in risk governance at the EU level defining the role of experts in regulatory processes is complicated. Policy-making powers have to be allocated between experts, member state representatives of regulatory authorities, European Commission regulators, members of the European Parliament and the Council of Ministers. Secondly, the institutional separation of legislative and policy responsibilities from scientific consultation has been a principle of EU food law since 1997.[22]

For some, including consumer groups, the BSE crisis did indeed highlight the need for an independent food agency (this argument has most clearly been made in the UK).[23] Others, including academic analysts conducting research on the role of experts in government decisions on health and environmental risks, warn against creating pockets of insulated expertize and placing too much faith in the objectivity of formal analysis.[24]

In summary, recent changes in the governance of food safety include the integration of oversight and coordination of decision-making processes across the food and animal feed industry sector at the EU level, and the clarification of clear lines of accountability by public and private sector entities involved in producing, distributing and regulating foods. The US and the EU could learn from each other as they reform and update their food safety systems.[25] This will also allow review of the allocation of government resources to food safety according to the importance of risks rather than investing resources in outdated practices such as 'poke and sniff' tests. Insights from recent developments in food safety systems in the EU might provide some helpful insights in this area. The EU, in turn, could learn lessons from the US on the merits and limitations of formal cost-effectiveness analysis of regulatory measures, and risk-ranking practices to guide the allocation of government resources for food safety.

European Food Hygiene Regulation

Since 1993, the Directive 93/43/EEC on the hygiene of foodstuffs provided one standard for hygiene across preparation, processing, manufacturing, packaging, storing, transportation, distribution and handling at the EU level. The harmonization of the standards across member states was considered essential for the functioning of the Single Market. The Framework Directive has now been repealed by the General Food Law. As a result of this policy reform, 11 product-specific sectoral directives complement the general horizontal regulatory provisions on food hygiene in the General Food Law.[26]

The general horizontal provisions on food hygiene of the General Food Law, and the previous Framework Directive, require that member state authorities ensure that manufacturers are in compliance with the directive through inspections and monitoring provisions that can include the following: requests for regular sampling to check analytical specifications; keeping of inspection records for two years; and prescriptions to establish a batch system that allows some control over a products origin along the food chain. Experts from the European Commission are entitled to perform spot-checks in collaboration with national competent authorities.

The individual vertical product directives provide product definitions, requirements for marketing that include compliance with hygiene rules, analytical specifications, health check requirements and, in some sectors, product-specific labeling provisions. Furthermore, the product directives re-emphazise the Hazard Analysis and Critical Control Points (HACCP) system provisions that also require recording of specific food attributes related to safety (biological and chemical hazards) across the food production and distribution chains as required in the production process.[27]

At the EU and national levels, the implementation of hygiene legislation is divided. The responsibility for the General Hygiene Directive lies with national regulatory authorities, while state veterinary inspection services and, at the EU level, the European Food and Veterinary Office[28] are usually responsible for the product specific legislation. However, the coexistence of the framework and product directives gave rise to criticisms of a lack of coherence of the system.[29] Therefore, simplification of general horizontal and product-specific vertical provisions has been a major goal of the revision of EU food law since 1997. At the present time, the goal is to establish a comprehensive and integrated policy covering all food from the farm to the point of sale to the consumer.

The European Commission has drafted a proposal for a Regulation of the European Parliament and of the Council on the Hygiene of Foodstuffs to reinforce and add to the general provisions on hygiene that are already contained in the General Food Law. This proposal focuses on defining the food safety objectives to be achieved, leaving the food companies responsible for adopting the safety measures to be implemented in order to guarantee food safety.[30] The proposal consists of the review of the systems for food hygiene, specific hygiene rules for food of animal origin, official controls on products of animal origin intended for human consumption, and animal-health rules governing the production, placing on the market and importation of products of animal origin intended for human consumption. This regulation seeks to ensure the hygiene of foodstuffs at all stages of the production process, from primary production up to, and including, sale to the final consumer.

This regulation also applies to food businesses, but not to the primary production of food for private domestic use or the domestic preparation of foodstuffs for private consumption. The final adoption of the comprehensive coordinated system for the implementation and enforcement of hygiene legislation across the EU will allow risk-based priority setting for resource allocation to food safety regulation. This is particularly important in the area of food hygiene, since the majority of adulterated food-related deaths and diseases occur due to microbiological contaminants.

III REGULATION OF HUMAN FOOD AND ANIMAL FEED SAFETY OF GENETICALLY MODIFIED ORGANISMS

The Novel Foods Regulation

Before 1997, foods and animal feeds containing genetically modified organisms were approved through Directive 90/220/EEC on the deliberate release and placing on the market of genetically modified organisms. Two genetically modified crops were approved for import and food use under this directive: Monsanto's herbicide-tolerant soybeans and Syngenta's insect-protected corn (developed by Ciba Geigy). In June 1999, five member states (Denmark, France, Greece, Italy and Luxembourg) declared: 'in accordance with the precautionary principle, new marketing authorizations shall be suspended'. The declaration called for the adoption of a more rigorous and transparent regulatory framework that, among other improvements, sets out provisions for monitoring requirements of transgenic crops. The consequence, although not officially declared, is a de facto moratorium on the commercial cultivation of transgenic crops in the EU.

The Novel Foods Regulation was introduced by the European Commission in 1997. This regulation provides an EU-wide regulatory approval system for novel foods that 'have not hitherto been consumed to a significant degree in the EU'. This includes foods derived from genetically modified organisms. Each EU member state has to appoint a national regulatory authority for administration of the law at the national level. The 1997 Novel Foods Regulation is being revised in order to adapt it to provisions of the 2002 General Food Law.

The 1997 Novel Foods Regulation provides for two alternative decision-making procedures for placing foods derived from, or containing, genetically modified organisms on the market: foods that are deemed 'substantially equivalent' to a conventional counterpart undergo a simple notification procedure requiring either an opinion delivered by a competent body of a member state, or available and generally recognized scientific evidence. The determination of 'substantial equivalence' of the novel food to an appropriate conventional counterpart with an accepted standard of safety by the member state serves as regulatory clearance for marketing of the product and is notified to the European Commission. Processed oil from genetically modified rape seed and cotton, and processed products derived from genetically modified corn, are among the products notified to the European Commission based on a determination of substantial equivalence under the Novel Foods Regulation.

Novel foods that are not deemed substantially equivalent need to undergo a more complex authorization procedure involving a review by all EU member states. A regulatory committee of representatives of member states' regulatory authorities makes the decisions through a weighted voting system. The European Commission Directorate for Health and Consumer Protection administers the review process. If the regulatory committee remains inconclusive since the Treaty of Amsterdam came into force, and if there is no qualified majority either in favor of or opposed to the Commission proposal, the question is referred to the Council of Ministers of Health. A range of processed food products derived from specific genetically modified crops, such as highly refined oil from herbicide-tolerant oilseed rape or insect-protected cotton, have been approved for food use under the Novel Foods Regulation.

A new regulation for human foods and animal feeds derived from genetically modified organisms was adopted by the Council after a second reading by the European Parliament in July 2003.[31] The new regulation provides for an authorization procedure that relies on a risk assessment conducted by experts of the European Food Safety Authority. The regulation now foresees a centralized system. The requests for approval will still be sent to a member state, which now, however, defers the risk assessment to the EFSA. The regulation also abolishes the notification procedure for products determined to be substantially equivalent to a non-modified counter part. Now the EU-wide authorization procedure applies to all products.

In the EU, there is one single authorization procedure for human food use, animal feed use and commercial release of genetically modified organisms. The so-called 'one-door-one key' regulatory strategy is in line with the European Commission's effort to integrate food and animal feed regulation across sectors and to enhance the efficiency and coherence of the review system. It is also hoped that this strategy will help to avoid fiascos such as the finding of Aventis's StarLink insect-protected corn in the food-chain, although it had only been approved for local cultivation and animal feed use in the US.

In response to the EU food safety policy reform, the US government filed a formal complaint in May 2003. Under the WTO dispute settlement procedure, the US government argued that the de facto EU moratorium is not in compliance with WTO agreements.[32] One main motivation of the US is to deter other countries, in particular in the developing world, from adopting a similar stance on GM crop approvals as the EU.

EU Food Labeling Laws

The European Commission's role in consumer protection has grown together with its increasingly political mandate since the Single European Act came into force in 1987. This priority has been further highlighted in the Treaty of Amsterdam and the recently published General Food Law. The provision of consumer information and choice through labeling and product information is considered an important element required to re-establish consumer trust in the EU food safety system after the BSE, dioxin and other food safety crises. Information should be provided not only on health-related issues, as in the US, but also on salient matters related to food production processes.

In the 1970s, the European Community law to harmonize member state approaches to labeling, presentation and advertising of foodstuffs, were established to protect against unfair competition (different label provisions across member states prevented free movement of goods), and to protect and provide information to the consumer through Council Directive 79/112/EEC on labeling. This directive is complemented by some sectoral product-specific requirements in EU law relating to hygiene or quality requirements for specific food products.

The labeling provisions were consolidated and simplified by Directive 2000/13/EC on the labeling, presentation and advertising of foodstuffs.[33] The Directive applies to prepackaged foodstuffs to be delivered as such to the final consumer or to restaurants, hospitals, canteens and other similar mass caterers. However, this regulation does not apply to products intended for export outside the European Community.

In terms of labeling provisions, the General Food Law requires that food labeling and product presentation should allow consumers to make informed choices and that consumers shall not be misled. The 1997 Novel Foods Regulation's Article 8 provides that food and food ingredients that are deemed to be no 'longer equivalent' to existing products need to be labeled for consumer information purposes, in addition to health, safety and nutritional considerations.[34] This labeling policy provides for consumer information on changes in composition due to production processes, even if such changes do not impact on human health.

On 2 July 2003, the Council of Ministers adopted a Commission proposal for legislation on labeling and traceability of foods derived from transgenic crops.[35] The intention is, among other things, to restore consumer trust through enhancing consumer information and choice.[36] According to the proposal, labeling shall be process based. Even highly refined oils that do not contain detectable traces of recombinant DNA or novel protein from genetically modified organisms, and hence are not materially distinguishable from other oils not derived from genetically modified organisms, must be labeled.

The new labeling provisions require the quantitative detection and management of information on product movements in the agro-food chain. The regulation concerning traceability and labeling of genetically modified organisms allows for a tolerance threshold of up to 0.9 per cent in case of the presence of technically unavoidable traces of genetically modified organisms that are approved for import into the EU in food and animal feed items. For genetically modified crops not approved in the EU a zero tolerance remains, unless they have already received a positive scientific opinion for marketing. In that case a threshold level of 0.5 per cent will apply.

Standardized and validated scientific methods are required to obtain representative samples and detection methods for genetically modified crops in diverse foodstuffs including commodities and processed food products. The development of such methods requires reference materials and product information for all genetically modified crops that are cultivated for commercial or testing purposes anywhere in the world.[37] The cost of implementing labeling requirements remains uncertain, since it depends on the nature of food product industry structure, international and local markets, and rapidly changing technologies for information management and inspection systems.

A particular area of concern is linking labeling and traceability systems between businesses as food is exported and imported. The implementation of labeling and traceability systems clearly requires more than just technical tools: international agreements on issues relating to detection and traceability are called for. The agreement in the Codex Alimentarius Commission on the Principles for Risk Analysis of Foods Derived from Modern Biotechnology, and its mention of food labeling as a risk management measure and trace back as a tool for its implementation and enforcement, was one step in this direction.

Some critics of the EU's labeling provisions question whether the current policy results in meaningful information for consumers. For instance, why should products be labeled in which there is no detectable trace of the recombinant DNA or the novel protein, if they are not materially different from counterparts not derived from genetically modified organisms. Process-based labeling that, for some products, cannot be verified, also increases the risk of fraud. When combined with the choice of stringent thresholds of contents of genetically modified materials for such labels, very extensive labeling requirements is the result.

In contrast to the EU, the US government argues that labeling should be strictly science based, that is, relate to health concerns. Furthermore, effectively enforced food safety performance standards are preferable to standards for product tracing processes. However, the US government and the Grocery Manufacturers of America view the regulations as discriminatory and inconsistent with the terms of trade agreements of the WTO. In this context, crushed soybean oil needs to bear a label, whereas European wines and cheeses made with enzymes produced from genetically modified organisms would not be covered when used as food production aids.

The Consumer Federation of America, however, does not concur with industry or the official position of the current US government.[38] The group strongly advocates mandatory labeling to help technology to gain the public trust that is essential to the fulfillment of its promise.[39] Consumer International that represents interest from national consumer groups at Codex meetings also lobbies for process-based labeling. The Transatlantic Consumer Dialogue (TACD), grouping 62 US and European consumer organizations, and whose secretariat is run by Consumers International, also adopted a resolution in favor of mandatory pre-market approvals and labeling of foods derived from or containing genetically modified organisms.

In conclusion, there are similarities and differences in the US and EU policies on labeling and traceability, in particular of food ingredients derived from genetically modified crops. The US and the EU administrations agree that there is no scientific evidence that would support the association of any health risks with transgenic crops that are currently cultivated in the United States and those that have been assessed as safe by scientific committees at EU level. Moreover, both seem to agree that the state of the art of current detection methods does not guarantee fully reliable verification of the contents of transgenic crops throughout the agro-food chain. But opinions on whether this is a suitable basis for establishing an international system for labeling and tracing genetically modified crops throughout the agro-food chain diverge. In contrast to the US, the EU considers such policies to be legitimate under the WTO Agreements on Technical Barriers to Trade and on Sanitary and Phytosanitary measures.

Traceability Requirements

The General Food Law has provisions for traceability, which is the ability to trace back to the origin, and to understand the distribution of foods and food ingredients. The traceability of human foods and animal feeds at all stages of production, processing and distribution is necessary to facilitate targeted food recalls related to product safety concerns, and to provide appropriate information to consumers or control officials, where necessary.

The traceability of foods and food ingredients, including imported foods, also requires the establishment of international systems for the traceability of traded food products.

The establishment of an international system that allows food safety regulators to trace back to the origin and to understand the distribution of foods requires agreement with at least three of the system's elements: each product must have a unique identifier (a bar code, lot identification number or container identification marking in case of commodities); guidance must be given on what specific information is recorded; and all points in the production and distribution chain at which this information is recorded must be reliably linked. Audits for verification of the implementation of the system are also required.

The EU regulation on traceability and labeling of genetically modified organisms contains three main provisions: food companies shall have in place a system and procedures to identify to whom and from whom products are made available; food companies shall transmit specified information concerning the identity of individual GMOs it contains or whether it is produced from GMOs; and food companies shall retain specified information for a period of five years and make it available to competent authorities on demand. The European Commission considers the provision of paper or electronic information on whether transgenic material is present in a food as one way to minimize current testing practices carried out in the European food industry to comply with current food labeling regulations.[40]

The potential advantages of an efficient traceability system must also be considered, since some of these procedures might result in cost savings for certain companies in the food industry. In the fall of 2000, the discovery of the transgenic StarLink corn in the food chain, although it had only been approved for feed use, effectively demonstrated that the absence of traceability systems for food ingredients back to farms can be very costly. On 1 November 2000, the US FDA reported the recall of over 300 corn-based food products due to potential contamination with StarLink GM corn.

In response to this recall, Frito Lay switched to non-transgenic supplies of corn for its food products, and foreign buyers like the Canadian distiller company Seagram started acquiring corn from non-US sources. During that period, US corn exports were valued at approximately US$1 billion a year. Several US farmers filed class action suits against the company Aventis (ironically an EU-based company) that produced StarLink, due to concerns about the future loss of export markets for their corn products.[41] Therefore, improved systems for risk management across the agro-food chain internationally will make supply chain and logistical management more effective.

Upon publication of the European traceability laws, the US government protested that compliance costs for US food companies with the European traceability and labeling regulations for genetically modified organisms will amount to approximately US$4 billion per year. The US government asserts that market forces, specific government performance standards for product safety, and liability regulations suffice as a basis for a self-organizing traceability system that reliably links the diverse players of the agro-food chain.[42]

The attitude of the US government with respect to mandatory registration and record-keeping of companies in the agro-food chain, however, seemed to change with the new awareness of vulnerability triggered by terrorist attacks on 11 September 2001. Recent provisions to enhance the security of the US food supply in the 2002 Bioterrorism Act include requirements for the registration of private entities and record-keeping in the agro-food production chain. This is also the case for proposed requirements for country of origin labeling requirements.

Over time, consumer groups, including those in the US, are now strong advocates of traceability regulations for food safety. The Consumer Federation of America, for example, commissioned a report that casts doubt on most official cost estimates of implementing traceability laws in the US. It also advocated the use of established identity preservation systems to assure 'transgenic-free' supplies of food to allow consumer choice, in spite of added cost. Finally, the Consumer Federation signed on to the position of Consumers International for Codex that advocates traceability as an essential tool in assuring the safety of foods derived from modern biotechnology.

The Precautionary Principle

Another point of contention between the EU and the US is the application of the precautionary principle in the governance of food safety. In both jurisdictions, the stringency of risk management measures that are adopted depends on the issue at hand, the interests at stake and the level of citizens' concerns. Both the US and the EU are more precautionary than most other countries; both can afford it. In fact, in some domains the US acts in a more 'precautionary' manner than the EU.[43]

In other areas the EU acts in a more precautionary manner than the US. In some cases, opinions between the EU and the US governments differ not only on the level of precaution that is appropriate for selection of risk management measures for specific issues. A major point of disagreement in negotiations on international guidelines on risk management is whether the term 'precautionary principle' should be enshrined in law and serve as a legal basis for adopting regulatory measures in situations of uncertainty.

In the EU, the General Food Law states that where uncertainty persists, provisional risk management measures to ensure a high level of health protection may be adopted, pending further information for a more comprehensive risk assessment. The regulatory measures adopted on this basis shall be proportionate and no more trade restrictive than is required to achieve this high level of protection, taking into account technical and economical feasibility of the chosen measure and other legitimate factors. A periodic review of the measure is also required, with the frequency of review depending on the nature of risk and further information needed for risk assessment.

The use of institutionalized forms of precaution, such as references to the precautionary principle in laws, are seen by its proponents as one resort for policy-makers to justify immediate costs associated with actions to mitigate or prevent potential future risks when it is difficult scientifically to evaluate the nature and extent of negative effects.[44] The European Commission's official position, backed by most EU member states, advocates the precautionary principle's use in legal texts as a tool to allow policy-makers to identify the most appropriate risk management measures in situations of uncertainty.[45] The legal trigger for application of the principle, they suggest, depends first, on the identification of a potentially adverse effect, secondly, on the impossibility of assessing the risk with sufficient certainty[46] and, thirdly, on the chosen level of protection within a jurisdiction.

The communication on the precautionary principle also emphasizes the need to take into account the costs and benefits of alternative regulatory measures. This requires a more systematic approach to the cost–benefit analysis of alternative regulatory actions at the EU level in the area of food safety and decision-making on foods derived from genetically modified organisms. Therefore, the EU is failing to properly implement its own precautionary principle as called for by the WTO SPS Agreement and TBT Treaties.[47]

Paradoxically, in international negotiations the US government has always emphasized the need to disregard factors other than sound science as a basis for risk regulation and international standards. This position is defended in spite of the fact that cost–benefit analysis has played in important role in shaping and implementing many regulations in the United States.[48] As a consequence, economic analysis can be seen as inherent in US regulatory frameworks.[49]

IV GLOBAL DIMENSIONS OF EU FOOD SAFETY POLICIES AND LAWS

EU Enlargement

The accession of Central and Eastern European countries enhances the EU's regulatory diversity in the areas of public health, agro-food production and environmental protection.[50] In cases where new entrant countries are not in a position to meet the EU's high standards for product safety, they can request transitional periods for adaptation in which their products cannot be exported to other EU countries. However, negotiations on matters related to food safety that fall under agricultural policy, such as animal nutrition, veterinary and plant health issues, were more difficult due to important socio-economic and financial implications. Nevertheless, Slovenia, Hungary, Estonia, the Czech Republic, Lithuania, Slovakia, Cyprus and Latvia have completed the negotiations.

There are three major concerns relating to food safety in negotiations on the EU accession of the new member states: the need for conformity with the European standards applicable to food manufacturers and animal welfare; observance of the strict health protection rules in relation to BSE; and the candidate countries' ability to guarantee sufficient controls at the border inspection posts situated at the future external frontiers of the European Union. The European Union provides financial and technical support to strengthen regulatory policy and administrative procedures, and upgrades infrastructures through financial credits and loans for rural development, giving priority to allocation of funds for addressing these three concerns.

On the one hand, the EU enlargement results in significant internal administrative challenges to the implementation of effective food safety regulations and policy processes with ten additional member states. On the other hand, a larger EU will have significantly more influence in international negotiations on the global coordination of food safety systems provided its members establish common interests and speak with one voice.

The Role of the EU in International Food Safety Negotiations

The European Commission's goal in international negotiations on food safety is to ensure that the rules of international trade help to maintain high standards of safety and quality. Therefore, a major goal is to ensure that common EU interests are taken into account in international rules and regulations pertaining to food safety, consumer protection, trade, public health and the environment. In this regard, most international guidelines and standards in these areas are established under the auspices of intergovernmental organizations such as the United Nations Food and Agricultural Organization, or the Organization for Economic Cooperation and Development.

For the EU, the ability to influence the development of guidelines and standards pertaining to food safety under the Codex Alimentarius Commission is of great importance. Several Committees under Codex work on the more controversial issues such as labeling, traceability and the precautionary principle. These include the Codex Committee on Food Labeling; the Codex Committee on General Principles; and the Ad Hoc Intergovernmental Task Force on Foods Derived from Biotechnology. The Codex Committee on Food Labeling is developing 'Guidelines for the labeling of foods obtained through certain techniques of genetic modification/genetic engineering'.

The Codex Ad Hoc Intergovernmental Task Force on Foods Derived from Biotechnology published consensus 'Draft Principles for the Risk Analysis of Foods Derived from Modern Biotechnology'.[51] The draft principles refer to traceability as a tool to facilitate the implementation and enforcement of risk management measures that are to be defined on a case-by-case basis, for the purpose of facilitating withdrawal of a product from the market when a risk to human health has been identified or to support post-market monitoring.

V CONCLUSIONS

The series of food safety crises in Europe in the mid-1980s and the 1990s, culminating with BSE, has been the single most important trigger for a complete overhaul of regulations, policy legislation and institutions for the governance of food safety in the EU. Until the mid-1990s, the European institutions served as a platform for the piecemeal coordination of different food laws of the member states that might hinder the creation of the Single Market. In response to these regulatory challenges, Jacques Santer, the President of the European Commission, established a coherent food safety system as a policy priority for the European Commission.

The new EU food safety system is being established in tandem with wider structural and political transformations in EU institutions. The EU policy reforms and institutional changes also influence its development, and comprise, at the political level of EU enlargement, new obligations under the successive EU treaties, such as the new emphasis on consumer protection in the Treaty of Amsterdam, and the EU's engagement in negotiations in the multilateral system for the global governance of food safety. The objectives of the complete overhaul of the existing set of EU legislation include rebuilding consumer trust in the governance of food safety in the European Union, providing a platform for better coordination of decisions on food safety among the member states and integrating food and animal feed safety management across industrial sectors.

The fundamental changes in laws, administrative institutions and the underlying regulatory philosophy for the governance of food safety at EU level started in 1997. New legislation such as the 1997 Novel Foods Regulation and the 2002 General Food Law, allocated a progressively greater role to institutions at the EU level. The BSE crisis highlighted that the integration of oversight and coordination of decision-making processes across the human food and animal feed sector at the EU level, and the clarification of accountability of public and private sector entities involved in regulating, producing and distributing foods in member states and at EU level was badly needed. The recent adoption of the 2002 General Food Law is an important step towards this goal.

The shift from creation of the Single Market to consumer protection has given direction to subsequent policies that were drafted since 1997. The EU's emphasis on protecting and informing consumers is one of the most fundamental differences in the governance of food safety between the EU and the US. These principles are reflected in the text of the 1997 Treaty of Amsterdam and in the EU common agricultural policy on agro-food production which emphasize quality, ethical and environmental considerations over high-quantity production at lowest possible cost. This difference also explains diverging regulatory policy approaches on such issues as labeling for consumer information purposes, traceability, the distribution of foods and food ingredients, and the role of the precautionary principle in policies and legislation.

The two most important institutional changes were the creation of the European Commission Directorate General for Health and Consumer Protection and the European Food Safety Authority. The need to restore consumer trust in the governance of food safety was an important determinant in the shift of legislative and administrative responsibilities from European Commission departments responsible for industry and agriculture (the producers) to the newly created Department for Health and Consumer Protection (the consumers). The legislation and policies developed since then support consumer interests that are given primacy over industry interests.

The stronger consumer voice in EU policy-making is also reflected in policies that explicitly refer to value-driven concerns such as the emphasis on quality, ethical and environmental considerations over high-quantity production at lowest possible cost. A shift in consumer preferences towards increasingly differentiated and identity preserved food products, and a willingness to pay for it, has been noted. These interests are voiced at EU level through consumer groups such as the BEUC.

The food industry also has influence on the EU's legislative and policy processes. The market and regulatory strategies of powerful players in the food industry both influences, and is influenced, by consumer preferences. New technologies changing production and information management practices are causing changes in the structure of the food industry, largely resulting in concentration and vertical integration. These, albeit slow, changes in EU agro-food industry structure and consumer preferences also support the adoption of an integrated approach to the governance of food and animal feed safety.

Negotiations under the auspices of multilateral organizations on international systems for food safety clearly reveal that there are core convictions reflected in EU policies relating to food production that are based on values shared by European countries. However, these values are not attributed the same importance in other countries and regions in the global system. The EU has been successful in recent years in introducing these issues into deliberations on systems and guidelines for the global governance of food safety under the auspices of intergovernmental organizations. The EU will have an even better chance to defend the common values that underlie these principles in a global marketplace if it speaks with one voice and as one market of 470 million consumers after the enlargement in May 2004. However, neither the EU nor the US pay sufficient attention to the international repercussions of their regulatory actions, and transatlantic food safety policy conflicts. In this context, trade frictions over hormones in beef are irrelevant now that the US administration has filed a case at the WTO against the European Union's de facto moratorium on genetically modified crops.

In order to resolve these transatlantic regulatory conflicts, closer US and EU policy coordination at the time of drafting legislation, and improved mutual understanding on values and interests at stake by diverse groups in each jurisdiction, is needed. Furthermore, the US FDA and the European Commission Directorate General for Consumer Protection could both benefit from more constant regulatory collaboration and interchange on issues pertaining to the global governance of food safety, and the modernization of their respective regional food safety systems. In this respect, closer collaboration between the US and EU governments and regulatory authorities will help to adapt their respective food safety systems, not only to diverse local values and interests, but also to more widely changing consumer preferences, and the changing structure of the global agro-food industry.

NOTES

* Acknowledgments: I would like to thank Antoine van der Haegen, Minister-Counselor for Agriculture, Fisheries and Consumer Affairs at the Delegation of the European Commission in Washington, DC, for his thorough review and helpful comments.

1. The Article provides the legal basis to protect the health, safety and economic interests of consumers. Related policies also emphasize the need to promote consumers' right to information and education, and to organize themselves in order to safeguard their interests.
2. The European Court of Justice is responsible for the interpretation of EU law. Three European institutions, the European Commission, the Council of Ministers and the European Parliament cooperate in EU legislative and policy-making processes. The European Commission is run by civil servants and spearheaded by a College of 20 Commissioners who are appointed by the member states (the number of parliamentarians has changed after the EU enlargement on 1 May 2004). The European Commission has the right of initiating legislative and policy processes by drafting proposals, either of its own accord or following a request from Parliament or Council. The Council of Ministers provides the institutional platform for deliberations on EU laws and policies among Ministers from the member states. The European Parliament is constituted of 626 European Parliamentarians who are locally directly elected in the member states for five-year terms (the number of Parliamentarians will change after the EU enlargement). European Union legislative processes, in particular since the 1990s, provide progressively greater powers to the European Parliament. There are four main types of legal instruments: regulations, directives, decisions and recommendations. Regulations are directly applicable and binding. Directives have to be transposed into national law by member states; European directives, however, have direct legal effect. Individuals can file complaints against governments of member states based on negligence of transposition or implementation of directives, provided they incur direct harm from such negligence. Citizens can claim reparations for member state failure to comply with Community measures since a ruling of the European Court of Justice in 1991 stating that remedy to individuals shall be available for failure by Italy to implement Directive 80/987 on the protection of employees in the event of insolvency of their employer. Decisions are rules that apply for a specific issue, they are often addressed to individuals, companies or member states; they are legally binding. Recommendations are the opinion of the issuing body; they are not legally binding. The body of EU law (or Acquis Communautaire) comprises these four types of legislation and the case law decided by the European Court of Justice.
3. For a thorough explanation of the legislative processes in the EU see Craig, P. and G. de Burca (2003), *EU Law: Text, Cases, and Materials*, New York and Oxford: Oxford University Press.
4. The Council must vote unanimously to change Parliament's amendments. If the Council and Parliament cannot agree on amendments proposed in the second reading of Parliament, a conciliation procedure is initiated whereby a consensus position between Council and Parliament has to be agreed upon within six months. If no agreement can be reached, a fresh start to the legislative process is required. Parliament's amendments can be rejected. During the second reading, the Parliament can approve, reject or amend the legislation, given the support of an absolute majority of Parliamentarians (314 out of 626 votes). After the second reading of Parliament, the Council votes on the proposal (the number of votes a member state has is largely determined by the gross domestic product and soon also by the population size). Support from a qualified majority of member states, that is, at least 62 out of a total of 87 votes, is required to adopt Parliament's amendments that have been accepted by the European Commission and to pass the law (the voting rules have changed after the EU enlargement). Exceptions to this rule are decisions concerning energy use, country planning and provisions of a fiscal nature, where unanimity is required.
5. Communication from the Commission *Towards a Reinforced Culture of Consultation and Dialogue: General Principles and Minimum Standards for Consultation of Interested Parties by the Commission*, COM (2002) 704. There are, however, no open and formal procedures comparable to, for example, the US procedural Statutes including the 1946 Administrative Procedure Act and the 1972 Federal Advisory Committee Act that ensure public notice, and opportunities to comment or actual face-to-face involvement, of those who wish to participate in rule-making.

6. The Commission often organizes roundtable discussions or creates ad hoc consultative committees of stakeholders and experts. The mechanisms and extent of consultation with interested parties is largely left to the discretion of officials involved in the decision-making process. This also holds true for the majority of the individual decision processes in the various member states.
7. In this regard, successful lobbying at national level can through well-briefed government representatives of the respective member states inject viewpoints into discussions of the Council of Ministers. The openness of member state governments to different stakeholder interests is significantly determined by the political appointees in concerned government departments, which in turn depends on the ruling party(ies) in member states. For instance, when Germany, France and Italy, the three largest member states were governed by red–green coalitions, as was recently the case, consumer and environmental groups had a stronger voice, both at EU level and in national governments.
8. Website at http://www.netlink.de/gen/Zeitung/970507.htm.
9. Lyon, J.D. (1998), 'Food systems and accountability mechanisms for food safety: a law and economics approach', *Food and Drug Law Journal*, **53**: 27.
10. Kalaitzandonakes, N. and J. Bijman (2003), 'Who is driving biotechnology acceptance?', *Nature Biotechnology*, **21** (4): 366–9.
11. O'Rourke, Raymond (1999), *European Food Law*, Bembridge: Palladian Law.
12. Case 178/84 Commission vs Germany [1987] ECR 1227; [1988] 1 CMLR 780; Case 120/78 Rewe-Zentrale AG v. Bundesmonopolverwaltung fuer Branntwein [1979] ECR 649, [1979] 3 CMLR 494.
13. O'Rourke (1999). Overall the main objective of helping to establish the Single Market was achieved, but the resulting set of Directives was often criticized as opaque, fragmented, incoherent and in general as not adding any benefit to existing EU member state legislation.
14. *Council Directive 89/107/EEC of 21 December 1988 on the Approximation of the Laws of the member states Concerning Food Additives for use in Foodstuffs Intended for Human Consumption*, amended by European Parliament and Council Directive 94/34/EC of 30 June 1994 (European Council 1988). *Council Regulation (EEC) No 315/93 of 8 February 1993 Laying Down Community Procedures for Contaminants in Food*, Official Journal L 37 of 13 February 1993 (European Council 1993). *Council Directive 90/220/EEC on the Deliberate Release and Placing on the Market of Genetically Modified Organisms* Official Journal L 117 of 8 May 1990, pp. 0015–0027. CORRIGENDUM: Official Journal L 074 of 19 March 1999, p. 0032 (European Council 1991a). *Council Directive 91/414/EEC of 15 July 1991 Concerning the Placing of Plant Protection Products on the Market*, Official Journal L 230 of 19 August 1991 pp. 0001–0032 (European Council 1991).
15. *Regulation (EC) No 258/97 of the European Parliament and of the Council of 27 January 1997 Concerning Novel Foods and Novel Food Ingredients*, Official Journal L 043 of 14 February 1997, pp. 0001–0006 (European Parliament/European Council 1997).
16. The need for legislation to be coherent, rational, consistent, simpler, user friendly and developed in full consultation with interested parties had been pinpointed and put to broader public discussion in the European Commission's (1997b) *Green Paper on The General Principles of Food Law in the European Union* (May 1997) COM (97) 176, Brussels: European Commission. These needs and the general principles of food law were then consolidated in the European Commission's (2000b) *White Paper on Food Safety in the European Union*, COM (2000), Brussels: European Commission.
17. Hulebak, K.L. and W. Schlosser (2002), 'Hazard Analysis and Critical Control Point (HACCP) history and conceptual overview', *Risk Analysis*, **22** (3): 547–52.
18. Directive 85/374/EEC on the liability for defective products. Amended in 1999.
19. FAO/WHO (1997) *Risk Management and Food Safety – Report of the Joint FAO/WHO Expert Consultation*, Rome 27–31 January, Rome: FAO, at http://www.fao.org/es/esn/risk/risktext.htm. Risk management is defined as the process of weighing policy alternatives in consultation with interested parties, considering risk assessment and other legitimate factors, and if need be selecting appropriate prevention and control options.

20. European Commission (2002c), *Regulation (EC) No 178/2002 of the European Parliament and of the Council of 28 January 2002 Laying Down the General Principles and Requirements of Food Law, Establishing the European Food Safety Authority and Laying Down Procedures in Matters of Food Safety*, Official Journal L 031 of 01 February 2002, pp. 0001–0024. Article 6(3) provides that the administrator in the European Commission, when writing the proposal for a decision that is to be voted upon by member states shall take into account the results of the risk assessment (in particular the opinions of the Authority), and other factors legitimate to the matter under consideration, and the precautionary principle (Article 7(1) in order to achieve the general objectives of food law established in Article 5).
21. Article 22 (2) of the General Food Law provides that the Authority shall provide scientific advice and technical support for the Community's legislation and policies in all fields, which have direct or indirect impact on human food and animal feed safety. It shall provide independent information on all matters within these fields and communicate on risks.
22. European Commission (1997a), *Communication of the European Commission on Consumer Health and Safety*, COM (97) 183 fin, at http://europa.eu.int/comm/food/fs/sc/index_en.html 'Consumer confidence in the legislative activities of the EU is conditioned by the quality and transparency of the scientific advice and its use on the legislative and control process.' At the peak of the BSE crisis, the then President of the European Commission, Jacques Santer, in a speech to the European Parliament, announced general principles for the management of food safety and consumer health. The subsequent European Commission Communication on Consumer Health and Safety announced these changes and placed emphasis on the excellence of the Committee members and the independence and transparency of the advice.
23. Davies, S. and S. Todd (1996), 'The need for an independent food agency', *Consumer Policy Review*, **6**: 82–6.
24. Jasanoff, S. (1997), 'Civilisation and madness: the great BSE scare of 1996', *Public Understanding of Science*, **6** (3): 221–32.
25. Taylor, M.R. (2002), 'Reforming food safety: a model for the future', *Food Technology*, **56**: 190. Michael Taylor, former administrator of the US Department of Agriculture's Food Safety and Inspection Service and Deputy Commissioner for Policy at the Food and Drug Administration, compellingly argued that the US food safety system would also benefit from an overhaul to achieve similar objectives. Two of his main goals are identical to the objectives of the General Food Law: improved integration of human food and animal feed safety aspects, and defining clearer lines of accountability among states and private sector entities.
26. The Framework Directive is based on Treaty provisions for the completion of the Single Market Article 95, whereas the sectoral legislation is based on Article 37 that provides for the Common Agricultural Policy. Separate product Directives exist for fresh meat, poultry meat, meat products, minced meat and meat preparations, rabbit, farmed and wild game, fish, eggs and egg products, milk and milk products, other products such as frogs' legs, snails and honey. Member states can introduce provisions that are more specific than those laid down in the Directive, provided they do not conflict with provisions in the Directive or restrict the free movement of goods and services in the internal market.
27. Hulebak and Schlosser (2002), pp. 547–52.
28. The European Food and Veterinary Office is based in Grange, Ireland. Its primary responsibility is the monitoring of the implementation of EU legislation on food hygiene, veterinary and plant health legislation in Europe and elsewhere.
29. O'Rourke, (1999).
30. *Proposal for a Regulation of the European Parliament and of the Council on the Hygiene of Foodstuffs*, COM (2000) 438 final, Official Journal C 365 of 19 December 2000 (European Parliament/European Council 2000b).
31. *Regulation (EC) No 1829/2003 of the European Parliament and of the Council on Genetically Modified Human Food and Animal Feed*, Official Journal L 268 of 18 October 2003, pp. 1–23 (European Parliament/European Council 2003a).
32. The World Trade Organization (WTO) was established in 1995 as the successor to the

Secretariat of the General Agreement on Tariffs and Trade (GATT). The WTO Agreements on the Application of Sanitary and Phytosanitary Measures (SPS Agreement) and on Technical Barriers to Trade (TBT Agreement) contain provisions that are relevant to the regulation of foods and crops derived from modern biotechnology. The TBT Agreement covers technical measures that seek to protect consumers from economic fraud and deception and measures concerning human, animal and plant life and health that are not covered by the SPS Agreement.

33. *Directive 2000/13/EC of the European Parliament and of the Council of 20 March 2000 on the Approximation of the Laws of the Member States Relating to the Labeling, Presentation and Advertising of Foodstuffs for Sale to the Ultimate Consumer*, Official Journal L 109 of 06 May 2000 (European Parliament/European Council 2000a).
34. In 1997 the European Commission introduced *Regulation EC No. 258/97 on Novel Foods and Food Ingredients*, which provides an EU-wide regulatory approval system for novel foods, including foods derived from genetically modified organisms. Food and food ingredients that are deemed to be no 'longer equivalent' to existing products need to be labelled for consumer information purposes, additionally to health, safety and nutritional considerations. Labeling is not required if the proportion of transgenic organism in a food or food ingredient does not exceed 1 per cent. Commission Regulation (EC) No 49/2002, Official Journal L 6/13 of 11 January 2000 (European Commission 2002a).
35. *Regulation (EC) No 1830/2003 of the European Parliament and of the Council Concerning the Traceability and Labeling of Genetically Modified Organisms and the Traceability of Human Food and Animal Feed Products Produced From Genetically Modified Organisms and Amending Directive 2001/18/EC*, Official Journal L 268 of 18 October 2003, pp. 24–8 (European Parliament/European Council 2003b).
36. *Proposal for a Regulation of the European Parliament and of the Council concerning Traceability and Labeling of Genetically Modified Organisms and Traceability of Human Food and Animal Feed Products Produced From Genetically Modified Organisms*, Official Journal C 304 E of 30 October 2001, p. 327 (European Parliament/European Council 2001).
37. Miraglia, K. (ed.) (2004), 'Detection and traceability of genetically modified organisms in the food production chain', *Journal of Food and Chemical Toxicology*, **42** (7): 1157–80. Also see König, A. (ed.) (2004), 'Assessment of the safety of foods derived from genetically modified (GM) crops, *Journal of Food and Chemical Toxicology*, **42** (7): 1047–88.
38. The Consumer Federation of America is an advocacy organization, working to advance pro-consumer policy, educational organization, disseminating information on consumer issues to the public and the media, as well as to policy-makers and other public interest advocates.
39. Remarks from Carol Tucker Foreman, former Assistant Secretary, USDA 77–81, representing the Consumer Federation of America, before the 2nd Joint CSL/JIFSAN symposium on Food Safety and Nutrition: current issues in Food Biotechnology July 2001. An analysis of various pools on acceptance of biotechnology in the US by the International Food Information Council, the Pew Foundation and the National Science Foundation concludes that in a generally technology and innovation supportive nation like the US biotechnology is in fact one of the least favorably viewed technologies, the levels of acceptance of which can be are comparable to those of nuclear energy.
40. As discussed in the section on labeling, major obstacles remain for the stringent implementation these laws: for instance, reliable test methods and reference materials have to be developed for all genetically modified organisms that are cultivated anywhere on the planet. The European Commission Joint Research Centre has been declared the Community Reference Laboratory, with responsibility for the ring testing and validation of detection methods and reference materials. A network of national reference laboratories will assist the Centre.
41. Sutter v. Aventis CropScience USA Holding Inc., 145 F. Supp. 2d 1050 (2001).
42. Sipress, A. and M. Kaufman (2001), 'US challenges EU's biotech food standards', *The Washington Post*, 26 August.

43. Wiener, J.B. and M.D. Rogers (2001), *Comparing Precaution in the United States and Europe*, Chapel Hill, NC: Duke University, Duke Center for Environmental Solutions.
44. In Principle 15 of the Declaration of the 1992 United Nations Rio Earth Summit the role of precaution in environmental regulation is defined as follows: 'In order to protect the environment the precautionary approach shall be widely applied by states according to their capabilities. Where there are threats of serious or irreversible damage, lack of full scientific certainty shall not be used as a reason for postponing cost-effective measures to prevent environmental degradation.'
45. European Commission (2000a), *Communication From the European Commission on the Precautionary Principle*, COM(2000)1-C5-014/2000, European Commission (2000c) *Comments from the European Commission Services to the Codex Secretariat*. Replies to the questions raised by the United States Codex Conference Room Document. At http://europa.eu.int/comm/food/fs/ifsi/eupositions/ccgp/ccgp 01_en.html.
46. In fact, according to the European Commission Communication on the Precautionary Principle, the precautionary principle should be understood as a dynamic concept, in which attention to scientific and technical progress should enable regulatory measures to be adapted to the evolving state of understanding of the risks, costs and benefits associated with such progress. The communication also places emphasis on concepts such as proportionality and non-discrimination that ensure consistency of the application of the principle with WTO Treaties. Scientific uncertainty, the Communication explains, may stem from lack of sufficient data, inconclusive or imprecise information, or divergent scientific opinions.
47. Jasanoff, S. (1983), 'Negotiation or cost–benefit analysis: a middle of the road for US policy?', *The Environmental Forum*, **2** (3): 37–43.
48. Since the adoption of the 'Quality of Life Review Procedure' in 1971, the White House Office of Management and Budget (OMB) regulatory review and systematic ranking of safety and environmental regulations in terms of cost-effectiveness is routine practice. The US Regulatory Flexibility Act also mandates US agencies to report on potential costs and benefits of regulation. Specific regulatory statutes can prescribe or preclude the explicit use of cost–benefit analysis in case-by-case regulatory decision-making. Since the implementation of the 1996 Food Quality Protection Act, regulatory decisions on pesticides may not be based on cost–benefit analysis any longer. Arguably, however, the continued broad use of pesticides might be considered as circumstantial evidence that the socio-economic context, in this case potential impacts on food production costs of sudden bans of classes of dangerous pesticides like organophosphates, is always taken into account in such regulatory decisions.
49. Hahn, R.W. (2000), *Reviving Regulatory Reform – a Global Perspective*, Washington, DC: AEI Press/Brookings Institute.
50. James, P., F. Kemper and G. Pascal (1999), *A European Food and Public Health Authority. The Future of Scientific Advice in the EU*, Brussels: the European Commission.
51. Codex Alimentarius Commission (2003), 'Principles for the Risk Analysis of Foods Derived from Modern Biotechnology', CAC/GL 44, http://www.codexalimentarius.net/download/standards/10007/CXG_044e.pdf.

REFERENCES

Codex Alimentarius Commission (2003), 'Principles for the Risk Analysis of Foods Derived from Modern Biotechnology', CAC/GL 44, http://www.codexalimentarius.net/download/standards/10007/CXG_044e.pdf.

Craig, P. and G. de Burca (2003), *EU Law: Text, Cases, and Materials*, New York and Oxford: Oxford University Press.

Davies, S. and S. Todd (1996), 'The need for an independent food agency', *Consumer Policy Review*, **6**: 82–6.

European Commission (1997a), *Communication of the European Commission on Consumer Health and Safety*, COM (97) 183 fin, at http://europa.eu.int/comm/food/fs/sc/index_en.html.

European Commission (1997b), *Green Paper on The General Principles of Food Law in the European Union* (May 1997) COM (97) 176, Brussels: European Commission.

European Commission (2000a), *Communication from the European Commission on the Precautionary Principle*, COM (2000)1-C5-014/2000, Brussels: European Commission.

European Commission (2000b), *White Paper on Food Safety in the European Union*, COM (2000). Brussels: European Commission.

European Commission (2000c), *Comments from the European Commission Services to the Codex Secretariat*, at http://europa.eu.int/comm./foods/fs/ifsi/eupositions/ccgp/ccgp 01_en.html.

European Commission (2002a), *Regulation EC No. 258/97 on Novel Foods and Food Ingredients Commission Regulation*, (EC) No 49/2002, Official Journal L 6/13 of 11 January 2000.

European Commission (2002b), *Towards a Reinforced Culture of Consultation and Dialogue: General Principles and Minimum Standards for Consultation of Interested Parties by the Commission*, COM (2002) 704.

European Commission (2002c), *Regulation (EC) No 178/2002 of the European Parliament and of the Council of 28 January 2002 Laying Down the General Principles and Requirements of Food Law, Establishing the European Food Safety Authority and Laying Down Procedures in Matters of Food Safety*, Official Journal L 031 of 1 February 2002.

European Council (1988), *Directive 89/107/EEC of 21 December 1988 on the Approximation of the Laws of the member states Concerning Food Additives for use in Foodstuffs Intended for Human Consumption*, amended by European Parliament and Council Directive 94/34/EC of 30 June 1994.

European Council (1991a), *Council Directive 90/220/EEC on the Deliberate Release and Placing on the Market of Genetically Modified Organisms.*

European Council (1991b), *Directive 91/414/EEC of 15 July 1991 Concerning the Placing of Plant Protection Products on the Market*, Official Journal L 230 of 19 August 1991, pp. 0001–0032.

European Council (1993), *Council Regulation (EEC) No 315/93 of 8 February 1993 Laying Down Community Procedures for Contaminants in Food*, Official Journal L 37 of 13 February 1993.

European Parliament/European Council (1997), *Regulation (EC) No 258/97 of the European Parliament and of the Council of 27 January 1997 Concerning Novel Foods and Novel Food Ingredients*, Official Journal L 043 of 14 February 1997.

European Parliament/European Council (2000a), *Directive 2000/13/EC of the European Parliament and of the Council of 20 March 2000 on the Approximation of the Laws of the Member States Relating to the Labeling, Presentation and Advertising of Foodstuffs for Sale to the Ultimate Consumer*, Official Journal L 109 of 6 May 2000.

European Parliament/European Council (2000b), *Proposal for a Regulation of the European Parliament and of the Council on the Hygiene of Foodstuffs*, COM (2000) 438 final, Official Journal C 365 of 19 December 2000.

European Parliament/European Council (2001), *Proposal for a Regulation of the European Parliament and of the Council Concerning Traceability and Labeling of*

Genetically Modified Organisms and Traceability of Human Food and Animal Feed Products Produced From Genetically Modified Organisms, Official Journal C 304 E of 30 October 2001.

European Parliament/European Council (2003a), *Regulation (EC) No 1829/2003 of the European Parliament and of the Council on Genetically Modified Human Food and Animal Feed*, Official Journal L 268 of 18 October 2003.

European Parliament/European Council (2003b), *Regulation (EC) No 1830/2003 of the European Parliament and of the Council Concerning the Traceability and Labeling of Genetically Modified Organisms and the Traceability of Human Food and Animal Feed Products Produced From Genetically Modified Organisms and Amending Directive 2001/18/EC*, Official Journal L 268 of 18 October 2003, pp. 24–8.

FAO/WHO (1997) *Risk Management and Food Safety – Report of the Joint FAO/WHO Expert Consultation*, Rome: FAO, at http://www.fao.org/es/esn/risk/risktext.htm.

Hahn, R.W. (2000), *Reviving Regulatory Reform – A Global Perspective*. Washington, DC: AEI Press/Brookings Institution.

Hulebak, K.L. and W. Schlosser (2002), 'Hazard Analysis and Critical Control Point (HACCP) history and conceptual overview', *Risk Analysis*, **22** (3): 547–52.

Jasanoff, S. (1983), 'Negotiation or cost–benefit analysis: a middle of the road for US policy?', *The Environmental Forum*, **2** (3): 37–43.

Jasanoff, S. (1997), 'Civilisation and madness: the great BSE scare of 1996', *Public Understanding of Science*, **6** (3): 221–32.

Kalaitzandonakes, N. and J. Bijman (2003), 'Who is driving biotechnology acceptance?', *Nature Biotechnology*, **21** (4): 366–9.

König, A. (ed.) (2004), 'Assessment of the safety of foods derived from genetically modified (GM) crops', *Journal of Food and Chemical Toxicology*, **42** (7): 1047–88.

Levidoff, L., S. Carr and D. Wield (2000), 'Genetically modified crops in the European Union: regulatory conflicts as precautionary opportunities', *Journal of Risk Research*, **3** (1): 189–208.

Lyon, J.D. (1998) 'Food systems and accountability mechanisms for food safety: a law and economics approach', *Food and Drug Law Journal*, **53**: 27.

O'Rourke, Raymond (1999), *European Food Law*, Bembridge: Palladian Law.

Miraglia, M. (ed.) (2004), 'Detection and traceability of genetically modified organisms in the food production chain', *Journal of Food and Chemical Toxicology*, **42** (7): 1157–80.

Sipress, A. and M. Kaufman (2001), 'US Challenges EU's Biotech Food Standards', *The Washington Post*, 26 August.

Tait, J. (2001), 'More Faust than Frankenstein: the European debate about the precautionary principle and risk regulation for genetically modified crops', *Journal of Risk Research*, **6** (3): 221–32.

Taylor, M.R. (2002), 'Reforming food safety: a model for the future', *Food Technology*, **56**: 190.

Wiener, J.B. and M.D. Rogers (2001), *Comparing Precaution in the United States and Europe*, Chapel Hill, NC: Duke University, Duke Center for Environmental Solutions.

5. Governance of food safety in the NAFTA region: regulatory cooperation by the United States, Canada and Mexico

Grace Skogstad and Reba A. Carruth*

I INTRODUCTION: REGIONAL COOPERATION FOR THE GOVERNANCE OF FOOD SAFETY IN NORTH AMERICA

The regionalization of North American food and agriculture industries reflects the rapid consolidation and integration of the Canadian, US and Mexican food systems. The emergence and integration of the North American agri-food industry and biotechnology sector are the result of regional market liberalization, tripartite policy cooperation, and trade liberalization through a series of bilateral trade agreements prior to the ratification of the North American Free Trade Agreement (NAFTA) in the early 1990s. The first bilateral trade arrangement came into effect in January 1989 through the enactment of the Canada–US Free Trade Agreement (CFTA). The CFTA liberalized and committed to the harmonization of technical standards and regulations in the dairy, poultry, eggs, cotton, sugar and sugar products sectors. During this period, a free trade agreement between Mexico and the United States, and a third agreement between Canada and Mexico, created a regional market and policy framework for the development of an integrated North American agri-food industry and food safety system.[1]

Since the implementation of NAFTA in 1994, food and agriculture trade within the North American region has grown significantly. To a large extent, this trend reflects the growing importance of agri-food industries and policies for the economies of Canada, the United States and Mexico, and the socio-economic integration of the NAFTA region.[2] As Table 5.1 shows, US food and agriculture exports to Canada and Mexico, accounted for 28 per cent of exports and 35 per cent of imports by the year 2000. This is a dramatic increase from the base year of 1990 when Canada and Mexico

Table 5.1 US agricultural trade with NAFTA (Mexico and Canada), 1992–2000: share of world (percentage)

Commodity	1993	1994	1995	1996	1997	1998	1999	2000
Agricultural exports to world	100.0	100.0	100.0	100.0	100.0	100.0	100.0	100.0
Exports to NAFTA:								
Agriculture, total	20.8	22.0	16.6	19.2	20.9	25.4	26.3	27.5
Animals and animal products	26.5	26.0	17.0	19.3	23.8	27.2	27.7	27.9
Grains and feeds	12.6	16.1	11.2	15.3	15.4	20.8	20.2	22.4
Fruits and preparations, ex. juice	35.9	33.5	29.9	30.5	31.6	34.6	37.2	37.9
Fruit juices, including frozen	36.9	34.7	32.8	35.8	34.6	39.0	35.6	39.0
Nuts and preparations	16.8	14.9	15.1	15.4	14.5	12.7	15.4	18.3
Vegetables and preparations	43.7	42.0	37.7	38.9	41.0	45.4	43.5	45.7
Oilseeds and products	n.a.	n.a.	n.a.	n.a.	n.a.	n.a.	n.a.	n.a.
Other	n.a.	n.a.	n.a.	n.a.	n.a.	n.a.	n.a.	n.a.
Forestry	n.a.	n.a.	n.a.	n.a.	n.a.	n.a.	n.a.	n.a.
Agriculture and forestry, total	n.a.	n.a.	n.a.	n.a.	n.a.	n.a.	n.a.	n.a.
Agric. and non-agric., total	n.a.	n.a.	n.a.	n.a.	n.a.	n.a.	n.a.	n.a.
Agricultural imports from world	100.0	100.0	100.0	100.0	100.0	100.0	100.0	100.0
Imports from NAFTA:								
Agriculture, total	29.4	30.3	31.3	31.5	32.0	33.8	34.1	35.2
Bananas and plantains	8.8	5.5	4.1	3.7	5.1	4.7	3.3	2.1
Coffee, including products	18.4	15.5	20.2	23.0	19.1	18.9	19.9	21.8
Animals and animal products	41.9	40.4	45.6	46.0	47.0	45.2	45.2	45.3
Cattle, live	100.0	100.0	99.7	100.0	99.6	100.0	100.0	100.0
Grains, products and feeds	57.0	59.6	60.7	62.8	62.9	59.3	60.7	60.7
Fruits and preparations	27.6	29.6	35.2	32.1	31.7	37.0	36.0	31.4

Fruit juices, including frozen	6.4	10.1	14.9	9.6	10.9	16.1	12.2	11.8
Vegetables and preparations	54.9	53.1	54.7	58.6	59.4	62.3	59.3	62.9
Tomatoes	95.4	94.7	94.0	91.9	88.8	88.1	88.4	89.5
Sugar and related products	22.4	26.0	22.8	18.8	21.0	26.8	31.1	32.1
Beverages, ex. fruit juices	19.0	20.7	20.2	20.8	21.1	22.8	23.4	25.2
Oilseeds and products	37.5	43.4	36.6	39.9	37.6	42.0	38.2	34.3
Cotton, ex. linters	0.1	0.	22.3	5.7	12.4	0.9	3.9	2.6
Seeds, field and garden	31.1	33.4	32.6	30.2	31.4	26.6	23.6	24.1
Cut flowers	4.8	5.0	6.0	5.2	6.5	6.6	7.2	7.8
Nursery stock, bulbs, etc.	37.9	37.5	37.9	40.9	45.3	48.6	48.8	51.1
Other								
Trade balance:	n.a	n.a	n.a	n.a	n.a	n.a	n.a	n.a
Agriculture with world	n.a	n.a	n.a	n.a	n.a	n.a	n.a	n.a
Agriculture with NAFTA	n.a	n.a	n.a	n.a	n.a	n.a	n.a	n.a
Forestry with NAFTA	n.a	n.a	n.a	n.a	n.a	n.a	n.a	n.a
Agric. and forestry with NAFTA	n.a	n.a	n.a	n.a	n.a	n.a	n.a	n.a
Agric. and non-agric. w/NAFTA	n.a	n.a	n.a	n.a	n.a	n.a	n.a	n.a

Note: n.a = not available or does not apply.

Sources: For forestry data, FAS BICO reports; for all other data, Foreign Agricultural Trade of the United States Economic Research Service, USDA, *The Effects of NAFTA on Agriculture and the Rural Economy*.

accounted for only 17 per cent of all US food and agriculture exports and 25 per cent of US agriculture imports.

By the mid-1990s, Canada became one of the largest markets for US processed foods, while Mexico received a growing amount of foreign direct investment (FDI) from US agri-food companies and industries.[3] As a result of North American agri-food industry growth, cross-border food and agriculture trade between the United States, Canada and Mexico accounted for over one-quarter of the total global agriculture trade by the year 2000. Figure 5.1 shows the growing scale and importance of North American food trade.

By the end of the 1990s, Mexican citizens spent approximately 35 per cent of their income on food, and accounted for a large share of the market for processed foods from the United States. In the Mexican food-processing industry, the production of tortillas, processed fruits and vegetables, and non-alcoholic beverages are major drivers of consumer demand in the national and North American agri-food markets and industries.[4] During this period, there was a notable consumer shift toward higher-value products such as meat, milk, fruit and vegetables relative to traditional grains and beans in the average Mexican diet. At the same time, national food retail chains in Mexico, such as Cifra, Grupo Gigante and Comercial Mexicana accounted for approximately 67 per cent of all national food sales. The remainder of national food sales was claimed by regional grocery stores such as Soriana, Chedraui, and Casa Ley and convenience stores.

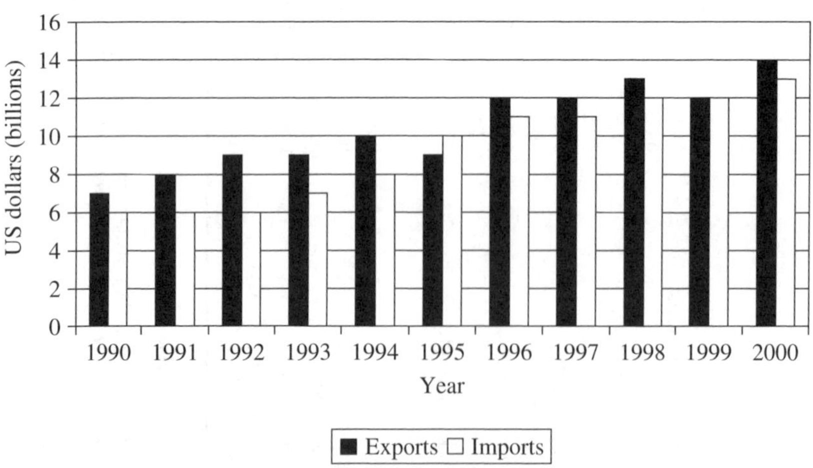

Sources: Foreign Agricultural Trade of the United States database, Economic Research Service, USDA; USDA (2002).

Figure 5.1 US agriculture trade with the NAFTA countries, 1990–2000

In the case of Canada, the Canadian market for US processed foods is one of the largest in the world. This market is projected to grow as the demand for high-value international products and packaged food increases in the years ahead. Since the implementation of the Canada–US Free Trade Agreement in 1989 and NAFTA in 1994, Canadian and US food consumption and demand trends are converging. As a result, the food and beverage processing industry is one of Canada's largest manufacturing sectors. While the largest producers are US and European agri-food companies, there are several Canadian companies such as McCain Foods, Molson Breweries and Maple Leaf Foods that are now world class food processors as a result of NAFTA.[5]

By 1999, US foreign direct investment in the Canadian food-processing industry had also increased from $1.8 billion in 1989 to $5 billion. The bulk of this cross-border investment and industry integration is in the production and processing of grains. In the case of Canada, baked goods are the largest category of Canadian FDI in the US food-processing industry. This FDI represents, almost entirely, the acquisition of the Best Foods Brands of baking products by George Weston, a company that manufactures baked goods in Toronto. This trend also reflects the maturity of the US food-processing industry and the liquidation of Seagrams, a large world-class spirits and beverage company in 1999.[6]

As a result of the regional free trade agreement, US foreign direct investment in the Mexican food-processing industry has doubled since the start of NAFTA. The largest part of this cross-border investment in the Mexican food-processing industry has gone to the production of pasta, candy and confectionary products, and canned and frozen meat. Since the start of this decade the Mexican food-processing industry is concentrated in the processed foods and beverages, grain milling and bakery product segments. In contrast, 5 per cent or less is targeted on processed fruits and vegetables. Therefore, most of the Mexican investment in the US is in the food and beverage processing segment which includes bread baking, corn milling and Mexican food products.

In the twenty-first century the NAFTA agreement serves as a driver for the integration of the North American food-processing industries.[7] Increasingly, US foreign direct investment is used to expand agri-food-processing facilities and biotechnologies, and to increase economic efficiencies across the North American region. In turn, food costs are lowered, product quality is standardized and consumer choices are converging in the NAFTA region. This trend is the result of cross-border investment, and the integration of North American agri-food industries and food systems.

The impact of NAFTA on the trade in food and agriculture products varies across items. Table 5.2 and 5.3 show that trade in fruits and preparations,

Table 5.2 *US agricultural trade with NAFTA (Mexico and Canada), 1992–2000: value ($ million)*

Commodity	1992	1993	1994	1995	1996	1997	1998	1999	2000
Agricultural exports to world	43 159	42 915	46 251	56 347	60 417	57 217	51 815	48 278	51 580
Exports to NAFTA:									
Agriculture, total	8 746	8 937	10 163	9 345	11 583	11 963	13 169	12 700	14 195
Animals and animal products	2 164	2 126	2 401	1 868	2 165	2 718	2 891	2 833	3 304
Grains and feeds	1 873	1 770	2 188	2 094	3 198	2 360	2 909	2 829	3 070
Fruits and preparations, ex. juice	785	839	871	794	809	881	880	935	1 041
Fruit juices, including frozen	166	170	184	210	227	229	256	267	278
Nuts and preparations	170	171	169	179	198	204	206	223	249
Vegetables and preparations	1 227	1 321	1 515	1 372	1 486	1 701	1 918	1 871	2 042
Oilseeds and products	1 006	1 028	1 184	1 193	1 562	1 770	1 626	1 563	1 599
Other	1 356	1 511	1 652	1 635	1 937	2 100	2 483	2 180	2 612
Forestry	n.a.	n.a.	1 635	379	1 538	1 878	1 908	2 067	2 251
Agriculture and forestry, total	n.a.	n.a.	11 978	9 724	13 121	13 841	15 077	14 767	16 446
Agric. and non-agric., total	n.a.	n.a.	165 282	173 518	189 345	221 502	233 162	253 509	290 290
Agricultural imports from world	24 799	25 137	27 031	30 263	33 520	36 160	36 908	37 737	38 991
Imports from NAFTA:									
Agriculture, total	6 522	7 384	8 194	9 467	10 556	11 561	12 482	12 881	13 740
Bananas and plantains	103	94	59	47	44	63	57	40	24
Coffee, including products	290	281	385	660	640	742	649	576	589
Animals and animal products	2 228	2 467	2 326	2 739	2 800	3 053	3 132	3 294	3 764
Cattle, live	1 245	1 341	1 151	1 409	1 121	1 119	1 144	1 000	1 152
Grains, products and feeds	828	1 008	1 372	1 403	1 669	1 862	1 707	1 815	1 875
Fruits and preparations	391	380	438	570	616	639	808	993	852

Fruit juices, including frozen	37	42	66	94	88	90	107	96	890
Vegetables and preparations	1072	1379	1491	1746	2066	2201	2727	2715	2977
Tomatoes	139	310	326	423	618	576	668	609	573
Sugar and related products	244	253	310	304	354	389	451	494	504
Beverages, ex. fruit juices	373	387	460	494	607	715	865	1019	1199
Oilseeds and products	361	440	663	641	814	800	872	707	636
Cotton, ex. linters	0	0	0	2	16	0	0	5	1
Seeds, field and garden	59	65	78	79	94	117	113	109	118
Cut flowers	16	19	21	31	30	39	41	43	47
Nursery stock, bulbs, etc.	90	103	110	131	155	185	227	248	281
Other	430	468	418	526	562	666	728	727	783
Forestry	n.a.	6539	7771	7400	9026	9908	10067	12187	11276
Agriculture and forestry, total	n.a.	13923	15965	16867	19582	21469	22549	25068	25016
Agric. and non-agric., total	n.a.	151133	177899	207032	229469	253881	269553	308432	366764
Trade balance:									
Agriculture with world	18361	17779	19220	26084	26897	21057	14907	10541	12588
Agriculture with NAFTA	2223	1553	1969	−122	1026	402	687	−181	455
Forestry with NAFTA	n.a.	n.a.	−6136	−7021	−7488	−8030	−8159	−10120	−9025
Agric. and forestry with NAFTA	n.a.	n.a.	−4167	−7143	−6462	−7628	−7472	−10301	−8570
Agric. and non-agric. w/NAFTA	n.a.	n.a.	−12617	−33514	−40124	−32379	−36391	−54923	−76474

Note: n.a = not available or does not apply.

Sources: For forestry data, FAS BICO reports; for all other data, Foreign Agricultural Trade of the United States Economic Research Service, USDA, *The Effects of NAFTA on Agriculture and the Rural Economy*.

Table 5.3 NAFTA food and agriculture trade volume by commodity

Commodity	Annual average of actual trade					Estimated change in trade volume due solely to NAFTA
	Value		Volume			
	1990–93	1994–2000	1990–93	1994–2000	Units	
Selected exports to Canada						
Beef and veal	349	317	85	92	mt	Increase-High
Wheat products#	22	48	27	66	mt	Increase-High
Cotton	62	91	42	60	mt	Increase-Medium
Processed tomatoes	71	109	–	–	–	Increase-Medium
Selected exports to Mexico						Increase-High
Rice	41	87	161	386	mt	Increase-High
Dairy Products	151	162	–	–	–	Increase-High
Cotton (including linters)	102	342	80	235	mt	Increase-High
Processed potatoes	6	19	8	28	mt	Increase-High
Fresh apples	28	61	54	112	mt	Increase-High
Fresh pears	16	26	31	51	mt	Increase-High
Corn	178	521	1 557	4 326	mt	Increase-Medium
Oilseeds	401	740	1 662	2 956	mt	Increase-Medium
Beef and veal	149	309	5	107	mt	Increase-Medium
Sorghum	402	307	3 687	3 083	mt	Decrease-High
Selected imports from Canada						
Wheat (excluding seed)	136	268	1 109	1 920	mt	Increase-High
Wheat products#	38	98	72	185	mt	Increase-High

Beef and veal	111	264	260	638	mt	Increase-High
Corn	21	30	218	268	mt	Increase-Medium
Fresh potatoes	51	85	274	380	mt	Increase-Medium
Processed potatoes	50	199	91	313	mt	Increase-Medium
Cattle and calves	741	857	1 063	1 185	no	Decrease-High
Selected imports from Mexico						
Wheat products#	4	14	6	21	mt	Increase-High
Cattle and calves	388	300	1 144	965	no	Increase-High
Peanuts (shelled and in shell)	*	3	*	4 323	mt	Increase-High
Sugar (cane and beet)	2	49	1	17	mt	Increase-High
Fresh tomatoes	264	470	322	608	mt	Increase-Medium
Processed tomatoes	15	16	–	–	–	Increase-Medium
Cantaloupe	40	47	120	136	mt	Increase-Medium

Notes:
mt = Metric tons.
no = Number.
* = Negligible.
# = Includes flour, bulgur wheat, starch, gluten, and uncooked pasta.
Estimates reflect changes in trade volume during 1994–2000 due solely to CFTA and NAFTA and are based on assessments of ERS analysts:
High = A change of more than 15 per cent, compared with what would have occurred without CFTA and NAFTA.
Medium = A change of 6 to 15 per cent.

Sources: Economic Research Service, USDA, *The Effects of NAFTA on Agriculture and the Rural Economy*; for trade data: Agricultural trade of the United States database.

non-frozen fruit juices, beef and veal, grain products and seeds, sugar and sugar products, fresh tomatoes, rice and cotton have grown significantly. The growth of these agri-food industries is due to the removal of trade barriers, regulatory compliance with WTO sanitary and phytosanitary standards (SPS) and harmonization of national food safety regulations. Consequently, NAFTA countries are creating a North American food safety system that is compatible with WTO SPS and Codex Alimentarius Commission standards to support the regional agri-food industry and biotechnology sector.

II REGIONAL REGULATORY COOPERATION AND INDUSTRY STANDARDS CONVERGENCE

Food Safety Regulation in the United States: The Federal Regulatory System

The US food system integrates food and agriculture markets, and uses science-based regulatory laws and industry standards to produce safe food for American consumers. In the US food system, the following goals serve as the basis for the regulation of food safety: provision of safe and wholesome foods for consumption, science-based regulation of food safety, regulatory enforcement, transparency of food safety regulation, review of regulations by US citizens and consumers, agri-food producers, processors and distributors that are required by law to comply with food safety standards, and assessment of corporate legal liability for failure to adhere to legally binding regulations and laws.[8] In this context, agri-food companies and industries seek to avoid liability to consumers, and play a major role in the protection of the national food system.[9]

The leading government agencies responsible for food safety regulation in the United States are as follows: the Food and Drug Administration (FDA) which is part of the Department of Health and Human Services (DHHS), the Food Safety and Inspection Service (FSIS), the US Department of Agriculture (USDA), the Environmental Protection Agency (EPA) and the National Marine Fisheries Services (NMFS) which is located in the Department of Commerce.[10]

In terms of regulatory responsibility and legal authority, the FDA is responsible for the protection of consumers and citizens from unsafe, impure and incorrectly labeled food and agricultural products.[11] The USDA is responsible for ensuring the safety of meat and poultry products, and has regulatory authority for food production and processing plants. In this context, the USDA works through a network of agencies and departments such as the Food Safety Inspection Service (FSIS), Grain Inspection,

Packers and Stockyards Administration (GIPSA) and the Animal and Plant Health Service (APHIS) to ensure the safety and quality of food through a variety of market surveillance, quality assurance and risk management programs.[12] The EPA is responsible for the regulation of pesticide use and licensing, and sets standards for pesticide residue tolerance in the air, water and ground, and food and animal feed chains.[13]

The federal regulatory agencies with food safety oversight have a supporting network of agencies and departments. In each case, the regulatory agencies have specific responsibilities for consumer safety and public health protection and are as follows: DHHS Center for Disease Control and Prevention (CDC), the National Institute of Health (NIH), the USDA Agricultural Research Service (AMS), the Economic Research Service, Education and Extension Services (CSREES), the Agricultural Marketing Service (AMS), the Department of Commerce National Marine Fisheries Service (NMFS) and the US Codex Alimentarius Office in the USDA.[14] In support of federal food safety regulation and agri-food industry governance, state and local health departments enforce FDA food standards, regulations and laws. In turn, states and local municipalities are responsible for the promotion of the FDA Food Code which provides science-based standards for the regulation of food safety in restaurants and food service organizations.[15]

Risk analysis and the precautionary model of the United States

In response to the globalization of agri-food industries, United States food safety regulators increased their focus on risk analysis and the management of microbial food pathogens that increasingly threaten 'farm to table' food systems. Moreover, the historical focus on food safety threats from additives, drugs, pesticides, chemicals and other hazards in the production, processing and marketing of food increase the importance of risk assessment, management and communication within US, North American food systems and global agri-food industries.[16]

In the case of risk assessment, past, present and emerging food safety threats are identified and addressed in the regulatory process. Therefore, in 1997 the President's Food Safety Initiative launched the Interagency Risk Assessment Consortium. Through interagency cooperation, microbial and other food safety risk assessments are collectively done to prevent the contamination of national food systems and agri-food industries. For example, US food safety regulators carried out risk analysis on *Salmonella enteritidis* in egg and egg products for the first 'farm to table' microbial risk assessment in the US food system. Likewise, food safety regulators are working in partnership with Harvard University to carry out risk analysis for BSE transmission in the national food system.[17]

Meat and poultry inspection

The first phase of meat and poultry inspection is carried out through FSIS, which requires all domestic and international food production and processing plants (that import food into the United States) to implement HACCP. In the second and third phases, FSIS enforces legally binding food safety standards for processing plants and agri-food industry implementation, and training requirements for plant inspectors. In support of this new strategy, FSIS was reorganized to strengthen its regulatory enforcement capabilities for agri-food producers and processors that fail to comply with US regulatory standards. Through the adoption of the pathogen reduction and HACCP regulations, the following regulatory and industry standards goals are achieved to ensure the safety of the US food system:

- All meat and poultry plants must develop and implement a system of HACCP controls to increase the safety of their food products.
- Pathogen reduction standards must be set for *Salmonella* in slaughterhouses and plants that produce raw meat products.
- All meat and poultry plants have to develop and implement written standard operating procedures for sanitation.
- Meat and poultry slaughter and processing plants must carry out microbial pathogen testing for *E. coli* and certify the prevention of fecal contamination of food.
- Finally, government intervention is legally justified when food system contamination occurs and threatens consumer safety and the public health which is the case for food recalls.[18]

In December 2003, the first case of Mad Cow disease was found in the United States. In this case, a cow in Washington state was found to be the source of the first documented case of BSE in the United States. While US government and beef industry officials were initially confident that the outbreak of BSE was contained, growing consumer pressure and international concern led to an expanded beef recall of meat from the infected cow in Oregon, California, Nevada and Washington. During this period, concerns were raised about the unidentified amount of meat from the same slaughterhouse that was sent to Alaska, Hawaii, Montana, Idaho and the Territory of Guam.[19] Eventually, three cases of BSE were found in Canada.

In an effort to contain the damage from the outbreak of BSE, the United States government and US beef industry associations went on the offensive with a public relations campaign.[20] In response to the news of the first reported case of Mad Cow disease in the United States, which is a leading exporter of beef, several countries banned US beef exports. Within a few days after the announcement of a positive finding of BSE over 30 countries including Japan, South Korea, Taiwan, Singapore, Vietnam, the Russian Federation, Mexico, Brazil, China, Hong Kong, Australia, Malaysia, South Africa, Thailand, Ukraine and the United Arab Emirates issued immediate bans on the importation of US beef. During this period, Canada issued a partial ban on US beef, while the European Union, which had earlier banned most US beef due to the use of growth hormones, was the least affected.[21]

As the Mad Cow crisis in the United States unfolds, the USDA and FDA are strengthening meat inspection, food safety certification regulations and risk management procedures. The goal of these regulatory policy changes is to restore consumer confidence and the trust of global trading partners. As part of the comprehensive review and reform of meat inspection and food safety procedures, the USDA launched the following new measures:

1. The immediate ban on non-ambulatory (downer) animals from inclusion in the food chain and human food supply was enacted.[22]
2. The immediate requirement of additional process controls for advanced meat recovery (AMR) to increase the detection of beef and meat pathogens was implemented.[23]
3. The holding of meat from cattle that have been tested for BSE until the test results confirm a negative finding is now a mandatory requirement.[24]
4. The USDA and FSIS inspectors will no longer mark cattle tested for BSE, or inspected, as passed until the cattle test returns negative.[25]
5. The FSIS prohibits the use of skull, brain, vertebral column, spinal cord, trigeminal ganglia, eyes and dorsa root ganglia of cattle 30 months of age or older, and small intestine of all cattle in the human food system. Furthermore, FSIS now requires that meat slaughterhouses and food processors remove, segregate and dispose of specified risk materials so they cannot enter the food chain.[26]
6. The use of air injection stunning to prevent portions of the brain from entering into tissues of beef carcasses during the human stunning of cattle in the slaughter process is now prohibited.[27]
7. The FDA issued a new set of regulations and standards to remove animal blood in livestock feed, which was not covered by the 1997 decision to remove cattle parts from animal feed. The use of cattle parts in the production of dietary supplements is now prohibited.[28]

In addition to these precautionary risk assessment and risk management measures designed to strengthen beef inspection measures, the USDA announced that an international scientific review panel would assess the department's BSE surveillance system. The recommendations of the review panel will determine future actions to increase the number of cattle tested for BSE.[29]

In the poultry industry, the USDA and FDA responded to recent outbreaks and spread of avian flu in Delaware and Maryland, and the subsequent banning of US poultry products by many major chicken importers.[30] In this regard, the USDA is significantly expanding the testing of poultry raised in the United States for avian flu. Through implementation of a $12.5million Poultry Improvement Program, the most dangerous forms of avian flu will be identified and controlled to protect food safety and public health. While this program is voluntary, the US poultry industry endorses the plan for all commercial chicken producers.[31]In terms of risk communication for the BSE and avian flu outbreaks in the United States, national media and open global information sharing, and cooperation with WHO, FAO the WTO, OIE, the EU and other food safety regulatory agencies are used as part of the official notification process.[32]

Regulation of biotechnology

The FDA has regulatory authority under the Federal Food, Drug and Cosmetic Act for the governance of food and food ingredients developed by genetic engineering and biotechnology. Through this policy, GM foods are regulated in the same way as their conventional counterparts. In 1990, the FDA published the first food safety regulation for the use of the recombinant DNA produced food ingredient – fermentation-derived chymosin (rennet). In an effort to support the interests of consumers and food producers, the FDA issued a policy statement in 1992 regarding the development and consumption of GM foods, grains, fruits and vegetables.[33]

The policy statement encouraged firms and industry to consult the FDA regarding potential safety concerns of new plant varieties intended for food use, and to provide government authorities with scientific data on the safety and nutritional assessment of GM food. However, companies are not required to notify the FDA before they place GM foods on the market. While most companies voluntarily comply with the FDA guideline, they do not need mandatory FDA approval to place GM food on the market. As the consumers grow increasingly concerned about GM food safety, the role of mandatory notifications are being discussed. However, the current voluntary system of notification remains in place.[34]

This regulatory framework vests legal responsibility and product liability in food producers and processors to ensure that the food sold to US consumers is safe and in compliance with food safety laws and standards. In addition, the FDA uses the food additive provisions under section 409 of the Act to ensure that substances introduced through biotechnology and genome manipulation are safe before pre-market approval is granted for the genetic modification of food crops for consumption. In spite of these measures, consumer concern over biotechnology food, and the voluntary nature of US regulation of novel agri-food products is growing in the United States. For example, the Center for Science and the Public Interest claims that government regulators do not always obtain the data they request of companies in their task of evaluating GM foods.[35] Therefore, in 2002, the US General Accounting Office (GAO), recommended random verification of industry-submitted data and greater transparency of FDA GM food safety evaluations.[36]

The FDA also uses the food additive provisions under section 409 of the Act to ensure that substances introduced through biotechnology and genome manipulation are safe before pre-market approval is granted for GM food products. However, GM food products can be removed from the market by the FDA in the event of food safety hazards or emerging public health risks.[37] In 2000, genetically modified StarLink corn, which was only approved for use as animal feed, was found in the human food chain. The restriction of StarLink corn to animal feed reflects the public health concerns over allergic reactions to GM corn in humans. As a consequence of the mixing of GM and conventional corn supplies, millions of taco shells at supermarkets and fast-food restaurants such as Taco Bell were recalled by Kraft Foods and government food safety authorities.[38]After the incident, agri-business and food companies worked with food safety authorities to prevent further contamination of the food supply.

Product labeling

The FDA has regulatory authority over the labeling of all food products.[39] Regulations require that information on food labels must be truthful, free of fraud and deception, that food be given a common and recognizable name, and that the information about the claims and consequences (good or bad) that may result from the consumption of the product is clearly stated. In addition, if the composition of a GM food differs significantly from conventional or non-GM food in terms of nutrient levels, for example, or if there are any potential safety concerns such as allergenicity, the label must indicate this for consumers. However, the 1992 FDA Biotechnology Act does not require that information be given by food producers on a 'consumer right to know' basis.[40]

In this context, food labeling is also mandated in regard to vitamin and mineral fortification to protect consumers and to prevent food safety hazards. Specifically, the establishment and enforcement of minimum levels of food nutrients in certain foods to reduce deficiency diseases, and the specification of maximum levels of vitamins and minerals to prevent the toxic side effects and health risks, are now requirements for food labeling. Furthermore, food producers must prove all claims of fortification and nutritional benefits relative to FDA science-based regulatory standards and laws.[41]

As globalization intensifies, the FDA is under increasing pressure from farmers, ranchers, selected food industry associations and consumer organization to implement mandatory country of origin labeling of food. At the present time, country of origin labeling is not mandatory. However, the FDA and USDA prohibit incorrect, false or misleading statements about the geographic origin of domestic and imported foods.[42] As the decade unfolds, US farmers and consumers are demanding mandatory country of origin labels to increase the quality of food product information to ensure rapid food recalls and traceability of food safety hazards.

Regulatory harmonization and international standards cooperation: FDA

In response to globalization of the food industry, and growing demand for imported and high-quality foods by American consumers, the FDA adopted the Food and Drug Administration Modernization Act in 1997.[43] Through the passage of this food and drug law reform, international cooperation and activities of the FDA gained more attention and importance. In turn, the FDA Modernization Act of 1997 makes international regulatory harmonization a major priority and policy goal of the FDA relative to domestic public health and consumer protection.[44] In this context, a formal framework for the achievement of Mutual Recognition of Good Manufacturing Practices (GMP) inspections is required within 180 days of the enactment of new laws. The types of international agreements for regulatory and standards harmonization include the following: Memoranda of Understanding (MOUs), Memoranda of Agreement or arrangements (MOAs), Memoranda of Cooperation (MOC) or Exchange of Letters (EOL).

At the next level, Mutual Recognition Agreements (MRAs) allow the US government to enter into agreements for reciprocal recognition and acceptance of regulations and regulatory systems of other nations. Through this regulatory procedure, US food safety authorities ensure that the standards and requirements of the importing countries are met. Furthermore, the FDA engages in the adoption and application of common regulatory policies through harmonization when the determination of equivalence is made that another country's regulatory system and laws, inspection procedures and enforcement provides, at a minimum, the same level of consumer protection as the US.[45]

In many cases, the FDA and USDA use food safety and GMP inspection standards harmonization to carry out its regulatory mandate.[46] One of the most important regulatory harmonization frameworks is Codex Alimentarius. The United States is an active member of the Codex Alimentarius Commission, and supports Codex standard-setting activities.

In this context the US participates in the Codex Committees and related multilateral food safety forums. Through the coordination of the US Codex Office, which is housed in FSIS, the United States is represented in Codex through the participation of the USDA, FDA and EPA.

In spite of these efforts, the FDA and USDA face growing concern over the principle of equivalency of regulations and food inspection systems. In some cases, regulatory harmonization through MRAs and inspection certification are viewed as marketing strategies by US companies and agri-food industries. Ultimately, growing concerns by citizens and consumers over market-driven and fast-track policy decisions to certify countries as having equivalent regulatory policies and food safety capacity confirms the need for faster harmonization and institutional convergence in North America.

III FOOD SAFETY REGULATION AND AGRI-FOOD MARKET GOVERNANCE IN CANADA

Food safety issues are a high priority in Canadian agri-food policy. Food safety is one of five pillars in Canada's Agricultural Policy Framework, the federal–provincial blueprint for agri-food policy, whose implementation commenced 1 April 2003. The Canadian government's objective is to make Canada the world leader in food safety.[47] To this end, there are ongoing initiatives to ensure that both levels of government and the agri-food industry work coherently to provide consumers with a high measure of protection. This policy goal is achieved by implementing food safety and inspection systems that are based on the latest technology and best practices. In this respect, Canada is committed to a domestic food safety system based on scientific standards and risk assessment principles, and supports regional and global harmonization of food safety regulations.

Canada's interest in regional and global harmonization of food safety measures stems from its relatively high dependence on export markets and, with the exception of wheat exports, its relatively small share of these same global markets. In fact, almost half of total Canadian primary production is exported directly, or indirectly in the form of processed products, and more than one-third of farm-gate receipts come from exported products.[48] Even while highly reliant upon export markets to absorb production surpluses for most commodities, Canada's share of world agri-food trade is only around 3 per cent.[49]

Table 5.4 provides further evidence of Canada's comparatively small share of global production and trade in various commodities. This export dependence gives Canadian governments strong incentives to engage in initiatives to prevent other countries' food safety measures from acting as

Table 5.4 Canada's share of global production and export trade

	% Global production*	% Global exports**
Wheat	4.6	21.1
Coarse grains+	2.8	3.5
Oilseeds	4.3	4.2
Pork	4.7	2.1
Beef and veal	4.6	2.6
Poultry	3.2	2.8

Notes:
* Agriculture and Agri-Food Canada, 2002–07, OECD database.
** See Agriculture and Agri-Food Canada, *Medium Term Policy Baseline: International and Domestic Markets*, September 2001, Ottawa: Government of Canada Tables B.4, B.5, and B.6, pp. B7–9 for data on wheat, coarse grains and oilseeds. Data on pork, beef and veal, and poultry exports as percentage of global exports are obtained from USDA, at website http//www.fas.usda.gov/dlp/dlp.html.
† Coarse grains include corn, barley, sorghum, oats, rye, mixed grains and millet.

non-tariff barriers that bar the entry of Canadian agri-food products. It also leads Canada to be a strong advocate of science-based food safety regimes in regional agreements like (NAFTA) and the multilateral World Trade Organization.

National Frameworks of Food Safety Regulation in Canada

Federal and provincial regulation

Achieving a high-quality food safety system is complicated by Canada's federal system that divides responsibility for food safety between the two levels of government. The national government sets food safety, quality and grading standards for products sold inter-provincially and internationally. The federal government also administers regulations aimed at preventing the production or sale throughout Canada of dangerous, adulterated or misbranded products. Provinces and municipalities are responsible for the intra-provincial aspects of the food industry, including local food-processing, the food service industry and the food retail industry.

At the national level and under the authority of the Food and Drug Act, the federal department of health, Health Canada, is responsible for ensuring that all foods, including those derived from biotechnology, are safe prior to their entering the Canadian food system. Health Canada also has legislative and administrative authority for policies regarding food labeling; labeling of food for health and safety reasons is mandatory. Inspection to ensure that food safety standards are enforced is the responsibility of the

Canadian Food Inspection Agency (CFIA). The CFIA inspects all meat and dairy processing facilities whose products are traded inter-provincially and internationally. The CFIA also conducts border inspections for foreign pests and diseases, and to prevent the introduction and spread of quarantine pests which could impact on Canada's grains and field crops sector. The CFIA also undertakes food safety investigations, issues recalls, and enforces regulations related to fraudulent labeling.

HACCP industry standards

In recent years, and in response to criticisms of gaps in food safety regulation,[50] the CFIA works closely with provincial governments and industry to develop a coherent and seamless food safety inspection system. The CFIA entered into agreements with provincial governments regarding procedures for food recalls, safe food-handling practices, inspection of non-federally registered food establishments, and sharing federal and provincial inspection activities in areas of food safety. The implementation of HACCP systems is technically and financially supported by the Government of Canada. Under the Food Safety Enhancement Program (FSEP), HACCP systems are being developed, implemented and maintained, with oversight by the CFIA in all segments of the food industry.

With scientific and technical advice from the CFIA, most, if not all, nationally regulated processors in the fish, meat, dairy and poultry sectors have implemented HACCP systems. The final step is on-farm food safety systems. Several industry groups, representing livestock, poultry, horticultural and field crops currently have plans to implement HACCP on-farm systems on a voluntary basis. Initiatives are also under way to implement tracing and tracking systems throughout the food production and processing chain.

Canada's endorsement of HACCP systems to ensure food safety in the production and processing sectors is consistent with international standards and is deemed necessary to ensure access to foreign markets for Canadian products. HACCP is recognized under Codex as an internationally accepted standard for food safety. The United States' requirement that imported meat and poultry be produced under HACCP in the country of origin was a major incentive for Canada to introduce HACCP at home. In turn, the United States accepts Canada's HACCP sanitation programs as equivalent to its own HACCP Rule.

Aligning safety standards and inspection systems with those in the US is very important to the Canadian agri-food industry. Over three-fifths of Canada's agri-food exports and imports are with the USA.[51] The Canadian fear is that export products will be denied entry to the large and important US market on the grounds that Canadian standards and inspection systems are not equivalent to American regulations. In the early 1990s, shipments of ultra high temperature (UHT) milk from Quebec to Puerto Rico were denied access for three years on the grounds that Canada's dairy inspection system was not equivalent to the US National Pasteurized Milk Ordinance (PMO).[52] This challenge gave Canada's dairy industry a strong incentive to harmonize Canadian export standards across provinces to create a national standard. However, Canada has yet to finalize equivalency negotiations on milk with the United States.

Protecting the safety of its domestic food supply results in a restrictive Canadian policy with respect to imports from countries affected with diseases or food safety problems. Two cases in point are the Canadian response to the Bovine Spongiform Encephalopathy (BSE) and Foot-and-Mouth disease crises. Canada is free of Foot-and-Mouth disease, and until 2003, was free of BSE. Like all countries free of these diseases, Canada takes action to prohibit imports from countries where an outbreak occurs. Imports of live ruminants and ruminant products from countries with cases of BSE are prohibited. The restrictions are lifted only when countries are determined to be free of BSE. The situation is similar for imports from countries with recorded cases of Foot-and-Mouth disease (FMD).

In March 2001, Canada suspended all import permits for susceptible products (live animals, embryos, semen, animal products) from countries with confirmed cases of FMD: that is, the members of the European Union and Argentina. Argentina opposed the import restriction, arguing that it was politically motivated, despite strong evidence that it was scientifically based on a precautionary approach. As it did with Argentina, Canada has lifted restrictions on imports from FMD countries once risk assessments demonstrate the country is free of the disease. In order to protect the health of Canadian livestock, travelers from countries susceptible to FMD were required to follow disinfectant procedures at Canadian international airports.

In May 2003, when a single case of BSE was found in the Canadian cattle heard, Canada was at the receiving end of other countries' precautionary regulatory approach. Virtually overnight, exports of Canadian beef and live cattle to the United States (the most important export market) and 33 other countries stopped. In early 2005, as the US border remained blocked to most Canadian beef products and live cattle, the losses to the Canadian cattle and beef sector were estimated at $5 billion. Although the US administration and American meat packers supported removal of the ban, and allowing Canadian meat and live cattle into the US, an organization representing American cattlemen, R-CALF, persuaded a US judge that doing so would put at risk the safety of the American food supply. In Canada, the Canadian government came under increasing pressure to launch a trade action against the US on the grounds that the import ban violated NAFTA and WTO rules. The rules require that restrictions on food imports must be backed by scientific evidence of their lack of safety.

Regulation of genetically modified foods

Canada's policies with regard to genetically modified (GM) foods are not specific to GM foods but, rather, are similar to those for other plants and foods with novel traits. Canada is alone among countries in regulating plants and foodstuffs on the basis of their novelty. Like the United States, Canada uses the concept of substantial equivalence as a guide to identify differences between conventional and novel crops. The net result is that Canada shares the US practice of regulating the products rather than the process of genetic engineering.

Both Health Canada and the CFIA share responsibility for the safety assessments and final approval of GM products. The Canadian Food Inspection Agency has responsibility for the regulation of products derived from biotechnology for non-food safety concerns, that is, any necessary field trials for crop plants (and their environmental effects) and for approval of any GM feed for animals. Since most crop plants will eventually become foodstuffs, Health Canada also must grant their approval.

The Novel Foods Regulation (under the Food and Drug Act) requires that the company that wants to sell the product notify the Health Products and Food Branch (HPFB) of Health Canada prior to the marketing or advertising of a novel food. Pre-market notification permits Health Canada to conduct a safety assessment of all biotechnology derived foods, using data submitted by the company, to determine that a novel food is safe and nutritious before it is allowed in the Canadian marketplace. This regulatory practice differs from that in the US where FDA rules do not require FDA pre-market notification and approval of GM foods.

In recent years, the regulation of GM products has been subject to some controversy, provoking several government-commissioned hearings, studies and reports. Two issues in particular have elicited attention: first, the adequacy of Canada's biotechnology regulatory framework and, second, whether GM products should be labeled and, if so, whether labeling should be voluntary or mandatory. The adequacy of Canada's biotechnology regulatory framework has been questioned, not only by mobilized environmental and consumer groups, but also in two government-commissioned reports by the independent Royal Society of Canada (2001)[53] and the Canadian Biotechnology Advisory Committee (CBAC, 2002). (The latter's members are appointed by the Government of Canada.) Both bodies find fault with certain features of Canada's GM regulatory framework.

The Royal Society is critical of the use of 'substantial equivalence' as a decision threshold to exempt GM agricultural products from rigorous scientific assessment, stating that the concept is scientifically unjustifiable and inconsistent with precautionary regulation of biotechnology. The concept of substantial equivalence is also used in the United States; GM food that is 'substantially equivalent' to conventionally produced food is 'generally recognized as safe'. The company that produces the GM food judges whether the product meets this 'generally recognized as safe' test on the basis of its own data.

The Royal Society further argues that the scientific basis for risk regulation in Canada is undermined in several ways: first, the same regulatory agency (the CFIA) has a mandate both to promote the development of agricultural biotechnologies and to regulate them, 'thereby putting itself in a potential conflict of interest. Second, there are barriers to confidentiality that compromise the transparency and openness to scientific peer review of the science upon which regulatory decisions are based'; and, finally, 'there are extensive and growing conflicts of interest within the scientific community due to entrepreneurial interests in resulting technologies and the increasing domination of the research agenda by private corporate interest are cited as major regulatory challenges.'[54]

The CBAC is also critical of the current regulatory system, arguing that it does not provide clear information about how GM products are regulated and regulatory decisions made, the roles of the regulatory bodies or the information considered during safety assessments.[55] Like the Royal Society, it faults vesting both promotional and regulatory functions in the CFIA, and calls for a number of organizational changes to avoid this and to provide greater coordination across regulatory bodies. However, both organizations recommend more public transparency of the scientific data and rationales on which regulatory decisions are based.

The Government of Canada responded to the criticisms and recommendations of the Royal Society Report with a number of initiatives that included review and clarification of the concept of substantial equivalence, strengthening of public transparency and confidence, including an external expert in all novel food decisions, and development of a strategy to identify the public health risks of biotechnology products, including GM foods.[56]

Food labeling

The second matter of debate is the labeling of GM foods. Currently, GM foods are treated like all novel foods: that is, labeling is mandatory to indicate any health or safety concern arising from allergens or a significant nutrient or compositional change. This labeling information does not disclose the process (of genetic engineering) by which the GM food is produced. Canadian labeling regulations are therefore identical to those in the United States. Public opinion surveys indicate that, like American consumers,[57] Canadian consumers want more non-safety related information about GM foods.[58] Neither the Royal Society nor the CBAC has recommended mandatory labeling for non-health and safety purposes, proposing instead voluntary labeling.[59] The CBAC suggests that a voluntary system be re-evaluated after five years to determine whether it gives consumers sufficient choice.

Consistent with their recommendations and to comply with consumers' wishes, the Government of Canada encouraged voluntary labeling by food manufacturers. A national voluntary standard was developed by a commitee that included representatives of food manufacturers, farmers, consumer and other interested parties under the auspices of the Canadian General Standards Board. The government and the food industry ruled out mandatory labeling of GM foods as an option because most Canadian farmers and food processors believe it would raise their costs and, like government officials, fear that the US would challenge mandatory labeling as a discriminatory non-tariff trade barrier.

IV FOOD SAFETY REGULATION IN MEXICO

The regulation of food safety in Mexico is carried out by the Secretary of Health in Mexico. The legal authorization of the Mexican food regulatory system is provided in the General Act for Health, which was enacted in 1984.[60] The Secretary of Agriculture, Livestock, Rural Development, Fishery and Food (SALRDFF) which was created in 1951, has authority over slaughterhouses and meat-processing plants in Mexico. Through the use of a federal inspection system, export standards are enforced in keeping with international agreements. Since that time, new regulations were developed to fill the gaps in sanitary and phytosanitary standards in the Mexican agri-food sector.

In 1988, the Secretary of Health and SALRDFF formed a cooperation to regulate imported meat standards and the quality of meat products. By 1990, the Mexican government launched a food safety training program through the National Fishery Institute in cooperation with the FAO. Through this cooperation arrangement, the HACCP system was introduced into the food safety system of Mexico. As a result of NAFTA, the Secretary of Economy used the Federal Act on Metrology and Normalization of 1992 to create mandatory standards and voluntary standards for Mexican Accreditation Entities (MAE) and private third-party accreditation and certification bodies for agri-food industry sanitary standards labeling. In 1992, the Mexican standards system was created with the participation of consumer, industry, university and government agency stakeholders.

During this period, Mexico became actively involved in Codex Alimentarius, which eventually led to strong participation of Mexican delegations in the Codex Committees. This process was carried out to support the fair food trade and sanitary regulation requirements of Mexican industries and markets. Later in 1993, the Federal Animal Hygiene Act was enacted to give authority and responsibility for sanitary standards enforcement, and food safety regulatory power over other animal livestock products. This Act required the creation of private standards monitoring agencies that are under the control and accreditation authority of SALRDFF.[61]

Prior to the creation of the new Food Safety Act, Mexico did not have an integrated food safety program. As a result, agricultural production was unregulated for food safety problems such as microbiological, chemical and physical risks in the agri-food industries.[62] At the present time, Mexican sanitary regulations and standards are under the control of the Secretary of Health. Through its federal, state and municipal action, sanitary regulations and standards are coordinated and implemented for the manufacture, importation, distribution, commercialization and provision of processed food, and raw agricultural commodities.

As the North American food system unfolds in the twenty-first century, the Mexican government is under increasing pressure to adopt and enforce Codex Alimentarius and WTO SPS standards for food safety regulation. In response to the policy and market convergence requirements of NAFTA, the Mexican government launched the National System for Food Safety through a cooperative arrangement between the Departments of Health and Agriculture. Through this institutional arrangement, the sanitary standards, food quality, security and integrity of Mexican agricultural, livestock and fishery products and food industries are now regulated in accordance with national and international standards.[63]

In July 2001, the Mexican Department of Health created a Federal Commission for Sanitary Risk Protection to integrate food safety regulations and agri-food industry standards. Within this cross-sectoral policy framework, pharmaceutical products, medical equipment, health supplies, environmental and occupational health, food, beverages and cosmetics are regulated under a merged institutional framework. Furthermore, efficient technical and scientific methods of risk analysis and risk management are used to support the role of SALRDFF as the leading sanitary and food safety regulatory authority in Mexico.

In an effort to increase consumer safety and representation, the National Service for Agriculture and Food Hygiene, Safety and Quality (NSAFHSQ) created a General Office for Consumer Communication. The goal of this consumer advocacy agency is to ensure that Mexican food safety goals, regulations and standards are effectively communicated to the public. The need for more regulatory enforcement, and increased public confidence in food safety regulation and agri-food industry governance, are growing concerns for Mexico and its North American partners.[64] In response to these concerns a National Forum on Food Safety was held, in 2002. During this meeting, there was a strong consensus that food safety should be a priority in Mexico, and that an exclusive agency was needed for 'farm to table' regulation of the agri-food sector.

Finally, a Master Plan for Food Safety was developed to coordinate and combine the regulatory and industry standards activities for Mexican agri-food companies and industries. Through this plan, an integrated food safety system provides a coherent policy framework for the launch of the following initiatives: Good Agricultural Practices; Good Production Practices; Standards for Sanitization Procedures; and Risk Analysis and Critical Control Points for the agricultural, livestock and fisheries producers and industries. As a result of these regulatory policy, industry standards and consumer initiatives, Mexico is moving rapidly to comply with the regulatory and industry standards requirements of NAFTA, the WTO SPS agreements, and Codex standards.

V THE EMERGING NORTH AMERICAN FOOD SAFETY SYSTEM

Emerging Tripartite Governance of Food Safety in North America

As the decade unfolds, the governments of Canada, the United States and Mexico are creating a regional food safety framework. The fundamental goals of this framework are to protect consumers, the public health and to promote safe cross-border food trade in North America. The legal basis for the creation of a North American policy cooperation framework for the regulation of regional food safety, agri-food industries and cross-border are found in Article 722 of the NAFTA Treaty. Through this provision, a NAFTA SPS Committee was created in 1994 to promote regulatory harmonization and industry standards convergence in accordance with the WTO SPS Agreement and Codex standards.

The formal tripartite process for North American food safety cooperation consists of working groups within the NAFTA SPS Committee, and the adoption of Codex Alimentaarius standards. The following working groups support the regulatory cooperation, regional certification, and industry standards convergence work of the NAFTA SPS Committee:

- Animal Health
- Dairy, Fruits, Vegetables and Processed Foods
- Fish and Fishing Product Inspection
- Food Additives and Contaminants
- Labeling, Packaging and Standards
- Meat, Poultry and Egg Inspection
- Pesticides
- Plant Health, Seeds and Fertilizers
- Veterinary Drugs and Feeds.

The discussion of regulatory procedures and the future work of the NAFTA SPS Committee was started in the first NAFTA SPS Committee meeting which took place in Washington, DC, in 1994.[65] Since the creation of this policy cooperation process, negotiation of pest-free zones and regionalization of pork, poultry and wheat inspections have come into force in the NAFTA region. By 1995, the governments of Canada, the United States, and Mexico signed a Memorandum of Cooperation in support of public health, drug, medical device, biotechnology and food safety regulatory cooperation.[66] Through this agreement, which was signed by the Food and Drug Administration of the United States, the Subsecretaria De Regulacion Y Fomento Sanitario of the United Mexican States and the Health Protection Branch of Canada, the North American governments agreed to cooperate on the following food safety regulation goals:

- exchange of information on the investigation of product, consumer and public health safety risks and threats
- exchange of information on legislation, regulations, technical and industry standards, product recalls and rejected food and drug products
- information on the evaluation of food and drug safety, nutritional quality of food, product approvals and withdrawal protocols
- exchange of information on the chemical and microbiological safety of foods and methods used for food safety testing
- exchange of information on the development of R&D protocols, and pre- and post-market surveillance activities
- communication on the development of consumer protection programs and health food fraud.[67]

During this period, the US and Mexico moved to establish guidelines for the recognition of disease and pest-free zones. In the case of Mexico, the declaration of disease and pest-free Mexican agriculture and livestock production in designated states became increasingly important for cross-border trade in North America. In a NAFTA meeting in June 1996, Mexico requested the US to certify that the Mexicali Valley in the United States was free from Karmal Bunt disease in an effort to prevent contamination during the rail transport of wheat and other grains across the US–Mexican borders.[68]

On 10 June 1998, the governments of the United States and Mexico entered into regulatory policy cooperation for food safety. In this agreement, the US Department of Health and Human Services, the US Department of Agriculture, the Secretariat of Health of Mexico, and the Secretariat of Agriculture, Livestock, Rural Development, Fish and Food of the United Mexican States, formally agree to work towards convergence and harmonization of food safety regulations and standards. The agreement provides a formal institutional mechanism for regulatory harmonization and industry standards convergence in the following food safety areas:

- processed and unprocessed foods and food products for human consumption
- animal feeds for food producing animals
- foods produced from biotechnology
- human food and animal feed additives
- pesticide residues and other contaminants in food and agricultural commodities
- veterinary drugs for food producing animals
- antimicrobial resistance
- Good Agricultural Practices
- Good Laboratory Practices
- biotechnology
- nutrition
- food product labeling requirements
- reports on disease outbreaks, health hazards, contamination, injury or emergency.[69]

In 1996, the Government of Canada requested more coordination between NAFTA and FTAA technical working groups in the areas of food safety regulations and industry standards convergence. In response to these concerns, the governments of the United States and Canada signed a Record of Understanding in December 1998 to resolve major agricultural trade and food safety issues. The key areas of focus for the United

States–Canada Action Plan for Agriculture Trade are grains, livestock, and red meat sectors, and the following regulatory issues:

1. Importation of Slaughtered Swine
2. Expansion of the Northwest Cattle Project
3. Restricted Feeder Cattle
4. Regionalization of Animal and Veterinary Public Health
5. Resolution of Current and Emerging Animal and Veterinary Health Issues
6. Exchange of Cattle Data
7. Control of In-Transit Movement of Grain by Rail
8. Wheat Access Facilitation Program
9. Phytosanitary Requirements for the Importation of US Wheat
10. Current and Emerging Grain Issues
11. Seed Trade
12. Export Subsidies for Oats
13. Veterinary Drugs
14. Pest Control Products
15. Horticulture
16. Joint US/Canadian Cooperation on Biotechnology
17. Labeling Sugar-Containing Products.[70]

By the end of the 1990s, weak consumer protection, public health and animal livestock and plant health regulation and agri-food industry standards in Mexico gave rise to food safety concerns in Canada and the US.[71] In response to these challenges, the NAFTA SPS Committee, and its working groups provide a framework for regulatory cooperation and industry standards convergence in North America. Through increased technical cooperation, regulatory transparency and industry standards convergence, a regional food safety inspection system is emerging in North America.

Regional mechanisms for regulation and governance of the agri-food industries

In contrast to the European Union, the NAFTA free trade agreement did not provide formal policy harmonization mechanisms for the governance of markets, the regulation of firms, or the protection of North American consumers, public health and public safety. On the contrary, the NAFTA Treaty relies on a voluntary tripartite policy cooperation framework for the governance of cross-border trade, foreign direct investment and market regulation.[72] Therefore, harmonization of Mexican food safety regulations and industry standards is a major goal of North American governments and agri-food industries.[73]

In the NAFTA region, food safety standards and regulatory harmonization are required to protect consumers and increase the competitiveness of Mexican agri-food industries.[74] Consequently, under increasing pressure from Mexican farmers and food industry producers, President Vincente Fox of Mexico called for the renegotiation of the agriculture section of the NAFTA agreement. In this context, the requested National Agreement on Agriculture will provide a regional policy and market framework for the restructuring of Mexican agriculture and agri-food industries, and increasing regulatory capacity.[75] The following regulatory harmonization goals support the competitiveness of Mexican farmers and food producers:

- formal harmonization of food inspection procedures
- simplification of border-crossing procedures and inspection of transport infrastructure
- removal of regulatory barriers and standards that make it easier for US and Mexican companies and industries to import food to Mexico, but at the same time, make it difficult for Mexico to import food to the United States.[76]

As the decade unfolds, there are growing complaints of unfair competition by US and Canadian food companies that sell lower-priced and substandard products on the Mexican market. Furthermore, Mexican meat and crop producers face a larger set of regulatory and market barriers due to the need for reform and restructuring of Mexico's agri-food industries.[77] Therefore, Mexican beef producers are lobbying for stronger meat certification standards to prevent unfair product and price competition from US and Canadian beef producers.[78]

VI REGULATING AND HARMONIZING REGIONAL AND GLOBAL FOOD SAFETY MEASURES

North American Participation in Codex

Canada is committed to cross-national harmonization of food safety measures on the basis of scientific principles and evidence, and is using risk assessment techniques. The Canadian government supported this principle in Chapter 7 of NAFTA which deals with sanitary and phytosanitary (SPS) measures, and in the Sanitary and Phytosanitary Agreement (SPS Agreement) of the World Trade Organization. In this regard, Canada has been aggressive in using the WTO SPS Agreement to disallow sanitary and phytosanitary measures that are inconsistent with its provisions.

With the passage of the SPS Agreement in 1995, Canada and the US were also a part of the majority of Codex Commission members who approved the use of the therapeutic hormones in 1995, over the objections of the EU member states. Shortly thereafter, they lodged a formal complaint with the WTO, arguing that the hormone import ban was inconsistent with the terms of the SPS Agreement. Their challenge was ultimately unsuccessful since a WTO Appellate Body ruled that the EU ban on hormone-treated beef contravened the SPS Agreement, and that the EU had failed to provide the scientific evidence needed to support it as a necessary measure to protect human health and food safety. Despite this favourable outcome, Canada failed in its effort to persuade WTO dispute settlement officials that the SPS Agreement required countries to *conform to* Codex standards, guidelines and recommendations where they existed.[79] The Appellate Body argued that a country's SPS measures could be based on international standards without conforming to them.

Canada's preference for international standard-setting as a basis for its own and other countries' food safety measures is also revealed in its strategy for biotechnology risk assessment and labeling policies. Canada is deeply engaged with the Codex committees working on these issues, including the Codex Ad Hoc Intergovernmental Task Force on Foods Derived from Biotechnology and the Codex Committee on Food Labeling (CCFL), which is chaired by a Canadian. Canada also made significant contributions to the Ad Hoc Task Force's 'Draft Principles for the Risk Analysis of Foods derived from Modern Biotechnology', and 'Draft Guidelines for the Conduct of Food Safety Assessment of Foods Derived From Recombinant-DNA Plants'. It also chaired the Ad Hoc Open-Ended Working Group on Allergenicity. The Canadian *Guidelines for the Safety Assessment of Novel Foods* are being revised to take into account the Codex 'Draft Guidelines' report.

Institutional mechanisms created under the 1989 Canada–US Free Trade Agreement (FTA), and continued under NAFTA, provide a forum for regulatory harmonization and the integration of the Canadian and American agri-food markets. Under Article 708 of the FTA, Canada and the United States agreed to establish eight working groups 'to harmonize their respective technical regulatory requirements and inspection procedures'. These working groups were carried forward under NAFTA. In terms of promoting regulatory harmonization, these working groups have had mixed results, with some much more active than others. The Pesticides NAFTA Technical Working Group has been one of the more successful examples of a collaborative intergovernmental approach among regulators from the three trading partners.[80] A similar intergovernmental exchange of information and cooperation characterizes biotechnology issues.

A final mechanism for intergovernmental cooperation and resolution of trade issues is the Canada–US Consultative Committee on Agriculture (CCA), established pursuant to the 1998 Canada–US Memorandum of Understanding on Agriculture.[81] Technical issues around grain, livestock, and red meats sectors are normally the focus of the CCA's biannual meetings. The United States–Canada Action Plan for Agriculture Trade targeted several matters for convergence, including importation of pork, exchange of cattle data, control of in-transit movement of grain by rail, wheat access and phytosanitary requirements for wheat imports, veterinary drugs, labeling and biotechnology.

V CONCLUSIONS

The governance of food safety in North American agri-food systems and industries is emerging through tripartite regulatory policy cooperation, and industry standards convergence in accordance with NAFTA obligations in the WTO SPS Agreement and Codex Alimentarius. In many ways NAFTA is a unique regional framework that promotes regional policy cooperation and market integration between two G8 nations and an emerging Latin American country. Through this regional agri-food market system, the challenges and requirements for more formal institutional cooperation is apparent. In this respect, Mexico is working to meet the WTO SPS and Codex food safety standards in compliance with the agri-food trade obligations of the NAFTA Treaty.

In this regard, the acknowledgement of regulatory and food inspection certification differences between Canada and the United States relative to Mexico, highlights the need for more extensive food safety capacity-building in North America and the Western Hemisphere in the run-up to the FTAA. At the same time the appearance of BSE in Canada and the United States underscores the market competition and public health risks that are collectively shared in the North American food system. Ultimately, more solidarity and collective policy action by North American governments, regulators, farmers and consumer organizations are needed to balance the extensive and expanding interests of US agri-business, processors and retailers in regional agri-food industries.

From a business and public policy perspective, North American agri-food market interests are currently unchecked by competing Canadian and Mexican food industry interests. As a result, more mobilization is needed at the regional level to balance and regulate the market power and potential threat to food safety that is arising from agri-food industry concentration and agri-food firm consolidation. In this respect, food safety regulation and industry standards harmonization in North America must become more transparent and open to agri-food industry stakeholder participation across Canada, the United States and Mexico. In addition, more financial and technical resources are needed to accelerate regulatory harmonization, Codex standards enforcement and food safety capacity-building in Mexico and the Western Hemisphere.

In North America, there is growing concern about the ability of Mexican consumers and regulators to withstand US and Canadian agri-food lobbying and industry mobilization. Likewise, there is inequality relative to the articulation, power and response of Mexican consumers and citizens in the governance of food safety in North America. In many cases, food safety threats can arise from a less regulated agri-food industry environment with cheaper labor costs and price structures, and relatively weak regulatory laws and institutions. Consequently, increasing technical assistance and financial resources are needed to strengthen food safety capacity, consumer protection, regulatory harmonization and inspection standards enforcement in Mexico.

The public policy aspects of North American food safety regulation and agri-food industry governance require more pragmatic, proactive and precautionary mechanisms for the harmonization of biotechnology and GM food, food labeling, traceability, HACCP, animal livestock health, plant health and food inspection regulations. Furthermore, a North American rapid alert food safety information system for risk identification, risk communication and risk management is needed. In order to facilitate the development of a formal North American food safety system, regulatory and industry standards organizations in Canada, the United States and Mexico should provide a fund for the training and development of HACCP food safety inspections systems for Mexican farmers, agri-food companies and industries. In turn, support for increased participation of Mexican regulators in Codex and international food safety meetings and the work of the Mexican Codex Committee and PAHO/WHO should be provided.

Finally, the United States has the most extensive regulatory cooperation and industry standards frameworks in the transatlantic region. In light of the extensive agri-food market integration and food system convergence that is occurring in North America between Canada, Mexico and the United States, a more aggressive program for food safety in the NAFTA and Western Hemisphere regions must become a comparable priority. Through the creation of North American and Western Hemisphere frameworks for regulatory harmonization and industry standards enforcement in keeping with the WTO SPS and TBT Agreement and Codex Alimentarius, emerging and developing countries in the region can rapidly be brought up to the level of global food safety standards.

NOTES

* Acknowledgments: The chapter authors express their thanks to Dr Albino J. Belotto, Chief Veterinary Public Health Unit, Pan American Health Organization/World Health Organization, and Dr Raul Vargas, Professor of Veterinary Medicine and Public Health, National Autonomous University of Mexico – Consultant for the Pan American Health Organization/World Health Organization, for their support and assistance in the preparation of this chapter.

1. Zahniser, Steven and John Link (2002), 'Effects of North American Free Trade Agreement on agriculture and the rural economy', *Agriculture and Trade Report*, United States Department of Agriculture, Washington, DC: USDA.
2. Ibid., p. 1.
3. Christine Bolling, Steve Neff, and Charles Handy (1998), *US Foreign Direct Investment in the Western Hemisphere Processed Food Industry*, Market and Trade Economics Division/Food and Rural Economics Division, ERS-USDA, AER Report No. 760, Washington, DC: USDA, pp. vii.
4. Ibid., pp. 28–9.
5. Ibid., pp. 18–19.
6. Ibid.
7. Ibid., pp. 22–5.
8. See FDA/USDA (2000), *United States Food Safety System*, US Food and Drug Administration, US Department of Agriculture, Rockville, MD and Washington, DC: FDA and USDA, p. 1.
9. In the US effective corporate and industry self regulation and ethical responsibility, combined with a strong rule of law and court system, and a free media serve to make the national food safety system one of the best in the world. In many instances, management and industry do not want legal liability or bad press over food safety problems. FDA/USDA (2000), 'Country Report Annex II: Precaution in the US Food Safety System', p. 40.
10. Institute of Medicine and National Research Council (1998), *Ensuring Safe Food: From Production to Consumption*, Washington, DC: National Academy Press, p. 26.
11. The FDA started as a Division of Chemistry in the US Department of Agriculture in 1862, and then became the Bureau of Chemistry in 1906. In 1906, the Federal Food and Drugs Act was passed by Congress and signed by President Theodore Roosevelt on 30 June 1906, and created the present day US FDA. See FDA website on history of the agency www.fda.gov/oc/historyoffda. Also see Kurian, George (ed.) (1998), *A Historical Guide to the US Government*, New York and London: Oxford University Press.
12. Ibid., p. 28.
13. Ibid, p. 27.
14. FDA/USDA (2000), p. 2.
15. Institute of Medicine and National Research Council (1998), p. 29.
16. FDA/USDA (2000), 'Country Report', p. 4. In 1938, the Food, Drug and Cosmetics Act was passed an required safe standards for unavoidable poisons in food, authorized standards for the indentification, quality assurance and fill of food containers, and authorization of food inspections.
17. Ibid., p. 4.
18. Ibid., pp. 16–17.
19. BBC News website, 28 December 2003, 'US government expands recall of beef after discovery of BSE infected cow', at http://news.bbc.co.uk/2/hi/europe/3346285.stm.

20. BBC News website, 24 December 2003, 'Russian Federation suspends beef exports' and BBC News website, 26 December 2003, 'More nations ban US beef imports', both at http://news.bbc.co.uk/2/hi/americas/33522911.stm.
21. Ibid. Also see USDA (2004), 'USDA Issues New Regulations to Address BSE', 8 January, http://www.fsis.usd.gov/oa/news/2004/bseregs.htm.
22. See USDA website, 'Food safety inspection service news release' 'USDA Issues New Regulations to Address BSE', *Federal Register*, Vol. 69, No. 7, pp. 1862–74; *Federal Register* (2004b), Docket no. 03-048N, 'Bovine Spongiform Encephalopathy Surveillance Program', Vol. 69, No. 7, p. 1892.
23. *Federal Register* (2004d), Docket No. 3-031F, 'Meat Produced by Advanced Meat Recovery (AMR) System', 12 January, Vol. 69, No. 7, pp. 1874–85. AMR is a food processing technology that removes muscle tissue from the bone of the beef carcasses under pressure without inclusion of the bone material.
24. *Federal Register* (2004c), Docket No. 7, 03-048N, 'Food Safety Inspection Service', 9CFR, parts 301, 318 and 320, 12 January, p. 1892.
25. *Federal Register* (2004a), 12 January, 'FSIS – Bovine Encephalopathy Surveillance Notice', 12 January, Vol. 69, No. 7.
26. *Federal Register* (2004f), Docket No. 03-0251F, 'Prohibition of the Use of Specified Risk Materials for Human Food and Requirements for the Disposition of Non-Ambulatory Disabled Cattle', 12 January 2004, Vol. 69, No. 7, p. 1862; Vol. 69, No. 7, 12 January 2004, 9 CFR, parts 309, 310, 311, 318 and 319.
27. *Federal Register* (2004e), Docket No. 01-0331F, – 'Prohibition of the Use of Certain Stunning Devices Used to Immobilize Cattle During Stunning', Vol. 69, No. 7, 12 January 2004, pp. 1885–91.
28. BBC News website, 27 January 2004, 'US acts against "Mad Cow" disease', at http://news. bbc.co.uk.
29. USDA news release, 'Veneman announces expanded BSE surveillance program', Washington, 15 March 2004, Release Number 0105.04.
30. In response to the outbreak of avian flu in Delaware and Maryland, several Asian countries such as Japan, South Korea, Malaysia, Singapore and Hong Kong, which are large importers of chicken and poultry products, introduced import bans.
31. Dreyfuss, Ira, 'Testing for bird flu to be expanded', *Washington Post*, 12 March 2004.
32. Ibid., p. 6.
33. 'FDA policy for foods developed by biotechnology' (1995), US Food and Drug Administration, Center for Food Safety and Applied Nutrition, CFSAN Handout, p. 2.
34. FDA (2002), *Animal Cloning and the Production of Food Production: Perspectives from the food Chain*, proceedings from a workshop sponsored by the Pew Initiative on Food and Biotechnology and the Center for Veterinary Medicine of the US Food and Drug Administration, 26 September, Rockville, MD and Washington, DC: FDA and PEW Initiative on Food and Biotechnology.
35. Randy Fabi (2003), 'FDA cannot ensure safety of biotech foods – US group', 7 January, Reuters online at http://foodhaccp.com/msgboard:my?parm_func=showmsg+parm.msgnum=1006593.
36. GAO (2002), *Genetically Modified Foods: Experts View Regimen of Safety Tests as Adequate, but FDA's Evaluation Process Could Be Enhanced*, GAO-02-566, Washington, DC: GAO.
37. 'FDA Policy for Foods Derived by Biotechnology' (1995), p. 2.
38. BBC Online News (2000), 'GM tacos recalled', BBC Tom Carver, 25 September, http://news.bbc.co.uk/1/hi/world/americas/940687.stm.
39. In 1907, the Certification of Color Act established regulations for the use of seven color additives in food. In 1954, the Food Additives Amendment was passed which prohibits approval of food additives that cause cancer in humans or animals. In 1960, the Color Additives Amendment was passed to require that manufacturers establish the safety of color additives in food, drugs, and cosmetics. In 1966, the Fair Packing and Labeling Act was passed, and was followed by the Nutrition Labeling and Education Act in 1990.

40. The regulation of food labeling is historically one of the most important elements of food safety regulation in the United States. See the FDA Food Labeling Website, http://www.cfsan.fda.gov/label/html. For information relative to the labeling of GM food, see the FDA guidance for industry at http://www.cfsan.fda.gov/~dms/biolabgu.html.
41. FDA/USDA (2000), p. 40.
42. FDA (1980), 'Country of Origin Labeling', FDA, Office of Regulatory Affairs, Sec. 560.200, (cpg 7119.02), issued 10/1/80. Revised 6/30/89.
43. Food and Drug Administration Modernization Act of 1997, Public Law 105–15, 21 November 1997.
44. FDA (1998), *Status Report on International Harmonization of Regulatory Requirements and Standards, Office of Policy*, Rockville, MD: FDA, p. 2.
45. See *Federal Register* notice, 'International Harmonization Policy on Standards', 60 Fed. Reg. 53,078 (Oct. 11, 1995), and Horton, Linda R. and Kathleen E. Hasting s (1998)', A plan that establishes a framework for achieving mutual recognition of good manufacturing practices inspections', *Food and Drug Law Journal*, **53** (3): 527–35.
46. Ibid., pp. 9–10.
47. Agriculture and Agri-Food Sector Canada (2003a), *An Architecture for Agricultural Policy in the 21st Century*, Ottawa: Government of Canada (and section on *Food Safety and Food Quality*), at http://www.agr.gc.ca/cb/apf/fs_e.html.
48. Agriculture and Agri-Food Sector Canada (2003b), *Overview of the Canadian Agriculture and Agri-Food Sector*, Ottawa: Government of Canada, at http://www.agr.gc.ca/cb/apf/bgd_overview_e.html.
49. Ibid.
50. In 2001, the Office of the Auditor-General warned that the Canadian food inspection system and the CFIA were understaffed, and that the CFIA had no strategy for putting resources into the areas of highest risk or for ensuring a national food-safety strategy. It drew attention to the fact that almost half food-processing plants are under provincial or municipal control and therefore not subject to stringent federal regulations.
51. See Agriculture and Agri-Food Sector Canada (2003b).
52. Government of Quebec (1993), *Matter of Puerto Rico Regulations on the Import, Distribution and Sale of UHT Milk from Quebec* , Final Report of the Panel, 3 June 1993 Quebec City: Government of Quebec. The US claimed that the Canadian regime was not equivalent to the US system since it lacked the federal oversight and verification elements in the US system. For their part, Canadians observed that many US states allow the sale of unpasteurized milk directly to the consumer, and that the notion of one US national system is thus suspect. The dispute was resolved when the plant in Quebec that was shipping UHT milk to the US was deemed to be in compliance with the US standards.
53. Royal Society of Canada (2001), *Elements of Precaution: Recommendations for the Regulation of Food Biotechnology in Canada*, Ottawa: Royal Society of Canada.
54. Royal Society of Canada (2001), p. ix.
55. Canadian Biotechnology Advisory Committee (2002), 'Improving the Regulation of Genetically Modified Foods and Other Novel Foods in Canada', Ottawa, http://www.cbac-ccab.ca/documents/en/cbac.report.pdf.
56. The Government's Progress Report (2002), 'Action Plan of the Government of Canada in Response to the Royal Society of Canada Expert Panel Report', 31 May, Ottawa: Government of Canada, http://www.hc-sc.gc.ca/english/pdf/royalsociety/progress_report_may.pdf.
57. An ABC News poll in mid-July 2003 reported that 92 per cent of Americans favor mandatory labeling of GM foods. A study by the National Science Board in 2002 put the figure at 85 per cent. See National Science Board, *Science and Engineering Indicators 2002*, Arlington MA: National Science Foundation, in addition, a poll commissioned by the government of Canada. See Pew Initiative for Food and Biotechnology (2005), 'Canadians suspicious of biotech foods despite lack of harm evidence', 26 January, http://pewagbiotech.org/newsroom/summaries/display.php3?NewsID=821.

58. A poll commissioned by the government and released in June 2002 indicated that more than three-quarters of Canadians polled want labels on genetically modified foods. See Sarah Staples, 'Public wants GM food labeled: poll finds majority willing to pay more to clearly identify modified products', *The Ottawa Citizen*, 12 June, p. A1.
59. Royal Society of Canada (2002), the Government's Progress Report (31 May 2002), entitled *Action Plan of the Government of Canada in Response to the Royal Society of Canada Expert Panel Report*, Ottawa: Government of Canada is available at http://www.hcsc.gc.ca/english/pdf/royalsociety/progress_report_may.pdf.
60. Joint FAO/WHO Food Standards Programme (2002), *Global Forum of Food Safety Regulation* , Joint FAO/WHO Meeting, Marrakesh, Rome: FAO, p. 196. As published in the *Diario Oicial de la Federacion*, Mexico City: Government of Mexico, 7 February 1984.
61. Joint FAO/WHO Food Standards Programme (2002), p. 197.
62. Ibid., p. 197.
63. Ibid., p. 198.
64. Ibid., p. 198
65. NAFTA SPS Committee (1996), 'Joint Minutes of the Fifth Meeting of the NAFTA SPS Committee on Sanitary and Phytosanitary Standards', 20 June, p. 1, Ottawa, http://www.far.usda.gov/itp/ofsts/nafatamtg.jun96.htm.
66. FDA (2001b), *Memorandum of Cooperation in the Scientific and Regulatory Fields of Health. International Cooperative Agreements Manual, Canada and Mexico*, IFDA Agreement number 225-96-4001, Rockville, MD: FDA, pp. 59–62.
67. Ibid., pp. 59–60.
68. NAFTA SPS Committee (1996), 'Joint Minutes of the Fifth Meeting of the NAFTA SPS Committee on Sanitary and Phytosanitary Standards', 20 June, p. 1, Ottawa, http://www.fas.usda.gov/itp/ofsts/nafatamtg.jun96.htm.
69. FDA/USDA (1988), *Mexico Food Safety, Cooperative Arrangement Among the Department of Health and Human Services and the Department of Agriculture of the United States of America and the Secretariat of Health of Mexico and the Secretariat of Agriculture, Livestock, Rural Development, Fish and Food of the United Mexican States*, Rockville, MD and Washington, DC: FDA and USDA, pp. 1–6.
70. USDA (1998), *Record of Understanding Between the Governments of the United States of America and Canada Regarding Areas of Agricultural Trade*, Washington, DC: USDA, pp. 1–14.
71. Gourlie, Katherine E. (1996), 'NAFTA countries: convergence and fracture', *Food and Drug Law Journal*, **51** (3): pp. 423–35.
72. Drache, Daniel (1996),'The limits of trade blocs, in international regulatory competition and cooperation', in Richard Stubbs and Geoffrey R.D. Underhill (eds), *Political Economy and the Changing Global Order*, New York: St Martin Press, pp. 420–31.
73. Ibid., p. 421.
74. Alpay, Ebru, Steven Buccola and Joe Kerkvliet (2002), 'Productivity growth and environmental regulation in Mexican and US food manufacturing', *American Journal of Agricultural Economics*, **84** (4): 887–901.
75. Mexican grower dissatisfaction over national agriculture accord', *Food Chemical News*, 7 July 2003, Vol. 45, No. 21.
76. 'Mexico's NAFTA consensus refuses to die', *Food Chemical News*, 28 July 2003, Vol. 45, No. 24. Also see 'Mexico seeks alternative to NAFTA renegotiation', *Food Chemical News*, 7 April 2003, Vol. 45, No. 8, and 'National agriculture agreement completed', *Food Chemical New*, 28 April 2003, Vol. 45, No. 11.
77. Burfischer, Mary E., Sherman Robinson and Karen Thierfelder (2002), 'Developing country gains from regionalism: links between trade and farm policy reforms in Mexico', *American Journal of Agriculture*, **84** (3): 736–48.
78. According to Jorge Felix Rodriquez, Head of the Regional Cattlemen's Union of Sinola, Mexico, unfair competition hurt Mexican beef producers through the depression of beef price imports, and the need for increased prices by Mexican producers. See 'Mexican

producers capitalize on Canadian beef restriction', *Food Chemical News*, 5 June 2003, Vol. 5, No. 107.

79. Canada was not happy with the discretion that the WTO Appellate Body afforded countries in terms of the scientific evidence they provided in support of their SPS measures. The WTO observed that food safety measures need not be based on mainstream scientific opinion but could reflect a minority view in the relevant scientific community.
80. At www.hc-sc.gc.ca/pmra-arla.
81. Reports of the CCA can be found on the USDA website at www.fas.usda./gv/itp/us-canada.html, and the website of Agriculture and Agri-Food Canada.

REFERENCES

Agriculture and Agri-Food Canada (2001), *Medium Term Policy Baseline: International and Domestic Markets*, September, Ottawa: Government of Canada.

Agriculture and Agri-Food Canada (2003a), *An Architecture for Agricultural Policy in the Twenty-first Century*, Ottawa: Government of Canada, at http://www.agr.gc.ca/cb/apf/fs_e.html.

Agriculture and Agri-Food Canada (2003b), *Overview of the Canadian Agriculture and Agri-Food Sector*, Ottawa: Government of Canada, at http://www.agr.gc.ca/cb/apf/bgd_overview_e.html.

Alpay, Ebru, Steven Buccola and Joe Kerkvliet (2002), 'Productivity growth and environmental regulation in Mexican and US food manufacturing', *American Journal of Agricultural Economics*, **84** (4): 887–901.

BBC News website (2000), 'GM tacos recalled', 25 September, http://www.news.bbc.co.uk/1/hi/world/americas/940687.stm.

BBC News website (2003a), 'Russian Federation suspends beef exports', 24 December, at http://news.bbc.co.uk.

BBC News website (2003b), 'More nations ban US beef imports', 26 December, at http://news.bbc.co.uk.

BBC News website (2003c), 'US government expands recall of beef after discovery of BSE infected cow', 28 December, at http://news.bbc.co.uk.

BBC News website (2004), 'US acts against "Mad Cow" disease', 27 January, at http://news.bbc.co.uk.

Bolling, Christine, Steve Neff and Charles Handy (1998), *US Foreign Direct Investment in the Western Hemisphere Processed Food Industry*, Market and Trade Economics Division/Food and Rural Economics Division, ERS-USDA, Washington, DC: UDSA.

Burfischer, Mary E., Sherman Robinson and Karen Thierfelder (2002), 'Developing country gains from regionalism: links between trade and farm policy reforms in Mexico', *American Journal of Agricultural Economics*, **84** (3): 736–48.

Canadian Biotechnology Advisory Committee (2002), 'Improving the Regulation of Genetically Modified Foods and Other Novel Foods in Canada', Ottawa, http://www.clboac-ccab.ca/documents/en/dcboac.report.pdf.

Diario Oicial de la Federacion (1984), 7 February, Mexico City: Government of Mexico.

Drache, Daniel (1996), 'The limits of trade blocs, in international regulatory competition and cooperation', in Richard Stubbs and Geoffrey R.D. Underhill (eds), *Political Economy and the Changing Global Order*, New York: St Martin Press.

Fabi, Randy (2003), 'FDA cannot ensure safety of biotech foods – US group', 7 January, Reuters online, at http://foodhaccp.com/msgboard.my?parm_func=showmsg+parm.msgnum=1006593.

FDA (1980), 'Country of Origin Labeling', FDA, Office of Regulatory Affairs, Sec. 560.200, (cpg 7119.02), issued 10/1/80. Revised 6/30/89.

FDA (1998), *A Status Report on International Harmonization of Regulatory Requirements and Standards, Office of Policy*, Rockville, MD: FDA.

FDA (2001a), 'FDA guidance for industry', at http://www.cfsan.fda.gov/~dms/biolabgu.html.

FDA (2001b), *Memorandum of Cooperation in the Scientific and Regulatory Fields of Health. International Cooperative Agreements Manual, Canada and Mexico*, IFDA Agreement number 225-96-4001, Rockville, MD: FDA.

FDA (2002), *Animal Cloning and the Production of Food Production: Perspectives from the Food Chain*, proceeding from a workshop sponsored by the Pew Initiative on Food and Biotechnology and the Center for Veterinary Medicine of the US Food and Drug Administration, 26 September, Rockville, MD, and Washington, DC: FDA and Pew Initiative on Food and Biotechnology.

FDA/USDA (1998), *Mexico Food Safety, Cooperative Arrangement Among the Department of Health and Human Services and the Department of Agriculture of the United States of America and the Secretariat of Health of Mexico and the Secretariat of Agriculture, Livestock, Rural Development, Fish and Food of the United Mexican States*, Washington, DC: FDA and USDA.

FDA/USDA (2000), *United States Food Safety System*, US Food and Drug Administration, US Department of Agriculture, Washington, DC: FDA and USDA.

Federal Register (2004a), 'FSIS – Bovine Encephalopathy Surveillance Notice', 12 January, Vol. bg, No. 7.

Federal Register (2004b), Docket No. 03-048N, 'Bovine Spongiform Encephalopathy Surveillance Program', Vol. 69, No. 7, p. 1892.

Federal Register (2004c), Docket No. 7, 03-048N, 'Food Safety Inspection Service', 9CFR parts 301, 318 and 320, p. 1892.

Federal Register (2004d), Docket No. 3-031F, 'Meat Produced by Advanced Meat Recovery (AMR) System', 12 January, Vol. 69, No. 7.

Federal Register (2004e), Docket No. 01-0331F, 'Prohibition of the Use of Certain Stunning Devices Used to Immobilize Cattle During Stunning', 12 January, Vol. 69, No. 7, 9 CFR.

Federal Register (2004f), Docket No. 3-0251F, 'Prohibition of the Use of Specified Risk Materials for Human Food and Requirements for the Disposition of Non-Ambulatory Disabled Cattle', 12 January, Vol. 69, No. 7, 9 CFR.

Federal Register notice (1995), 'International Harmonization Policy on Standards', 60 Fed. Reg. 53,078 (11 October 1995).

Food Chemical News (2003a), 'Mexico seeks alternative to NAFTA renegotiation', 7 April, Vol. 45, No. 8.

Food Chemical News (2003b), 'National agriculture agreement completed', 28 April, Vol. 45, No. 11.

Food Chemical News (2003c), 'Mexican modules capitalize on Canadian beef restrictions', 5 June, Vol. 5, No. 107.

Food Chemical News (2003d), 'Mexican grower dissatisfaction over national agriculture accord', 7 July, Vol. 45, No. 21.

Food Chemical News (2003e), 'Mexico's NAFTA consensus refuses to die', 28 July, Vol. 45, No. 24.

GAO (2002), *Genetically Modified Foods: Experts View Regimen of Safety Tests as Adequate, but FDA's Evaluation Process Could Be Enhanced*, GAO-02-566, Washington, DC: GAO.

Gourlie, Katherine E. (1996), 'NAFTA countries: convergence and fracture', *Food and Drug Law Journal*, **51** (3): 423–35.

Government of Quebec (1993) *Matter of Puerto Rico Regulations on the Import, Distribution and Sale of UHT Milk from Quebec*, Final Report of the Panel, 3 June 1993, Quebec City: Government of Quebec.

Health Canada (1994), *Guidelines for the Safety Assessment of Novel Foods*, Vol. 1, Preamble and Guidance Scheme for Notification, Ottawa: Health Canada.

Horton, Linda R. and Kathleen Hastings (1998), 'A plan that establishes a framework for achieving mutual recognition of good manufacturing practices inspections', *Food and Drug Law Journal*, **53** (3): 527–35.

Institute of Medicine and National Research Council (1998), *Ensuring Safe Food: From Production to Consumption*, Washington, DC: National Academy Press.

Joint FAO/WHO Food Standards Programme (2002), *Global Forum of Food Safety Regulation*, Joint FAO/WHO Meeting, Marrakesh, Rome: FAO.

Joint FAO/WHO Food Standards Programme (2004), *Codex Alimentarius Commission – Foods Derived from Modern Biotechnology*, Rome: FAO/WHO.

Kurian, George (ed.) (1998), *A Historical Guide to the US Government*, New York and London: Oxford University Press.

NAFTA SPS Committee (1996), 'Joint Minutes of the Fifth Meeting of the NAFTA SPS Committee', 20 June, Ottawa, http://www.fas.usda.gov/itp/ofsts/nafatamtg.jun96.htm.

National Science Board (2002), *Science and Engineering Indicators 2002*, Arlington, MA: National Science Foundation.

Pew Initiative for Food and Biotechnology (2005), 'Canadians suspicious of biotech foods despite lack of harm evidence', 26 January, http://pewagbiotech.org/newsroom/summaries/display.php3?NewsID=821.

Royal Society of Canada (2001), *Elements of Precaution: Recommendations for the Regulation of Food Biotechnology in Canada*, Ottawa: Royal Society of Canada.

Royal Society of Canada (2002), *Action Plan of the Government of Canada in Response to the Royal Society of Canada Expert Panel Report*, The Government's Progress Report (31 May 2002), available at www.hc-sc.gc.ca/english/pdf/royalsociety/progress_report_may.pdf.

Staples, Sarah (2002), 'Public wants GM food labelled: poll finds majority willing to pay more to clearly identify modified products', *The Ottawa Citizen*, June, p. A1.

USDA (1998), *Record of Understanding Between the Governments of the United States of America and Canada Regarding Areas of Agricultural Trade*, Washington, DC: USDA.

USDA (2002), 'The Effects of NAFTA on Agriculture and the Rural Economy', WRS-0201, http://www.ers.usda.gov/publications/wrs0201a.pdf.

USDA (2004), 'USDA Issues New Regulations to Address BSE', 8 January, http://www.fsis.usd.gov/oa/news/2004/bseregs.htm.

USDA news release (2004), 'Veneman announces expanded BSE surveillance program', Washington, 15 March, Release Number 0105.04.

Zahniser, Steven and John Link (2002), 'Effects of North American Free Trade Agreement on agriculture and the rural economy', *Agriculture and Trade Report*, United States Department of Agriculture, Washington, DC: USDA.

6. Globalization and the emerging rule of law on regulatory standards: transatlantic corporate compliance and governance of food safety

Linda R. Horton*

I INTRODUCTION

With globalization, people around the world are exposed more and more to the gastronomic traditions of diverse cultures and nations. Today, food is traded on a scale inconceivable only a few years ago. In this regard, the nature of food trade is also changing. In the past, bulk commodities such as coffee, cocoa, grains, and sugar dominated world food trade. In the twenty-first century, however, food trade is increasingly made up of raw or minimally processed fruits, vegetables, seafood and meat, as well as canned, packaged and frozen goods. Therefore, food safety regulation is essential because pathogens or other contaminants may lurk in food, undetectable even by discerning consumers.

As people and goods move across national borders, food producers and regulatory agencies can no longer afford to think of their challenges, or opportunities, solely in national terms. Increasingly, industries are global and companies sell products around the world. This presents difficulties because, as of today, food regulatory requirements are only partially harmonized. As a result, global marketing requires food companies to cope with a labyrinth of multiple regulatory systems.

II THE NEW PRIORITY OF FOOD SAFETY

In recent years, food safety issues became front-page news in many countries. The revelation in 1996 that ten young British citizens had died due to the transmission to humans of 'Mad Cow' disease (Bovine Spongiform Encephalopathy or BSE) was a watershed event in European food regulation. The discovery of BSE in cattle in other countries, including Japan in 2001, as well as Canada and the United States in 2003, showed that no part of the world could consider itself exempt from this scourge.

Among the many daunting food safety issues presented to the food industry and food regulators in the twenty-first century are microbial pathogens, parasites and deadly prions. The pathogens and prions might be present in meat from certain countries. Likewise, traces of unlabeled allergens, such as nuts, that can kill sensitive individuals. Finally, chemical contaminants such as heavy metals, illegal residues of pesticides, food or color additives, animal drugs, and environmental contaminants such as polychlorinated biphenols and dioxins, can pose serious threats to consumer safety and the public health.

Challenges of Regulatory Harmonization: Prospects for Improvement

The international harmonization of food regulation is difficult to achieve. People from different countries do not easily agree on the 'right way' to produce, prepare, or even regulate food and its components. However, people care deeply about food issues, not only because food can contain concealed hazards, but also because it is so much more than just nourishment. Rather, food has social, cultural and even religious importance. Consequently, people around the world hold very strong opinions about the food they eat.

Nevertheless, governments and industry around the world need to embrace both regulatory harmonization and food safety as international goals. However, unjustified regulations that do nothing to improve food safety or consumer protection should be eliminated. In this context, two multilateral institutions are working to achieve these goals. The United Nations Food Standards Programme within the context of the Codex Alimentarius Commission is making progress toward global food safety, public health and consensus on consumer protection norms. The World Trade organization (WTO) provides the means to increase global food trade and challenges unjustified regulations. These institutions are important because there is no global food safety regulator.

The Challenge of Global Food Trade for Food Safety Regulators

Many countries find food safety regulation difficult. This is particularly true for imported food, due to the impracticality of conducting, in other countries, the inspections that regulators routinely conduct of domestic food establishments. Good practices in the production and processing of food are essential to producing food that is safe and free from unwanted contaminants. Good practices include Good Agricultural Practices (GAPs), Good

Manufacturing Practices (GMPs), and the Hazard Analysis Critical Control Points food safety system (HACCP). These practices recognize that safety must be 'built into the product' through the process by which food is grown or prepared. Although finished product testing has a place in food safety assurance programs carried out by processors, governments or private laboratories as part of border checks, testing alone is no substitute for good practices. A major impediment to the effectiveness of border checks is the lack of rapid and practical methods for testing food samples for pathogens and other contaminants. Another problem is the inadequacy of sampling methods, and the risk of missing pathogens or other contaminants. This is particularly true if the adulterant is not distributed uniformly in a shipment. Therefore, there is no substitute for good practices in food production. Moreover, safe food production ranges 'from farm to table', or, more poetically, 'from farm to fork', 'from plough to plate', or for seafood 'from boat to throat' in scope.

Like domestic foods, imports must meet national requirements for food labeling, vitamin or mineral fortification, standards for food identity, defect action levels for filth, and other important regulations. Some of these aspects of food regulation can be adequately checked through physical examination or sample testing at the border, while others, such as deviation from a food standard, would rarely have health implications. For example, the lack of required nutrition labeling can be corrected through supervised relabeling of the product. Still, food regulatory agencies lack sufficient resources to perform border checks and oversight of corrections while maintaining adequate surveillance to block imports that present food safety issues.

Globalization as a Positive Force for Food Safety

It is now common for consumer organizations in the United States, Europe, Japan and other developed countries to attack globalization, trade, and even regulatory standards harmonization activities. Very often, the concern is that food products produced elsewhere are not as safe as those produced in one's own country. Moreover, it is feared that global trade and the competitive pressures it engenders, will cause a regulatory policy 'race to the bottom' that might drive down food safety standards. Even harmonization is viewed with suspicion because it is thought to consist of 'harmonization downward' towards the least common denominator, rather than 'harmonization upward' towards safer food. At the same time, today's robust food trade benefits consumers. Through global food trade, consumers are able to have a rich variety of products all year round, and at cheaper prices than if they rely on local producers shielded from international competition.

In contrast to the views of some consumer organizations, the food industry believes that, with the right forces in play, globalization can actually promote food safety. These forces are science-based regulation oriented to public health protection; producer responsibility; rule of law; transparency and stakeholder involvement; and international cooperation and harmonization. Very often global companies make foreign direct investments in developing countries, and actually export best practices in safe food production to their overseas production and manufacturing sites.

Currently, these food safety forces must operate principally at the national level, due to the lack of a world food and drug administration or global food regulator. Instead, there are literally hundreds of national and sub-national food regulatory systems. Increasingly, these national and sub-national food regulatory systems are linked together through a web of bilateral and multilateral trade agreements, as well as intergovernmental policy cooperation frameworks with international organizations. However, these agreements have virtually no direct role in the day-to-day control of food safety. As a consequence of this fact, global food safety rests principally upon the efforts of producers and governmental institutions in individual nations to assure food safety, and support global food standards compliance.

Interdependence and Attributes of National Food Safety Systems

With globalization, international cooperation – on a bilateral, regional and multilateral basis – is the key to both global food safety and ample supplies of safe food and water. If nations can ensure that their food producers and regulators can take more responsibility for the safety of foods they produce and export, trading partners in other countries can import food with some measure of confidence that it is safe and meets consumer protection requirements. Since good practices in food production are essential, and food testing at the border ineffectual, all countries have an interest in how food is grown or produced in another country. However, even the transatlantic and OECD countries cannot afford to carry out foreign inspections of food producers except on a very limited scale.

Consequently, foreign inspections of food producers is relatively rare, except in the case of meat and poultry, where a combination of circumstances have led to a tradition of foreign inspections by regulators in the United States, the European Union and other countries.[1] Even in this special case, there is a trend away from 'inspections' of individual foreign processors, and increasing use of 'audits' of foreign food production systems.

As a result of these trends, science-based regulation and food safety laws, oriented to public health protection, are very important. Moreover, food safety measures are required by trade agreements to be scientifically justified, either on the basis of Codex Alimentarius standards or public health risk assessments. In this context, it is important that food safety regulations are not issued unless there is a need. If the marketplace is adequately attending to an issue, a regulation on that issue is unnecessary. Ultimately, governmental action and regulatory interventions taken to address a legitimate food safety concern must be reasonable and proportionate given the facts of the case.

III CORPORATE RESPONSIBILITY IN GLOBAL AGRI-FOOD INDUSTRIES

Any aspiration to the ideal of food safety that does not include the concept of producer responsibility is doomed to failure. Fundamentally, producers must internalize, as a cost of production, the measures necessary to ensure food safety, including food quality control procedures such as HACCP, employee training, and physical production standards for clean water and adequate refrigeration. In this context, regulation, enforcement, and the rule of law, work hand in hand with legal concepts of producer liability to ensure that the forces of competition do not unfairly reward those who do not take responsibility for making the necessary investment in food safety.

One issue that must be addressed is the extent to which a product liability system, such as that of the United States, might contribute to regulatory food safety efforts. Although the US food safety system may help instill in producers a heightened sense of responsibility for their products, the downside is that damage awards are relatively infrequent, and do not necessarily correlate directly with seriousness of harm. Therefore, the American food industry supports efforts to make the US tort system fairer and more rational.

A stronger force in favor of high standards by global companies is brands: these firms have global brands to protect. For example, liberal return policies, and vigilance during food recalls and similar threats to brand names, helps to support consumer-oriented international norms and corporate consumer protection policies. In fact, the corporate drive to protect brands, corporate policies emphasizing food safety, and cooperation with governments and consumers, and where necessary, third-party private sector conformity assessment programs, can supplement under-funded or weak governmental food safety infrastructures. In many cases, stronger controls by exporting producers, overseen by regulators in exporting countries, along with checks by importers in destination countries, can also strengthen food safety. Therefore these measures can reduce consumer and public health risks from imported food.

Global Food Companies and Improvement of Local Safety Standards

Many countries lack legal systems that both encourage producers to take corporate responsibility for the safety of their food, and provide consequences for non-compliance through a rule of law. Therefore, direct foreign investment by quality-conscious companies can actually enhance producer responsibility across nations if local governments can match private sector improvements with upward harmonization, and compliance with multilateral food safety standards. For example, global companies can improve infrastructure in middle-income and developing countries by providing employee training and sanitary standards, clean facilities, refrigerated trucks and warehouses as well as political support for transportation improvements. Thus, the 'export' of corporate quality standards to production facilities in developing countries can showcase Best Practices in product quality, and help raise local consumers' expectations of product quality for imported or domestic foods.

Transparency and Stakeholder Involvement

The global agri-food industries need to be able to participate in the formulation of food safety requirements affecting their products by participating in rule-making. Of course, what every company would like best is for governments to issue only rules that can be met immediately, without costly changes in processing facilities, product composition or product labeling. This is rarely the ideal case because participation by other members of the public, including consumers, is also important. Therefore, regulatory bodies should publish a general notice inviting comments and suggestions even before a proposed food safety regulation is published. Likewise, public meetings help facilitate dialogue and understanding among regulators, industry and interested stakeholders. While the relationship between industry and its governmental regulators seems strained, in fact the two need each other. In reality regulation benefits industry by helping to protect honest sellers against dishonest competitors.

Food Markets and Regulation: Complementary Forces in Food Safety

A central question in food regulation is, 'Who sets food safety rules – Codex Alimentarius, the WTO, national regulatory agencies such as the US Food and Drug Administration (FDA), or the market?' The answer, not surprisingly, is 'all of the above'. The global marketplace is older than Codex, FDA and its counterparts, and goes back to the dawn of civilization. In the marketplace, consumer demands and industry standards rule. However, while market-driven standards are important, they are insufficient to protect consumers against invisible threats to food safety. As a result, regulations are needed so that competition among food producers occurs on a level playing field where producers take responsibility for the safety of their products, and ensures consequences for those who fail. The divergence of national food safety regulations raise food costs, often with no real benefits to consumers. Conversely, global food safety rules enhance food safety and reduce unnecessary costs due to inconsistent requirements.

IV WTO AND CODEX ALIMENTARIUS: MULTILATERAL ORGANIZATIONS AND THE GLOBAL HARMONIZATION OF FOOD SAFETY STANDARDS

Since 1962, two United Nations bodies, the Food and Agricultural Organization (FAO) and the World Health Organization (WHO), have administered the UN Food Standards Programme through the Codex Alimentarius Commission. The main work product is the multi-volume code of authoritative guidance known as the Codex Alimentarius, which serves as the principal source of international standards for foods. The stated purposes of Codex are twofold: to facilitate world food trade and to promote consumer protection.[2] Since its creation in the early 1960s, Codex, has contributed to the development of national food regulatory systems by enabling expert dialogue and providing a useful body of food norms for countries to use at the national level.

With the creation of the WTO in 1995, two trade agreements were put in place that are of special interest to food regulators, consumers, and industry: the Agreement on the Application of Sanitary and Phytosanitary Measures (SPS Agreement) and a revised version of a 1979 Agreement on Technical Barriers to Trade (TBT Agreement). The SPS Agreement marked the beginning of a new era for Codex. This agreement makes Codex standards the reference standards – the 'safe harbor' standards – for national food safety regulations.[3] Harmonization – the establishment, recognition and application of common measures by different countries[4] – is explictly encouraged by the SPS Agreement.

A WTO member country has a sovereign right to establish a more stringent food safety regulation than a Codex standard to meet its own level of protection.[5] However, if a nation becomes embroiled in a WTO challenge brought by another country whose products are being excluded by the regulation, it can be called upon to produce a risk assessment[6] justifying the use of a regulation more stringent than the Codex standard. If the country loses the case in the WTO, it must either change the controversial regulation or suffer the imposition of extra tariffs on its exports to the prevailing country (or countries) that won the case. If the defending country simply based its regulation upon the Codex food safety standard, it is difficult for another country to challenge the regulation. Consequently, it is a delicate task to ensure that countries can protect their own consumers without using regulatory policies as a protectionist device unfairly to strengthen the competitive advantage of their own producers.

The revised TBT Agreement encourages countries to use standards produced by international standards organizations as the basis for their national technical regulations. Unlike the SPS Agreement, the TBT Agreement does not refer to Codex Alimentarius by name. Nevertheless, the Codex Alimentarius Commission would surely qualify as a relevant international standards organization as that term is used in the TBT Agreement. Indeed, one WTO panel has so held, in a case in which Peru and other countries[7] successfully challenged a European Union (EU) regulation that was at odds with a Codex standard of identity for sardines.[8]

The TBT agreement encourages harmonization. The TBT agreement provides that, where a technical regulation is required, and a relevant international standard exists or its completion is imminent, WTO-member countries shall use the standard, or the relevant parts of it, as a basis for their technical regulations. An exception is provided for when the international standards are an ineffective or inappropriate means for the fulfillment of the legitimate objectives pursued (TBT Agreement, Art. 2.4).

The core obligation under both agreements is that WTO members' regulations achieve their legitimate objectives in a manner no more restrictive of trade than is 'required' (SPS Agreement, Article 5.6), or 'necessary' (TBT Agreement, Article 2.2). Here again, a mechanism by which countries can satisfy these criteria is reliance upon Codex standards in the formulation of national requirements. In both instances, the SPS and TBT agreements measures share five core principles: non-discrimination, harmonization, avoiding unnecessary trade barriers, equivalence or mutual recognition, and transparency. Sanitary and phytosanitary measures are subject to an additional requirement that regulations be scientifically justified, either on the basis of Codex standards or a risk assessment.

Although the TBT Agreement imposes no requirement that technical regulations be scientifically justified, it forbids regulations that are unjustified or more trade restrictive than necessary.[9] Under both agreements, countries have a right to place health considerations above trade. However, member countries may be called upon to explain and defend their food safety requirements. Furthermore, member countries are required to notify the WTO relative to new SPS measures, as well as new technical regulations subject to the TBT Agreement. The notification requirement also increases the transparency of requirements for food products or production methods, and facilitates comments on proposed requirements by other members.

In another far-reaching change by the WTO Agreements, a dispute resolution procedure[10] gave 'teeth' to a process that previously resulted in decisions easily evaded by a GATT member that lost a dispute. For example, with the new binding procedures introduced in 1995,[11] a WTO dispute panel can find that a member country has failed to justify its food safety measure under the requirements of the SPS Agreement. If a WTO appellate body upholds the panel decision, the member country must either change that measure or be subject to a form of compensation. This compensation could take the form of a lump sum or periodic cash payment, paid by the losing country to the prevailing country. Very often, the prevailing country may apply sleep tariffs to imports from the country that lost the WTO case, but that refuses to comply with the WTO order.

Several cases involving food regulation have been the subject of WTO disputes, and in each case the measure of the importing country was held to be in violation of the WTO SPS or TBT agreement: (1) United States v. the EU on hormones in beef cattle (sanitary/human health issue); (2) Canada v. Australia on restrictions on imports of salmon (sanitary/animal health issue); (3) United States v. Japan on varietal testing requirements for fruits (phytosanitary/plant health issue); and (4) Peru v. EU on sardine standard (technical regulation held inconsistent with the TBT Agreement because it was not based on Codex standard).

The most interesting example of WTO dispute resolution in the food safety area was the 1998 WTO appellate body's decision against the EU, in the case brought by Canada and the United States. The case was filed by the US and Canada following an EU ban on meat from cattle treated with hormones for growth promotion.[12] The appellate body ruled that the EU failed to produce a risk assessment justifying its refusal of the meat. When the EU refused to eliminate its ban, both Canada and the United States were allowed to put into effect steep tariffs on EU products.

The ruling against the EU was based in part upon the fact that the Codex Alimentarius Commission had established standards for five of the six hormones in question. The EU was unable to produce a risk assessment or justify its continued ban of these hormones in the face of these international standards of Codex, the relevant food safety standards body under the SPS Agreement. Therefore, the WTO permitted the United States and Canada to impose sanctions on EU exports. The sanctions consist of increased tariffs on a list of European goods exported to North America and total \$116.8 million for the United States and C\$11.3 million for Canada per year.

In late 2003, the long-running saga of the transatlantic beef war took on a new twist. In October 2003, the European Commission published new legislation that cited new updated scientific information supporting its refusal to allow imports of beef from cattle treated with hormones. The next day, the Commission called upon the United States and Canada to lift the trade sanctions authorized by the WTO as compensation for the EU's refusal to amend the ban. During this official communication, the Commission stated its belief that the EU now complies with the WTO recommendations and that the United States and Canada should withdraw the sanctions. Furthermore, the Commission argued that the EU had carried out a 'thorough and careful appraisal of the scientific evidence available' leading to the new directive, which EU member states have a year to implement. The Office of the United States Trade Representative (USTR) disagreed with the position of the European Commission.[13]

Controversy, Consensus and Adoption of Codex Food Safety Standards

The increasingly important status of Codex Alimentarius as the food safety reference organization for the WTO SPS Agreement has motivated the representatives of many member countries to seek greater convergence between their domestic regulatory laws and Codex standards. Many countries, especially developing countries, are willing to accept Codex standards in their national regulations or allow free distribution of products that meet Codex standards. However, the United States, the EU and others seem interested in first moving Codex closer to their own regulatory approaches.

For example, EU countries appear to be unmotivated to adopt Codex standards unless they match EU regulatory policy approaches that are reached through a difficult internal market harmonization process.[14] In a similar way, the United States wants Codex standards to mirror US approaches, a view supported by domestic consumer and industry groups.[15] If the EU and the United States have already adopted variant regulatory approaches before Codex takes up an issue, these two global powers can easily polarize Codex's discussion into two-sided policy debates.

One of the most important benefits of global harmonization is the fact that regulatory consistency with a Codex standard provides a safe harbor from WTO disputes. However, a national government that has already issued a regulation, or decided whether to approve it in substance, would consider it ideal for Codex to adopt a standard that matches its regulation, approval of a substance, or disapproval decision. Since members countries want Codex standards to describe how they produce food, an effect of Codex standards' status as reference norms under the WTO Aggrements is to raise the stakes in Codex participation.

In Codex meetings, it is not uncommon for member country delegates to arrive with instructions to seek Codex standards that match their domestic regulations, or food product characteristics. However, members countries can gain the benefit of Codex's status as a safe harbor, or even to secure advantages for its food producers. While Codex's procedures call for decisions to be made by consensus to the maximum extent possible, voting procedures are also provided in the rules. For example, at the 1993 Codex Alimentarius Commission meeting, the EU strongly opposed Codex standards for hormones used for growth promotion in beef cattle, and won a vote by a lop-sided margin.[16] At the next meeting in 1995 the EU lost the vote, by a close margin.

The result of this voting process was that the EU was vulnerable, a few months later, when the United States and Canada initiated the WTO case about the EU's refusal to allow the importation of meat from hormone-treated beef. During the formal complaint process, the United States and Canada were able to cite Codex standards for hormones. (As has been discussed, when the EU could not produce a risk assessment justifying its refusal, it ultimately lost the case before both the WTO panel and the WTO appellate body.)

Later, in 1997, the EU won a close vote (33–31) on a bitterly contentious issue on the proposed standard for bottled mineral water, which was also a WTO TBT Agreement issue.[17] The close Codex votes on the hormone and water standards meant that the losing side, in each case, did not accept the legitimacy of the outcome of the vote. Since these sessions of the Codex Alimentarius Commission, the organization has renewed efforts to resolve issues through consensus rather than through voting.

Adoption and National Acceptance of Codex Standards

After the Codex Alimentarius Commission decides to 'adopt' a standard that is at the final step of the Codex process, member countries must decide whether to 'accept' the standard.[18] One option available to any member country is the ability to accept 'free distribution' of food meeting Codex standards without the need to change its own requirements in order to be harmonized with Codex standards. After free distribution became a category of Codex acceptance, the number of acceptances of pesticide and veterinary drug residue Maximum Residue Levels (MRLs) rose significantly: 34 per cent of countries notified Codex as to full acceptance, 40 per cent notified Codex that it would allow free distribution of food that meets the standard, and 26 per cent notified Codex that the new standard was not accepted.[19]

As a result of the growing importance of Codex, US lawmakers included provisions in national legislation to ensure that the public is aware of Codex activities. The US government is now required to publish information on these activities each year in the *Federal Register*, as a result of a provision in the 1994 Uruguay Round Agreements Act, Section 491(a) of the Trade Agreements Act (19 U.S.C. §§ 1202–2582), Pub. L. 103–465. Through this legislation, the President of the United States must 'designate an agency to be responsible for informing the public of the sanitary and phytosanitary standard-setting activities of each international standard-setting organization.' The President has designated the United States Department of Agriculture (USDA) to be responsible for informing the public of both Codex activities, and certain other international sanitary and phytosanitary standard-setting activities discussed above (Proclamation No. 6780 of 23 March, 1995 (60 FR 15845, 27 March, 1995)). The annual *Federal Register* notice is published by 1 June each year, and these now serve as useful sources of information on US Codex activities. Through the publication of these annual *Federal Register* notices, the public is informed of Codex activities.

In spite of substantial investment in Codex, US food agencies often find it difficult to accept Codex standards. In response to this situation, the FDA initiated a process to increase acceptance of Codex standards that meet the United States' high level of domestic consumer protection in 1997. During this period, the FDA published a notice inviting public comments on steps the agency can and should take to accept Codex standards.[20]

One impediment to US acceptance of Codex standards is that Codex's priorities, and US agencies' priorities, often seem unsynchronized. For example, in 1992 US agencies succeeded in overhauling nutrition labeling rules. As of 2003, Codex was still at the earliest stage of considering how to update a 1985 Codex standard that had been based upon the 1972 version, now replaced, of the FDA's nutrition labeling rule. While US agencies needed to take steps to deal decisively with pathogens and parasites such as *E. coli 0157:H7* in meat,[21] *cyclospora* in raspberries or *salmonella enteriditis* in eggs and egg products, Codex's work on these topics has lagged.

With so many compelling public health priorities, national food safety regulators find it difficult to make a case for 'harmonization for harmonization's sake'. The US government[22] and consumer groups[23] strongly oppose 'harmonization downward'. When there is no adverse health consequence, government officials may be willing to consider raising a numerical limit for a pesticide or animal drug residue. For example, the FDA may bring its limit in line with a Codex maximum residue level (MRL). Consumers, however, tend to view such changes as realization of their worst fears about Codex and food standards harmonization. In this regard, consumers generally[24] favor 'harmonization upward'. For example, they would like US agencies to adopt Codex's labeling guidance on quantity of fill in canned food,[25] a proposal to list hazardous herbs, or its stricter pesticide limits in about half of the Codex MRLs.[26]

In some cases, US regulators find it difficult to simply adopt the Codex rule. For example, quantity-of-fill labeling may be a low priority. Furthermore, the FDA's authority to regulate herbal dietary supplements is limited. Although some Codex pesticide MRLs may look stricter than the corresponding EPA tolerances, the process that preceded the Codex numbers may not be as scientifically rigorous as the EPA's. In some cases, tolerances may be based on different underlying assumptions, and make streamlined regulation acceptance difficult.[27]

The Food and Drug Administration Modernization Act of 1997 (FDAMA)[28] directed the FDA to participate in harmonization activities to reduce the regulatory burden. The FDAMA also amended the FDA's mission statement to include a requirement that the FDA 'participate in appropriate processes with representatives of other countries to reduce the burden of regulation, harmonize regulatory requirements, and achieve appropriate reciprocal arrangements'.[29] The FDA shall also 'regularly participate in meetings with representatives of other foreign governments to discuss and reach agreement on methods and approaches to harmonize regulatory requirements'.[30]

In this context, the FDA is also mandated to

> support the Office of the United States Trade Representative, in consultation with the Department of Commerce, in meetings with representatives of other countries. The goals of the meetings are to discuss methods and approaches to reduce the burden of regulation, and to harmonize regulatory requirements if the FDA determines that such harmonization strengthens consumer protections consistent with the purposes of [the Federal Food, Drug, and Cosmetic Act].[31]

In order to facilitate harmonization, the FDA has progressively changed its regulations[32] on sharing documents with officials of foreign counterpart agencies and international organizations. Therefore the FDA can now share drafts of proposed regulations and other non-public documents with foreign regulators to promote cooperation and harmonization, even before those documents are made public.[33]

A significant impediment to the FDA finding another country's food safety measure to be equivalent is a set of requirements imposed under the 1994 US law that implemented the WTO agreements.[34] If the FDA Commissioner proposes to issue a determination of the equivalency of a foreign country's SPS measure to an FDA SPS measure, the agency must use rule-making (as to a measure that is required to be promulgated as a rule under a statute administered by the FDA), or it must publish a notice in the *Federal Register* on the proposed determination (as to a measure that is not required to be promulgated as a rule under a statute administered by the FDA). In either case, the public is guaranteed the opportunity for comment on the proposed equivalence determination. However, the overall procedure is so burdensome that the FDA is reluctant to use it.

Another challenge to the development of a single regulatory approach to harmonization is that the Federal Food, Drug, and Cosmetic Act reflects a balkanized approach to regulatory policy making. In some cases, different provisions apply under various clauses of the 'adulteration' definition. Special provisions govern a substance, depending upon whether it is a food additive, a substance that is generally recognized as safe, a color additive, a contaminant, an animal drug residue, and so on. In some cases, highly prescriptive special provisions govern nutrition labeling,[35] infant formula[36] and dietary supplements.[37] Paradoxically, many of the most important regulations – those controlling pathogens – come from some of the most nonspecific provisions in the law relative to regulations,[38] food adulteration[39] and control of communicable diseases.[40]

The Codex General Standard on Food Additives is an example of how US acceptance of Codex standards can be difficult. The Codex General Standard lists several additives that are either not allowed, or are restricted in, the United States: (1) food additives prohibited by regulation (for example, the artificial sweetener, cyclamate); (2) substances that are the subject of pending food additive petitions; (3) food additives that have broader uses in the Codex standard than in the FDA regulation; (4) food additives covered by the Codex standard that may be 'generally recognized as safe' (GRAS) and therefore not a 'food additive' under US law, but for which the FDA has not promulgated a GRAS regulation; (5) color additives prohibited by regulation either because of delisting, for example, Amaranth and carbon black, or cancellation of certification, for example, Red 2G, Guinea Green B; and (6) color additives that are not approved in the United States, for example, Brilliant Black PN, Chryosoine. Codex may also set allowable limits for food additives that cannot be approved in the United States because they have been shown to cause cancer in humans or animals, and therefore would violate the 'Delaney clause' of the US law.[41]

Another impediment to harmonization is that many US food laws contain detailed processes for decisions on food standards, contaminants, food and color additives, and other matters.[42] With two possible exceptions, these provisions do not easily accommodate reliance upon international standards, scientific reviews performed by international scientific bodies, or provide a shortcut for adoption of Codex standards. The two possible exceptions involve pesticide residues and veterinary drug residues. In this instance the 1996 statutory changes[43] might facilitate acceptance of Codex standards. The EPA and the FDA, respectively, are still implementing these amendments, so the contribution that they make to regulatory harmonization is still unclear. (The FDAMA included a streamlined process for the FDA to recognize voluntary consensus standards for medical devices,[44] but no similar provision was included for streamlined recognition of Codex standards.)

Codex Commodity Standards and US Food Standards

Codex commodity standards sometimes conflict with US food standards[45] or they contain elements not dealt with in US standards. The last time the FDA formally notified Codex of its acceptance of a standard was in 1986. Each time the FDA notified Codex of its acceptance of a Codex commodity standard, it did so with specified deviations. For example, many years ago, when the FDA accepted the Codex canned green bean standard it specified several deviations: the FDA has quantitative limits on fibrous material, limits on the length of the cut, allows margarine as well as butter, allows more choice of sweeteners and emulsifiers, bars artificial coloring, has no minimum fill requirement, requires labels to meet the FDA's general regulations, and requires low-acid food registration and filing of the heat process.[46] This one mundane example illustrates the complexity of acceptance of international standards.

The FDA has long had a regulation[47] for the acceptance of Codex standards, and promulgated them when Codex's principal output was recipe-type commodity standards. These standards, as a regulatory approach, were in their in its heyday when Codex was founded in 1962. Indeed, even before Codex began, the FDA had gone a long way towards standardizing a large proportion of staple products in the American food system, such as bread, milk, and popular canned goods. However, the US was not alone in adopting an ambitious food standards program. For example, in the 1960s, the earliest European Economic Community directives were food standards for products such as jams.

By the 1970s food standards began to fall into disfavor in the United States. During that period, nutrition experts and regulatory reformists pronounced them overly prescriptive, oriented toward unimportant aspects of food regulation, and even barriers to entry of new products that might offer significant health advantages (for example, low-fat substitutes for traditional ice cream).[48] In the United States, labeling was often viewed as providing a better way to communicate information about a food's key characteristics, and aid consumers in making wise and safe food choices. After the marathon food standards proceedings that defined 'peanut butter', and unsuccessful attempts to impose limits and labeling requirements on vitamin and mineral products, the FDA was criticized. The basis for this criticisim of the FDA was its investment of resources in these matters, and the law requiring the use of cumbersome trial-type procedures.[49]

In the early 1970s, the FDA began to adopt the recommendations of a 1969 White House Conference on Food, Nutrition and Health.[50] The conference recommendations supported the inclusion on the food label of much more information about nutrition, as well as regulatory alternatives to food standards. Eventually, the agency adopted a more lenient interpretation of the statute's 'imitation' food provisions. The provisions focused on the nutritional equivalence or superiority of the innovation,[51] and nutritional and common name labeling with additional information on characterizing ingredients, such as shrimp in shrimp cocktail.[52] Over the next several years, the FDA increased resources for food safety, but reduced resources for economic regulation such as food standards.

In spite of these, efforts many old food standards remained in the US Code of Federal Regulations, either because they still served a useful purpose[53] or because revoking them was so difficult. During this period, there was an extensive cutback in regulation writers in the FDA food standards program. Eventually, a statutory change in 1990 simplified the process for amending most food standards so they could be more easily revoked.[54] By 1995, the FDA had proposed to eliminate many of its standards of identity as a 'Reinventing Government' initiative.[55]

Despite the movement away from standards of identity that began in the 1970s, due to its earlier activism, the FDA still has many more standards of identity for key food groups than Codex has commodity standards. For example, a 1996 study by the Grocery Manufacturers Association showed that for milk and cream the FDA had 31 standards of identity, 13 of which were targeted for revocation, while Codex had nine commodity standards.[56] For the 22 types of canned fruits for which the FDA had standards of identity, in content, Codex only had nine commodity standards. But Codex had another ten standards for canned fruits for which the FDA had no standards of identity. However, the FDA has no need or desire to promulgate many new mandatory standards because some products subject to Codex standards, for example, mango chutney, are more commonly eaten in other countries than in the United States.

While the FDA was moving away from launching new food standards, Codex continued to produce new commodity standards. However in 1991, a major conference reoriented Codex toward horizontal standards, that focused on food safety. During this period, the FDA's principal use of its regulation on acceptance of Codex standards was to publish, for each Codex standard, an advance notice of proposed rule-making that included the text of the standard. The accompanying preamble explained that the agency would need to receive comments justifying the promulgation of a mandatory food standard based upon that Codex standard. Then, after receipt and consideration of comments, the FDA typically published a notice announcing that it was not pursuing the rule-making. Instead, the agency was allowing the marketing of a food that conformed to the Codex standard, as well as the FDA requirements. This regulation has fallen into disuse, yet the FDA still has not adopted a replacement for it.

V INCREASING EU ACCEPTANCE OF CODEX STANDARDS: THE IMPLICATIONS OF EUROPEAN FOOD SAFETY CHALLENGES IN THE 1990S

To understand the hypersensitivity in Europe to food safety issues, one must understand the impact of the Mad Cow crisis. In 1989, scientists reported that British cows had developed a disease known as Bovine Spongiform Encephalopathy (BSE), apparently the result of feeding cows rations that include a large proportion of neural tissue (brains, spinal cords, and so on) from sheep infected with a common disease known as scrapie. During this period, the US agricultural quarantine agency (the Animal and Plant Health Inspection Service) barred British beef from the US market. To this day, British beef is excluded from the US market, along with that of Switzerland and the other EU member countries after the reporting of BSE cases in Portugal, France, the Netherlands, Denmark and other countries that had imported British animal feed.

In April 1996, scientists in Scotland reported that a dozen young British citizens had died of a new variant form of a human neurological disease known as Creutzfeld-Jakob disease (CJD). The global scientific community verified these results, and confirmed that the causative agents in the transmission of the disease are deadly proteins known as prions. The regulatory policy impact of this food safety crisis was extensive, and continues to have a major impact on food safety standards.

Meanwhile, in Europe, the European Parliament investigated the Mad Cow crisis, and issued a report blaming both the British government and the European Commission for inaction, particularly in the 1989–96 time period. Thereafter, the Commission's food regulatory programs were quickly reorganized. In mid-1996, a Directorate General (DG) on Consumer Protection – then known as DG XXIV and since 1999 known as 'DG Health and Consumer Protection' or 'DG SANCO' for short – was established. The new EU food safety agency was given certain responsibilities for food safety: management of scientific committees on the safety of food and other products, and auditing the food control systems of member states and so-called 'third countries' such as the United States that ship food to Europe.

In 1997, the competence and independence of the European Commission's scientific committees were strengthened. The previous advisory committees were influenced by trade or political considerations, and were considered major weaknesses in the previous system. By early 2000, all food safety officials moved from the former DGs III (on industry) and VI (on agriculture) to the Health and Consumer Protection DG. The 1998 Amsterdam Treaty amending the Treaty of the European Community included provisions on consumer protection, health, and increased transparency in EU institutions. Eventually, all of the additional provisions in the Amsterdam Treaty were influenced by the Mad Cow crisis in the EU.

Another consequence of the European Mad Cow crisis was intense interest in the 'FDA model' as possibly worthy of adoption in Europe. The interest in the FDA model started in 1996, and continued into the start of this decade. The, European Union institutions, the Commission, Parliament and auditors, and those of EU member countries, consulted with FDA officials to ascertain which features of the US system might deserve consideration. Thereafter, the United Kingdom and Ireland created food safety agencies independent of their Ministries of Agriculture to allay concerns that the placement of food regulatory authority in the Ministry of Agriculture may have impeded the governmental response to the BSE crisis.

The French government also enacted legislation that created an independent risk assessment agency, but left risk management responsibility in its Ministry of Agriculture. For example, in 1999 the European Commission permitted one British beef-packer to resume shipping meat outside the UK. However, the French risk assessment agency issued a scientific report advising that France should continue to exclude British beef. The agency found the beef presented a risk of BSE, and therefore of causing human CJD, in orders of magnitude greater than that presented by beef from France and other EU countries. The French Ministry of Agriculture promptly announced that its 'risk management' decision was to follow the advice of the French risk assessors. Eventually the European Court of Justice ordered France to accept the British beef found safe by EU authorities.

In June 1999, news exploded across Europe that Belgian chicken feed producers had added industrial oil to feed, and that sewage sludge was routinely included in French animal feeds.[57] At that time, angry consumers expressed dismay that reorganizations and new laws – at the national and European Community level – still were failing to protect the public. The government of Belgium fell, in part due to the controversy surrounding this food safety scandal. As a result, Belgians[58] joined the ranks of Europeans who consulted the FDA in the mid 1990s about how to structure and empower a consumer protection agency.[59]

Many in the EU viewed the Mad Cow and dioxin chicken crises as evidence of betrayal of trust by public servants, both at the national level (UK, France), and at the European Union level. During this period, consumer alarm escalated over other food safety issues, for example, genetically modified organisms (GMOs). At the same time, there were protests when the United States and Canada won the WTO hormones and beef case. In this case, the WTO gave the US permission to impose high tariffs on European exports due to EU refusal to allow the importation of North American beef following the WTO appellate body decision.

In this regard, many European officials believe consumer concerns are one of several 'other legitimate factors', besides science, upon which to base food safety policy decisions. The EU member states' bans of food products due to safety concerns about content or mode of production would be judged under the SPS Agreement. Therefore, food bans needed to be justified and, in many cases, either based upon an international standard or risk analysis. On the other hand, an EU member country ban on a food product due to consumer concerns would probably be judged under the TBT Agreement. Under either agreement, a food product ban would encounter an issue about whether there was a less trade restrictive way to achieve the country's food safety objectives. For example, other countries could argue that labeling would be considered one way to satisfy a 'consumer right to know' that food was produced through the use of biotechnology, where there is no scientific basis for a safety concern.

In response to the growing concerns of European consumers and policymakers, the EU favors a 'precautionary principle' as an appropriate concept in food safety regulation and law. In 2000 the European Commission issued a formal communication explaining the precautionary principle. In response to the position of the European Union, the United States, Australia and other countries insisted that sanitary and phytosanitary measures be supported by science. Furthermore, these countries also expressed concern over ambiguous concepts, such as the precautionary principle, being added to the norms governing international trade and food standards.

In early 2000, the European Commission issued a White Paper on a proposal to establish a European Food Safety Authority (EFSA).[60] The publication of the White Paper was followed by legislative enactment of a regulation establishing this agency, a law and a regulation on food and feed controls. By 2005, the EFSA started operations in Parma, Italy.

The Changing Context of Food Safety in the European Union

After several food safety crises in the 1990s, there was a widespread view that neither member state regulators nor European Union officials had taken appropriate precautions to prevent animal diseases from spreading to humans. As result, consumers in Europe no longer trusted their food regulators. From an American perspective, the European concern about biotech food containing genetically modified organisms, that was found safe by respected expert bodies such as the FDA, was viewed as odd. For example, in 1989, American regulators exercised precaution in barring British beef – six years before ten UK deaths stimulated EU action on BSE. So why were Europeans wary of beef from hormone-treated cattle – or of grains containing GMOs – that were found safe by the same trusted US agencies?[61] The answer to this question lies in the fact that many Europeans saw a link between BSE and GMOs, and viewed industrialization of agriculture as the common culprit.[62] The continued impasse over the EU's moratorium on approvals of food derived from biotechnology led to the initiation of a WTO case by the United States and other countries that was still pending as of 2005.

Another area of difficulty involves the 1999 EU–US 'framework agreement' on equivalence that remains unimplemented, many years later. The goal of this agreement is achievement of 'equivalence determinations' concerning the EU and US systems for regulating meat, poultry, seafood, dairy products, eggs and other 'veterinary products'. However, until this agreement becomes operational, the EU is auditing the FDA and the USDA Food Safety Inspection Service. These food safety agencies are principally responsible for US regulation of meat, poultry and egg products, for compliance with EU directives. Consequently, the United States has asked that the benchmark for review be 'equivalence' as stated in the SPS Agreement and the bilateral agreement.

In summary, the European food safety crises have strengthened both cooperation and autagonisim between the FDA and EU governments. Furthermore, both sides of the Atlantic now face serious challenges in achieving, in the near term, greater harmonization in their regulatory approach to many food safety issues, through Codex Alimentarius or other international fora.

VI REGULATORY CHALLENGES FOR THE FUTURE: MULTINATIONAL HARMONIZATION OF FOOD SAFETY STANDARDS AND NATIONAL ENFORCEMENT

As the new millennium unfolds, many challenges face Codex and other international bodies in the food regulatory arena. Fortunately, Codex is implementing changes to ensure that its food safety standards program keeps pace with the times. Following a report assessing Codex, an extraordinary session of Codex was held in early 2003 to map the organization's future. Through the assessment process launched at that conference, consumer protection, food standards development, regulatory harmonization and the facilitation of global food trade are being strengthened.

A remaining challenge is that the Codex process requires more effective ways to deal with rapidly emerging food safety problems, for example, Transmissible Spongiform Excephalopathies (TSEs), and the process for producing Codex standards must be accelerated and streamlined. Expert consultations called by the WHO, FAO and the Joint FAO/WHO Food Standards Programme are filling, to some degree, the need at the global level for expert advice. Nevertheless, the process used has been much less open than Codex meetings and standards procedures. In this regard, the Codex ad hoc committees on animal feeding and biotechnology can be viewed as examples of pilot efforts for the use of ad hoc committees, following normal open Codex processes to respond to emerging problems. Furthermore, improvement of the methods for achieving consensus in Codex must continue to be a priority, particularly if Codex takes on cutting-edge problems where controversy is likely. At both the national and global Codex levels, there should be continued strengthening of the processes for involving all countries, particularly developing countries and former Communist countries, as well as consumers, industry and academia.

At a time when international harmonization should be accelerated, food regulators in developed countries such as the US and EU must also confront new challenges, such as products derived from recombinant DNA biotechnology, unique food additives and the ever-present issue of dietary supplements. In fact, the sheer number of individual substances for use in food or processes for food such as pesticides, veterinary drugs, aids in processing, direct food additives, irradiation technologies and food packaging materials – and the tendency of the FDA, the FSA and other advanced regulatory agencies to make decisions on these substances on a one-by-one basis – magnify the number of decisions lacking international uniformity. Ultimately, the importance of Codex's activities cannot be overstated.

VII CONCLUSIONS: FUTURE OPTIONS FOR INCREASED FOOD SAFETY STANDARDS HARMONIZATION

In conclusion, enhanced US–EU regulatory cooperation on food safety standards harmonization, will provide Codex with a strong foundation for food safety standards leadership upon which to build – instead of the transatlantic competition and conflict now seen. Clearly, existing fora such as the bilateral meetings between the FDA and the European Commission, and initiatives led by the Office of the US Trade Representative such as Transatlantic Economic Partnership (TEP) and US–EU Regulatory Cooperation, are useful mechanisms for transatlantic progress on food safety.

The past efforts of the FDA and the European Commission that were quite successful included the FDA's sharing of safety data on flavors and extracts that was compiled by the Flavors and Extracts Association. In this case, both governments collaborated effectively in the Codex ad hoc Task Force on Foods Derived from Biotechnology, particularly on the risk assessment guideline.

Finally, the current 'disharmony' means that food manufacturers and importers bear a heavy burden of corporate responsibility for global food safety. Therefore, compliance with the requirements of all the different nations to which food may be shipped is a potentially daunting task for food producers. As a consequence, the global food industry is a strong supporter of international harmonization of food regulatory standards through the Codex Alimentarius Commission.[63]

NOTES

* Acknowledgments: Since 2002, the author has been a partner in the global law firm Hogan & Hartsan, LLP, first in its Washington, DC office and now in its Brussels office. She represents clients in the food, animal health, pharmaceutical, and medical device industries, and works with both clients and governments on regulatory legislative frameworks. From 1968 to 2002, Ms Horton served the US Food and Drug Administration (FDA) in a range of legislative, legal, and international policy positions. This chapter reflects the author's personal views based on her experience in the FDA and now the private sector.

1. Among major food groups, meat and poultry are relatively high-risk products; they present animal disease issues as well as human disease concerns; and they often are processed under assembly-line conditions by workers with minimal skills. Moreover, regulatory norms began a century ago that included antemortem inspection of cattle by veterinarians, continuous inspection of each processing establishment by a government employee stationed in the plant, and highly prescriptive hygiene requirements. Also, a fair number of food trade issues seem to involve meat, for example, the hormone case and BSE.
2. FAO/WHO (2003), *Codex Alimentarius Commission Procedural Manual, 12th edition*, Rome: FAO. Much of this section of the chapter summarizes, without specific citations, provisions of the Codex manual.
3. The SPS Agreement may be accessed at http://www.wto.org and defines 'international standards, guidelines and recommendations' as: (a) for food safety, the standards, guidelines and recommendations established by the Codex Alimentarius Commission relating to food additives, veterinary drug and pesticide residues, contaminants, methods of analysis and sampling, and codes and guidelines of hygienic practice; (b) for animal health and zoonoses, the standards, guidelines and recommendations developed under the auspices of the International Office of Epizootics; (c) for plant health, the international standards, guidelines and recommendations developed under the auspices of the Secretariat

of the International Plant Protection Convention in cooperation with regional organizations operating within the framework of the International Plant Protection Convention; and (d) for matters not covered by the above organizations, appropriate standards, guidelines and recommendations promulgated by other relevant international organizations open for membership to all Members, as identified by the Committee.
4. SPS Agreement, Annex C, http://www.wto.org.
5. According to the SPS Agreement Annex A, an '[a]ppropriate level of sanitary or phytosanitary protection' is 'The level of protection deemed appropriate by the Member establishing a sanitary or phytosanitary measure to protect human, animal or plant life or health within its territory'.
6. Risk assessment, according to the SPS Agreement, Annex A, is '[t]he evaluation of the likelihood of entry, establishment or spread of a pest or disease within the territory of an importing Member according to the sanitary or phytosanitary measures which might be applied, and of the associated potential biological and economic consequences; or the evaluation of the potential for adverse effects on human or animal health arising from the presence of additives, contaminants, toxins or disease-causing organisms in food, beverages or feedstuffs'.
7. Peru, Canada, Chile, Ecuador, United States and Venezuela.
8. WTO (2002), 'European communities – trade description of sardines, report of the appellate body', 26 September, Geneva, at WTO, at www.wto.org.
9. WTO TBT Agreement, Art. 2.2.
10. Consumer organizations criticize the WTO decision process on several grounds. First, trade specialists sit as a panel in judgment of a country's health and environment laws. Second, WTO panels meet behind closed doors in sessions that cannot be attended by members of the public – or even representatives of WTO member governments other than the parties. Third, although the US and a few other countries make their WTO filings public, the general WTO processes allow briefs to be secret, and draft panel reports are kept secret until the parties have commented on them. Fourth, amicus curiae briefs are not explicitly allowed, although the US government was allowed to attach amicus briefs prepared by environmental advocacy groups to its own brief in a challenge to a US environmental law to protect sea turtles caught in shrimp nets.
11. Understanding on Rules and Procedures Governing the Settlement of Disputes (DSU).
12. The WTO panel decision and the WTO appellate body decision may be found at http://www.wto.org.
13. Relevant filings by the European Commission and the Us government may be found at http://www.wto.org.
14. Lister, C. (1995), *A Sad Story Told Sadly: The Prospects for US–EU Food Trade Wars*, Washington, DC: Food and Drug Law Institute Annual Education Conference. '[T]he EU's policymaking regarding foodstuffs is motivated almost entirely by goals other than international harmonization.'
15. The Center for Science in the Public Interest suggests that the United States instruct its Codex delegations 'to officially object to the development of any Codex standard that falls below US regulatory requirements' to build a record in case of a trade dispute. Center for Science and the Public Interest (1997), *Threats and Opportunities for the US Food and Drug Administration and the US Department of Agriculture: International Harmonization of Food Safety and Labeling Standards*, Washington, DC: Center for Science and the Public Interest. The Center urged that when the US cannot block a weaker Codex standard, 'it should make a concerted effort to record its position in the minutes [on] why the US believes the Codex standard does not accord sufficient protection for consumers, and call for a vote on standards that fall below US regulatory requirements'.
16. http://www.fao.org/catalog/ed/cat/cate062.htm is the address for ordering copies of archived reports of Commission meetings, such as the 1993 report: ALINORM 93/40 (1993), *Report of the 20th Session of the Joint FAO/WHO Food Standards Programme Codex Alimentarius Commission*, Geneva, ISBN 92-5-103379-X, Rome: FAO.
17. Joint FAO/WHO Food Standards Programme, Codex Alimentarius Commission (1997), *Report of the 22nd Session. ALINORM 97/37*, Rome: FAO, pp. 14–15.

18. FAO/WHO, Codex Alimentarius Commission (1999), *Procedural Manual, 10th edition*, Rome: FAO
19. CX/EXEC 96/43/7, Application of Residue Limits.1996. Transmitted by the government of Australia for consideration at the Codex Executive Committee.
20. 7 July 1997, 62 FR 35243.
21. Contaminated hamburgers at a 'Jack in the Box' fast-food restaurant in Washington state killed two children and left hundreds seriously ill due to hemolytic uremic syndrome caused by infection from *E. coli 0157H7*
22. Office of the United States Trade Representative (1997), 62 FR 64619.
23. Center for Science in the Public Interest (1997), op. cit. The Center expressed concern about lower Codex standards on pasteurization of dairy products, food additives, mineral content of bottled water, meat inspection and lead contamination. Ibid. p. 10.
24. The view is sometimes expressed that harmonization encroaches upon domestic regulatory prerogatives and fails to take into account local differences. Therefore, the Center for Science and the Public Interest, a strong supporter of nutrition labeling, believes that dietary problems are so different around the world that specific labeling requirements may never be able to be harmonized internationally. However, Codex should institute a basic requirement that each country develop a mandatory nutrition labeling law suited to its needs. Center for Science and the Public Interest (1998), *Food Labeling for the 21st Century: A Global Agenda for Action*, Washington, DC: Center for Science and the Public Interest, p. 43.
25. Ibid.
26. Conversation between Marc Silbergeld, Consumers Union, and author 4 March 1996, Washington, DC.
27. EPA (1991), *Chemicals in Foods: US Perceptions of Codex Pesticide MRL Acceptance Issues*, Washington, DC: The EPA. See also Government Accounting Office (1991) *International Food Safety: Comparison of US and Codex Pesticide Standards*, 4 GAO/PEMD-91-22, Washington, DC: GAO. The EPA assumes that a risk exists at any level of a carcinogenic pesticide and focuses its quantitative risk assessment on whether the risk is acceptable at given exposure levels. The Codex process calculates a threshold level called a 'no observed effects level' which then serves as a basis for an acceptable daily intake level. Thus, it is extremely difficult to make direct comparisons between Codex numerical limits and EPA tolerances.
28. 21 November 1997, Pub. L. 105–15.
29. Section 903(b)(3) (21 U.S.C. 393(b)(3)).
30. Section 803(c)(3) (21 U.S.C. 383(c)(3)). The FDA is also required to 'support the Office of the United States Trade Representative, in consultation with the Department of Commerce, in efforts to move toward the acceptance of mutual recognition agreements' with the EU relating to, *inter alia*, the regulation of foods, food additives, and color additives, and the regulation of GMPs: section 803(c)(2). The harmonization and mutual recognition provisions in section 803(c) do not apply to dietary supplements, due to an express Congressional exemption in section 803(c)(5) (21 U.S.C.383(c)(5)). Apparently the dietary supplement industry, fearful that the FDA may undertake to harmonize toward the EU's stricter regulatory approach, persuaded Congress to include this exemption. Personal communication to the author dated 6 January 1998, from a colleague involved in drafting the FDAMA.
31. Section 803(c)(1) (21 U.S.C. 383(c)(1)).
32. 21 CFR 20.89.
33. 9 December 1995. 60 FR 63372; 63 FR 40069, 27 July 1998.
34. 19 U.S.C. 2578a (b), (c).
35. 21 U.S.C. 343(q)–(r).
36. 21 U.S.C. 350a.
37. 21 U.S.C. 350.
38. 21 U.S.C. 371(a).
39. 21 U.S.C. 342.

40. 42 U.S.C. 264, the interstate and foreign quarantine provisions of the Public Health Service Act.
41. Three provisions of the FFDCA include a Delaney clause which bars approval of a substance found to cause cancer when ingested by humans or other animals: the food additive provision, section 409(c)(3)(A) (21 U.S.C. 348(c)(3)(A)); the animal drug provision, section 512(d)(1)(I) (21 U.S.C. 360b(d)(1)(I)); and the color additive provision, section 721(b)(5)(B) (21 U.S.C. 379e(b)(5)(B)).
42. 21 U.S.C. 341, 346, 348, 379e.
43. The Food Quality Protection Act of 1996, Pub. L. 104–70 amended section 408 of the Federal Food, Drug, and Cosmetic Act (FFDCA) to add a new subsection (b)(4) (21 U.S.C. 346a(b)(4)) to facilitate adoption of Codex MRLs in pesticide tolerances set by the Environmental Protection Agency (EPA) and enforced by the FDA. The Animal Drug Availability Act of 1996, Pub. L. 104–250 amended the FFDCA to add a new section 512(a)(6) to allow the FDA to establish import tolerances for veterinary drugs used in other countries, if found safe by the FDA, including use of Codex standards for these tolerances.
44. Pub. L. 105–115, new section 514(c) (21 U.S.C. 360d(c)).
45. FDA food standards are promulgated under section 401 of the FFDCA (21 U.S.C. 341).
46. Codex Alimentarius/Acceptances/Part I – Rev.2. 1983.
47. 21 CFR 130.6, 564.6.
48. Merrill, R.A. (1974). 'Like mother used to make: an analysis of the FDA food standards of identity', *Columbia Law Review*, **74**: 561.
49. Hamilton, R.W. (1972), 'Rulemaking on a record by the Food and Drug Administration', *Texas Law Review*, **50**: 1132.
50. Meyer, J. (ed.) (1970), *White House Conference on Food, Nutrition, and Health – Final Report*, Washington, DC: White House.
51. Section 403(c) (21 U.S.C. 343(c)). 38 FR 20702, 2 August 1973. McNamara, S. (1975), 'Some legal aspects of providing a sufficient food supply for a hungry population', *Food Drug Cosmetic Law Journal*, 38: 527.
52. *American Frozen Food Institute*, v. *Mathews*, 413 F. Supp. 548 (D.D.C. 1976), aff'd sub nom., *American Frozen Food Institute* v. *Califano*, 555 F. 2d 1059 (D.C.Cir. 1977).
53. Letter to FDA Commissioner Kessler from International Jelly and Preserves Association, 4 December 1995, arguing that elimination of FDA's fruitspread standards would open the way for unethical producers to reduce the amount of fruit in the product and replace fruit with inferior substitutes.
54. The Nutrition Labeling and Education Act, Pub. L. 101–535, amending section 701(e) of the FFDCA (21 U.S.C. 371(e)).
55. National Performance Review (1996), *Reinventing Food Regulations*, Washington, DC: White House, pp. 18–19.
56. Grocery Manufacturers Association (1996), *An Inventory of Food Standards Established by US Regulatory Agencies and the Codex Alimentarius Commission*, Department of Science and Technology, Washington, DC: Grocery Manufactures of America.
57. Erickson, B.E. (1999), 'Dioxin food crisis in Belgium', *Analytical Chemical News & Features*, 1 August, p. 541A.
58. Lallemand, A. (1999), 'The American food and drug administration, a model?' *Independent – Le Soir* [a companion article is an interview with the author], Brussels.
59. These countries included the UK, whose government consulted in 1996 with former FDA and USDA official Michael Taylor; and France, whose officials visited FDA in 1996, followed by invitations for FDA officials to address the French Senate.
60. A debate has raged over whether this body should have far-reaching powers similar to those wielded by the FDA or more limited responsibilities similar to those of the European Medicines Evaluation Agency EMEA Commission Plans Radical Overhaul of food safety Laws, (1999), European Voice, 5(45), 9 December, http:// www.european-voice.com.
61. The FDA handles human and animal health aspects of hormones and human health aspects of GMOs. The Animal and Plant Health Inspection Service (APHIS) of USDA handles plant health aspects of GMOs. Also, the Environmental Protection Agency reviews the human health and environment aspects of crops that have pesticide action.

Hence, the 'Round-Up-ready' soybeans and corn that prompted EU consumers' ire had been reviewed and found acceptable by three US regulatory agencies. The FDA regulates human health aspects of BSE. Both the FDA and APHIS have authority over the animal health aspects of BSE, with APHIS focused on protecting American agriculture from a deadly animal disease, and the FDA charged with assuring the safety of food for animals, as well as food for humans.

62. See interview with Belgian Public Health Minister Magda Aelvoet, 16 September 1999, *Independent – Le Soir*, Brussels.
63. 'FDA told to increase focus on international food regulation' (1998), *World Food Reg. Review*, p. 9.

REFERENCES

A European Food and Public Health Agency: The Future of Scientific Advice in the EU (1999), December, Brussels: Advice to European Commission by expert panel.

American Council on Science and Health (1999), *Microbes, Not Chemicals, are the Major Source of Foodborne Illness*, New York: American Council on Science and Health.

Avery, N., M. Drake and T. Lang (1992), *Cracking the Codex: An Analysis of Who Sets World Food Standards*, London: National Food Alliance.

Buzby, J. (2001), *Effects of Food-Safety Perceptions on Food Demand and Global Trade. Changing Structure of Global Food Consumption and Trade*, ERS-WRS-01-1 USDA 55, Washington, DC: USDA.

Center for Science and the Public Interest (1997), *Threats and Opportunities for the US Food and Drug Administration and the US Department of Agriculture: International Harmonization of Food Safety and Labeling Standards*, Washington, DC: Center for the Public Interest.

Center for Science in the Public Interest (1998), *Food Labeling for the 21st Century: A Global Agenda for Action*, Washington, DC: Center for Science in the Public Interest.

Consumers Union (1992), *Understanding GATT: Is the Uruguay Round a Benefit to Consumers Or a Threat to Food Safety and The Environment?* Washington, DC: Consumers Union.

Cooper, K. (1996), 'The US–EC hormone dispute: aspects of the complaint under the SPS Agreement', seminar paper, Ann Arbor, MI: University of Michigan Law School.

Coote, B. with C. LeQuesne (1992), *The Trade Trap, Poverty and the Global Commodity Markets*, London: Oxfam Publications.

Costarica, M. (1997), *The Codex Alimentarius : Trade and Food Security*, RIMSA 10/11, X Inter-American Meeting, at the Ministerial Level on Health and Agriculture, Washington, DC: PAHO/WHO.

Croley, S. and J. Jackson (1996), 'WTO dispute procedures, standard of review, and deference to national governments', *American Journal International Law*, **90**: 193–213.

Echols, M. (1996), 'The international tower of Babel: the small business perspective', *Food Drug. Law Journal*, **51** (1): 175–90.

Echols, M. (1998a), ' Food safety regulation in the European union and the united states: different cultures, different laws', *Columbia Journal European Law*, **4**(3): 525–40.

Echols, M. (1998b), 'Sanitary and phytosanitary measures', in American Bar Association, Section on International Law and Practice (ed.), *The Multilateral Trade Framework for the 21st Century and US Implementing Legislation*, Washington, DC: American Bar Association.

Eldred, J. and Coffield, S. (1998), 'What every food manufacturer needs to know: realizing the impact of globalization on national food regulation', *Food and Drug Law Journal*, **52** (1), 31–8.

EPA (1991), *Chemicals in Food: US Perceptions of Codex Pesticide MRL Acceptance Issues*, Washington, DC: EPA.

Erickson, B.E. (1999), 'Dioxin food crisis in Belgium', *Analytical Chemical News & Features*, p. 541A.

Esty, D. (1994), *Greening the GATT, Trade, Environment, and the Future*, Washington, DC: Institute for International Economics.

European Voice (1999), 9–15 December, p. 1.

FAO (1998), *FAO Technical Assistance and the Uruguay Round Agreements: The Uruguay Round Agreements and FAO*, Rome: FAO.

FAO (1999), *Food Quality, Safety and International Trade: Codex Alimentarius and the SPS and TBT Agreements*, Rome: FAO, at http://www.fao.org/ur/fact/foodqual.htm.

FAO/WHO (1995), *Application of Risk Analysis to Food Standards Issues. Expert Consultation*, Geneva WHO.

FAO/WHO (1997), *Risk Management and Food Safety; Expert Consultation*, Rome: FAO.

FAO/WHO (1999a), *Codex Alimentarius Commission – Procedure Manual, 10th edition*, Rome: FAO.

FAO/WHO (1999b), *This is Codex Alimentarius*, Rome: FAO.

FAO/WHO (1999c), *Understanding the Codex Alimentarius*, Rome: FAO.

FAO/WHO (2002a), 'Improving efficiency and transparency in food safety systems – sharing experiences', *Global Forum of Food Safety Regulators Conference Proceedings*, Rome: FAO.

FAO/WHO (2002b), *Global Forum of Food Safety Regulators Conference*, 28–30 January 2002, Marrakesh, Rome: FAO.

FAO/WHO (2003), *Codex Alimentarius Commission Procedure Manual, 12th edition*, Rome: FAO.

FAO/WHO – Codex Alimentarius Commission (1999), *Codex Guidelines for the Development of Equivalence Agreements Regarding Food Import and Export Inspection and Certification Systems, Rome*, Rome: FAO.

FDA (1995a), *International Harmonization; Policy on Standards*, 60 FR 53078, Rockville, MD: FDA.

FDA (1995b), *International Memoranda of Understanding; Compliance Policy Guide*, 60 FR 13485, Rockville, MD: FDA.

FDA (1995c), *Procedures for the Safe and Sanitary Processing and Importing of Fish and Fishery Products; Final Rule, 21 CFR 123.12, Special Requirements for Imported Products*, Rockville, MD: FDA.

FDA (1996), *Cooperative Agreement Between the Food and Drug Administration and New Zealand Covering Seafood*, 61 FR 7112, Rockville, MD: FDA.

FDA (1997a), *Advance Notice of Proposed Rulemaking, Consideration of Codex Alimentarius Standards*, 62 FR 36243 (6 July 1997) (as of October 2003, there had been no further FDA action on this initiative), Rockville, MD: FDA.

FDA (1997b), *Draft Guidance on Equivalence Criteria for Food*, 62 FR 30593 (as of

October 2003, the final guidance had not been issued by FDA), Rockville, MD: FDA.
FDA (1997c), *Food Safety from Farm to Table: A New Strategy for the 21st Century*, Rockville, MD: FDA.
FDA (1999), *United States–European Union Veterinary Agreement*, Rockville, MD: FDA. Available at http://www.fda.gov/oia/Agreements/euvet.pdf
Flamm, E. (1995), 'Codex Alimentarius: a primer', in *Compilation of International Laws*, Washington, DC: Food and Drug Law Institute.
Food and Drug Law Institute (1996), *Compilation of International Laws*, Washington, DC: Food and Drug Law Institute.
Food Safety Inspection Service (FSIS) (2005), *International Standard-Setting Activities*, Washington, DC: USDA.
Frawley, J. (1987), 'Codex alimentarius: food safety – pesticides', *Food Drug Cosmetic Law Journal*, **42** (1): 168–73.
Gaull, G. and R. Goldberg (1993), *The Emerging Global Food Safety System: Public and Private Sector Issues*, New York: John Wiley.
Gerth, J. and T. Weiner (1997), Imports swamp US food-safety efforts', *New York Times*, p. A1.
Goldman, P. (1994), 'The democratization of the development of United States trade policy', *Cornell International Law Journal*, **27** (3): 631–97.
Goldman, P. and R. Wiles, (1994), *Trading Away US Food Safety*, Environmental Working Group, Washington, DC: Public Citizen.
Goldstein, S. (1999), 'US importation of French cheeses: trade protectionism or consumer protection', master's thesis, Blacksburg, VA: Virginia Polytechnic Institute.
Government Accounting Office (1991), *International Food Safety: Comparison of US and Codex Pesticide Standards*, 4 GAO/PEMD-91-22, Washington, DC: GAO.
Grocery Manufacturers Association (1996), *An Inventory of Food Standards Established by US Regulatory Agencies and the Codex Alimentarius Commission*, Department of Science and Technology, Washington, DC: Grocery Manufacturers of America.
Hamilton, R.W. (1972), 'Rulemaking on a record by the Food and Drug Administration', *Texas Law Review*, **50**: 1132.
Horton, L. (1995), 'International harmonization and compliance', in R. Shapiro (ed.), *Nutrition Labeling Handbook*, New York: Marcel Dekker.
Horton, L. (1997a), 'The Food and Drug Administration's international harmonization, enforcement, and trade policy activities; international harmonization of food and veterinary medicine regulation', in R. Brady, R. Cooper, and R. Silverman (eds), *Fundamentals of Law and Regulation: An In-Depth Look at Foods, Veterinary Medicines, and Cosmetics*, Washington, DC: Food and Drug Law Institute, pp. 99–159.
Horton, L. (1997b), 'International harmonization of food and veterinary medicine regulation', in R. Brady, R. Cooper and R. Silverman (eds), *Fundamentals of Law and Regulation: An In-Depth Look at Foods, Veterinary Medicines, and Cosmetics*, Washington, DC: Food and Drug Law Institute, pp. 381–484.
Horton, L. (1997c), 'The United States Food and Drug Administration: its role, authority, history, harmonization activities, and cooperation with the European Union', *European Food Law Review*, 8, Frankfurt: International Business Press.
Horton, L. (1998a), 'Food from developing countries: steps to improve compliance', *Food Drug Law Journal*, **53** (1): 139–71.

Horton, L. (1998b), 'Mutual recognition agreements and harmonization', *Seton Hall Law Review*, **29** (2): 708–29.
Horton, L. and K.E. Hastings (1998), 'A plan that establishes a framework for achieving mutual recognition of Good Manufacturing Practices Inspections, *Food Drug Law Journal*, **53** (3): 527–36.
Horton, L., M. Pendergast and L. Weinstein (1993), *Regulation of Food, Cosmetics, and Medical Products: Legislative Concepts*, Rockville, MD: FDA.
Huggett, A., B. Petersen, R. Walker, C. Fisher, H. Notermans, F. Rombouts, P. Abbott, M. Debackere, S. Hathaway, E. Hecker, A. Knaap, P. Kuznesof, I. Meyland, G. Moy, J. Narbonne, J. Paakkanen, M. Smith, D. Tennant, P. Wagstaffe, J. Wargo and G. Wurtzen (1998), 'Towards internationally acceptable standards for food additives and contaminants based on the use of risk analysis', *Environmental Toxicology and Pharmacology*, **5** (4): 227–36.
Jackson, J. (1992), *The World Trading System, Law and Policy of International Economic Relations*, Cambridge, MA, and London: MIT Press.
Joint FAO/WHO Food Standards Programme (1993), *Codex Alimentarius Commission – Report of the Twentieth Session*, ALINORM 93/40, Rome: FAO.
Joint FAO/WHO Food Standards Programme (1997), *Codex Alimentarius Commission Report of the 22nd Session. ALINORM 97/37*, Rome: FAO.
Kaferstein, F. (1997), *The Codex Alimentarius and its Importance for Public Health*, X Inter-American Meeting, at the Ministerial Level, on Animal Health, RIMSA 10/12, Washington, DC: PAHO/WHO.
Kellam, J. and Guarino E.T. (eds) (2000), *International Food Law*, Washington, DC: Food and Drug Law Institute.
Kettle, M. (1999), 'A world of difference: making peace is easy compared with making dinner', *Washington Post*.
Lefferts, L. (1997), *Risk Management and the Codex Process: a Consumer Perspective*, Washington, DC: Consumers Union.
Leiss, W. (2000), *Governing Food: Science, Safety and Trade; Rapporteur's Report*, The Canada–UK Colloquia, School of Policy Studies, Queen's University.
Lewis, C., A. Randell and F. Scarbrough, (1996), *Nutrition Labeling of Foods: Comparisons Between US Regulations and Codex Guidelines*, Washington, DC: FDA and Rome: FAO.
Lister, C. (1993), 'The proposed new EC rules for food claims', *World Food Regulation Review*, **3** (6): 16–8.
Lister, C. (1994), 'Discord and change: an assessment of the European Community's food packaging laws', *Food Drug Law Journal*, **48** (4): 589–630.
Lister, C. (1995), *A Sad Story Told Sadly: The Prospects for US–EU Food Trade Wars*, Washington, DC: Food and Drug Law Institute Annual Education Conference.
Lister, C. (1996), 'A world out of tune: the prospects for harmonizing international food law', *World Food Regulation Review*, **6** (1): 19–21.
McNamara, S. (1975), 'Some legal aspects of providing a sufficient food supply for a hungry population', *Food Drug Cosmetic Law Journal*, **38**: 527.
Merrill, R.A. (1974), 'Like mother used to make: an analysis of the FDA food standards of identity', *Columbia Law Review*, **74**: 561.
Merrill, R.A. (1998), 'The importance and challenges of mutual recognition', *Seton Hall Law Review*, **29** (2): 736–54.
Meyer, J. (ed.) (1970), *White House Conference on Food, Nutrition, and Health – Final Report*, Washington, DC: White House.

National Performance Review (1996), *Reinventing Food Regulations*, Washington, DC: White House.

Office of the US Trade Representative, in conjunction with FDA, USDA and EPA (1994), *The Uruguay Round and US Food Safety* [responding to Public Citizen and Environmental Working Group (1994), *Trading Away US Food Safety*], Washington, DC: USTR.

Public Citizen (1997), *NAFTA's Broken Promises: Fast Track to Unsafe Food*, Washington, DC: Public Citizen.

Public Citizen (1998), *Comments on the US Preparations for the 1999 World Trade Organization Ministerial*, Washington, DC: Public Citizen.

Public Citizen (1999a), *A Citizen's Guide to the World Trade Organization*, Washington, DC: Public Citizen.

Public Citizen (1999b), *Whose Trade Organization?* Washington, DC: Public Citizen.

Public Citizen and Environmental Working Group (1994), *Trading Away US Food Safety*, Washington, DC: Public Citizen.

Rees, N. and D. Watson (eds) (2000), *International Standards for Food Safety*, Gaithersburg, MD: Aspen.

Roberts, D. (1998a), *Implementation of the WTO Agreement on the Application of Sanitary and Phytosanitary Measures: The First Two Years*, International Agricultural Trade Research Consortium, Geneva: USTR Mission to the WTO.

Roberts, D. (1998b), 'Preliminary assessment of the effects of the WTO Agreement on sanitary and phytosanitary trade regulations, *Journal of International Economic Law*, **1** (3): 377–405.

Ruff, J. (1996), 'The globalization of a food processor', *Food and Drug Law Journal*, **51** (4): 727–34.

Schwartz, M. (2003), *How the Cows Turned Mad*, Berkeley, CA: University of California Press.

Sikes, L. (1998), 'FDA's consideration of Codex Alimentarius standards in light of international trade agreements', *Food and Drug Law Journal*, **53** (2): 327–36.

Silverglade, B. (1995), *Using Food Labeling to Improve Diet and Health in the United States*, Tokyo, WHO 15th Annual Conference of the International Union for Health Promotion and Education, Geneva: WHO.

Silverglade, B. (1998a), 'The impact of international trade agreements on US food safety and labeling standards', *Food and Drug Law Journal*, **53** (2): 537–42.

Silverglade, B. (1998b), 'What is the true price of free trade?', *44th Annual Conference of the American Council on Consumer Interests*, Conference Proceedings, Washington, DC: American Council on Consumer Interests.

Smith, M. (2000), 'Consumers, industry, science, openness: key hall marks of US food regulation', *World Food Regulation Review*, Washington, DC: Bureau of National Affairs.

Speer, L. (1999), 'Biotechnology, food labeling key issues before international delegates to Rome', *World Food Regulation Review*, **9** (3): 17–24.

Stewart, T. and D. Johanson (1999), 'The SPS Agreement of the World Trade Organization and the international trade of dairy products', *Food Drug Law Journal*, **54** (1): 55–72.

The Economist (1999), 'Genetically modified government', p. 56.

US Government (1994a), *Equivalence Determinations, Enacted as Part of the Uruguay Round Agreements Act*, 19 U.S.C. 2578a4, Public Law 103–465, Washington, DC: US Government.

US Government (1994b), *Notice of United States Participation in International Standard-Setting Activities, Uruguay Round Agreements Act*, 19 U.S.C. 2578 (a), Washington, DC: US Government.

US Government (1995), *United States v. 2998 Cases . . . Food* [*Canned Mushroom Case*], 64 F.3d 984 (5th Cir. 1995), Washington, DC: US Government.

US House of Representatives (1994), *Message from the President of the United States Transmitting The Uruguay Round Trade Agreements, Texts of Agreements Implementing Bill, Statement of Administrative Action and Required Supporting Statements*, 103d Congress, 2d Sess., H. Doc. 103–316, 776–93, Washington, DC: Government Printing Office.

Victor, D. (1999), *Risk Management and the World Trading System: Regulating International Trade Distortions Caused by National Sanitary and Phytosanitary Policies*, New York: Council on Foreign Relations.

Vogel, D. (1995), *Trading Up: Consumer and Environmental Regulation in a Global Economy*, Cambridge, MA: Harvard University Press.

Wehr, M. (1997a), 'Codex Committee on Food Hygiene sets promising course for the future', *World Food Regulation Review*, **7** (7): 25–8.

Wehr, M. (1997b), 'Update on issues before the Codex Alimentarius', *Food Drug Law Review*, **52** (4): 531–6

World Food Reg. Review (1998), 'FDA told to increase focus on international food regulation', p. 9.

WTO (1998a), *EC Measures Concerning Meat and Meat Products, Report of the Appellate Body*, Geneva: WTO, at www.wto.org.

WTO (1998b), *Sanitary and Phytosanitary Measures: The International Agreement Series*, Geneva: WTO.

WTO/GATT Secretariat (1994), *The Results of the Uruguay Round of Multilateral Trade Negotiations*, Geneva : WTO.

Young, J. (1983), 'Food and Drug Administration (FDA)', in D.R. Whitnah (ed.), *Government Agencies*, Westport, CT: Greenwood Press.

INTERNET ADDRESSES:

Codex (FAO) http://www.codexalimentarius.net
FAO http://www.fao.org
EPA http://www.epa.gov
FDA http://www.FDA.gov
FSIS http://www.fsis.usda.gov
ISO http://www.iso.ch/iso/en/ISOOnline.openerpage
OECD http://www.oecd.org
US Codex http://www.fsis.usda.gov/OA/codex
US food safety http://www.foodsafety.gov
US food safety system annex on precaution in US system
http://www.foodsafety.gov/~fsg/fssystem.html
WHO http://www.who.org
WTO http://www.wto.org.

PART III

Regional and Global Regulatory Harmonization and Governance of Food Safety

7. Governance of food safety in the Western Hemisphere

Fernando Robles*

I INTRODUCTION: GLOBAL FOOD TRADE AND FOOD SAFETY IN THE WESTERN HEMISPHERE

Food safety is emerging as the single most pressing issue in global food trade and global food industries in the twenty-first century.[1] At the present time, concerns over the potential sabotage of food supplies from bioterrorism, contamination of global food industries and increased awareness of the link between health and economic development, have triggered increased interest in the governance of national food systems (Buzby 2001; USDA 2003a; Veneman 2003). In spite of the number of global agreements in agricultural trade protecting public health and safety (WTO SPS), and food safety standards (Codex), there is confusion over diverse national standards. In many cases, countries are guided by their domestic policy goals of protecting the public health and the global market interests of their farmers and food industries.

As a result of different national food safety standards, global trade in agriculture and competition in global agri-food industries can be restricted. Furthermore, market access can be restricted because of high levels of standards, multiple standards, lack of information on regulations, high costs of testing and verification procedures, lack of scientific data and inconsistent application of procedures. Consequently, there is increasing interest in harmonizing diverse national food safety standards (Stanton 2003).

The importance of making progress in food safety standards and regulations is not trivial for Western Hemisphere countries. The region's agricultural trade totals $200 billion, and accounts for about 30 per cent of world trade in agriculture.(Sawaya et al. 2002) In the global food markets, the region is a major exporter of agricultural commodities and beef to the world. At the present time, the following five countries in the Western Hemisphere rank among the top 15 largest agricultural exporters: the United States, Canada, Brazil, Argentina and Mexico. The agricultural exports from these five countries alone accounted for 36 per cent of world agricultural exports or $100 billion (USDA 2003b). Conversely, Mexico is the sixth largest import market of agricultural products, while five Latin American countries are net food importers with high levels of food insecurity: Haiti, the Dominican Republic, Cuba, Peru and Honduras. In sum, restrictions to agricultural trade emerging from food safety regulations and standards have a detrimental impact on export revenue generation and food security in the Western Hemisphere.

In this chapter we explore the issues of food safety standard harmonization in the Western Hemisphere. Section II explores food safety within the larger context of food security and trade.[2] Section III provides an assessment of food security. Section IV focuses on agricultural trade in the Western Hemisphere in the context of regional integration. Sections V, VI and VII discuss food safety standards harmonization in the Western Hemisphere. Section VIII addresses the future of food safety standards harmonization in the Western Hemisphere.

Food Safety Harmonization in Latin America: A Conceptual Framework

The analysis of food safety harmonization is very complex. Therefore, harmonization of diverse national food safety regulations and standards must be studied within the larger framework of agricultural trade liberalization, national food security and free trade negotiations. In each case, the implications of technical regulations and standards for human health, animal health and food quality for food safety standards harmonization must be examined (Diaz-Bonilla et al. 2002b).

The implementation of food safety standards is also determined by bilateral and regional free trade agreements. Clearly, the European Union followed a different regulatory approach to food safety standards for modern biotechnology and genetically modified food than the US. Nevertheless, the Free Trade Agreement between the United States and Chile includes a chapter on food standards. In this respect, groups of countries may share common goals and approaches to harmonization depending on their situation as net food exporters or importers, levels of economic development or membership in a regional trade group.

The starting point is the goal established by the 1996 World Food Summit; that countries should provide access to safe and nutritious food to meet the dietary needs and food preferences of all citizens and nations (FAO 1996). Clearly, this World Food Summit goal commits all countries to work towards securing the availability of a sustainable food supply for all – not only privileged groups – and meet minimum per capita levels of daily calories and proteins. In other words, the goal is for national governments and regulators to provide safe and secure food systems.

As a result of WTO multilateral negotiations, world agricultural trade has expanded greatly in recent years to reach a level of $525 billion in 2001 (WTO 2002). However, growing concerns about the consumer protection, animal and plant health, and public health impacts of food safety, led to the landmark WTO Sanitary and Phytosanitary (SPS) Agreement in 1995. In cases where scientific evidence is not fully developed, such as the case of biotechnology, governments can use precautionary regulatory policies, such as the banning of GM food, until information is available to reach consensus on food safety (Burnquist et al. 2002). Finally, the implementation of Codex standards by countries varies depending on national risk assessments, different levels of scientific knowledge and available technologies (Wilson 1999).

II FOOD SECURITY IN THE WESTERN HEMISPHERE

Latin America is far from being a homogenous group of nations in terms of food security, public health and agricultural development. At one extreme, countries such as Argentina and Uruguay exhibit food production and public health indicators at the levels of highly developed countries. On the other extreme, countries such as Haiti and the Dominican Republic are among the poorest countries in the region in terms of food security and public health standards. Therefore, there is a need to distinguish the different levels of food security and agriculture in this region.

On average, the region's per capita food consumption was 2407 calories in 1999, exceeding the recommended minimum level of 2100 calories. The number of undernourished people has declined from 60 million in 1995 to 55 million in 2000, and is expected to reach 30 million in 2011 (FAO 2002a; USDA 2003b). The majority of the undernourished population is concentrated in six Latin American countries. However, Haiti is the only country in the region that does not reach the minimum recommended level of calories per capita. This country's critical level of poverty is reflected in malnourishment levels of more than 35 per cent of its population. Likewise, in Nicaragua, the Dominican Republic, Bolivia, Guatemala and Honduras between 20–34 per cent of their population suffer from malnutrition (FAO Health Indicators; see also Table 7.1).

The improvement in the region's average food consumption levels reflects increased food imports rather than increases in regional agricultural and food production. The volume of food imports have increased from levels of 6.3 million tons in 1992 to 10.7 million tons in 2000, representing approximately 44 per cent of domestic food supplies (USDA 2003b).

Table 7.1 Nutritional profile in the Western Hemisphere by regional group

Trade group	Countries	% of population undernourished (1996–98)	Per capita dietary energy supply	% urban population	Agriculture as % of GDP
NAFTA	Canada	—	3083*	77	4
	Mexico	5	3150	74	5
	United States	—	3800	77	2
	Average group	1.66	3344	76	3.6
MERCOSUR	Argentina	—	3180	90	7
	Brazil	10	2960	81	8
	Paraguay	14	2540	55	25
	Uruguay	3	2850	91	8
	Average group	6.75	2882.5	79.2	12
Ancom	Bolivia	23	2210	62	16
	Colombia	13	2570	73	13
	Ecuador	5	2680	64	12
	Peru	11	2600	72	7
	Venezuela	21	2280	87	4
	Average group	14.6	2468	71.6	10.4
CACM	Costa Rica	5	2780	48	18
	Guatemala	25	2160	39	21
	Honduras	22	2390	52	23
	Nicaragua	29	2240	56	34
	El Salvador	14	2460	46	13
	Average group	19	2406	48.2	21.8
CARICOM	Antigua and Barbuda		2396	36	

	Bahamas		2443	88	
	Barbados		3022	50	
	Dominica		2994	70	
	Grenada		2764	37	
	Jamaica	9	2680	56	
	St Kitts and Nevis		2685	34	
	St Lucia			38	
	St Vincent and Grenadines		2579	55	
	Trinidad and Tobago	12	2720	90	
	Average group		2698	63	
Others	Chile	4	2850	85	8
	Cuba	13	2560	80	
	The Dominican Republic	26	2310	64	12
	Haiti	50	2040	40	
	Panama	18	2410	56	7

Source: Food, Nutrition and Health Indicators, FAO; World Development Indicators, World Bank; *Díaz-Bonilla et al. (2002b).

Since income is poorly distributed, the region suffers from inadequate food consumption in lower-income segments of the population. As a region, Latin America has become dangerously dependent on imports to meet its local food security needs. The increased level of food imports can be attributed to increased trade liberalization in the region, as well the reduction of agricultural commodity prices. However, increased dependence on food imports increases vulnerability to food safety hazards in the region. The risk is greater for food importers who must balance the trade-offs of food security and the high cost of stringent regulations for food safety.

As the decade unfolds, the traditional Latin American production system of small farmers geared to the domestic market is being replaced by networks of large agri-business geared to export sectors (Spoor 2000). On the other hand, the liberalization of exchange rates and trade coupled with investment incentives brought a large inflow of foreign investment that favored large export-oriented agri-food industries. For example, US foreign direct investments in the food-processing industries in NAFTA and MERCOSUR free trade areas was 37 per cent of its total global investment of $32 billion in 1995 (Bolling et al. 1998). Furthermore, productivity in the agri-food industries improved to the point that some sectors, such as sorghum, in the Southern Cone countries of Brazil and Argentina, are among the world's leading food-producing nations (Spoor 2000). The transformation of the agricultural sector is most impressive in early reformers where agricultural exports grew 18 per cent in Argentina, 11.5 per cent in Chile and 12.5 per cent in Mexico in the 1990–98 period (Quiroz 2000).

Food Security Groups

The different food security and agricultural sector strategies in Latin America suggest different national food security situations. It is argued here that the food safety approach may depend on the type and similarities of the food security situation in each country. In this regard, analysis of heterogeneity of food security situations in the world suggest the existence of 11 clusters or profiles ranging from very food insecure to food secure. The Latin American countries are represented in six of the clusters described in Table 7.2.

The first cluster of Latin American countries represents the most food insecure countries in the region, and the second lowest level of food security in the world. Haiti is in a group by itself and is one of the poorest nations in the world. The second group includes Cuba, the Dominican Republic, Peru, El Salvador and Nicaragua (FAO 2002b). These countries use close to 20 per cent of their total export earnings for food imports. The Latin American countries in this group are a mix of rural and urban populations.

Table 7.2 Food security clusters

Global food security cluster	Latin American countries		Global averages					Western Hemisphere averages	
	Net food importers	Net food exporters	Calories per capita	Proteins per capita (grams)	Food production per capita ($)	Food imports as % of exports	Urban population %	Calories per capita (grams)	Urban population
1	Haiti		1989	48	82	20	23	1930	34
2	Cuba, the Dominican Republic, Honduras, Peru	El Salvador, Nicaragua	2229	59	118	19	71	2230	58
3		Bolivia, Guatemala,	2244	53	120	7	41	2270	50
4		Grenada, St Kitts and Nevis, Saint Vincent, Grenadines	2581	71	157	21	39	2676	n.a.
5	Jamaica, Trinidad and	Brazil, Colombia, Costa Rica,	2602	66	210	9	75	2664	67

Table 7.2 (continued)

Global food security cluster	Latin American countries		Global averages					Western Hemisphere averages	
	Net food importers	Net food exporters	Calories per capita	Proteins per capita (grams)	Food production per capita ($)	Food imports as % of exports	Urban population %	Calories per capita (grams)	Urban population
	Tobago, Venezuela	Ecuador, Paraguay						.	
6		Antigua	2673	73	124	5	41	2396	n.a.
7	Barbados	Bahamas, Dominica, Mexico	2976	83	135	11	82	2719	74
8		Chile, Panama	2828	78	233	4	83	2860	85
10		United States	3272	98	304	3	93	3800	77
11		Argentina, Canada, Uruguay	3303	103	521	6	93	3037	94

Source: adapted from Díaz-Bonilla et al. (2002a).

Since food insecurity in urban and rural settings may lead to different policies, food safety standards in this group will be different (Garret and Ruel 2000).

The third cluster of food insecurity includes the Latin American countries of Bolivia and Guatemala. In contrast to the first cluster, they only use 7 per cent of export revenues on food imports. This group of countries is characterized as food consumption vulnerable but food import neutral (Díaz- Bonilla et al. 2002b). Guatemala is mostly rural and therefore faces a different situation than Bolivia which has a large urban population. In many cases, food imports can be expanded to increase food security. However, the ability to increase food export revenue is limited since these countries do not have export-led agri-business and agri-food industry strategies.

The fourth cluster group consists of small Caribbean countries. Since these Caribbean economies are primarily dependent on tourism, their food security and food safety is tied to flows of people attracted to these popular Caribbean destinations. In contrast, the fifth food security cluster is the largest in terms of countries and total population. This cluster comprises a large and diverse group of Latin American countries, and includes Brazil, Colombia, Costa Rica, Ecuador and Paraguay. This group is characterized by higher calorie and protein intake per capita than previous groups. However, most of these countries are net food exporters, and have large agri-business and agri-food industry sectors. Therefore, this group is food secure and food trade neutral (Díaz-Bonilla et al. 2002b).

III FOOD SECURITY AND REGIONAL TRADE INTEGRATION

Regional Trade and Market Integration

For the past 15 years, Latin America has embarked on an intense process of economic and trade liberalization and market integration.[3] Embracing a doctrine defined as the 'new regionalism', Latin America has been described as a 'spaghetti bowl' of trade agreements (Devlin and Estevadeordal 2001). Consequently, more than 30 major bilateral, regional and multilateral trade agreements coexist with the major WTO trade liberalization efforts (IDB 2003). The major regional trade and economic integration groups in the Western Hemisphere are as follows; the North American Free Trade Agreement (NAFTA), the Southern Cone Common Market (MERCOSUR), the Andean Community (ANCOM), the Caribbean Community (CARICOM) and the Central American Common Market (CACM).

Since 1994, the region has been negotiating a Free Trade Area of the Americas (FTAA) with the hope of achieving consensus by 2005 (OAS 2002). During this period, intra-regional growth in the Western Hemisphere (8.5 per cent) was three times the rate of growth of extra-regional trade (2.6 per cent) (IDB 2002). Latin American exports, excluding the US and Canada, almost tripled from \$135 billion in 1991 to \$318 billion in 2001. This represents a growth rate of 9 per cent per year. For the Latin American countries, both intra- and extra-regional exports grew at the same rate of 9 per cent per year.[4]

By the end of the decade, trade liberalization brought changes in food-processing and retail industries when food imports were placed on the shelves of expanding supermarket retail chains (WHO 1999). During this period, global food retailers entered the region with force in Latin American markets such as Argentina, Brazil and Chile. Eventually, national food retailers consolidated through cross-border mergers and acquisitions, and expanded into local markets. In turn, food safety risks increased in the region. For example, the fish industry in Peru suffered \$700 million losses during an outbreak of cholera in 1991. The cholera crisis in Peru also affected its tourism industry since many visitors feared that the Peruvian regulatory authorities could not guarantee public health and consumer safety.[5]

Regional Agricultural Trade Integration and Market Liberalization

World agricultural exports were estimated to be \$547 billion in 2001, and accounted for approximately 9 per cent of world merchandise trade (FAO 2002a). Agricultural trade is very important in the Western Hemisphere region, which includes the United States and Canada, and accounted for \$166.5 billion or about 30 per cent of total global exports. At the start of the decade, Latin American exports totaled \$62.7 billion in 2001, and represented 11 per cent of the world's agricultural exports (see Table 7.3). The major markets for Latin American agricultural exports are North America (US and Canada), the European Union and within Latin America. In fact, increasing trade integration in the region may explain the growing share of Latin American exports to the US and within Latin America (Jerardo 2002). As Table 7.4 shows, the combined share of Latin American exports to the US and within Latin America rose to 44.4 per cent in 2001 from 37.3 per cent in 1990.Therefore, agricultural trade in Latin America grew at an annual rate of 8 per cent per year.

As argued before, the approach to food safety policy depends on the food security situation of the country, and whether the country is a net food exporter or importer. However, regional trade integration is also a major factor in food safety standard harmonization due to common market

Table 7.3 Latin American agricultural exports to the world ($ billion)

Group	To the world	North America	Latin America	Western Europe	Central Europe/CIS	Africa	Middle East	Asia
Raw materials	7.59	2.53	0.95	2.13	0.04	0.06	0.06	1.79
Food	55.12	14.55	9.82	15.58	2.17	2.15	2.76	7.84
Total	62.71	17.08	10.78	17.71	2.21	2.21	2.82	9.63

Source: UNCTAD.

Table 7.4 Structure of Latin American agricultural exports, 1990–2001 (percentage)

Region	1990	2001	Average annual growth 1990–2001
World	100.0	100.0	4
Western Europe	33.5	28.2	3
North America	26.0	27.2	5
Latin America	11.3	17.2	8
Asia	10.1	15.4	8
Middle East	3.1	4.5	8
Africa	2.5	3.5	7
Central Europe/CIS	13.2	3.5	−8

Note: Totals do not add up to 100 per cent due to regions omitted from the list or rounding up errors.

Source: WTO (2002).

regulations, tariffs and non-tariff barriers. Table 7.5 shows the agricultural trade balances by country and sub-regional trade groups. A trade group surplus or deficit in agricultural trade may influence the group's position regarding food safety.

The MERCOSUR group surpasses NAFTA with an $18.9 billion surplus against $16.2 billion for the latter. All members of MERCOSUR reached a trade surplus whereas Mexico runs an agricultural deficit in NAFTA. The Andean Common Market also managed to run a surplus in agricultural goods mostly because of good performances by Colombia, Ecuador and Bolivia. Chile, which is only an associate member of MERCOSUR, also had an agricultural trade surplus. On the other hand, the CARICOM nations were net agricultural importers in 2000.

Table 7.5 Agricultural trade balances by country and regional group, 2000

Trade integration group	Country	Agricultural trade balance ($ million)
NAFTA	Canada	4 142
	Mexico	−2 101
	United States	14 237
MERCOSUR	Argentina	9 494
	Brazil	8 050
	Paraguay	302
	Uruguay	579
ANCOM	Bolivia	169
	Colombia	1 441
	Ecuador	1 117
	Peru	−258
	Venezuela	−1 309
CACM	Costa Rica	1 241
	Guatemala	919
	Honduras	98
	Nicaragua	141
	El Salvador	−90
CARICOM	Antigua and Barbuda	−73
	Bahamas	−615
	Barbados	−94
	Dominica	−8
	Grenada	−19
	Jamaica	−133
	St Lucia	−43
	St Kitts and Nevis	−27
	St Vincent	−4
Others	Chile	1 567
	Dominican Republic	−327
	Panama	−67
	Haiti	

Source: Inter-American Development Bank (2003).

Regional trade integration may have different impacts on food security. For example, as a group, CACM countries expanded export growth at the high levels of 11 per cent per year. Intra-CACM exports have been growing at a faster rate than extra-regional trade. Except for El Salvador, all of the countries run a surplus in agricultural trade. As a regional trading group, the CACM wants to meet the food safety standards imposed by their main agricultural export markets.

In contrast to the CACM group, CARICOM countries have not been as successful in creating large volumes of intra-regional trade. The extra-CARICOM trade has not been phenomenal either, and all CARICOM member countries have agricultural trade deficits. Furthermore, certain CARICOM countries such as Grenada, Saint Kitts and Nevis, Saint Vincent and Grenadines, use as much as 21 per cent of their export revenues on food imports. However, the CARICOM countries, do not face the same level of malnutrition as some of the CACM countries.

As illustrated by the two examples above, WTO trade liberalization increased Western Hemisphere agricultural trade with the world. However, intra-regional food trade integration has been minimal. In this respect, analysis of the destination of food trade of selected key countries reveals that trade patterns are relatively stable, and are mostly aligned with extra-regional trade markets. (See Tables 7.6 and 7.7.) For example, the share of Argentina's exports to different trade groups does not vary much during this period. In terms of trade, Argentina's key markets for food exports are the European Union followed by the MERCOSUR regional trading group. In contrast, the NAFTA region only accounts for about 3 per cent of Argentine food exports, while MERCOSUR is the principal source of food imports followed by the European Union.

In light of these trends, food safety standards harmonization by Argentina with the rest of the world should take place in the context of further regional trade and market integration with MERCOSUR, and the implementation of MERCOSUR's free trade agreement with the European Union. In the case of Brazil, which has a greater share of its food exports going to Europe, and most of its food imports coming from MERCOSUR countries, food safety standards harmonization is driven by trade relations with the European Union.

On the other hand, NAFTA is a major destination of food exports and source of food imports. More than a quarter of Mexico's food exports and imports take place within NAFTA, with the United States market being the main destination and source of regional food trade. During the period between 1994 and 2000, Mexico's total food exports and imports to and from the United States continued to grow in absolute terms. Therefore, there is no other country or region that rivals the strong trade relationship of these two NAFTA member countries.

In the case of Chile, which is not a member of any given group but is characterized by entering into bilateral agreements with many other countries, there are clear benefits from an open trade strategy. Food exports in Chile have increased from $8.2 billion in 1994 to $11.1 billion in 2000. Although the largest share of Chilean exports are to the United States, the country has been able to diversify its trade with other export markets. On the other hand,

Table 7.6 Agricultural exports of key Latin American countries by regional group, 1994–2000

Country	Year	Total	% of total exports					
			NAFTA	MERCOSUR	Ancom	CACM	European Union	Others
Argentina	1994	13 697	3	11	2	0	16	68
	1998	22 699	0	11	2	0	12	75
	2000	20 643	17	3	10	2	0	68
Brazil	1994	9 205	20	5	0	0	48	27
	1998	10 358	12	6	1	1	42	38
	2000	9 227	12	2	3	0	43	40
Chile	1994	8 272	11	3	2	0	7	77
	1998	11 518	11	3	3	0	6	77
	2000	11 103	12	2	3	0	6	77
Mexico	1994	14 112	23	0	0	0	1	76
	1998	21 516	23	0	0	0	2	75
	2000	23 768	23	0	0	0	1	76
Peru	1994	1 346	20	0	4	0	31	45
	1998	1 201	27	0	6	0	36	31
	2000	1 635	17	0	4	0	30	49

Table 7.7 Agricultural imports of key Latin American countries by regional group, 1994–2000

Country	Year	Total	% of total imports					
			NAFTA	MERCOSUR	Ancom	CACM	European Union	Others
Argentina	1994	2 820	3	15	3	0	6	73
	1998	3 577	3	16	3	0	5	73
	2000	3 110	3	16	4	0	4	73
Brazil	1994	9 199	5	20	0	0	4	71
	1998	13 540	3	23	0	0	3	71
	2000	9 203	2	24	0	0	3	71
Chile	1994	1 935	8	15	4	0	2	71
	1998	3 062	7	17	3	0	2	71
	2000	3 331	5	19	3	0	2	71
Mexico	1994	17 828	22	0	0	0	2	76
	1998	19 673	23	0	0	0	1	76
	2000	24 537	22	0	0	0	2	76
Peru	1994	843	28	25	11	3	9	24
	1998	980	36	23	11	5	6	19
	2000	741	35	31	9	0	5	20

the principal source of food imports for Chile is MERCOSUR. Therefore Chile's position on food safety is largely influenced by MERCOSUR on the import side and NAFTA on the export side.

The case of Peru is important since this country is a net food importer and has high vulnerability in food security. As Table 7.5 shows, Peru is a net food exporter. Peru's main food export markets are the European Union and the United States. However, Peru's export shares to these two important markets are not as stable as the other Latin American markets. For example, in the period 1994–2000, Peru's food exports to these two important markets fluctuated widely. On the other hand, Peru's main sources of food imports, MERCOSUR and the United States, are constant and very stable, while food trade with ANCOM is very low. Consequently, for Peru, the important forum to discuss food safety standards harmonization is not ANCOM, but the United States, Europe and MERCOSUR.

IV GOVERNANCE OF FOOD SAFETY IN THE WESTERN HEMISPHERE AGRI-FOOD INDUSTRIES

Sub-Regional Trade Groups and the Regulation of Food Safety

NAFTA

The NAFTA agreement requires implementation of the WTO SPS standards to regulate food safety in North American agri-food trade. However, special NAFTA provisions have insulated certain agricultural sectors from the challenges of free trade (Burfisher et al. 1998). In support of the creation of a North American food system, the NAFTA SPS committee established working groups for the implementation of the Codex Alimentarius standards in the region. At a subsequent meeting in 1998, the NAFTA member countries signed a regulatory cooperation agreement on food safety.[6] The progress of NAFTA on the coordination of common food safety standards for agri-food industries, is one of the most comprehensive in the Western Hemisphere.

Andean Community

In light of the importance of agriculture for the socio-economic development and global market integration of Andean Community member countries, the presidents of the region met in November 1990 to discuss the launch of an Andean Common Agricultural Policy. The goals of this Common Agricultural Policy are as follows: to increase the competitiveness of the Andean Community (ANCOM) countries in regional and global agri-food markets, the development of common policy positions in international forums, the harmonization of export policies, creation of a regional free trade zone and strengthening of consumer safety and public health in the region.[7] To achieve these goals, the Andean Community must harmonize trade policy and consumer safety, public health and plant health regulations in accordance with the WTO SPS agreement.[8]

MERCOSUR

In terms of food safety standards and regulations in the MERCOSUR region, COSAVE serves as the regional technical standards organization for the regional trade group. For example, COSAVE developed pest risk analysis, quarantine protocols and phytosanitary standards for the production, processing and marketing of agricultural products. In this context, COSAVE provides certification of biotechnologies used to produce food crops, and regulatory guidelines for the use of pesticides in the MERCOSUR region.[9] Moreover, the phytosanitary standards issued by COSAVE are used to harmonize plant protection measures, operating procedures and agri-food industry standards in the MERCOSUR region.[10]

CARICOM

The CARICOM nations are harmonizing regulations for consumer safety, public health, animal and plant health, and food safety in Caribbean agri-food industries.[11] In response to the BSE threat to the Caribbean food system, tourism and agri-food industries, regional animal livestock surveillance and meat inspection measures were implemented.[12] Furthermore, a CARICOM Agricultural Health and Food Safety Agency (CAHFSA) was created to reform regulations and mandatory industry standards for the certification of agri-food products and commodities.

Chile–United States Free Trade Agreement

Chapter six of the Chile–US Free Trade Agreement includes provisions to protect human, animal and plant health, and provides a forum to address sanitary and phytosanitary issues that may affect bilateral agricultural trade. The chapter reaffirms the rights and obligations of the WTO SPS Agreement, and calls for the establishment of a committee. The goals of this chapter are as follows: to enhance mutual understating of SPS measures and regulatory processes, provide a framework for consultation on matters related to the application of food safety measures, coordinate common positions in international organizations, creation of a regional framework for cooperation programs and the establishment of ad hoc working groups (USTR 2003).

V REGIONAL FOOD SAFETY CAPACITY-BUILDING PAHO/WHO, FAO AND CODEX ALIMENTARIUS

Governance of Food Safety in the Western Hemisphere: The Role of PAHO/WHO

At the regional level, the main food safety organization for the Western Hemisphere is the Pan American Health Organization/World Health Organization (PAHO/WHO). As a multilateral institution, and the regional office of WHO, PAHO was created in 1902 to respond to animal health crises and food trade disruption in the Western Hemisphere. Within PAHO/WHO, food safety and animal health are the primary responsibilities of the Veterinary Public Health Unit. The PAHO/WHO unit serves as the lead agency for the food safety and animal health activities and programs in the region.[13]

The regional food safety activities of PAHO/WHO are carried out with the support of PANAFTOSA in Brazil, INPPAZ in Argentina, and a network of advisors in the member states. In addition, the regional food safety and veterinary public health programs of PAHO/WHO are implemented through the following advisory bodies and collaborating centers in the Western Hemisphere;

- Inter-American Meeting, at the Ministerial Level, of Health and Agriculture (RIMSA)
- Hemispheric Committee for the Eradication of Foot-and-Mouth Disease (COHEFA)
- Pan American Commission for Food Safety (COPAIA)
- South American Commission for the Control of Foot-and-Mouth Disease (COSALFA)
- Pan American Foot-and-Mouth Disease Center (PANAFTOSA).

Through the strong and proactive leadership of PAHO/WHO, regulatory cooperation between ministries of health and agriculture, and food safety standards harmonization is achieved. In many cases, PAHO/WHO works through strategic partnerships with FAO, OIE, the Inter-American Institute for Cooperation on Agriculture (IICA), non-governmental organizations (NGOs), universities, research institutes, associations of livestock breeders, food producers and consumers (Berrios 2003). In the region, PAHO/WHO provides leadership in the following food safety activities:

- mobilization of member nations for the production and consumption of safe foods

- strengthening of food safety regulations and policies
- creation of national food safety programs
- setting of national and regional food safety standards
- harmonization of regulations and legislation
- professional and human resource training in Good Manufacturing Practices (GMP), HACCP methodologies and process inspection programs, information dissemination and provision of direct technical assistance
- eradication of Foot-and-Mouth disease in South America through surveillance, control, and vaccination of cattle in some regions of the Western Hemisphere
- creation of local animal health committees to improve sanitary conditions, and increase livestock production in rural communities
- risk identification, risk assessment, risk communication and risk management for the prevention and control of new and recurring animal diseases such as BSE and Foot-and-Mouth disease.[14]

In preparation for the FTAA, regulatory harmonization with Codex food safety standards is under way in Latin American and Caribbean nations. In order to achieve regional harmonization with the Joint FAO/WHO Food Standards Programme, PAHO/WHO collaborated with the Regional Committee of Codex Alimentarius, the USDA and FDA to strengthen the work of National Codex Committees.[15] In this context, the Memorandum of Understanding (MOU) between PAHO/WHO and USDA that was signed in 2004 represents a new phase of regional regulatory harmonization. In this agreement, foods safety standards harmonization for the protection of regional food systems, animal livestock and agri-food industries are the goals for the Americas.[16] Furthermore, the governments agree to cooperate on the development of regional animal, health, food safety and biosecurity capacity.[17] To achieve these regulatory harmonization goals, the MOU increases the exchange of scientists and government food safety officials, and mobilizes resources for capacity-building in the Western Hemisphere.[18]

Regulatory Harmonization, Policy Cooperation and Food Safety Capacity-Building in the Western Hemisphere: The Central Role of PAHO/WHO

The Inter-American Meeting, at the Ministerial Level, of Health and Agriculture (RIMSA)

The first framework for regional food safety cooperation is the Inter-American Meeting, at the Ministerial Level, of Health and Agriculture (RIMSA). The high-level food policy forum of senior public health, agricultural regulators and government officials was launched in 1968. The high-level RIMSA meetings are held every two years, and serve as the formal food safety standards harmonization mechanism for PAHO/WHO member countries (PAHO 2001a). In the 1980s, Western Hemisphere governments convened the first Inter-American Conference on Food Protection. The main outcome of this meeting was consensus on food industry standards for the region, and the Regional Program for Food Protection 1986–90.[19] The five-year plan developed by PAHO/WHO initiated the process of regulatory harmonization and industry standards convergence in accordance with the WTO SPS Agreement and Codex Alimentarius.[20]

The Pan American Institute for Food Protection and Zoonoses (INPPAZ)
By the start of this decade, some countries in the region had adequate laboratory and food-testing facilities. However, many countries lacked the resources to invest in state-of-the-art technologies or the ability to update their national food safety laboratory facilities. Consequently, food safety in the Americas was strengthened by the creation of the Inter-American Network of Food Analysis Laboratories (INFAL). Since its creation in 1997, INFAL supports 39 laboratories in 19 countries in the Western Hemisphere, harmonization of food analysis methodologies, and promotes acceptable frameworks for the certification of agri-food product equivalence. INFAL also works on the development of mutual recognition agreements for regional and global markets.[21] In the region, the Latin American Network for the Epidemiological Surveillance of Food Bourne Disease established the following regional centers in the late 1990s: the Pan American Institute for Food Protection and Zoonoses (INPPAZ), United Food and Drug Laboratory (LUCAM) and Caribbean Network of Laboratories for the Quality Control of Food.[22]

In response to the growing threat of food safety hazards and the important role of international food trade for the economic growth of countries in the Western Hemisphere, the Pan American Institute for Food Protection and Zoonoses was created in 1991 to replace the Pan American Zoonoses Center (CEPANZO). In its role as a major part of the Veterinary Public Health Unit of PAHO/WHO, INPPAZ was responsible for the regional development and harmonization of food safety and food surveillance programs.[23]

At the present time, the food safety capacity of the region is strengthened through the creation of a regional information system for epidemiological surveillance (SIRVEDA). This information system is now available for food safety regulators and governments in the Americas. The SIRVEDA system was so successful that it was adopted as a model for 47

European and Asian countries. In addition, a computerized food legislation system (BIREME) now provides access to information on food safety regulations and policies across the Western Hemisphere.[24] Through PAHO/WHO support of BIREME, the food safety regulations and policies of Bolivia, Argentina, Brazil, Chile, Colombia, Guatemala, Paraguay, Peru, Uruguay, Mexico, ANCOM and MERCOSUR are now available on-line. Currently, Panama and other countries are being added to the BIREME system.[25]

Finally, INPPAZ participated in a Codex Committee Meeting on General Principles, and represented the interests of the Americas on food traceability, risk analysis, and modification of the Code of Ethics for global food trade. The Pan American Institute for Food Protection and Zoonoses also initiated forums on food additives and pesticides, the Codex Commission, the Committee on Imports and Exports, and the Committee on Food Hygiene. In this context, regional positions are developed for the Codex Coordinating Committee for Latin America and the Caribbean, and the food standards harmonization work of the Codex Alimentarius Commission.[26]

The Pan American Foot-and-Mouth Disease Center (PANAFTOSA)

In the Americas, the Pan American Foot-and-Mouth Disease Center (PANAFTOSA) was created in 1950. The center is part of a larger project of the Organization of American States (OAS) to prevent Foot-and-Mouth disease.[27] In 1968, PANAFTOSA became a major and permanent part of the Veterinary Public Health Unit of PAHO/WHO, and is now recognized by the OIE and FAO as the reference center for vesicular animal diseases in the Americas.[28] The official mission of PANAFTOSA is to provide technical cooperation for the prevention, control and eradication of Foot-and-Mouth disease.[29]

The center also works to protect the disease-free status of Argentina, Brazil, Colombia, Chile, Paraguay and Uruguay.[30] In this regard, PANAFTOSA is implementing regional projects and goals to eradicate Foot-and-Mouth disease in South America.[31] In order to eradicate Foot-and-Mouth disease in the Western Hemisphere, a high-level conference was convened in March 2004. As the decade unfolds PAHO/WHO in cooperation with FAO, OIE and IICA are rapidly moving to eradicate Foot-and-Mouth disease in the Americas by 2007.

The Pan American Commission for Food Safety (COPAIA)

The Pan American Commission for Food Safety was created in the late 1990s.[32] By 2000, high-level meetings were held between officials of the Government of the United States, FDA, USDA, the Government of Brazil, the Secretary of Agriculture of the State of Sao Paulo, Brazil and PAHO/WHO, to discuss the launch of COPAIA. During these meetings the US and Brazilian governments, regulatory authorities and PAHO/WHO agreed that COPAIA now serves as a formal institutional mechanism for regional food safety policy cooperation. In 2001, during the RIMSA XII meeting in Sao Paolo, Brazil, COPAIA was formally launched.

As the decade unfolds, COPAIA is emerging as the regional institutional mechanism for the following food safety policy measures: regulatory harmonization, food safety cooperation, governance of food production chains and agri-food industries, inter-sectoral coordination, the strengthening of laboratories and implementation of Codex Alimentarius principles of risk assessment and risk management.[33] In this context, COPAIA is mandated to serve as an advisory body of RIMSA, and promotes food safety programs of the Codex Alimentarius Coordinating Committee for Latin America and the Caribbean, the Inter-American Development Bank, the World Bank, FAO, the FDA, IICA, RIOPPAH, USAID and USDA. Finally, COPAIA is responsible for coordination of regional food safety standards in regional trade and market integration blocs such as NAFTA, CARICOM, CAFTA, the Andean Community and MERCOSUR.

Regional Risk Assessment and Risk Management Infrastructure

HACCP

The strengthening of national and regional inspection capability is now a priority for PAHO/WHO. In this regard, the use of HACCP inspection programs for the detection of food hazards in agri-food industries is growing in the region. At the start of the decade, extensive food inspection, management compliance and industry training programs were implemented across the region. Since that time, PAHO/WHO-sponsored HACCP training programs were attended by over 120 food safety officials and industry inspectors in the region. In these training programs for red meat, chicken and seafood industries, HACCP methodologies and guidelines were discussed.

In response to the growing demand for in-country training programs, a collaboration with the International HACCP Alliance and the HACCP Seafood Alliance was organized by the Veterinary Public Health Program of PAHO/WHO. Through this cooperation, the Second Pan American Meeting of National Services and Institutions for the Inspection and Quality Control of Seafood Products was sponsored by INPPAZ in cooperation with FAO and INFOPESCA.[34] The development of regional training programs, infrastructure, guidelines for the adoption of Good Manufacturing Practices (GMP), standard procedures for the cleaning and disinfection of food, and HACCP process control programs are increasingly mandated for the inspection of agri-food industries in the Americas.[35]

In response to rapid globalization, regional free trade and market integration in the Western Hemisphere, the INPPAZ Center for Food Safety was reorganized in 2005.[36] The goals of the reorganization are as follows: to decentralize regional capacity building, strengthen National Centers of Excellence and networks for food safety and to increase technical cooperation across the entire food chain. Therefore, National Centers of Excellence in food safety are being created to strengthen member country capacity to implement food safety policies, programs and projects.[37] In this context, regional food safety policies, programs and projects will be strengthened by the continued support of the following regional and global WHO networks:

- WHO Global Salm-Surv (GSS): A Global Salmonella Surveillance Network
- Latin American Molecular Subtyping Network for Foodborne Disease (PulseNet)
- Codex Commitee for Latin America and the Caribbean (CCLAC)
- Inter-American Network on Food Analysis Laboratories (INFAL)
- Pan-American Network of Fish Inspection and Quality Control
- Regional Surveillance System for Foodborne Diseases
- Modern Food Inspection and Quality Control Systems
- International Food Safety Authorities Network (INFOSAN).[38]

In the strategic reorganization of INPPAZ, a technical food safety team will be established in the PANAFTOSA Center in Rio de Janeiro, Brazil. In turn, regional networks of food safety and animal health regulators will be supported from PANAFTOSA in Brazil, under the control of the Veterinary Public Health Unit in PAHO/WHO. Ultimately, the reorganization of INPPAZ will increase the effectiveness, efficiency and integration of training, risk analysis, epidemiological surveillance, laboratory quality assurance, and the monitoring of food safety across food production chains.[39]

VI VETERINARY PUBLIC HEALTH AND FOOD SAFETY IN THE WESTERN HEMISPHERE

Beef and Cattle Industries: BSE Risk Management and Food Safety Regulation

In the Western Hemisphere, beef and cattle industries are very important for the economies of the North American (NAFTA) and South American

(MERCOSUR) countries. According to FAO, South America accounted for approximately 20 per cent of the entire global cattle population, and an estimated 15 per cent of global beef exports at the start of the decade.[40] At the present time, Latin American countries such as Argentina, Brazil, Uruguay and Paraguay are world beef exporters, while the English-speaking Caribbean region is a net importer of beef. Therefore, PAHO/WHO works to protect food safety and animal livestock health in regional beef and cattle industries.

The first veterinary public health measures and food safety policies to prevent the spread of BSE in Latin America were adopted in 1989.[41] From 1988 to 2001, Argentina, Brazil, Chile, Colombia, Paraguay and Uruguay implemented the following food safety regulations and BSE control measures: animal and genetic material import bans, ruminant material feed bans, meat and bone meal import ban, and epidemiological and laboratory surveillance.[42] During this period, governments in the region worked in cooperation with PAHO/WHO, FAO and OIE to introduce scientific infrastructure, harmonize BSE surveillance measures and strengthen meat-processing industry regulations.[43] In light of the potential collapse of beef and cattle industries in the Western Hemisphere, PAHO/WHO convened a meeting of health and agriculture ministers and BSE experts in Uruguay in 2001. As a result of this meeting, PAHO/WHO in cooperation with FAO, OIE and governments in the Americas are implementing the measures to prevent BSE.[44]

VII GOVERNANCE OF BIOTECHNOLOGY AND THE SAFETY OF GM FOODS IN THE AMERICAS

Biotechnology and GM Food Safety Regulation

As the decade unfolds, governments, farmers and agri-food industries in the Western Hemisphere are evaluating the use of genetically modified foods to increase food security, agricultural productivity and competitiveness in global markets. However, consumers in Latin America and the Caribbean mistrust biotechnology and question the safety of GM foods. Consequently, growing public resistance to GM food is resulting in delayed adoption of beneficial biotechnology innovations in Latin American and Caribbean agri-food industries. In response to this growing food safety issue, PAHO/WHO, FAO and PANAFTOSA convened a meeting in February 2004 to discuss the production and regulation of GM food.[45] The following food safety capacity-building measures are needed in the Western hemisphere:

- development of international and regional frameworks for risk assessment of genetically modified organisms (GMOs) used in food products
- evaluation of all new GM crops and food for health risks such as allergenicity, toxicity and the development of antibiotic resistance
- improvement in infrastructure and human resources for applied research and technology in developing countries in the Western Hemisphere.[46]

As the globalization of food industries accelerates, negative public perceptions and resistance to biotechnology and GM foods by consumers, farmers and governments in the region must be addressed (Paarlberg 2002). In this regard, more analysis of consumer preferences and attitudes in Latin America and the Caribbean is needed to gain public confidence in the safety of foods derived from biotechnology (Nugent 2003). Nevertheless, some Latin American food-producing countries are adopting biotechnology to strengthen their competitiveness in global agri-food industries. For example, Chile, one of the largest global suppliers of salmon, is considering the adoption of GM species that grow four times as fast as conventional salmon. Through the adoption of GM food production, Chile is also positioning itself in the global kiwi fruit, blueberry, organic food and seed industries.[47]

In a similar way, Argentina ended its moratorium on GM crops and animals in the late 1990s, and is now the world's second leading commercial GM food producer after the United States. In support of Argentina's GM crop production, scientific evaluation and regulation of biotechnology is carried out by the following regulatory agencies; the National Commission on Livestock Biotechnology (CONABIA), the Advisory Committee of SENASA, which controls human food and animal feeds, and the Office of the Director of Markets of the Secretariat of Agriculture, Livestock, Fishing and Foods which controls the sale and marketing of food. In keeping with international standards of Codex Alimentarius and OECD food safety regulatory authorities, the Government of Argentina carries out risk assessments of GM foods.[48]

The regulation of biotechnology in Brazil is carried out through the National Technical Commission of Biosafety, which is linked to the Ministry of Science and Technology. The regulatory responsibilities of the Commission are to carry out environmental risk assessment, animal and plant health, food safety risk assessment, and public health risk analysis. However, GMO safety is evaluated by the National Agency for Sanitary Surveillance (ANIVISA) to ensure that all food is safe for consumption with no risk to human health. In this regard, ANIVISA enforces the labeling and traceability regulation of GM food products, especially plants and GM crops.[49] As the decade unfolds, Brazil has a major stake in biotechnology. Therefore, the regulatory and food safety oversight of GM food by ANVISA is increasing.[50]

To summarize, countries in the Western Hemisphere are strengthening the regulation of GM crops, livestock and food production in accordance with Codex guidelines and expert scientific advice from the Joint FAO/WHO Food Standards Programme. In this regard, the Codex Coordinating Committee for Latin America and the Caribbean provides the framework for regional food safety standards and the regulation of biotechnology. In the Codex Regional Committee, Latin American and Caribbean governments are developing traceability and product segregation regulations in the emerging risk management strategy for GM food and biotechnology.[51]

VIII CONCLUSIONS: FUTURE REGULATORY HARMONIZATION SCENARIOS IN THE WESTERN HEMISPHERE

In conclusion, the Western Hemisphere is far from homogenous in any aspect of food security and food safety regulation. Given this level of heterogeneity, is regulatory harmonization and food safety standards convergence possible? The review of the major determinants of food safety standards harmonization suggest that Western Hemisphere countries range from high levels of food insecurity and food supply vulnerability, to high levels of food security and affordability.

In the case of free trade areas such as NAFTA, MERCOSUR, CARICOM and the Andean Community, regional trade integration has not had a major impact on agricultural trade patterns. The shares of the main markets for Latin American agricultural exports, that is, Western Europe and the United States, remain relatively stable over time. However, significant progress in the implementation of food safety standards and regulations, and animal livestock health standards, have been achieved at the regional and sub-regional trade group levels.

The growing success and progress in food safety standards and regulatory harmonization in the Western Hemisphere are due to the noble and outstanding efforts of PAHO/WHO and the Codex Coordinating Committee for Latin America and the Caribbean, which are noted in this chapter. At the sub-regional level, some trade groups have made considerable progress in harmonizing their food safety standards and have developed working committees to coordinate their efforts. In contrast, other sub-regional trading groups are not as developed due to varying levels of food safety regulatory infrastructure and food security policy priorities.

In this regard, efforts are currently under way to develop a regional framework for food safety regulation in the Western Hemisphere to support the creation of the FTAA. In light of the scale and scope of food trade and agri-food industry evolution in the region, PAHO/WHO and USDA signed a Memorandum of Understanding for food safety capacity-building in the Western Hemisphere. The goals of this historic agreement are to strengthen the protection of regional food systems, agri-food industries, animal and plant health and livestock from contamination.

Given this situation, what are the prospects for further regulatory harmonization of food safety standards in the Western Hemisphere? It can be argued that progress in the years ahead will depend on the food safety situation, the pressure to secure market access for net food exporters and the ability to secure affordable sources of food supply in the case of net food importers. The deterioration or progress on these three dimensions may accelerate or retard the rate and level of success in harmonizing national food safety standards. Ultimately, the regulatory policy approach and urgency to harmonize food safety will be different for countries that are more interested in having increased global food market access for their food exports than countries whose main goal is to provide affordable food to their citizens.

At the present time, a commonality of interests across sub-regional trade groups is emerging in correlation with the food security situation of countries in the Western Hemisphere. Therefore, regulatory harmonization within these groups may emerge first before full Western Hemisphere food safety standards convergence is achieved. One of these clusters is made up of food-insecure nations mostly in the Andean, Central America and Caribbean regions: Bolivia, Peru, Honduras, El Salvador, Nicaragua, Guatemala, Cuba and the Dominican Republic. The food safety concerns in this group relate to potential contamination from food imports, strict regulations for national food producers and the risks associated with food distribution to poor and rural populations. Risk assessment in this group may be taken in the context of food supply constraints and scarcities rather than food safety regulations for agri-food exporters.

At the other extreme, we have a group of countries that are mostly net food exporters from the NAFTA and MERCOSUR blocs plus Chile, Costa Rica, Colombia and Ecuador. This group of countries has well-developed agricultural sectors and secure food supplies. Agricultural producers in these countries increasingly harmonize food safety standards to meet the requirements of their export markets. Therefore, the countries in this group may be more interested in harmonizing global food safety standards and regulations that allow market access for their agricultural exports, rather than achieving sub-regional harmonization. To this end, adoption of WTO SPS and Codex Alimentarius standards drive harmonization at the regional level.

The third group consists of the CARICOM countries. This group is between the two other groups in all respects. Although these countries are food secure with adequate levels of dietary food intake, all of these countries show an agricultural trade deficit. With relatively small populations and land mass, these countries may be able to manage their food supply distribution efficiently. However, to afford food imports, these countries depend on tourism revenues.

Finally, the policy agendas and market interests of the three distinct groups of countries outlined above underscore the need for rapid progress in regulatory harmonization and food safety standards in regional and global forums such as FAO, WHO and Codex Alimentairus as well as OIE and IPPC. Ultimately, rapid mobilization of Latin American, Central American and Caribbean governments, farmers, agri-food industry interests and consumers is needed to accelerate the harmonization of regional food safety regulations through PAHO/WHO in accordance with Codex Alimentarius standards and WTO SPS Agreement requirements.

NOTES

* Acknowledgments: The author and editor would like to express their gratitude and thanks to Dr Albino J. Belotto, Chief-Veterinary Public Health Unit, and Dr Genaro Garcia, Manager Veterinary Public Health Unit, of the Pan American Health Organization/World Health Organization in Washington, DC, for their guidance in the preparation of this chapter.

1. WHO (1999), *Food Safety Report*, EB105/10, 2 December, Geneva: WHO.
2. USDA (2003a), *Global Food Security: Overview, Food Security Assessment*, Agriculture and Trade Report, No. GFA-14, Washington, DC: USDA.
3. Staut, J.V. and J. Ugaz-Pereda (1998), 'Western Hemisphere trading blocs and tariff barriers for United States agricultural exports', in Mary Burfischer and Elizabeth Jones (eds), *Regional Trade Agreements and United States Agriculture*, ERS/USDA, AER-771, Washington, DC: USDA.
4. Inter-American Development Bank (2002), *Integration and Trade in the Americas*, periodic note, December, Washington, DC: Inter-American Development Bank.
5. Ibid.
6. For a comprehensive treatment of the evolution of agricultural reforms in NAFTA, see Chapter 4 in this volume, 'Governance of food safety in the NAFTA region'.
7. Andean Community/Economic Policies/Agricultural Policy.
8. Andean Community/Technical Regulations.
9. Ibid.
10. Southern Cone/MERCOSUR Standards – COSAVE at www30.brinkster.com/cosave/stand_ing.htm.

11. Sabaroche, Hon. Herbert (2003), *Carribean Food Safety Initiative: Challenges in the English-Speaking Caribbean*, XIII Inter-American Meeting, at the Ministerial Level, on Health and Agriculture, RIMSA 13, Washington, DC: PAHO/WHO. CARICOM website: www.CARICOM.org/cvo-recommendations.htm.
12. Ibid.
13. Ibid.
14. PAHO/WHO (2001b), *Report of the PAHO Program on Veterinary Public Health on Compliance with the Strategic and Programmatic Orientations (SPO), 1999–2000*, XII Inter-American Meeting, at the Ministerial Level, on Health and Agriculture, RIMSA 12, Sao Paolo, Brazil, 2–4 May, Washington, DC: PAHO/WHO, pp. 6–7 and 10–15.
15. Ibid.
16. See PAHO press release (2004), 'PAHO and USDA sign agreement on food systems capacity building', Washington, DC, 24 June.
17. Ibid.
18. Ibid.
19. PAHO/WHO (2000), *Food Protection*, 126th Session of the Executive Committee, Washington, DC: PAHO/WHO.
20. Ibid.
21. Ibid.
22. Ibid.
23. PAHO/WHO (2003a), *Proposed Plan of Action for the Pan American Institute for Food Protection and Zoonoses (INPPAZ)*, XIII Inter-American Meeting, at the Ministerial Level, On Health and Agriculture, RIMSA 13/5, 17 March/24–25 April, Washington, DC: PAHO/WHO, pp. 7–11.
24. Ibid.
25. Ibid., pp. 8.
26. PAHO/WHO (2003a), pp. 11–12.
27. PANAFTOSA (2003), *Situation of Foot and Mouth Disease Eradication Programs – South America – 2002*, Rio de Janeiro: PANOFTOSA.
28. PAHO/WHO (2001a), *Proposed Action Plan for the Pan American Foot and Mouth Disease Center (PANAFTOSA) 2002–2003*, XII Inter-American Meeting, at the Ministerial Level on Health and Agriculture, RIMSA 12/5, 12 March, Sao Paolo, Brazil, 2–4 May, Washington, DC: PAHO/WHO, p. 3.
29. Ibid. Also see PAHO/WHO (1999), *Pan American Foot and Mouth Disease Center PANAFTOSA*, XI Inter-American Meeting at the Ministerial Level, on Animal Health, RIMSA 11/6, 19 March/13–15 April, Washington, DC: PAHO/WHO, pp. 3–6.
30. Ibid., pp. 8–10.
31. Ibid., p. 7.
32. COPAIA was created from a proposal presented by Dr Joao Carlos de Souza Meirelles, Secretary of Agriculture, State of Sao Paolo, Brazil, and approved by Ministers of Health and Agriculture at the Inter-American Meeting, at the Ministerial Level, on Health and Agriculture (RIMSA XII) in 2001. See PAHO/WHO (2001a), *Proposed Regulation of the Pan American Commission of Food Safety (COPAIA)*, XII Inter-American Meeting, at the Ministerial Level, on Health and Agriculture, 2–4 May, Sao Paolo, Brazil, Washington, DC: PAHO/WHO.
33. PAHO/WHO press release (2001), 'New pan American food safety commission starts work', Buenos Aires, 31 July.
34. PAHO/WHO (2001a), pp. 9–10.
35. PAHO/WHO (2005b), *Proposed PAHO/WHO Plan of Action for Technical Cooperation in Food Safety 2006–2007*, XIV Inter-American Meeting, at the Ministerial Level, on Health and Agriculture, RIMSA 14, Mexico City, 21–22 April, Washington, DC: PAHO/WHO.
36. PAHO/WHO (2005a), *46th Directing Council Strategy for the Future of the Pan American Centers – Current Status of the Center*, Washington, DC: PAHO/WHO, p. 19.
37. Ibid., pp. 20–21.

38. Ibid., pp. 18–19.
39. Ibid., pp. 19–21.
40. Van Gelderen, C., E.J. Gimeno and A.A. Schudel (2003), 'Bovine spongiform encephalopathy in South America: a regional preventive approach', *Review of Science and Technology*, **22** (1): 227–36. The origin of the beef and cattle industry in Latin American can be traced back to the early settlement of the region in the sixteenth century. During this period, cattle and sheep were first introduced to the region by Spanish colonists, and rapidly emerged as a very lucrative agri-food industry sector. By the twentieth century, many South American cattle breeds were introduced from Europe, and eventually, North America.
41. Ibid.
42. Van Gelderen et al., pp. 229–33.
43. PAHO/WHO (2001d), *Report of the PAHO/WHO Consultation on Bovine Spongiform Encephalopathy BSE – Scientific Bases for Policy Decisions in the Americas*, Montevideo, 9–11 April, Washington, DC: PAHO/WHO, pp. 52–80.
44. PAHO/WHO (2001d), http:/www.paho.org/english/ad/dpc/vp/alimentos.htm.
45. PAHO/WHO food safety website.
46. Ibid.
47. Ibid.
48. PAHO/WHO (2003b), *Report on the Regional Meeting on Genetically Modified Foods*, XIII Inter-American Meeting, at the Ministerial Level, on Health and Agriculture, RIMSA 13, 24–25 April, Washington, DC: PAHO/WHO, pp. 223–42.
49. Ibid., pp. 233–42.
50. Ibid., p. 237.
51. Ibid., pp. 223–42.

REFERENCES

Andean Community (Ancom), Agricultural Policy: http://www.comunidadandina.org/ingles/politcs/paca.htm.

Berríos, M. (2003), *Participación y Compromiso Cívicos en la Estrategia de Reducción de la Pobreza*, RIMSA 13/17, Washington, DC: PAHO/WHO.

Bolling, C., S. Neff, and C. Handy (1998), *United States Foreign Direct Investment in the Western Hemisphere Food Processing Industry*, AER-760, ERS/USDA, Washington, DC: USDA.

Burfisher, M.E., S. Robinson and K. Thierfelder (1998), 'Farm policy reforms and harmonization in the NAFTA', in Mary Burfisher and Elizabeth Jones (eds), *Regional Trade Agreement and United States Agriculture*, ERS/USDA, AER77, Washington, DC: USDA.

Burnquist, H.L., G. Barros, S. de Miranda and J. da Cunha (2002), *SPS in Agricultural Trade: Issues and Options for a Research Agenda*, paper presented at the Conference on Agricultural Liberalization and Integration: What to Expect from the FTAA and the WTO?, Washington, DC: Inter-American Development Bank.

Buzby, J.C. (2001), 'Effects of food-safety perception in food demand and global trade', *Changing Structure of Global Food Consumption and Trade*, ERS/USDA, WRS-01-1, Washington, DC: USDA.

COSAVE: www30.brinkster.com/cosave/stand_ing.htm.

Devlin, R. and A. Estevadeordal (2001), 'What's new in the regionalism in the Americas?', in V. Bulmer-Thomas (ed.), *Regional Integration in Latin America and the Caribbean: The Political Economy of Open Regionalism*, London: ILAS.

Díaz-Bonilla, E., M. Thomas and S. Robinson (2002a), *On Boxes, Contents, and Users: Food Security and the WTO Negotiations*, Washington, DC: International Food Policy Research Institute-IFPRI.
Díaz-Bonilla, E., M. Thomas and S. Robinson (2002b), *Trade Liberalization, WTO, and Food Security*, Washington, DC: International Food Policy Institute.
FAO (1996), *Rome Declaration of World Food Security and World Food Summit Plan of Action. World Food Summit*, Rome: FAO.
FAO (2002a), *The State of Food Insecurity in the World*, Rome: FAO.
FAO (2002b), *Safe Food and Nutritious Diet for the Consumer, World Food Summit– Five Years Later*, Rome: FAO, at www.fao.org/worldfoodsummit/sideevents/papers/WEF-en.htm.
FAO, Food Nutrition and Health Indicators: http://www.fao.org/DOCREP/Meeting/004/Y644e01.htm.
Garret, J.L. and M. Ruel (2000), *Achieving Urban Food and Nutrition Security in the Developing World*, Washington, DC: International Food Policy Research Institute.
Inter-American Development Bank (2002), *Integration and Trade in the Americas*, periodic note, December, Washington, DC: Inter-American Development Bank.
Inter-American Development Bank (2003), *Beyond Borders: The New Regionalism in Latin America*, Washington, DC: Inter-American Development Bank.
Jerardo, A. (2002), *The Import Share of United States Consumed Food Continues to Rise*, FAU-66-01, ERS/USDA, Washington, DC: USDA.
Nugent, Donal (2003), 'Battling over biotechnology', *Perspectives in Health Magazine*, **8** (3), pp. 18–22.
Organization of American States (2002), *Free Trade Area of the Americas – Chapter on Agriculture, Draft Agreement*, Washington, DC: OAS, at http://www.sice.oas.org/ftaadraft/eng/ngage%5F2.asp.
Paarlberg, R.L. (2002), *Governance and Food Security in an Age of Globalization*, Washington, DC: International Food Policy Research Institute.
PAHO/WHO (1999), *Pan American Foot and Mouth Disease Center PANAFTOSA*, XI Inter-American Meeting, at the Ministerial Level, on Animal Health, RIMSA 11/6, 19 March/13–15 April, Washington, DC: PAHO/WHO.
PAHO/WHO (2000), *Food Protection*, 126th Session of the Executive Committee, Washington, DC: PAHO/WHO.
PAHO/WHO (2001a), *Proposed Regulation of the Pan American Commission for Food Safety (COPAIA)*, XII Inter-American Meeting, at the Ministerial Level, on Health and Agriculture, RIMSA 12/11, 2–4 May, Sao Paolo, Brazil, Washington, DC: PAHO/WHO.
PAHO/WHO (2001b), *Proposed Action Plan for the Pan American Foot and Mouth Disease Center (PANAFTOSA) 2002–2003*, XII Inter-American Meeting, at the Ministerial Level on Health and Agriculture, RIMSA 12/5, 12 March 2001, Sao Paolo, Brazil, 2–4 May, Washington, DC: PAHO/WHO.
PAHO/WHO (2001c), *Report of the PAHO Program on Veterinary Public Health on Compliance With the Strategic and Programmatic Orientations (SPO), 1999–2000*, XII Inter-American Meeting, at the Ministerial Level, on Health and Agriculture, RIMSA 12, Sao Paulo, 2–4 May, Washington, DC: PAHO/WHO
PAHO/WHO (2001d), *Report of the PAHO/WHO Consultation on Bovine Spongiform Encephalopathy BSE – Scientific Bases for Policy Decisions in the Americas*, Montevideo, 9–11 April, Washington, DC: PAHO/WHO.
PAHO/WHO (2001e), 'New Pan American Food Safety Commission Starts Work', Buenos Aires: PAHO/WHO.

PAHO/WHO (2003a), *Proposed Plan of Action for the Pan American Institute for Food Protection and Zoonoses (INPPAZ)*, XIII Inter-American Meeting, at the Ministerial Level, on Health and Agriculture, RIMSA 13/5, 17 March, 24–25 April, Washington, DC: PAHO/WHO.

PAHO/WHO (2003b), *Report on the Regional Meeting on Genetically Modified Foods*, XIII Inter-American Meeting, at the Ministerial Level, on Health and Agriculture, RIMSA 13, 24–25 April, Washington, DC: PAHO/WHO.

PAHO/WHO (2004), 'PAHO and USDA sign agreement on food systems capacity building', press release 24 June, Washington, DC: PAHO/WHO.

PAHO/WHO (2005a), *46th Directing council strategy for the Future of Pan American Centers – Current Status of the Center*, Washington, DC: PAHO/WHO.

PAHO/WHO (2005b), *Proposed PAHO/WHO Plan of Action for Technical Cooperation in Food Safety 2006–2007*, XIV Inter-American Meeting, at the Ministerial Level, on Health and Agriculture, RIMSA 14, Mexico City, 21–22 April, Washington, DC: PAHO/WHO.

PANAFTOSA (2003), *Situation of Foot and Mouth Disease Eradication Programs – South America – 2002*, Rio de Janeiro: PANOFTOSA.

Quiroz, J.A. (2000), *Agriculture and the Macroeconomy in Latin America During the 1990s*, paper presented at the Development of the Rural Economy and Poverty Reduction in Latin America and the Caribbean, Inter-American Development Bank, 24 March, Washington, DC: Inter-American Development Bank.

Sabaroche, Hon. Herbert (2003), *Carribean Food Safety Initiative: Challenges in the English-Speaking Caribbean*, XIII Inter-American Meeting, at the Ministerial Level, on Health and Agriculture, RIMSA 13, Washington, DC: PAHO/WHO.

Sawaya, M., I. Fuchsloch and G. Kutas (2002), *Agricultural Liberalization in Multilateral and Regional Trade Negotiations*, paper presented at the Conference on Agricultural Liberalization and Integration: What to Expect from the FTAA and the WTO?, 1–2 October, Washington, DC: Inter-American Development Bank.

Spoor, M. (2000), *Two Decades of Adjustment and Agricultural Development in Latin America and the Caribbean*, Economic Commission for Latin America and the Caribbean (ECLA), LC/L 1352, Washington, DC: ECLA.

Stanton, G.H. (2003), *Food Safety and Trade: Regulations and Transparency in a Global Market Economy*, XIII Inter-American Meeting, at the Ministerial Level, on Health and Agriculture, RIMSA 13/12, Washington, DC: PAHO/WHO.

Staut, J.V. and J. Ugaz-Pereda (1998), 'Western Hemisphere trading blocs and tariff barriers for United States agricultural exports', in Mary Burfisher and Elizabeth Jones (eds), *Regional Trade Agreements and United States Agriculture*, ERS/USDA, AER-771, Washington, DC: USDA.

USDA (2003a), *Global Food Security: Overview, Food Security Assessment*, Agriculture and Trade Report, No. GFA-14, Washington, DC: USDA.

USDA (2003b), *Latin America and the Caribbean: Global Food Security Assessment*, Agricultural and Trade Report, No. GFA-14, Washington, DC: USDA.

USDA (2003c), *A Competitive Agricultural System*, Washington, DC: USDA, at http://www.ers.usda.gov/Emphases/Competitive/.

USDA (2003d), *Global Agricultural Trade*, ERS, Washington, DC: USDA, at http://www.usda.gov/briefing/AgTrade/commoditytrade.htm.

USTR (2003), 'United States – Chile Free Trade Agreements', Washington, DC: United States Trade Representative, at http://www.ustr.gov/Trade_Agreements/Bilateral/Chile_FTA/Section_Index.htm.

Van Gelderen, C., E.J. Gimeno and A.A. Schudel (2003), 'Bovine spongiform encephalopathy in South America: a regional preventive approach', *Review of Science and Technology*, **22** (1): pp. 227–36.

Veneman, A.M. (2003), *Food Safety – A Key to Harmonization of Trade in the Americas – Keynote Address*, XIII Inter-American Meeting, at the Ministerial Level, on Health and Agriculture, RIMSA 13, 24 April, Washington, DC: PAHO/WHO.

WHO (1999), *Food Safety Report*, EB105/10, 2 December, Geneva: WHO.

Wilson, S.R. (1999), 'The impact of standards on industrial development and trade', *Quality Progress*, **32** (7):, pp. 71–5.

WTO (2002), *International Trade Statistics 2002*, Geneva: WTO.

8. Regulatory development and regional institutional reform for food safety in Africa

Cheikh Ndiaye and Reba A. Carruth

I THE EMERGING CONTEXT OF FOOD SAFETY IN AFRICAN COMMODITY AND AGRI-FOOD INDUSTRIES

Introduction: African Agricultural Commodities Competition and Integration in Global Agri-Food Industries

At the start of the twenty-first century, African governments are engaging in regional policy cooperation and transatlantic free trade agreements to strengthen the safety and competitiveness of African agri-food products (Mengu 2003). The goals of these regional integration strategies are to develop regulatory capacity for food safety and the modernization of agri-food industries (Oramah and Abou-Lebot 1998). Through the harmonization of food safety regulations, African nations are strengthening the competitiveness of their products in global agri-food industries.

In the past, the lack of agri-food industry diversification and modern infrastructure, and colonial ties prevented regional food market integration in Africa.[1] As a consequence of these historical facts, the African region was not a profitable location for FDI from transatlantic food and beverage industries.[2] As a result, African farmers are often marginalized in global agri-food industries.[3] Nevertheless, Table 8.1 shows that agricultural commodities provide a platform for integration of African farmers and products in global agri-food industries (Daviron and Gibbons 2002).

Transatlantic free trade agreements

At the present time, African agri-food products are less competitive in transatlantic markets and OECD food industries due to lower quality and food safety standards.[4] Nevertheless, the EU is the largest importer of African agri-food products due to preferential Lome agreements. However,

*Table 8.1 Agricultural commodity trade flows from the Africa region to global markets**

	2001 (%)			2000 (%)			1999 (%)		
Commodity	Production	Export	Food	Production	Export	Food	Production	Export	Food
Cereals excluding beer:									
Rice	9.97	24.43	31.60	11.09	16.09	12.85	10.93	14.96	12.66
Maize	37.52	32.60	29.49	41.82	42.18	29.18	39.21	39.42	28.91
Millet	11.99	1.51	8.56	11.94	1.15	9.12	12.73	0.95	9.22
Sorghum	18.90	0.34	12.79	17.54	4.77	13.05	17.19	12.34	13.29
Starchy roots:									
Cassava	57.55	3.44	60.12	57.43	2.81	59.75	57.34	1.81	60.19
Yams	21.33	1.38	15.29	21.82	3.01	16.03	22.16	2.17	16.32
Sugar crops*		0.005	5.91		0.01	5.65		0.005	3.72
Tree nuts		32.69	72.01		34.06	70.99		46.32	70.11
Oil crops:									
Groundnuts (shelled)	34.85	15.56	40.76	34.91	9.98	41.26	32.85	8.67	40.08
Cotton seed	14.82	18.35	—	12.52	20.79	—	12.98	25.10	—
Coconuts incl. copra	9.97	13.36	16.19	10.05	13.33	15.74	10.11	15.71	15.70
Palm kernels	5.69	2.56	0.13	5.73	12.19	0.14	5.15	1.43	0.17
Vegetable oils									
Soya bean oil	3.00	2.39	13.57	2.51	1.64	12.60	2.24	1.18	11.04
Groundnut oil	24.10	19.88	15.00	22.89	16.94	15.60	20.69	13.95	15.11
Palm oil	34.19	32.74	28.20	36.16	26.23	29.39	34.43	28.95	28.91
Fruits:									
Oranges, mandarines	9.98	39.35	9.33	10.40	35.50	10.60	10.24	39.09	9.96
Lemons	1.09	2.77	1.17	1.02	2.46	1.11	0.95	2.24	1.08

Table 8.1 (continued)

	2001 (%)			2000 (%)			1999 (%)		
Commodity	Production	Export	Food	Production	Export	Food	Production	Export	Food
Citrus, other	6.25	0.53	7.38	6.25	1.13	7.44	6.27	1.55	7.43
Bananas	11.84	12.48	11.97	11.39	13.30	11.25	11.20	10.99	11.19
Plantains	36.86	—	32.53	36.78	—	32.12	37.36	—	33.19
Pineapples	4.27	10.17	4.48	4.23	11.13	4.47	4.19	10.05	4.46
Stimulants:									
Coffee	31.27	24.59	50.38	29.93	29.71	48.57	33.05	26.38	49.40
Cocoa beans	57.96	63.77	18.18	59.62	58.82	16.95	56.17	62.02	16.91
Tea	11.05	11.64	31.43	10.45	11.47	34.49	10.78	11.61	33.69

Note: * Values are a percentage of total production and consumption respectively.

Source: FAOSTAT, agricultural data, at http://apps.fao.org.

the termination of the Lome Agreement in 2006, will result in the loss of preferential access to EU markets.[5] In turn, US and EU agri-food industries remain protected by rising food safety regulations and market barriers to African food products.[6]

In response to the globalization of agri-food industries, African nations are trying to increase their share of transatlantic food markets (Hertel et al. 1998). For example, the South African Development Community (SADC) countries support the creation of an EU-South Africa free trade area. Likewise Morocco is negotiating a North African–EU free trade area with the EU.[7]

In this context, African countries are also aggressively pursuing intra-regional and transatlantic free trade agreements with the United States. In this regard, the African Growth and Opportunity Act (AGOA) is 'extending the transatlantic marketplace' to include Africa in the twenty-first century.[8] Moreover, AGOA also provides opportunities for African countries to integrate into global agri-food industries through strategic alliances with US agri-businesses and food-processing companies. Therefore, transatlantic free trade agreements promote regulatory capacity-building, and harmonization with Codex, OIE and IPPC and WTO SPS food safety standards by African countries.[9]

African Agri-Food Industries and Food Safety in the African Region

In global agri-food industries, US and EU food processors and food retailers use exclusive supply arrangements for washing, chopping and shelf-ready packaging in Africa.[10] In turn, African agricultural commodity and food-processing industries target value-added food markets.[11] In many cases, African farmers are shifting to organic foods, premium chocolate and high-quality coffee.[12] Consequently, transatlantic markets and global agri-food industries provide a tremendous growth opportunity for African farmers and food producers.

By the start of the 2000s, FDI in African agricultural commodity chain industries and agri-food-processing operations started to grow.[13] As a result, South Africa is now a growing base for supermarket chain extension across Africa. For example, the South African supermarket chain, Shoprite, is the largest food retailer in Africa, with approximately 981 stores and franchises across the region, and $2 billion in sales revenue.[14] In the African region, the South African business model is rapidly expanding across African agri-food industry sectors. By 2002, an African food processor entered the top 100 list of global companies.[15] Table 8.2 shows the African countries that are becoming bases for global food company expansion.

As Table 8.2 shows, FDI by global food companies in Africa is concentrated in Ghana, Kenya, Nigeria, Mozambique and Tanzania.[16] The main

Table 8.2 Slected global food and beverage companies in Africa

Multinational food producer	location
Cadbury	Ghana, Kenya, Nigeria
Schweppes	Ghana, Kenya, Nigeria
DIAGEO	Ghana, Kenya, Nigeria, Tanzania
Nestlé	Ghana, Kenya, Nigeria, Tanzania, Mozambique, Zimbabwe
South African Breweries	Ghana, Kenya, Tanzania, Mozambique, Zimbabwe
The Coca Cola Company	Ghana, Kenya, Nigeria, Tanzania, Mozambique, Zimbabwe
Pepsico	Ghana, Nigeria
Proctor and Gamble	Ghana, Kenya, Nigeria
Unilever	Ghana, Kenya, Nigeria, Tanzania, Zimbabwe

Source: www.rase.org.uk/communications.

regulatory and food safety challenges for the less developed African countries are as follows:

- the need for modern food laws and food safety regulations
- the need for modernization of privatized African agri-businesses
- underinvestment and modernization of farming cooperatives
- the weakness of the private sector and market systems
- limited capital for public and private agri-business and food-processing investment
- inadequate scientific and technical infrastructure for food quality and new product research and development (R&D)
- the lack of reliable data and information
- limited capacity to effectively control and monitor food safety and comply with WTO SPS and Codex Alimentarius standards.[17]

As a result of these challenges, developing countries in Africa have difficulties in attracting high levels of FDI. In many cases, African food companies are unable to achieve economies of scale and scope in transatlantic markets and global agri-food industries.[18] Consequently, many African nations are working to improve food quality, food safety and the competitiveness of farmers and food-processing industries.[19]

Africa and the global coffee industry

In the global coffee industry, many small African farmers and food producers now face rapid globalization of agricultural commodity supply chains.[20]

Overtime, US and EU food companies control the global coffee industry through concentrated buyer/supplier chains, value-added processing of high-quality beans and strong global brands.[21] In this market system, profits shift from African farmers to global food producers that roast, freeze dry, flavour, blend, transport, store and retail branded coffees.[22] Moreover, rising food quality and food safety standards exclude many African farmers from premium coffee markets.[23] Ultimately, food safety and quality standards compliance, and value-added competition by African farmers and food producers, is required in global coffee industries.[24]

Africa and the global fresh fruit and vegetable produce industry

At the start of the twenty-first century, African countries emerged as major suppliers of fresh fruit and vegetable produce in transatlantic food markets and global agri-food industries. During this period, South Africa, Egypt, Morocco, Kenya and Zimbabwe emerged as large-scale producers and suppliers of fresh fruits and vegetables for transatlantic agri-businesses and global food retailers.[25] In the UK and EU, food retailers such as Tesco and Sainsbury are increasing their reliance on exclusive suppliers in Kenya and other African countries. Through this market arrangement, primarily with large White and Asian owned farms in Africa, fresh produce is supplied to UK food retailers in accordance with strict EU food safety and quality standards. However, small African farmers are excluded due to lack of access to the following resources:

- national and regional state-of-the-art transport and air cargo infrastructure
- modern agricultural commodity and food supply chain investment, management, agri-food product R&D and information technologies
- food-processing and hygiene standards capacity-building for the washing, chopping, peeling and packaging of fresh produce products[26]
- high-quality and reliable production of fresh produce
- food traceability and food safety standards compliance
- mandatory HACCP, food pathogen and food control systems.[27]

Food safety, animal livestock health and African meat and livestock industries

In the African region, animal livestock production provides the basis for socio-economic development for many nations. Furthermore, the demand for meat and diary products is growing faster than industry supply in many African countries.[28] Table 8.3 shows, meat production and consumption in the African region is increasing.

Table 8.3 Production and consumption of meat, dairy products and livestock

Item	Production			Consumption (1000MT)		
	2001	2000	1999	2001	2000	1999
Meat:						
Beef and veal	39.17	39.08	38.24	39.62 (41.90)*	40.00	38.01
Mutton and goat	16.77	17.13	17.24	16.15	16.43	16.82
Poultry	26.90	26.71	27.19	27.59	27.34	28.18
Pork	6.36	6.23	6.27	6.44	6.20	6.44
Other	10.79	10.85	11.06	10.20	10.03	10.55
Dairy products: Total (MT)						
Butter ghee	0.69	0.69	0.72	0.98	1.02	1.02
Cream	0.01	0.01	0.01	0.04	0.06	0.03
Milk	92.43	92.54	92.36	93.52	93.49	93.47
Eggs	6.87	6.76	6.91	5.46	5.42	5.48

Notes: * Figures in brackets are a percentage of total production.

Source: FAOSTAT, agricultural data, http://apps.fao.org.

At the regional level, African farmers and food producers are increasing animal livestock and diary production to meet growing consumer demand. For example, South Africa is a large milk and meat producer, and an emerging competitor in global meat and livestock industries.[29] However, trans-boundary livestock diseases reduce the safety of African meat and diary products, and competitiveness in global meat and livestock industries.[30]

In African countries, weak meat inspection standards compliance and limited veterinary services pose serious challenges for African food safety regulators. For example, in 2003, over 52 000 Australian sheep were stranded at sea due to the refusal of Saudi Arabia and the other Gulf Cooperation Council (GCC) countries to accept the shipment.[31] At that time, the Australian government faced public outrage, and threats of boycotts over animal cruelty.[32] Eventually, the Government of Eritrea agreed to take the infected sheep due to chronic food shortages. However, Eritrea required veterinary and food safety assistance from OIE and WHO to carry out risk assessments of the sheep due to limited food safety infrastructure and regulatory capacity.[33]

In the African region, animal livestock contamination with diseases from wild animals increases food safety risks. Therefore, animal livestock traceability systems are urgently needed in African countries to identify the source of animal livestock diseases that threaten food safety and the public health.[34] In contrast to North America, Europe and Japan, there are no reported cases of BSE or avian flu in Africa. However, indigenous animal diseases threaten food safety in African meat and livestock industries.[35] Consequently, African nations must control African animal livestock diseases through national and regional harmonization of Codex and OIE standards.

Plant health and food safety: the challenge of mycotoxin, pesticide and chemical contamination

Mycotoxin contamination of agricultural commodities and food crops As the century unfolds, primary and processed agricultural commodities are the main drivers of global trade, economic growth and socio-economic development in African countries.[36] However, plant health and food safety risks from indigenous trans-boundary pests and crop diseases are significant. In the case of mycotoxins, food contamination and diet concentration have been found in Ghana, Sierra Leone, Nigeria, Sudan, the United Arab Emirates, South Africa and East Africa.[37] In a recent incident, the entire maize supply of a village in Kenya was contaminated with mycotoxins.[38] The contamination was caused by improper storage of maize.[39] Eventually, the Ministry of Public Health called for the immediate disposal of maize in grocery stores and the entire stored crop of the village.[40]

At the regional level, food safety and food security in Africa are at risk from high levels of mycotoxin contamination and other plant crop diseases.[41] In turn, the contaminated food products are sold to African consumers, global agri-business and food-processing companies.[42] Therefore plant crop health and mycotoxin contamination are major threats to food safety and food trade in African countries.

Chemical pesticide contamination The major source of chemical contamination of agricultural food and feed crops in Africa is the extensive use of dangerous unregulated pesticides. In many cases food safety is at risk due to ineffective pest management of locusts, insects, malaria-carrying mosquitos and microbial plant diseases by African farmers.[43] Currently, large stocks of the following dangerous chemical pesticides are sold and donated to African countries through Western foreign aid packages: DDT, Dieldrin, Endrin, HCH, Fenitrothion, Lindane, Malathion and Parathion.[44] As a result, chemical contamination of food and feed crops is a major food safety threat in Africa.

In response to this growing threat to food safety and food trade, the World Bank Africa Stockpiles Program initiative was launched. The goals of this World Bank program are to reduce the use of dangerous chemicals and pesticides, and to clean up and destroy all dangerous chemical pesticide stockpiles during the next 15 years. At the present time, the following African countries participate in this World Bank program: Ethiopia, Mali, Morocco, Nigeria, South Africa, Tanzania and Tunisia. Eventually, other African countries will be included.[45] In this regional initiative, African governments develop regulatory capacity to comply with transatlantic regulations and Codex standards for maximum chemical and pesticide levels.

Modern biotechnology and GM food production in Africa As the decade unfolds, African farmers are evaluating modern biotechnology for crop production and animal livestock quality.[46] However, the rejection of GM food aid by Zambia shows that many African countries do not want unregulated GM food and agriculture.[47] In the meantime, US government and agri-food industries are lobbying for rapid adoption of GM food in Africa.[48] In an effort to increase the acceptance of modern biotechnology in Africa, the Rockefeller Foundation, the Agency for International Development and its counterpart in the United Kingdom launched the African Agricultural Technology Foundation in Nairobi, Kenya.[49]

The goal of the foundation is to identify the main crop production problems facing small farmers and African agri-food industries. Through this initiative, African governments will establish partnerships with the following consortium of US and EU agri-businesses: Monsanto (USA), DuPont (USA), Syngenta (Switzerland) and Dow Agro Sciences (USA).[50] The consortium companies will donate patent rights, seeds, laboratory training and technical support. In this project, the consortium companies work with small African farmers to develop GM seeds and crop traits to resist drought, insects and plant diseases.[51] Ultimately, the development of new varieties of African food crops such as cassava, sweet potatoes, cowpeas, chickpeas, bananas and corn are major goals of this collaboration.

II REGULATORY DEVELOPMENT AND INSTITUTIONAL REFORM FOR FOOD SAFETY IN AFRICA

In the transatlantic and OECD countries, food safety liability laws and consumer protection regulations place responsibility onto corporations and food producers.[52] In contrast, African food safety regulations focus on adulteration, contamination and processing hazards.[53] In this respect, the main goals of food safety regulation in Africa are the protection of consumers from unsafe food and the regulation of markets.[54] However, food safety in Africa now requires new regulatory policies and institutional frameworks for inspection, product certification, product liability, standards enforcement and modern laboratory services.[55] In each African country, food safety standards must now comply with WTO SPS, Codex, OIE and IPPC standards.

Food Safety Regulation in Africa: The Case of South Africa, Kenya and Morocco

The case of South Africa

Prior to the 2000s, the Republic of South Africa (RSA) had no basic food law, and relied on a set of regulations across several departments of government to regulate food safety. At that time, regulations, policy legislation and laws governing food production and regulation in South Africa was fragmented. In many cases, different aspects of food safety regulation are handled by several departments and agencies. For example, the certification of meat safety and quality was controlled by the Department of Agriculture. However, the South African Bureau of Standards (SABS) was given responsibility for the mandatory compliance of canned meat with national food safety standards. Therefore, food safety regulation in South Africa was the primary responsibility of the health and agricultural departments and industry sectors.

In South Africa, the Department of Health (DOH) has the overall responsibility for food safety, and operates at the national, provincial and local levels. In South Africa, a number of regulations, policies, laws, statutes and directives govern food safety. In this context, several government agencies performed the following roles and regulatory functions: the regulation of weights and measures, the movement of plants and plant products, and control of plants and products that are capable of spreading quarantine and regulated non-quarantine pests. The institutional responsibility for various food safety laws, regulations and standards is shown in Table 8.4.[56]

In South Africa, the Food, Drugs and Disinfectants Act, No. 13: 1929 is supported by two regulations on solvents in foods, labelling and advertising. Foods standard development in South Africa involves the following organizations: DOH, SABS, NDA, DTI, DTA and MCMCEAT (see Table 8.5 for full organization titles). The general regulations cover the following food safety measures: pre-market approval, permits, licensing, registration of new food products, regulation of organic food, food import/export regulation, food labelling, food additives, food contaminants, pesticide and

Table 8.4 Laws acts and directives governing the food control system in South Africa

Law	Implementing agency
Foods, Cosmetics and Disinfectants Act. No. 54: 1972	Department of Health (DOH)
Health Act, No. 63: 1977	Department of Health (DOH)
Food, Drugs and Disinfectants Act, No.13: 1929	Department of Health (DOH)
Standards Act, No. 29: 1993 (Amended)	South African Bureau of Standards (SABS)
Animal Diseases Act, No. 35: 1984	National Department of Agriculture (NDA)
Abattoir Hygiene Act No. 121: 1992	National Department of Agriculture (NDA)
Agricultural Pest Act, No 36: 1983	National Department of Agriculture (NDA)
Agricultural Products Standards Act, No. 119: 1990	National Department of Agriculture (NDA)
Liquor Products Act, No. 60: 1989	National Department of Agriculture (NDA)
Trade Metrology Act, No. 77: 1973	Department of Trade and Industry (DTI)
Perishable Products Export Control Act, No. 9: 1983	Department of Transport Affairs (DTA)
Marine Living Resources Act, No. 8: 1998	Marine and Coastal Management Component of Environmental Affairs and Tourism (MCMCEAT)

veterinary drug residues in foods. The structure of the food control system in South Africa is shown in Table 8.5.[57]

In response to globalization, and regional free trade in the South African Development Community (SADC) and the rest of Africa, the Department of Health, Directorate of Food Control developed guidelines for food safety. In this regulatory framework, the following food safety guidelines for the control and inspection of imported foods are carried out in accordance with WTO SPS and Codex standards to:

- create uniform control procedures for implementation
- ensure that the various health authorities within the national health system meet their obligations for food safety control and inspection of imported foods entering the country through land ports of entry

Table 8.5 Structure of food control systems in South Africa

Function	Responsible agency
Operation of food control system at the National Provincial and Local authority levels	DOH, SABS, NDA, DTI, DTA, MCMCEAT
Inspection units and inspection programmes at domestic level	DOH, SABS, NDA, DTI, DTA
Import/export inspection system	DOH, SABS, NDA
Certification authority	DOH, SABS, NDA
Laboratory services	DOH, SABS, NDA
Laboratory accreditation	SANAS, DOH, SABS, CSIR
Compliance mechanisms	DOH, MCMCEAT, CSIR
Training of food control officers	DOH, SABS, Environmental Health
Control of consumer organizations	DOH, SABS, NDA, DTI
Consumer education, information service	DOH, SABS, NDA, DTI
In-plant control quality assurance and management	DOH, SABS, NDA, DTI
Industry trade associations	SABS
Advice, assistance to industry	DOH, SABS, NDA, DTI

- establish cooperation between the major government agencies within the health sector and other authorities involved in border control.[58]

The provisions and applications of the Food, Cosmetic and Disinfectants Act, 1972 (Act 54/1972) are the most important public health regulations for the governance of the safety of all foods manufactured, sold or imported into South Africa. The Minister of Health is responsible for the implementation of regulations on food safety issues specified in the Act. However, the Director-General of the Department of Health implements policies for imported foods.[59]

At the national level, the South African food safety guidelines take into account provisions of the Codex Alimentarius Commission, the WTO SPS and TBT agreements and related matters. However, public health authorities at the national, provincial and district levels are responsible for the enforcement of the Act. In this regard, food safety regulations for imported foods provide the mechanism for the implementation of the guidelines, and support free food trade within the SADC and African regions.

The case of Kenya[60]

The food safety system of Kenya is governed by the Basic Food, Drugs and Chemical Substance Act Cap 254, and is supported by other relevant

Table 8.6 Laws and regulations governing food control in Kenya

Law	Responsible institution
Public Health Act Cap 242	Government Chemist Department
Agriculture Act Cap 318	Ministry of Agriculture
Plant Protection Act Cap 324	Kenyan Plant Health Inspectorate Service
Fertilisers animal Foods Act Cap 345	Ministry of Agriculture
Meat Control Act Cap 356	Food quality and safety Unit, Ministry of Health
Pig Industry Act Cap 361	Ministry of Agriculture
Import Inspection Directive	Kenya Bureau of Standards
Fish Industry Act Cap 378	Fisheries Department
Standards Act Cap 496	Kenya Bureau of Standards
Regulations	**Lead agency**
Licensing and Registration of Food Establishments	Public Health Department
Food import/Export Regulations	WHO NEP for TBT Agreement and SPS Measures
Street Foods	Public Health Department
Food Labelling	Kenya Bureau of Standards (KBS)
Food Additives	Kenya Bureau of Standards
Food Contaminants	Kenya Bureau of Standards
Pesticides/Veterinary Drug Residues	Department of Veterinary Services

regulations, laws, and policies. The following Acts of government govern the food safety system in Kenya: (1) Food, Drugs and Chemical Substances Act Cap 254, (2) Public Health Act Cap 242 and (3) Standards Act Cap 496. At the present time, many government agencies are involved in the implementation of laws. However, no lead agency has full responsibility for food safety regulations in Kenya. The responsibility for various supporting laws is shown in Table 8.6.

In Kenya, the Kenyan Bureau of Standards (KBS) is the lead agency for consumer protection and education. The Ministry of Agriculture and the consumer information network serve as collaborating agencies. While 12 institutions are involved in food safety, the Food Quality and Safety Unit in the Ministry of Health (MOH) is responsible for inspection of foods produced in Kenya. The KBS has direct responsibility for certification and laboratory services. The laboratories of the KBS are accredited for the analysis of pesticide residues, mycotoxins, heavy metals and microbial contaminants. In the future, the KBS laboratories will be accredited for the analysis of veterinary drug residues. Currently, the following food safety measures and goals are being implemented: the establishment of a Kenyan Accreditation Service, and the integration of street foods into the formal sector and food safety reguations.

In terms of the national food safety system, the following are major food safety concerns and challenges for Kenya: lack of a food safety policy, inadequate prevention and control of food-borne disease, limited food safety infrastructure, outdated food safety regulations, policies and laws, and inadequate funding for food safety programs and trained professionals. In an effort to ensure food quality and food safety in Kenya, the government launched a food safety improvement program with the following regulatory goals and objectives:

- the development of a modern national food law with enabling regulations
- the establishment of a national food safety standards system
- the creation of a national food inspection program and a national food quality assurance network
- the acceleration of capacity-building for selected laboratories, and the upgrading of equipment to support the food safety and a quality management program
- the assessment of the street food situation and improvement of street food safety
- the development of capacity-building programs and food control systems to train food control officials to administer the food quality and safety management systems on a sustainable basis.

The case of Morocco[61]

In Morocco, the food safety system operates under two main laws (adopted in 1977 and 1984) and a series of regulations related to food safety and food trade. In 1989, a new food safety law for the inspection of live animal imports and exports, and food products of animal origin was enacted. This food safety law concentrates regulatory authority and power to the Ministry of Agriculture. Therefore, the Ministry of Agriculture is responsible for all food safety regulations on the rejection and recall of food products that present risks to human health.

In Morocco, several government ministries including Health, Interior and Industry, are also involved in food safety regulation (Table 8.7). In an effort to improve communication and relations with international organizations such as Codex Alimentarius and OIE, a new system is being developed. In this system, a formal contact for international food safety standards cooperation in the Moroccan government is designated. The

Table 8.7 Structure of food control systems in Morocco

Function	Responsible agency
Operation of food control system at the National Provincial and Local authority levels	DOH, SABS, NDA, DTI, DTA, MCMCEAT
Inspection units and inspection programmes at domestic level	DOH, SABS, NDA, DTI, DTA
Import/export inspection system	DOH, SABS, NDA
Certification authority	DOH, SABS, NDA
Laboratory services	DOH, SABS, NDA
Laboratory accreditation	SANAS, DOH, SABS, CSIR
Compliance mechanisms	DOH, MCMCEAT, CSIR
Training of food control officers	DOH, SABS, Environmental Health
Control of consumer organizations	DOH, SABS, NDA, DTI
Consumer education, information service	DOH, SABS, NDA, DTI
In-plant control quality assurance and management	DOH, SABS, NDA, DTI
Industry trade associations	SABS
Advice, assistance to industry	DOH, SABS, NDA, DTI

Moroccan government is currently implementing the following comprehensive reform of the national food safety system:

- formation of a single network in charge of food safety control at border checkpoints
- establishment of industry self-regulation and management-based regulations at the company and manufacturing levels based on HACCP and Good Manufacturing Practices
- reform and modernization of the basic law on food fraud
- creation of an independent scientific assessment agency for food safety hazards, regulatory policy reform and the management of food contamination hazards.

The major component of the regulatory reform process by the Moroccan government is the development of an integrated food safety system. The goal of the integrated food safety initiative is to increase the participation of all Moroccan stakeholders in setting regulatory standards, risk management, and communication of food safety risks and food quality issues. The following policy recommendations for regulatory and institutional reforms are designed to strengthen food safety in Morocco:

- creation of an independent scientific body for food safety and risk assessment and development of a structure for risk assessment to split risk assessors and risk managers
- development of a rapid alert system
- development of a coordination system for all consumer and agri-food industry stakeholders
- separation of processing and development aspects from the official food safety controls
- reform of procedures and regulations for the adoption of legal texts regarding food safety
- development of food safety regulations and control systems across the entire food chain
- development of a traceability system to guarantee the recall of unsafe food
- establishment of an independent food safety inspection and control agency
- improvement and capacity-building for national laboratory facilities
- workforce training and human resource development programs for inspectors and professionals in the field of food safety regulation
- provision of assistance to small and medium-size food companies and industries to produce high-quality and safe foods through management-based regulations and inspection programs
- creation of an ongoing awareness program for all stakeholders from 'farm to table'
- scientific evaluation and assessment of food safety, nutritional quality of traditional food, ground waters, sewage treatment infrastructure, domestic and industrial wastes, and the economic impact of urban pollution on food safety.

Regional Regulatory Harmonization of Food Safety Policies in Africa

As the twenty-first century unfolds, African nations are harmonizing regulatory standards, and developing regional institutional frameworks to govern food safety. The goals of regional food safety authorities and regulatory policy harmonization frameworks for consumer protection, public health, GM food safety, animal livestock health and plant health in the African region are as follows:

- coordination and governance of food safety issues at the national, sub-regional and regional levels in Africa
- formulation and harmonization of food safety legislation for the African region

- development of a regional rapid alert system for Africa
- provision of a central inquiry point about WTO SPS and TBT standards and requirements for African countries and the region
- risk analysis support and training for African countries
- accreditation of sub-regional laboratories, and development of metrology inspection and national laboratory networks across Africa.[62]

In an age of globalization and regional free trade, African governments accept the need for regional regulatory harmonization and independent food safety regulators. Therefore, the harmonization of food safety regulations is emerging in the Regional Committee of Codex for Africa. For example, in the fourteenth session of the Codex Coordinating Committee for Africa in November 2000, the South African government announced its consideration of an independent food safety regulator, and harmonization of food safety regulations and laws in SADC. In Uganda, the National Bureau of Standards announced the development of 67 new food standards, of which 47 are Codex based and include the labelling of prepackaged food through the East African standards organization.[63]

Regional animal livestock health and food safety in African

At the regional level, the African Union provides the framework for animal livestock health and food safety standards harmonization. In cooperation with FAO, OIE, the European Commission, and transatlantic aid agencies, the African Union–Inter African Bureau for Animal Resources (AU–IBAR) provides the following regional framework for animal livestock health and food safety standards harmonization;[64] Pan African Programme for the Control of Epizootics (PACE), Farming in Tse Tse Controlled Areas (FITCA) and Regional Action for Livestock Production in Eastern Africa (RALEA).[65] The regulatory standards harmonization goals of AU–IBAR are as follows:

- improvement of animal health in Africa through the control and eradication of trans-boundary animal diseases
- improvement in animal livestock breeding, management and food industry productivity
- improvement of veterinary public health through quality assurance of animal livestock health, certification of meat and livestock products and the regulation of food safety
- improvement of the marketing and trade of animal livestock products in Africa and global meat and livestock industries

- harmonization of policies and regulations for animal livestock health, production and management in Africa
- collection and dissemination of information for the improvement of African animal livestock and food industry resources.[66]

In the Southern African region, SADC has a formal relationship with OIE for the harmonization of animal livestock health, production and trade regulations.[67] In SADC, the following sub-committees protect animal livestock industries and regulate food safety: Animal Health, Veterinary Laboratory Diagnostic Services, Animal Production and Marketing and Veterinary Public Health and Food Safety.[68] The following animal livestock health goals are achieved in SADC: protection of animal livestock health, promotion of safe and high-quality livestock production, promotion of safe livestock trade and enforcement of compliance with animal livestock regulations and standards.[69]

Regional harmonization of plant health, crop protection and pesticide safety

In African countries trans-boundary pests can destroy the value, health and safety of African agri-food products.[70] Therefore, the African Union works through the Inter-African Phytosanitary Council (IAPSC) to regulate plant health, and certify the pest-free zone status of countries in the region. The IAPSC also serves as the regional African Plant Protection Organization (AU–APPO), and works to prevent the spread of plant pests.[71] In the case of chemical pesticides, the IAPSC harmonizes registration, certification and training for pest management workers and officials. The IAPSC also trains national plant protection organizations in the following areas: pest risk analysis, phytosanitary inspection, certification of pest-free zones and pest surveillance.

Regional regulation of GM food safety and traceability: the case of SADC and the African Union

In many cases, African countries must certify the GM-free status of food as a prerequisite for access to EU markets and global agri-food industries.[72] For example, the government of Zambia rejected GM corn in food aid to protect its status as a GM-free zone. Therefore, regional regulatory frameworks for the governance of GM food and modern biotechnology, and investment in food safety capacity infrastructure are emerging. The goals of these frameworks are to ensure compliance with mandatory GM food traceability, segregation and labelling regulations, development of national and regional regulatory frameworks for GM seeds and foods, comprehensive GM food labelling laws and creation of a high-level Bio-Ethics Commission for Modern Biotechnology for the African region.[73]

At the regional level, the African Union/NEPAD is creating an African biotechnology policy harmonization framework. The goals of the regional biotechnology policy harmonization framework are as follows: development of expertise in targeted areas of high growth modern biotechnology, harmonization of biotechnology to develop Africa's rich biodiversity, improvement of agricultural productivity, and development of pharmaceutical products.[74] By 2002, SADC launched a biotechnology policy framework for the Southern African region.[75] The goals of the SADC framework for GM food safety and biotechnology regulation are as follows: to develop and adopt proactive policies for current and emerging modern biotechnology, market governance and food safety regulation, and adoption of policies and market strategies to address modern biotechnology.[76]

III THE GROWING ROLE OF HACCP AND MANAGEMENT-BASED FOOD SAFETY REGULATION AND HACCP

In the African region, fish and aquaculture are a major source of food in many countries. However, approximately 50 per cent of all fish exports come from Africa and other developing countries with limited HACCP process inspection capacity.[77] As a consequence, many African fish processors have financial losses due to the spoilage of fish and seafood. In turn, the low-quality fish products are used for animal feed. Therefore, HACCP process inspection is needed to increase the safety and value of African fish and seafood industries.

In the case of Kenya, the fish-processing industry began in the Lake Victoria region of the country in the 1980s. During that period, Nile perch fish accounted for approximately half of all fish caught in Kenya.[78] Eventually, salmonella contamination and a cholera outbreak resulted in an EU ban on chilled fish products from Lake Victoria fish-processing plants. The source of this food safety hazard was poor food hygiene in the fish-processing plants. As a result of the ban, the Kenyan fish-processing industry lost approximately 66 per cent of its exports to the EU and 32 per cent of its foreign exchange earnings.[79] In response to this crisis, the Government of Kenya created new food safety agencies for the fish-processing industry.[80]

In the case of agricultural commodities, the high level of mycotoxin contamination results in the detention and rejection of African agri-food products. However, large amounts of investment are needed for mycotoxin reduction. In this regard, the African Groundnut Council, which represents the Gambia, Mali, Niger, Nigeria, Sudan and Senegal, estimates the projected investment costs at approximately $7.5 million.[81] Therefore, African countries are developing mycotoxin eradication standards, bio-controls and HACCP strategies for food-processing plants to comply with transatlantic regulations and Codex food safety standards.

IV THE GROWING ROLE OF FAO, WHO AND CODEX ALIMENTARIUS IN AFRICAN CAPACITY-BUILDING

The WTO SPS Agreement requires countries to base public health and food safety regulations and standards on sound science and appropriate risk assessment (Bankole et al. 2000). In this respect, many African countries view the WTO SPS Agreement as the correct framework for the protection of food safety, public health, animal livestock and plant health.[82] Therefore, the following food safety, consumer protection and food production issues must be addressed in African countries:[83]

- stronger reliance on consumer demand, product benefits, food safety and food security needs for national food system and agri-food industry modernization
- growing focus on the impact of rapid urbanization on food demand and the growth of value-added food products and food service requirements
- protection of consumers through the increase of African consumer power and sovereignty over food markets and supply chain industries
- increasing use of emerging food safety technologies such as pathogen detection and HACCP process inspection systems
- increasing governance and regulation of competition by small farmers, large agri-businesses, food cooperatives and agri-food-processing industries to strengthen product choice, consumer protection, animal livestock and plant health, and public health standards for food safety
- development of a regulatory framework for modern biotechnology and GM food production.

In Africa, food safety capacity increases the competitiveness of African food products in global agri-food industries.[84] However, the widespread reliance of African consumers on street food, limited food hygiene and public infrastructure increase food safety risks.[85] Therefore, the African

Development Bank and the World Bank are providing financial assistance for national and regional regulatory capacity-building and food safety infrastructure through FAO, WHO and Codex.[86]

In 2001, FAO and WHO launched a framework for capacity-building in SPS issues with the World Bank, OIE and WTO.[87] At the national level, FAO works with African governments to improve the quality, safety and hygiene of street foods and imported foods.[88] During the 2000–03 period, support was given for the development of SPS and Codex compliant national food regulatory systems to the governments of Senegal, Gambia, South Africa, Swaziland, Uganda and Zimbabwe.[89] At the regional level, WHO promotes the use of Codex national food standards and Codes of Practice. In support of these goals, WHO disseminates consumer and public information for food safety education in African countries. In this context, WHO launched 'Healthy Marketplace' programs in Tanzania and Nigeria to improve food safety practices of street food vendors.[90]

Finally, HACCP training and capacity-building projects are under way in Africa. In September 2000, a training course on Good Manufacturing Practices and HACCP was held in Tanzania for participants from food industries, government regulatory agencies and universities in Zimbabwe, Botswana, Ethiopia, Uganda, Kenya and Tanzania.[91] In 2001, FAO launched a regional project to train small private firms and medium-sized agri-food industries in HACCP, Good Hygiene Practices and Good Manufacturing Processes in Senegal, Benin, Burkina Faso, Ivory Coast, Mali and Niger.[92] During this period, a conference was held on agricultural commodity safety, mycotoxin contamination and HACCP.[93]

V CONCLUSIONS

In conclusion, the African region is emerging as an important agricultural commodity producer and processed-food supplier for transatlantic regional markets and global agri-food industries. The globalization of African agricultural commodity chains, transatlantic free trade and regional market agreements, contract farming and exclusive supplier alliances are now integrating Africa into global agri-food industries.[94] As a result, African farmers and food producers are working to increase the quality and safety of their agri-food products for domestic customers and global markets. Therefore, rapid regulatory harmonization, product certification and mandatory HACCP food inspection standards are needed for mutual recognition of African food safety standards (Tsunehiro et al. 2001).

To accomplish these goals, regional laboratory certification standards, conformity assessment certification, national and regional frameworks for the regulation of modern biotechnology, GM food labelling, food traceability, certification of food inspection systems, harmonization of animal livestock and plant health, mandatory HACCP programs, agri-food industry standards and Best Practices must become national regulatory priorities for African governments. Ultimately, African governments, farmers, consumers and agri-food industries must participate in regional and multilateral food safety standards organizations.

In the African region, the lack of government investment in public goods, rural infrastructure and agricultural extension is undermining food safety in national food systems and agri-food industries. Moreover, food production, processing, storage and transport requires modern public infrastructure. Therefore, African governments, multilateral institutions, transatlantic aid agencies and agri-food companies must work in partnership to rapidly develop clean water, public health and modern public infrastructure systems. In this context, the access by consumers, small farmers, farming cooperatives, food processors, rural and urban communities and all African countries to public infrastructure must be a food safety and public health priority for the region.

Finally, limited regulatory capacity and weak market governance institutions are major threats for African consumers, farmers, agri-food industries and governments. In this regard, food safety capacity is required for the competitiveness of African farmers and food producers in global markets.[95] As a consequence, investment in modern agriculture, food-processing and farming extension services are urgently needed.[96] Ultimately, African governments must collectively harmonize Codex, OIE and IPPC food safety standards to protect African and global consumers, and to strengthen food safety in global agri-food industries.

NOTES

1. Hanik, M. and Henry J. Owusu (1998), 'Has ECOWAS promoted trade among its members?', *Journal of African Economies*, 7 (3): 363–70. While South–South trade was promoted by Sir Arthur Lewis, a Nobel Prize winning economist in the 1980s, the feasibility of intra-regional free trade and market cooperation between developing and emerging regions was not possible until the 1990s when regional market integration and policy cooperation became a legitimate strategy of transatlantic, trilateral and OECD nations.
2. Sheldon, Ian M. (1996), *Industrial Organization and Trade in Food Industries*, Boulder, CO: Westview Press, pp. 197–212. According to Sheldon, US food-processing industries view profit maximization and growth as the criteria for FDI rather than product trade.
3. Dixon, John and Aidan Gulliver (2001), *Farming Systems and Poverty*, Joint FAO and World Bank Study, Rome: FAO.
4. Ibid.

5. Otsuki, Tsunehiro, John S. Wilson and Mirvat Sewadeh, *Saving Two in a Billion: A Case Study to Quantify the Trade Effect of European Food Safety Standards on African Exports*, policy paper, Development Research Group, Washington, DC: World Bank.
6. Bruinsma, Jelle (ed.) (2003), *World Agriculture Towards 2015/2030 – An FAO Perspective*, London and Rome: FAO/Earthscan.
7. See World Bank Standards–Africa Trade Standards Project, and Agriculture Initiative for Market Access, at www.worldbank.org.
8. The African Growth and Opportunity Act (AGOA) was signed into law on 18 May 2000 under Title I of the Trade and Development Act in the United States Department of Commerce. The policy provides coordinated market access and development assistance as incentives for market reform, and market governance in accordance with WTO trade liberalization goals. President Bush has announced his intention to extend the Act in 2008.
9. Oyejide, T. Ademala (1999), *Agriculture in the Millennium Round of Multilateral Trade Negotiations: African Interests and Options*, paper prepared for the World Bank in Cooperation with the World Trade Organization, Geneva: WTO, pp. 6–7.
10. Friis-Hansen, Esbern (2000), *Agricultural Policy in Africa After Adjustment, CDR Policy Paper*, Centre for Development Research, Copenhagen, Demark: CDR, pp. 43.
11. Oyejide, T. Ademola (2001), *Agriculture in the Millennium Round of Multilateral Trade Negotiations: African Interests and Options*, Washington, DC: World Bank.
12. Dixon and Gulliver (2001).
13. UNCTAD (2003), *World Investment Report 2003 – FDI Policies for Development*, Geneva: UNCTAD, at www.unctad.org/wir.
14. Reardib, Thomas, Julio A. Berdegue and John Farrington (2002), 'Supermarkets and farming in Latin America: pointing directions for elsewhere?', National Resource Perspectives No. 81, London: ODI.
15. Jaffee, Steven, Ron Kopicki, Patrick Labaste and Iain Christie (2003), *Modernizing Africa's Agri-food Systems: Analytical Framework and Implications for Operations*, African, Region Working Papers, series No. 44, Washington, DC: World Bank, p. 14. Also see *Food Engineering*, October 2002 list of the world top 100 food processors.
16. Report of the First Commonwealth Agricultural Seminar, at www.rase.org.uk/communications.
17. Jaffee et al. (2003), pp. 9–20.
18. Ibid.
19. Ibid.
20. For a good economic history analysis of the global coffee commodity chain see William Gervase Clarence-Smith and Steven Topic (eds) (2003), *The Global Coffee Economy in Africa, Asia and Latin America 1500–1989*, Cambridge: Cambridge University Press.
21. Kaplinsky, R. and R. Fitter (2004), 'Technology and globalization: who gains when commodities area de-commodified?', *International Journal of Technology and Globalization*, **1** (1): 5–28.
22. Ibid.
23. Ibid.
24. Fitter, Robert and Raphael Kaplinsky (2001), *Can an Agricultural 'Commodity' be De-Commodified, and If So Who Is to Gain?*, Discussion Paper No. 380, Institute of Development Studies, Sussex: IDS, pp. 21–5.
25. Dolan, Catherine, John Humphrey and Clara Harris-Pascal (1999), *Horticultural Commodity Chains: The Impact of the UK Market on the African Fresh Vegetable Industry*, Discussion Paper No. 96, Institute of Development Studies, Sussex: IDS.
26. Jaffee et al. (2003), op. cit., pp. 18–29.
27. Dolan (1999), op. cit., pp. 36–7.
28. Ibid.
29. Malzbender, David (2003), *EU, CAP Reform and Southern Africa, No. 8/2003*, Trade Law Centre for Southern Africa (TRALAC), Stellenbosch, South Africa, p. 3–5.
30. Sidibe, A.S. (2003), 'The present and future organization of veterinary services in Africa', *Review of Science and Technology – Office of International Epizootics*, **22** (2): 473–84.

31. Environmental News Network-Reuters, 'Animal rights groups want unwanted Gulf sheep killed fast', 17 September 2003.
32. *Sydney Morning Herald*, 'Stranded sheep'not bound for our dinner table', 3 November 2003.
33. *Sydney Morning News*, 'Odyssey of Australian sheep to end in Eritrean pots', 28 October 2003.
34. Vosloo, W., A.D.S. Bastos, A. Michel and G.R. Thomson (2002), 'Tracing movement of African buffalo in Southern Africa', *Science and Technical Review – Office of International Epizootics*, **20** (2): 630–9.
35. See SADC website at http://SADC.org, Animal health.
36. Collier, P. (2002), 'The future of perennial crops', *African Development Review*, **14** (2): 237–50.
37. Bhat, Ramesh V. and Siruguri Vasanthi (2003), *Food Safety Issues in Food Security and Food Trade: Mycotoxin Food Safety Risk in Developing Countries*, Brief 3 of 17, July, 2020 Vision for Food, Agriculture and the Environment, Washington, DC: IFPRI.
38. *BBC News*, 'Mouldy maize kills 80 Kenyans', 7 June 2004.
39. Ibid.
40. *BBC News*, 'Killer maize sparks Kenyan alarm', 13 June 2004.
41. Bhat and Vasanthi (2003), op. cit.
42. Ibid.
43. *News and Highlights of the Food and Agricultural Organization of the United Nations*, 'Cleaning up the pesticides nobody wants', 24 May 1999.
44. Ibid.
45. According to Africa Stockpiles, a starting fund of $50 million is now available to launch this new World Bank initiative which will increase the acceptance of African agricultural commodities and food products. At the same time, this project will improve public health and consumer safety. See www.Africa Stockpiles.org.
46. Ibid.
47. Consumers International, 'African consumer leaders adopt a critical position with respect to GMOs and their implications for food security in the region', press release, 26 November 2002, at www.consumersinternational.org.
48. There is a growing transatlantic conflict over the role of GM food production in Africa as a solution for hunger, food insecurity, increasing agricultural productivity and competitiveness in transatlantic and global agri-food industries.
49. Pew Initiative on Food and Biotechnology (2003), 'Biotech firms share technology to help Africa', *News in Brief*, Washington, DC: Pew Initiative on Food and Biotechnology, 28 March, http://www.pewagbiotech.org/buzz/print.php 3?Story 10–99.
50. Ibid.
51. Ibid.
52. National Food Control Systems Assuring Food Safety-GF/CRD FAO-1. Conference room document proposed by FAO, FAO/WHO Global Forum on Food Safety Regulators, Marrakech, 28–30 January 2002, at www.fao.org/docrep.
53. Woteki, C.E. (2000), *Food Safety: HACCP and Future Regulation*, FSIS/USDA, Washington, DC: USDA.
54. Boutrif, Ezzeddine and Catherine Bessy (1999), 'Basic approaches to consumer protection', Conference on International Food Trade Beyond 2000: Science Based Decisions, Harmonization, Equivalence and Mutual Recognition, Melbourne, 11–15 October 1999, Rome: FAO, at www.fao.org/docrep.
55. The benefits of this regulatory and food safety standards strategy include increasing safety, quality and competitiveness of African agri-food products in global markets. Likewise, more efficient food safety controls for food production, processing, retailing and marketing systems are implemented through compliance with Codex standards and the WTO SPS Agreement.
56. Baptist, G.O. (2002), *Mission Report – Food Control Country Profiles for Botswana, Lesotho, Namibia, South Africa and Swaziland*, Rome: FAO, pp. 29–38.
57. Ibid.

58. 'Guidelines for Food Safety Control of Imported Foods Entering South Africa through Land Ports of Entry', Department of Health, Food Control Directorate, at www.doh.gov.za/docs.
59. Ibid.
60. Yankey, L.E. (2003), *Mission Report – Food Control Country Profiles for Kenya*, Rome: FAO. Also see FAO (2002), *Awareness Training Workshop on Food Safety Concerns in the Africa Region, Food Safety Issues and Challenges – Mali and Kenya 2002*, Rome: FAO.
61. *FAO/WHO Global Forum of Food Safety Regulators* (2002), 'Improving efficiency and transparency in food safety systems – sharing experiences', Mamdouh Gabr, Professor of Pediatries, University of Cairo, FAO/WHO Global forum of Food Safety Regulator Proceedings, Rome: FAO, pp. 77–81.
62. See the Inter-African Phytosaniatry Council, African Union, The African Plant Protection Organization (APPO), Regulatory & Quality Infrastructure Development for Food Safety and Food Quality, Awareness Raising Programme for East and West African Countries, Sweden, 28 September–24 October 2003.
63. FAO/WHO (2000), *Harmonization and Cooperation in Food Legislation and Control Activities*, Codex Coordinating Committee for Africa, 14th Session, Kampala, 27–30 November, Rome: FAO.
64. African Union interafrican Bureau for Animal Resources, Pan American Program for the Control of Epizootics, www.au-iba.org.
65. Ibid.
66. Ibid.
67. SADC website, Animal health.
68. Ibid.
69. Ibid.
70. Locusts and trans-boundary pests destroy crops in a matter of minutes in Africa.
71. See the AU–APPO website, at www.AU-APPO.org and the Inter-African Phytosanitary Council website which is the Regional Plant Protection Organization for Africa, at www.ippc.int/id/16384.
72. See Paarlberg, Robert L. (2001), *The Politics of Precaution: Genetically Modified Crops in Developing Countries*, Baltimore, MD: Johns Hopkins University Press. According to the author, African governments fear the loss of agricultural commodity markets in the EU due to their inability to implement mandatory food labelling, segregation and traceability requirements.
73. Consumers International (2002).
74. See NEPAD (2001), *The New Partnership for Africa's Development*, Dakar: NEPAD, p. 36.
75. Mugabe, Dr John (2003), *Biotechnology and Sustainable Development in Africa: Towards Regional Consensus and Common Strategy*, Dakar: NEPAD, pp. 1–10.
76. Ibid.
77. Abila, Richard O. (2003), *Food Safety Issues in Food Security and Food Trade, Case Study: Kenyan Fish Exports*, 2020 Vision for Food, Agriculture and the Environment, Focus 10, Brief 8 of 17, July, Washington, DC: International Food Policy Research Institute.
78. Ibid.
79. Ibid.
80. Ibid.
81. Ibid.
82. Billy, Thomas J. (2000), *Factors Driving Food Safety Policy and Their Implications in the Harmonization of Food Standards*, FSIS/USDA, Washington, DC: USDA, at www.fsis.usda.gov.
83. Jaffee et al. (2003), op. cit., pp. 10–11.
84. Unnevehr, Laurian and Nanc Hirschorn (2003), *Food Safety Issues in the Developing World*, Washington, DC: World Bank.
85. Tinker, Irene (1997), *Street Foods: Urban Food and Employment in Developing Countries*, New York and London: Oxford University Press.

86. African Development Bank (2000), *Agricultural and Rural Development Sector Paper*, Bank Group Policy, Nairobi: African Development Bank.
87. Ibid.
88. Joint FAO/WHO Food Standards Programme (2002), *Capacity Building for Food Standards and Regulations*, FAO/WHO Coordinating Committee for Africa, Fifteenth Session, Kampala, Codex Alimentarius Commission, 26–29 November, Rome: FAO, p. 2.
89. Ibid.
90. Ibid.
91. Ibid., p. 5.
92. Ibid., p. 4.
93. Ibid., p. 2. Also see FAO (2001), *Manual on the Application of the HACCP System in Mycotoxin Prevention and Control*, FAO Food and Nutrition Paper No. 73, FAO and the International Atomic Energy Agency (IAEA), Rome: FAO, pp. 1–24.
94. Wilson, John S. and Victor O. Abiola (2003), *Standards and Global Trade: A Fair Voice for Africa*, Washington, DC: World Bank.
95. Ibid.
96. Jaffee et al. (2003), op. cit., pp. 22–7. African governments and multilateral aid agencies must provide integrated packages of extension services and modernization of agricultural sector producers and food-processing industries to meet global food safety and food quality standards.

REFERENCES

Abila, Richard O. (2003), *Food Safety Issues in Food Security and Food Trade, Case Study: Kenyan Fish Exports*, 2020 Vision for Food, Agriculture and the Environment, Focus 10, Brief 8 of 17, July, Washington, DC: International Food Policy Research Institute.

African Development Bank (2000), *Agricultural and Rural Development Sector Paper*, Bank Group Policy, Nairobi: African Development Bank.

AU–APPO website. At www.AO-APPO.org.

Bankole, Abiodun, Olawale Ogunkoba and T. Ademola Oyejide (2000), *Quantifying the Trade Impact of Sanitary and Phytosanitary Standards: What Is Known and Issues of Importance for Sub-Saharan Africa*, paper for World Bank Workshop on Quantifying the Trade Effects of Standards and Regulatory Barriers: Is It Possible? Washington, DC: World Bank.

Baptist, G.O. (2002), *Mission Report – Food Control Country Profiles for Botswana, Lesotho, Namibia, South Africa and Swaziland*, Rome: FAO.

BBC News (2004a), 'Killer maize sparks Kenyan alarm', 13 June.

BBC News (2004b), 'Mouldy maize kills 80 Kenyans', 7 June.

Bhat, Ramesh V. and Siruguthi Vasanthi (2003), *Food Safety Issues in Food Security and Food Trade – Mycotoxin Food Safety Risk in Developing Countries*, Brief 3 of 17, July, 2020 Vision for Food, Agriculture and the Environment, Washington, DC: IFPRI.

Billy, Thomas J. (2000), *Factors Driving Food Safety Policy and Their Implications in the Harmonization of Food Standards*, FSIS/USDA, Washington, DC: USDA, at www.fsis.usda.gov.

Boutrif, Ezzeddine and Catherine Bessy (1999), 'Basic approaches to consumer protection', Conference on International Food Trade Beyond 2000: Science Based Decisions, Harmonization, Equivalence and Mutual Recognition, Melbourne, 11–15 October, Rome: FAO, at www.fao.org/docrep.

Bruinsma, Jelle (2003), *World Agriculture Towards 2015/2030 – An FAO Perspective*, London and Rome: FAO/Earthscan.

Clarence-Smith, William Gervase and Steven Topic (eds) (2003), *The Global Coffee Economy in Africa, Asia and Latin America 1500–1989*, Cambridge: Cambridge University Press.

Consumers International (2002), 'African consumer leaders adopt a critical position with respect to GMOs and their implications for food security in the region', press release, 26 November, at www.consumersinternational.org.

Daviron, B. and P. Gibbon (2002), 'Global commodity chains and African export agriculture', *Journal of Agrarian Change*, **2** (2): 137–61.

Dixon, John and Aidan Gulliver (2001), *Farming Systems and Poverty*, Joint FAO and World Bank Study, Rome: FAO.

Dolan, Catherine, John Humphrey and Clara Harris-Pascal (1999), *Horticultural Commodity Chains: The Impact of the UK Market on the African Fresh Vegetable Industry*, Discussion paper No. 96, Institute of Development Studies, Sussex: IDS.

Environmental News Network-Reuters (2003), 'Animal rights groups want unwanted sheep killed fast', 17 September.

FAO (2001), *Manual on the Application of the HACCP System in Mycotoxin Prevention and Control*, FAO Food and Nutrition Paper No. 73, FAO and the International Atomic Energy Agency, Rome: FAO.

FAO (2002), *Awareness Training Workshop on Food Safety Concerns in the Africa Region, Food Safety Issues and Challenges – Mali and Kenya 2002*, Rome: FAO.

FAO/WHO (2000), *Harmonization and Cooperation in Food Legislation and Control Activities*, Codex Coordinating Committee for Africa, 14th Session, Kampala, 27–30 November, Rome,: FAO.

FAO/WHO Global Forum of Food Safety Regulators (2002), *Improving efficiency and Transparency in Food Safety Systems*, Mamdouh Gabr, Professor of pediatrics, University of Cairo, FAO/WHO Global Forum of Food Safety Regulators Proceedings, Rome: FAO, pp. 77–81.

Fitter, Robert and Raphael Kaplinsky (2001) *Can an Agricultural 'Commodity' Be De-commodified, and If So Who Is to Gain?*, Discussion Paper No. 380, Institute of Development Studies, Sussex: IDS.

Friis-Hansen, Esbern (2000), *Agricultural Policy in Africa After Adjustment, CDR Policy Paper*, Centre for Development Research, Copenhagen: CDR.

'Guideline for Food Safety Control of Imported Foods Entering South Africa through land Ports of Entry', Department of Health, Food Control Directorate, at www.doh.gov.za/docs.

Hanik, M. and Henry J. Owusu (1998), 'Has ECOWAS promoted trade among its members?', *Journal of African Economies*, **7** (3): 363–70.

'Harmonization of International Standards – Current NASDA Policy', at www.nasda-hq.org.

Hertel, Thomas W., William A. Masters and Elbehri, Aziz (1998), 'The Uruguay Round and Africa: a global general equilibrium analysis', *Journal of African Economics*, **7** (2): 208–29.

Inter-African Phytosanitary Council website, at www.ippc.int/id/16384.

Jaffee, Steven, Ron Kopicki, Patrick Labaste and Iain Christie (2003), *Modernizing Africa's Agro-food Systems: Analysitical Framework and Implication for Operations*, African Region Working Papers, No. 44, Washington, DC: World Bank.

Joint FAO/WHO Food Standards Programme (2002a), *Capacity Building for Food Standards and Regulations*, FAO/WHO Coordinating Committee for Africa, Fifteenth Session, Kampala, Codex Alimentarius Commission, 26–29 November, Rome: FAO.

Joint FAO/WHO Food Standards Programme (2002b), *Report of the Evaluation of Codex Alimentarius, FAO and WHO Standards Work*, Rome: FAO.

Kaplinsky, R. and R. Fitter (2004), 'Technology and globalization: who gains when commodities area de-commodified?', *International Journal of Technology and Globalization*, **1** (1): 5–28.

Malzbender, David (2003), *EU CAP Reform and Southern Africa, No. 8/2003*,Trade Law Centre for Southern Africa (T/R/AL/AC), Stellenbosch, South Africa.

Mengu, Moses (2003), *Food Quality and Safety in the African Agri-Food Industry: Some Policy Implications*, WAITRO, Denmark: Danish Technological Institute.

Mugabe, Dr John (2003), *Biotechnology and Sustainable Development in Africa: Towards Regional Consensus and Common Strategy*, Dakar: NEPAD.

National Food Control Systems Assuring Food Safety-GF/CRD FAO-1 (2002), Conference room document proposed by FAO, FAO/WHO Global Forum on Food Safety Regulators, Marrakech, 28–30 January, at www.fao.org/docrep.

NEPAD (2001), *The New Partnership for Africa's Development*, Dakar: NEPAD.

News and Highlights of the Food and Agricultural Organizations of the United Nations (1999), 'Clening up the pesticides nobody wants', 24 May.

Oramah, B.O. and C. Abou-Lebof (1998), 'Commodity composition of African trade and intra-African trade potential', *Journal of African Economies*, 7 (2): 263–7.

Otsuki, Tsunehiro, John S. Wilson and Mirvat Sewadeh, *Saving Two in a Billion: A Case Study to Quantify the Trade Effect of European Food Safety Standards on African Exports*, policy paper, Development Research Group, Washington, DC: World Bank.

Oyejide, T. Ademala (1999), *Agriculture in the Millennium Round of Multilateral Trade Negotiations: African Interests and Options,* paper prepared for the World Bank in Cooperation with the World Trade Organization, Geneva: WTO.

Oyejide, T. Ademola (2001), *Agriculture in the Millennium Round of Multilateral Trade Negotiations: African Interests and Options*, Washington, DC: World Bank.

Paarlberg, Robert L. (2001), *The Politics of Precaution: Genetically Modified Crops in Developing Countries*, Baltimore, MD: Johns Hopkins University Press.

Pew Initiative on Food and Biotechnology (2003), 'Biotech firms share technology to help Africe', *News in Brief*, Washington, DC: Pew Initiative on Food and Biotechnology, 28 March, http://pewagbiotech.org/buzz/print.ph3? Story 10–99.

Reardib, Thomas, Julio A Berdegue and John Farrington (2002), 'Supermarkets and farming in Latin America: pointing directions for elsewhere?', National Resource Perspectives No. 81, London: ODI.

SADC website, at http://SADC.org, Animal health.

Sheldon, Ian M. (1996), *Industrial Organization and Trade in Food Industries*, Boulder, CO: Westview Press.

Sidebe, A.S. (2003), 'The present and future organization of veterinary services in Africa', *Review of Science and Technology Office of International Epizootics*, **22** (2): 473–84.

Sydney Morning Herald (2003), 'Stranded sheep not bound for our dinner table', 3 November.
Sydney Morning News (2003), 'Odyssey of Australian sheep to end in Eritrean pots', 28 October.
Tinker, Irene (1997), *Street Foods: Urban Food and Employment in Developing Countries*, New York and Oxford: Oxford University Press.
Tsunehiro, Otsuki, John S. Wilson and Mirvat Sewadeh (2001), *A Race to the Top? A Case Study of Food Safety Standards and African Exports*, World Bank Research Paper, No. 2563, Washington, DC: World Bank.
UNCTAD (2003), *World Investment Report, 2003 – FDI Policies for Development*, Geneva: UNCTAD, at www.unctad.org/wir.
Unnevehr, Laurian and Nanc Hirschorn (2003), *Food Safety Issues in the Developing World*, Washington, DC: World Bank.
Vosloo, W., A.D.S. Bastos, A. Michel and G.R.Thomson (2002), 'Tracing movement of African buffalo in Southern African', *Science and Technology Review – Office of International Epizootics*, **20** (2): 630–9.
Wilson, John S. and Victor O. Abiola (2003) *Standards and Global Trade: A Fair Voice for Africa*, Washington, DC: World Bank.
World Bank Standards–Africa Trade Standards Trade Project, and Agriculture Initiative for Market Access, at www.worldbank.org.
Woteki, C.E. (2000), *Food Safety: HACCP and Future Regulation*, FSIS/USDA, Washington, DC: USDA.
Yankey, L.E. (2003), *Mission Report – Food Control Country Profiles for Kenya*, Rome: FAO.

9. Regulatory standards and food safety in South Asia: the growing role of SAARC

Reba A. Carruth*

I INTRODUCTION: REGIONAL COOPERATION THROUGH SAARC AND SAFTA: IMPLICATIONS FOR THE REGULATION OF FOOD SAFETY

At the start of the twenty-first century, South Asian nations are strengthening the regulation of food safety in national and regional food systems, and agri-food industries. To a large extent, national regulation and regional governance of food safety is directly linked to the dominant role of farming, agricultural commodity production and food-processing industries in South Asian economies. However, growing food safety risks threaten food security, food systems, agri-food trade and South Asian food-processing industries.

The South Asia region has historical and cultural precedents for increased intra-regional food trade, agri-food industry integration and policy cooperation. During the British colonial period, India, Pakistan, Bangladesh and Sri Lanka were a unified economic and trade region. In this regional system, domestic food demand and production were met by intra-regional farming and agri-food market systems. However, the closed economy and import substitution policies during the early independence period, resulted in low levels of complementarity in South Asian agri-food industries.[1]

In light of the global trend in regional free trade, market integration, and policy cooperation, the South Asian Association for Regional Cooperation (SAARC) serves as the regional institutional framework for collective action.[2] The goals of SAARC are socio-economic development, increasing living standards and effective governance of South Asian nations.[3] In SAARC, South Asian countries are developing frameworks for regulatory harmonization and food safety standards for the agri-food sector.[4]

In accordance with the global trend in regional free trade areas, SAARC member governments launched the South Asian Free Trade Area (SAFTA) in January 2006.[5] As SAFTA evolves, the Government of India proposes the adoption of an EU model of regional market integration, a common currency, policy cooperation and a South Asian Economic Union by the year 2015.[6] However, the SAARC region has low levels of intra-regional trade. Consequently the EU and NAFTA regions are the major trading partners for SAARC countries.[7]

II SOUTH ASIAN FOOD PRODUCTION AND AGRI-FOOD INDUSTRIES

Changing Structure of Indian and South Asian Agri-Food Industries

Historically, farming and agriculture in SAARC countries is carried out by large numbers of small farmers and traditional food producers.[8] In response to these trends, agriculture and food production in South Asia underwent change and transformation at the start of the 2000s.[9] In turn, structural changes occurred in South Asian farming, agriculture and agri-food industries.[10]

As the decade unfolds, agriculture and food-processing industries are the basis of socio-economic development and global market integration for SAARC countries.[11] In light of the strategic importance of agriculture and agri-food industries, SAARC nations unilaterally reduced trade barriers and implemented policy reforms during the Uruguay Round Agriculture Agreement (URAA) (Stern and Mattoo 2003). However, South Asian agri-food products failed to gain increased access to transatlantic markets.[12] Therefore, global agricultural market liberalization in the WTO increases the importance of SPS and Codex standards.[13]

In South Asia, agriculture and food production is undergoing modernization and change due to the growing use of contract farming. However, the position of the South Asian region in the global economy is declining due to the following factors: decreasing comparative advantage in agriculture, agri-food product rejection, growing SPS barriers, agri-food industry protection and subsidies in the OECD countries.[14] Therefore, the strengthening of food safety regulations is a priority for SAARC countries.[15]

In South Asian agri-food industries, SAARC farmers and food producers have limited scale and scope of operation, and low levels of efficiency and productivity. Consequently, many SAARC agri-food industries are fragmented, and lack modern supply chain management and food safety infrastructure.[16] In this sector, India is a leading global producer of cereals, pulses, edible oils, meat, poultry, eggs and dairy products.[17] India is also the sixth largest global poultry producer after the United States, Brazil, the EU, China and Mexico.[18] Finally, India is a major producer of fresh and processed fruits, vegetables and fish.

Table 9.1 Food and agricultural production in the SAARC countries

	1991	2001
Marine capture fisheries: production (1000 MT)		
Bangladesh	258.9	330.0
Bhutan	N/A	N/A
India	2353.2	2787.9
Maldives	90.1	125.8
Nepal	N/A	N/A
Pakistan	399.6	426.9
Sri Lanka	174.2	249.8
	1992	2002
Hen egg production (1000 MT)		
Bangladesh	67.5	133.5
Bhutan	0.3	0.2
India	1262.0	2000.0
Maldives	N/A	N/A
Nepal	17.7	25.0
Pakistan	231.0	345.6
Sri Lanka	46.1	53.6
Total meat production (1000 MT)		
Bangladesh	325.8	433.2
Bhutan	7.1	6.5
India	4232.7	5743.5
Maldives	0.8	1.1
Nepal	190.1	246.1
Pakistan	1473.7	1838.6
Sri Lanka	70.4	119.3
Chicken production (million heads)		
Bangladesh	100.6	140.0
Bhutan	0.1	0.2
India	284.0	823.5
Maldives	N/A	N/A
Nepal	13.5	21.4
Pakistan	82.0	153.0
Sri Lanka	8.7	10.7

Source: Selected Indicators of Food and Agriculture Development in the Asia-Pacific Region (1992–2002), FAO Regional Office for Asia and the Pacific Region-Bangkok 2003, pp. 128–9, 137–8 and 166.

Table 9.2 South Asian crop production

	1992	2002
Rice paddy production (1000 MT)		
Bangladesh	27 510.4	38 134.0
Bhutan	43.0	44.3
India	109 001.2	116 580.0
Maldives	N/A	N/A
Nepal	2 584.9	4 130.0
Pakistan	4 674.2	6 343.0
Sri Lanka	2 339.7	2 794.0
Wheat production (1000 MT)		
Bangladesh	1 065.1	1 606.0
Bhutan	5.0	4.4
India	55 689.5	71 814.3
Maldives	N/A	N/A
Nepal	762.0	1 258.1
Pakistan	15 684.2	18 226.1
Sri Lanka	N/A	N/A
Cereals production (1000 MT)		
Bangladesh	2 8654.3	39 811.0
Bhutan	105.8	106.9
India	201 468.4	213 590.1
Maldives	0.0	0.0
Nepal	4 901.8	7 212.2
Pakistan	22 123.4	26 767.9
Sri Lanka	2 373.9	2 827.1

Source: Selected Indicators of Food and Agriculture Development in the Asia-Pacific Region (1992–2002), FAO Regional Office for the Asia-Pacific, Bangkok, October 2003, pp. 21, 24 and 33.

In the fruit and vegetable processing industry sector, India is increasingly attracting joint ventures and FDI from US, Swiss, Dutch and German food companies. The main products for joint venture processing are mushrooms, purees, jams, jellies, fruit juices, fruit concentrates, freeze dried vegetables, onions and frozen vegetables. Through these joint ventures and strategic alliances, financial investment and technology transfer is rapidly building Indian food-processing industries. The main markets for India's processed foods are Saudi Arabia, Kuwait, the United Arab Emirates, the Netherlands, Hong Kong, the United States, Germany, the United Kingdom and Russia.

The Indian food-processing industry has the following range of product

Table 9.3 Global dairy food producers in Indian dairy food industry

Company	Brands	Major Products
Nestlé India Limited	Milkmaid, Cerelac, Lactogen	Sweetened condensed milk and milk powder
Milkfood Limited	Milkfood	Ghee, ice cream, and other milk products
SmithKline Beecham Limited	Horlicks	Malted milkfood, ghee, butter, powdered milk, milk fluid and other milk-based baby foods.
Indodan Industries Limited	Indana	Condensed milk, skimmed milk powder, whole milk powder, dairy milk whitener, chilled and processed milk
Gujarat Co-operative milk Marketing Federation Limited	Amul	Butter, cheese and other milk products
H.J. Heinz Limited	Farex, Complan, Glactose, Bonniemix, Vitamilk	Infant milkfood, malted milkfood
Cadbury	Bournvita	Malted food

Source: Indian Ministry of Food Processing, 'Industry Specific Information for Milk and Milk Products', at http://mofi.nic.in/industryspecific information/milk/milk players/milk players.htm.

categories: food grain milling, dairy products, poultry, eggs and fish processing, breakfast foods, confectionary and baked goods, biscuits and soft drinks. In order to increase the safety and quality of processed foods, India implements ISO 9000 quality standards through the support of the Ministry of Food-Processing Industries. For example, cold chain technologies are built to reduce post-harvest losses through spoilage and food contamination.[19] In this regard, SAARC countries are increasing the competitiveness of their food-processing industries. At the same time, FDI by transatlantic and global food companies supports the modernization of South Asian food-processing plants and cold chain infrastructure. Consequently, FDI in the Indian agri-food industry sector has multiplier effects in the SAARC region (Ingco 2003).

Food Safety in SAARC Agriculture and Agri-Food Industries

In OECD countries, strong government and business relations, 'market friendly' regulations and food safety standards strengthen the competitive position of US and EU agri-food firms and industries. In turn, transatlantic food safety regulations protect US and EU agri-food products from competition by processed food industries in South Asia (Gupta 2002). Consequently, SAARC spice, tea, rice and oilseed industries face rising regulatory standards in value-added transatlantic and OECD markets.[20]

In this regard, the lack of water and rural infrastructure systems, limited public funding and private resources for national public health systems, rapid urbanization, and food contamination resulting in diarrhea linked illnesses pose 'multidimensional' challenges for South Asian countries. Food-borne illnesses are the leading cause of illness and death in many developing nations and the South Asian region.[21] As a result of limited investment in rural infrastructure and public health resources, food safety risks are high for SAARC consumers. For example, poultry and meat, eggs, raw milk, dairy, cooked and processed foods with contaminated raw food ingredients can pose serious food safety risks in some South Asian countries.[22] Therefore, SAARC countries face the following barriers to competition in global agri-food industries:

- high cost of SPS, Codex and HACCP standards compliance
- perceived irrelevance of foreign food safety standards to South Asia
- inadequate information on new standards and enforcement timetables, product testing, conformity assessment and certification problems
- and inadequate scientific data in global food markets.[23]

In response to these challenges, the Government of India requests that SAARC countries receive longer periods of time for compliance with WTO SPS and Codex food safety standards. Moreover, the Government of India calls for more participation of SAARC countries in the development of food safety standards, regulatory equivalence and MRA agreements in transatlantic agri-food industries.

III CRITICAL FOOD SAFETY ISSUES IN THE SAARC REGION

The environmental contamination of agriculture, animal livestock and food products with chemical, pesticide and microbial agents is a growing threat to food safety in South Asia.[24] Therefore, the governance of food safety in South Asian agri-food industries and food systems requires preventative public health policies and regulations to eradicate food contamination.[25] In this respect, the following food safety threats are emerging as major consumer protection and public health issues in the SAARC member countries (Karki 2002).

Street Foods

Street foods provide an easy and cheap source of nourishment for a large number of people in the South Asian region. The growing use of street food reflects socio-economic trends toward urbanization, and changing consumption patterns in the region. In terms of benefits, street foods provide an inexpensive, convenient and nutritious source of food for both rural and urban consumers. In addition, street foods provide a major source of income for poor people, especially women, and often provide a mechanism for self-employment in SAARC member countries.[26]

In spite of these benefits, street foods pose major food safety risks to consumers. In most cases, a wide range of foods is sold on carts and stalls. However, there is poor food hygiene due to the lack of access to clean water, sanitation infrastructure, toilets and contamination by food handlers.[27] Therefore, street food risks are directly related to the lack of food safety infrastructure, that is, electricity, clean water, refrigeration, certification of vendors and food inspection. As a result, street foods present major food safety risks to consumers, and threaten public health in the SAARC region.

The lack of food safety education, microbial surveillance, standards enforcement and HACCP food-processing inspection are also increasing the health risks for South Asian consumers. In response to these street food safety risks, SAARC member governments are developing regulations and standards to control this sector of the national food system. To achieve these goals, South Asian street food vendors and consumers must be educated and trained to recognize and prevent food contamination. Likewise, regulation, registration and licensing are needed, along with street food vending infrastructure, such as HACCP training for small enterprises.[28]

Pesticides and Food Chemical Contamination

By the start of the decade, low food quality due to product contamination and the lack of food safety enforcement was on the rise.[29] In many cases, the contamination of agricultural commodities and adulteration of processed food products are due to the lack of compliance with Codex maximum residue standards. For example, Germany rejected tea imports from Nepal due to high levels of pesticide residues. Similar incidents also occurred with Sri Lankan and Indian tea exports. Therefore, a major food safety concern in SAARC member countries is the protection of South Asian consumers from residues in agri-food products.

In this respect, there is a growing threat to food safety due to environmental contamination of agri-food industry supply chains in SAARC member countries. For example, in Nepal, the Kinely brand of bottled water, which is produced by Bottler Nepal for Coca-Cola, was declared unsafe due to chemical residue contamination.[30] As a result of chemical residues, many SAARC agricultural commodity and processed food products face high rates of rejection in transatlantic markets and global agri-food industries.[31]

In South Asia, there are common food industry specific standards for milk and diary products, grains, vegetables edible oils, spices, sugars, tea and coffee.[32] However, SAARC countries need more regulation and Codex standards harmonization for the monitoring of food additives such as emulsifying and stabilizing agents.[33] In many cases, high levels of adulteration, and food safety risks exist due to the dilution of expensive oils with cheaper substitutes that may contain high levels of trace elements.[34] Ultimately, the lack of common standards for food preservatives, colors, emulsifying agents and antioxidant additives reduces the safety of SAARC food products. Since most SAARC countries have generic standards, India is developing maximum limit standards for selected food stabilizing, buffering, flavoring and anti-caking food additives.[35]

In the case of food coloring, the regulation of food safety is very important in the SAARC region.[36] Since traditional foods are widely consumed in South Asia, natural colors, inorganic pigments and artificial food colors are often used. In the case of natural food colors, carotens, carotenoic acids, saffron, tumeric, curucumin are some of the major regulated food substances in SAARC countries. In the case of synthetic colors, India, Bangladesh Nepal, Sri Lank and Pakistan have different regulations. As a result of converging food preparation and coloring practices, Codex standards for food coloring should be adopted and harmonized by SAARC countries.[37]

Food Packaging and Labeling

In the area of food labeling, SAARC countries are not in compliance with Codex standards. The Codex labeling standards require that the name of the food, list of all ingredients, net contents, country of origin, lot identification, date of production and expiration, storage and usage instructions, and the name and address of the food product producer appear on the label. While India complies with Codex food labeling standards, most SAARC countries do not. As a result, South Asian food product detention and rejection problems are growing in transatlantic markets and global agri-food industries.

Mycotoxins

Mycotoxins represent a major food safety and public health threat in the SAARC region.[38] In terms of incidence, South Asian climate factors result in the rapid growth of fungus before and after the harvesting of agricultural commodities.[39] At the regional level, SAARC farmers and agri-food industries face high levels of mycotoxin contamination due to their growing production and processing of the following commodities: cereals and grains (sorghum, maize and millet), nuts (peanuts and pistachios), dried fruits, chillies peppers and oilseeds.[40] As a result, SAARC agricultural commodity and food product rejection is growing in transatlantic markets and global agri-food industries.

Metal Residues

In South Asia, heavy metal residues pose food safety risks for Indian and SAARC consumers.[41] In the case of heavy metal residues in food, Codex recommends standards for lead, cooper, arsenic, tin, zinc and iron. In light of diverging standards for metal residues in the SAARC region, regulatory harmonization through the Codex framework is urgently needed. Through the use of Codex standards for heavy metal residues, SAARC member countries can increase the safety of their national food systems and agri-food industries. In support of the adoption of common standards, SAARC countries are developing a regional database for the surveillance of food additives, heavy metal and chemical pesticide residues in food.[42]

Biotechnology and GM Foods in South Asia and the SAARC Region

At the present time, SAARC member countries face decreasing government investment in agriculture, growing food contamination risks and changing consumer demand. As a result, modern biotechnology and innovative agriculture and animal livestock management strategies are needed in SAARC countries. Through investment in R&D and modern biotechnology, 'post-Green Revolution' problems arising from stagnant crop and animal livestock productivity and soil depletion due to intensive farming practices by small farmers can be addressed.[43]

IV FOOD SAFETY REGULATION, INDUSTRY STANDARDS AND FOOD CONTROL SYSTEMS IN THE SAARC REGION

National Food Safety Regulation in SAARC Countries

At the start of this decade, SAARC member countries had diverse food safety regulations, regulatory institutions and agri-food industry standards.[44] With the exception of India, most South Asian countries, even countries with food control agencies like Bangladesh, Pakistan and Sri Lanka, had limited regulatory capacity and infrastructure for risk assessment, food hygiene and food safety surveillance.[45] In turn, regulatory capacity problems threaten food safety in SAARC countries.[46] As a result of these regulatory and industry standard challenges, many SAARC food products are rejected in international markets.[47] Moreover, many SAARC food producers face growing liability for product safety, and the rejection of food products.[48] Therefore, SAARC countries carried out an extensive review of national food laws and food safety regulations in the late 1990s.[49]

Bangladesh

The Bangladesh Pure Food Ordinance, is taken from the East Pakistan Pure Food Ordinance of 1959. Later in 1994, Bangladesh's Food Safety Law was revised, but not implemented by the year 2000. The law does not address many current and emerging WTO SPS Agreement and Codex food safety standards. In Bangladesh's current food safety system, approximately 52 food commodities are covered, and require mandatory certification. In Bangladesh, food inspection and quality control are carried out by the Food Inspection Agency. The Food Inspection Agency has a laboratory for the analysis of pesticides and food contaminants.[50]

Bhutan

In 1980, the Government of Bhutan implemented the Livestock Act to address food safety issues related to increased chicken and fish importation from India. The Livestock Act also regulates animal slaughter and meat inspection. By the year 2000, Bhutan had no formal food safety legislation. Instead, food safety problems were addressed by the Department of Animal Husbandry in the Ministry of Agriculture. While a veterinary laboratory monitors animal health in Bhutan, food safety laboratories in the Indian Veterinary Research Institute are the reference standard. As a result of high levels of food imports from India, and the lack of national food laws, Bhutan relies on India's food safety regulations system.[51]

India

As the largest, richest and most technologically advanced member country in SAARC, India has a federal and state level system of food safety regulation. The basic food law for India is the Prevention of Food Adulteration Act of 1954. This food law is reviewed and amended by the federal government to meet public health, consumer safety and food market governance objectives. The Prevention of Food Adulteration Act was amended in 1964, 1976 and 1986. The goal of these amendments is to address emerging food safety regulation issues on a wide range of food standards including surveillance of food additives and contaminants.[52]

In the Indian food safety system, regulations and laws focus on food quality, consumer protection and the promotion of regional and global trade on behalf of farmers and agri-food industries.[53] For example, India has the Agriculture Produce Grading and Marketing Act, a BIS-Certification Marks Act, a Fruit Products Order, and the Export Quality Control and Inspection Acts.[54] In addition, several food safety regulations cover agri-food commodity production, distribution, storage and marketing. Consequently, India has the most comprehensive regulatory framework for food safety in the SAARC region.[55]

In 2002, the Government of India revised food regulations and launched a comprehensive program to harmonize food safety regulations with Codex standards.[56] In this process, the National Codex Committee was strengthened through the implementation of FAO technical assistance programs, and increasing awareness of Codex stakeholders.[57] During this period, the Government of India negotiated a comprehensive food safety capacity-building project with the World Bank, and launched a national HACCP implementation program in cooperation with industry, universities and technical organizations.

Maldives

By the start of this decade, the Government of the Maldives had not implemented food safety laws. Instead, the Consumer Protection Act of 1996 was enacted to protect consumer safety and public health in the Maldives food system. Through this Act, provisions for food labeling are provided. In terms of food inspection and monitoring, the Public Health Department under the Ministry of Health is responsible for surveillance of food safety in the production, processing and marketing of food.

Pakistan

In Pakistan, provincial governments are responsible for the regulation of food safety. However, by the year 2000, there was no federal or national system of food safety regulation in Pakistan. The Pakistan Standard Institute (PSI) develops voluntary food safety standards for agri-food products. The Ministry of Agriculture is responsible for the regulation of agricultural produce and animal livestock. The Ministry of Agriculture is also responsible for mandatory certification of selected foods such as fish products, oil cakes, dry whole chillies, onions, potatoes, citrus fruits, mangoes and eggs. In the case of food imports and exports, the Federal Ministry of Health monitors food safety and quality for Pakistan's agri-food industry and food system. In spite of these efforts, Pakistan is under pressure to comply with the WTO SPS Agreement and Codex standards.[58]

In 2002, the Pakistan Standards Quality Control Authority (PSQCA) was created under the Ministry of Science and Technology. Since that time, over 250 food safety standards have been developed for a wide range of agri-food products. However, many food safety standards are voluntary. During the same period, the Pakistan Food Quality Control Council (PFQCC) was reactivated, and the Pure Food Law was updated to meet mandatory WTO SPS/TBT rules. The Pakistan Ministry of Food, Agriculture and Livestock also strengthened food safety regulation, and developed a National Food Safety Plan that includes biological hazards, risk analysis, HACCP industry standards, chemical food hazards and regulatory capacity-building.[59]

Nepal

In Nepal, the Food Act 1966 and the Food Regulation 1970 serve as the national food safety framework. In Nepal's regulatory framework for food safety, consumer protection and governance of the national food system is carried out by an extensive food control system. The food safety system consists of inspection services, laboratories and enforcement programs. In Nepal, determination of adulterated food, food bans, misbranded and mislabeled food, product liability, licensing, development of food standards and laboratory analysis of food are major components of food safety regulation.[60]

In 2002, the Government of Nepal revised several food laws and regulations, and drafted new food safety policies and legislation to converge with Codex regulatory standards and WTO SPS guidelines. Through this process, Nepal is rapidly developing a comprehensive food safety and quality management system for the entire food chain. In this regulatory framework, Codes of Good Practices for food-processing and small slaughterhouses, GMP, HACCP and GAP to reduce pesticide hazards in vegetables were adopted.[61]

Sri Lanka

The Sri Lankan food safety system is governed by the Food Act. By 2002, Sri Lanka revised 23 food safety regulations as required by Codex. During that period, the Government of Sri Lanka introduced regulations for genetically modified food to comply with Codex food safety standards. At that time, an integrated 'farm to table' strategy was developed, and food certification systems were improved to strengthen the regulation of imported and exported foods. In order to finance the development of a strong food safety system, the Government of Sri Lanka requested multilateral aid and financial support.[62]

Strengthening Regulatory Standards in SAARC Countries

In support of regulatory reform and regulatory harmonization, International Life Sciences Institute (ILSI) India, provided a series of timely and important workshops, seminars and conferences on food safety issues. The following ILSI programs were held for public health, food safety and agri-food industry leaders in SAARC member countries: 1997 – Report on the Proceedings of the Seminar on the Harmonization of Food Laws, Food Safety Evaluation and Food Colors, Report on the Proceedings of the Conference on SPS/TBT Agreements and Codex; 1998 – Report on the Proceedings of the International Conference on New Technologies in Food-Processing, Report on the Workshop on Science Based Approaches to Harmonization of Regulatory Food Quality and Safety Measures in SAARC; and 2002 – South Asian Conference on Food Safety.[63]

The rejection of SAARC agri-food products due to adulteration and contamination is a growing problem for South Asian countries.[64] As a consequence, SAARC countries agreed to harmonize food safety and quality standards in accordance with WTO SPS and Codex requirements.[65] For the first phase of this process, India, Bangladesh, Sri Lanka and Nepal will harmonize food standards and regulations.[66] In this context, India is moving to rapidly improve the food quality and safety.[67] In 2005, the food safety and quality standards for milk and dairy, cereals, edible oils and fresh fruits and vegetables were harmonized. In the second phase, the SAARC countries will harmonize pesticide residue and food pathogen contamination standards by 2007.[68]

Agri-Food Product Traceability and Mandatory Labelling

The concerns over BSE, avian flu, mycotoxin contamination and GMO food safety risks are growing in SAARC agri-food industries. Consequently, animal livestock identification, agri-food product traceability and GM food segregation are rapidly emerging food safety issues for SAARC countries. In recognition of the growing urgency of animal livestock identification, food product labeling, traceability and GM food segregation, SAARC governments are developing a regulatory framework in the Codex Regional Committee for Asia. However, the Government of India is concerned about the regulatory capacity and time frame for SAARC countries to develop and enforce strict animal livestock identification, food product labeling and traceability standards.

The outbreaks of avian flu and BSE in the EU, Japan, Canada and the United States increase the urgency of animal livestock food traceability and product labeling in the South Asian region.[69] In response to these global food safety risks, SAARC member countries are developing frameworks for risk assessments that are to be used for mandatory product labeling, animal livestock identification and traceability regulations. However, the Government of India is requesting that Codex standards for product labeling and traceability not be used as a regulatory barrier. Therefore, SAARC governments are requesting specific Codex guidelines for the regulation of animal livestock identification and food traceability across the food chain.[70]

Governance of Biotechnology in SAARC Countries

In the South Asian region, modern biotechnology and GM food production are emerging areas of agriculture and agri-food industry innovation. However, SAARC countries have diverse regulatory policies for modern biotechnology and GM food production. Therefore, the regulation of modern biotechnology must address the following food safety issues:

- the application of genome science and modern biotechnology to South Asian farming and agriculture production to help poor farmers
- the potential risks and negative impacts of GM food production and modern biotechnology for SAARC food systems and agri-food industries
- the public health and food safety risks of GMOs and modern biotechnology for consumer safety in SAARC member countries
- potential risk of modern biotechnology and GMO foods being tested on South Asian nations as part of the global expansion of multinational food companies
- the risk of modern biotechnology and genome science creating a 'genetic divide' with little or no focus for staple crop improvement and small farmer input.[71]

In response to these challenges, SAARC governments are developing national and regional regulatory frameworks for GM food safety, scientific risk assessment, risk analysis, risk management and risk communication capacity.[72] In these biotechnology policy frameworks, GM crop and animal livestock safety, labeling, segregation and traceability regulations are emerging in South Asia.

HACCP Standards in the SAARC Region

In response to limited food safety infrastructure in the SAARC region, the US, EU and other OECD countries develop and maintain lists of high-risk food exporters. As a result, SAARC agricultural commodities and processed food products are evaluated on their compliance with Codex and HACCP standards, and the following food safety risk factors: insect/rodent/bird filth, low acid canned food, microbial contamination, incorrect labeling, food decay, pesticide residue, food additives, mould, heavy metals and other reasons. In many cases SAARC food exports and food products are often rejected and placed on automatic food detention in transatlantic and other OECD countries.[73]

The Case of HACCP Inspection in Bangladesh's Shrimp-Processing Industry

The case of Bangladesh's shrimp export industry illustrates the importance of HACCP standards for the competitiveness of SAARC food-processing industries.[74] In the late 1970s, Bangladesh expanded its seafood-processing industry into transatlantic and global markets. However, substandard seafood-processing resulted in automatic detention, and a FDA ban on shrimp exports to the US.[75] In spite of efforts to correct these problems, the EU banned the importation of fishery products from Bangladesh after inspection of seafood plants revealed continued food safety risks.[76] In response to this situation, the Government of Bangladesh invested in new food safety laboratories, employee training and new HACCP inspection technologies. By the 1990s, the value of Bangladesh's processed shrimp exports increased, and the competitive position of Bangladesh's seafood processors was strengthened in transatlantic and global food markets.[77]

HACCP Food Safety Compliance and Management-Based Regulation

In SAARC countries, industry standards, management-based regulation and self-regulation are new and emerging frameworks for food safety. In this regard, agri-food product equivalence, import/export inspection, and industry specific Best Practices and standards are needed to regulate SAARC agri-food industries.[78] However, SAARC countries need technical assistance and financial resources to customize HACCP process inspection systems.[79]

In the SAARC region, the seasonal nature of fresh fruit and vegetable farming, also serve as barriers to HACCP inspection compliance. In many cases SAARC food processors handle several food lines and lack resources for individual plans and programs for each product category.[80] In contrast to the transatlantic region, small South Asian companies have limited access to modern management, capital and technology for food-processing. Therefore HACCP and risk management capacity-building efforts are under way in SAARC countries to assist small farmers and medium size food processors.[81]

Very often, these companies have limited resources for participation in HACCP inspection programs, GAP, GMP and other management-based regulations. Furthermore, HACCP programs are difficult to implement in SAARC countries due to the large numbers of small food producers.[82] Therefore, the Government of India is working through the National Codex Committees and Regional Codex Committee for Asia to develop HACCP compliance programs for small and medium-sized firms in the SAARC region.

Harmonization of Codex and HACCP Food Inspection Standards in India

In response to growing pressure for compliance with transatlantic, WTO SPS and Codex standards, the Government of India is reforming the national food safety system. Through this reform process, the Directorate General of Health Services and the Ministry of Health and Family Welfare in India is adopting and harmonizing national regulations with the WTO SPS Agreement and Codex food safety standards.[83] The national food regulations and laws are reformed to strengthen food safety standards in the following areas: pesticide residues, veterinary antibiotic residues, heavy metals, mycotoxin and food pathogen contamination.[84]

In the case of food-processing inspections, Codex standards for HACCP and food hygiene standards were adopted by the Indian Bureau of Standards. As a result, over 1000 Indian companies are certified for HACCP inspection, and approximately 400 are under mandatory export certification.[85] Currently, attention is given to improving the quality of rice, milk and dairy products. However, Indian agri-food-industries and food-processing companies are only requested to 'voluntarily adopt' HACCP inspection standards. Therefore, harmonization with mandatory transatlantic Codex food safety and HACCP standards are required by the Government of India and SAARC agri-food industries.[86]

In India, the Export Inspection Council (EIC) is responsible for the certification of Indian agri-food exports, and establishes mutual recognition agreements in the transatlantic and OECD countries.[87] For example, the EIC is the designated regulatory authority for fish and seafood products by the European Commission. In the United States, the EIC is the designated regulatory authority for black pepper. In Sri Lanka, the Government of India signed agreements through EIC for 86 food products. In Australia, an agreement was reached for fish and seafood products.[88] As the decade unfolds, bilateral regulatory agreements are under way with Italy and

Singapore to provide information exchange on the following issues: agri-food product specifications, methods of sampling, inspection, testing, rejection procedures and appeals of rejection decisions.

V GOVERNANCE OF FOOD SAFETY IN SAARC: CAPACITY-BUILDING AND REGULATORY STANDARDS HARMONIZATION

The governance of food safety in South Asia represents a multidimensional public health and market regulation challenge for SAARC governments, citizens and agri-food industries (Khallil 2000). Consequently, SAARC member countries need more technical assistance for the reform of food laws, regulatory harmonization, and the adoption of Codex standards, Good Manufacturing Practices, Good Hygiene Practices and Good Agricultural Practices.[89] However, regulatory harmonization in SAARC countries is often delayed due to the following challenges:

- difficulties in trade with the US, EU and OECD countries due to increasing food safety standards for the production, processing, inspection and certification of food products
- low levels of participation in CAC, OIE and IPPC activities and meetings
- lack of accurate and timely regional data for multilateral standard-setting
- limited resources for SPS compliance, data communication and information exchange at the regional level
- undeveloped networks for regional laboratory, product conformity assessment and product safety certification.[90]

In response to the need for increased risk management, SAARC countries are modernizing laboratories, and developing regional risk identification, management and communication systems and food quality assurance plans.[91] At the request of the Government of India, the European Commission and FAO provide funding and technical assistance for regulatory capacity-building, laboratory upgrading, and the development of a database for importing country regulations and food standards.

Regional Food Safety: Risk Assessment and Risk Management Infrastructure

In South Asia, a Regional Action Plan on Standards, Quality Control and Measurement was developed through SAARC. The goal of this plan is to support compliance with the WTO SPS Agreement by countries in the South Asian region. Through this framework, SAARC member countries are adopting the following regulatory measures for consumer protection, food safety and public health:

- identification of agri-food products where intra-SAARC trade is at risk due to divergent national food safety standards and regulations
- harmonization of specific product standards as a platform for the development and implementation of regional standards
- regional consultations and development of common positions for the SAARC countries and South Asia region for international and multilateral standards to ensure consideration and protection of regional interests
- access to food and agri-food product certification strategies and programs of all SAARC countries including the exchange of information on regulations, laws and mandatory industry standards that affect national and regional certification
- increase of intra-SAARC trade through the regional exchange of information between regulators and industry associations in the area of agri-food products
- development and implementation of mutual recognition agreements and mutual acceptability of product certifications by SAARC countries
- establishment of a regional accreditation system that allows all SAARC countries to comply with international requirements and certification guidelines
- sharing of accreditation facilities and bodies to avoid duplication of efforts, resource depletion and to gain recognition from international accreditation bodies
- identification of state-of-the-art agri-food testing, certification and calibration facilities across the region to promote cooperation and regional access
- promotion of mutual acceptability of laboratory accreditation processes
- regional food safety cooperation through the SAARC Secretariat
- creation of a regional list of food safety, food control and HACCP experts
- exchange of experts for food safety, risk management and HACCP training among SAARC countries.[92]

Finally, regulatory capacity-building at the national and regional levels is the most urgent goal of SAARC governments.[93] As a result, infrastructure modernization, and policy support for food regulatory harmonization is growing in SAARC countries.[94]

VI MULTILATERAL COOPERATION AND FOOD SAFETY CAPACITY-BUILDING IN SOUTH ASIA: THE GROWING ROLE OF FAO, WHO AND CODEX ALIMENTARIUS

Codex Standards and Infrastructure in the SAARC Region

Codex Alimentarius standards are now the normative and technical framework for the regulation and governance of food safety. However, the lack of resources and food safety infrastructure results in the exclusion of SAARC countries from scientific data collection, and the development of multilateral food safety standards. Therefore, the full participation of SAARC countries, South Asian regional institutions and networks are required for the collection of scientific data. In turn, SAARC food safety experts must increase their participation in international standard-setting meetings to protect consumers and public health in South Asian food systems and agri-food industries.[95]

In response to WTO SPS and Codex food safety standards, SAARC countries are working with transatlantic and multilateral organizations to build regulatory capacity. Through international cooperation, regulatory and industry standards enforcement capacity is growing in SAARC countries. However, SAARC countries must be given full access and representation in the food safety standard-setting process through strengthened national Codex infrastructure. Therefore, SAARC governments are working through their National Codex Committees and Contact Points to create regional networks of food safety regulators and control agencies in the region.[96]

In this context, SAARC countries need rapid access to information on current and emerging regulations, food trade standards, and enforcement systems in other nations. While bilateral assistance is offered by the US and EU, it is driven by the interests of the transatlantic governments and agri-food industries instead of the collective needs of SAARC countries. Therefore, the US and EU must give more technical assistance as called for by the WTO SPS Agreement to support the compliance of SAARC countries with Codex standards. Finally, regulatory equivalence agreements with SAARC governments should support MRA approvals in the transatlantic and OECD countries.[97]

Regional Training and Human Resource Development for Food Control

In the SAARC member countries, food safety risk communication training is now an important area of national and regional capacity-building. Therefore, SAARC and FAO/WHO are establishing a network of universities and institutes. For example, FAO implemented a Technical Cooperation Program (TCP) to assist SAARC governments to strengthen national food systems, and to enhance laboratory facilities and scientific analysis capabilities as required by the WTO SPS Agreement.[98]

In 2000, FAO launched a multi-year TCP project to strengthen the Indian National Codex Committee and National Codex Contact Point. Through this project, the Government of India increased the effectiveness of Codex at the national level, and India's participation in international food safety forums. In a similar initiative, the Government of India in cooperation with FAO, provides training for government officials, industry and consumer groups. The goal of this training program is to strengthen food safety and food quality through the National Codex Committee. Finally, a national action plan for the harmonization of national food standards and regulations is available in India through the support of FAO and recommendations from the Codex Alimentarius Commission.[99]

In the South Asian region, FAO, WHO, and SAARC work in cooperation with the ILSI to convene high-level workshops, seminars and conferences (ILSI 2001). The goals of these regional conferences are to identify and establish an SAARC-wide system for the identification, management and communication of food safety risks in accordance with WTO SPS/TBT agreements and Codex Alimentarius standards. The first conference was a joint FAO/ILSI South Asian Conference in 1998. In 2000, the first conference on food safety was convened by ILSI in cooperation with FAO and SAARC. In the conference, regional regulatory harmonization, compliance with Codex and WTO SPS standards and scientific risk analysis were cited as priority policy areas in South Asia.[100]

In December 2002, FAO and ILSI jointly sponsored the Regional Meeting on Modernizing Food Control systems in the SAARC Region in Kathmandu, Nepal. The goal of this conference was to examine the regulatory and industry standards requirements for food safety. The main areas of discussion were as follows: microbiology, food additives, biotechnology, nutraceuticals and micronutrient fortification of foods. The growing role of HACCP, scientific risk analysis, and GMP for agri-food production, processing, transport, trade and marketing were also central themes for regulators and agri-food industries.

During the meeting on 'Modernizing Food Control Systems in SAARC Countries' that was jointly sponsored by FAO, ILSI and SAARC, a comparative study of national food safety regulations in SAARC countries and regional food industries was carried out.[101] In this seminar, the regulatory capacities of SAARC countries and requirements for modernization and reform of food safety regulations were reviewed. In the same period, the governments of Pakistan and Bangladesh requested technical assistance from FAO for food quality and food safety capacity-building.[102]

VII CONCLUSION

In conclusion, SAARC member governments are strengthening food safety regulation in national and regional food systems and agri-food industries. As the decade unfolds, the start of SAFTA increases the role of agriculture and agri-food industries in the socio-economic development of SAARC countries. In this respect, the protection of consumers and public health in SAARC countries requires convergence with transatlantic and multilateral food safety regulations. To achieve these goals, the modernization of agriculture, investment in HACCP process inspection systems, and agri-food industry infrastructure are under way in the SAARC countries. In turn, the safety of South Asian agri-food products and industries is growing in accordance with WTO SPS and Codex standards.

As the decade unfolds, the SAARC region is increasing intra-regional and inter-regional agri-food trade, and competition in global agri-food industries. Therefore, SAFTA will provide a market system for regional integration, modernization and consolidation of fragmented South Asian agri-food industries. However, regional regulatory reform and food safety standards harmonization are required to protect consumers and public health in South Asian food systems and agri-food industries.

In global agri-food industries, the urgency of this issue is growing. In this context, transatlantic and multilateral aid and technical assistance must be increased and strategically deployed to support national and regional Codex standards and HACCP process inspection systems. To accomplish these goals, investment in food production, processing technologies, food storage, refrigeration, transport networks and information systems for SAFTA and SAARC are urgently needed.

Finally, the national and regional Codex Committees are necessary institutional components in the harmonization of food safety regulations and industry standards in SAARC member countries. Therefore, SAARC regulatory capacity-building must be coordinated through FAO, WHO and Codex to ensure regional harmonization of food safety standards. Ultimately, consumer protection and the public health in SAARC countries will be strengthened through harmonization with the WTO SPS and Codex food safety standards.

NOTES

* Acknowledgments: The author wishes to thank Dr Deepak Gupta who served as Chairman, of the National Codex Committee of India, and Joint Secretary for Food Safety in the Ministry of Health, Government of India, for his review, comments and assistance in the preparation of this chapter. Dr Gupta contributed the views on India for the preparation of this chapter, and is a strong proponent of recognition of developing country needs, conditions, and priorities in Codex. The author also wishes to thank Mrs Rekha Sinha, Executive Director of ILSI India, for reviewing and commenting on this chapter.

1. Mehta, R., M. Saquib and J. George (2002), *Assessing Sanitary and Phytosanitary Agreements: A Case Study of Select Processed Food Products in India*, Research and Information System for the Non-Aligned and Other Developing Countries (RIS) DP#39/2002, New Delhi: RIS, p. 4.
2. Dutta, M. (1999), *Economic Regionalization in the Asia-Pacific: Challenges to Economic Cooperation*, Aldershot, UK and Brookfield, US: Edward Elgar, pp. 275–86.
3. Charter of SAARC – Article I – Objectives; see SAARC website, www.SAARC-sec.org. Also see Khan, S.M. and Z.S. Khan (2003), 'Asian economic integration: a perspective on South Asia', *Journal of Asian Economies*, **13** (6): 767–85.
4. Sachdeva, Sujata Dutta (2004), 'Unification', *Times of India*, 4 January.
5. Jain, S.C. (1999), 'Prospects for a South Asian free trade agreement: problems and challenges', *International Business Review*, **8** (4): 399–419. Also see Nirmala George, 'South Asia nations move toward free-trade zone', *Washington Post*, 3 January 2004, p. E01.
6. Paranjpe, S.S. (2002), 'Development of order in South Asia: towards a South Asian Association for Regional Cooperation parliament, *Contemporary South Asia*, **11** (3): 345–56. Also see Sachdeva (2004).
7. Asaduazzaman, M., Nazeen Ahmed, Sharif M. Hossain and Subrata Sarker (2003), *South Asian Free Trade Area – An Analysis for Policy Options for Bangladesh*, Dhaka: Bangladesh Institute of Development Studies, pp. 3–7. Also see, Siriwardana, M. (2001), 'Looking beyond SAARC: some trade liberalization options for Sri Lanka', *Asian Studies Review*, **25** (4): 453–77.
8. Dorjee, Kinlay, Sumiter Broca and Prabhu Pingali (2003), *Diversification in South Asian Agriculture: Trends and Constraints*, ESA Working Paper No. 03–15, July, FAO, Agriculture and Developing Economies Division, Rome: FAO, p. 11.
9. Ibid., pp. 1–3.
10. Ibid., pp. 4–5.
11. Tsunehiro, Otsuki and John Wilson (2001), *Global Food Trade and Food Safety: Winners and Losers in a Fragmented System*, Agricultural Trade – South Asia, World Bank, Washington, DC: World Bank.
12. Ibid.
13. *The Kathmandu Post*, 10 December 2002, 'SAARC essays to harmonise food standards', 10 December, 2002.
14. Athukorala, Prema-Chandra (1999), *Agriculture and the New Trade Agenda in WTO 2000 Negotiations: Interests and Policy Options for South Asia*, 1–2 October, Geneva: WTO, p. 1.
15. Dixon, John and Adian Gulliver (2001), *Farming Systems and Poverty*, FAO/World Bank Publication, Rome: FAO.
16. See 'Can farmers switch gears in South Asia?', IFPRI Forum, December 2003, Washington, DC: IFPRI. This topic was addressed in a high-level conference sponsored by IFPRI on Agricultural Diversification and Vertical Integration in South Asia, held in New Delhi in 2003.
17. Price, Gregory K., Rip Landes and A. Govindan (2003), *India's Pulse Sector: Results of Field Research*, WRS-03-01, ERS, electronic report, Washington, DC: USDA, pp. 2–10; see USDA website www.ers.usda.gov.
18. Landes, Maurice, Suresh Persaud and John Dyck (2004), *India's Poultry Sector–Development and Prospects*, WRS-04-03, ERS, Washington, DC: USDA, pp. 1–4.

19. ILSI India (1998a), *Report on the Proceedings of the International Conference on New Technologies in Food Processing*, New Delhi: ILSI India.
20. Government of India (1999), *General Counsel – Communications from India – Preparations for the 1999 Ministerial Conference – June 14, 1999 (99-2363)*, Geneva: WTO. Also see Gulati, Ashok (2003), 'India', in Merlinda Ingco (ed.), *Agriculture, Trade and the WTO in South Asia*, Washington, DC: World Bank, pp. 189–220. Also see Khan, Safray (2003), 'Pakistan', in ibid., pp. 141–80, and Kelegama, Saman (2003), 'Sri Lanka', in ibid., pp. 96–130.
21. FAO/WHO Global Forum of Food Safety Regulators (2002), 'Capacity Building and Technical Assistance – New Approaches and Building Alliances', Deepak Gupta, Ministry of Health and Family Welfare, Government of India, *FAO/WHO Global Forum of Food Safety Regulators Proceedings 2002*, Rome: Italy, pp. 178–87.
22. Karki, Tika Bahadur (2002), *Sanitary and phytosanitary measures in SAARC Countries*, discussion paper, South Asia watch on Trade, Economics and Environment (SAWTEE) and the center for International Trade Economics and Environment (CUTS-CITEE), Kathmandu: SAWTEE.
23. Mehta et al. (2002).
24. Food contamination with pesticides and heavy metals is a serious food safety and food trade threat for SAARC countries. Karki (2002), op. cit., pp. 30–31.
25. WHO (1996), *Essential Safety Requirements for Street Vendor Foods-Revised Edition*, Geneva: WHO, p. 2.
26. Ibid.
27. Ibid., p. 3.
28. Ibid., p. 22.
29. Karki (2002).
30. The contamination of agricultural commodities and agri-food products with chemical and pesticide residues is a growing challenge for India, Nepal and Sri Lanka. See Poudel, Keshab (2004), 'South Asia initiative for uniform food standards', *One World South Asia*, 22 March, at www.oneworld.com.
31. Karki (2002).
32. Ibid.
33. SAARC food additive regulations are needed, and should be harmonized at the regional level and with the Codex standards.
34. Food safety and global food trade by SAARC countries requires food oil standards to reduce the risk of food adulteration with chemical contaminants. Karki (2002), pp. 34–9.
35. Ibid.
36. ILSI India (1997), *Food Safety Evaluation and Food Colors*, New Delhi: ILSI India.
37. Natural and synthetic food coloring are important elements of food preparation in the SAARC region. However, food safety standards for natural and synthetic food colorings are needed, and must be harmonized with Codex standards to protect consumers in the South Asia region, and to strengthen global food trade. Karki (2002), pp. 31–2.
38. FAO (2001), *Manual on the Application of the HACCP System in Mycotoxin Prevention and Control*, FAO Food and Nutrition Paper 73, Rome: FAO, p. 1.
39. Bhat, Ramesh V. and Siruguri Vasanthi (2003), *Food Safety Issues in Food Security and Food Trade–Mycotoxin Food Safety Risk in Developing Countries*, 2020 Vision, Brief 3 of 17, July, Washington, DC: IFPRI.
40. FAO (2001), pp. 4–5.
41. *BBC News Website*, 'High lead levels in Delhi spinach', Rajyasri Rao (BBC Correspondent in New Delhi), http://news.bbc.co.uk/2hi/south_asia/2891587.stm. 27 March, 2003. According to a joint study by Toxics Link and the Imperial College in London, there is a growing threat to food safety and the public health in New Delhi and the rest of India due to growing water and air pollution. As a result, food chain contamination, due to the unregulated expansion of Indian manufacturing into rural areas, and the need for increased food safety capacity are now major threats to the public interest of consumers and citizens.

42. In support of SAARC standards, regional databases are needed for food additives, metal and chemical residue levels to provide a baseline for regulatory harmonization with Codex standards.
43. See biotechnology page of SAARC Secretariat at http://www.saarc-sec.org/main.php?t=2.7.
44. See Haque, M. Shamsul (2001), 'Recent transition in governance of South Asia: contexts, dimensions and implications', *International Journal of Public Administration*, **24** (12): 1405–36. Also see Huque, Ahmed Shafiqul (2001), 'Governance of public management: the South Asian context', *International Journal of Public Administration*, **24** (12): 1289–97.
45. Karki (2002). Also, see 'South Asian initiative for Uniform Standards', 23 March 2004, http://foodhaccp.com/msgboard.mv?parmfunc=showmsg+parm_msgnum=1014204.
46. The regulatory capacity challenges that face the SAARC countries must be addressed across a range of food safety issues to facilitate compliance with Codex standards. Ibid.
47. Ibid.
48. In spite of high rates of food rejection in South Asia, the regulation of food safety is a challenge for many SAARC countries even though efforts are underway to reform policies and to modernize infrastructure. Ibid., pp. 3–6.
49. See the following reports ILSI India (1997c), *Report on the Proceedings of the Seminar on the Harmonization of Food Laws*, New Delhi: ILSI India. Also see ILSI India (1997b), *Report on the Proceedings of the Conference on SPS/TBT Agreements and Codex*, New Delhi: ILSI India.
50. See the Twenty Sixth Codex Asia Report Item #125, Joint FAO/WHO Food Standards Program (2003a), Codex Alimentarius Commission, Rome, 30 June–5 July 2003, Codex Commission for Asia Report – Kuala Lumpur, 17–20 September 2002, Rome: FAO.
51. Bhutan is a very small country, with very limited regulatory and financial resources. Therefore, Bhutan sometimes works through India's food safety infrastructure. Ibid., pp. 8–9.
52. Sareen, Shashi (2003), *Case Study: India Responds to International Food Safety Requirements*, Food Safety in Food Security and Food Trade, Brief 11 of 17, 2020 vision, Washington, DC: IFPRI.
53. The Indian food safety regulations are the reference point for the other SAARC countries and the South Asia region. In turn, India increasingly serves as the regional leader and negotiator on behalf of the SAARC governments, farmers and agri-food industries' interests on transatlantic and multilateral food safety standards.
54. Sareen (2003).
55. Ibid.
56. India is implementing regulatory reforms to accelerate harmonization with Codex food safety standards.
57. Sareen (2003).
58. The government of Pakistan is under pressure to accelerate regulatory reform, and to strengthen food safety capacity harmonization with transatlantic and Codex standards.
59. Karki (2002).
60. The government of Nepal is working to converge its food safety regulations with Codex standards.
61. Karki (2002).
62. Ibid.
63. ILSI India (1998b), *Report on the Workshop on Science Based Approaches to Harmonization of Regulatory Food Quality and Safety Measures in SAARC*, New Delhi: ILSI India.
64. The problem of food rejection is a major economic challenge for SAARC governments, farmers and agri-food industries. However, the SAARC countries are working to meet the high standards required by the transatlantic food safety regulators and Codex.
65. See 'SAARC level seminar on food products kicks off', Kathmandu, 16 March 2004, www.Gorkhapatra.org.np.

66. See Poudel, Keshab (2004), 'South Asia initiative for uniform food standards', *One World South Asia*, 22 March.
67. Mehta et al. (2002), pp. 20–28.
68. Ibid.
69. FAO/WHO (2003b), *Joint FAO/WHO Food Standards Programme - Codex Alimentarius Commission, Capacity Building for Food Quality and Food Safety*, Activities of the Food and Agriculture Organization (FAO) and the World Health Organization (WHO), Twenty-sixth session, 30 June – 7 July, Rome: FAO, http://www.fao-org/DOCREP/Meeting/006/y9805e.htm.
70. The Government of India is requesting that more specifications be given for mandatory traceability, product labeling requirements and standards requirements by the US and EU.
71. See FAO press releases, Regional Office for Asia and the Pacific: 'Food production declining in Asia', 24 December 2000, RAP 02/03, 'Agriculture biotechnology must be pro-poor farmer', 26 March 2002, RAP 02/07, 'Renowned farm scientist calls for bridging "genetic divide"' 16 January, RAP 02/01.
72. Karki (2002).
73. Food detention and rejection on the basis of bird filth, rodents, microbial contamination and unhygienic practices is a problem for many developing countries that lack modern infrastructure and regulatory capacity.
74. Cato, James C. and S. Subasinge (2002), *Food Safety Issues in Food Security and Trade Case Study: The Shrimp Export Industry in Bangladesh*, 2020 Vision for Food, Agriculture and the Environment, Focus 10, Brief 9, Washington, DC: IFPRI.
75. Ibid.
76. Ibid.
77. Ibid.
78. The mandatory adoption of HACCP and other Best Practices for food inspection, processing and retailing are now required for compliance with transatlantic and Codex food safety standards.
79. Gupta (2002), p. 181.
80. According to the Government of India, small and medium-sized food producers need an HACCP program that meets food production realities of South Asia.
81. Gupta (2002), p. 182.
82. FAO/WHO, (2003a), *Joint FAO/WHO Food Standards Programme – Codex Alimentarius Commission – Codex Committee on Food Hygiene* – Thirty-Fifth Session, Orlando USA, 27 January–1 February, Rome: FAO, p. 8. The position of the Government of India is that HACCP standards require a considerable amount of regulatory capacity, financial investment, and human resources from SAARC and other developing countries.
83. Sareen (2003).
84. Ibid.
85. Ibid.
86. Ibid.
87. Ibid.
88. Ibid.
89. Ibid.
90. The countries in the SAARC region need financial and technical resources to fully develop food safety capacity and to meet the requirements for transatlantic food market regulations and Codex standards harmonization.
91. Sareen (2003), p. 182.
92. See 'Key elements of regional action plans on standards, quality control and measurement', SAARC Secretariat website, at www.SAARC-sec.org.
93. Ibid.
94. Ibid.
95. Verma, D.P.S. (2002), 'Developments in consumer protection in India', *Journal of Consumer Policy*, **25** (1): 117–23.

96. Gupta (2002), pp. 182–3.
97. Ibid., pp. 185–6.
98. FAO/WHO (2003b).
99. Ibid.
100. Science-based regulatory policies are needed to comply with transatlantic food trade and market access requirements, the WTO SPS Agreement and Codex food safety standards.
101. FAO/WHO (2003b).
102. Ibid.

REFERENCES

Asaduazzaman, M., Nazeen Ahmed, Sharif M. Hossain, and Subrata Sarker (2003), *South Asian Free Trade Area – An Analysis for Policy Options for Bangladesh*, Dhaka: Bangladesh Institute of Development Studies.

Athukorala, Prema-Chandra (1999), *Agriculture and the New Trade Agenda in WTO 2000 Negotiations: Interests and Policy Options for South Asia*, 1–2 October, Geneva: WTO.

BBC News website (2003), 'High lead levels in Delhi spinach', by Rajyasri Rao, 27 March, http://news.bbc.co.uk/2hi/south-asia/2891587.stm.

Bhat, Ramesh V. and Siriguri Vasanthi (2003), *Food Safety Issues in Food Security and Food Trade – Mycotoxin Food Safety Risk in Developing Countries*, 2020 Vision, Brief 3 of 17, July, Washington, DC: IFPRI.

'Can farmers switch gears in South Asia' (2003), IFPRI Forum, December, Washington, DC: IFPRI.

Cato, James C. and S. Subasinge (2002), *Food Safety Issues in Food Security and Food Trade Case Study: The Shrimp Export Industry in Bangladesh*, 2020 Vision for Food, Agriculture and the Environment, Focus 10, Brief 9, July, Washington, DC: IFPRI.

Charter of SAARC – Article 1 – Objectives, SAARC website, at www.SAARC-sec.org.

Dixon, John and Adian Gulliver (2001), *Farming Systems and Poverty*, FAO/World Bank Publication, Rome: FAO.

Dorjee, Kinlay, Sumiter Broca and Prabhu Pingali (2003), *Diversification in South Asian Agriculture: Trends and Constraints*, ESA Working Paper No. 03–15, July, FAO, Agriculture and Developing Economies Division, Rome: FAO.

Dutta, M. (1999), *Economic Regionalization in the Asia-Pacific: Challenges to Economic Cooperation*, Aldershot, UK and Brookfield, US: Edward Elgar.

FAO (2001), *Manual on the Application of the HACCP System in Mycotoxin Prevention and Control*, FAO Food and Nutrition Paper 73, Rome: FAO.

FAO Regional Office for Asia and the Pacific (2000), 'Food production declining in Asia', press release 24 December, RAP 02/03.

FAO Regional Office for Asia and the Pacific (2002a), 'Agriculture biotechnology must be pro-poor farmer', press release 26 March, RAP 02/07.

FAO Regional Office for Asia and the Pacific (2002b), 'Renowned farm scientist calls for bridging "genetic divide"', press release 16 January, RAP 02/01.

FAO/WHO (2003a), *Joint FAO/WHO Food Standards Programme – Codex Alimentarius Commission – Codex Committee on Food Hygiene*, Thirty fifth session, Orlando, USA, 27 January–1 February, Rome: FAO.

FAO/WHO (2003b), *Joint FAO/WHO Food Standards Programme – Codex*

Alimentarius Commission, Capacity Building for Food Quality and Food Safety, Activities of the Food and Agriculture Organization (FAO) and the World Health Organization (WHO), Twenty-Sixth session, 30 June–7 July, Rome: FAO, http://www.fao.org/DOCREP/meeting/006/y9805e.htm.

FAO/WHO Global Forum of Food Safety Regulators (2002), 'Capacity Building and Technical Assistance – New Approaches and Building Alliances', Deepak Gupta, Ministry of Health and Family Welfare, Government of India, *FAO/WHO Global Forum of Food Safety Regulators Proceedings 2002*, Rome: Italy, pp. 178–87.

Government of India (1999), *General Counsel – Communications form India – Preparations for the 1999 Ministerial Conference – June 14, 1999 (99-2363)*, Geneva: WTO.

Gulati, Ashok (2003), 'India', in Merlinda Ingco (ed.) *Agriculture, Trade and the WTO in South Asia*, Washington, DC: World Bank.

Gupta, Deepak (2002), 'Capacity building and technical assistance – new approaches and building alliances', *FAO/WHO Global Forum of Food Safety Regulators Proceedings 2002*, Rome: Secretariat of the FAO/WHO Global Forum of Food Safety Regulators/FAO, PP. 178–87.

Haque, M. Shamsul (2001), 'Recent transition in governance of South Asia: contexts, dimensions and implications', *International Journal of Public Administration*, **24** (12): 1405–36.

Hugue, Ahmed Shafiqul (2001), 'Governance of public management: the South Asian context', *International Journal of Public Administration*, **24** (12): 1289–97.

IFPRI (2003), 'Can farmers switch gears in South Asia?', DIFRRI Forum, Washington, DC: IFPRI.

ILSI India (1997a), *Food Safety Evaluation and Food Color*, New Delhi: ILSI India.

ILSI India (1997b), *Report on the Proceedings of the Conference on SPS/TBT Agreements and Codex*, New Delhi: ILSI India.

ILSI India (1997c), *Report on the Proceedings of the Seminar on the Harmonization of Food Laws*, New Delhi: ILSI India.

ILSI India (1998a), *Report on the Proceedings of the International Conference on New Technologies in Food Processing*, New Delhi, India: ILSI India.

ILSI India (1998b), *Report on the Workshop on Science Based Approaches to Harmonization of Regulatory Food Quality and Safety Measures in SAARC*, New Delhi: ILSI India.

ILSI India (2001), *South Asian Conference on Food Safety*, New Delhi: ILSI India.

Ingco, Merlinda (ed.) (2003), *Agriculture, Trade and the WTO in South Asia*, Washington, DC: World Bank.

Jain, S.C. (1999), 'Prospects for a South Asian free trade agreement: problems and challenges', *International Business Review*, **8** (4): 399–419.

Karki, Tika Bahadur (2002), *Sanitary and Phytosanitary Measures in SAARC Countries*, discussion paper, South Asia Watch on Trade, Economics and Environment (SAWTEE) and the Center for International Trade, Economics and Environment (CUTS-CITEE), Kathmandu: SAWTEE.

Kelegama, Saman (2003), 'Sri Lanka', in Merlinda Ingco (ed.) *Agriculture, Trade and the WTO in South Asia*, Washington, DC: World Bank.

'Key elements of regional action plans on standards, quality control and measurement', SAARC Secretariat website, at www.SAARC-sec.org.

Khallil, J.K. (2000), 'Food composition activities in developing countries: SAARCFOODS perspective', *Journal of Food Composition and Analysis*, **13** (4): 669–84.

Khan, Safray (2003), 'Pakistan', in Merlinda Ingco (ed.) *Agriculture, Trade and the WTO in South Asia*, Washington, DC: World Bank.
Khan, S.M. and Z.S. Khan (2003), 'Asian economic integration: a perspective on South Asia', *Journal of Asian Economies*, **13** (6): 767–85.
Landes, Maurice, Suresh Persaud and John Dyck (2004), *India's Pulse Sector: Results of Field Research*, WRS-03-01, ERS, Washington, DC: USDA, USDA website at, www.ers.usda.gov.
Mehta, R., M. Saquib and J. George (2002), *Assessing Sanitary and Phytosanitary Agreements: A Case Study of Select Processed Food Products in India*, Research and Information System for the Non-Aligned and Developing Countries – RIS DP#39/2002, New Delhi: RIS.
Paranjpe, S.S. (2002), 'Development of order in South Asia: towards a South Asian Association for Regional Cooperation parliament, *Contemporary South Asia*, **11** (3): 345–56.
SAARC Secretariat at http://www.saarc-sec.org/main.php?t=2.7.
'SAARC level seminar on food products kicks off' (2004), Kathmandu, 16 March, at www.Gorkhapatra.org.np.
Sachdeva, Sujata Dutta (2004), 'Unification', *Times of India*, 4 January.
Sareen, Shashi (2003), *Case Study: India Responds to International Food Safety Requirements*, 2020 Vision, Food Safety in Food Security and Food Trade, Brief 11 of 17, Washington, DC: International Food Policy Research Institute (IFPRI).
Siriwardana, M. (2001),'Looking beyond SAARC: some trade liberalization options for Sri Lanka', *Asian Studies Review*, **25** (4): 453–77.
Stern, Robert M. and Aaditya Mattoo (2003), *India and the WTO*, Washington, DC: World Bank and Oxford University Press.
The Kathmandu Post (2002), 'SAARC essays to harmonise food standards', 10 December.
Tsunehiro, Otsuki and John Wilson (2001), *Global Food Trade and Food Safety: Winners and Losers in a Fragmented System*, Agricultural Trade – South Asia, World Bank, Washington, DC: World Bank.
Verma, D.P.S. (2002), 'Developments in consumer protection in India', *Journal of Consumer Policy*, **25** (1): 117–23.
WHO (1996), *Essential Safety Requirements for Street Vendor Foods – Revised Edition*, Geneva: WHO.

10. Food safety standards harmonization in the Asia-Pacific region

Lee Ann Jackson

I INTRODUCTION

This chapter examines the food safety regulatory environment of Japan, China, Australia and New Zealand due to their dominant roles in the regional trade economy. The Asia-Pacific region includes countries at both ends of the spectrum of economic development. Although many countries in the region suffered from the Asian financial crisis in the late 1990s, the region has experienced dramatic economic improvements over the past decade due to increased global and regional integration.[1]

The rapid industrialization and the corresponding movement of resources out of agricultural production, particularly in China, has raised concerns about food production and distribution in the region (Anderson et al. 1996). By the end of the 1990s, the percentage of GDP represented by trade in the Asia-Pacific region was one and a half times the world average. Table 10.1 presents data on various indicators for 1997 that reflect agricultures' economic contribution in the region. Food exports represent nearly 8 per cent of the region's merchandise exports, while food imports represent almost 6 per cent of the region's merchandise imports.

The share of food products in both merchandise exports and imports declined over the 1990s, reflecting the slower growth of the agricultural sector as compared to the rest of the economy. Nevertheless, the livestock sector grew rapidly in the 1990s. While the proportion of total labour in agriculture also declined in the 1990s, a large proportion (45.9 per cent) of the region's total labour force continues to work in the agricultural sector.

While developing countries' food safety issues are also important, this chapter does not address the distributional impacts of food safety harmonization in the region. Will developing countries such as Vietnam, Lao PDR and Cambodia experience net positive returns from enhanced value of food production, or will they bear burdensome regulatory costs in order to

Table 10.1 Selected development indicators for East Asia and Pacific countries, OECD countries and the world in 1997

Development indicators	Asia and Pacific	OECD	World
Agricultural raw materials exports (% of merchandise exports)	2.43	2.16	2.15
Agricultural raw materials imports (% of merchandise imports)	3.75	2.45	2.49
Food exports (% of merchandise exports)	7.90	8.09	8.40
Food imports (% of merchandise imports)	5.78	8.79	8.49
Labor force in agriculture (% of total)	45.91	4.09	—
Livestock production index (1989–91 = 100)	186.39	—	134.18
Rural population (% of total population)	66.65	21.92	54.27

Source: World Bank (2002).

participate in the new global food economy? In many cases, small farmers in developing countries lack the ability to comply with international food safety standards. Therefore, food safety standards harmonization may put Asian-Pacific farmers and agri-food industries at a competitive disadvantage in global food markets.

On the other hand, agricultural trade liberalization and the resulting reduction in traditional trade barriers can provide benefits to some sectors of the economy. At least one study concludes that processed food sectors in South Asia could benefit substantially from reduced agricultural input costs driven by agricultural trade liberalization (Rae and Josling 2003). However, further study is needed to understand under what conditions the national benefits of food safety harmonization lead to improved trade efficiency and outweigh the costs associated with achieving improved food safety in small developing countries.

While the WTO SPS and TBT Agreements encourage harmonization of food policies at the international level, regional and bilateral harmonization efforts also shape the system of food policy and thus play an important role in trade and food safety outcomes. A variety of formal and informal institutional arrangements within the Asia-Pacific region creates possibilities for food safety policy harmonization. Existing regional organizations such as the Asia-Pacific Economic Cooperation (APEC) and the Association for South East Asian Nations (ASEAN) provide opportunities for countries to engage in regional harmonization of food safety regulations, agri-food industries and agricultural trade policies. Furthermore, ongoing trade liberalization activities and the globalization of agricultural trade may lead to new pressures and opportunities for the food safety regulatory systems in the Asia-Pacific region. While Asian-Pacific agricultural trade is concentrated within the region, free trade agreements (FTAs), particularly the US–Australia FTA, are creating new trade opportunities with countries outside the region.

At the same time, this FTA and market integration through APEC and ASEAN are likely to create pressures for member countries to harmonize their regulatory and agricultural policies. This is likely to be the case with the trade-inhibiting SPS regulations, food inspection and quarantine measures used extensively by Australia. In addition, China's accession to the WTO, further enhances the current evolution of its agricultural sector and food safety regulations.

As countries become more integrated into the global economy, they may voluntarily adopt higher food safety standards in order to enter foreign markets.[2] In turn, as consumers' incomes expand, they prefer safer foods and increased food safety standards and regulations. However, inappropriate incentives and safeguards liberalizing trade could potentially produce opportunities for countries to 'dump' less-safe products in countries with more relaxed food safety regulatory systems.

This chapter focuses on food safety policies in the Asia-Pacific region, with special attention to China, Japan, Australia and New Zealand. The following section discusses the role of agriculture in each country's economy, and the general food safety regulatory structure. Next, the beef industry and national regulatory frameworks for controlling Bovine Spongiform Encephalopathy (BSE) are presented. The section following the discussion on BSE policies focuses on production of several crops that have been genetically modified (GM), and the types of food safety regulation approaches that countries have implemented to manage the introduction and adoption of genetically modified crops. The section on emerging regulatory harmonization on BSE and GM policies highlights current evidence of policy coordination in the Asia-Pacific region. The chapter concludes with a discussion of the challenges for achieving regulatory harmonization in this region, and stresses the importance of understanding the distributive impacts of regulatory policy harmonization.

II NATIONAL AGRICULTURAL PRODUCTION AND FOOD SAFETY POLICIES IN THE ASIA-PACIFIC REGION

Within the region there is a wide variation in trade of food and live animals (see Table 10.2). In 2000, Australia/New Zealand and China provide more than half of the regions exports of food and live animals, and about 9 per

Table 10.2 Food and live animal exports and imports of selected countries in 2000

Country	Exports (1000 US$)	Percentage of world exports	World rank
USA	38 721 522	13.55	1
France	23 664 912	8.28	2
Australia	10 966 869	3.84	8
China	12 281 714	4.30	9
Thailand	9 687 066	3.39	11
New Zealand	5 590 683	1.96	19
Indonesia	3 503 016	1.23	23
Japan	1 764 170	0.62	36
Malaysia	1 702 725	0.60	35
Philippines	1 286 449	0.45	44
World total	285 828 830		
Country	**Imports (1000 US$)**	**Percentage of world imports**	**World rank**
Japan	41 097 098	13.55	1
USA	39 619 024	13.06	2
Korea Republic	6 496 498	2.14	13
China	4 758 318	1.57	16
Malaysia	2 995 467	0.99	24
Indonesia	2 782 240	0.92	25
Philippines	2 253 301	0.74	29
Australia	2 524 086	0.83	31
Thailand	2 073 507	0.68	33
New Zealand	851 017	0.28	49
World total	303 286 530		

Source: UNCTAD/WTO (2000).

cent of the total world value of exports. Countries in the Asia-Pacific region tend to concentrate their agricultural trade in the region.

In this regard, food safety issues related to fish are also important due to the role of fish and seafood in the diet of many countries in the Asia-Pacific region. Aquaculture supplies the bulk of fish produced in the region while marine fisheries contribute a smaller amount to regional fish production. In 1995, the region produced over 87 per cent of total world food fish production from aquaculture, compared with only 36 per cent of animal livestock and meat products for the same year (FAO 1997). Small-scale rice

Table 10.3 Total fish catch, value of imports and value of exports in Asian-Pacific countries in 1999

	Total fish catch (million tons)	% of world fish catch	Value imports ($1000)	Value exports ($1000)
Australia	250 075	0.2	16 755	316 714
China	41 512 698	32.9	804 978	715 515
Indonesia	4 797 060	3.8	1 484	248 341
Japan	5 937 427	4.7	2 388 504	114 077
Korea, Dem. Rep.	278 500	0.2	689	59 952
Malaysia	1 406 895	1.1	117 560	54 238
New Zealand	685 734	0.5	1 701	108 667
Philippines	2 198 825	1.7	1 518	63 083
Singapore	9 081	0.0	110 255	95 489
Thailand	3 607 707	2.9	12 193	119 508
Vietnam	1 794 910	1.4	351	126 872
Total	62 478 912	49.5	3 455 988	2 022 456

Source: FAO (2003).

farmers dominate the freshwater aquaculture for fish production (World Fish Center 2002).

Table 10.3 shows the relative importance of fisheries in the trade economy of selected countries in the region. China's fish production in 1999 accounted for nearly 33 per cent of the world's total fish catch. Other countries in the region also contribute to a lesser extent, including Indonesia (4 per cent), Japan (5 per cent) and Thailand (3 per cent). Several countries in the region, particularly Japan, play important roles in the world fish trade. The value of Japanese fish imports is nearly 22 times the value of the country's fish exports.

Food safety issues related to aquaculture include trematode infections, food-borne diseases associated with pathogenic bacteria and viruses, residues of agro-chemicals, veterinary drugs and heavy-metal organic or inorganic contamination (FAO 1997). One incentive to harmonize food safety standards for fish products comes from the adoption of mandatory HACCP requirements by large importers like the USA and the European Union.[3] However, small-scale, subsistence aquaculture systems in the Asia-Pacific region challenge food safety regulatory mechanisms.

Australia and New Zealand

Agricultural sectors in Australia and New Zealand have a strong export focus. In the last decade, agricultural exports grew 104 per cent in nominal value terms, to exceed $32 billion in 2001–02 in Australia (DFAT 2001). Currently, 65–70 per cent of Australian domestic agricultural production is exported. From this amount, more than 40 per cent of Australian agricultural exports go to regional trade partners including China, Japan, Malaysia, Indonesia, Thailand, the Republic of Korea and New Zealand.

In the case of New Zealand, the agricultural sector also plays an import role in the country's trade portfolio, accounting for nearly 50 per cent of New Zealand's total exports (MAF 2002). Like Australia, a high percentage of New Zealand's agricultural exports go to regional trade partners, especially Japan, Australia and China. In order to support their reputations as dependable sources of high-quality agricultural products, both Australia and New Zealand maintain strict SPS food standards and quarantine measures, which can inhibit access of trading partners to their markets.

Australia and New Zealand have a supranational food standards agency which uses a bilateral approach to harmonization of food standards (Hooker 1999). In 1996, these two countries developed a bi-national food regulatory agency to cover these issues. The Australia New Zealand Food Authority was renamed Food Standards Australia New Zealand (FSANZ) in 2002. However, under the terms of the agreement, Australia and New Zealand continue to have separate food safety systems (Roche 2002). The joint Australia New Zealand Food Standards Code sets composition and labelling standards for the two countries, but specifically excludes food hygiene issues from the activities the FSANZ undertakes for New Zealand.

The FSANZ provides a focus for cooperation between governments, industry and civil society to harmonize food standards between the two countries, reduce compliance costs for industry and help remove regulatory barriers to food trade. Australian states and territories adopt, without variation, food standards that are approved by the Australia New Zealand Food Standards Council (ANZFSC), which is the Ministerial Council representing all jurisdictions, including New Zealand. While Australia and New Zealand are working towards the establishment of harmonized food standards in many areas, they have maintained separate regulatory structures for maximum residue limits, food hygiene provisions and export requirements relating to third-country trade. Under this regulation, New Zealand can opt out of a joint standard for exceptional reasons relating to health, safety, environmental concerns or cultural issues. These exemptions may hinder the development of harmonized policies for biotechnology and GM food products.

The main intergovernmental governing body in Australia is the Council of Australian Governments (COAG), which consists of the Prime Minister, State Premiers, Territory Chief Ministers and the President of the Australian Local Government Association. The COAG initiates, develops and monitors the implementation of policy reforms which are of national significance, and which require cooperative action by Australian governments. New Zealand Ministers may participate in policy deliberations when matters affecting New Zealand are being considered. In a meeting of the COAG, ministers agreed to sign a revised Food Regulation Agreement to ensure consistency with the Food Standards Australia New Zealand Act 1991 and the Joint Food Standards Treaty with New Zealand. In contrast with Australia, New Zealand does not have state territories within its national boundaries, and therefore has a smaller voice in the deliberations and policy decisions of the COAG.

In Australia, other governmental departments, particularly the Department of Agriculture, Fisheries and Forestry Australia (AFFA), contribute to food safety regulation. The AFFA organizational mandate includes the promotion of agricultural and food industries that are protected from diseases and have increased market access. Towards this end, the department has responsibilities for food-processing, food regulation policy, supply chain policy development, trade assistance, and enhancement of agricultural cooperation with key trading partners. In order to enhance agricultural cooperation with key trading partners, AFFA has representatives in Australian missions in Beijing, Brussels, Jakarta, Rome, Seoul, Tokyo, Washington, and the Australian permanent delegation to the OECD in Paris help to identify and pursue trade barriers faced by agriculture and food exporters.

China

The Chinese economy has undergone dramatic changes since the country initiated economic liberalization and structural changes in the late 1970s. While China continues to be the world's largest producer and consumer of agricultural products, growth in the agricultural sector lags behind the industrial and service sectors. Over the past two decades, the share of agriculture in the Chinese economy has declined, from 30 per cent in 1980, to 16 per cent in 2000 (Huang and Rozelle 2002). During the same period, agricultural trade has also changed dramatically. In fact, the share of food exports in total exports fell from 17 per cent in 1980, to 5 per cent in 2000 (Huang and Rozelle 2002). However, rapid growth in China's non-agricultural economy, and rising urban incomes, have led to growing demand for meat, fruits, vegetables and other high-value commodities.

The Development Research Center of the State Council (DRC) assisted China's central government in establishing an institutional framework governing all aspects of food safety and quality. In China, the 'Food Hygiene Law of the People's Republic of China' governs food safety. The Ministry of Health and local governments are primarily responsible for the enforcement of food safety regulations. On some issues, special meetings are conducted to obtain advice and comments from industry, but the regulatory system is primarily controlled by government agencies. In some cases, Chinese provincial governments have the right to develop standards where no food safety regulations and national standards exist. However, overlapping jurisdictions have led to a complex, and potentially conflicting, system of food safety regulations.

Japan

Japan is the world's largest food importer. From 1995 to 2001 Japan's annual food imports averaged US$40 billion. In 2000, Japan individually represented over 65 per cent of the total value of regional imports of these products, and more than 13 per cent of the total value of world imports of these products. The next largest importer in the region, China, imported only one-tenth of the value imported by Japan. Japan's dependence upon food imports means that their regulatory system must focus on defending against food products that pose health and environmental threats.

In Japan the Department of Food Safety within the Ministry of Health, Labour and Welfare is primarily responsible for food safety under the Food Sanitation Law. The law covers foods and drinks, food additives such as flavouring agents and equipment used for handling, manufacturing, processing or delivering food. The Ministry of Health, Labour and Welfare can establish standards on specific foods without revising the law. However, under the Food Sanitation Law, food manufacturers and processors establish sanitary control methods based upon the HACCP system, then the ministry confirms whether these methods achieve the appropriate standards.

In Japan, local governments have the authority to monitor businesses to ensure they meet appropriate standards (Ushio 2002). In response to the first domestic case of BSE, Japanese food safety regulators began promoting 'farm to table' food safety control systems. However, competing policy interests pose challenges to tracking food safety through Japanese food production and distribution channels (Ushio 2002).

III BEEF INDUSTRY AND BSE REGULATION IN THE ASIA-PACIFIC REGION

The first reported case of BSE in the Asia-Pacific region occurred in Japan in 2001 (OIE 2002). Since then, six additional Japanese cases have been confirmed. At the same time two countries in the region, Australia and New Zealand, are two of only five countries in the world that are recognized as BSE-free. While the rest of the region has not yet reported any cases, rapidly changing regional demand and production in the livestock industry could bring about new risks of disease introduction. National governments in the region are developing regulations to protect their countries from the introduction of this disease. However, regional cooperation on BSE policies is minimal.

Beef Production and Consumption Trends

Table 10.4 provides an overview of the sources of domestic supply and domestic consumption of bovine meat in Australia, China, Japan and New Zealand. The table also provides an indication of the change in self-sufficiency and the ratio of domestic production to total domestic supply in these products over the 1990s. Higher self-sufficiency index ratios indicate a larger proportion of domestic production being exported.

Australia and New Zealand

Australia is the world's largest exporter of grass-fed beef, but has recently begun expanding its grain-fed herd (USDA 2002b). Because periodic drought decreases the availability of forage for Australia's primarily grass fed herd, annual bovine beef production is highly variable. In 1997 Australia's beef production represented only 5 per cent of total world production. Nevertheless Australia's beef and veal exports represent 24 per cent of total world exports in the same year (ABARE 2004).

By the mid-1990s, exports to Asia represented about 60 per cent of all Australian beef exports, compared with 25 per cent in the late 1980s. Japan is Australia's primary market for beef in the region. From 1995 to 2001, beef exports from Australia to Japan steadily rose. Domestic consumption accounts for 31–35 per cent of annual beef production in Australia. Australia ranked fourth in the world for beef consumption per person in 2001, behind Argentina, Uruguay and the US (Meat and Livestock Australia 2003). While Australian annual beef and veal consumption decreased in 2000, coinciding with the first case of BSE in the Asia-Pacific region, consumption in 2004 was projected to exceed 1999 levels (FAS, 2002b).

China

According to the FAO figures, in the 1990s China experienced the largest change in annual bovine meat supply – 360 per cent from 1990 to 2000. In China, beef production and consumption have increased proportionately faster than all other meats over the last two decades (Brown et al. 2002). While pork and poultry are a much larger proportion of total meat production in China, the share of beef in total meat production in China

Table 10.4 Domestic supply of bovine beef (1000 MT)

Country	Year	Supply				Domestic consumption			Self-sufficiency index
		Production	Imports	Stock changes	Exports	Waste	Other	Food	
Australia	1991	1760	5	0	993	0	0	771	2.28
	2000	1988	7	0	1240	0	0	755	2.63
China	1991	1579	117	1	316	0	2	1380	1.14
	2000	5352	170		72	0	2	5448	0.98
Japan	1991	575	486	33	5	23	0	1068	0.54
	2000	531	940	−148	3	31	0	1289	0.36
New Zealand	1991	540	2	−8	422	0	0	112	4.51
	2000	572	13	48	508	0	0	126	7.45

Source: FAO (2003), author's calculations.

increased 150 per cent between 1983 and 1993 (Delgado et al. 1998). Currently, China is self-sufficient in beef, but imports are increasing due to population growth and increased affluence (Bingsheng 2002).

In China, small farmers produce the vast majority of beef cattle. In 1996, farms with more than 100 head of cattle accounted for less than 1 per cent of the total beef herd in China (Bingsheng 2002). The Chinese government is actively promoting the beef cattle industry as a means of raising incomes for poor farm households and as an efficient use of crops and grains (Brown et al. 2002). The Chinese beef industry sector has been protected, but since its accession to the WTO, China has initiated tariff reductions on fresh/chilled beef and frozen beef cuts. Household slaughtering accounts for around 90 per cent of all slaughtering, but produces low-quality beef under conditions of extremely variable hygiene (Brown et al. 2002).

Rising incomes and increasing population are driving increases in demand for red meat in China. In the 1990s, Chinese demand for beef increased nearly 300 per cent, from 1.1 kg/capita to 4 kg/capita (Bingsheng 2002). While a small sub-segment of the consumer market is willing to pay a premium for beef that is perceived to be safe, the vast majority of the beef sold in China is of low price, low value and low quality (Brown et al. 2002). Meat sold in urban state stores and larger supermarkets often carries labels indicating that the meat was processed under government supervision and inspected, anticipating increased demand for safe and higher-quality beef products (Brown et al. 2002).

Japan

During the 1990s Japanese consumers increasingly switched to Western diets with growing consumption of beef. In the first half of the 1990s, Japanese production of beef grew. However, since the mid-1990s beef consumption stagnated and production has steadily declined. Imports play an increasing role in satisfying domestic demand, and currently account for about two-thirds of all beef consumption in Japan (USDA 2002b). In 2002, the drop in demand for beef was due to the discovery of the first case of BSE.

Beef Food Safety and BSE Regulations

Australia and New Zealand

In the 1990s co-regulation of the Australian beef industry, a system in which industry self-regulates through approved programs with strong legislative underpinning, gained acceptance. During this period, the governments moved from uniform regulatory approaches to more industry and management based regulatory approaches such as HACCP and other food product certification systems. While the national framework for food safety is moving towards co-regulation, states and territories maintain the right to develop more prescriptive regulations for food safety.

In January 2001, in response to the increased risk of BSE introduction through food trade, the Australian government temporarily suspended imports of beef and beef products from 30 European countries. In addition, the FSANZ developed a certification system to replace import suspension, while continuing to ensure that imported beef products are safe for human consumption. Currently Australia and New Zealand are following the European Commission's risk categorization of countries exporting beef products, known as the Geographical BSE Risk (GBR) assessment.

China

In China meat distribution channels have diversified rapidly in the last decade, and create challenges for regulators seeking to effectively control hygiene and cleanliness (Brown et al. 2002). The Chinese government implemented regulations in response to public concerns about the safety of meat products sourced from non-inspected slaughter premises. However, monitoring and enforcement of food safety regulations are variable and are unevenly implemented by local governments.

The 1992 Rules and Regulations of Livestock and Poultry Epidemic Prevention issued by the Ministry of Agriculture sought to prohibit the sale of uninspected meat. However, the provisions of this regulation were largely ignored. In 1997, in response to growing consumer concerns about meat safety, the government adopted the Animal Epidemic Prevention Law of the People's Republic of China. The law established requirements for veterinary public health quarantine inspection of meat and restricted slaughter activities to specified plant locations (Brown et al. 2002). The Industry Commerce and Administration Bureau monitors the registration of beef processors and cattle slaughterhouses. However, in many cases food safety inspections are not conducted (Brown et al. 2002).

Japan

In response to the first case of BSE in Japan, the Japanese government (Ministry of Agriculture, Forestry, and Fishery) ordered on-site inspection of all 146 000 dairy and beef cattle farms (USDA 2002b). In addition, the Japanese Ministry of Health issued a directive to food manufacturers to stop using animal parts such as brain, spinal cord, eyes and small intestines. While the directive does not entail a legal obligation to cease using these products, the ministry plans to publicize a list of violators. In spite of the Japanese government's action to allay consumer fears, beef consumption declined by nearly 50 per cent. By 2003, six additional cases were confirmed, but Japanese imports of beef indicate a return in consumer confidence in beef safety.

In December 2001, the Japanese Ministry of Agriculture introduced a voluntary scheme to slaughter more than 5000 animals that were fed animal feeds that potentially carry the disease (BSE Review 2002). Farmers who voluntarily destroyed their cattle were compensated for this loss. In 2002, Japan adopted a new set of regulations, including testing and feeding requirements, to control BSE in the domestic beef industry. The cattle testing is implemented on all beef cattle over the age of 24 months that die of disease or injuries. In addition, Japanese food safety regulations introduced a ban on feeding meat and bone meal feed to cattle. Finally, a food traceability system including tagging and recording cattle movements, is being implemented in Japan (Clemens 2003).

IV BIOTECHNOLOGY, GENETICALLY MODIFIED CROPS AND GM FOOD LABELLING

In the past two decades several governments in the region devoted significant financial and human resources to develop new agricultural biotechnologies. The range of products varies from rice and maize to high-value specialty crops like vanilla and orchids. While GM foods are approved in several countries in the region, as of 2003 only the Philippines had publicly announced its intention to produce GM food.[4] The delayed marketing of GM foods produced in Asia is due to concerns over access to global food markets.

The Asian-Pacific countries that are dependent on their export markets for national income consider the trade-offs between GM food production, and potential restrictions on market access. Some governments, like Australia, are promoting food traceability along the entire food supply chain to ensure that products meet the GM content regulations and food safety standards of importing countries. However, large industry solutions are costly, and the benefits depend on global consumer preferences for differentiated food products.

Production and Consumption Trends

The following analysis focuses on the rice, maize and wheat industry sectors since these crops include GM varieties that are already adopted, or are likely to be adopted in the near future.

Tables 10.5–10.7 show the changes in supply sources and demand composition for wheat, maize and rice during the 1990s in Australia, New Zealand, China and Japan. In general, wheat and rice was consumed

Table 10.5 Domestic supply and consumption of maize (1000 MT)

Country	Year	Supply				Domestic consumption						Self-sufficiency index
		Production	Imports	Stock changes	Exports	Feed	Seed	Processing	Waste	Other	Food	
Australia	1991	193	38	4600	12044	669	410	133	151	535	1253	1.13
	2000	406	11	−18	51	242	1	1	11	4	89	1.11
China	1991	97214	5587	−7312	3408	51557	1302	1264	8359	585	29013	0.98
	2000	106180	5059	16481	10593	78211	1741	1223	10103	2376	2372	1.05
Japan	1991	1	16015	86	0	12303	0	1361	5	1261	1172	0.00
	2000	0	16125	−430	2	11662	0	1815	3	687	1528	0.00
New Zealand	1991	162	42	5	1	182	0		6	9	10	0.80
	2000	181	10	−8	13	145	0		6	15	4	1.02

Source: FAO (2003), author's calculations.

Table 10.6 Domestic supply and consumption of wheat (1000 MT)

Country	Year	Supply				Domestic consumption						Self-sufficiency index
		Production	Imports	Stock changes	Exports	Feed	Seed	Processing	Waste	Other	Food	
Australia	1991	150 66	36	−300	11 645	799	323	161	151	522	1 201	4.77
	2000	96	1 100	18 106	2 135	526	110	233	956	1 320	420	4.20
China	1991	98 232	13 974	−2504	243	3 304	4 952	2 000	4 963	257	93 984	0.90
	2000	99 636	2 620	4 794	504	606	3 928	0	2 202	213	99 597	0.94
Japan	1991	952	5 558	184	434	613	24	146	155	0	5 321	0.15
	2000	689	6 054	16	424	446	19	185	164	0	5 522	0.11
New Zealand	1991	188	195	−10	6	63	5	56	7	3	234	0.51
	2000	326	255	−75	23	128	11	60	11	6	268	0.67

Source: FAO (2003), author's calculations.

Table 10.7 Domestic supply and consumption of rice (1000 MT)

Country	Year	Supply				Domestic consumption						Self-sufficiency index
		Production	Imports	Stock changes	Exports	Feed	Seed	Processing	Waste	Other	Food	
Australia	1991	525	32	12	456		9	1	6	0	98	4.65
	2000	734	59	32	665		10	2	7	0	150	4.58
China	1991	123 857	603	−55	921	2 567	3 013	1 016	5 912	10	110 965	1.00
	2000	126 606	630	4 078	3 102	2 201	2 647	1 552	6 263	9	115 544	0.99
Japan	1991	8 007	19	751	0	22	59	549	163	1	7 983	0.91
	2000	7 913	610	−57	38	255	47	408	154	14	7 550	0.94
New Zealand	1991	0	17	0	0	0	0	0	0	0	16	0.00
	2000	0	32	−4	1	0	0	0	0	0	27	0.00

Source: FAO (2003), author's calculations.

as human food while maize was used as livestock feed in these four countries.

Australia and New Zealand

Australian wheat and maize annual production increased during the 1990s. The average annual Australian wheat production over the last five years was 21.1m tonnes (about 4 per cent of world output). Most of the wheat produced in Australia was exported, and more than 40 per cent of wheat exports in 2000 went to regional trading partners, such as Indonesia, Japan and Korea. Australia is the third main world exporter of wheat behind the US and Canada (AFFA 2002a).

In contrast, maize and rice are produced in much smaller amounts than wheat.[5] New Zealand exhibits a similar pattern of production, with wheat surpassing maize and rice production throughout the 1990s. Australia produces only 0.2 per cent of world rice, but accounts for about 3 per cent of global trade in rice. Major export markets for Australian rice include Papua New Guinea Japan, Hong Kong, the Middle East and Pacific countries such as New Zealand and Fiji (AFFA 2002b). In the case of Australia, wheat consumption steadily increased in the 1990s, but the primary consumption destination shifted from domestic food to livestock feed in the late 1990s.

In the case of maize, consumption also increased over the 1990s, peaking in 1997, then dropping to lower levels. Livestock feed was the primary use for maize in Australia during this decade. The use of maize as livestock feed increased during the first part of the decade, then fell as export demand for livestock in Asia decreased due to the Asian financial crisis. During this period, New Zealand maize and wheat consumption remained fairly constant throughout the 1990s.

China

The Chinese grain sector, is still characterized by small farms and labor-intensive management methods (Rozelle 2001). In 2000, rice accounted for 37 per cent of all cereals produced in China, while wheat and maize combined accounted for 60 per cent of cereal production. During this decade, Chinese maize production increased more than the production of rice and wheat. Eventually, maize production exceeded aggregate wheat production, and now ranks second only to rice in total agricultural production. Over the decade, the share of domestic wheat consumption for food increased. In China, demand for maize increased in conjunction with rapid increases in meat production.

Japan

In contrast to the beef industry which was increasingly liberalized in the 1990s, Japanese grain and rice industries are still heavily protected. Japanese farmers have not increased production despite high levels of protection. In Japan the state is heavily involved in trading agricultural commodities. In turn, industry evolution, and an integrated food supply-chain approach is constrained (Trewin et al. 2000). In terms of agri-food industry sectors, Japanese agricultural production is dominated by rice.

During this period, Japan produced only small volumes of wheat and maize, supplementing domestic production of these commodities with imports primarily from Australia. Both wheat and maize production also decreased during the 1990s in Japan. However, Japanese wheat and maize consumption remained fairly constant during the 1990s. The share of wheat and maize consumption in livestock feed and food also remained relatively constant over the decade. In contrast, total rice consumption has been falling in Japan since the 1970s (Flukudo et al. 2003).

GM Food Regulations

Australia and New Zealand

The regulatory system for biotechnology and GM food is evolving to govern the production and trade of GM products separately from conventional food products.[6] In June 2001, Australia adopted a new regulatory regime governed by the Gene Technology Act 2000. The Act regulates all research, field trials, manufacturing, production and imports of GM food products (Ernst and Young et al. 2001). As an independent regulatory office, the Gene Technology Regulator (OGTR), governs the implementation of the Gene Technology Act, maintains a public record of genetically modified products and licenses the intentional release of GM organisms into the environment. The Australian Quarantine and Inspection Service (AQIS), also regulates the importation of all animal, plant and biological products into Australia that could introduce pests or disease. Therefore, OGTR has jurisdiction over GM food imports.

Australia is currently conducting field trials on over 17 GM crops. The marketing of some of these GM crops is expected over the next five years. Consequently, the Australian government is developing a traceable and auditable food traceability system and testing regime to allow for the segregation of GM food products. The agricultural industry works with government agencies to develop and implement a policy of coexistence of GM, conventional and organic crops (AFFA 2001). This type of food traceability system enhances the effectiveness of national food labelling regulations. A separate agency, the FSANZ, controls GM product labelling. From

December 2001, the FSANZ required labelling of all food and food ingredients that meet the following criteria:

- novel DNA or novel protein are present in the final food
- food nutritional or allergenicity characteristics differ from the conventional food counterpart
- foods that are exempt from the food labelling regulations
- highly refined foods that do not contain novel DNA or proteins
- food additives and processing aids
- flavors that are present in a concentration no more than 1g/kg in the final food and
- food prepared at point of sale.

Labels for single ingredient products that are genetically modified must include the phrase 'genetically modified', and the name of the product. Packaging of multi-ingredient foods must identify GM ingredients by including the phrase 'genetically modified' immediately after any ingredient that requires a label (Ernst and Young et al. 2001). In New Zealand, two agencies have mandates relating to GM crops. Food Standards Australia New Zealand develops GM food standards for Australia and New Zealand.

The Environmental Risk Management Authority (ERMA) controls the genetic modification of plants, animals and other living things under the Hazardous Substances and New Organisms Act of 1996. In 2001, New Zealand's Royal Commission on Genetic Modification implemented a two-year constraint period during which the ERMA did not accept applications for the release of GMOs. The only exceptions to the GM food approval moratorium are products with direct human or animal health benefits (Ministry for the Environment 2001a). The law exempts several types of products including medicines that are, or contain, live GMOs for human use, veterinary medicines that are, or contain, approved live GMOs, and GMOs approved under the Hazardous Substances and New Organisms Act of 1996 (Bridges 2002).

Since the law focuses on GMOs intended for release into the environment, it does not relate to GM foods and ingredients. Nevertheless, it has clear implications for New Zealand exporters, who claim GM-free status, and access global markets for GM-free products. The government stresses 'preserving opportunities' through the governance of the economic and environmental impacts of GM crop releases (Ministry for the Environment 2001b).

China

China has rapidly built up scientific programs for agricultural biotechnology over the past 15 years. In November 2002, the Chinese government announced the intention of quintupling government agricultural biotechnology research funding by 2005 (CropBiotech Update 2002).[7] These investments support rapid advances in the development of genomic studies and transformation technologies in China.

A national committee established in 1996 accepts applications twice a year for biosafety evaluation of genetically improved crop plants, farm animals and micro-organisms (ADB 2001).[8] Official regulatory restrictions on the planting of other GM crops may mask the true adoption of these crops, as rural farmers often use informal marketing channels to acquire seeds (ISAAA 2001).

Despite the many new seed varieties in China, the Chinese regulatory agencies only allowed the widespread planting of Bt Cotton (Huang et al. 2004). While China invests heavily in GM crop development, the country maintains strict regulations on GM food trade and labelling. In 2001, China adopted restrictive regulations on GM food imports, requiring that importers of GM products obtain safety permits. Since China is the largest importer of US soybeans, and 70 per cent of US soybeans were GM, these regulations disrupted US–China trade. By April 2002, China issued temporary safety permits to allow imports of GM food and to resolve the US–China conflict (Reuters 2002). China also adopted regulations that require all foods containing GM ingredients to be labelled. Processed foods that do not contain detectable modified DNA or proteins must state on the packaging that some of the product source is GM (AFFA 2001).

Japan

The Ministry of Health, Labor and Welfare (MHLW) and the Ministry of Agriculture, Forestry, and Fisheries share the responsibility for the regulation of food labelling. The MHLW administers the Food Sanitation Law, and the Ministry of Agriculture, Forestry and Fisheries administers the Law concerning Standardization and Proper Quality Labelling of Agricultural and Forestry Products. Both ministries imposed labelling requirements for GM foods, including prepackaged processed foods, food additives and ingredients (MHLW 2001). In the Japanese system, only ingredients in which GM DNA or proteins are present as the top three ingredients in food, or at more than 5 per cent by weight, are subject to this regulation.

The Japanese labelling system has three broad categories. All foods that have been genetically modified and identity preserved must be labelled 'genetically modified'. Products that have not been handled in a food traceability system must be labelled 'not segregated from GM product'.

A non-GM food using a food traceability process may be labelled 'not genetically modified'. In addition, manufacturers may state on the label when the government approved the GM ingredient (Asian Food Information Centre 2002).

V EMERGING REGIONAL REGULATORY HARMONIZATION AND INSTITUTIONAL CONVERGENCE FOR FOOD SAFETY

National policy frameworks, as well as regional groups, influence emerging regulatory policy harmonization for food safety. In the Asia-Pacific, regional groups such as APEC and ASEAN, contribute to food safety standards harmonization by facilitating interaction among countries, initiating policy dialogue across national borders and supporting consensus-building activities through workshops and policy discussions. Due to the difficulty in achieving consensus across diverse groups of countries, these activities are very useful in situations of rapid technological change or increasing health concerns. The food regulatory issues addressed in this chapter, are rapidly changing due to technological advances in GM crops, and potential global public threats in the case of BSE.

National Policies

The four Asia-Pacific countries examined in this chapter are not actively seeking to harmonize their approaches to BSE. This is due to their unique economic and governmental characteristics. Japan, a major importer of beef, has already experienced its first case of BSE. Therefore, current Japanese food safety regulations emphasize the control of BSE within national borders. While China's imports of beef are growing, they represent a small proportion of Chinese imports. Nevertheless, growing domestic demand for beef products means that China must face this food safety issue in light of new cases of BSE in Canada and the United States. In contrast, Australia and New Zealand are exporters of beef, and have long traditions of enforcing strict quarantine standards. Australia looked to the EU for guidance on the regulation of beef trade, and control of BSE food safety threats. The EU country classification system categorizes countries by the type of food safety threat posed by beef imports and provides one effective mechanism for regulatory harmonization. In turn, the EU system provides the best mechanism for regulatory harmonization for BSE.

An effective and broadly adopted GM food labelling system would support variable national regulations on biotech food segregation and adoption. To date national food labelling systems are extremely diverse, and include broad ranges in threshold GM ingredient content levels, and definitions of products that require labelling. In the Asia-Pacific region, the FSANZ is the only example of a bilateral and fully harmonized labelling approach. This regulatory agency works due to the close relationship of Australia and New Zealand, and depends upon the food safety and trade policy objectives of these two countries.

Both countries have long traditions of strict quarantine laws to control the introduction of pests and disease. Consequently, the regulation of the safety of imported GM material in agri-food products fits into their existing policy priorities of strict food safety control. In addition, both countries have strong export focus and are eager to maintain access to global markets. While consumers in these countries do not have a strong aversion to GM food, industry is concerned that segregation decisions will impact access to global food markets.

At the present time, the Chinese have relatively simple food labelling regulations, and have instituted border controls that limit trade in GM products. In the future, China will become more dependent on imports to meet domestic food demands. Therefore, the Chinese government is currently improving the productivity of agricultural industry sectors to meet the needs of a growing population. In this new environment of food security and food production, China is aggressively developing new GM food and biotechnology. However, the Chinese government is adopting a conservative approach to the production and trade of GM food products.

Corporate and Civil Society Interests

The reaction of consumers in the Asia-Pacific region to GM foods is varied and difficult to measure. According to several surveys, Australian consumers are moderately concerned about the food safety risks associated with GM foods. One survey, conducted by Biotechnology Australia (2001) found that while Australians are concerned about the food safety of GM products, about half are willing to eat GM foods. In that same survey just over half of the consumers surveyed believed that GM crop safety risks outweigh the benefits.

By the late 1990s, Japanese consumers were aware of genetically modified foods, but one in five opposed the use of GM products in agriculture (Hoban 1999). The best indication of Asian-Pacific consumer aversion to GM food products in wealthy countries is whether consumers are willing to pay extra for 'non-GM' products. One measure of Japanese price premiums for non-GM products, the Tokyo Grain Exchange, indicated that monthly prices between GM and non-GM soybeans ranged from \$18 to \$36 per tonne in

2001 (Bullock and Desquilbet 2001). In contrast, in lower-income countries more consumers accept GM food products and may even believe that they will benefit from consuming them (Khong et al. 2002).

Asian-Pacific governments across the region acknowledge the importance of input and participation by national consumer groups in food safety standard-setting. In a food safety regulators forum convened by the FAO, China, the Philippines, Indonesia, Australia, New Zealand, Japan, and Thailand provided information about food safety regulatory systems, and efforts to include consumers in food safety activities (FAO 2002). In this context, Consumers International has several regional offices, including one that concentrates on Asian-Pacific consumer issues. In turn, Consumers International, which represents consumer interests in the Codex Alimentarius, is strengthening consumer organizations' participation in food safety policy-making in many international forums.

During the 1990s, multinational corporations increased their participation in Asian agri-food industries, and now play an important role in the regional agri-food systems (DFAT 2001). Since these corporations act as another type of demand for agricultural products, they can influence Asian-Pacific industry standards through their acceptance of food products and ingredients. For example, several Japanese firms adopted strict food labelling regulations for their products. Eventually, some companies removed GM ingredients rather than adopting labelling systems (Phillips and Foster 2000). For example, in the year 2000 several Japanese tofu producers (National Tofu Manufacturers Association), soy sauce producers (Kikkoman and Taihei Company), and breweries (Kirin and Sapporo), announced that they would only use non-GM ingredients in their products (Phillips and Foster 2000). During this period, some Japanese food companies switched from corn to wheat in the processing facilities to avoid the GM food safety controversy. (See Table 10.8 for US and European MNCs' GM product strategies.)

From 1995–2001, European and American multinational food companies increased their investment and expanded their Asian operations. By the start of this decade, the majority of leading global agri-business and multinational corporations had at least one manufacturing operation in China and Thailand (DFAT 2001). For example, Nestlé has food/beverage processing plants throughout Asia including China (11), Japan (4), Philippines (8), Thailand (8), Malaysia (9) and Australia (12). Currently, Cargill owns and operates food-processing plants in the Philippines, Indonesia, Malaysia, China, Japan, Vietnam and Australia.

As the decade unfolds, rapid consolidation of the Asian-Pacific agri-food industry sector is expected to lead to regional food markets dominated by fewer and larger corporations. This industry structure trend is expected to

Table 10.8 US and European agri-food MNCs' GM product strategies

Company	Country of headquarters	Net profit (US$million)	Products/activities	GM policies
Cargill	USA	358	Agri-inputs, trading, processed foods	Will continue to accept and market genetically enhanced, conventionally bred crops and specialty grains[1]
Coca-Cola	USA	2177	Non-alcoholic beverages	Source all their ingredients from GMO-free crops for the food and drink they sell in Europe
Heineken	Netherlands	572	Beer brewing	Has a policy of not using GM raw materials[2]
Heinz	USA	478	Processed foods	Stated that policy is for products to be GM-free
J. Sainbury	United Kingdom	397	Food retailing supermarkets	Stated that has eliminated GM ingredients from own brand products
Nestlé	Switzerland	3412	Processed foods, beverages, petfood	Will continue to use GM ingredients, but may be considering offering GM-free products in Europe
Unilever	United Kingdom/ Netherlands	1018	Processed foods	In some markets has removed GM inputs from products

Notes:
1 Cargill website, 'Cargill's biotechnology position', 2003, http://www.cargill.com/news/issues/biotechnology.htm.
2 Heineken website, 'About Heineken FAQs, 2003, http://www.heinekeninternational.com/faqs/about/index.jsp?page=4.

Source: Adapted from tables in DFAT (2001) pp. 6 and 66.

accelerate food safety regulation harmonization efforts, particularly in the area of GM food labelling. Ultimately, industry consolidation trends will lead to a more homogeneous agri-food industry sector with fewer participants in the Asia-Pacific region. When multinational corporations (MNCs) set policies in the Asia-Pacific region, they reflect the US and European principles of the headquarters in the home country of the firms. (See Table 10.8 for example with GM food marketing strategies).[9]

Regional Food Safety Institutions

APEC has several committees and sub-committees that conduct work relevant to the regional and multilateral harmonization of food safety standards. The APEC Sub-committee on Standards and Conformance (SCSC) was established in 1994, with the goal of providing a framework for reducing the negative effects on trade and investment in the region due to differing standards and product conformance systems (APEC 2002c). Several action areas under the SCSC involve food safety regulations, including the APEC MRA on conformity assessment of foods in 2002.[10]

Through the food MRA, countries voluntarily minimize food safety inspection controls at the border of importing countries. Official inspection and certification systems provide assurance that imported products have met minimal safety requirements. An umbrella arrangement includes general food safety provisions, and encourages member countries to cooperate on specific sectoral arrangements. While APEC provides guidelines for the development of sectoral arrangements, member governments develop sectoral arrangements on a government-to-government basis. However, the smaller countries in the Asia-Pacific region have few shared food safety regulations, but are affected by the food trade standards. Furthermore, trade between China and the ASEAN countries increased dramatically in the past decade. The smaller countries are eager to expand their regional free trade agreements with China.

Biotechnology policy received more attention than beef safety regulations in the regional trade agreements. In 1996, APEC created the Agricultural Technical Cooperation Experts' Group (ATCEG) to focus on agricultural technical cooperation, including joint activities to enhance extension of agricultural biotechnology. During 2001 and 2002, APEC funded three ATCEG projects, two of which were directly related to cooperative activities related to biotechnology: Capacity-building, Safety Assessment, Communications in Biotechnology and a workshop on Technical Cooperation and Information Exchange on Safety Assessments in Agricultural Biotechnology (APEC 2002b). These are voluntary activities, but may promote information exchange and the development of expertise that will support the harmonization of biotechnology and food safety regulatory policies within the region.

The International Life Sciences Institute – Southeast Asia Region (ILSI SEA) brings together ASEAN policy-makers and regulators to discuss and share experiences of risk assessment in order to promote harmonization of food safety standards. In 1999, ILSI SEA organized a seminar and workshop on Risk Assessment and Harmonization in Malaysia to encourage the harmonization of regional food safety and control regulations with Codex standards. At the conclusion of the meetings participants proposed the establishment of an ASEAN framework on food safety and risk assessment. Since that time several meetings, many held in conjunction with the annual ASEAN Food Conference, were held targeting various topics including microbial risk assessment, risk assessment and the impact of food-borne pathogens. In 2003, the Eighth ASEAN Food Conference emphasized trade obligations, and the acceptance of GM food in member countries.

In response to the 1999 ILSA SEA recommendation, ASEAN developed a food safety improvement plan targeting regulatory policy harmonization in member countries. In 2002, the ASEAN Working Group on Food Safety Standards Harmonization, comprising key regulators and scientists from member countries, analysed ASEAN country data in order to align these standards with Codex standards. In 2003, the working group addressed the harmonization of additives including flavors, antioxidants, emulsifiers and stabilizers. To accelerate the harmonization of ASEAN food safety standards, the working group is developing a regional standards database.

At the regional level, the APEC and ASEAN food safety harmonization and trade facilitation efforts of the Pacific Islands Forum (PIF), provide a mechanism for member countries to cooperate for the promotion of Asian-Pacific food products in global markets.[11] The forum has trade offices in Australia, Japan, New Zealand and China. Many members of PIF ratified the following complementary trade agreements to facilitate trade and technical assistance programmes: the Pacific Island Countries Trade Agreement (PICTA) and the Pacific Agreement for Closer Economic Relations (PACER). Currently PACER is developing trade facilitation programmes in three priority areas – customs procedures, SPS measures, and standards and conformance – and providing financial and technical assistance to forum island countries.

VI CONCLUSIONS

The ability of countries to achieve effective harmonization of food safety standards depends upon the national characteristics of Asia-Pacific regulatory systems, the structure of food and agricultural industries and the nature of government and industry relations. Ultimately, wide variation in regulatory policies, industry structure and Asia-Pacific market integration pose challenges to food safety standards harmonization. In some countries, the structure of regulatory systems, the relationship among different levels of government and their assigned regulatory responsibilities affect the adoption of food safety standards. For example, in Australia, new laws and regulatory offices were created to handle GM regulations. In Japan, existing regulatory agencies govern GM crops under existing food regulations. In the case of China, the Ministry of Agriculture has responsibility for the national regulation of GM food production. However, the provinces implement and oversee some aspects of national food safety regulations.

Industry structure, limited land and labor scarcity will also effect GM food safety standards implementation. However, some countries are exploring the potential of food traceability systems to address consumer concerns over GM crop safety. If these types of biotechnology regulatory systems are implemented in some but not all countries, harmonization of GM food standards will be more difficult. In the case of BSE regulations, national beef-processing facilities will determine how industry structure will influence the regional harmonization of BSE policies. While small farmers and beef processors dominate the Chinese beef industry, large farm holders and meat processors dominate the Australian beef industry.

Since both regulatory policy and industry structure are important for the implementation of effective food safety regimes, the relationship between regulators and industry play an important role in the standards harmonization process. For example, Australia stresses the importance of co-regulation where industry works directly with regulators to develop flexible regulatory policies and management-based regulations. In this context, Australian agri-food industries are working with the government to analyse the potential trade-offs of food traceability systems. In contrast, China's communist history led to a regulatory system in which government tightly controls industry output and functions. These policy differences have major implications for regulatory harmonization, and will determine Asian-Pacific countries' food safety regulations.

The evolution of a global system of agriculture trade, agri-food industry consolidation and food safety standards harmonization creates conducive conditions for regulatory cooperation in the Asia-Pacific region. The influence of Europe and the US will grow in the region due to the consolidation of the agri-food industry and the increased regional investment by US and EU multinational food companies. China's recent WTO accession links it with other countries in the system of WTO rights and obligations for SPS food safety standards. Given China's key role in the world economy, these evolving relationships provide an important foundation for regulatory harmonization.

The development of new free trade agreements, including PACER, PICTA and the US–Australian FTA, support the harmonization of regulations and industry standards as countries negotiate to achieve transparent and open food-safety systems. Nevertheless, the proposed harmonization of agricultural, animal livestock health and food safety standards may generate contentious debate. For example, in the case of BSE policy, food safety risks are more immediate and demonstrable. The categorization of countries by levels of BSE risk creates incentives for countries to develop effective internationally recognized food safety standards. Therefore, it is easier to consider regulatory harmonization that will support more consistent food safety approaches in the beef industry.

In contrast, GM foods that reach the commercial approval stage probably pose no greater risk than conventional food products (Gasson and Burke 2001). Even if the food safety benefits of harmonized GM food policies are negligible, regulatory harmonization is desirable if it enhances global food market efficiency. In many cases, economic efficiency is difficult to measure in the global food system and competing agri-food industries. However, if consumers care about food product differences, and producers incur minimal costs for implementing the food safety standards, efficiency benefits are likely to arise from harmonization. In contrast, when trading partners have widely different policies on GM foods, regulatory harmonization may be inefficient (Jackson 2002).

The costs of identity segregation that allows labelling of GM food products throughout the food chain are under examination. Sectors that are dominated by smaller farms are likely to experience higher costs of food traceability across food supply chains. This has equity implications since lower-income Asian-Pacific countries with small farms will incur higher costs in implementing GM food segregation strategies than will higher-income countries. In turn, lower-income countries might refuse to adopt potentially beneficial GM food and biotechnology to maintain access to export markets, rather than adopting regulations with excessive costs. If labelling and food traceability leads to the refusal to adopt GM products by developing countries, the potential productivity benefits from GM crop adoption will never be realized.

While the region contains the only example of successful bilateral food safety standards harmonization in the FSANZ, diverse trading strategies and stages of economic development are challenging extensive regulatory harmonization. Australia and New Zealand will adopt strategies that enhance their market access while maintaining their strict quarantine policies for the protection of food safety, and animal livestock and plant health. In contrast, large food importers, like Japan, are primarily concerned with the introduction of disease and unsafe products into their food chain.

In the years ahead, China will play a critical role in the regional food system and Asia-Pacific agri-food industries. The decisions made in China on food safety standards have large impacts on the rest of Asia-Pacific region. While there are tangible public health and economic benefits from the harmonization of BSE regulations, the benefits from harmonized GM policies are less clear. Ultimately, the question of who will bear the costs, and who will benefit from food safety policy harmonization in the Asia-Pacific region deserves careful consideration.

NOTES

1. China experienced steady 8.2 per cent annual economic growth between 1996 and 2000, while other countries showed negative growth.
2. Some developing countries may produce products entirely for export and will invest in monitoring and certification to meet standards of trade partners. Foods that are grown to satisfy export market standards may be unacceptable domestically for cultural or economic reasons. Thus, developing countries may divert resources from domestic food safety controls to improve food safety for export products but still experience few domestic food safety spill overs.
3. The Codex Alimentarius, a joint commission of FAO and WHO, develops food standards and guidelines.
4. Philippine farmers expected to begin commercially planting GM maize in 2003.
5. Public debate within Australia increased a shipment of US GM maize intended for animal feed was accepted. Currently animal feed is not affected by labelling regulations, but feed companies may adopt voluntary GM-free labels.
6. By 2002 the food safety regulatory agency had approved 17 applications for GM foods, including corn, canola, soybeans and potatoes. Food manufacturers have avoided using these products as ingredients.
7. Genetically modified crops being tested in China in the late 1990s included rice, wheat, maize, cotton, tomatoes, pepper, potatoes, cucumbers, papaya, and tobacco. More than 90 per cent of Chinese field trials target insect and disease resistance, reducing the need for expensive and dangerous pesticides.
8. By mid-1998 the committee had received 75 applications for field testing of transgenic crops and granted permission to 53 for commercial production, environmental release or small-scale field testing.
9. For more descriptive information and data on major food producers, processors and distributors in the Asian-Pacific agro-food industries and markets see DFAT (2001), also at http://www.dfat.gov.au/publications/agrifoodasia/index.html, and see the DFAT Subsistence to Supermarket Series.
10. The APEC MRA on Conformity Assessment of Foods and Food Products calls for consistency with SPS and TBT requirements as well as with Codex standards, including the recommendations of the Codex Committee on Food Import and Export Certification Systems.
11. The Pacific Island Forum is composed of representatives from Australia, the Cook Islands, Federated States of Micronesia, the Fiji Islands, Kiribati, Nauru, New Zealand, Niue, Palau, Papua New Guinea, the Republic of Marshall Islands, Samoa, Solomon Islands, Tonga, Tuvalu and Vanuatu.

REFERENCES

Agriculture, Fisheries and Forestry – Australia (AFFA) (2002a), *Biotechnology Strategy for Agriculture, Food and Fibre*, Canberra: AFFA Science Policy.

Agriculture, Fisheries and Forestry – Australia (AFFA) (2002b), *The Rice Industry*, Canberra: Commonwealth of Austrialia, at www.affa.gov.au.

Agriculture, Fisheries and Forestry – Australia (AFFA) (2001), *Report – Agricultural Biotechnology Workshop 2001*, Canberra: Commonwealth of Australia, at http://www.affa.gov.au.

Anderson, K., B. Dimaranan, T. Hertel and W. Martin (1996), 'Asia-Pacific food markets and trade in 2005: a global, economy-wide perspective', *Australian Journal of Agricultural and Resource Economics*, **41** (1): 19–44.

Asia-Pacific Economic Cooperation (APEC) (2002), *Convenor's Summary Report on Standards and Conformance*, Singapore: APEC, at www.apecsec.org.

Asian Development Bank (ADB) (2001), *Agricultural Biotechnology, Poverty Reduction and Food Security*, Manila: Asian Development Bank.

Asian Food Information Centre (2003), *Food Biotechnology: A Review Paper*, at http://www.afic.org.

Australian Bureau of Agricultural Resource Economics (2004), *Australian Commodity Statistics*, Australian Government, Canberra.

Biotechnology Australia (2001), *Biotechnology Public Awareness Survey, Final Report*, at http://www.biotechnology.gov.au.

Bingsheng, K. (2002), *Perspectives and Strategies for the Livestock Sector in China Over the Next Three Decades*, Livestock Policy Discussion Paper No. 7, Rome: FAO.

Bridges Weekly Trade News Digest (2002), 'New Zealand notifies EMO law to the WTO', *Bridges*, **6** (29).

Brown, C., J. Longworth and S. Waldron (2002), 'Food safety and development of the beef industry in China', *Food Policy*, **27**: 269–84.

BSE Review (2002), 'Japan confirms fifth case of BSE', *BSE Review*, at http://www.bsereivew.org.uk.

Bullock, D. and M. Desquilbet (2001), 'The economics of non-GMO segregation and food traceability', *Food Policy*, **27** (1): 81–99.

Cargill website (2003), 'Cargill's biotechnology position', http://www.cargill.com/news/issues/biotechnology.htm.

Clemens, Roxanne (2003), 'Meat traceability in Japan', *Iowa AG. Review*, **9** (4): 4.

CropBiotech Update (2002), 'China gears up for biotech', *International Service for the Acquisition of Agri-biotech Applications*, Ithaca, NY: Cornell University, at http://www.isaaa.org/.

Delgado, C., C. Courbois and M. Rosegrant (1998), *Global Food Demand and the Contribution of Livestock as We Enter the New Millennium*, MSSD Discussion Paper No. 21, Washington, DC: International Food Policy Research Institute.

Department of Foreign Affairs and Trade (DFAT) (2001), 'Agrifood globalisation and Asia – Volume I', *Agrifood Multinational Corporations in Asia*, Canberra: Commonwealth of Australia.

Ernst and Young, Reehills and the Department of Industry, Science and Resources (2001), *Australian Biotechnology Report*, Canberra: Ernst and Young.

Food and Agriculture Organization (FAO) (1997), 'Review of the state of the world of aquaculture', FAO Fisheries Circular No. 886 FIRI/C886 (Rev.1), Rome: FAO.

Food and Agriculture Organization (FAO) (2002), 'Improving efficiency and transparency in food safety systems', FAO/WHO Global Forum of Food Safety Regulators – Marrakesh – Conference Proceedings, Rome: FAO, downloadable at http://www.foodsafetyforum.org/global/index_en.htm.

Food Agricultural Organization (FAO) (2003), *FAOSTAT. FAO Statistical Databases*, at http://faostat.fao.org/faostat/collections?subset=agriculture.

Foreign Agricultural Service (2002a), 'Dairy, livestock and poultry market report: the Japanese beef market', *International Agricultural Trade Report*, Washington, DC: USDA.

Foreign Agricultural Service (FAS) (2002b), 'Livestock and poultry: world markets and trade', DL&P 2-02 Circular Series, Washington, DC: USDA.

Gasson, M. and D. Burke (2001), 'Scientific perspectives on regulating the safety of genetically modified foods', *Nature Review*, **2**: 217–22.

Heineken website (2003), 'About Heineken FAQs', http://www./heinekeninternational.com/faqs/about/index.jsp?page=4.

Hoban, T. (1999), 'Consumer acceptance of biotechnology in the United States and Japan', *Food Technology*, **53** (5): 50.

Hooker, N. (1999), 'Food safety regulation and trade in food products', *Food Policy*, **24** (6): 653–68.

Huang, J. and S. Rozelle (2002), *China's Accession to WTO and Shifts in the Agriculture Policy*, Department of Agricultural and Resource Economics Working Paper No. 02-0002, Davis, CA: University of California Davis.

Huang, J., R. Hu, C. Pray and S. Rozella (2004), 'Plant biotechnology impacts in China: public investments and impacts on farmers', in *New Directions for a Diverse Plant, Proceedings of the 4th International Crop Science Congress*, 26 September–1 October, Brisbane.

Hukudo, H., J. Dyck and J. Stout (2003), 'Rice sector policies in Japan', RCS 03-03-01, USDA, Economic Research Service, Washington, DC, electronic outlook report accessed on 1 August 2005, at http://www.ers.usda.gov/publications/rcs/mas 03/rcs 030301/rcs 0303-01.pdf.

ISAAA (2001), 'Agricultural biotechnology, poverty reduction, and food security', Ithaca, NY: ISAAA.

Jackson, L. (2002), *Is Regulatory Harmonization Efficient? The Case of Agricultural Biotechnology Labelling*, Discussion Paper 206, Centre for International Economic Studies, Adelaide: University of Adelaide.

Meat and Livestock Australia (2003), *Australian Beef Industry*, Canberra: Commonwealth of Australia, at: http://www.mla.com.au/content.cfm?sid=28.

Ministry for the Environment (2001a), Royal commission on genetic modification – summary of key government decisions', Wellington: Government of New Zealand, at http://www.mfe.govt.nz.

Ministry for the Environment (2001b), *Royal Commission on Genetic Modification: Government Response*, Wellington: Government of New Zealand, at http://www.mfe.govt.nz.

Ministry of Agriculture and Forestry (MAF) (2002), *International Trade Statistics*, Wellington: Government of New Zealand, at http://www.maf.govt.nz/statistics/internationaltrade/exports/index.htm.

Ministry of Health, Labor and Welfare (MHLW) (2001), 'Mandatory labelling of genetically modified foods and foods containing allergens', Tokyo: Government of Japan, at http://www.mhlw.go.jp/English/topics/qa/gm-food/gm4.htm.

Phillips, P. and H. Foster (2000), 'Labelling for GM foods: theory and practice', ICABR Conference in Ravello, Italy.

Rae, A. and T. Josling (2003), 'Processed food trade and developing countries: protection and trade liberalization', *Food Policy*, **28** (1): 147–66.

Roche, G. (2002), 'The development and implementation of the new Australian food safety standards', *FAO/WHO Global Forum of Food Safety Regulators Conference Proceeding*, Marrakesh, 28–30 January, Rome: FAO, at http://www.fao.org/docrep/meeting/004/y2003E.htm.

Rozelle, S. (2001), 'China's corn economy: a brief introduction', *Report to the National Research Initiative Committee*, Davis, CA: University of California, at http://www.agecon.ucdavis.edu/facultypages/rozelle/.

Trewin, R., M. Bosworth and P. Drysdale (2000), 'Moving Japanese agriculture forward', ch. 1 in *Issues, Options and Strategies for Improving Japanese Agricultural Trade Policies*, RIRDC Publication No. 00/176, Canberra: RIRDC.

UNCTAD/WTO (2000), *PC-TAS Trade Analysis System on Personal Computer 1996–2000 SITC3*, International Trade Centre United Nations Statistics Division, Geneva: UNCTAD/WTO.

United States Department of Agriculture (USDA) (2002), *International Agricultural Trade Report*, 6 February, Washington, DC: USDA.

Ushio, M. (2002), 'Food safety regulatory issues', *FAO/WHO Global Forum of Food Safety Regulators Conference Proceeding*, Marrakesh, Morocoo, 28–30 January, Rome: FAO, at www.fao.org/docrep/meeting/004/y2003E.htm.

World Bank (2002), *World Development Indicators*, Washington, DC: World Bank.

World Fish Center (2002), 'Strategies and options for increasing and sustaining fisheries and aquaculture production to benefit poor households in Asia', *Semi Annual Progress Report (March–August 2002)* , Malaysia: World Fish Center.

Zhong, F., M.A. Marchant, Y. Ding and K. Lu (2002), 'GM foods: a Nanjing case study of Chinese consumers' awareness and potential attitudes', *AgBioForum*, **5** (4): 136–44, at http://www.agbioforum.org.

PART IV

Regulated Competition in Global Food and Agriculture Industries

11. Governance of biotechnology: emerging regulation of GM crops and livestock in global food industries and food systems

Jørgen Schlundt*

I INTRODUCTION: BIOTECHNOLOGY AND THE GLOBAL FOOD SYSTEM

The globalization of national food markets, food systems and global food industries is unfolding within the context of modern livestock, fish and agricultural biotechnology revolutions. From a socio-economic perspective, the driving forces in these food and agriculture market revolutions are rapid population growth and food security issues in developing countries, increasing global consumer demand for high-quality fresh produce, livestock products and processed foods, increasing land productivity pressure on farmers and agricultural sectors, and growing pressure to protect the environment and biodiversity. In response to these socio-economic factors, modern biotechnology is emerging as a science and public policy issue, and a driving force in the regulation of national agricultural systems and global food industries.

Historically, agriculture and livestock production are modified through a combination of traditional farming methods and technological innovations. The goals of these innovations are as follows:

- to increase animal livestock and crop productivity
- to remove plant and livestock pathogens and pests
- to increase food security through animal livestock, crop and fisheries yield stability
- to raise the market value of agricultural commodities, livestock and processed food.

In many cases, the transfer of different species of plants and animals is carried out to restore depleted and destroyed crops and livestock herds. In other cases, the transplantation of plant and animal species improves the genetic stock, crop management, livestock breeding and agriculture.[1] Ultimately, biotechnology historically improves livestock breeding and crop management capabilities of farmers and food producers.

By the mid-twentieth century, the Green Revolution emerged as an innovative biotechnology strategy for Asian governments, farmers and Western agri-businesses. The first goal of the Green Revolution was to increase the agricultural productivity of rural Asian farmers. The second goal of the Green Revolution was to increase food security in rapidly growing Asian nations. However, the introduction of new biotechnologies for food production and market development is insufficient for the governance of biotechnology.[2] On the contrary, normative consensus and collective policy action by governments on behalf of farmers and rural communities are needed to integrate modern biotechnology into agriculture and socio-economic systems.[3]

By the 1980s, US agri-business and food industries became early adopters of modern biotechnology. At that time, the United States of America developed the first generation of GM seeds and crops. During that decade, the first transgenic plant cell was developed, and the first field test of GM plant crops was conducted. By 1990, the first insect-protected crop plants were created and the first field test of Bt corn was carried out. Finally, in 1996, food safety studies were conducted and led the way for GM seed and food sales in the US.[4] The boxed text shows the main GM products by the year 2001.

In the 1990s, the importance of modern biotechnology for new product innovation, socio-economic change, and growth of food and drug industries became apparent. During this period the market and wealth creation aspects of modern biotechnology, and food and pharmaceutical industry innovation, attracted the attention of stock-market speculators, corporate investors and policy-makers in the US, EU and Japan.[5] Eventually, modern biotechnology emerged as a strategic policy and industry sector for market

BOX 11.1 MAIN GM CROPS BY FOOD CATEGORY – 2001

1. Soybean – 63 per cent
2. Maize/corn – 19 per cent
3. Cotton – 13 per cent
4. Canola – 5 per cent

Source: ISAAA (2001), in Bruinsma (2003), p. 320.

economies in these OECD countries.[6] At the start of the twenty-first century, modern biotechnology provides new sources of competitive advantage in global food industries.[7] The following benefits of GM food production are emerging in national food systems and global food industries:

- increased product quality
- increased attractiveness of food for consumers
- increased productivity of farms and food industries
- promotion of biodiversity and sustainability
- environmental protection
- increased food safety through pathogen and pest identification and destruction.[8]

In the context of rising food demand and food insecurity in developing nations, modern biotechnology can be a public and private good that can increase food production. Furthermore, modern biotechnology can increase the value of food production both for small farmers and industrial food producers through the reduction of pests and weeds, and increases in crop and livestock productivity.[9] In global food-processing industries, modern biotechnology is used to increase the attractiveness of food consistency, enhance the smell and extend the shelf life of processed foods. For example, fresh fruits and vegetables are treated with delayed ripening agents that are inserted into GM seeds. Consequently, all stakeholders potentially benefit from this agricultural innovation.

Genome Technology and Value-Added Production of Biotechnology Food

As a growing field of biotechnology, genomics is revolutionizing farming, agriculture and livestock management and, hence, the evolution of global food industries. In global food industries, genomics provides an economically efficient input for food production. Through the use of genome science, productivity, profitability and competitiveness are increasing in national agricultural systems and global food industries. In turn, farmers, agribusiness and food companies can respond more efficiently to growing consumer demand and national food security needs through the use of selected GM seeds, crops, fish and livestock.[10]

In global food industries, genome science and modern biotechnology can support the growth of food markets through the development of novel GM food products. Through the application of new food traits, food-processing and storage capabilities, GM food products are sourced across the globe in supermarkets. For example, food additives and microbial fermentation agents, that is, bacteria, yeasts, gums, starches and delayed ripening agents are used by food companies to expand into global markets. Furthermore, the US Biotechnology Industry Organization reports that over 55 enzymes are used in global food-processing industries and more enzymes are under development.[11]

At the present time, genome science and modern biotechnologies are used in the production of following novel foods: milk and diary products, soybeans, tomatoes, corn, potatoes, cantaloupe, squash, cucumbers, canola, grapes, peppers, peas, tropical fruits such as papaya, sunflowers and peanuts. In food markets, biotech companies and agri-businesses such as Syngenta with long shelf life bananas, and Calagene with its delayed ripening tomatoes, are increasing the consumer benefits of GM foods in second and third generation products. Along the same lines, Monsanto, Syngenta, DuPont and Bayer Crop Science are extending the range and product traits of a widening group of foods including, wheat, strawberries, rice, lettuce, apples and alfalfa.[12]

Genome science and modern biotechnology are also used to differentiate branded food products in global food markets. In many cases, branded food products are marketed on their quality, safety and attractiveness to global consumers, as well as the product taste, color and texture. But more important, genome science and modern biotechnology allow government and industry to increase the security of food supply chains in response to the threat of bioterrorist sabotage of national food systems and global food industries.[13]

In terms of food safety, genome science and modern biotechnology can be used proactively to reduce the risk of microbial, fungal and parasite contamination of food products. For example, new biotechnology agents and techniques developed from genome science can strengthen food safety through the use of antibody tests, biosensors, polymerase chains reactions (PCR) and DNA probes that identify the presence of dangerous food pathogens and toxins. In this way, deadly strains of *E. coli 0157:H7*, which caused several deaths in the United States in food contamination incidents a few years ago, can now be easily identified and distinguished from harmless strains of *E.coli*.[14] Finally, in the case of *Salmonella*, modern biotechnology can confirm its presence within 36 hours. This is a major improvement from the three-to-four-day waiting period of the past.

The Challenge of Food Safety: GM Food and Modern Biotechnology

From a socio-economic perspective, food biotechnology and genome science can be used to improve livestock quality, crop management and the safety of the global food system. Therefore, proponents of modern biotechnology and GM food argue that consumer welfare is maximized, and efficiency is increased through this innovation.[15] Table 11.3 shows the range of commercial applications for GM crop production.

In this context, there are growing concerns over the safety of genetically modified food, the potential risks of genetic pollution of conventional plant crops and the environment, and endangerment of biodiversity. Furthermore, there are ethical and competition policy concerns over the exclusion of independent farmers and developing countries from novel food R&D. In many cases, small and independent farmers and developing countries do not benefit from patents, that is, the collection of rents and profits from patented modern biotechnologies and GM food products. As a result, the main beneficiaries of GM food and modern biotechnologies at the moment are primarily transatlantic agri-business and food industries.

In response to global food industry trends, US food safety regulators developed a voluntary registration system for GM food. Through this market friendly regulatory approach, US regulators argue that GM food is safe for commercialization and consumption. Therefore, the FDA and USDA rejected mandatory regulation of novel food products in the early phase of the GM food development. In contrast, the EU Commission and member governments placed a moratorium on the approval of GM foods. By the late 1990s, EU regulators assigned corporate responsibility and liability for food safety risks and environmental damage from GM food and biotechnology agriculture. The EU moratorium on GM foods remained in place until May 2004 to allow for the development of a science-based and precautionary regulatory system. The boxed text shows the main GM food producing countries at the start of the 2000s.

In response to growing concerns over the impact of modern biotechnology on food safety, many public policy and industry competition issues are under review. The goal of these policies and market regulations are to fully inform consumers about the true content of food, and to

BOX 11.2 MAIN GM CROP COUNTRIES, 2001

1. United States – 69 per cent
2. Argentina – 22 per cent
3. Canada – 6 per cent
4. China – 3 per cent
5. Australia – 0 per cent
6. South Africa – 0 per cent

Source: ISAAA (2001), in Bruinsma (2003), p. 320.

enable them to exercise their right to choose (or not) GM foods and biotechnology agriculture. The following issues are regulatory policy considerations:

- the need for clear GM food product and ingredient labeling
- the need for GM product segregation, and ingredient traceability in food and animal feed supply chain systems and industries
- the need for GM product segregation to protect consumer food product choice
- economic concerns relative to the loss of labor cost advantages and competitiveness of small and independent farmers in conventional food and agricultural production
- access to consumer safety information and control of patented information
- promotion of effective competition by independent farmers and organic food producers to reduce market concentration and restriction of food product choice
- assignment of food safety, public health, animal and plant health, and environmental liability for GM contamination of conventional agricultural systems.[16]

In this context, the FAO calls for more focus on the farming, agricultural and food industry problems of developing countries to increase the global benefits of GM food production.[17] However, the lack of information and long-term scientific risk assessment of GM food safety, and dependence on small farmers and traditional agriculture systems are major challenges for GM food production in developing countries. For example, the limited role of developing countries in the ownership and development of GM food products and applications prevents the rapid adoption of modern biotechnology in African, Latin American and Asian nations. Furthermore, the lack of effective regulation of modern biotechnology weakens the confidence of global consumers, farmers and national governments in the safety of GM food.

Table 11.1 Selected commercial varieties of GM crops and plants – 2001

GMO category	GM change	Purpose of GMO	Primary beneficiary
Corn/maize	Insect resistant	Reduced insect damage	Farmers
Soybean	Herbicide tolerance	Weed control	Farmers
Cotton	Insect resistance	Reduced insect damage	Farmers

Source: ISAAA (2001), in Bruinsma (2003), p. 317.

Therefore, national governments are increasingly working with the FAO and WHO through the FAO/ WHO Codex Alimentarius Commission to develop standards for the regulation of foods derived from modern biotechnology.

II BIOTECHNOLOGY AND GLOBAL AGRICULTURAL PRODUCTION

The use of modern biotechnology to develop high-quality foods, and increasing crop yields is now an emerging competitive strategy in global food industries. As a result, a growing number of farmers and food producers in the Western Hemisphere, Australia, South Africa and China are adopting GM food production and agriculture. Therefore, late adopters of GM crops and livestock face long-term market risks as governments effectively regulate the safety of foods derived from modern biotechnology.

In many cases, agri-businesses, food companies and biotechnology firms must recover high R&D costs through high levels of market share and profits in global food markets. Furthermore, the rapid mobilization of latent consumer demand, the development of high-quality global food brands, and market access in developing countries with growing national food security needs are driving GM food production. In this regard, the gradual lifting of the EU moratorium on novel food products and GM food production will have a major impact on competition in national food systems, and global food industries. In light of global food industry trends, GM crop, livestock and food production must focus on the needs of small farmers, consumers, food trade and food security in developing nations.

In regard to applications, modern biotechnology is used to increase productivity and profitability in global cereal, grains, fruits and vegetables industries. For example, the first generation of GM food and feed crops was used to manage producer costs and productivity. As a result, the most important product traits and producer benefits of first generation GM crops were the development of herbicide tolerant (Ht), and insect resistant (Bt) food crops. Since the development of first generation GM food and feed crops, new combinations of traits are emerging to increase the value for farmers, agri-business and food processors in the form of herbicide resistant corn and maize. Ultimately, insect resistant GM crops that are 'stacked' with herbicide tolerance represent the next generations of value-added producer traits for farmers and global food industries.

While some first generation GM crops had higher yields, this was due to built-in pesticides that reduced crop losses in Bt/Ht corn/maize. In addition, the genetic modification of seeds allowed crops to grow in agricultural environments that were previously unsuitable for food production. In contrast, the second generation of GM crops increased productivity and food quality benefits for consumers. Consequently, developing countries can benefit from first and second generation GM crops as they move to increase food production and food security in the their national food systems.[18]

Since the start of this decade, increasing government regulation of pesticide and fertilizer use, and growing demands for sustainable agriculture, are forcing farmers and agri-business to find new ways to increase productivity. In this regard, modern biotechnology can be used to reduce the need for pesticides, chemicals and water resources.[19] Furthermore, small farmers in developing countries can increase their productivity on marginal farmland through the use of GM seeds and food crops. Since, national food security and consumer access to high-quality food comes from increasing crop yields, many OECD food producers are investigating the potential use of the following GM food and feed crops.

Soybeans:

- Soybeans with less saturated fat, high oleic content, and no need for hydrogenation allows the product to be marketed to 'health'-conscious consumers.
- Soybeans with improved nutritional value for animal feeds and higher levels of lysine and methionine reduces the need for expensive protein meals and animal feeds.
- Higher sucrose content soybeans provide better taste and easier digestion.

Rapeseed canola:

- Higher lauric content varieties of rapeseed are now used to produce oil with 40 per cent lauric acid for the chemical and cosmetic industry products.
- High stearate varieties of rapeseed are used to produce oils that remain solid at room temperature without the need for hydrogenation. The oils can then be used by the baking, margarine and confectionary food industries that cannot use liquid oils.

Corn/maize:

- New GM research in corn and maize products is increasing the nutritional value of corn for animal and livestock feed. In addition, there is also vitamin A enriched maize and rice for human consumption.
- Through the increase in energy values, protein content and better amino-acid levels in GM corn/maize, there will be a declining need for expensive supplemental feeds.

As the century unfolds, modern biotechnology is creating new emerging markets in environmental protection and biodiversity support. In this regard, species preservation, land reclamation from salt and acid saturation, and the transformation of non-productive farmland that was historically given to the poor marginalized farming communities, represent new applications for biotech agriculture. Through these innovations, poor farmers in developing countries could be able to increase their agricultural productivity and improve indigenous livestock management.[20]

III BIOTECHNOLOGY AND THE GLOBAL MEAT AND FISH INDUSTRY

Biotechnologies for Global Animal Livestock and Fish Industries

In the global meat industries, FAO reports that the livestock revolution is fuelled by growing demand for milk, meat and eggs in developing countries. According to FAO, approximately 82 per cent of all food and agriculture production will take place in developing countries by the year 2020.[21] As a major sector in the global food industry, livestock production is growing faster than other sectors due to value-added meats, meat products, eggs and diary foods. The major drivers of the global livestock industry are as follows:

- shifting livestock production from cool and dry climates to warm/humid regions
- shifting livestock production from family farms and agricultural activities to market driven and integrated industrial production
- increasing pressure on land for livestock production and management
- increasing shift to industrial production of livestock located closer to urban areas
- growing shift and consumer demand for livestock such as pigs and poultry, and the decreasing role of ruminants in the global livestock markets and industries
- dramatic and rapid increase in the use of cereal based animal feeds for the production of livestock for human consumption.[22]

In many countries, the demand for meat, livestock products and animal feed grains is growing in global poultry, pork, and diary industries.[23] By the year 2000, the FAO reported that approximately 20 per cent of the protein in the diet comes from animal products.[24] Therefore, OECD countries improve the quality of domestic livestock herds through selective breeding, improved animal feed, prophylactic veterinary medicines, control of contagious animal livestock diseases, and improved hygiene and sanitation practices.[25] However, meat and livestock production in OECD and developing countries requires regulation of modern biotechnology.[26]

Fish and aquaculture

At the start of the 2000s, fish production and aquaculture emerged as one of the fastest growing sectors of national food systems and the global food industry.[27] According to the FAO, aquaculture is the farming of aquatic organisms, including fish and seafood, and aquatic plants for food.[28] The importance of this segment of the global food industry is the growing role of fish and seafood products as a major source of dietary protein for many consumers and nations.

By the start of this decade, China, India, Japan, the Republic of Korea, the Philippines, Indonesia, Thailand, Bangladesh and Taiwan, China were among the largest fish producers in the world.[29] While Norway, the United States and France are among the leading fish-producing countries in the world, approximately 90 per cent of all global aquaculture production is based in Asia. In this regard, fish and aquaculture products are major sources of small farmer income, and global food trade for many Asian, African and Western Hemisphere nations. Therefore, fish farming and industrial aquaculture represent an important and growing area of modern biotechnology innovation in the global food industry.[30]

In the case of salmon and other commercially farmed fish species, GM fish are modified to increase the rate and speed of growth. At the same time, GM fish are used to improve the productivity and profitability of commercial fisheries and the global fishing industry. However, food safety and biodiversity risk concerns are being raised over the use of biotechnology to manipulate the growth and production fish stocks. In spite of these concerns, GM fish and aquaculture species provide a new and growing resource for the industrial production of fish as a source of food protein for many nations (FAO 2000).

A growing number of genes are being inserted into livestock for the development of GM animals and fish. In contrast to GM crops, livestock and fish biotechnology are strongly resisted on the grounds of animal welfare and ethical consideration partly due to earlier problems with impaired animal physiology, breeding and reproduction. However, there is now in some societies growing acceptance of food and pharmaceutical products derived from GM animals and fish.[31]

Artificial Insemination (AI)

Since the 1950s, biotechnologies for artificial insemination, embryo transfer, including oestrus synchronization and multiple ovulation, are widely used to improve the quality and efficiency of animal livestock breeding in global livestock industries. The goal of reproductive biotechnologies is to improve the efficiency of animal breeding and livestock management, and to improve the quality, quantity and value of food products. In the case of artificial insemination, cattle, sheep, goats, pigs and poultry production have been improved through the use of this animal biotechnology by transatlantic farmers and OECD food industries.[32]

Embryo Transfer (ET)

In many cases, animal biotechnology such as embryo transfers, are used to accelerate the reproduction process in female livestock. In this processes, premium genetic material can be strategically placed into animals to get the desired food industry products and offspring. Through the use of freezing, low-cost transport technologies and innovative conservation techniques, animal livestock can be cross-bred to meet market specifications. Ultimately, embryo transfer and other sophisticated animal livestock production technologies can be used to develop value-added meat and livestock products to meet global consumer demands. However, animal livestock technology is primarily used in the transatlantic region and OECD countries. Therefore, increasing access to modern animal biotechnology is needed to improve the quality of meat and livestock products in developing countries.[33]

Ovum Pick Up (OPU) and In Vitro Maturation and Fertilization (IVM/IVF)

Through this animal biotechnology, livestock are able to receive immature eggs without any risk to the animals. By increasing and extending the fertility of female livestock, food producers and farmers can increase the productivity of their animals, and produce more food for national food systems and global food industries.[34]

Sexing

In this reproduction biotechnology, the sex of embryos can be selected to allow the mass production of animals with desired characteristics, and food production traits. This technology is often used for semen products to increase the genetic stock of animals and livestock herds that are raised for food production. Through the application of this livestock biotechnology, food producers are able to remove unwanted livestock traits, and produce desired meat and livestock products for global food industries.[35]

Cloning

The use of animal cloning technology in livestock breeding allows farmers and industrial food producers to increase the number of 'founder' animals that are used as gene types for new livestock herds. In the case of cattle, sheep and pig production, the splitting of embryos to produce genetically identical animals, requires the introduction of embryonic cells into enucleated zona to produce clones that differ in cell makeup. Through the use of this technology, the quality of meat and livestock products such as milk and eggs, can be improved through the creation of 'model' herds derived from copying the genetic information of a single 'perfect' animal.

Animal livestock cloning is also used as a genetic conservation technology to prevent the loss and depletion of poultry and mammal livestock. For example, livestock in developing countries, which are at risk of extinction, can be revived and improved for food production through the transfer of genetic material from 'perfect' animal herds in developed countries.[36] Therefore, the benefits of this animal biotechnology are important for meat and livestock producers in OECD and developing nations.

Molecular biotechnologies: DNA technology, animal health and breeding

The growing use of genome science is an important innovation in livestock breeding, animal health and food safety in national food systems and global food industries. Through the use of genome biotechnology, the production and processing of food products is increasingly protected through the use of the following food safety measures:

- production of monoclonal antibodies
- production of vaccines
- production of enzymes to improve animal nutrition and livestock performance
- manipulation of DNA to make livestock animals resistant or tolerant of selected diseases and improving their food traits through market assisted selection, gene introgression and, in the future, transgenesis
- improvement of livestock animal forages and rumen fermentation
- use of molecular markers for pedigree livestock identification, identification of genetic differences between animal breeds, increased understanding and knowledge of animal physiology, production and adaptation for food industry production.[37]

Genome science and DNA biotechnologies play a major role in improving livestock gene pools, controlling animal disease and increasing access to global food markets. Moreover, genetic modification of animals increases the value of livestock products through increased disease resistance and tolerance traits, better food intake and body growth, increasing egg production and fertility, and lifespan extension.[38] Table 11.2 shows the scale and scope of GM animal and fish production, and the regulatory implications of animal livestock biotechnology for food safety.[39]

The growing importance of food safety in global animal livestock and fish industries increases the value and importance of genome science and modern biotechnology. In many cases, contagious animal diseases result in economic costs and productivity losses, and serve as barriers to meat, fish and livestock product trade in global food markets. However, developing countries are less able to manage the long-term impact of contagious animal livestock diseases on their national food and public health systems. Therefore, animal livestock biotechnology can improve the health and quality of animal livestock in OECD and developing countries.

Environmental protection and food safety

As the scale and scope of animal livestock biotechnology innovation increases, food safety in global food industries is increasingly threatened by potential hazards from the unregulated release of GM animals, fish and their transgenes into the environment.[40] For example, GM animals and fish can pose serious threats to the environment and food safety through their unintended effects on biodiversity. Therefore, unregulated production and release of GM animals and fish can result in the contamination of conventional species, and destruction of the environment and food chain.

As a consequence, national governments are regulating the traceability and segregation of GM animal livestock, fish, crops and processed foods. However, these efforts sometimes fail to prevent contamination of national food systems and food industries. When contamination occurs, the purging of GM animals and fish and their transgenes from conventional species, the environment and the food supply chain can take one or more generations to complete. Therefore, food safety risk assessments must be carried out on a case-by-case basis to address the following issues:

- assessment of whether the GM animal or fish, when compared with its conventional counterpart, has a lower, equal or greater potential for gene flow to wild or feral animals and fish in the ecosystem
- assessment of whether GM animal or fish, when compared with its conventional counterpart has a lower, equal or greater potential to invade and establish itself as an alien species when wild or feral relatives are absent.

Table 11.2 Applications of animal livestock and fish gene transfers

Application	Intended outcome	Example	Comments
Improved animal production	Increased yield by accelerated growth rate or improved feed conversion rate	Growth hormone gene in Atlantic salmon, common carp and Nile tilapia	
	Improved disease resistance	Lactoferrin gene in carp, cecropin gene in channel catfish	
	Increased tolerance of environmental conditions, such as low temperature	Antifreeze protein in Atlantic salmon and goldfish	Cold tolerance was improved in goldfish but not in salmon
	Improved digestibility of feed ingredients	Phytase gene in pig	Approach could also be used to adapt carnivorous fishes to a plant-based diet
Improved product quality	Change in nutritional profiles	Reduced lactose concentration in milk	
	Remove allergens from food	Knock-out gene for allergenic protein in shrimp	
	Novel ornamental animals	Fluorescent protein genes expressed in zebrafish	
Novel products	Pharmaceuticals for human and veterinary use	Genes for monoclonal antibodies, lysozyme, growth hormone, insulin, and so on, expressed in milk or blood of farm animals	

	Industrial products	Spider silk expressed in milk of goats	
Bioindicators	Sensors for pollution	Expression of reporter genes linked to metallothionein promoter in topminnows exposed to heavy metal ions	
Human health	Cells, tissuess and organs for xenotransplantation	Knock out of galactosyl transferase gene in pig	Cloning may also be needed
Animal health	Prevention of transmissible spongiform encephalopathies	Knock out Prn-p gene of cattle and sheep	Prevention of mad cow disease and scrapie
Biocontrol	Pesticide-resistant beneficial insects	Introduction of pesticide resistance gene into predators and parasitoids	Ability to use both chemical and biological means of insect pest control
	Control transmission of disease	Introduce genes for resistance to Plasmodium parasite to Anopheles mosquito	Could reduce transmission of malaria
	Reproductive and sex control	Introduce anti-sense gene for GnRH or aromatase	Could be used to control invasive exotic species

Source: FAO/WHO (2003), p. 9.

The control of GM animal and fish contamination requires effective regulation, and protection of conventional livestock species. In most cases, the prevention and reduction of GM animal and fish escape is achieved through sterilization and removal of reproductive capability. In addition, biological, mechanical, physical and chemical confinement and control measures, and multiple confinement methods should be used to reduce the chance of GM gene transfer. Through this approach, the probability of GM animal and fish escape is greatly reduced. At the same time, proactive risk management is achieved for the protection of the environment and food system safety.

Finally, the identification and transfer of animal livestock and fish genes can produce benefits for consumers, agriculture and global food industries. For example, human health can be improved through the creation of new species of animals that model human disease, express pharmaceutical proteins and develop genetic lines for xenotransplantation. Therefore, risk assessment, risk management and risk communication must be strengthened to ensure effective regulation of food safety as food companies commercialize GM animal and fish production in global food, pharmaceutical and biotechnology industries.

Animal biotechnology and the global meat and livestock industries

At the start of the twenty-first century, meat and livestock producers in the transatlantic region and OECD countries are improving their competitiveness in global food industries. In many cases, the increasing competitiveness of GM products is achieved through productivity gains and cost reductions from the use of animal and fish biotechnologies. As the decade unfolds, agri-businesses and food companies in OECD countries are adopting the following biotechnologies for animal health and food safety:

- the use of animal biotechnology tools to more quickly diagnose infectious livestock diseases through DNA and antibody tests for *brucellosis*, *pseudorabis*, scours, Foot-and-Mouth disease, bluetongue, avian leucosis, Mad Cow disease and *trichinosis*
- the use of new biotechnology derived vaccines for shipping fever, lung infections in pigs, enzootic pneumonia, hemorrhagic septicemia, fowl cholera, cultivated fish infections, Newcastle disease of poultry and rabies
- genetic analysis of animal pathogens to improve the control in livestock herds.[41]

Unfortunately, many animal livestock and fish biotechnologies are beyond the reach of most small farmers, rural communities and the infrastructure capabilities of developing nations. In many ways, these problems are directly linked to the following global food industry and market challenges: corporate agri-business and food company R&D, patents and intellectual property rights, the need for capital investment, industrial production of livestock in developed countries, and the lack strategic policy frameworks for the regulation of food safety and livestock biotechnology in developing nations. As a result, the animal and fish biotechnology divide is growing between the OECD and developing nations which now have the fastest growing demand for meat, fish and animal livestock products.[42]

At the present time, many farmers in developing countries manage livestock with traditional technologies and agricultural resources. However, developing countries need genome science to improve the breeding and food quality of indigenous livestock. For example, the low quality and market value of indigenous breeds of animal livestock and fish, and inadequate breeding weaken the competitiveness of developing countries in global food markets. Furthermore, developing countries face food safety risks from tropical and traditional livestock diseases, and the lack of veterinary vaccines and medicines.[43] The consequence of these trends is the inability of small farmers and food producers to compete with OECD-based competitors.[44] Therefore, the following food safety and global food industry issues and requirements are emerging:

- proactive national and regional livestock development policies and multilateral regulatory standards to support the use of animal biotechnology in OECD and developing nations
- adaptation of animal biotechnology to the needs of local and regional farming and agriculture systems, livestock and aquaculture industries, rural communities and national food systems
- increased access to livestock management and animal biotechnology information by governments, regulators, farmers, universities, consumers and developing nations
- management of animal livestock and fish biotechnology costs, transparent intellectual property rights, and small farmer access to new and emerging technologies
- increased participation and incorporation of small farmer and livestock producers into modern animal biotechnology developments, regulatory policies and food safety programs.[45]

IV FOOD SAFETY REGULATION: THE GOVERNANCE OF ANIMAL LIVESTOCK AND FISH BIOTECHNOLOGY IN GLOBAL FOOD INDUSTRIES

Regulatory Oversight of Animal Biotechnology

As the decade unfolds, seed, crop, animal livestock and fish biotechnologies are exclusively controlled and driven by world-class agri-businesses, food companies and food industries based in the transatlantic region and OECD countries.[46] However, growing domestic and global demand for high-quality and safe meat, fish, poultry and dairy products increase the need for livestock biotechnology by farmers and food industries in developing countries. Therefore, the following applications for transgenic and cloned animals and fish are driving the food safety and food industry regulation concerns of governments, consumers and farmers:

1. *Production of new products in milk*
   - pharmaceutical products
   - blood proteins
   - antigens for vaccine production
   - new food products
2. *Industrial production of xenotransplant organs without human rejection*
3. *Food production animals improved with value-added traits for farmers and consumers*
   - disease resistance
   - environmental adaptation
   - environmental contamination.[47]

The effective regulation and governance of animal biotechnology in global food supply chain industries requires proactive, science-based risk assessment. For example, in the case of xenotransplantation, human health and food safety are at risk due to the fact that pigs and humans can easily transmit diseases to each other. In this case, pigs may become hosts for the evolution of new human pathogens and food-borne diseases. In turn, animals developed for organ transplantation could enter the human food supply.[48] Therefore, mandatory regulation of GM fish and animal livestock production is urgently needed.

Food safety and aquaculture

The development of transparent food safety standards for the commercialization of GM animal livestock and fish, and science-based risk management, are emerging areas of focus for national governments and the FAO/WHO Food Standards Programme and its active arm, the Codex Alimentarius Commission. In light of the growing importance of aquaculture and fish products in national food systems, food trade and global food industries, the FAO convened a conference that adopted the Code of Conduct for Responsible Fisheries in 1995.[49] Later, in 1999, a joint FAO/NACA/WHO report on food safety issues associated with products from aquaculture was published (WHO 1999).

The major outcome of the joint FAO/NACA/WHO report was acknowledgement of the need for increased food safety controls and regulation of aquaculture and fish farming. The report cited the growing consumer protection, food safety and public health risks associated with fish and seafood products due to chemical, biological and food pathogen contamination. Likewise, growing food safety risks due to the consumption of raw and inadequately processed fish and seafood products increase the need for more effective regulation of aquaculture and fish farming, particularly in developing countries.[50]

In the case of GM salmon, fish producers are capitalizing on the industrial production of fish that grow twice as fast as its conventional counterpart. In the case of Atlantic salmon, the use of growth hormones increases cold-water tolerance. In other fish species, such as GM tilapia, carp and trout, modern biotechnology offers new opportunities for fish and aquaculture industries.[51] However, there are growing concerns over the safety of GM fish for consumers, public health and the environment. Consequently, the regulation of GM fish and aquaculture is a growing area of food safety regulation.[52] Therefore, mandatory government regulations and policies are needed to govern the following socio-economic impacts and food safety risks posed by GM crops, animal livestock and fish products:

- increased access and participation of poor and marginalized rural communities and developing nations to affordable and safe GM meat, fish and animal protein foods
- regulation of sustainable environments, livestock management, aquaculture and agriculture production through public policies and special programs to assist small-scale and traditional farmers and rural communities
- identification and management of the public policy, market risks and industry opportunities for GM crops, animal livestock and aquaculture production, management, trade and food-processing relative to selected breeds and species of animals, fish and crops
- public and private sector investment in livestock and fisheries R&D to support the public goods aspects of animal and fish livestock

production and food safety in national, regional and global food systems
- more efficient and equitable management of animal genetic resources, modern biotechnology and sustainable livestock and fisheries production systems in the transatlantic region, OECD countries and developing regions.[53]

In this emerging regulatory framework, government policy, infrastructure and pubic health investments have major roles in the governance of food safety. At the same time, farmers and agri-business in OECD and developing countries are under increasing pressure to increase the quality, productivity and value of their food products. Therefore, national governments and multilateral organizations such as the FAO, WHO and the FAO/WHO Codex Alimentarius Commission are developing regulatory guidelines for GM livestock, crops and fish.

Consumer Protection, Competition and Food Biotechnology Regulation

Consumer protection

From the point of view of many consumers, food product choice, animal and plant health, and environmental protection are the emerging context for the mandatory regulation of modern food biotechnology.[54] However, novel foods and GM food production are not perceived as mutually beneficial for nations, consumers, farmers and global food industries. Furthermore, the global introduction of Monsanto's novel seeds and crops with terminator genes, and the StarLink GM corn contamination incident, led to growing consumer distrust of GM food production. Consequently, the production of GM animals is increasing public fears over consumer health and food safety.

In the context of public health and consumer protection, several issues emerge in the governance of GM food safety in national food systems and global food industries. First is the issue of exclusive control of patent rights for GM crops, animal livestock and fish by agri-businesses and food companies. Second, the inability of farmers and agri-business to ensure the segregation of GM crops and livestock requires more regulation of global food industries. Finally, the risk of 'sleeper genes' that are dangerous when exposed to certain changes in plants, livestock or humans, needs more public health risk assessment and food safety surveillance. As the number of gene transfers grow, food safety risks require more regulatory oversight.[55]

Ultimately, many consumers in OECD and developing countries do not see GM food quality benefits. Moreover, OECD consumers with the strongest food market demand are not willing to push GM food into developing countries. In turn, the lack of perceived benefits from GM animals and crops, is resulting in a lack of willingness by developing countries to assume the potential risks of GM food production.[56] As a result of these considerations in OECD and developing countries, a multilateral framework for the regulation of GM food safety is emerging through Codex.

Regulation of GM food and biotechnology agriculture competition

From a business and public policy perspective, modern biotechnology requires mandatory regulation of farming, agriculture, food firms and global food industries. In this respect, the costs and benefits of modern food biotechnologies must be balanced. Furthermore, the interests of all stakeholders of national food systems and global food industries must be addressed to ensure equity relative to GM food production and biotechnology agriculture. As the decade unfolds, food biotechnology poses economic costs for small and independent farmers. In contrast, food biotechnology is controlled by a small number of private transatlantic companies. As a result, there is growing pressure for more focus on the collective good and broader socio-economic goals of GM food and biotechnology agriculture.[57]

A specific consideration of plants, animals and essential biological processes within the patent, trademark and trade secrets domain is necessary to protect the interests of developing countries and farmers. In other cases, animal livestock biotechnology patents are only permitted for medical and pharmaceutical research. As a result, the development of patents for novel food products, that is, seeds, livestock, plants, microorganisms, insects and processed foods, is increasingly regulated (Bruinsma 2003). In turn, the rights and obligations of biotechnology patent holders and GM food producers should be balanced with the overriding socio-economic goals of nations, and the regulatory policy frameworks of governments to protect food safety as called for in the Cartagena Protocol.

V THE NEW MULTILATERAL FRAMEWORK FOR THE REGULATION OF BIOTECHNOLOGY AND GM FOOD SAFETY

The New Challenge for Global Food Industries

As the use of modern biotechnology intensifies, the FAO/WHO Codex Alimentarius Commission is working in cooperation with national governments to develop multilateral frameworks for the regulation of GM food safety. Through the development of scientific risk assessment and risk management standards for national regulators, the WHO is suggesting a science-based framework for the evaluation of biotechnology and its impact on food safety and public health.[58]

In regard to consumer safety and public health, FAO and WHO experts stress the need for scientific risk assessments of the indirect and unintended effects of gene transfer on food preparation and digestion.[59] In 1999 the Codex Alimentarius Commission established the Ad Hoc Intergovernmental Task Force on Foods Derived from Biotechnology to develop guidelines and recommendations on GM food. The task force successfully completed its mandate in July 2003 with the international adoption of the 'Principles for the Risk Analysis of Foods Derived from Modern Biotechnology', the 'Guideline for the Conduct of Food Safety Assessment of Foods Derived from Recombinant-DNA Plants', and the 'Guideline for the Conduct of Food Safety Assessment of Foods Produced Using Recombinant-DNA Micro-organisms'.[60] In support of this initiative, the following series of joint FAO/WHO expert consultations were convened to provide the scientific basis for some of the issues raised by the task force:

- Safety Aspects of Genetically Modified Foods of Plant Origin (WHO, Geneva, 2000)
- Allergenicity of Genetically Modified Foods (FAO, Rome, 2001)
- Safety Assessment of Foods Derived from Genetically Modified Micro-organisms (WHO, Geneva, 2001).[61]

The growing range of modern biotechnologies and GM food and animal feed products complicates the development of national regulations and multilateral standards for GM food safety. For example, the role of GM micro-organisms in the processing and preparation of food is a new dimension of food biotechnology regulation. According to the FAO and the WHO, approximately one-quarter of all food produced and processed uses microbial fermentation.[62] The bread and baked goods, yoghurt, cheese, sour milk, cream and dairy, fermented meat, vinegar, wine and beer industries are expected to increasingly use genetically modified micro-organisms (GMM) to improve the quality of bacteria and yeasts for industrial food production and processing. Consequently, the following food safety issues are emerging in the regulation of biotechnology and GMMs:

- the food safety impacts of foods and food ingredients with live GMM
- the food safety impacts of foods and food ingredients with dead GMM
- the food safety impacts of foods and food ingredients produced with fermentation from GMM which have been removed from the end product.[63]

In this context, the scientific expert consultation recommends stronger analysis of the gastrointestinal (GI) tract microflora to get a better understanding of their biology and function. Through this process, food safety regulators and public health authorities will develop more accurate assessments of the potential impacts of GMM on food safety and public health.[64] In this context, the FAO is examining the food safety and food security impacts of modern biotechnology on the needs and market interests of farmers and producers in developing countries.[65]

In light of the rapid growth of food biotechnology, national governments are developing legally binding multilateral frameworks. In 1992, the UN Convention on Biological Diversity (CBD) was agreed to at the World Summit to protect agricultural plant and animal biodiversity. The Cartagena Protocol on Biosafety protects the environment from risks arising from the movement of Living Modified Organisms (LMOs) in national food systems and global food industries. Through this legally binding agreement, the obligations and standards for the transfer and distribution of LMOs through global food industries and food trade are established in the following areas: scientific risk assessment, risk management, advance informed agreement, technology transfer and regulatory capacity development.

The Cartagena Protocol requires that national governments indicate their acceptance of imports of GM crops through the Internet-based Biosafety Clearing House. Ultimately, companies must label all shipments of GM food commodities.[66] In this legally binding agreement, nations retain control over their plant and animal genetic resources. In turn, nations have the right to regulate access, benefits, revenue sharing and commercial use of these resources by agri-business and global food industries.[67] As the decade progressed, developing and OECD countries also created the International Treaty on Plant Genetic Resources for Food and Agriculture (ITPGRFA). The ITPGRFA was adopted by the FAO Member States in 2001 to protect the rights of small farmers and indigenous people relative to GM food and novel product development.

In this context, the Advanced Informed Agreement (AIA) is a precautionary food safety measure for seeds, live fish, attenuated vaccines and other LMOs that are introduced into the environment. Under the agreement, exporting companies must provide detailed information for each importing country before the first shipment. The importing country must obtain authorization for GM food shipments within one year.[68] In the event that importing countries are unable to pay the costs of risk assessment, the importing country can require the applicant company to pay for the GM food product risk assessment costs.

FAO/WHO Food Safety Assessments of Foods Derived from Genetically Modified Animals

In 2003, a joint FAO/WHO Expert Consultation on the Safety Assessment of Food Derived from Genetically Modified Animals Including Fish was held in Rome.[69] The goal of the expert consultation was to provide scientific advice to FAO and WHO member governments on the safety of GM animals and fish.

As the decade unfolds, governments need food safety standards and regulatory capacity for the governance of GM animal livestock and fish safety. In support of the regulation of GM food safety, global databases for public health and food safety regulators are needed. In the global databases, national and regional regulatory information can be provided for the following food safety measures: food risk detection, identification methods,

Table 11.3 Business and public policy implications of GM animal livestock and fish production

Ethical matrix for GM fish	Welfare as eliminating negative utilities	Welfare as promoting positive utilities	Dignity/ autonomy	Justice/ fairness
Small producers	Dependence on nature and corporations	Adequate income and work security	Freedom to adopt or not to adopt	Fair treatment in trade
Consumers	Safe food	Nutritional quality	Respect for consumer choice (labeling)	General affordability of food product
Treated fish	Proper animal welfare	Improved disease resistance	Behavioral freedom	Respect for natural capacities (telos)
Biota	Pollution and strain on natural resources	Increasing sustainability	Maintenance of biodiversity	No additional strain on regional natural resources

Source: FAO/WHO (2003), p. 22.

and reference materials for GM food products in the market and under development.[70] The joint FAO/WHO Expert Consultation also called for increased capacity-building in developing countries, and more global food industry stakeholder and public involvement in the early phases of GM animal livestock, fish and crop production.

Finally, there is increasing emphasis on the ethical and food quality assurance aspects of GM animal livestock and fish. In the future, national governments must develop capacity to regulate modern food biotechnology on behalf of farmer and consumer interests. Ultimately, the regulation of animal livestock and fish biotechnology must address the need for public debate, transparency, ethics, animal welfare, and the clear assignment of liability to GM food producers, agri-business and biotechnology companies.[71]

As a consequence of these emerging business, public policy and market governance issues (Table 11.3), industry self-regulation and management-based regulation are now major components of GM food safety regulation. Therefore, post-market surveillance, testing and evaluation are needed to ensure the medium and long-term safety of animal livestock and fish biotechnology in national food systems and global food industries.

Codex Principles for Risk Analysis of Foods Derived from Modern Biotechnology

In July 2003, the Codex Alimentarius Commission adopted the Codex Principles for the Risk Analysis of Foods Derived from Modern Biotechnology.[72] In this multilateral regulatory framework, governments are given guidelines for risk analysis of food safety, and nutritional aspects of GM foods. In the Codex guidelines, GM food product traceability is an important risk management tool for governments. The major components of the Codex framework for the regulation of GM food safety are as follows:

- pre-market approval on a case-by-case basis for foods derived from biotechnology using sound science and food safety assessments that withstand scientific peer review
- food safety assessment based on comparative analysis with conventional animal and fish counterparts to ensure that GM food is as safe as non-GM foods
- risk management measures that are proportional to food industry and food system risks, and may include labeling, post-market monitoring, and product tracing
- use of definitions in Codex texts and the Cartaegena Protocol on Biosafety which are the same and compatible with national environmental protection goals.[73]

Codex Guidelines for the Conduct of Food Safety Assessment of Foods Derived from Recombinant-DNA Plants

The food safety assessment guideline for GM crops and plants is based on the general principles for risk assessment under the risk analysis principles (see above) and should include an evaluation of food allergy potential in new GM plant and crop varieties.[74] The safety assessment of a food derived from a recombinant-DNA plant follows a stepwise process of addressing relevant factors that include:

A) Description of the recombinant-DNA plant;
B) Description of the host plant and its use as food;
C) Description of the donor organism(s);
D) Description of the genetic modification(s);
E) Characterization of the genetic modification(s);
F) Safety assessment:
  a) expressed substances (non-nucleic acid substances);
  b) compositional analyses of key components;
  c) evaluation of metabolites;
  d) food processing;
  e) nutritional modification; and
G) Other considerations.

In certain cases, the characteristics of the product may necessitate development of additional data and information to address issues that are unique to the product under review.

Experiments intended to develop data for safety assessments should be designed and conducted in accordance with sound scientific concepts and principles, as well as, where appropriate, Good Laboratory Practice. Primary data should be made available to regulatory authorities at request. Data should be obtained using sound scientific methods and analysed using appropriate statistical techniques. The sensitivity of all analytical methods should be documented.

The goal of each safety assessment is to provide assurance, in the light of the best available scientific knowledge, that the food does not cause harm when prepared, used and/or eaten according to its intended use. The expected endpoint of such an assessment will be a conclusion regarding whether the new food is as safe as the conventional counterpart taking into account dietary impact of any changes in nutritional content or value. In essence, therefore, the outcome of the safety assessment process is to define the product under consideration in such a way as to enable risk managers to determine whether any measures are needed and if so to make well-informed and appropriate decisions.

Codex Guidelines for the Conduct of Food Safety Assessment of Foods Produced Using Recombinant-DNA Micro-organisms
These guidelines are based on the principles for risk assessment under the risk analysis principles (see above).

The new Codex intergovernmental Task Force on Food Derived from Biotechnology (2005–08) will develop Guidelines for the conduct of food safety assessment of foods derived from recombinant-DNA animals, probably available from 2008.

In summary, modern biotechnology is driving consumer concern and collective policy action by governments to regulate the safety of GM food products. The regulation of food biotechnology by governments is directly linked to the role of farmers and food industries in the socio-economic development of nations. Therefore, government regulation of GM food and modern biotechnology is a growing area of food policy in the twenty-first century. Codex Principles and Guidelines will enable better international coordination in this area, as well as specific support to developing countries in the evaluation of this new technology.

VI CONCLUSIONS: GOVERNANCE OF FOOD SAFETY IN FOOD INDUSTRY BIOTECHNOLOGY INDUSTRIES

In conclusion, as the globalization of food trade and food markets accelerates, modern biotechnology increasingly serves as a driver of global food industry innovation. In global food industries, GM micro-organisms, animal livestock, fish and crops have multiple industry uses and applications as bio-indicators, biological and environmental controls, pharmaceutical products and xenotransplantation for medicine and health care. Therefore, GM food ingredients must be regulated to ensure consumer protection, public health, animal health, plant health, and environmental safety.

In the twenty-first century, the important role of the FAO, WHO and the FAO/WHO Codex Alimentarius Commission in the multilateral regulation of GM food safety is growing. Through the work of the Joint FAO/WHO Food Standards Programme, national governments, particularly in developing countries, now have a framework in which to regulate the safety of foods derived from modern biotechnology. In this context, the Joint FAO/WHO Food Standards Programme provides expert advice and regulatory policy guidance for governments as they harmonize science-based risk assessment and risk management frameworks.

In the FAO/WHO Codex Alimentarius framework, capacity-building for the regulation of GM foods derived from modern biotechnology is supported by a network of multilateral institutions such as the FAO, the WHO, the OIE and the IPPC, which are actively involved in the harmonization of food safety, public health, animal health and plant health standards. Through the development of standards for the regulation GM food safety and modern biotechnology in global food industries, pre- and post-market surveillance, and the pooling of data and information for national food safety regulators, are now available for countries in the Americas, Europe, Asia, Africa and the Middle East.

Finally, more public and private sector partnerships are needed to redirect the goals and uses of modern biotechnology and GM food production in global food industries. In the years ahead, concerns over long-term food safety, market benefits and public policy impacts of food biotechnology will continue to grow. As a result, the need for multilateral frameworks for food safety standards harmonization for GM animal livestock, fish, crop and food segregation, and product traceability is rapidly increasing. In this respect, multipurpose agriculture and environmental protection are now important areas of GM food safety regulation. Ultimately, national regulation of GM food safety requires multilateral harmonization of scientific risk assessment and precautionary standards to govern food safety in global food industries in the twenty-first century.

NOTES

* The opinions expressed in this chapter are those of the author and do not imply any statement of World Health Organization policy.

Acknowledgments: The author would like to thank Dr Kele Lekoape, Scientist and Biotechnology Specialist in the Department of Food Safety at WHO in Geneva, Switzerland, for her review, comments and assistance in the writing of this chapter.

1. In some instances, crops are transferred from one place to another agricultural environment to replace depleted and diseased crops. Through this process, the health and genetic quality of agricultural crops and livestock are improved. PEW Initiative on Food and Biotechnology (2001), *Harvest on the Horizon: Future Uses of Agricultural Biotechnology*, September, Washington, DC: PEW Initiative on Food and Biotechnology, pp. 4–13, 19–44 and 71–80. Also see FAO (2004), *The State of Food and Agriculture 2003–2004 – Agricultural Biotechnology: Meeting the Needs of the Poor?*, Rome: FAO, pp. 31–9 and 87–98.
2. Asian Development Bank (2001), *Agricultural Biotechnology, Poverty Reduction and Food Security*, Manila: Asian Development Bank.
3. OECD (1993), *Safety Evaluations of Foods Derived from Modern Biotechnology: Concepts and Principles*, Paris: OECD. FAO (2002), *World Agriculture: Towards 2015/2030*, Rome: FAO.
4. Biotechnology Industry Organization website, at http://www.bio.org.

5. Oliver, Richard (2003), *The Biotech Age: The Business of Biotech and How to Profit from IT*, New York: McGraw Hill.
6. Teitelman, Robert (1989), *Gene Dreams, Wall Street, and the Rise of Biotechnology*, New York: Basic Books.
7. Galsford, James D. (ed.) (2001), *The Economics of Biotechnology*, Aldershot, UK and Brookfield, US: Edward Elgar.
8. Agricultural Production Applications, Biotechnology Industry Organization website, at http://www.bio.org/er/agriculture.asp.
9. FAO (2000), *Modern Biotechnology and the Management of Animal Genetic Resources: Policy Issues*, Intergovernmental Technical Working Group on Animal Genetic Resources for Food and Agriculture, Commission on Genetic Resources for Food and Agriculture, Second Session, 4–6 September, Rome: FAO, pp. 7–8.
10. Ibid., p. 7.
11. See the Biotechnology Industry Organization website for an overview of the role of food biotechnology, at http://www.bio.org/er/food.asp.
12. Ibid., see Agricultural Products on the Market in the Food and Agriculture section of Biotechnology Industry Organization website, at www.bio.org/er/agri-products.asap.
13. Ibid.
14. Ibid.
15. Sheldon, Ian M. (2002), 'Regulation of biotechnology: will we ever freely trade GMOs', *European Review of Agricultural Economics*, **29** (1): 155–76.
16. Bruinsma, Jelle (ed.) (2003), *World Agriculture: Toward 2015/2030 An FAO perspective*, Rome: FAO.
17. FAO (2004), pp. 3–39. According to FAO, modern biotechnology can improve food safety and food security.
18. Consumer benefits of second generation GM crop traits are designed to increase the value of biotechnology foods for end-users and customer. The first generation of GM food was developed for agri-business. Bruinsma (2003), pp. 318–19.
19. In many countries, contamination of food is occurring through the use of pesticides to control plant pests, and crop diseases. Consequently, certain targeted and restricted GM seeds, food crops food industry applications could be of benefit for developing countries that now face public health and economic hardship from transboundary pests (locusts), and deadly mycotoxin crop and food contamination. FAO (2004), pp. 11–23, 25–31 and 87–106. Also see Bruinsma (2003), pp. 318–19.
20. See Bruinsma (2003). The development of GM crops and biotechnology food industry products provides a new market opportunity to produce agriculture products for non-food industries. For example, corn can be used for the development of alternative energy products. As a result of the widening scope of biotechnology innovation by global agri-businesses and food companies, new uses for crops and agriculture are giving way to new markets through multiple sector production of pharmaceuticals, energy, biodegradable plastics, alternative fuels and other industrial products from traditional food crops. However, the growing trend in diverse and competing uses of food and livestock requires mandatory regulation of biotechnology agriculture.
21. Bruinsma (2003), p. 2.
22. Ibid., p. 1.
23. Joint FAO/WHO Food Standards Programme (2003), *Report of the Fourth Session of the Ad Hoc Intergovernmental Codex Taste Force on Animal Feeding*, Codex Alimentarius Commission, Rome: FAO.
24. The FAO World Agriculture report confirms the shifting trends and structure of global food production. Bruinsma (2003), pp. 5–23 and 274–9.
25. Ibid., p. 2
26. At the present time, developing countries are applying modern biotechnology innovations to the productivity challenges facing the global meat and livestock industries. In a growing number of cases, genome science is now used to improve breeding, animal health and nutrition, and livestock management. FAO (2000), pp. 1–4 and 11–13.

27. Joint FAO/NACA/WHO Study Group (1999), *Food Safety Issues Associated with Products from Aquaculture*, WHO Technical Report Series No. 883, WHO, Geneva: WHO, p. 2.
28. According to the FAO, fish and aquaculture are among the fastest growing global food segments. Josupeit, Helga (2006), 'Aquaculture production and markets', Rome: FAO, at http://www.GLOBEFISH.org-index.php?id=2713.
29. Joint FAO/NACA/WHO Study Group (1999), p. 5.
30. Ibid., p. 4.
31. PEW Initiative on Food and Biotechnology (2002), *Biotech in the Barnyard: Implications of Genetically Engineered Animals*, 24–25 September, proceedings from a workshop sponsored by the Pew Initiative on Food and Biotechnology, Washington, DC: Pew Initiative on Food and Biotechnology.
32. Ibid.
33. Ibid.
34. Ibid., p. 5.
35. Ibid.
36. Ibid.
37. Ibid., p. 6.
38. Ibid., p. 7.
39. FAO/WHO (2003) *FAO/WHO Expert Consultation on the Safety Assessment of Foods Derived from Genetically Modified Animals Including Fish, Report*, 17–21 November 2003, Rome: FAO, pp. 9.
40. The unintended release of GM species must be controlled through regulation. FAO/WHO (2003), pp. 6–9.
41. Biotechnology Industry Organization, Agricultural Production Applications, at http://www.bio.org/er/agriculture.asp.
42. According to the FAO (2000, pp. 1–2) developing nations are becoming the largest producers and consumers of meat, fish and livestock products.
43. Ibid., pp. 3–8.
44. Ibid.
45. Ibid., p. 4.
46. FDA (2002), *Animal Cloning and the Production of Food Production: Perspectives from the Food Chain*, proceedings from a workshop sponsored by the Pew Initiative on Food and Biotechnology and the Center for Veterinary Medicine of the US Food and Drug Administration, 26 September, Rockville, MD and Washington, DC: FDA and Pew Initiative on Food and Biotechnology.
47. PEW Initiative on Food and Biotechnology (2002), p. 7.
48. Ibid., p. 22.
49. Ibid., p. 3.
50. Ibid.
51. PEW Initiative on Food and Biotechnology (2002), 'Spotlight Section – Biotech in the Deep Blue Sea', **2** (3), 27 March, at http://pewagbiotech.org/buzz/display.php3?storyID=47.
52. Ibid.
53. Ibid., pp. 2–5.
54. Consumer protection concerns are growing as a result of the limited regulation of GM food production, and the possible long-term and socio-economic implications of biotech agriculture and livestock production. At the same time, global food industries are increasing the use of GM seeds, micro-organisms, crops, animal livestock and fish in the production of food. Bruinsma (2003), pp. 323–7.
55. Consumer protection, public health and food safety concerns over sleeper genes and food allergies are real, and require more scientific risk assessment and precautionary regulation. WHO (2005), *Modern Food Biotechnology, Human Health and Development: An Evidence-Based Study*, Geneva, pp. 48–57.
56. Ibid., pp. 326–30.
57. There are growing firm and industry competition concerns over the concentration of

food biotechnology in the hands of a relatively small number of transatlantic and OECD firms and food industries. Asian Development Bank (2001), p. 12.

58. Joint FAO/WHO Food Standards Programme (2003b), *Risk Analysis Policies of the Codex Alimentarius Commission*, Codex Alimentarius Commission, Twenty-Sixth Session, 30 June–7 July, Rome: FAO.
59. The WHO and FAO expert consultations provide important information that is needed for regulatory policies and food safety standard harmonization for GM food. WHO (2005), pp. 25–32.
60. FAO/WHO (2000b), *Joint FAO/WHO Expert Consultation on Safety Aspects of Genetically Modified Foods of Plant Origin*, Geneva: WHO.
61. See FAO/WHO (2000a), *Report of Joint FAO/WHO Expert Consultation on Foods Derived from Biotechnology*, 21 May –2 June, Geneva: WHO. In this report, the criteria for determining substantive equivalence as a valid component of science-based risk assessment was addressed. At this meeting of WHO and FAO expert scientists, it was decided that several dimensions of risk assessment must be included to ensure that food safety was protected throughout the evolution of food in the production, processing, cooking and human digestion and metabolism process.
62. FAO/WHO (2001a), *Joint FAO/WHO Expert Consultation on Safety Assessment of Foods Derived From Genetically Modified Microorganisms*, 24–28 September, Geneva: WHO.
63. Ibid.
64. FAO/WHO (2002), *Guidelines for the Evaluation of Probiotics in Food*, Report of a Joint FAO/WHO Working Groups on Drafting Guidelines for the Evaluation of Probiotics in Food, 30 April –1 May, London, Ontario, and Geneva: WHO, pp. 3–10.
65. FAO (2000), p. 8
66. The Articles in the Cartagena Biosafety Protocol give specific normative guidelines for national regulatory policies and laws for the governance of the environmental, socio-economic and market impacts of biotechnology. See Preamble and Articles 1–19, http://www.biodiv.org/convention/articles.asp.
67. See Cartagena Protocol on Biosafety – Text of Protocol, Article 61 Transit and Contained Use, http://www.biodiv.org/biosafety/protocol.asp.
68. Ibid.
69. This meeting examined the food safety, environmental and ethical implications of GM animals and fish. See the FAO/WHO (2003).
70. Ibid.
71. FAO/WHO (2003), pp. 20–25. See meeting report summary and conclusion.
72. Ibid., p. 18.
73. Ibid., p. 19.
74. FAO/WHO (2003), *FAO/WHO Expert Consultation on the Safety Assessment of Foods Derived from Genetically Modified Animals, Including Fish*, Rome: FAO/WHO, p. 19.

REFERENCES

Asian Development Bank (2001), *Agricultural Biotechnology, Poverty Reduction and Food Security*, Manila: Asian Development Bank.

Biotechnology Industry Organization website, at http://www.bio.org.

Bruinsma, Jelle (ed.) (2003), *World Agriculture: Toward 2015/2030 – An FAO Perspective*, Rome: FAO.

FAO (2000), *Modern Biotechnology and the Management of Animal Genetic Resources: Policy Issues*, Intergovernmental Technical Working Group on Animal Genetic Resources for Food and Agriculture, Commission on Genetic

Resources for Food and Agriculture, Second Session, 4–6 September, Rome: FAO.
FAO (2004), *The State of Food and Agriculture 2003–2004 – Agricultural Biotechnology: Meeting the Needs of the Poor?*, Rome: FAO.
FAO/WHO (2000a), *Report of Joint FAO/WHO Expert Consultation on Foods Derived from Biotechnology*, Geneva: WHO.
FAO/WHO (2000b), Joint *FAO/WHO Expert Consultation on Safety Aspects of Genetically Modified Foods of Plant Origin*, Geneva: WHO.
FAO/WHO (2001a), *FAO/WHO Expert Consultation on Safety Assessment of Foods Derived from Genetically Modified Microorganisms*, 24–28 September, Geneva: WHO.
FAO/WHO (2001b), *Guidelines for the Evaluation of Probiotics in Food, Report of a Joint FAO/WHO Working Groups on Drafting Guidelines for the Evaluation of Probiotics in Food*, London, Ontario, and Rome: FAO.
FAO/WHO (2003), *FAO/WHO Expert Consultation on the Safety Assessment of Foods Derived from Genetically Modified Animals Including Fish, Report*, 17–21 November, Rome: FAO.
FDA (2002), *Animal Cloning and the Production of Food Production: Perspectives from the Food Chain*, proceedings from a workshop sponsored by the Pew Initiative on Food and Biotechnology and the Center for Veterinary Medicine of the US Food and Drug Administration, 26 September, Rockville, MD and Washington, DC: FDA and PEW Initiative on Food and Biotechnology.
Galsford, James D. (ed.) (2001), *The Economics of Biotechnology*, Aldershot, UK and Brookfield, US: Edward Elgar.
ISAAA (2001), *Global Review of Commercialized Transgenic Crops*, ISAAA Brief 23, Cornell, NY: International Service for the Acquisition of Agri-biotech Application (ISAAA).
Joint FAO/NACA/WHO Study Group (1999), *Food Safety Issues Associated with Products from Aquaculture*, WHO Technical Report Series No. 883, Geneva: WHO.
Joint FAO/WHO Food Standards Programme (2003a), *Report of the Fourth Session of the Ad Hoc Intergovernmental Codex Task Force on Animal Feeding*, Codex Alimentarius Commission, Rome: FAO.
Joint FAO/WHO Food Standards Programme (2003b), *Risk Analysis Policies of the Codex Alimentarius Commission*, Codex Alimentarius Commission, Twenty-Sixth Session, 30 June –7 July Rome: FAO.
Josupeit, Helga (2006), 'Aquaculture production and markets', Rome: FAO, at http://www.GLOBEFISH.org-index.php?id=2713.
OECD (1993), *Safety Evaluations of Foods Derived from Modern Biotechnology: Concepts and Principles*, Paris: OECD.
Oliver, Richard (2003), *The Biotech Age: The Business of Biotech and How to Profit from IT*, New York: McGraw Hill.
PEW Initiative on Food and Biotechnology (2001), *Harvest on the Horizon: Future Uses of Agricultural Biotechnology*, September, Washington, DC: PEW Initiative on Food and Biotechnology.
PEW Initiative on Food and Biotechnology (2002), *Biotech in the Barnyard: Implications of Genetically Engineered Animals*, proceedings from a workshop sponsored by the Pew Initiative on Food and Biotechnology, 24–25 September, Rockville, and Washington, DC: FDA and PEW Initiative on Food and Biotechnology.

Sheldon, Ian M. (2002), 'Regulation of biotechnology: will we ever freely trade GMOs', *European Review of Agricultural Economics*, **29** (1): 155–76.

Teitelman, Robert (1989), *Gene Dreams, Wall Street, and the Rise of Biotechnology*, New York: Basic Books.

WHO (2005), *Modern Food Biotechnology, Human Health and Development: An Evidence-Based Study*, Geneva.

12. Multilateral governance of food safety in global food industries and food systems: the role of FAO, WHO and Codex Alimentarius in regulatory harmonization

Genaro Garcia and Reba A. Carruth*

I INTRODUCTION: CODEX ALIMENTARIUS: THE MULTILATERAL FRAMEWORK FOR THE GLOBAL GOVERNANCE OF FOOD SAFETY

In the twenty-first century, the globalization of food companies and food industries, changing consumer demand, international food trade and the growing need for food security are serving as integrating forces in the global food system. The changing trends in food production and distribution are creating an environment in which known and new food-borne diseases are becoming prevalent. In a growing number of cases, spectacular outbreaks and an increase in the general incidence of food-borne disease is documented in many countries over the past decades.[1]

As nations, citizens and consumers increasingly rely on global market forces for year-round supplies of fruit, vegetables, meat, dairy and fish products, national governments, corporate management and industry are under increasing pressure to protect the collective good of society through the harmonization of food safety standards. Consequently, the globalization of food markets is increasing the need for the multilateral regulation of food safety, consumer protection, public health and competition by all nations and food supply chain industries in the global food system.[2]

As the decade unfolds, the globalization of food production and trade, growing consumer demand and genetically modified foods increase the need for collective regulatory policy action and scientific risk assessment across the global food chain. As a consequence, the protection of food safety in national food systems and global food industries requires normative consensus and increased regulatory capacity-building, especially in developing countries, to ensure compliance with national and international standards. In this changing food system, governments are under increasing pressure to maximize efficiency through the modernization of agriculture and food industries. However, the ability of national governments to regulate food safety as they simultaneously move to increase food security presents many challenges.

The necessary changes in food production systems should be matched with the food safety lessons learned through the developments in the industrialized food-producing countries. There is no need to repeat the food safety mistakes in these countries in other parts of the world. These challenges can only be addressed through the pooling of technical, public health and financial resources at the regional and international levels. In response to globalization, governments are developing regulatory standards to address the public goods and free market aspects of food industry regulation in the twenty-first century.

Through the socio-economic transformation of nations, changing food systems, global food trade and food industry integration, a new multilateral system for food safety and food security is emerging. The major determinant of this system is the precautionary regulation of food safety. In the unfolding system, precautionary regulation requires science-based risk analysis, risk assessment and risk communication as the basis for transparent decisions and policy-making.

At the present time, governments are forced to acknowledge the inability of nations to unilaterally regulate domestic food systems and food industries. When confronted with growing levels of international food trade, cross-border competition, increasing corporate power and consolidation of global food industries, national governments are engaging in collective policy action at the multilateral level to protect citizens. Therefore, the success of Codex Alimentarius – a subsidiary body of FAO and WHO, as the multilateral framework for global food safety, is the result of the global scale and scope of over 200 regulatory standards, 40 codes and guidelines for food production and processing, maximum recommended levels of approximately 500 food additives and approximately 2700 maximum levels of residue limits for pesticides in food products.[3]

Codex Structure and Process for Regulatory Harmonization

The main goals of Codex are the protection of consumer health, and the facilitation of global food trade through the harmonization of food safety standards. As the leading multilateral institution for the harmonization of food safety regulations, the Codex Alimentarius Commission relies on intergovernmental policy cooperation and collective action by nation-states.[4]

Membership in Codex is universal and open to all member nations and associate members of FAO and WHO. At the present time, 169 nations and the European Union are members of Codex, and are invited to participate in Commission meetings that are held once a year, alternatively in Rome and Geneva.[5]

In terms of management structure, Codex is a subsidiary body of FAO and WHO. The Codex Alimentarius Commission (CAC), was created in 1963, and is the central administrative body of Codex. The Executive Committee consists of two subsidiary bodies. The subsidiary bodies include the Codex committees which prepare and draft standards for submission and review by the Codex Alimentairus Commission. The Codex committees are organized as General Subject or Commodities Committees. The General Subject Committees work on food standards that are relevant across all food commodities, and are designated as horizontal committees. The Commodity Committees are responsible for developing standards for specific foods, classes of foods and food industry segments, and are designated as vertical committees. The other subsidiary body of the Codex Alimentarius Commission consists of the regional coordinating committees, which are responsible for the coordination and development of regional food safety standards.

The Executive Committee works between sessions on behalf of the Codex Commission, and is comprised of a chairperson, vice chairpersons and seven members elected by the Codex Commission from each of the regions: Africa, Asia, Europe, Latin America and the Caribbean, the Near East, North America and South-West Pacific. There are six regional coordinators appointed by the Codex Commission for each of the seven regions. The exceptions are the North America and South-West Pacific regions, where a single Coordinator is appointed to advise the Codex Commission of the views of government and NGOs in the region. In this multilateral framework for regulatory harmonization, Codex drafts and consults on texts for international standards based on the work of subsidiary bodies and working groups. The Codex committees and ad hoc task forces prepare draft standards for submission and approval by the Commission for adoption. Codex food safety standards are developed through the following eight-step process:

1. Decision to elaborate a standard.
2. Preparation of proposed draft standards by the Secretariat or Committee.
3. Circulation of standards draft for review and comment.
4. Committee discusses the comments and revises the proposed draft standard before submitting the draft to the Codex Commission or Executive Committee.

5. Submission to the Commission or Executive Committee for adoption as a draft standard including an assessment of economic impacts of the standard.
6. Step 6 is a repeat of step 3.
7. Step 7 is a repeat of step 4 in a second and final round of proposed standard review and amendments prior to approval.
8. Upon adoption of a proposal by the Codex Commission, the draft becomes a Codex standard.[6]

In this context, Codex represents collective policy action and multilateral cooperation through the joint activities of FAO and WHO which focus on the following consumer protection, public health and food safety goals:

- increasing the impact of food safety standards for the protection of consumer health and safety
- increasing linkage of food safety standards to the expressed and emerging needs of consumers, food producers, food industries and governments in developing and emerging nations
- increased consensus and convergence of product information labeling relative to health and safety issues.[7]

FAO and WHO Cooperation in Codex: The Role of the Joint FAO/WHO Food Standards Programme

In light of the importance of the food standards setting and normative consensus building work of the Codex Alimentarius Commission, the FAO and WHO formally cooperate on national and regional implementation and compliance activities through the Joint Food Standards Programme. The FAO /WHO Food Standards Programme was created through the passage of the resolution to establish the Codex Alimentarius Commission at the Eleventh Session of the Conference of the FAO in November 1961. Later in 1963, the WHO approved and adopted a founding resolution at the Sixteenth World Health Assembly. The Secretariat of the Codex Commission, which is located in the FAO headquarters in Rome, provides the office for the Joint FAO/WHO Food Standards Programme. The Secretary of the Codex Alimentarius Commission is a senior FAO official, who also serves as the Chief of the Joint FAO/WHO Food Standards Programme.

Since the creation of the Codex Alimentarius Commission and Joint FAO/WHO Food Standards Programme in the early 1960s, FAO and WHO work in cooperation to support food safety standards development and harmonization in Codex. Through the mobilization of their respective scientific and food safety expertise, FAO and WHO historically provide technical assistance, financial resources and administrative support through their secretariats. The FAO and WHO, as the parent bodies of Codex Alimentarius, are actively engaged in the provision of capacity-building support and standards implementation assistance for national governments and regions through the work of the Joint FAO/WHO Food Standards Programmes.

In this context, FAO and WHO are increasing their scientific, financial and technical support for developing countries. Furthermore, FAO and WHO actively mobilize increasing support from developed countries for food safety capacity-building and standards implementation programs. The following overview of food safety capacity-building in FAO and WHO confirms the complementary and critical role of the Joint FAO/WHO Food Standards Programme in the work of Codex.

FAO: governance of food security and food safety

As a parent body of Codex Alimentarius, and a major institution in the multilateral food safety system, FAO was founded in 1945. The mandate of FAO is to raise the level of nutrition, increase standards of living, improve agricultural productivity and increase the quality of life for rural populations.[8] The FAO is now one of the largest specialized agencies of the United Nations system, and currently has 183 member countries and one member organization, the European Union. In this context, FAO supports sustainable agriculture and rural development, efficient food production, food security, food safety and environmental conservation.

One of the major activities of FAO is development assistance, which includes practical policy advice, and technical assistance to governments, especially developing countries, in the area of food and agricultural production, food security and food safety. The FAO also collects, analyses, interprets and disseminates information on nutrition, food, agriculture, forestry and fisheries. By 1962, the Codex Alimentarius Commission was created by FAO and WHO to set international food safety standards. In the 1980s, FAO appointed representatives in developing member countries. During this period, AGROSTAT was launched. The department was later renamed FAOSTAT, and is now the leading global source of agricultural information and statistics. In 1991, the International Plant Protection Convention (IPPC) was ratified by 92 signatory countries, and is now a supporting agency of FAO for plant health, food safety and food security.

Later, in 1994, FAO launched the Special Program for Food Security which targets low income food deficit countries (LIFDC). During that time, the Emerging Prevention System for Transboundary Animal and Plant Pests and Diseases (EMPRES), was launched to reduce livestock diseases and contagious plagues which can destroy global food trade and threaten public health, particularly in developing countries. In that year, FAO was reorganized to decentralize operations, streamline procedures and reduce costs.

Finally, in 1998, FAO brokered the legally binding Convention to Control Trade in Pesticides and other hazardous trade in chemicals at a conference in Rotterdam. At the start of the twenty-first century, FAO adopted the legally binding Treaty on Plant Genetic Resources for Food and Agriculture to support the rights and interests of farmers and breeders in global markets and food systems. The result of this meeting was the launch of an FAO Trust Fund to support ongoing work on food security, prevention of trans-boundary pests and animal livestock and plant diseases, project funding and program studies.[9] In this respect, FAO is strengthening food safety in national food systems and global food industries through 'farm to table' and 'boat to throat' strategies.[10]

WHO: governance of public health and food safety

As a major and well recognized UN agency, WHO has a historical and specific public health role in the governance of food safety. Through the mobilization of resources at the national, regional and global levels, WHO works to achieve its core mission of 'the attainment by all people of the highest possible level of health'. In this regard, the following institutional goals are identified in the 1948 WHO Constitution for the governance of public health and food safety:

- assist governments in strengthening health services relating to food safety
- promotion of improved nutrition, sanitation and other aspects of environmental hygiene
- development of international standards for food
- assistance in developing informed public opinion among peoples on matters of food safety.[11]

Many of WHO's food safety programs and policies are carried out in collaboration with FAO, and are institutionalized through the Joint FAO/WHO Food Standards Programme. This formal collaboration between FAO and WHO was approved by the Sixteenth World Health Assembly in 1963.[12] The main institutional mechanism and structure of this program is the Codex Alimentarius Commission, which is charged with the protection of consumer health and safety, and the development of global food safety standards.[13]

By 1978, the World Health Assembly formally requested the Director-General of WHO to develop a food safety program to govern the public health aspects of food-borne diseases and food system contamination. In this regard, the normative role of WHO in the development of international standards for risk assessment, risk management and risk communication of food safety is rapidly growing. Through these coordinated policies and technical assistance programs, scientific, quantitative and sometimes qualitative assessments of microbiological, biotechnological and chemical risks to food safety are carried out by WHO. The assessments are often carried out in collaboration with FAO.

By the end of the 1990s, WHO developed and implemented an extensive system of technical support for national governments as they moved to address the impact of food industry globalization, regional market integration and free trade agreements on food safety. Within this realm of institutional and multilateral policy cooperation, WHO is increasing its support for capacity-building in member countries to govern the safety of food systems, global food trade and food industries. Furthermore, WHO provides increasing levels of support for training in the areas of sanitation, community public health and 'healthy markets' programs. In this context, WHO cooperates with national, regional and international organizations and regulatory agencies to develop global standards for risk analysis and food safety. In this regard, WHO assists governments in developing and implementing food safety programs and policies to legally enforce the monitoring, information collection and reporting of food safety hazards.[14]

In response to globalization, WHO's policies are implemented to reduce the risks, systemic threats and economic costs of food-borne illness and contamination of food systems and markets. Moreover, WHO works through Codex Alimentarius to reduce the dangers posed by unacceptable levels of food contamination. Ultimately, WHO works through policy cooperation and technical assistance to countries and regions to ensure the quality and safety of national and global food systems.[15]

As the decade unfolds, WHO is increasing its support of food safety regulation and global governance of food market systems. In May 2000, the fifty-third World Health Assembly unanimously supported resolution WHA53.15 on food safety. Through this resolution, WHO confirms the central role and importance of food safety for the public health at national, regional and global levels. Furthermore, the resolution reaffirms the importance of multi-sectoral and multidisciplinary plans of action for the governance of global food systems, food markets and industries. In 2002, WHO's Executive Board approved the WHO Global Strategy for Food Safety. The WHO strategy was developed with the support of technical experts, regional advisors in food safety, international stakeholders and partners in the regulation and governance of food industries. The main goals of this initiative are to rapidly increase food safety, and attain regulatory harmonization for the reduction of food contamination, and public health threats in food systems.

WHO global strategy for food safety

The globalization of food firms and industries is increasing the systemic risk of food contamination, consumer injury and public health hazards in the twenty-first century. When viewed in this context, WHO believes that traditional approaches to the governance of food safety are no longer efficient or effective for preventing food contamination and food hazards in national food systems, global food trade and food industries. Consequently, WHO is developing a global framework for the systematic implementation of risk assessment, risk management and risk communication of public health threats posed by food contamination in national food systems and food markets.[16]

The successful achievement of these goals requires increasing WHO cooperation with national governments for capacity-building. Through capacity-building programs, the coordination of scientific assessments of food safety hazards, food contamination risks, public health protection through prevention programs and harmonization of regulatory policies and food safety standards are carried out by WHO. In this context, the following measures are the priority areas of the WHO Global Strategy for Food Safety:

- development of science-based measures across the entire food production, processing and distribution industry supply chain to prevent dangerous and unacceptable levels of chemical, biological and microbial contamination of food
- increased support and technical assistance for the development of risk-based, sustainable and integrated food safety systems
- stronger assessment, communication and management of food safety risks and cooperation across regulatory and industry sectors[17]
- reduction of the socio-economic costs of food contamination and food industry hazards for consumers, communities, society and nations.[18]

Enhancing the Scientific and Public Health Roles of WHO in Codex

As the recent outbreaks of BSE in the European Union, Japan, Canada and the United States, and avian flu in Asia, North America and Europe show, the globalization of food systems and food industries increases consumer safety and public health risks in all nations. In turn, the harmonization of food safety regulations is needed to govern cross-border competition and market integration in global food industries. Therefore, WHO is increasing the scientific and public health components of global food safety standards in Codex Alimentarius.[19] In light of these global food market and regulatory policy trends, WHO is working to ensure that consumer health and food safety concerns are more fully integrated and reflected in the regulatory standards and harmonization work of the Codex Alimentarius Commission. In this context, WHO views the mobilization of science as important for the regulation of public health and consumer safety in national food systems and global food industries.[20]

Strengthening the Surveillance Systems for Food-borne Disease and Food Product Contamination

The WHO is now urging member states' governments to develop epidemiology and laboratory-based systems for the surveillance of food contamination, disease outbreaks, sporadic cases and the monitoring of chemical and microbial food contaminants. In this regard, the monitoring of food-borne disease agents of microbiological or chemical origin across the entire food and feed chain is the goal for all countries, regions and food supply chain industries in the global food system.[21]Therefore, WHO is helping national governments build epidemiological capacity and public health laboratories for the surveillance of public health threats to food systems and global food industries.[22]

One important example of such ongoing work is the WHO Global Salm-Surv (GSS): a global network of laboratories and individuals involved in isolation, identification and antimicrobial resistance testing of *Salmonella*. Initiated in January 2000, the program is targeted at microbiologists and epidemiologists who work in public health, veterinary services, food-related services or environmental health. The extension of GSS to other major food-borne pathogens is in progress, notably *Campylobacter* is now included in the training program. The GSS is part of WHO's endeavors to strengthen the capacities of its member states in the surveillance and control of major food-borne diseases, and to contribute to the global effort to contain antimicrobial resistance in food-borne pathogens.

At the present time, WHO is working with national governments to develop and coordinate a global approach for food-borne disease reporting that will be used to inform scientific risk assessment and policy-making at the national, regional and global levels. The reporting system and regulatory policy information is used by national governments to strengthen the global regulation of food safety, consumer protection and public health. Upon the request of member states, WHO now supports capacity-building for information collection, surveillance systems and the creation of common global standards for the harmonization of food safety database systems. The WHO is also developing web-based systems for the collection, reporting and communication of food safety hazards, risks and data. Through this system, governments can control and prevent food-borne disease and food product contamination in global food trade and food industries.

The conclusion of the Uruguay Round, and the successful negotiation of the SPS Agreement in the WTO, increases the work of FAO and WHO. Through their Joint Food Standards Programme, and the work of the Codex Alimentarius Commission, FAO and WHO, are actively involved in the global harmonization of food safety regulatory standards. In this regard, FAO, WHO and Codex Alimentarius serve as positive examples of successful multilateral policy cooperation through the United Nations system. Furthermore, decades of FAO, WHO and Codex Alimentarius food safety standards work underscores the growing need for multilateral regulatory policy cooperation by governments in response to the globalization of food markets and industries.

It should not be forgotten, however, that this international food standards work contributes significantly to general public perceptions of food safety improvement in many countries. This trend is also true in many developing countries, which do not necessarily have the expertise, infrastructure and food safety system at hand to develop the most recent scientific knowledge for food safety advice and regulation. Currently, developing nations and regions are moving to comply with WTO trade and SPS Agreement obligations to govern the impact of food industry and food trade globalization on food safety. As a result, the work of Codex in establishing a basis for food safety standards and regulatory harmonization continues to grow in importance.

The continued high level of food-related burdens of disease is a cause for concern in many countries. However, many food-borne hazards and their related human health risks are preventable, and the newest food safety improvements and measures will enable action towards risk reduction at the national as well as international levels. Therefore, emerging new biotechnologies and food-processing innovations are challenging traditional agriculture and food industries as they move to comply with SPS standards.

At the present time, national governments and food industries are under pressure to adopt and enforce ISO and HACCP food process inspection standards for consumer protection, food product safety and public health in global food markets. The growing risk of national food system contamination and systemic food safety hazards due to inadequate food control and inspection systems increase the need for a global rule of regulatory law and legally binding standards. Therefore, the roles of FAO and WHO through the work of Codex Alimentarius Commission as the central multilateral framework for the regulation and governance of food safety is growing in the twenty-first century.

II INTERNATIONAL NORMATIVE CONSENSUS ON RISK ASSESSMENT: THE JOINT FAO/WHO FOOD STANDARDS PROGRAMME, EXPERT COMMITTEES AND CONSULTATION

The protection of consumer health in national food systems and global food industries, and the promotion of global food trade through regulatory standards harmonization, requires international normative consensus on risk assessment. As the globalization of food trade and food industries intensifies, the surveillance of food-borne risks and government capacity for risk assessment are now requirements for the regulation of food safety in national, regional and global food systems. As the framework for food standards development and harmonization, international normative consensus on risk assessment through the Joint FAO/WHO Food Standards Programme requires agreement on the following steps in food safety regulation:

- normative agreement on food safety hazard identification
- normative consensus on food safety hazard characterization
- normative agreement on food risk exposure assessment
- normative consensus on food risk characterization.[23]

As the structure of national food systems and global food industries change in response to consumer demand for a wider variety of fresh vegetables, fruits, meats and fish products, collective policy action and support of food safety risk assessment is needed. In this regard, the rapid spread of food-borne hazards now requires well-developed regulatory standards harmonization capacities by governments and industries and global risk surveillance systems. Moreover, growing demand for organic foods, the integration of global food industries and increasing use of modern biotechnology requires more sophisticated and sensitive laboratory detection equipment, and more frequent review of food standards.[24] Therefore, normative agreement on food safety goals and regulatory standards is required to protect consumers and the public health in global food industries.

In contrast to the past, national and global food system and food industry risk assessment increasingly relies on process standards and regulations instead of end-product standards. Therefore, the development of science-based risk assessment procedures and infrastructure at national, regional and global levels supports the interests of government, farmers, food industries and consumers. Ultimately, international normative consensus on risk assessment through cooperation between FAO and WHO provides the basis for food safety, consumer protection and public health in the twenty-first century.[25]

The Work of the Joint FAO/WHO Food Standards Programme, Expert Committees and Consultation

As the multilateral institutional mechanism for food safety, FAO and WHO and their subsidiary body, the Codex Alimentarius Commission, view the harmonization of food safety regulatory standards as the responsibility of national governments. Through the harmonization of regulations and regulatory standards and risk assessment of food safety hazards, the Joint FAO/WHO Food Standards Programme, in its capacity as the implementation arm of Codex Alimentarius Commission, is working to protect consumers and support national governments as they move to collectively regulate national and global food markets. In order to achieve these goals, national governments must be able to ensure that imported and locally produced food is safe, and does not weaken consumer health. Therefore, the Joint FAO/WHO Food Standards Programme provides science-based guidance for national governments as they develop and reform mandatory regulations and industry standards to protect consumers and food safety.[26]

For the implementation of these goals and mandates, Codex Committees through their ongoing work with the FAO/WHO Food Standards Programme, collaborate through joint expert committees and consultations. In these expert committees and consultations, FAO and WHO address emerging food safety hazards, food standards and regulatory guidelines for the protection of consumers and the public health. Through these working groups, FAO, WHO and Codex Alimentarius Commission collaboration on scientific studies are carried out in the fields of food chemistry, food technology, food microbiology, mycology, pesticide and veterinary drug residues with scientists, laboratories, institutes and universities. In the mid-1990s, the following Joint FAO/WHO expert consultations were convened to provide guidance for food safety standards:

1995 FAO and WHO Consultation on Risk Assessment and Food Safety

1997 Joint FAO/WHO Consultation on the Application of Risk Management and Food Safety

1998 Joint FAO/WHO Consultation on the Application of Risk Communication to Food Standards and Safety Matters.[27]

The FAO and WHO also work together to provide scientific guidance on pesticides through the Joint Meeting on Pesticide Residues (JMPR). The

Joint FAO/WHO Meeting was created in 1963 as an independent group that advises the Codex Alimentarius Commission on maximum residue levels for pesticides and environmental contaminants in food products. The JMPR also provides guidance and leadership in sampling methodologies, and analysis of food safety and public health data related to pesticides contamination of food.

In the case of food additives, FAO and WHO created a Joint Expert Committee on Food Additives (JECFA) in 1955 to study the impact of food additives, including veterinary drugs, chemicals and toxins on human health and consumer safety. As an independent group, JECFA advises the Codex Commission and other Codex bodies on current and emerging consumer health and food safety issues relative to food additives.[28] More recently, the problems of microbial contaminants in food have resulted in the creation of a Joint FAO/WHO Expert Meeting on Microbiological Risk Assessment (JEMRA). Since 2000, this body in collaboration with the Codex Committee on Food Hygiene, initiated risk assessment work on a number of important food-borne pathogens (for example, *Salmonella*, *Campylobacter*, *Listeria* and *Vibrio*).

III INTERNATIONAL NORMATIVE CONSENSUS ON RISK MANAGEMENT: THE WORK OF THE CODEX ALIMENTARIUS COMMISSION

Governance of Food Safety and Public Health in Food Systems

The Codex Alimentarius Commission, as a subsidiary body of FAO and WHO, is one of the most important and successful multilateral institutional mechanisms for regulatory harmonization and food safety standards cooperation in the global system. The success of FAO, WHO and the Codex Alimentarius Commission is the result of normative agreement, and sustained work on global food trade, industry globalization and regulatory policy harmonization. Furthermore, the clear definition and the separation of the scientific advice provided by the FAO and WHO expert groups, and the management decisions suggested by the Codex Committees, have contributed significantly to this success. Therefore, the multilateral normative consensus-building activities of Codex in food safety risk management is being strengthened the twenty-first century.

Historically, national governments have the legitimate role and responsibility for setting and enforcing food safety standards for consumer protection and public health. However, FAO, WHO and the Codex Alimentarius Commission acknowledge that food safety standards must be enforced through multi-level networks of regulations to protect consumers in global food markets. Ultimately, policy cooperation and regulatory harmonization are accepted and promoted by the Codex Alimentarius Commission to increase the effectiveness and efficiency of food contaminants monitoring and food-borne illness surveillance across the global food system.[29] In turn, Codex standards are based on risk assessment and risk management and reflect the growing trend of process regulations and regulatory standards for food trade and global food industries.[30]

The Strategic Framework of Codex Alimentarius 2003–07: Food Safety Goals and International Normative Risk Management Priorities

As the globalization of food markets and trade accelerates, the role of the Codex Alimentarius Commission is growing as the multilateral framework for the governance of food safety. In response to this growing challenge, the Codex Alimentarius Commission is increasing its capacity to support and strengthen food safety and risk management capacity in national and global food systems. In support of consumer protection, public health and global food trade promotion goals, the Codex Alimentarius Commission is strengthening its risk management function through the following procedures:

- improvement of regulatory policy alternative analysis
- expansion of stakeholder consultations
- strengthening of food hazard prevention and control.[31]

The risk management activities of the Codex Alimentarius Commission are increasingly focused on balancing the costs and benefits of incremental food safety and food quality. In this context, the international normative risk management work of the Codex Alimentairus Commission is increasingly directed to strengthening the participation of developing countries in the international standard-setting process, increasing regulatory capacity-building activity and prioritizing standards work.[32]

In a recent evaluation of Codex Alimentarius by an independent group of experts, the growing importance and role of Codex for normative consensus, regulatory harmonization and convergence of food regulatory standards emerged as central goals and achievements for the twenty-first century. Specifically, the surveillance of food-borne diseases, monitoring of food contaminants, risk management, risk communication and the protection of consumer health are cited as the most important functions for Codex. In this respect, the harmonization of food safety standards is occurring in the context of national farming and agricultural sectors, and the globalization of food markets and industries.[33] Therefore, the strengthening of food safety in the global food market and food systems is now a priority for Codex Alimentarius.

In light of the importance of normative consensus in the management of food safety risks, the Codex Alimentarius developed a Strategic Framework for 2003–07. In this framework, a strategic vision was created to provide an institutional context for the development and implementation of the highest food safety standards and consumer protection goals for the Codex Alimentarius Commission. The fundamental objective of Codex is to provide guidelines for the regulation of food safety in national, regional and global food control systems in accordance with the following strategic goals:

1. The promotion of effective regulatory frameworks, standards and guidelines for food safety, nutrition, labeling, import and export inspections, and certification.
2. The promotion of science as the basic foundation for food safety, national food control system regulation and risk analysis.
3. The promotion of networks and cooperation between Codex and other multilateral institutions, regulatory agreements and conventions in the area of food safety standards and regulation.
4. The strengthening and increase of regulatory capacity in all nations and regions to respond to new food safety issues and food pathogen threats.
5. The full participation of all Codex member countries, and incorporation of all regions in the food safety standard-setting work.
6. The promotion and facilitation of national, regional and global adoption and implementation of Codex regulatory standards, guidelines and recommendations.

Through the establishment of food safety and regulatory standards priorities, the changing realities of global food system protection and consumer health are fully addressed by Codex. Moreover, the Codex Strategic Framework facilitates more efficient and effective targeting of national regulatory capacity and food safety protection goals through increased mobilization of the Codex parent organizations, FAO and WHO. In the course of the increasing mobilization of FAO and WHO, the integration of food safety into public health regulation, and the public policies of nations and regions will be achieved. As a consequence, the principles of the Codex Strategic Framework strengthen the efficiency and effectiveness of governments and food industries.

In support of food safety standard-setting and regulatory harmonization work in Codex Alimentarius, and the need for more participation of developing nations in the international standard-setting process, risk analysis capacity-building is now a core objective and goal of the Codex Strategic

Framework. In turn, Codex promotes risk assessment, risk management and risk communication as part of the risk analysis process. The following national scientific risk analysis, regulatory capacity-building, food safety standards development and implementation measures are in the Codex Strategic Framework:

- promotion of consistent use and application of risk analysis principles in all of the work of Codex and its subsidiary bodies
- strengthening of national, regional and global capacity for risk assessment including microbiological hazards and emerging food safety pathogens
- improving the capacity of national governments and developing countries to understand risk management concepts, principles and applications across the entire food system
- promotion of greater transparency of the entire risk analysis process
- improvement of the understanding of the role of precaution and scientific uncertainty in the risk analysis process
- strengthening of risk communication
- collection of information from developing countries and all regions to ensure that risk analysis is based on global food system conditions and requirements for food safety. (FAO and WHO 2002a)

At the present time, food safety capacity-building is a central feature of FAO, WHO and the Codex Alimentarius Commission activities and programs. This central focus of Codex reflects the growing integration of developing countries in global food production, trade, consumption and industry globalization in the twenty-first century. Through the growing focus on regulatory capacity-building by FAO and WHO, emerging regions and developing countries are given access to regulatory standards which are science based, focused on consumer protection, sustainable agriculture and public health, and in compliance with the WTO SPS/TBT Agreements. In response to the growing role of markets in national food systems, Codex is addressing the need for greater food safety, and more effective regulation of food markets through the following organizational changes:

- increased speed and efficiency in the development and dissemination of expert scientific advice in Codex
- more rapid, equitable and efficient integration of developing and emerging countries into Codex standards development and enforcement
- increased relevance of Codex standards relative to needs and importance of consumers and governments in member countries

- increased efficiency and effective capacity-building for the development of national food safety, risk management and surveillance systems.[34]

In terms of the scope of global food safety standards, Codex Alimentarius serves as the legal framework for regulatory and legal standards harmonization in all processed, semi-processed and raw foods industries in the global food system. Consequently, Codex provides a multilateral framework for normative consensus and regulatory standards harmonization for the following areas of food safety:

- food safety standards for the setting of maximum levels of pesticide residues, additives and contaminants (including microbial) that can be found in food
- standards on processes and procedures for Codes of Practice for HACCP, management-based regulation of food safety and other food industry surveillance processes
- standards for labeling for health (allergens, nutritional labeling) consumer protection against fraud (weights and measures, date marking), consumer information (halal, kosher, organic)
- commodity and product standards to define and specify food products (spices), or how products are made (cheddar cheese, corned beef, and so on)
- standards for quality descriptions of food products for grading of products by color.[35]

In the past, member governments of Codex Alimentarius were under no obligation to use Codex standards for the regulation of food safety, consumer protection and public health. However, Codex standards gained enhanced legal status with the creation of the WTO SPS Agreement in response to the growth of global food trade and market globalization. Therefore, member governments must justify the adoption of regulations more stringent than Codex standards, in accordance with well-defined criteria for non-adoption.

In this regard, there is a growing need for regulatory coordination and institutional cooperation between Ministries of Agricultural, Public Health, Trade and Industry to strengthen food safety on a 'farm to table' and 'boat to throat' basis. Therefore, precautionary regulation and science-based risk analysis are viewed by member governments of Codex as new requirements for effective regulation of food safety in national food systems and global food industries. Currently, member countries do not have to adopt all Codex standards. However, Codex is gaining power as the multilateral framework for food law and regulatory standards harmonization in the twenty-first century.[36]

Consumer safety and food standards harmonization

In the growing mandate of Codex for the regulation of food safety in national food systems and global food industries, the role of consumer interests and input is an important issue. Increasingly, consumers are more knowledgeable and aware of technological innovations in food production, food marketing strategies, the growing role of food additives and nutritional supplements, and the risks of food contamination. Therefore, Codex is increasing its focus and activities in food packaging, processing, labeling and marketing, which are the basis for the regulation of consumer protection, public health and product safety in national food markets and global food industries.[37]

At the present time, growing consumer demand for food safety and food quality are driving regulation and regulatory standards harmonization. However, global food trade and food industry integration relies on legal recognition and enforcement of Codex food safety standards.[38] Consequently, the harmonization of food quality standards within the context of food safety and national food security is a growing area of regulatory policy cooperation. In this regard, collective policy action is occurring at the multilateral levels through ISO (for spices), UN ECE (for fruit and vegetables) and, increasingly, Codex in its work on health and non-health related features of food products and food systems.[39]

Improving risk assessments

Through the work of the Codex Alimentarius Commission, a global framework for risk analysis, including risk assessment, risk management and risk communication, is rapidly emerging at the national, regional and global levels. In turn, the capacity of national governments to regulate food safety is strengthened through the implementation of scientific risk assessment, and the development of science-based standards for global food trade and food industries. In this area, WHO has a historical leadership role in the provision of scientific assessments of chemical food contamination risks to Codex and its member states. Furthermore, the Joint FAO/WHO Expert Committee on Food Additives (JECFA) and the Joint FAO/WHO Meeting on Pesticide Residues (JMPR) are now recognized by national government, industry and consumer stakeholders of the global food system as the leading authority on the food safety risks of chemicals in food.

As a result of these joint food safety initiatives, the risk assessment work of WHO and FAO is being strengthened to ensure more rapid analysis, dissemination of findings to governments, improved quality, consistency of risk assessment and transparency to prevent conflicts of business and policy interests. At the same time, FAO and WHO are launching a new program for the analysis and management of risks across the 'farm to table' food chain. Finally, FAO and WHO are working to increase the participation and representation of developing countries in the evaluation of food safety risks and public health hazard exposure through food trade and global food industries.[40]

Assessment of food safety in biotechnology

As the twenty-first century unfolds, the modern biotechnology revolution is accelerating the growth and integration of GM food products in national food systems and global food industries. Since 1990, WHO and FAO are working to develop consistent standards and criteria for the scientific risk assessment of GM food safety. In this regard, the safety of GM food and food ingredients derived from genetic engineering are a major area of focus for the regulation of consumer protection and food safety in Codex. In 2000, the Joint FAO/WHO Expert Consultation on Foods Derived from Modern Biotechnology developed a framework to support risk assessment and analysis of GM food. This framework led to Codex Principles and guidelines for risk analysis and risk assessment of foods derived from modern biotechnology, adopted by the Commission in 2003.[41]

As the decade unfolds, transatlantic regulatory policy and market conflict over GM food is growing into a global controversy over the governance of food safety. Therefore, WHO and FAO are addressing the food allergy risks of GM food, and the long-term implications of modern biotechnology for the governance of food safety in national food systems and global food industries. In addition to GM crops, FAO is working on the assessment of modern biotechnology and the management of animal genetic resources. In support of this initiative, an Intergovernmental Working Group on Animal Genetic Resources for Food and Agriculture was convened. The Working Group examined the implications of modern biotechnology for animal livestock reproduction through artificial insemination, embryo transfer, ovum pick up (OPU) and in vitro maturation and fertilization (IVM/IVF), sexing and cloning.[42]

Enhancing risk communication and consumer protection advocacy

In an age of firm and market globalization, information is a critical factor in consumer choice, public health, risk assessment, risk management and risk communication of food safety hazards. In this respect, product patents, private intellectual property rights, and product liability are growing areas of concern for corporate management and shareholders. However, WHO and FAO recognize the need for more transparency, good communication and information access for all stakeholders of global food industries. Therefore, WHO and FAO promote pragmatic dialogues between governments, food industries and consumers for the governance of food safety in the twenty-first century.

In the area of food safety risk communication, WHO and FAO are aggressively moving to ensure that national governments and consumers are correctly informed of the product safety and public health consequences of improper preparation, packaging and storage of food. At the same time, national governments are working with WHO and FAO to find more efficient and effective ways of communicating the public health risks associated with globalization of food systems and food industries. In light of the speed and scope of public health pandemics, the socio-economic impacts of food safety hazards and the rejection of food trade, rapid risk communication is critical for the governance of food safety. In this respect, the increased risk associated with delays in communication between governments, consumers, industry and regulators as witnessed by the Mad Cow, dioxin animal feed and avian flu crises, increases the importance of risk communication in the regulation of global food industries.

The new mandate for FAO, WHO and the Codex Alimentarius Commission

The globalization of food production and consumer demand requires collective action by governments, companies, industries, farmers, consumers and civil society to effectively govern food safety in national food systems and global food industries. To this end, FAO and WHO are increasing their cooperation to meet the growing challenges and threats posed by food firms and industry globalization, and the integration of national and regional food supply chains. In this respect, the Joint FAO/WHO Food Standards Programme is intensifying its work in the area of food regulatory standards-setting, regulatory harmonization and mandatory regulatory standards compliance.

At the twenty-sixth session of the Codex Alimentarius Commission that was held in 2003, a groundbreaking agreement was adopted on consumer protection and food safety relative to GM foods and modern biotechnology.[43] The guidelines for consumer protection and food safety were developed by FAO and WHO, and were designed to standardize risk analysis and risk management across nations and regions. Through the harmonization of GM food safety regulations, national governments and regulatory authorities are able to compare and use the science-based risk assessment results of other nations.[44]

As the decade unfolds, Codex is undergoing organizational and management reform to increase its efficiency, speed and effectiveness as the multilateral framework for the global regulation of food safety. During the twenty-sixth meeting of the Codex Alimentarius Commission, a suggested reform of Codex to speed up food standards development and harmonization was approved. The urgent need to open Codex standard-setting to developing countries, regional bodies and other international organizations was approved. At the meeting, the creation of the FAO/WHO Trust Fund for increased participation in Codex was confirmed. The Trust Fund, which is hosted in Geneva, became operational in February 2004, and supports the participation of more than 50 delegates from developing countries to Codex meetings every year. The FAO and WHO also requested that Codex prioritize requests for scientific advice. In exchange, FAO and WHO will strengthen their efforts to provide scientific advice in an efficient manner.[45]

General subject, commodity and regional committee reforms

Since its creation over 40 years ago, the role of the Codex Alimentarius Commission and its official committees have grown in importance, scale and scope in keeping with the globalization of the food industries and the integration of national food systems. As a result of the growing importance of Codex as the leading food safety standard-setting organization for national food systems and global food industries, the work of commodity committees and general subject (horizontal) committees have become more important. In some cases, committees have been disbanded or changed to task forces as new food safety standards issues emerge. As the following list shows, FAO, WHO and Codex Alimentarius are providing regulatory guidance for food safety in global food trade, and across the full range of agricultural product categories and food-processing sectors:

General Subject Committees

Codex Committee on Food Additives and Contaminants
Codex Committee on Food Hygiene
Codex Committee on Food Import and Export Inspection Certificates
Codex Committee on Food Labeling
Codex Committee on General Principles
Codex Committee on Methods of Analysis and Sampling
Codex Committee on Pesticide Residues
Codex Committee on Residues of Veterinary Drugs in Food
Codex Committee on Nutrition and Foods for Special Dietary Uses

Commodity Committee

Codex Committee on Cocoa Products and Chocolate
Codex Committee on Fats and Oils

Codex Committee on Fish and Fish Products
Codex Committee on Fresh Fruits and Vegetables
Codex Committee on Milk and Milk Products
Codex Committee on Processed Fruits and Vegetables
Codex Committee on Meat Hygiene

Regional and Geographical Committees

FAO and WHO Coordinating Committee for Africa
FAO and WHO Coordinating Committee for Asia
FAO and WHO Coordinating Committee for Europe
FAO and WHO Coordinating Committee for Latin America and the Caribbean
FAO and WHO Coordinating Committee for the Near East
FAO and WHO Coordinating Committee for North American and the South West Pacific

Ad Hoc Intergovernmental Task Forces

Animal Feeding
Food Derived From Biotechnology
Fruits and Vegetable Juices

In keeping with the priorities of Codex standards-setting on consumer protection and public health, developed and developing country commodities, and non-health related labeling, general and commodity (vertical) working groups continue to develop standards for the protection of food safety. In addition to these committees, informal task forces are created to address time-sensitive issues, while ad hoc cross-committee task forces are created to increase the efficiency and effectiveness of the Codex standards work.[46] In some cases, the Codex Committees are updating and revising existing standards.

This is the case with recent work of the Codex Committee on Pesticide Residues, which is developing new methodologies for point estimates and analysis of residues, revision of pesticide lists to include standards for new products, regulations for ready to eat foods, and new rules for tropical fruits and vegetable commodities.[47] In addition, a draft Code of Practice on Good Animal Feeding was produced by the Ad Hoc Intergovernmental Codex Task Force on Animal Feeding. The draft code is currently under revision in light of the growing concern over animal feed safety in the global food industries. The new direction in Codex standard-setting reflects the work of committees, and includes rules for the regulation of content requirements of fruit and vegetable juices and nectars as addressed in the Ad Hoc Codex Intergovernmental Task Force on Fruit and Vegetable Juices.[48] Likewise, the thirty-first session of the Codex Committee on Food Labeling is considering standards for prepackaged foods that include nutrition and GM labeling.[49]

In Codex Regional Committees, some member countries depend on regional standards as the first step in international regulatory harmonization. As a consequence of the growth of regional market integration and free trade agreements between developed and developing countries, Codex acknowledges the growing importance of regional committees in the regulatory capacity-building process. In fact, regional regulatory capacity-building is the focus of many FAO, WHO and Codex activities, and is often included in workshops and conferences. In regional committees, developing member countries are more represented than other Codex standard-setting activities.[50] Therefore, Codex is expanding the success and role of regional standard-setting work and consultation to increase the participation of developing countries and NGOs. In order to increase the effectiveness of regional committees, Codex, FAO and WHO have identified the following issues as priority areas for improvement:

- management of intra-regional diversity, capacity and standards enforcement
- increase resources for regional representatives to work between regional meetings
- increase Codex support for developing regions
- justification for existing focus and activities of regional committees
- formalization and clarification of regional committee mandates
- development of flexible ad hoc sub-regional structures within regions to address geographical and economic systems such as MERCOSUR and SADC
- consolidation of roles and tasks of regional representatives and coordinators to represent the region at the Executive Board and to serve as the secretary of the regional committee, with the funding of expenses for representatives from developing countries
- increase systemic capacity-building in developing regions through seminars, briefings and conferences on trade and domestic consumer protection.[51]

Reform of Codex committees and working group procedures

For the last five decades, FAO and WHO, through the Codex Alimentarius Commission, have built a multi-level system for the governance of food safety and regulatory standards harmonization. The basic institutional mechanism for regulation and regulatory standards harmonization are formal committees and ad hoc working groups. In response to requests by member governments, Codex is increasing the focus and specialization of committees. Through this change in Codex committees, delegates can focus on issues that they are trained to address, greater efficiency is achieved, and conflict between general and commodity committee standards can be avoided.

At the present time, Codex is rationalizing the work, roles and responsibilities of committees to ensure timely goal attainment and completion of standard-setting programs.[52] In terms of Codex committee structure and procedures, Codex is streamlining the standards-making process. Through the streamlining process, more focus and resources will be devoted to emerging issues of food safety regulation.[53] In addition, task forces are used to facilitate the work of committees. In the case of regional committees, goal-directed mandates that address the needs of regional food systems and food industries are being implemented.[54] In all cases, the work of committees and task forces are given timetables for completion and dissemination of findings to member countries.

At the present time, the Joint FAO/WHO Food Standards Programme is increasing collaboration with the WTO to support the adoption and implementation of SPS standards for the governance of global food trade.[55] The FAO and WHO are also mobilizing a network of multilateral institutions and universities for the governance of food safety in global food industries. The multilateral institutions included in this collaboration include the UN Environmental Program (UNEP), the UN Development Program (UNDP), the International Labor Organization (ILO), the Organisation for Economic Cooperation and Development (OECD), Consumers International (CI), the International Association of Consumer Food Organizations (IACFD), the Industry Council for Development (ICD), the International Life Sciences Institute (ILSI) and regional development banks.

Codex cooperation with WTO, OIE and IPPC

Through the work of Codex, the WTO is able to build an open food trading and liberal market system that is based on a rule of law. In turn, the WTO SPS/TBT Agreements strongly urge national governments to use international standards in conformity with the legal obligations of signatory countries. However, some stakeholders of global food industries argue that Codex and the WTO can have a negative effect on food safety through a regulatory 'race to the bottom'. This is the case because the WTO SPS Agreement permits national governments to determine the level of food safety regulation and standards for consumer protection and public health in national food systems.

At the present time, there is concern about the political tensions that exist within Codex as a result of WTO market conflicts. In some cases, there are competing food industry, biotechnology, trade and regulatory policy interests among member countries and regions. In turn, concerns about political tensions are reinforced by the fact that most of the representation outside of national governments in Codex committees comes from corporations, industry and trading interests in the global food market system. Furthermore, some food exporters in developing countries argue that OECD countries require compliance with standards that are sometimes stricter than Codex. In some cases, requirements for exporting developing countries are inconsistent and are the result of the lack of regulatory harmonization. In turn, industrialized countries set standards faster than the multilateral process in Codex.

In spite of these challenges, removal or weakening of Codex standards is politically unacceptable to governments, consumers and regulators in OECD countries. Therefore, it is suggested that the number and influence of technical specialists who can work in an inclusive and politically neutral way to promote the development and adoption of Codex standards be increased.[56] In this regard, Codex acknowledges the need for more input from consumers on acceptable levels of food safety regulation, and regulatory standards in national food systems and global food industries.[57]

In many ways, food safety is now a national food system and global food industry management challenge. The need for more control over plant and animal health requires more cooperation with OIE and IPPC. At the present time, Codex and IPPC are physically based in the FAO headquarters in Rome. While Codex is mandated to address the regulation and governance of food safety in global food trade and food industries, the OIE is mandated to reduce food-borne risks to food safety and public health from animal livestock diseases.[58] However, there are areas in food safety standard-setting that are not addressed by Codex or OIE. In response to an OIE resolution in May 2002, FAO, WHO and Codex are establishing stronger working relationships with OIE on the following areas:

- risk analysis
- certification of exported products of animal origin and efficiency of the certification agencies
- animal feed safety
- inspection of food products of animal origin starting at the farm production and processing levels
- safety of animal products in regards to veterinary drugs
- thermal treatment methods for milk to reduce food pathogens
- biotechnology applications, vaccines, veterinary drugs and biological tests
- traceability of food products of animal origins.[59]

Expert advice and scientific risk assessment in Codex

As part of its ongoing process of scientific and technical support to member governments, Codex provides an increasing amount of policy advice for regulators on the development of global risk assessment and risk management standards for food safety. In their role as scientific and public health advisors to national governments, regulators, industry and consumer organizations, FAO, WHO and Codex are clarifying the distinction between risk assessment, which is carried out by scientific experts on committees and consultative working groups, and risk management, which is carried out by the Codex committees. Through this realignment of committee functions and roles, Codex will increase the efficiency, speed of delivery and adoption of regulatory standards based on scientific advice and expert consultations.

The realignment of risk assessment, provided by FAO and WHO expert bodies, and risk management functions in Codex committees, is important for the development of consumer protection guidelines and standards for member governments, industry and NGOs. As the globalization of food firms and markets accelerates, the importance of risk management is growing relative to food safety regulation and the governance of food systems. In turn, risk management increasingly requires the balancing of economic costs and political interests with consumer safety and public health risks in ways that might affect the affordability and availability of food. Consequently, the role of science in the determination of food safety standards, consumer protection and public health regulations requires more, not less, consensus and transparency given the socio-economic, and institutional interests of Codex member governments and stakeholders.[60]

In response to growing demands by national governments, industry, consumers and international organizations, FAO and WHO are increasing resources, independence and transparency within Codex. Through this realignment of committee functions, risk management and risk assessment activities of committees and working groups are currently being differentiated. The result of this realignment of committee functions is increasing efficiency and effectiveness of experts that carry out risk assessment, and Codex committees that carry out risk management. Furthermore, Codex committees are addressing the management options and outcomes of clearly developed risk assessment and risk management programs. Therefore, trust and communication between Codex, government regulators, standards organizations and consumer groups is increasing.

At the present time, FAO, WHO and Codex are considering the creation of a scientific committee of eminent scientists to provide the Codex Alimentarius Commission with multi-functional scientific advice on existing and emerging food safety risks and challenges for the governance of food safety. The new risk assessment procedures and strategies provide increased budget support and quality control for the Joint Expert Committee on Food Additives and Contaminants (JECFA), the Joint Expert meetings on Microbiological Risk Assessment (JEMRA) and the Joint Meeting on Pesticides Residues (JMPR).[61] Under this, still potential, scenario, a joint coordination function could be housed in WHO. Through this organizational change, proposals and review processes for food-borne hazards can be expedited and strengthened.

IV INTERNATIONAL CAPACITY-BUILDING: FAO, WHO AND THE JOINT FAO/WHO FOOD SAFETY STANDARDS PROGRAMME

Capacity-Building: The Joint FAO/ WHO Food Standards Programme

As the twenty-first century unfolds, FAO and WHO are increasing their focus on national and regional capacity-building through the Joint FAO/ WHO Food Standards Programme in accordance with the goals and mandates of the Codex Alimentarius Commission. In this regard, FAO and WHO are actively involved in the following capacity-building goals:

- provision of technical assistance for the review and analysis of food control regulations, laws and policies, regulatory agencies and institutions
- evaluation of food safety regulation and control system effectiveness
- identification of food safety system weaknesses
- development of recommendations and proposals for the creation of Good Food Control Systems that are harmonized with the WTO SPS and Codex standards
- training of food control officials, technical staff, food analysts, food inspectors and managers
- strengthening of food control laboratory capacity
- support and strengthening national Codex committees
- policy advice and creation of food safety regulatory frameworks.[62]

The inability of some national governments to comply with Codex food safety standards is jeopardizing public health, consumer protection and the global market interests of traditional farmers and developing countries.[63] However, regulatory harmonization and global regulatory standards enforcement require more focus and investment in the reform of regulatory institutions, public policy processes and market governance systems in developing countries. Therefore, regulatory capacity-building for food safety in developing countries and emerging regions is now an important area of focus for Codex and the Joint FAO/WHO Food Standards Programme.[64]

The goals of FAO and WHO cooperation are national and regional capacity-building for regulatory harmonization and enforcement of WTO SPS, Codex, OIE and IPPC food safety standards.[65] In support of this effort, a new Codex Trust Fund is being created by FAO and WHO to enable more participation and to increase attendance at meetings by developing countries.[66] In addition, a Joint FAO/WHO initiative is proposed to fund and coordinate bilateral capacity-building. In this initiative, FAO and WHO are strengthening Codex contact points, and national and regional Codex committees.

Joint FAO/WHO capacity-building initiatives

At the global level, FAO and WHO are rapidly increasing the capacity of food safety regulators to comply with Codex standards. In 2002, FAO and WHO convened the Global Forum of Food Safety Regulators, in Marrakech, Morocco. Through this conference, FAO and WHO brought together food safety regulators from every region, and many Codex member countries, to discuss their experiences and global food concerns.[67] As a result of the overwhelming success of this conference, FAO and WHO organized a second Global Forum of Food Safety Regulators. The theme of the second forum at the end of 2004 was 'Building effective food safety systems'.

In support of capacity-building, FAO and WHO prepared the *Training Manual on Risk Analysis* in cooperation with ICD and ILSI. The goal of the training manual is to support capacity-building, improve food safety, and facilitate global food trade through the application of practical risk analysis. The second training manual addressed risk assessment, risk management and risk communication. Finally, WHO/ICD in cooperation with FAO published the *HACCP Principles and Practice Teachers Handbook* for food safety regulators and food quality managers. In the area of food safety and food quality, FAO and WHO jointly published *Assuring Food Safety and Quality Guidelines for Strengthening National Food Control Systems* in 2003.[68] This publication provides governments and food safety regulators with the latest information and advice on food control systems, public health protection, food fraud, food adulteration and food trade. In this regard, the *Guidelines for Strengthening Food Control Systems and Guidelines for National Food Legislation* was published by WHO and FAO to support national regulatory policy development.

Africa

In Africa, FAO and WHO are working together to provide technical support and regulatory capacity-building training at the national and regional levels. In 2002, FAO and WHO in cooperation with ILSI, convened a workshop on 'Applying food safety risk analysis in Africa – practical approaches', in Kampala, Uganda.[69] In 2003, FAO and WHO jointly convened an international seminar entitled 'Acrylamide in food: current state of affairs', in Arusha, Tanzania.

Asia

In 2001, FAO and WHO, in cooperation with ILSI, convened a training program entitled 'Food safety seminar for Central Asian republics'. The seminar provided Central Asian food safety authorities and regulatory officials with a framework for understanding food safety, the regional implications and requirements for regulatory policy and legislation, standards enforcement, food system management and inter-ministerial cooperation.[70] During this period, the WHO Food Safety Programme launched a multi-country public health project to train food safety officers of the Central Asian republics at the Kazakhstan School of Public Health. The five training modules include food legislation, epidemiology, food microbiology, chemical analyses of foods and risk analysis.

In 2002, FAO, ILSI and WHO collaborated on the 'Workshop on microbiological risk analysis' that was held in Beijing, China. In this workshop, microbiological risk assessment and food safety risk analysis was discussed. During the same year, FAO and WHO in collaboration with ILSI, sponsored a workshop on 'Applying food safety risk analysis in Asia – practical approaches', in Kuala Lumpur, Malaysia. The conference was hosted by the Ministry of Health and the Government of Malaysia, and examined the role of risk analysis in food safety and the importance of developing country participation in Codex Regional Coordinating Committee meetings.[71] In a follow-up to the first Global Forum of Food Safety Regulators, FAO and WHO convened the first Regional Forum on Food Safety and Quality for Asia and the Pacific, in Malaysia in May 2004.[72]

Europe

In Europe, FAO and WHO are working to strengthen food safety system development, regulatory standards harmonization, and risk analysis capability in Central and Eastern European countries. In support of this capacity-building effort, WHO held regional workshops on 'Intersectoral development of food and nutrition action plans in South East Europe' in Malta in 2000 and Bulgaria in 2001. During the same year, a workshop on the 'Development of the food and nutrition action plan for the Nordic and

Baltic Countries' was held in Latvia. In 2002, the first WHO and FAO workshop on 'Food and nutrition action plans for countries in Southern Europe' was held in Rome, Italy.[73]

During this period, FAO launched a project on 'Training on meat inspection and meat technology' for Albania, Croatia, the Czech Republic, Slovakia and Slovenia. The goal of this food safety capacity-building project is to provide technical support to improve meat and livestock quality in accordance with EU, HACCP and Codex standards.[74] In 2003, FAO in cooperation with the Slovak Agricultural University held a workshop for Eastern and Central European countries on the 'Internet portal on food safety – communication systems to strengthen food safety and build consumer confidence' in Slovakia. The workshop covered food safety communication, the Internet portal for food safety, the EU rapid food safety alert system and emerging risk identification systems.

Latin America and the Caribbean

In the Latin American and Caribbean regions, FAO and WHO, in cooperation with ILSI, organized the Risk Analysis and Exposure Assessment Meeting in 2001. During this period, PAHO/WHO assisted Central American countries in creating and strengthening national Codex committees, and the application of Codex guidelines and recommendations. In 2002, a similar project for the strengthening of National Codex committees and application of the Codex Alimentarius standards in the Andean region was launched. Finally, a project to 'Strengthen phytosanitary capabilities in the Caribbean Community (CARICOM) region' was launched to strengthen phytosanitary capacities, pest exclusion capacity, capacity and compliance with the WTO SPS Agreement and Codex standards in CARICOM countries.

Near East

In the Near East region, FAO and WHO in cooperation with the Arab Federation of Consumers (AFC) held a workshop on 'Emerging food safety issues and consumer protection', in Jordan in 2001.[75] In 2002, FAO and WHO, in cooperation with the International Atomic Energy Agency (IAEA), organized a regional training workshop on the 'Development of quality assurance for mycotoxin analysis' in Cairo, Egypt. The goal of the workshop was to develop quality assurance systems for mycotoxin analysis in accordance with international guidelines, current science and standards for the accreditation of mycotoxin analysis in laboratories. In 2003, FAO and WHO organized a 'Food control system workshop' for food safety officials in the United Arab Emirates (UAE), and the Gulf Cooperation Council (GCC).

Food Safety Capacity-Building in FAO and WHO

FAO capacity-building

As the decade unfolds, FAO is working in cooperation with member governments and regions to develop and strengthen food security, ensure food safety and facilitate global food trade. In response to the globalization of food trade, FAO, in cooperation with the European Union and other donor countries, developed and implemented the Umbrella Programme for Training on the Uruguay Round and Future Negotiations on Agriculture. The goals of this project are to provide training on multilateral trade, improve understanding of WTO agreements and increase participation in trade negotiations.[76]

In December 2000, FAO launched a global project, in cooperation with the University of Surrey in the UK, and the Center for Agro-Economic Cooperation and Research for Development (CIRAD) entitled 'Enhancement of coffee quality through prevention of mould formation'. The goals of this food safety capacity-building program are as follows: identification of mould formation, creation of optimal coffee drying conditions, adoption of Good Manufacturing Practices and HACCP standards across the coffee production and processing chain, and prevention of mould contamination in coffee production. The program was completed in 2004, and was implemented in the Ivory Coast, Uganda, Brazil, Colombia, India, Indonesia and Kenya. The project funding was provided by the Common Fund for Commodities and the Dutch Government.[77]

In regard to food quality, FAO initiated a two-year project to improve the quality and safety of fresh fruits and vegetables through the Global Inventory, Reference Materials and Food Safety Training Programme for Improving the Quality and Safety of Fresh Fruits and Vegetables in 2002. The goal of this FAO initiative is to improve access to information and training to improve the quality and safety of fresh produce industries. In 2003, FAO held a symposium on 'Food safety and quality: issues for developing countries' in New Delhi, India. During this conference, the nutrition of GM foods, food safety risk analysis and infrastructure for food control systems were discussed.[78]

WHO capacity-building

As the need for science-based risk analysis and food-borne pathogen surveillance capacity grows, WHO is working in cooperation with governments to build food safety capacity, food regulation and laws, and laboratory accreditation reviews. In this regard, WHO is preparing modernization assessments in African, Latin American, Asian, Middle Eastern and Central and Eastern European member countries. In Africa, the WHO regional office promotes the 'Healthy Market' initiative for food safety, sanitation and wholesome food production and trade. In support of this initiative, WHO launched the 'Healthy Settings' concept in Africa, and provides public health and technical assistance for beverage additive safety and training of street food vendors in safe handling and promotion of wholesome food trade. In cooperation with the governments of Tanzania and Nigeria, the Buguruni Healthy Market Initiative was launched, and is expanding across the African region.[79]

In Europe, the WHO Food Safety Programme is working with member countries to develop National Food Safety Strategies for Action in Europe. In this initiative, WHO/Regional Office for Europe (WHO/EURO), in collaboration with the Council for Europe, prepared a sub-regional project to strengthen food safety and nutrition services in South East Europe. Through this project, WHO/EURO is collaborating with the signatory countries of the Stability Pact – Albania, Bosnia and Hercegovina, Bulgaria, Croatia, the Republic of Macedonia, Romania, Slovenia and Yugoslavia – to build food safety regulatory capacity.[80]

In the Near East, WHO worked with national governments to develop the regional plan of action, and held a regional workshop on 'New challenges in food safety: the regional action plan', in Dubai, United Arab Emirates, in December 1999. In 2001, WHO convened a meeting on the 'Promotion of food safety: regional food safety network' in Jordan. During this meeting, there was strong consensus on the urgent need for a regional network for food safety communication, food pathogen outbreaks, food rejection and recalls, risk analysis data and tools, and the harmonization of food safety procedures.[81]

In 2001, the WHO/Eastern Mediterranean Office (WHO/EMRO) organized a Regional Consultation on Food-borne Disease Surveillance. In this program, the WHO Global Salmonella Surveillance Program (GSS), and WHO/EMRO collaborated with WHO headquarters in Geneva, the Center for Disease Control (CDC) in Atlanta, Georgia (USA) and the Danish Veterinary Institute to organize a regional training course on the 'Surveillance of salmonella and antimicrobial resistance in food-borne pathogens'. By 2002, a special study on the burden of food-borne diseases was launched, and a manual on *Developing Food Legislation for Food Control Systems in Countries of the Eastern Mediterranean* was prepared.[82]

In the Asia-Pacific region, a WHO regional strategy for food safety was launched to increase policy support for national food safety programs. In support of public health and food safety initiatives, WHO is working with the governments of Mongolia, Vietnam, Papua, Cambodia and the South Pacific Islands to develop seminars for ministries involved with food safety policies and national plans of action.[83] In the case of HACCP standards, WHO is working in cooperation with the Malaysian Agriculture and

Research Development Institute (MARDI), the Australia–New Zealand Food Safety Authority (FSANZ), and the governments of Malaysia, Brunei Darussalam, Vietnam, Mongolia, Laos and China to strengthen Good Hygiene Practices and HACCP programs for small businesses and meat and dairy industries.[84]

V CONCLUSION: FUTURE PERSPECTIVES ON GLOBAL REGULATION OF FOOD SAFETY

At the start of the twenty-first century, national food system integration and the globalization of food trade and food industries are increasing the need for the harmonization of global food safety standards. In the absence of regulatory policy harmonization at the multilateral level, consumer safety, public health and animal and plant health are exposed to increasing risks from a wide range of food contaminants, pathogens and food safety hazards in global food industries and food trading systems. While government regulation and regulatory standards may protect specific segments of the population and food consumers, voluntary action by small numbers of companies, governments and food industries will not detect and manage emerging food safety risks in national food systems and global food industries. Therefore, regulatory harmonization is now required to govern food safety in national food systems and global food industries.

In this context, Codex provides the platform for the development of an international 'rule of regulatory law' by nations in the area of food safety. In its role as the center of the multi-level and multilateral framework for food safety standards harmonization, Codex is reforming its operations. Through this reform process, Codex is addressing the historical, current and emerging food safety, food security, global food trade and food industry needs of member governments, consumers and farmers.[85] Ultimately, food safety standards and regulatory harmonization are increasing in importance due to the production of foods derived from modern biotechnology, the global threat of bioterrorism and the growing need for national food security in the twenty-first century.

As the century unfolds, market competition and free trade agreements are increasing the scale and scope of food and biotechnology firms in global food industries. Therefore, national governments are increasing collective policy action through Codex to extend the reach of consumer protection, product safety, public health, animal livestock health, plant health, and product liability laws and regulations. Consequently, the twenty-first century is now witnessing unprecedented multilateral policy cooperation on behalf of food safety, consumer protection, public health, animal livestock and plant health, through regulatory harmonization and multi-jurisdictional regulatory enforcement.

In this multilateral and multi-level system of regulatory standards harmonization for food safety, the economic efficiency goals of national agriculture and food systems and global food industries are balanced. Increasingly, the supremacy of consumer power, public health, food safety and consumer welfare maximization serve as the primary goals of firm and industry competition in national food systems and global food industries. As a consequence, the roles of FAO, WHO and the Codex Alimentarius Commission in the global regulation of food safety are growing rapidly in the twenty-first century.

In the future, the work of FAO, WHO and Codex Alimentarius will change in keeping with scientific discoveries, modern biotechnology innovations, changing consumer perceptions, emerging public health needs, global food trade and the integration of global food industries. Therefore, the work of Codex will become more focused on the food safety implications of changing patterns of food demand and consumption, consumer attitudes, government and industry perceptions and values, and new approaches to food control and regulation. In this regard, food safety, food quality and the impact of modern biotechnology on the food system will increasingly serve as the focus of the normative consensus, and multilateral standard-setting activities of the Codex Alimentarius Commission and the Joint FAO /WHO Food Standards Programme.

Finally, the consolidation and concentration of global food companies and food supply chain industries requires more, not less, enforcement of food safety standards in keeping with food system integration. Therefore, in the future, the food safety work and the regulatory standard-setting activity of Codex requires closer intergovernmental cooperation at the national and regional levels. At the same time, stronger coordination of food industry self-regulation, management-based regulation, and mandatory government regulation of food systems and food industries are needed in the years ahead.

NOTES

* Acknowledgments: The chapter co-authors and book editor thank Dr Jørgen Schlundt, Director, Department of Food Safety, Zoonoses and Foodborne Diseases in the World Health Organization, Geneva, Switzerland for his review and comments on this chapter.

1. WHO (2002), *Global Strategy for Food Safety*, Food Safety Program, Geneva: WHO.
2. Ibid., p. 13. See Vogel, David (1995), *Trading Up: Consumer and Environmental Regulation in a Global Economy*, Cambridge, MA: Harvard University Press. In addition, see Held, David (1999), *Global Transformation*, Palo Alto, CA: Stanford University Press, pp. 55–7.

3. Braithwaite, John and Peter Drahos (2000), *Global Business Regulation*, Cambridge: Cambridge University Press, p. 401.
4. According to Professor Cary Coglianese at the John F. Kennedy School of Government at Harvard University, globalization of markets and industries is driving the trend and need for international coordination, multilateral institutions and collective policy action by national governments, regulatory authorities and public policy-makers. Therefore, multilateral institutions are being strengthened at the request of civil societies, industries and nation states in the twenty-first century. See Coglianese, Cary (2000), 'Globalization and the design of international institutions', in Joseph S. Nye and John D. Donahue (eds), *Governance in a Globalizing World*, Washington, DC: Brookings Institution Press, pp. 297–315.
5. Joint FAO/WHO Food Standards Programme (2000), *Report of the Evaluation of the Codex Alimentarius and Other FAO and WHO Food Standards Work*, 15 November Rome: FAO, p. 162. WHO (2002), p. 16. The Codex Commission allows for an annual meeting, but has held biannual meetings since 1968.
6. WHO (2002) p. 19.
7. Ibid., p. 6.
8. In 1943, forty-four governments met in Hot Springs, Virginia, to create a permanent multilateral organization for food and agriculture. At the end of the Second World War, the first FAO conference was held in Quebec City, Canada, to formally launch FAO as a specialized UN agency. In 1957, FAO headquarters was moved from Washington, DC, to Rome, Italy, www.FAO.org, 'A short history of FAO'. See FAO and WHO (1999), *Understanding the Codex Alimentarius*, Rome: FAO Also see FAO and WHO (2002a), *Codex Alimentarius Commission Strategic Framework 2003–2007*, Rome: FAO.
9. The FAO Trust Fund was lunched with $500 million. See 'FAO trust fund for food security', FAO News Room, Rome, 22 August 2002.
10. See 'From farm to table: a new global approach to food safety', FAO News Room, Rome, 31 March 2003.
11. WHO (2002), p. 10.
12. This collaboration was reaffirmed officially in WHO (2000), *Resolution by the 105th Session of Executive Board of WHO on January 28, 2000.-E B105.R16 – Food Safety*, Geneva: WHO. Also see WHO (1999), *Food Safety Report of the Director General, EB 105/10*, 2 December, Geneva: WHO. In this report, WHO stresses the normative role and public health leadership of WHO in risk assessment, risk management and risk communication, pp. 3–5.
13. Joint FAO/WHO Food Standards Programme (2000), p. 11.
14. WHO (2002), p. 11.
15. Ibid., p. 12.
16. In her address to the Codex Alimentarius Commission on 2 July 2001, Dr Gro Harlem Bruntland, Director-General of WHO, confirmed that consumers were losing confidence in the safety of their food. Therefore, she urged WHO, FAO and Codex Alimentarius to improve food safety, regain consumer confidence through global food standards, and pre-market approval of GM foods, and to confirm their safety and true improvement over conventional food products.
17. Ibid.
18. Ibid.
19. In addition to BSE, the dioxin crisis required extensive scientific consultation through Codex to assess and manage public health risks associated with dioxin contamination of poultry feed and related products in global food markets. See Joint FAO/WHO Food Standards Programme (2001b), *Position Paper on Dioxins and Dioxin Like PCBs, Codex Committee on Food Additives and Contaminants, Joint FAO/WHO Food Standards Programme, Thirty-third Session*, 12–16 March, The Hague, Rome: FAO.
20. 'Codex Biotech Task Force could gain second lease on life', *Food Chemical News*, 24 February 2003, **45** (2). The US and EU expressed gratitude to the Biotech Task Force, and Japanese leadership during times of great tension and controversy. In this instance, Japan served as a neutral and effective third party in the negotiation and eventual

adoption of the task force report. Also see, 'Japanese food safety official appointed new Codex Secretary', *Food Chemical News*, 6 August 2003, **5** (150). A senior Japanese food safety official, Kazuaki Miyagishima, from WHO was appointed as the new Codex Secretary effective 1, October 2003. In this new job, Dr Miyagishima has great skill from his work with the WTO and WHO. He is also very effective in pushing for greater involvement of developing nations in Codex activities and the WTO.

21. WHO (2001), *Global Surveillance of Food-borne Disease: Developing a Strategy and Interaction with Risk Analysis*, Report of a WHO Consultation, World Health Organization, Department of Communicable Disease Surveillance and Response, and Department of Protection of the Human Environment, Geneva.
22. FAO and WHO (2002b), *Principles and Guidelines for Incorporating Microbial Risk Assessment in the Development of Food Safety Standards, Guidelines and Related Texts, Report of the Joint FAO/WHO Consultation*, 18–22 March, Kiel, Geneva. WHO. In this report, the issue of 'appropriate levels of protection' emerge relative to the cost–benefit assessment of food safety standards through HACCP and other pathogen surveillance systems for national and global food chains and systems.
23. Joint FAO/WHO Food Standards Programme (2000), *Report of the Evaluation of the Codex Alimentarius and Other FAO and WHO Food Standards Work*, 15 November, Rome: FAO, p. 12.
24. Ibid., p. 13.
25. WHO (2002c), p. 13.
26. Ibid., p. 24.
27. Ibid., p. 28.
28. Ibid., pp. 28–9.
29. Joint FAO/WHO Food Standards Programme (2000), p. 12.
30. WHO (2002), p. 12.
31. Joint FAO/WHO Food Standards Programme (2000), p. 12.
32. Ibid., p. 13.
33. Joint FAO/WHO Food Standards Programme (2000), p. 5.
34. Ibid., p. 6.
35. Ibid., p. 16.
36. Ibid., p. 14.
37. Ibid., p. 6.
38. Ibid., p. 14.
39. Ibid.
40. WHO (2002), p. 14.
41. See Joint FAO/WHO Food Standards Programme (2001c), *Report of the Second Session of the Codex Ad Hoc Intergovernmental Task Force on Foods Derived from Biotechnology, Joint FAO/ WHO Food Standards Programme, Codex Alimentarius Commission, Twenty-Fourth Session*, 2–7 July, Geneva: WHO.
42. FAO (2000), *Commission on Genetic Resources for Food and Agriculture, Inter-governmental Technical Working Group on Animal Genetic Resources for Food and Agriculture, Second Session*, 4–6 September, Rome: FAO, pp. 4–8.
43. 'Codex Alimentarius Commission adopts more than 50 new food standards', FAO News Room, Rome, 9 July 2003.
44. Ibid.
45. Ibid.
46. Ibid., pp. 36–9.
47. See meeting report, Joint FAO/WHO Standards Programme (2003d), *Codex Committee on Pesticide Residues, Thirty Fifth Session*, 31 March–5 April, Rotterdam, Rome: FAO.
48. The meeting was held in Salvador, Brazil, 6–10 May 2003. The meeting and report focus on the need to improve the quality and real fruit and vegetable content of fruit and vegetable juices and nectars. See Joint FAO/WHO Food Standards Programme (2003a), *Ad Hoc Task Force on Fruit and Vegetables*, 6–10 May, Salvador, Brazil, Rome: FAO.
49. See Joint FAO/WHO Food Standards Programme (2003c), *Codex Committee on Food Labeling, Meeting Report, Thirty First Session*, Ottawa, 28 April–2 May, Rome: FAO.

50. Joint FAO/WHO Food Standards Programme (2000), p. 41.
51. Ibid., pp. 40–41.
52. Ibid., p. 39.
53. 'Codex adopts middle of the road stance toward evaluation report', *Food Chemical News*, 3 March 2003, **45** (3). To avoid problems related to dramatic and radical institutional change, some of the recommendations of the evaluation report were sent for further discussion and review. However, moderate changes in the structure and management of Codex are being implemented immediately.
54. Ibid., p. 7.
55. Ibid., p. 17.
56. Ibid., p. 33.
57. The issue of consumer protection standards was dropped from the Codex Committee on General Principles since very few guidelines have been put forward by member governments. Therefore it is recommended that Codex develop guidelines to determine acceptable levels of protection to guide risk assessment and advisory committees in Codex and the WTO. Ibid., p. 33.
58. At the Codex Alimentarius Commission meeting in July 2001, the Director-General of OIE, Dr Bernard Vallat, informed the Commission, that 158 countries were members. However, he stressed the fact that closer cooperation and collaboration is needed between OIE and Codex to help governments comply with the WTO SPS Agreement, and to increase scientific and technical support. See Joint FAO/WHO Food Standards Programme (2001a), *Joint FAO/WHO Food Standards Programme – Codex Alimentarius Commission – Capacity-Building for Food Quality and Food Safety Report of the Twenty-Fourth Session*, 2–7 July, Geneva, Rome: FAO, p. 5.
59. Ibid., p. 35.
60. Ibid., pp. 41–2.
61. Ibid., p. 8.
62. Ibid.
63. Ibid., p. 7. In response to the conference recommendations made at the Conference on International Food Trade Beyond 2000, the Codex Commission endorsed recommendation No. 13 which calls for Codex to give official guidance on equivalence; recommendation No. 14 – consideration of the special needs of developing nations; recommendation No. 16 – standards development for food composition, sensory quality and safety; recommendation No. 17 – to prevent Codex standards from becoming too prescriptive or stringent; recommendation No. 18 – promotion and extension of the General Principles of Food Hygiene and HACCP to the entire food chain; and recommendation No. 21 – increased effectiveness in the use of written comments, p. 7.
64. Joint FAO/WHO Food Standards Programme (2003b), *Joint FAO/WHO Food Standards Programme – Codex Alimentarius Commission – Capacity Building for Food Quality and Food Safety, Twenty Sixth Session*, 30 June–7 July, Rome: FAO.
65. Ibid., p. 1.
66. 'Codex trust fund launched by FAO and WHO', *Food Chemical News*, 20 February 2003, **5** (33), FAO and WHO have launched a $40 million trust fund to support the participation of developing countries in Codex activities and meetings. In spite of strong resistance to industry contributions by Consumer International and other consumer advocacy groups who claimed that solicitation of corporate funds violated WHO conflict of interest guidelines, FAO and WHO will continue as planned and review each donation.
67. Joint FAO/WHO Food Standards Programme (2003b), p. 2.
68. Ibid., p. 4.
69. Ibid., p. 4.
70. Ibid., p. 8.
71. Ibid., p. 8.
72. Ibid., p . 11.
73. Ibid., p. 12.
74. Ibid., p. 12.

75. Ibid.
76. Ibid., pp. 2–3.
77. Ibid.
78. Ibid., p. 9.
79. Ibid., p. 6.
80. Ibid., p. 12.
81. Ibid., p. 18.
82. Ibid., p. 19.
83. Ibid., p. 9.
84. Ibid., p. 9.
85. For a more detailed overview of the strategic direction of Codex Alimentarius over the next five years, see FAO and WHO (2002a).

REFERENCES

Coglianese, Cary (2000), 'Globalization and the design of international institutions', in Joseph S. Nye and John D. Donahue (eds), *Governance in a Globalizing World*, Washington, DC: Brookings Institution Press, pp. 297–315.

FAO (2000), *Commission on Genetic Resources for Food and Agriculture, Intergovernmental Technical Working Group on Animal Genetic Resources for Food and Agriculture, Second Session*, 4–6 September, Rome: FAO.

FAO and WHO (1999), *Understanding the Codex Alimentarius*, Rome: FAO.

FAO and WHO (2002a), *Codex Alimentairus Commission – Strategic Framework 2003–2007*, Rome: FAO.

FAO and WHO (2002b), *Principles and Guidelines for Incorporating Microbial Risk Assessment in the Development of Food Safety Standards, Guidelines and Related Texts, Report of the Joint FAO/WHO Consultation*, Kiel, 18–22 March, Geneva: WHO.

FAO News Room, Rome (2002), 'FAO trust fund for food security', 22 August, Rome: FAO.

FAO News Room, Rome (2003), 'Codex Alimentarius Commission adopts more than 50 new food standards', 9 July, Rome: FAO.

Food Chemical News (2003a), 'Codex trust fund launched by FAO and WHO', 20 February, **5** (33).

Food Chemical News (2003b), 'Codex Biotech Task Force could gain second lease on life', 24 February, **45** (2).

Food Chemical News (2003c), 'Codex adopts middle of the road stance toward evaluation report', 3 March, **45** (3).

Food Chemical News (2003d), 'Japanese food safety official appointed new Codex Secretary', 6 August, **5** (50).

Held, David (1999), *Global Transformation*, Palo Alto, CA: Stanford University Press.

Joint FAO/WHO Food Standards Programme (2000), *Report of the Evaluation of the Codex Alimentarius and Other FAO and WHO Food Standards Work*, 15 November, Rome: FAO.

Joint FAO/WHO Food Standards Programme (2001a), *Joint FAO/WHO Food Standards Programme – Codex Alimentarius Commission – Capacity Building for Food Quality and Food Safety Report of the Twenty-Fourth Session*, 2–7 July, Geneva, Rome: FAO.

Joint FAO/WHO Food Safety Standards Programme (2001b), *Position Paper on Dioxins and Dioxin Like PCBs, Codex Committee on Food Additives and Contaminants, Joint FAO/WHO Food Standards Programme, Thirty-third Session*, 12–16 March, The Hague, Rome: FAO.
Joint FAO/WHO Food Standards Programme (2001c), *Report of the Second Session of the Codex Ad Hoc Intergovernmental Task Force on Foods Derived from Biotechnology, Joint FAO/WHO Food Standards Programme, Codex Alimentarius Commission, Twenty–Fourth Session*, 2–7 July, Geneva: WHO.
Joint FAO/WHO Food Standards Programme (2003a), *Ad Hoc Task Force on Fruit and Vegetables*, Salvador, Brazil, 6–10 May.
Joint FAO/WHO Food Standards Programme (2003b), *Joint FAO/WHO Food Standards Programme – Codex Alimentarius Commission – Capacity Building for Food Quality and Food Safety, Twenty Sixth Session*, 30 June–7 July, Rome: FAO.
Joint FAO/WHO Food Standards Programme (2003c), *Codex Committee on Food Labeling, Meeting Report, Thirty First Session*, 28 April–2 May, Ottawa, Rome: FAO.
Joint FAO/WHO Food Standards Programme (2003d), *Codex Committee on Pesticide Residues, Thirty Fifth Session*, 31 March–5 April, Rotterdam, Rome: FAO.
Vogel, David (1995), *Trading Up: Consumer and Environmental Regulation in a Global Economy*, Cambridge, MA: Harvard University Press.
WHO (1999), *Food Safety Report of the Director General, EB 105/10*, 2 December, Geneva: WHO.
WHO (2000), *Resolution by the 105th Session of Executive Board of WHO on January 28, 2000.-E B105.R16 – Food Safety*, Geneva: WHO.
WHO (2001), *Global Surveillance of Food-borne Disease: Developing a Strategy and its Interaction with Risk Analysis*, Report of a WHO Consultation, World Health Organization, Department of Communicable Disease Surveillance and Response, and Department of Protection of the Human Environment, Geneva.
WHO (2002), *WHO Global Strategy for Food Safety*, Food Safety Program, Geneva: WHO.

PART V

Conclusions

13. Regulated competition and food safety in global agri-food industries

Reba A. Carruth

I REGULATION OF COMPETITION IN GLOBAL AGRI-FOOD INDUSTRIES

In the twenty-first century, globalization, market integration and regional free trade increase the need for regulated competition in global agri-food industries. In many food markets, the failure of competition occurs through weak government regulation of firms, and oligopolistic competition in national and global food industries. As a result, regulatory capture by corporations, industry and competing government policy interests, threaten consumer protection food safety and product choice.[1] Therefore, regulatory policies and industry standards that promote consumer welfare, free trade and effective market competition are required to govern firm and industry globalization (Yoffie 1993.)

According to classical and neoliberal economic theories, the rational self-interest of consumers and producers results in market equilibrium and consumer welfare.[2] In national food markets and global agri-food industries, consumers have more food product choices, through 'survival of the fittest' competition, biotechnology innovation and FDI by global food companies.[3] However, the WTO SPS/TBT Agreements strengthen food safety and consumer welfare in global food trade and agri-food industries (Hahn 1996).[4] In this respect, the moral dimension of firm and industry competition is important for the regulation of competition in global markets.[5]

In reality, food firm and global food industry competition are a form of market conflict that must be 'encapsulated', contained and regulated.[6] However, the encapsulation of competition requires normative consensus on policy standards and market goals for national food systems and global agri-food industries.[7] Ultimately the 'embedding' of competition in the broader socio-economic context of national food systems and global agri-food industries is needed to regulate food safety. Therefore, collective policy action by national governments, food safety regulators and public health authorities are required to govern food safety across nations, regions and global agri-food industries.[8]

II REGULATED COMPETITION IN GLOBAL AGRI-FOOD INDUSTRIES

Supplier Power and Concentration in Global Agri-Food Industries

Since the 1980s, cross-border merger and acquisition activity is accelerating integration and concentration across global agri-food industries.[9] During the 1980s, US food manufacturing industries had high levels of concentration.[10] By the 1990s, the EU food industry experienced regional consolidation, and globalization.[11] While industry concentration is negatively correlated with consumer welfare gains, producer benefits and supplier power appear to be positively correlated with increasing market share growth.[12] In this regard, FDI in the APEC region is growing as US and EU agri-business and processed food industries consolidate their power in transatlantic Asian and global food markets.[13]

By the end of the twentieth century, the growing power of food additive companies, that is, Archer Daniels Midland (ADM) and cartels with price-fixing capability, confirmed the dangers of oligopolistic competition.[14] For example, in 1996, US antitrust regulators cited the ADM company for its role in creating an international citrus acid food and animal feed additive cartel. In this case, two Swiss, one French and one Dutch firm were also indicted. At the same time, the US antitrust regulators moved on ADM to break up another collusive food market arrangement. This time a Lysine cartel that consisted of ADM, two Japanese and one South Korean company were cited for collusion in the global agri-food industry.[15] Therefore, agri-food industry governance now requires collective antitrust and competition policy cooperation to regulate the market, corporate power and to protect consumers.[16] Box 13.1 summarizes the Structural School framework for the regulation of agri-food firm and industry competition.[17] (Baron 2003)

In some cases, production efficiency maximizes consumer welfare by increasing the range of products that are available to a wider range of global consumers.[18] In this context, consumers and governments must choose between production efficiency, consumer protection or product choice as the primary goals of global agri-food industries.[19] However, biotechnology innovation, food branding, product advertising and FDI force the exit of smaller competitors in OECD and developing countries.[20] Therefore, the regulation of oligopolistic competition in global food industries must address the impact of supplier power on food safety, food security and consumer choice.[21]

BOX 13.1 STRUCTURAL SCHOOL OF REGULATED COMPETITION IN THE AGRI-FOOD INDUSTRY

Agri-food markets are socio-economic systems that affect public policy and market governance.

Market forces cannot be left to determine the normative goals and enforce the rules set by society to uphold the collective good.

Collective regulatory action is needed to protect consumers and farmers from supplier power in global agri-food industries.

Consumers need more information to understand food safety, product quality and health effects of globally sourced agri-food products.

Globalization of agri-food industries and national food chains accelerates the conduct of competition and will have to be regulated through global standards enforcement.

Globalization is decreasing competition and concentrating ownership of food producers.

Public health and consumer protection are the priority before economic efficiencies and profits for concentrated agri-business and industries.

Market power is increasingly derived from undocumented vertical alliances across border and regions, and through contract farming arrangements.

Decreasing profits can also drive global agri-food firm and industry concentration.

Oligopolistic and monopolistic competition can increase windfall profits.

Clear and strong multi-level and multi-jurisdictional enforcement of regulations is needed.

Note: Concerns over systemic risks to consumers and the safety of national food and agriculture systems are increasing due to growing consumer demand for more diverse foods, and increasing global food trade.

Source: Author's view of Structural School model of global agri-food industry regulation.

Agri-business and biotechnology firms' strategic alliances

The globalization of food and agriculture industries is characterized by the rapid commercialization of seed, plant, crop and animal biotechnologies.[22] The growing consolidation of global agri-business and food processors such as Cargill, ADM and ConAgra, and biotechnology innovators such as Monsanto and Norvartis gave rise to consumer, farmer and regulator concerns over supplier power.[23] By the twenty-first century, the growing power of food chain clusters in global agri-business, processed food and biotechnology industries emerged as a competition and food safety concern for consumers, farmers, regulators and governments (Heffernan et al. 1999). Figure 13.1 illustrates the scale and scope of food chain clusters in national and global agri-food industries.

As the decade unfolds, mergers and acquisitions, joint ventures and informal strategic alliances for sales and marketing are increasingly viewed as collusive.[24] In a growing number of cases, intellectual property rights and contract farming restrict competition in national and global agri-food industries.[25] In this context, global food conglomerates such Cargill, Monsanto, ConAgra and ADM, and large tobacco and pharmaceutical companies, are powerful global food producers.[26] Over time, powerful 'food chain clusters' (Figure 13.1) with vertical strategic alliances or informal agreements exert strong influence over product choice in national food systems and global food industries. Therefore, government regulation is needed ensure that market agreements do not weaken consumer protection, food safety competition and product choice in global agri-food industries.

Finally, there are market asymmetries between world-class food processors and retailers in the US, EU and Japan, and potential competitors in emerging nations, that is, Thailand, South Africa, Mexico and Brazil.[27] In this regard, many countries in the Western Hemisphere, Africa and Asia lack comprehensive regulations or competition policies for agri-food industries. In turn, developing countries have limited or no ability to regulate competition by domestic and foreign firms, or industry structure on behalf of food safety. Consequently, intensive multi-level lobbying and regulatory capture by powerful agri-business and global agri-food industry interests can threaten food standards harmonization.[28]

Transatlantic regulatory reciprocity and mutual recognition

As global competition in agri-food industries intensifies, institutional cooperation, regulatory harmonization and industry standards convergence are increasing.[29] A major trend in regional and multilateral regulation of competition in global agri-food industries is the growing use of mutual recognition frameworks.[30] As the previous chapters show, government-to-government recognition of regulatory systems and food safety standards is required for the governance of agri-food industries. The goal of regulatory reciprocity agreements is to strengthen the capacity of governments to regulate food safety, consumer protection and public health as shown in Box 13.2.

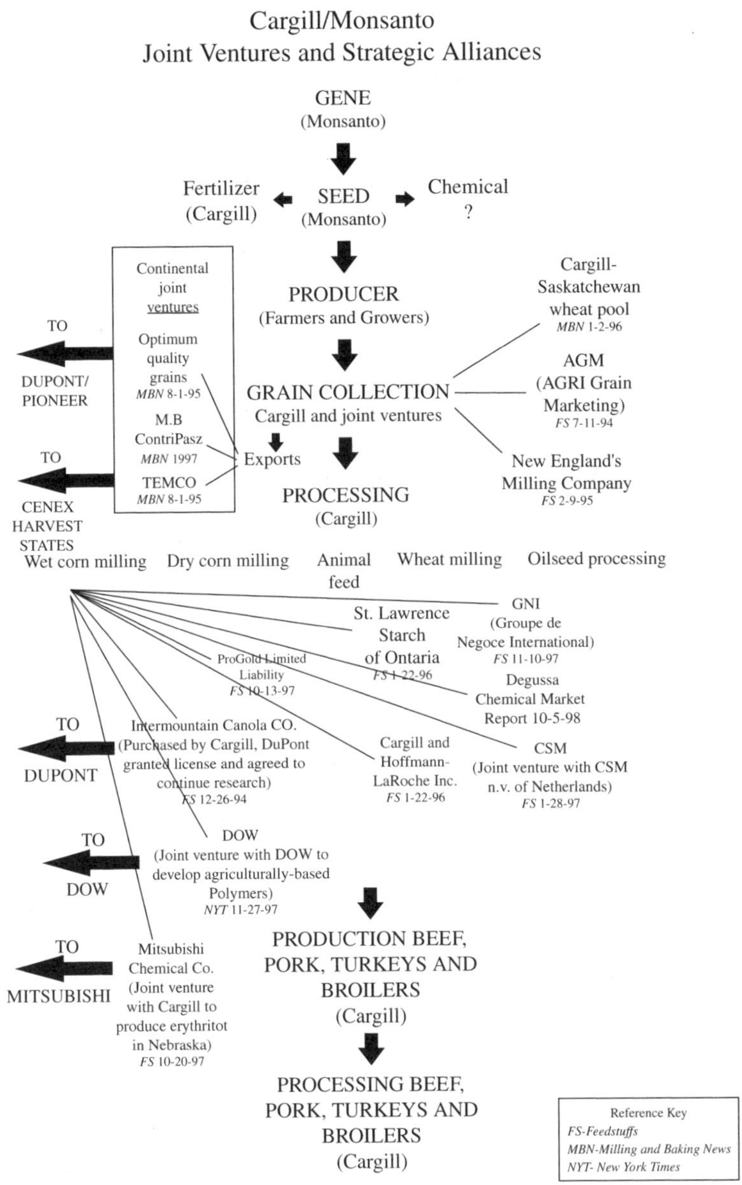

Source: Heffernan et al. (1999).

Figure 13.1 Cargill and Monsanto food chain cluster

BOX 13.2 REGULATORY RECIPROCITY, HARMONIZATION AND MUTUAL RECOGNITION

Government-to-Government
Public Health
Consumer Protection
Product Safety
Animal and Plant Health

Government-to-Industry
Management-Based Regulations
HACCP and ISO Quality Standards
Acceptance of Conformity Assessment Process
Best Practices – GMP/GAP/GHP
Post-Market Surveillance of Regulatory Compliance

Industry-to-Industry
Convergence of National Agri-Food Industry Standards
Global Standards Organizations
Food Producer, Processor and Retailer Declaration of Conformity with Global Industry Standards
Global Agri-Food Product Test Standards
Tested Once Accepted Everywhere

The transatlantic harmonization of US and EU regulations, and mutual recognition is carried out through the Transatlantic Economic Partnership (TEP) institutional mechanism. In the TEP, the US and EU are expanding regulatory reciprocity for food safety. Through this transatlantic policy framework, the FDA and the EU Directorate – General of Health and Consumer Protection of the European Union (DG SANCO), and the FDA and the FSA are increasing policy cooperation in the area of food safety. As a result, the US Consumer Product Safety Commission and DG SANCO now have a formal regulatory dialogue for product safety cooperation.

In the transatlantic region, regulatory harmonization frameworks require the adoption of science-based food safety standards, and consumer protection, public health, animal and plant health and GMP inspection regulations. At the same time, regulatory reciprocity requires industry standards harmonization and mandatory GMP for firms and agri-food industries. In the private sector and food industry, standards harmonization requires the convergence of US and EU product safety, consumer protection and conformity assessment requirements through the Transatlantic Business Dialogue (TABD). Through this formal institutional mechanism, the TABD provides the government-to-industry frameworks for conformity assessment and mutual recognition of firm and industry standards. Finally, transatlantic mutual recognition and regulatory cooperation requires the adoption of WTO SPS, Codex, OIE and IPPC standards to govern food safety in national markets and agri-food industries.

Veterinary Public Health and Food Safety

Antibiotics and animal feeds

The regulation of animal livestock health is a growing area of food safety regulation in global meat and livestock industries. The urgent need for rapid harmonization of animal feed and animal livestock health regulations is due to growing food safety and public health threats such as BSE, and deadly pandemic risks, such as avian flu.[31] According to WHO, approximately half of all antibiotics produced by the pharmaceutical industry are used for animal feed, animal diseases and rapid growth promotion in global meat and livestock industries.[32] Currently, the EU regulates the use of antibiotics through mandatory registration and licensing arrangements, while the US monitors the use of antibiotics in animal feeds. However, many nations do not regulate veterinary antibiotics.

In response to these food safety and public health threats, WHO in collaboration with FAO and OIE, is working with governments and veterinary public health authorities to control the use of veterinary antibiotics.[33] In this respect, regulation of animal feed safety requires multi-level and multilateral regulation of global animal livestock and feed industries.[34] Therefore, animal feed safety is addressed in Codex standards for meat hygiene and in maximum residue limits for veterinary drugs and pesticides.

Food Traceability and Mandatory Country-of-Origin Labeling

Mandatory country-of-origin labeling

The globalization of food production requires country-of-origin labeling for national and global food traceability, food recall and biosecurity.[35] From the point of view of independent farmers, ranchers and consumer organizations, country-of-origin labels are required to ensure food product safety since some food-bourne diseases spread through the importation and sale of contaminated meat and produce.[36] In this regard, country-of-origin labels increase the safety and competitiveness of domestic and foreign food products by disclosing accurate information at the point of sale.

In the United States, supermarkets and their industry association, the Grocery Manufacturers of America, oppose mandatory country-of-origin labeling regulations. Through an alliance of the leading food producers – the United Fresh Fruit and Vegetable Association (UFFVA), the National Cattlemen's Beef Association (NCBA), the National Pork Producers Council (NPPC), the National Fisheries Institute (NFI), the Food Marketing Institute (FMI) and the Grocery Manufacturers of America (GMA) – the demands of US consumers are being challenged. In each case, mandatory labeling is opposed due to costs, limited consumer benefit, excessive burdens for small food processors and disagreement over the types of food to be labeled.[37]

In contrast, farmer and consumer organizations correctly argue that country-of-origin labels can help consumers select safe food based on the reputation of food suppliers.[38] For example, the Snow Bird Company, a leading Japanese food supplier, caused the BSE crises by using false 'Japanese Beef' labels on illegally imported Australian and American beef.[39] Eventually, the Snow Bird Company applied for compensation for losses and food liability claims through a government buyback program. As a result of these scandals, Japanese consumers are demanding regulatory change to ensure the 'Made in Japan' label is correct. Ultimately, Japanese consumers want food labels to identify ingredients and processing locations since fish and food products are often produced in other countries, and only processed in Japan.[40]

Traceability: the new system for global animal identification and food recalls

From ancient times to the present, farmers and food traders rely on systems of food traceability and livestock identification.[41] In many ways, the movement and multiple uses of crops and livestock products increases the potential for food safety and public health risks. Furthermore, the vast production, processing and distribution of food and feed crops and animal livestock products across national and global food supply chains confirms the need for food traceability and recall capacity. The following diagram of the movement of corn in food and feed systems (Figure 13.2) illustrates the complexity of product traceability and food recall in agri-food industries.

In the twenty-first century, the globalization of food systems and agri-food industries requires harmonization of animal livestock and food traceability, and food product recall regulations across the entire food chain.[42] As a consequence, the leading global food retailers are rapidly adopting and promoting food traceability as a 'non-competition' issue relative to food safety.[43] The following types of food traceability are promoted

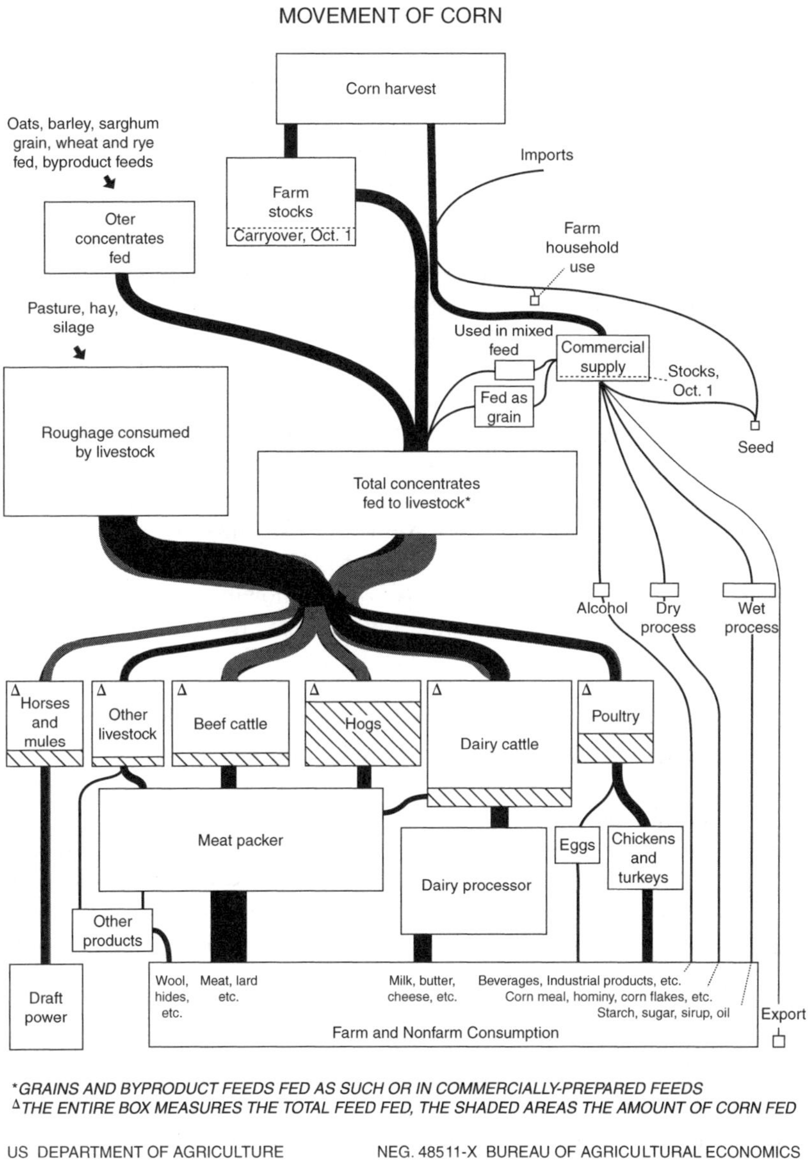

Figure 13.2 Movement of corn in food systems and global food and feed industries

through the Global Food Safety Initiative (GFSI) for companies in the global food retailing industry:

- *traceability* – according to ISO 9001:2000 standards traceability is defined as the ability to trace the history, application and location of products under consideration for product safety and consumer protection purposes
- *chain traceability* – the ability to trace the history, application or location of food products through recorded identification systems across the entire food chain
- *internal traceability* – the tracing of food product lots or batches in one company or unit.[44]

In the FAO, WHO and Codex Alimentarius framework for 'farm to table' and 'boat to throat' governance of food safety, traceability is a critical tool for government regulation and management-based regulation of food safety. In this regard, Codex Alimentarius is now the global framework for the regulation of competition across food systems and industries on behalf of food safety (FAO 1999).[45] The following goals are achieved through mandatory food traceability regulations and standards in global agri-food industries:

- guarantee fast national and global food product withdrawal or food recall to protect consumers and public health
- reduction and minimization of the impact of food safety hazards and food product recalls
- reduction of costs of targeted food product withdrawals and food recalls on specific brands, lots and batches versus an entire agri-food commodity
- proactive system to protect against food terrorism and deliberate sabotage of food industries
- increase consumer confidence through management-based systems of food safety regulation and traceability at the company and industry levels
- establishment of internal logistical and quality information systems to improve efficiency
- strengthen corporate and industry responsibility and liability identification in food companies and global agri-food industries
- protection of company reputation and food brands
- provide reliable information for business, consumers, government inspectors, regulators and financial auditors
- transparent distribution strategies to improve food supply chain efficiency and cooperation.[46]

III RAPID FOOD SAFETY ALERT: THE ROLE OF THE INTERNATIONAL FOOD SAFETY AUTHORITIES NETWORK (INFOSAN)

The globalization of agri-food industries, cross-border food trade and growing food safety risks require collective policy action by food safety regulators. In response to this need, WHO implemented a new International Food Safety Authorities Network (INFOSAN) at the second FAO/WHO Global Forum of Food Safety Regulators that was held in Bangkok, Thailand in October 2004. The creation of INFOSAN complements the existing WHO alert and response system to combat the spread of disease and global public health threats.[47]

The INFOSAN system provides a rapid alert and response system to improve communications among WHO and member countries. Through the INFOSAN network, global food safety information and public health emergencies are identified, verified and communicated to prevent the spread of food-borne diseases such as BSE, avian flu and deliberate bioterrorist contamination of national food systems and agri-food industries. For example, INFOSAN was used to disseminate information on salmonella (June 2004), avian flu (December 2004) and *Enterobacter Sakazakii* in baby food (January 2005).

The organizational and institutional structure of INFOSAN originates in WHO Geneva and works through the regional offices and official contact points in national ministries of health. In order to strengthen the capacity of INFOSAN to protect national, regional and global food systems, the WHO requests the designation of one or more focal points, and one INFOSAN EMERGENCY Contact Point in each country. The following WHO Global INFOSAN Network organizational structure is used for food recalls and collective regulatory policy action by national and regional food safety regulators:

WHO Global INFOSAN Network

- INFOSAN Focal Point in Agricultural Sector
- INFOSAN Focal Point in Health Sector
- INFOSAN Focal Point in Food Safety Authority
- INFOSAN Focal Point in Trade Sector
- INFOSAN Focal Point in Other Sectors.

By February 2005, 135 countries were full participants in INFOSAN, and had designated focal points and INFOSAN EMERGENCY Contact Points. At the present time, the WHO is working to obtain the participation of the remaining member countries and the designation of emergency contact officials. In support of the expansion of INFOSAN, an external advisory system is being developed to provide rapid and timely expert advice and guidance for INFOSAN and INFOSAN Emergency Contact Points. Furthermore, the WHO is preparing formal guidelines for INFOSAN Emergency Contact Points that are reviewed by member governments. Finally, a secure website for INFOSAN Emergency Contact Points is being continually upgraded to strengthen the regulation of food safety, consumer protection and public health in national food systems and global agri-food industries.[48]

IV. MANAGEMENT-BASED REGULATION OF FOOD SAFETY

The growing food safety risks in the transatlantic, OECD and developing countries confirm the need for moral agreement and normative consensus by government regulators, corporate management and global agri-food industries.[49] The failure of competition to prevent food safety hazards, and growing product liability for consumer illness and death, increases the need for management-based regulations.[50] Therefore, regulatory oversight of consumer protection, product safety and public health in global agri-food industries now require management-based regulations.[51]

For example, the USDA is aggressively enforcing food company compliance with the Advanced Meat Recovery (AMR) systems in light of the discovery of BSE in the United States and Canada. The reason for this review of management-based regulations is a USDA survey finding that showed that more than 75 per cent of all US beef plants were not complying with standards prohibiting the use of spinal cord tissue in food products. Figure 13.3 illustrates the challenges of meat inspection regulation in the United States.

Under the new procedures the Food Safety and Inspection Service (FSIS) will discard all mislabeled food and products that are no longer 'meat' due to the presence of spinal cord tissue.[52] However, the need for more government inspectors, in addition to management-based regulations, is now a growing business, public policy and food safety issue. Ultimately, mandatory government regulation and oversight is needed to strengthen management-based regulation.

Best Practices for management-based regulation of global agri-food industries

The governance of food safety requires the harmonization of Best Practices across global agri-food industries. The mandatory use of Best Practices by

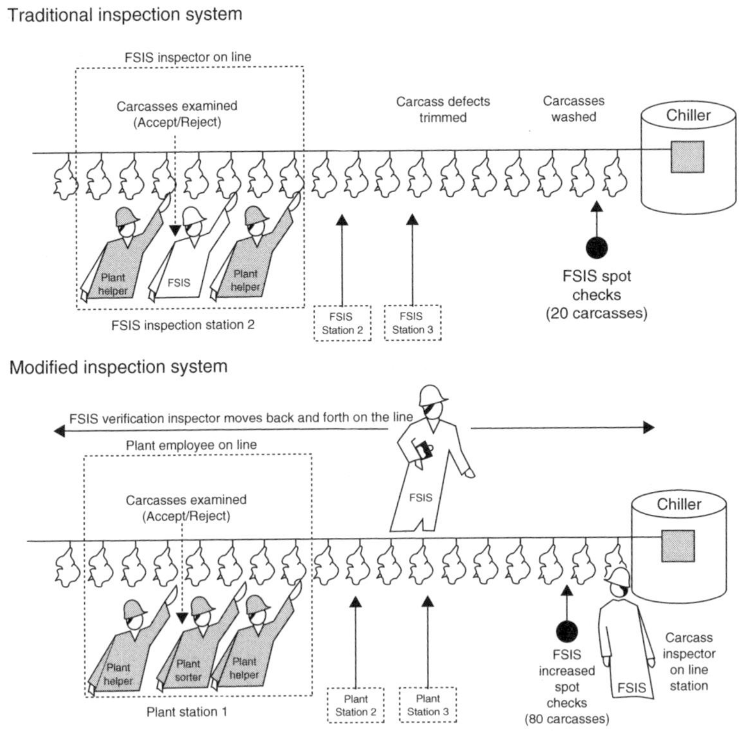

Source: GAO (2001), p. 8.

Figure 13.3 USDA meat inspection: traditional and modified inspection systems on a chicken slaughter line

farmers, agri-business, food processors and global agri-food industries increases food and feed safety across nations.[53]

ISO and HACCP meat, seafood and grain inspection

The major management based regulations, and global agri-food industry standards are HACCP, ISO and Codex Best Practices for GAP, GMP and GHP.[54] As the risk of food contamination and bioterrorist sabotage grows, global grain companies such as Cargill are now upgrading the HACCP inspection processes for foods derived from cereals and grains.[55] Moreover, NAFTA, the EU and transatlantic MRAs require mandatory compliance with HACCP and Best Practices for agricultural and livestock production, food-processing and food safety.[56] Therefore, mandatory compliance with

ISO, HACCP and Best Practices should be assessed relative to economic efficiency and competition in global agri-food industries.[57]

Good Agricultural Practices (GAP) for animal livestock and crop production

The goal of Good Agricultural Practice (GAP) is to strengthen the safety and quality of foods. In the case of animal livestock production, the following outcomes are achieved:

- placement of animal livestock facilities to avoid negative effects on waste management, landscape, environment and animal welfare
- avoidance of biological and chemical contamination of pasture, feed, water and the environment
- frequent monitoring of the health condition of animal livestock, animal feed and water supplies
- prevention of veterinary drug residues and chemicals in animal feeds and the food chain
- minimal use of antibiotics for non-therapeutic use
- integration of animal livestock and agriculture to avoid problems related to waste removal, nutrient loss and greenhouse gas emissions
- development of good records on animal stock acquisitions, breeding, diseases, illness, deaths, sales, feeding plans, feed acquisitions and sales.

In the case of agricultural commodities, GAP guidelines for farmers, agribusinesses and food companies require the following practices to ensure plant health and crop safety;

- use of resistant plant and crop species, crop sequences, and maximum use of biological prevention of pests and diseases
- maintenance of healthy balance between pests, diseases and beneficial organisms
- adoption of organic controls when and where possible
- application of pest and disease forecasting techniques
- minimal use of agrochemicals
- regulation and management of the storage of agrochemicals
- restriction of the use of agrochemicals by trained workers
- strict management of the use and storage of agrochemicals in accordance with safety and maintenance standards
- development of strict and accurate records of agrochemical use in agricultural production.[58]

Good Manufacturing Practices (GMP)

The following regulatory goals and industry standards are emerging as the national and multilateral framework for the governance of food safety in global agri-food industries:

- Stronger and more science-based goals for the assessment, analysis, management and communication of public health and consumer safety risks
- Expansion of the scale and scope of industry regulation relative to food safety
- Shift focus and adoption of mandatory HACCP for firms and industry specific standards
- Mandatory HACCP and performance standards for agri-food products and food industries
- National, regional and global reliance on conformity assessment, product certification and food traceability for GM and non-GM foods across the food chain and agri-food industries
- Increasing requirement for greater transparency for national and regional regulations and
- Shift of regulatory responsibility, liability, compliance and enforcement to exporting countries.[59]

Good animal feed practice

In the case of animal feed safety, FAO launched a Code of Practice for Good Animal Feeding for the production, manufacturing, processing and storage of all animal feeds. The Global Principles for the Containment of Antimicrobial Resistance framework provides regulatory guidelines for the following veterinary public health measures:

- mandatory prescriptions for all antibiotics used for disease control in food-producing animals and livestock
- termination and rapid phasing out of antibiotics for rapid growth and weight gain
- development of national regulatory systems to monitor antibiotic use in food-producing animals and livestock
- mandatory pre-licensing safety evaluation of antibiotics relative to the potential for antibiotic resistance in humans
- monitoring of antibiotic resistance to identify and correct emerging public health and food safety risks
- guidelines for veterinarians to reduce antibiotics in food-producing animals.[60]

Biosecurity regulatory framework for food safety

According to the WHO, the deliberate contamination of food with deadly chemical, radiological and biological contaminants can rapidly spread across national food systems, supply chains and global agri-food industries.[61] Therefore mandatory biosecurity regulation of food firms and agri-food industries is required.[62] The following seamless regulatory framework for biosecurity in national food systems, supply chains and global agri-food industries is unfolding:

- mandatory registration of any factory, warehouse or food business by the owner, operator, or licensed agent in charge of domestic or foreign establishments
- mandatory record-keeping and authorized access to records if there is a risk of food safety hazards, bioterrorist sabotage or serious threat to the health and life of animals and humans
- prior notification of imported foods including information on the product, manufacturer, shipper, grower, country of origin, country of shipment and port of entry destination
- prohibition of food importers and people convicted of felonies related to food production and trade that pose a threat to health and the lives of animals and humans
- clear marking of refused food imports and rejected food at importer and exporter expense with grants to states and Native American tribes to examine, inspect and investigate food
- mandatory detention through the authorization of the FDA to hold food in the event of a serious food safety threat to the public health and animal life
- delegation of authority to government to authorize and commission federal officers to assist in the examination and inspection of food.[63]

V CONCLUSIONS: REGULATED COMPETITION AND FOOD SAFETY

The effective regulation of competition on behalf of food safety, consumer protection, animal livestock and plant health, and public health in global agri-food industries is a major policy challenge for governments in the twenty-first century. As the decade unfolds, food safety is at risk due to cross-border competition, biosecurity threats, agri-food firm consolidation, limited regulatory capacity, industry concentration and unregulated supplier power in developing and developed countries. In this regard, the growing power of transatlantic and Asia-Pacific agri-business and food processors challenge national governments through multi-level lobbying and regulatory capture. As a result, competition in global agri-food industries must be governed in the context of food safety and the collective good of nations.

As the twenty-first century unfolds, regulated competition and multilateral governance of food safety in global agri-food industries requires normative agreement between national governments and industry regulators. Furthermore, regulated competition increasingly requires that agribusiness and global agri-food industries adopt mandatory management-based regulations. In this framework, industrial food production and processing requires mandatory firm and factory level surveillance of food safety hazards. Consequently, antitrust and competition policy enforcement, management-based regulations and corporate responsibility are required to regulate food safety and competition in global agri-food industries. Ultimately, collective policy action by governments, and the regulation of competition, strengthens food safety standards harmonization and the governance of global agri-food industries.

NOTES

1. Vietor, Richard (1994), *Contrived Competition – Regulation and Deregulation in America*, Cambridge, MA: Belknap/Harvard University Press, pp. 2–22.
2. According to Professor Razeen Sally at the London School of Economics, economic liberty and freedom is addressed by Adam Smith within the context of, market forces, free trade and a rule of law to uphold property rights and enforce contract. See Sally, Razeen (1998), *Classical Liberalism and International Economic Order: Studies in Theory and Intellectual History*, London: Routledge.
3. Hahn, Robert W. (1996), *Risks, Costs and Lives Saved: Getting Better Results from Regulation*, New York and London: Oxford University Press.
4. Sally (1998).
5. Buchanan, James M. (1978), 'Markets, states and the extent of morals', *American Economic Review*, **68** (2): pp. 364–8.
6. Ibid., pp. 199–216. Failure to regulate the power large corporations and industry interests can result in the collapse of socio-economic systems and markets.
7. Ibid., p. 179. At the global level, rational choice theory is inadequate and fails to explain regulatory and policy capture by large corporate and industry interests. As a result, the collective good is lost due to the exertion of political and economic power by big corporate and industry interests.
8. Etzioni, Amitai (1988), *The Moral Dimension*, New York and London: Free Press/Macmillan, p. 199. According to Etzioni, competition is a form of market conflict that must be contained and encapsulated with rules and moral principles to achieve the collective goals of individuals and communities.
9. Connor, John M. (2003), *The Changing Structure of Global Food Markets: Dimensions, Effects and Policy Implications*, OECD Conference on Changing Dimensions of the Food Economy: Exploring the Policy Issues, 6–7 February, The Hague, pp. 1–3.
10. Connor, John M. (ed.) (1985), *The Food Manufacturing Industries: Structure, Strategies, Performance, and Policies*, Lexington, MA: Lexington Books.
11. The rise of FDI and cross-border competition in Asia-Pacific agri-food industries from

the 1990s onwards increases the need for regional governance of food safety. While US and EU agri-food companies and processors such as Nestlé, Grand Metropolitan and Unilever are major competitors in Asian-Pacific food markets, large world-class Asian companies are now competing for growing shares of regional markets.

12. Lopez, Rigoberto A. (ed.) (2002), 'Market power and/or efficiency: a structural approach', *Review of Industrial Organization*, **20**: 115–26.
13. Bolling, Curis, Charles Handy and Steve Neff (1997), 'US direct investment in the APEC food-processing sector', *Economic Research Service/USDA*, APEC/WRS-97-4, Washington, DC: USDA.
14. Connor (2003), pp. 5–6.
15. Ibid., pp. 163–4, 171.
16. Wells, Wyatt (2002), *Antitrust and the Formation of the Postwar World*, New York: Columbia University Press.
17. Concerns over systemic risks to consumers and the safety of national food and agriculture systems are increasing due to growing consumer demand for more diverse foods, and increasing global food trade.
18. Lopez, Rigoberto A. and Carmen Liron-Espara (2003), 'Social welfare and market power efficiency trade off in US food processing: a note', *Journal of Agricultural and Food Industrial Organization*, **1** (1): Article 5.
19. Whitley, John (2002), 'The gains and losses from agricultural concentration: critical survey of the literature', *Journal of Agricultural and Food Industrial Organization*, **1** (1): Article 6.
20. Sutton, John (2003), *Understanding the Rise in Global Concentration in the Agri-Food Sector: A Background Paper*, OECD Conference on Changing Dimensions of the Food Economy: Exploring the Policy Issues, 6–7 February, The Hague. Also see chapters 1–3 of Sutton, John (1991), *Sunk Costs and Market Structure*, Cambridge, MA: MIT Press.
21. Heffernan, William, M. Hendrickson and R. Gronski (1999), *Consolidation in the Food and Agriculture System – Report to the National Farmers Union*, 5 February, Columbia, MO: Department of Rural Sociology, University of Missouri. p. 1. Dobson, Paul W. (2003), *Buyer Power in Food Retailing: The European Experience*, OECD Conference on Changing Dimensions of the Food Economy: Exploring the Policy Issues, 6–7 February, The Hague, pp. 1–2.
22. WHO (2005b), *Modern Food Biotechnology, Human Health and Development: An Evidence-Based Study*, 23 June, Food Safety Department, World Health Organization, Geneva: WHO, pp. 3–10.
23. See National Farmers Union charts on the concentration in US Agricultural Markets, February 2002, and Livestock Market Reform slides on the Legislation link of NFU website, http://www.nfu.org.
24. Dobson (2003).
25. Ibid., p. 3.
26. Alfred D. Chandler Jr, (1986), 'The evolution of modern global competition', *Competition in Global Industries*, Boston, MA: Harvard Business School Press, in M. Porter (ed.), pp. 405–47. According to Chandler at the Harvard Business School, the rise of MNCs and global companies is a turning point in globalization of industry structure and the conduct of competition. In addition to cross-border and global market expansion through subsidiaries and manufacturing facilities, American management increased economic efficiencies through economies of scale and scope, rationalization of supply chains and the use of technology to increase cost savings.
27. Kotler, Philip, Somkid Jatusripitak and Suvit Maesincee (1997), *The Marketing of Nations*, New York: Free Press, pp. 33–50. According to Kotler, developing nations face barriers to market entry and effective competition in global markets because of the weak infrastructure, regulatory and public policy processes, and weak recognition as legitimate producers of high-quality, value-added products and services.
28. WHO and tobacco industry and WHO and sugar lobby.
29. Lazer, David (2001), 'Regulatory interdependence and international governance', *Journal of European Policy*, **8** (3): 474–92.

30. Using the Heckscher–Ohlin product life-cycle model, Michael Porter acknowledged that each nation has comparative advantages that must be leveraged through corporate strategy and policies that reward innovations in global markets. Porter, Michael (1990), *The Competitive Advantage of Nations*, New York: Free Press. Yoffie, David B. (ed.) (1993), *Beyond Free Trade – Firms, Governments and Global Competition*, Boston, MA: Harvard Business School Press, pp. 7–9. In addition, globalization is in fact a form of oligopolistic competition that requires strategic alliances, policy cooperation and defensive countermoves by firms, industries and governments at the national and regional levels. Ibid. pp. 434–7.
31. Baros, L.O. (2001), 'Recent developments in animal identification and the traceability of animal products in international trade', *Review of Science and Technology*, **20** (2): 640–51.
32. See WHO 'Use of antimicrobials outside human medicine', at http://www.who.int/emc/diseases/zoo/antimicrobial.html.
33. Ibid.
34. FAO, press release 97/24, 'Code of practice for good animal feeding proposed to counter health threat to humans from contaminated meat, FAO reports', 11 June 1997. Also see, FAO press release 99/36, 'FAO urges better control of animal feed contamination problems, 10 June 1999.
35. Organic Consumers Association (2003), 'US food giants fight country origin labeling', by Scott Kilman, *Wall Street Journal*, 26 June, http://www.organicconsumers.org/ge/062303_origin_labeling.cfm.
36. The Honorable Tom Harkin (2002), Americans for country of origin labeling – an alliance of food producers and consumer advocates', United States Senate, Washington, DC, 6 March.
37. See the United Chamber of Commerce – Country of Origin Labeling, Government and Legal Issues website, at http://www.uschamber.com/issues/index/agriculture/origin.htm.
38. The Honorable Tom Harkin (2002).
39. See *BBC News*, Japanese firm admits BSE cash scam', BBC World Business Report, Doreen Walton, 24 January 2002, at http://news.bbc.co.uk/2/hi/business/1779666.stm.
40. *Food Chemical News*, 1 September 2003, **45** (29).
41. MacDonald, H.A. and Sheridan, M.K. (2001),'Traceability of animals and animal products', *Review of Science and Technology*, **20** (2): 420–5.
42. Vitello, D.J. and A.M. Thaler (2001), 'Animal identification: links to food safety', *Review of Science and Technology*, **20** (2): 598–604.
43. WHO (2004), *Joint FAO/WHO Workshop on Enterobacter Sakazakii and other Microorganisms in Powdered Infant Formula*, Geneva: WHO.
44. See the Global Food Safety Initiative (2004), *Guidance Document – Fourth Edition*, Paris: Global Food Safety Initiative (GFSI), at http://www.ciesnet.com/pdf/globalfood/CFSI_Guidance_Document_4th_edition.pdf.
45. FAO (1999), *Understanding the Codex Alimentarius*, Food Agriculture Organization of the United Nations and the World Health Organization, Rome: FAO.
46. Ibid., p. 8.
47. INFOSAN was created to WHO provide national, regional and global food recall capacity. See WHO (2005a), *International Food Safety Authorities Network (INFOSAN)*, 28 February, Geneva: WHO.
48. Ibid. Also see INFOSAN website, at http://www.who.int./foodsafety/fs_management/infosan/en/.
49. Gunningham, N. and J. Rees (1997), 'Industry self regulation: an institutional perspective', *Journal of Law and Policy*, 19: 363–414.
50. Unnevehr, Laurian, Lawrence Haddad and Christopher Delgado (2003), '*Food Safety Issues in Food Security and Food Trade: Food Safety Policy Issues for Developing Countries*, 2020 Vision for Food, Agriculture and the Environment, Focus 10, Brief 17 of 17,Washington, DC: International Food Policy Research Institute.
51. Coglianese, Cary and David Lazar (2002), *Management Based Regulation: Prescribing Private Management to Achieve Public Goals*, Working Paper 02-11, Washington, DC:

Brookings Institution. According to the authors, food safety regulations can and often do have multiple purposes which include information collection to improve the monitoring of product safety and consumer health risks. The collection of data to certify compliance with regulatory standards also requires the collection of information to enforce regulatory standards. When technology and performance based regulations are not the best solution for the governance of firms and industries, innovative management-based approaches are needed. Also see, Coglianese, Cary, Jennifer Nash and Todd Olmstead (2002), *Performance Based Regulation: Prospects and Limitations in Health, Safety and Environmental Regulations*, Working Paper, John F. Kennedy School of Government.

52. The USDA will not allow products with spinal cord tissue to be labeled as meat or food.
53. Global Food Safety Initiative (2004), pp. 1–18.
54. Organic Consumers Association (2003).
55. FAO (2001), *Manual on the Application of the HACCP System in Mycotoxin Prevention and Control*, FAO and International Atomic Energy Agency, FAO Food and Nutrition Paper 73, Rome: FAO, pp. 1–41.
56. The Canadian Food Inspection Agency is making HACCP program registration, implementation and compliance mandatory for all domestic and imported meat and poultry producers in Canada.
57. Muth, Mary K., Michael K. Wohlgenant, Shawn A. Karns and Donald Anderson (2003), 'Explaining plant exit in US meat and poultry industries', *Journal of Agricultural and Food Industrial Organization*, **1** (1): Article 7. According to the authors, US pathogen reduction and HACCP food regulations may increase costs for meat and poultry producers and result in corporate failure and industry exit.
58. FAO (2003), *Committee on Agriculture – Development of a Framework for Good Agricultural Practices – Seventeenth Session*, 4–31 March, Rome: FAO, at http://www.fao.org/DOCREP/MEETING/006/Y8704e.HTM. Also see Global Food Safety Initiative (2004), pp. 19–20.
59. Global Food Safety Initiative (2004), pp. 21–8. Also see Caswell, Julie A. (2003), *Food Safety Standards and Regulation: Implications for Developing Countries*, Focus 10, Brief 4 of 7, 2020 Vision for Food, Agriculture, and the Environment, Washington, DC: International Food Policy Research Institute.
60. FAO (1997), *Animal Feeding and Food Safety – Report of an FAO Expert Consultation*, 10–14 March, Rome: FAO.
61. WHO (2002), *Food Safety Issues – Terrorist Threats to Food – Guidelines for Establishing and Strengthening Prevention and Response Systems*, Geneva, pp. 4–16.
62. See WHO (2002), *Fifty-fifth World Health Assembly Adoption of Resolution WHA 55.16 on May 18, 2002*, Geneva: WHO.
63. Ibid.

REFERENCES

Baron, David P. (2003), *Business and Its Environment*, 4th edition, Englewood Cliffs, NJ: Prentice-Hall.

Baros, L.O. (2001), 'Recent developments in animal identification and the traceability of animal products in international trade', *Review of Science and Technology*, **20** (2): 640–51.

BBC News (2002), 'Japanese firm admits BSE cash scam', BBW World Business Report, Doreen Walton, 24 January, at http://news.bbc.co.uk/2/hi/business/1779666.stm.

Bolling, Chris, Charles Handy and Steve Neff (1997), 'US direct investment in the APEC food-processing sector', *Economic Research Service/USDA*, APEC/WRS-97-4, Washington, DC: USDA.

Buchanan, James M. (1978), 'Markets, states and the extent of morals', *American Economic Review*, **68** (2): 364–8.

Buchholz, Eugene (1992), *Business Environment and Public Policy*, 4th edition, New York: Simon and Schuster.

Caswell, Julie A. (2003), *Food Safety Standards and Regulation: Implication for Developing Countries*, Focus 10, Brief 4 of 7, 2020 Vision for Food Agriculture, and the Environment, Washington, DC: International Food Policy Research Institute.

Coglianese, Cary and David Lazar (2002), *Management Based Regulation: Prescribing Private Management to Achieve Public Goals*, Working Paper 02-11, Washington, DC: Brookings Institution.

Coglianese, Cary, Jennifer Nash and Todd Olmstead (2002), *Performance Based Regulation: Prospects and Limitations in Health, Safety and Environmental Regulations*, Working Paper, John F. Kennedy School of Government, Cambridge, MA: Harvard University.

Connor, John M. (ed.) (1985), *The Food Manufacturing Industries: Structure, Strategies, Performance, and Policies*, Lexington, MA: Lexington Books.

Connor, John M. (2003), *The Changing Structure of Global Food Markets: Dimensions, Effects and Policy Implications*, OECD Conference on Changing Dimensions of the Food Economy: Exploring the Policy Issues, 6–7 February, The Hague.

Dobson, Paul W. (2003), *Buyer Power in Food Retailing: The European Experience*, OECD Conference on Changing Dimensions of the Food Economy: Exploring the Policy Issues, 6–7 February, The Hague.

Etzioni, Amitai (1988), *The Moral Dimension*, New York and London: Free Press/Macmillan.

FAO (1997), 'Code of practice for good animal feeding proposed to counter health threat to humans from contaminated meat, FAO reports', press release 97/24, 11 June.

FAO (1999a), *Understanding the Codex Alimentarius*, Food Agriculture Organization of the United Nations and the World Health Organization, Rome: FAO.

FAO (1999b), 'FAO urges better control of animal feed contamination problems', press release 99/36, 10 June.

FAO (2001), *Manual on the Application of the HACCP System in Mycotoxin Prevention and Control*, FAO and International Atomic Energy Agency, FAO Food and Nutrition Paper 73, Rome: FAO.

FAO (2003), *Committee on Agriculture – Development of a framework for Good Agricultural Practices – Seventeenth Session*, 4–31 March, Rome: FAO, http://www.fao.org/DOCREP/MEETING/006/48704e.HTM.

Food Chemical News (2003), 1 September, **45** (29).

GAO (2001), *Food Safety – Weaknesses in Meat and Poultry Inspection Pilot Should Be Addressed Before Implementation*, Washington, DC: GAO.

Global Food Safety Initiative (2004), *Guidance Document – Fourth Edition*. Paris: Global Food Safety Initiative (GFSI), http://www.ciesnet.com/pdf/globalfood/CFSI_Guidance_Document_4th_edition.pdf.

Government Accounting Office (GAO) (2001), *Food Safety – Weakness in Meat and Poultry Inspection Pilot should be Addressed before Implementation*, Washington, DC: Government Accounting Office.

Gunningham, N. and J. Rees (1997) 'Industry self regulation: an institutional perspective', *Journal of Law and Policy*, **19** (4): 363–414.

Hahn, Robert W. (1996), *Risks, Costs and Lives Saved: Getting Better Results From Regulation*, New York and London: Oxford University Press.
Harkin, The Honorable Tom (2002), 'Americans for country of origin labelling – an alliance of food producers and consumer advocates', Unites States Senate, Washington, DC, 6 March.
Heffernan, Dr William, M. Hendrickson and R. Gronski (1999), *Consolidation in the Food and Agriculture System – Report to the National Farmers Union*, 5 February, Columbia, MO: Department of Rural Sociology, University of Missouri.
INFOSAN website, at http://www.who.int/foodsafety/fs_management/infosan/en/.
Kotler, Philip, Somkid Jatusripitak and Suvit Maesincee (1997), *The Marketing of Nations*, New York: Free Press.
Lazer, David (2001), 'Regulatory interdependence and international governance', *Journal of European Policy*, **8** (3): 474–92.
Lopez, Rigoberto A. (ed.) (2002) 'Market power and/or efficiency: a structural approach', *Review of Industrial Organization*, **20** (2): 115–26.
Lopez, Rigoberto, A. and Carmen Liron-Espara (2003), 'Social welfare and market power efficiency trade off in US food processing: a note', *Journal of Agricultural and Food Industrial Organization*, **1** (1): Article 5.
MacDonald, H.A. and Sheridan, M.K. (2001),'Traceability of animals and animal products', *Review of Science and Technology*, **20** (2): 420–5
Muth, Mary K., Michael K. Wohlgenant, Shawn A. Karns and Donald Anderson (2003), 'Explaining plant exit in US meat and poultry industries', *Journal of Agricultural and Food Industrial Organization*, **1** (1): Article 7.
National Farmers Union website, at http://www.nfu.org.
National Farmers Union (2002), 'Concentration of Agricultural Markets – Legislation', available at http://www.nfu.org.
National Farmers Union Livestock Market Reform, at http://www.nfu.org.
Organic Consumers Association (2003), 'US food giants fight country of origin labeling', by Scott Kilman, *Wall Street Journal*, 26 June, at http://www.organic-consummers.org/ge/062303_origin_labeling.cfm.
Porter, Michael (ed.) (1986), *Competition in Global Industries*, Boston, MA: Harvard Business School Press.
Porter, Michael (1990), *The Competitive Advantage of Nations*, New York: Free Press.
Sally, Razeen (1998), *Classical Liberalism and International Economic Order: Studies in Theory and Intellectual History*, London: Routledge.
Sutton, John (1991), *Sunk Costs and Market Structure*, Cambridge, MA: MIT Press.
Sutton, John (2003), *Understanding the Rise in Global Concentration in the Agri-Food Sector: A Background Paper*, OECD Conference on Changing Dimensions of the Food Economy: Exploring the Policy Issues, 6–7 February, The Hague.
Unnevehr, Laurian, Lawrence Haddad and Christopher Delgado (2003), *Food Safety Issues in Food Security and Food Trade: Food Safety Policy Issues for Developing Countries*, 2020 Vision for Food, Agriculture and the Environment, Focus 10, Brief 17 of 17, Washington, DC: International Food Policy Research Institute.
Vietor, Richard (1994), *Contrived Competition – Regulation and Deregulation in America*, Cambridge, MA: Belknap/Harvard University Press.
Vitello, D.J. and A.M. Thaler (2001), 'Animal identification: links to food safety', *Review of Science and Technology*, **20** (2): 598–604.

Wells, Wyatt (2002), *Antitrust and the Formation of the Postwar World*, New York: Columbia University Press.

Whitley, John (2002), 'The gains and losses from agricultural concentration: critical survey of the literature', *Journal of Agricultural and Food Industrial Organization*, **1** (1): Article 6.

WHO (2002), *Fifty-fifth World Health Assembly Adoption of resolution WHA 55.16 on May 18, 2002*, Geneva: WHO.

WHO (2002), *Food Safety Issues – Terrorist Threats to Food – Guidelines for Establishing and Strengthening Prevention and Response Systems*, Geneva, pp. 4–16.

WHO (2004), *Joint FAO/WHO Workshop on Enterobacter Sakazakii and other Microorganisms in Powdered Infant Formula*, Geneva: WHO.

WHO (2005a), *International Food Safety Authorities Network (INFOSAN)*, 28 February, Geneva: WHO.

WHO (2005b), *Modern Food Biotechnology, Human Health and Development: An Evidence-Based Study*, 23 June, Food Safety Department, World Health Organization, Geneva: WHO, pp. 3–10.

Yoffie, David (ed.) (1993), *Beyond Free Trade – Firms, Governments and Global Competition*, Boston, MA: Harvard Business School Press.

14. Conclusions: transatlantic and multilateral governance of food safety in global agri-food industries

Reba A. Carruth

I GLOBAL GOVERNANCE OF FOOD SAFETY

In conclusion, the globalization of agri-food industries increases the regulatory and moral responsibilities of government to citizens and nations in the twenty-first century.[1] As the twenty-first century unfolds, agriculture and food production are the foundation for socio-economic development and global market integration. The importance of food industry globalization lies in the growing dependence of citizens and nations on market forces for safe food.[2] However, small independent farmers in the OECD and developing countries now face oligopolistic competition in national food systems and global food markets. Consequently, the primary role and responsibility of farmers for food safety is under threat.[3]

In this context, the transatlantic, NAFTA, Western Hemisphere, African, SAARC and Asia-Pacific chapters show that free trade and market competition are insufficient to protect food safety.[4] Therefore, national governments have a moral obligation to implement and enforce strict mandatory food safety, public health, and consumer protection policies. To achieve this goal, national governments must work collectively at the regional and global level to strengthen management based regulation of agri-food industries and enforce competition and antitrust regulations within and across food systems and markets.[5]

Finally, national governments and multilateral institutions must uphold the socio-economic roles of farmers and the collective good of nations in the twenty-first century.[6] The governance of food safety in national and global agri-food industries requires the mobilization of resources to uphold the traditional role of farmers, and the regulation of agriculture, animal livestock health and plant health. To accomplish this goal, multi-level, multi-jurisdictional and multilateral frameworks for regulatory harmonization are needed to regulate global agri-food industries.[7] Therefore, stronger democracy, transparency and multilateral institutional mechanisms are needed for the harmonization of food safety, consumer protection, animal livestock and plant health, and public health regulations.[8]

II TRANSATLANTIC AND REGIONAL GOVERNANCE OF FOOD SAFETY

Transatlantic Cooperation and Multilateral Food Standards Harmonization

In the global food system, the transatlantic region is the driving force in the regulation of competition and food safety in global agri-food industries.[9] In this regard, the United States and the European Union are the core nations in the multilateral regulation of food safety.[10] Ultimately, transatlantic mutual recognition, HACCP and GMP standards harmonization are needed to regulate food safety in global agri-food industries.[11] Therefore, regulatory harmonization and institutional cooperation objectives between the US, EU and the multilateral food safety standards of Codex, OIE and IPPC are needed to achieve the following goals:[12]

- development of common transatlantic food safety policy positions to support the regulatory capacity-building work, biosecurity and food safety standards programs of FAO, WHO, Codex Alimentarius, OIE and IPPC
- removal of transatlantic regulatory competition in the area of food safety and the regulation of farming, animal livestock health, plant health, modern biotechnology, agri-business, food companies and agri-food industries
- development of complementary business and public policy frameworks for the regulation of transatlantic food companies and agri-food industries
- strengthening of the TEP, TACD and TABD frameworks, and the development of comparable regulatory reciprocity, GMP and industry standards harmonization frameworks for the Western Hemisphere, Africa, South Asia and the Asia-Pacific regions
- development of strong domestic leadership and policies to support and regulate small, independent and industrial farming, agriculture, food system and rural community development in the context of national and regional food safety policies
- consolidation and coordination of regional market integration and free trade agreements to rapidly and fully integrate emerging countries

in Eastern Europe, the Western Hemisphere, Africa, South Asia and the Asia-Pacific regions into the global agri-food industry, food safety standards-setting and regulatory capacity-building activities of Codex Alimentarius, OIE and the IPPC in accordance with the WTO SPS Agreement.

In the years ahead, the transatlantic region's central role in regulatory reciprocity, mutual recognition, management-based regulation, Best Practices, industry standards and multilateral harmonization will continue to grow in global agri-food industries.[13] Therefore, transatlantic support and partnership is needed for regulatory capacity-building in developing countries and multilateral regulatory harmonization with Codex standards.[14]

Regulatory Harmonization and Regional Free Trade Agreements

In the global market system, APEC, ASEAN, SAARC, SADC, NEPAD, the EU, NAFTA, MERCOSUR, CARICOM, CAFTA and the Andean Community are developing regional frameworks for food safety standards and multilateral regulatory harmonization. These regional regulatory policy cooperation, free trade and market integration trends are necessary due to the rapid integration of OECD and developing country food systems, and global agri-food industries.[15] Therefore, regional regulatory capacity-building requires harmonization of WTO SPS/TBT, Codex Alimentarius, OIE and IPPC food safety standards.[16]

As the decade unfolds, the Western Hemisphere is embarking on a historic phase of free trade that requires the rapid harmonization of national food safety regulations. In the Western Hemisphere, consumer protection and welfare maximization, food safety, public health, animal livestock health, plant health and public health regulations are highly developed in the NAFTA region. Therefore, comparable regional regulatory systems are needed in CARICOM, the Andean Community, CAFTA, MERCOSUR and the pending FTAA which serve as critical components of the global food safety system and agri-food industries.

In the Western Hemisphere, the role of regulated competition is becoming increasingly important as the FTAA unfolds. As the launch of the FTAA draws closer, PAHO/WHO is collaborating with national governments, the FDA and USDA to harmonize food safety regulations, and to establish regional infrastructure for inspection, HACCP process control programs in national food systems and regional agri-food industries. As a consequence, PAHO/WHO is strengthening the role of COPAIA as the regional framework for food safety regulation in the Western Hemisphere.

The Asia-Pacific region represents a vast and growing area of food demand and production in global agri-food industries. However, diverse national regulatory systems and limited regional regulatory capacity threaten food safety, consumer protection and public health in national food systems and global agri-food industries. In the Asia-Pacific region, developed nations in the region, such as Japan, Australia, New Zealand and Singapore, have strong regulatory systems and food safety frameworks. However, the strategic importance of food and agricultural imports and global food exports for socio-economic development in countries such as China and Thailand, underscore the importance and urgency of regulatory capacity-building and Codex standards harmonization in the Asia-Pacific region (Caswell 2003).

In the Asia-Pacific region, collective policy action for food safety is emerging through the APEC and ASEAN regional frameworks. In both, regional policy cooperation frameworks, Asia-Pacific governments are increasingly concerned with food safety impacts on food trade, rising FDI by transatlantic-based food companies, GM food safety and the competitiveness of labor-intensive farming and regional agri-food industries. In this regard, Asian-Pacific governments, APEC and ASEAN are working in cooperation with FAO, WHO and Codex to strengthen the regulatory capacity for food safety, animal livestock health, plant health and public health in food systems across the region. In this context, ASEAN and APEC provide the framework for regional regulatory capacity-building and harmonization with Codex, OIE and IPPC standards.

In the South Asian region, regulatory cooperation for food safety is carried out through SAARC in cooperation with FAO, WHO and Codex. The launch of SAFTA, and increasing dependence on expanding food trade in US and EU markets and global agri-food industries requires food safety standards harmonization with Codex, OIE, IPPC and the WTO SPS Agreement. Consequently, South Asian food producers and agri-food industries are rapidly moving to adopt ISO, GMP and HACCP food-processing standards to raise the quality and competitiveness of South Asian food products in transatlantic markets and global agri-food industries (Porter 1990).

Currently, SAARC governments, food safety regulators and food industries are working with FAO, WHO and Codex to implement regulatory reforms and to develop scientific risk assessment, risk management and risk communications capacity at the national and regional levels. In this regard, the Government of India is strengthening the role of national and regional Codex committees, and is working to increase the participation of SAARC countries in multilateral food safety meetings and international standard-setting processes.

In the African region, the African Union/NEPAD and SADC provide regional institutional mechanisms for food safety capacity-building and regulatory harmonization with the WTO SPS Agreement and Codex, OIE and IPPC standards. As the century unfolds, the WHO is working in cooperation with African governments to develop and strengthen national food safety systems, regulatory capacity and the safety of African food markets. Through the development of food safety capacity, African governments are able to strengthen food safety, consumer protection and the public health of African citizens. In turn, African farmers and agri-food producers are able to effectively compete in value added food processing industries in the US and the EU, and global agri-food industries.

At the present time, Morocco, South Africa, Kenya and SADC countries have the most advanced regulatory and market governance systems for food safety in the African region. In this regard, the pending transatlantic free trade agreements between the US and SACU, US and Morocco and AGOA, and the EU, Morocco, SADC and Kenya, provide economic incentives for regulatory capacity-building, food safety standards harmonization and HACCP compliance in African countries.

III MULTILATERAL REGULATORY HARMONIZATION OF FOOD SAFETY

The Role of FAO, WHO, Codex Alimentarius, OIE and IPPC

In the twenty-first century, FAO, WHO, Codex Alimentarius, OIE and IPPC, now serve as the multilateral framework for the harmonization of agri-food and animal livestock safety standards. The benefits of multilateral food safety standards harmonization through FAO, WHO, Codex Alimentarius, OIE and IPPC are as follows;

- governments work with a specific set of science-based regulatory standards for risk assessment, risk analysis, risk management and risk communication
- requirements for state-of-the-art food inspection procedures, certification and enforcement systems, mobilization of technical, financial and regulatory resources at national, regional and global levels are standardized
- food safety regulations and institutions have priority and intensive focus by governments
- common nomenclature to facilitate collective policy action by governments and food regulators is available

- common standards for food inspection auditing, written reports and qualification of auditors, and common standards for quality systems and GMP requirements are developed
- confidence-building at the national, regional and multilateral levels among food safety regulatory authorities, institutions, industry standards and market governance systems is achieved
- a common framework for the establishment of equivalence between national and regional food safety regulatory authorities can be developed to facilitate the harmonization of regulations.[17]

BOX 14.1 MULTILATERAL REGULATORY HARMONIZATION FRAMEWORK FOR FOOD SAFETY

MULTILATERAL INSTITUTIONS – GLOBAL REGULATORY STANDARDS
WTO SPS Agreement
FAO, WHO-Codex Alimentarius – OIE – IPPC
REGIONS, REGIONAL INSTITUTIONS and MARKET SYSTEMS
The Americas – Western Hemisphere, NAFTA, MERCOSUR, CARICOM, Andean Group, Central American Free Trade Area
Europe – European Union
Asia-Pacific – APEC, ASEAN
South Asia – SAARC
Africa – African Union/NEPAD, SADC
Codex Regional Committees
NATION-STATES – NATIONAL GOVERNMENTS
Food Safety Regulators
Public Health Authorities
Animal Livestock Health Regulators
Plant Health Regulators
Food and Agriculture Industry Standards
Antitrust and Competition Policy Authorities
Consumer Protection
Farmer Organizations
Codex National Committees
STATES – PROVINCES – LOCAL GOVERNMENTS

In the twenty-first century, Codex, OIE and IPPC food safety standards increasingly focus on food production, processing and retailing practices in global agri-food industries.[18] In this respect the Joint FAO/WHO regional and global food safety regulator forums are emerging as institutional mechanisms for greater collective action in support of regulatory harmonization. However, the growing need for seamless food safety and biosecurity regulatory systems requires rapid regulatory harmonization and institutional convergence. In turn systematic enforcement and verification of compliance by governments, farmers, agri-business, food companies and agri-food industries must be implemented across national, regional and global food systems and supply chains. Therefore, Codex, OIE and IPPC must work in partnership with the US, EU and OECD countries to accelerate regulatory policy cooperation, capacity-building, mutual recognition and institutional convergence in developing countries and regions.

Management-Based Regulation of Food Safety in Global Agri-Food Industries

The global agri-food market system is increasingly characterized by the provision of food products as private goods for individual consumption and the collective good of nations. In this model, individual self-interest and 'rational choice' affect consumption in food markets.[19] However, the true historical reality is that national food industries provide public goods for citizens, societies and nations.[20] On this point, the previous chapters show that food safety regulation in the transatlantic region and OECD countries requires management-based regulations and corporate responsibility. Therefore, globalization of agri-food industries is accelerating theCadoption of HACCP process inspection, ISO standards and Best Practices for GMP, GAP and GHP in the Western Hemisphere Africa, Asia-Pacific and South Asian regions.

Ultimately, mandatory standards for management-based regulation must be harmonized to strengthen food safety in global agri-food industries.[21] Through the adoption of mandatory regulations and industry standards, governments are increasing the security of national food systems and global agri-food industries.[22] In this respect, the strengthening of corporate responsibility, and firm and industry self-regulation by agri-business, food processors and global agri-food industries, increases food and feed safety and quality across nations.[23]

Transatlantic and Multilateral Cooperation for Food Safety

The harmonization of national, transatlantic, regional and multilateral systems of food safety regulation is required to govern food safety in global agri-food industries. The benefit of this multi-level, multi-jurisdictional and multilateral system is comprehensive and seamless regulation across national food systems, regional free trade areas and global agri-food industries (Lazer 2001). The absence of collective regulatory action by governments increases consumer, public health and biosecurity risks from food safety hazards. At the same time, regulatory capture and market failure in national food systems and global agri-food industries can have catastrophic impacts on food safety and food security in all nations. Therefore, governments must reach normative consensus on food safety, competition and regulation in global agri-food industries in the twenty-first century.

As the decade unfolds, regulatory policy reform, regional institutional convergence and the strengthening of independent food safety regulators confirm the success of transatlantic and multilateral food safety frameworks. In this respect, the chapters of this book confirm the need for immediate multilateral regulatory harmonization with Codex Alimentarius, OIE and IPPC standards and WTO SPS/TBT Agreement requirements. Ultimately, multilateral regulatory harmonization requires transatlantic policy cooperation and financial support for capacity-building, mutual recognition, GMP and HACCP capability in developing countries, free trade agreements and regions.

Finally, Codex, OIE and IPPC must strengthen their partnership with transatlantic governments, multilateral aid organizations and global agri-food industries to implement a ten-year plan for regional regulatory reform, food safety capacity-building and management-based regulation in each nation, region and free trade group in Europe, the Americas, South Asia, the Asia-Pacific and Africa. Through collective policy action by governments and multilateral institutions, global consumers will be protected from systemic food safety risks and bioterrorist threats in global agri-food industries in the twenty-first century.

IV CONCLUSION: REGULATORY HARMONIZATION: THE EMERGING CONCEPTUAL MODEL FOR MARKET REGULATION AND GOVERNANCE OF GLOBAL INDUSTRIES

From a conceptual point of view, the regulatory harmonization policy model provides a pragmatic framework for understanding the governance of markets and society in the context of globalization. To be specific, this conceptual model confirms the central role of socio-economic goals, normative consensus and institutional convergence as the requirements for effective regulation of firms, industry and global markets. At the same time, the regulatory harmonization model provides a framework for the assessment of domestic and external policy and market forces as they affect consumer protection, welfare maximization and the control of the unintended externalities of economic production. In this respect, regulatory harmonization is the emerging framework for the strengthening of government roles and responsibilities to citizens and nations in the twenty-first century.

In contrast to traditional theories of economic and market regulation, the regulatory harmonization model confirms the need for multi-level, multilateral and multi-jurisdictional policy cooperation. Without question, nations and national governments remain the basic units of order and governance in an age of globalization. However, the ability of national governments to rule and govern firms, markets and civil society depends on the regulatory capacity of other countries and regions. In this respect, the growing role of regional and global regulatory forums, and collective action for food safety, consumer protection and public health through global product recalls and rapid alert systems confirm the validity of multilateral regulatory harmonization. In turn, mandatory management-based regulations, industry standards, Best Practices and market-based governance mechanisms now require verification and enforcement by national governments through regional and global certification bodies.

In many ways, the chapters of this book confirm the conceptual power, intellectual rigor and fundamental relevance of the Structural School model of public interests regulation of firms, markets and industry structure. Furthermore, the power of the regulatory harmonization model is the central role of the Structural School approach in the governance of consumer protection, public safety and competition in global industries. Likewise, the Chicago School and New Industrial Organization School models of firm and industry competition and regulation also make valuable contributions to the concept of firm and industry governance in an age of free markets and global trade. However, the socio-economic context within which markets develop and society exists are absent in these conceptual models of firm and industry regulation.

As the century unfolds, global firm concentration and industry consolidation increasingly undermine the consumer welfare and public interest benefits of networked industries and global supply chain industries. But more important, cross-border competition, industry integration, free trade and market globalization increase consumer safety and public health risks in all nations. Therefore, the regulatory harmonization model is needed to provide a conceptual framework for collective policy action by national governments and nations in the context of multilateral institutions in the twenty-first century.

In terms of institutional mechanisms, the regulatory harmonization model confirms the need for strong government policy and effective institutions for the provision of public and private goods. In this respect, this conceptual model confirms the need for regulatory harmonization through formal regional and multilateral organizations and policy cooperation institutions. In the absence of formal institutional mechanisms for policy cooperation, regulatory harmonization and mandatory enforcement of management-based regulations and industry standards, national governments are unable to govern markets and society in an age of firm and industry globalization. Therefore, the regulatory harmonization model confirms the need for multi-level institutional convergence by national regulatory authorities.

In conclusion, the regulatory harmonization model provides new and innovative concepts of government policy making, market governance and multi-jurisdictional enforcement of regulations and laws. Consequently, formal transatlantic, regional and multilateral policy frameworks for standards harmonization, mutual recognition agreements, regulatory reciprocity and verification of management-based regulations are urgently needed. Finally, the regulatory harmonization model confirms the need for stronger normative consensus between governments, independent regulatory authorities and market governance institutions. Ultimately, governments must engage in multilateral and regional regulatory harmonization and institutional convergence to protect consumers, public safety and the collective good of nations.

NOTES

1. See Etzioni, Amitai (2004), *From Empire to Community: A New Approach to International Relations*, New York and Basingstoke: Palgrave Macmillan.
2. Bhagwati, Jagdish (1991), *Political Economy and International Economics*, Cambridge, MA: Cambridge University Press. According to the author, problems occur for government, consumers and nations due to the failure to abide by the rules of free trade in national industries and global markets.
3. Hoekman, Bernard and Michel M. Kostecki (1995), *The Political Economy of the World Trading System*, London and New York: Oxford University Press.
4. Vietor, Richard (1994), *Contrived Competition – Regulation and Deregulation in America*, Cambridge, MA: Belknap/Harvard University Press, pp. 328–30.
5. Pick, Daniel H., Denis R. Henderson, Jean Kinsey and Ian M. Sheldon (1998), *Global Markets for Processed Foods: Theoretical and Practical Issues*, Boulder, CO: Westview Press, p. 26.
6. Etzioni, Amitai (1992), *The Moral Dimension: Toward a New Economics*, New York: Free Press, pp. 217–51. According to Professor Etzioni, when the goal of policies are to change behavior, normative and economic factors must be addressed. Since perfect competition does not exist in global markets, firms and industries must be embedded in the broader socio-economic systems.

7. Ibid., pp. 199–216. The failure of government to regulate the power of large corporations and industry interests can result in the collapse of socio-economic systems.
8. Skogstad, Grace (2001a), 'Internationalization, democracy and food safety measures: the (i) legitimacy of consumer preferences, *Global Governance*, **7** (3): 293–316.
9. Nicolaidis, K. and M. Egan (2000), 'Transnational market governance and regional policy externality: why recognize foreign standards?', *Journal of European Public Policy*, **8** (3): 454–73.
10. Majone, G. (2000), 'Crisis of community regulation', *Journal of Common Market Studies*, **38** (2): 273–302.
11. There is an urgent need for more just and equitable mobilization of agricultural technology.
12. Skogstad, Grace (2001b), 'The WTO and food safety regulatory policy innovation in the European Union', *Journal of Common Market Studies*, **39** (3): 485–505.
13. Bruinsma Jelle (ed.) (2003), *World Agriculture: Toward 2015/2030 – An FAO Perspective,* FAO/Earthscan, Rome: FAO, pp. 232–64.
14. There is growing concern over the lack of consumer protection, anti-trust and competition policy and public health regulations and market governance institutions outside of the transatlantic and OECD nations.
15. Hollingsworth, J. Rogers, Karl H. Muller and Ellen Jane Hollingsworth (eds) (2002), *Advancing Socio-Economics – An Institutional Perspective*, Lantham, MD: Rowan and Littlefield, pp. 17–35. According to Hollingsworth, market and societal governance is complicated due to the embedding of local and national systems into multi-level systems. As a result, governments and citizens must increasingly expand their spheres of policy and market mobilization in an age of globalization and regional free trade.
16. Ibid., p. 26.
17. See the Response of FAO management and the Report of the Director-General of the WHO to the WHO Executive Board in FAO (2003), *Evaluation of the Codex Alimentarius and Other FAO and WHO Food Standards Work*, Eighty-ninth session, 5–9 May, Rome: FAO, http://www.Fao.org/DOCREP/MEETING/006/Y8820e.HTM.
18. Wilson, John and Tsunehiro Otsuki (2003), *Food Safety Issues in Food Security and Food Trade: Balancing Risk Reduction and Benefits from Trade in Setting Standards*, 2020 Vision for Food and Agriculture, and the Environment, Focus 10, Brief 6 of 17, July, Washington, DC: International Food Policy Research Institute.
19. Stigler, George J. and Gary S. Becker (1977), 'De Gustibus non est disputandum', *American Economic Review*, **67** (2): 76–90. According to this view, values are not the main considerations for consumer choice and self-interest maximization. Also see Becker, Gary (1976), *The Economic Approach to Human Behavior*, Chicago, IL: University of Chicago Press.
20. Buchholz, Eugene (1992), *Business Environment and Public Policy – Implications for Management Strategy*, Englewood Cliffs, NJ: Prentice Hall, pp. 72–7.
21. Coglianese, Cary and David Lazar (2002), *Management Based Regulation: Prescribing Private Management to Achieve Public Goals*, Working Paper 02–11, Washington, DC: Brookings Institution. Also see, Coglianese, Cary, Jennifer Nash and Todd Olmstead, (2002) *Performance Based Regulation: Prospects and Limitations in Health, Safety and Environmental Regulations*, Working Paper, John F. Kennedy School of Government, Cambridge, MA: Harvard University.
22. Ibid., pp. 73–85.
23. See FDA Guidance for Industry (1998), 'Guide to minimize microbial food safety hazards for fresh fruits and vegetables', 26 October, www.foodsafetyogov/dms/prodguid.htm. See also FDA Guidance for Industry (2003), 'Food producers, processors and transporters: food security preventative measures guidance', 21 March, www.cfsan.fda.gov/dms/secguid6.html.

REFERENCES

Becker, Gary (1976), *The Economic Approach to Human Behavior*, Chicago, IL: University of Chicago Press.

Bhagwati, Jagdish (1991), *Political Economy and International Economics*, Cambridge, MA: Cambridge University Press.

Bruinsma, Jelle (ed.) (2003), *World Agriculture: Toward 2015/2030 – An FAO Perspective*, FAO/Earthscan, Rome: FAO, pp. 232–64.

Buchholz, Eugene (1992), *Business Environment and Public Policy – Implications for Management Strategy*, 4th edition, Eaglewood Cliffs, NJ: Prentice Hall.

Caswell, Julie A. (2003), *Food Safety Standards and Regulation: Implications for Developing Countries*, Focus 10, Brief 4 of 7, 2020 Vision for Food, Agriculture, and the Environment, Washington, DC: International Food Policy Research Institute.

Coglianese, Cary and David Lazar (2002), *Management Based Regulation: Prescribing Private Management to Achieve Public Goals*, Working Paper 02–11, Washington, DC: Brookings Institution.

Coglianese, Cary, Jennifer Nash and Todd Olmstead (2002), *Performance Based Regulation: Prospects and Limitations in Health, Safety and Environmental Regulations*, Working Paper, John F. Kennedy School of Government, Cambridge, MA: Harvard University.

Etzioni, Amitai (1992), *The Moral Dimension: Toward a New Economics*, New York: Free Press.

Etzioni, Amitai (2004), *From Empire to Community: A New Approach to International Relations*, New York and Basingstoke: Palgrave Macmillan.

FAO (2003), *Evaluation of the Codex Alimentarius and other FAO and WHO Food Standards Work*, Eighty-ninth session, 5–9 May, Rome: FAO.

FDA Guidance for industry (1998), 'Guide to minimize microbial food safety hazards for fresh fruits and vegetables', 26 October, www.foodsafety.gov/dms/prodguid.htm.

FDA Guidance for Industry (2003), 'Food producers, processors and transporters: food security preventative measures guidance', 21 March, www.cfsan.fda.gov/dms/secguid6.html.

Hoekman, Bernard and Michel M. Kostecki (1995), *The Political Economy of the World Trading System*, London and New York: Oxford University Press.

Hollingsworth, J. Rogers, Karl H. Muller and Ellen Jane Hollingsworth (eds) (2002), *Advancing Socio-Economics – An Institutional Perspective*, Lantham, MD: Rowman and Littlefield.

Lazer, David (2001), 'Regulatory interdependence and international governance', *Journal of European Policy*, **8**, 474–92.

Majone, G. (2000), 'Crisis of community relations', *Journal of Common Market Studies*, **38** (2): 273–302.

Nicolaides, K. and M. Egan (2000), 'Transnational market governance and regional policy externality: why recognize foreign standards?', *Journal of European Public Policy*, **8** (3): 454–73.

Pick, Daniel H., Denis R. Henderson, Jean Kinsey and Ian M. Sheldon (1998), *Global Markets for Processed Foods: Theoretical and Practical Issues*, Boulder, CO: Westview Press.

Porter, Michael (1990), *The Competitive Advantage of Nations*, New York: Free Press.

Skogstad, Grace (2001a), 'Internationalization, democracy and food safety measures: the (i) legitimacy of consumer preferences, *Global Governance*, **7** (3): 293–316.

Skogstad, Grace (2001b), 'The WTO and food safety regulatory policy innovation in the European Union', *Journal of Common Market Studies*, **39** (3): 485–505.

Stigler, George J. and Gary S. Becker (1977), 'De Gustibus non est disputandum', *American Economic Review*, **67** (2): 76–90

Vietor, Richard (1994), *Contrived Competition – Regulation and Deregulation in America*, Cambridge, MA: Belknap/Harvard University Press.

Wilson, John and Tsunehiro Otsuki (2003), *Food Safety Issues in Food Security and Food Trade: Balancing Risk Reduction and Benefits from Trade in Setting Standards*, 2020 Vision for Food and Agriculture, and the Environment, Focus 10, Brief 6 of 17, July, Washington, DC: International Policy Research Institute.

Index